Lecture Notes in Computer Science 14900

Founding Editors

Gerhard Goos
Juris Hartmanis

AF173135

The series Lecture Notes in Computer Science (LNCS), including its subseries Lecture Notes in Artificial Intelligence (LNAI) and Lecture Notes in Bioinformatics (LNBI), has established itself as a medium for the publication of new developments in computer science and information technology research, teaching, and education.

LNCS enjoys close cooperation with the computer science R & D community, the series counts many renowned academics among its volume editors and paper authors, and collaborates with prestigious societies. Its mission is to serve this international community by providing an invaluable service, mainly focused on the publication of conference and workshop proceedings and postproceedings. LNCS commenced publication in 1973.

Simon Foster · Augusto Sampaio
Editors

The Application
of Formal Methods

Essays Dedicated to Jim Woodcock
on the Occasion of His Retirement

 Springer

Editors
Simon Foster 🆔
University of York
York, UK

Augusto Sampaio 🆔
Universidade Federal de Pernambuco
Recife, Pernambuco, Brazil

ISSN 0302-9743   ISSN 1611-3349 (electronic)
Lecture Notes in Computer Science
ISBN 978-3-031-67113-5   ISBN 978-3-031-67114-2 (eBook)
https://doi.org/10.1007/978-3-031-67114-2

Jim Woodcock

Preface

This book contains 14 chapters on the application of formal methods, in the form of essays dedicated to Jim Woodcock on his retirement. These essays present original contributions on formal methods from international academics in eight countries. The contributions were invited, and each paper was peer-reviewed by at least two expert academics. Jim Woodcock received a copy of this book on the 4th of September 2024, at an event held at the University of York, UK, when the authors presented their work.

Jim has significantly contributed to the history and consolidation of Formal Methods as an engineering discipline. Jim's contributions cover strong theoretical work, practical techniques and tools, teaching, and industrial applications of significant impact. He is the author of more than 240 papers, which include collaborations with more than 170 colleagues. He has always acted as an ambassador for our field, being able to see beyond the present, and across geographical frontiers, to disseminate Formal Methods worldwide.

While pursuing his PhD on software verification at the University of Liverpool under the supervision of Prof. Mike Hennell, Jim Woodcock already demonstrated his potential to contribute to software development as an engineering discipline; his PhD work provided the mathematical basis for prototype tools that became part of the spin-out company LDRA's testbed software. LDRA is now a global market leader in testing tools. He then joined the Telecoms Laboratory of GEC's Hirst Research Centre where he worked on a novel distributed telephone exchange, and pioneered the use of mathematical modelling at GEC to produce a service specification of a PABX exchange. He applied this new approach to the distributed exchange, verifying its routing algorithm; and subsequently to the System X telephone exchange. He also made contributions to a CCITT international standard for a trunk exchange protocol. The approaches he pioneered continued to be applied in GEC after he left.

Jim realised he could contribute even more to our field as an academic, while still keeping close interaction with industry. He joined Oxford's Programming Research Group in 1985, where he worked with the IBM Hursley Laboratories on the use of mathematical modelling in essential maintenance of one of the most successful systems the software industry has ever developed: CICS. This transaction processing system was IBM's most profitable product: 99 of the Fortune 100 companies were running on CICS, along with the vast majority of Fortune 500 companies. CICS continues to be used as a key component of IBM's Websphere product family. He worked with IBM engineers to devise mathematical techniques for design and coding from specifications, ensuring correctness of the final product. Together, they have also shown how to integrate these advanced ideas into IBM's development processes, and proved the correctness of key modules within CICS, which resulted in substantial savings in development costs (about 9%) and reduced errors. In 1992, they received the Queen's Award for Technological Achievement for "the use of software engineering mathematics in specifications using the Z notation".

The Z techniques were also central in a 10-year consultancy contract with the Communications-Electronics Security Group of GCHQ. Jim worked on a confidential project to develop a secure office automation system (T-Net), early work on the government's cyber-security strategy. The group also used Z to develop a secure version of the widely used UNIX operating system, and built a Z tool for type-checking and proof support with a powerful and sophisticated user interface. During this time, Jim made significant contributions to the semantics of Z and to its ISO standardisation committee.

As further contributions to proof methodologies, in 1996, Jim collaborated with the Smith Institute and BR Research to develop a technique for verifying the safety of Solid State Interlocking (SSI) railway signalling systems, the *de facto* signalling technology in the UK, still in use today. His work was extended by others at Oxford and York, and used commercially by Praxis Critical Systems. More recently, he used similar techniques for the verification of safety-critical control systems in collaboration with the Nuclear Installation Inspectorate and British Energy. Then, in 1998, Jim acted as a consultant and researcher in the development, verification, and certification of a smartcard-based electronic cash system, Mondex. It was crucial that the security of the card could not be broken, and the Bank of England required Mondex to be certified to the highest standard available: ITSEC Level E6. Proof of correctness required a technique beyond those that had become commonplace in the verification community after the CICS work. Jim developed a technically complete theory of correctness for Z, verified its soundness from first principles, and completed the verification of Mondex. This was the first application of a general theory of program correctness to an industrial product, and Mondex became the first product to be certified to ITSEC Level E6. This has proved to be a highly influential work.

In the early 2000s, following the release of Tony Hoare and He Jifeng's significant book on *Unifying Theories of Programming*, Jim began a two decade long endeavour to develop formal UTP semantics for a wide variety of modelling paradigms, and make the accompanying techniques applicable in industry. In 2001, he designed the *Circus* language with a UTP semantics, which has at its core a flexible combination of Z, Dijkstra's guarded command language, and an algebra for concurrent systems. Jim has also overseen the development of a suite of accompanying tools, including model checking and theorem proving support, and most recently the Isabelle-based semantic framework and verification tool, Isabelle/UTP.

Further research on *Circus* has produced a family of languages, with many extensions to the core notation and important industrial applications. There are versions to cover real-time, object orientation, synchronicity, mobility, probabilism, and data sharing. Industrial applications have focused on control systems and tool support has followed. Recently, hybrid systems have been included, with continuous dynamics and discrete events. Many have joined in the effort to develop *Circus*, including colleagues in the UK, Brazil, China, France, USA, Ireland, and Singapore. The work on *Circus* and UTP is also at the heart of the RoboChart language for modelling mobile and autonomous robots.

Jim has actively participated in promoting Formal Methods worldwide. Particularly, in 2003, he became a leader of the international grand challenge Verified Software Initiative, and has coordinated its experimental work. He has collected and promoted a series of industrial pilot projects and had considerable impact. An international team of researchers have contributed to the following projects: Apache web server, cardiac pacemaker, POSIX flash-memory (space-flight) file store, FreeRTOS real-time operating system, various hypervisors, Mondex, and Tokeneer ID Station. Companies like Google, Amazon, Microsoft, IBM, Intel, and Oracle are using these techniques.

Also in 2003, Jim joined the University of York, where he led the High-Integrity Systems Engineering research group, which combines research in system verification with safety and risk analysis, and was a world-leading group in this area. His work on heterogeneous language semantics has provided the technical foundations for a series of large projects that formed the basis of the RoboStar centre of excellence on software engineering for robotics.

In recognition of Jim's exceptional contributions to the engineering field, he was made a Fellow of the Royal Academy of Engineering (FReng) in 2011.

Currently, he is tackling robotics, addressing an important shortcoming in the industrial development of controllers for mobile and autonomous robots: modern software engineering techniques are not used by roboticists to improve product quality. He is using UTP results to underpin practical notations of relevance to this domain, and verification based on simulation and testing. New theories are required to deal with probabilistic and hybrid behaviour. He is also working on a UTP theory of probabilistic programs, with application to robotics. This involves the control and behaviour of robots in environments subject to unforeseeable events and other uncertainties, covering the application of automated proof techniques to practical control algorithms. He now has a novel theory to produce a practical verification tool to prove such results correct.

It was a great pleasure to organise this Festschrift in honour of Jim Woodcock. We especially thank the invited authors for their contributions, as well as the Program Committee for the important feedback they provided during the review process. The celebratory event was only possible due to the support of the Department of Computer Science at the University of York, and the RoboStar centre. We are appreciative of EasyChair for the seamless assistance during the submission and review process, as well as for the production of this volume. Finally, we are indebted to Springer for their cooperation and support in publishing this book.

September 2024   Simon Foster
                                                                   Augusto Sampaio

Dedications

Dedication from Augusto

Jim is a gentleman in every sense and is especially generous in sharing his extensive knowledge. Interactions with Jim have had a profoundly transformative effect on me. I first met Jim in Oxford in 1989, shortly after I arrived for my DPhil. I was finishing a paper on the Z language, and Jim, barely knowing me, kindly offered to help by meticulously revising it. Since then, Jim has been a great source of inspiration, providing many opportunities and much support to promote my academic career. He has also greatly contributed to enhancing the area of Formal Methods in Recife through several academic visits and by leading the organisation of international schools; more broadly, in Brazil, he has participated in several international events and played a crucial role in consolidating the Brazilian Symposium on Formal Methods. Undoubtedly, Jim has been the primary international influencer in shaping our field in Brazil! Congratulations, Jim, for having dedicated most of your life to the several facets of a brilliant academic career. I am confident that even more outstanding contributions are yet to come!

Dedication from Simon

I first met Jim in my interview for the COMPASS EU project back in 2011. I had never heard of UTP at the time, but following my PhD I was excited to pursue this new direction, and was delighted to be accepted onto the project. We have been working together ever since. I can still remember the first UTP tutorial that Jim gave in York in March 2012, which served to enthuse me and made a lasting impression on my career over the past 12 years. I came to appreciate the care and attention he dedicates to his mathematical work, particularly his hand-written proofs, which display both rigour and beauty. Working under Jim on three research projects was a great pleasure. He always gave me guidance, encouragement, and creative freedom, which enabled me to grow as a researcher and teacher. Together we have published more than 25 papers. He also opened up many exciting opportunities for me, particularly in teaching at international postgraduate schools, which has been formative of my teaching abilities, and he has also allowed me to take a central role in shaping future research directions. I believe he cares very deeply for all his postdocs, and proactively endeavours to help them flourish. Without Jim's support, both academically and practically, I am sure I would not have been awarded my EPSRC-UKRI fellowship, CyPhyAssure. More recently, since becoming a lecturer, we have developed both an undergraduate module and a professional course based on our research, which I believe have both been successful. Thank you Jim for all that you have done for me, and I wish you well in your retirement and future research adventures!

Organization

Program Committee

Alan Burns	University of York, UK
Michael Butler	University of Southampton,UK
Andrew Butterfield	Trinity College Dublin, Ireland
Deepak D'Souza	Indian Institute of Science, India
Jim Davies	University of Oxford, UK
Jin-Song Dong	National University of Singapore, Singapore
John Fitzgerald	Newcastle University, UK
Simon Foster	University of York, UK
Leo Freitas	Newcastle University, UK
Peter Gorm-Larsen	Aarhus University, Denmark
Wen-Ling Huang	University of Bremen, Germany
Cliff Jones	Newcastle University, UK
Thierry Lecomte	CLEARSY, France
Annabelle McIver	Macquarie University, Australia
Alvaro Miyazawa	University of York, UK
Carroll Morgan	University of New South Wales, Australia
Colin O'Halloran	University of Oxford, UK
Jan Peleska	TZI, Universität Bremen, Germany
Pedro Ribeiro	University of York, UK
Bill Roscoe	University of Oxford, UK
Augusto Sampaio	Universidade Federal de Pernambuco, Brazil
Steve Schneider	University of Surrey, UK
Andrew Simpson	University of Oxford, UK
Kangfeng Ye	University of York, UK
Frank Zeyda	Independent Researcher, Mexico
Huibiao Zhu	East China Normal University, China

Contents

Denotational and Algebraic Semantics for the SMrCaIT Calculus Based
on UTP 1
    Ningning Chen, Huibiao Zhu, and Jifeng He

Specifying Fault-Tolerant Mixed-Criticality Scheduling 22
    Alan Burns and Cliff B. Jones

Clarifying Assumptions 43
    Cliff B. Jones

PCSP# Denotational Semantics with an Application in Sports Analytics 71
    Zhaoyu Liu, Murong Ma, Kan Jiang, Zhe Hou, Ling Shi,
    and Jin Song Dong

Towards the Composition of Digital Twins 103
    Peter Gorm Larsen, Prasad Talasila, and John Fitzgerald

Formal Modelling of Peercoin and Proof-of-Stake Protocols 123
    Kent Leeding, Steve Schneider, and Helen Treharne

On the Unification of Conformance Notions 144
    Jan Peleska, Wen-ling Huang, and Robert Sachtleben

Abstracting and Verifying Decentralised Systems in CSP 172
    A. W. Roscoe, Pedro Antonino, and Jonathan Lawrence

Towards an Algebra for Unifying Theories of Concurrent Programming
(UTCP) 203
    Andrew Butterfield

Static Race Detection for Periodic Real-Time Programs with IPCP Locks 233
    Varsha P. Suresh, Rekha Pai, Deepak D'Souza, Meenakshi D'Souza,
    and Sujit Kumar Chakrabarti

A Tour Through the Programming Choices: Semantics and Applications 261
    Pedro Ribeiro, Kangfeng Ye, Frank Zeyda, and Alvaro Miyazawa

I Kaptured the System 306
    Colin O'Halloran, William Simmonds, and Nick Tudor

Proving B with Atelier B 329
    Thierry Lecomte

Semantics Formalisation – Modelling and Proving Strategies Using
Event-B Versus Theories 346
    Thai Son Hoang, Colin Snook, Karla Vanessa Morris Wright,
    Laurent Voisin, and Michael Butler

Author Index 375

Denotational and Algebraic Semantics for the SMrCaIT Calculus Based on UTP

Ningning Chen[1], Huibiao Zhu[2($\boxtimes$)], and Jifeng He[3]

[1] University of Shanghai for Science and Technology, Shanghai, China
nnchen168@163.com
[2] East China Normal University, Shanghai, China
hbzhu@sei.ecnu.edu.cn
[3] Shanghai Academy of AI Industrial Technology, Shanghai, China
jifeng@sei.ecnu.edu.cn

Abstract. The rapid development of the Internet of Things (IoT) has generated a global demand for related technologies, especially in improving system quality and security. In response, our recent work proposes SMrCaIT, a secure mobile real-time process calculus explicitly designed for IoT systems. Using SMrCaIT, we can model and verify IoT systems before implementation, enhancing system reliability and security.

To provide a rigorous mathematical explanation of the meaning of the SMrCaIT program and explore its properties, this paper gives the denotational and algebraic semantics of this calculus based on the Unifying Theories of Programming (UTP). To facilitate the algebraic exploration of parallel expansion laws, we extend the SMrCaIT calculus with three types of guarded choices, allowing us to convert any SMrCaIT program into a unified form (i.e., a guarded choice form).

Keywords: SMrCaIT calculus · IoT · UTP · Denotational semantics · Algebraic Semantics

1 Background

Jifeng He and Jim Woodcock worked together with Professor Sir Tony Hoare at the Programming Research Group within the Oxford University Computing Laboratory during the 1980s and 1990s. Jifeng and Tony developed the *Unifying Theories of Programming* (UTP) approach [1]. Subsequently, Jim set up a research direction based on UTP at the University of York and in 2006 founded the UTP symposium series [2,3]. During this time, Jim has spent much of his research effort on UTP-related activities, such as the development of *Circus*, a concurrent language for refinement; unifying imperative CSP, Z, and the refinement calculus, with a UTP-based formalisation. In 2013, Jim and Huibiao co-organised Jifeng's 70th birthday Festschrift symposium [4], thank you, Jim. We dedicate this paper to Jim on the occasion of his formal retirement at York. Happy "retirement" Jim, and we hope that you enjoy many more years of fruitful research.

S. Foster and A. Sampaio (Eds.): *The Application of Formal Methods*, LNCS 14900, pp. 1–21, 2024.
https://doi.org/10.1007/978-3-031-67114-2_1

2   Introduction

The Internet of Things (IoT) refers to networks of interconnected entities that possess distinct device identification, embedded software intelligence, as well as sensing and acting capabilities [5]. So far, IoT has achieved the goal of enabling anything (such as people, devices, and sensors) to be connected to the Internet anytime and anywhere [5]. As IoT devices rapidly integrate into daily life, the global demand for IoT applications and technologies has surged [6,7]. In response, several promising technologies (e.g., 5G, machine learning, and edge computing) are used in the IoT paradigm. However, with the increasing complexity of IoT systems, theoretical modeling and analysis of these systems becomes increasingly significant, especially from the perspective of formal methods [8]. Using formal methods (especially process calculus) enables us to model IoT systems before they are actually implemented, thus guaranteeing their quality, reliability, and security.

To the best of our knowledge, there are few works on modeling and analyzing IoT systems from a process calculus perspective, including only IoT-calculus [9], IoT-LYSA [10], and CaIT [9]. However, neither IoT-calculus nor IoT-LYSA supports the description of timed behavior [9]. Additionally, CaIT only supports point-to-point communication, not broadcast communication which is more common in IoT systems. When using CaIT to describe node movement, nodes cannot decide where to move: external agents move them to arbitrary locations, causing the migration trajectories of entities (even attackers) to become unpredictable. Thus, our recent work presents a secure mobile real-time process calculus for IoT systems, called SMrCaIT, with the following features [11]. Firstly, SMrCaIT introduces parametric mobility models to determine migration trajectories of nodes, while strictly separating process actions and mobility modeling. Secondly, SMrCaIT inherits the constructs of the applied pi calculus [12] for communication, concurrency, and scope. In detail, SMrCaIT binds each name (usually a channel) to a specific scope to ensure that the environment (e.g., an attacker) cannot access the name that is not explicitly given, namely channel restriction. The scope can be changed through scope extrusion. Finally, SMrCaIT provides real-time constraints to handle the dynamic evolution of real-time IoT systems.

As described in Hoare and He's Unifying Theories of Programming (UTP) [1], the semantics of a programing language can be represented through operational semantics [13], denotational semantics [14], and algebraic semantics [15]. The UTP approach aims to merge the strengths of these three methods, offering a comprehensive theoretical framework for programming language descriptions. UTP has been applied in the communicating processes with shared variables, where the proposed UTP semantics is encoded into the PVS theorem prover [16]. We previously investigated the operational semantics of SMrCaIT in our recent work [11]. Denotational semantics explains *what a program does* from a purely mathematical perspective, having the following superiorities.

– Using the denotational semantics, we can predict the behavior of each program without actually executing it on a computer [17].

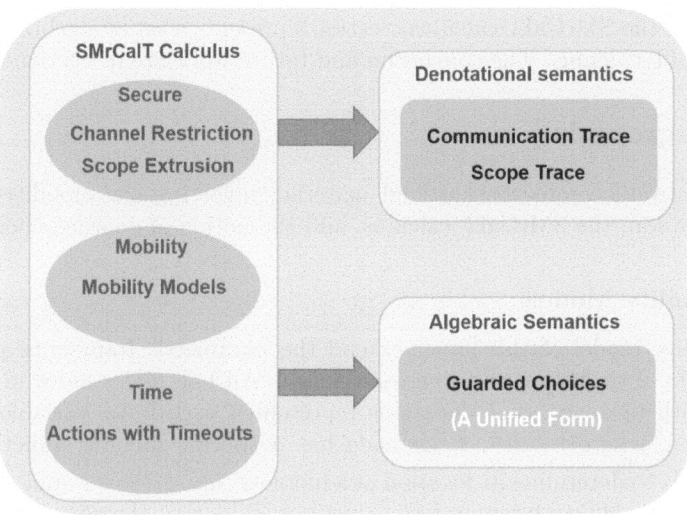

Fig. 1. Main Contributions

- The powerful mathematical theory can support our reasoning about programs, such as proving the equivalence among programs (see [17]).

Algebraic semantics consists of a series of algebraic laws (usually equations), which is well-suited for the symbolic calculation of parameters and structures of an optimal design [1,15]. Algebraic semantics does not explain the meaning of a program but focuses on describing the properties of programs. For example, we can use algebraic semantics to express two programs with the same meaning but different forms in terms of equations (i.e., the equivalence relationship). When denotational semantics is used to explore certain properties of programs, these properties can also be expressed as algebraic laws. Therefore, it is valuable to study the denotational and algebraic semantics of SMrCaIT in conjunction.

The main contributions of this paper are shown in Fig. 1, and the details are as follows:

- We explore the denotational semantics of the SMrCaIT calculus, which covers basic commands (or statements) and parallel compositions. Our denotational semantics has two types of traces: communication traces for message exchange and scope traces for implementing channel restriction and scope extrusion.
- We explore the algebraic semantics of the SMrCaIT calculus, especially the algebraic laws for parallel compositions, channel restriction, and scope extrusion. As a result, any SMrCaIT program can be described in a unified form (i.e., guarded choice form) with the help of the achieved algebraic laws.

The rest of this paper is organized as follows. Section 3 presents some backgrounds, including the mobility models, the scope extrusion, the SMrCaIT calculus, and the notion of guarded choices. Section 4 explores the denotational semantics of the SMrCaIT calculus. Section 5 presents a set of algebraic laws for the SMrCaIT calculus. The conclusion and future work are in Section 6.

3   Backgrounds

We now introduce some background material, involving our mobility models, scope extrusion, the SMrCaIT calculus, and the notion of guarded choices.

3.1   Mobility Models

The mobility model of this paper extend the parametric framework proposed in [18,19] by introducing real-time constraints. All IoT nodes move in a global area A, with its inaccessible locations represented as $\mathbf{bd}(A)$. Variable t is the global clock, where $t \in R^+$. Each node has a specific mobility function (i.e., $f : R^+ \to A$) to determine its location at a moment, i.e., $f(t) = \overrightarrow{l}$ and $\overrightarrow{l} \in A$ for $t \in R^+$. Each mobility function has a time out $T_f \in R^+ \cup \{\infty, \diamond\}$. **(1)** $T_f \in R^+$ means that f describes the trajectory of a node until f is replaced by a new function at $t = T_f$. **(2)** $T_f = \infty$ makes f never change. **(3)** $T_f = \diamond$ allows replacing f at any time in the future. **(4)** $f(t) \in \mathbf{bd}(A)$ means that the node reaches the boundary at t, and the mobility function must be replaced now.

A new mobility function with its timeout can be generated from the mobility model (denoted as Ω). Here, the vector $\overrightarrow{l_0}$ and t_0 are the current location of a node and the current time, respectively. And Vel and Dir are the sets of speed and direction, respectively.

$$\Omega(\overrightarrow{l_0}, t_0) =_{df} \{(f, T_f) \mid f(t) = \overrightarrow{l_0} + v \cdot \overrightarrow{\alpha} \cdot (t - t_0), \ v \in Vel,$$
$$\overrightarrow{\alpha} \in Dir, T_f \in R^+ \cup \{\infty, \diamond\}, \ t \in [t_0, T_f]\}.$$

Example 1. In Fig. 2, we establish a mobility model for node n. At the initial time 0, n follows the mobility function f_1. When the global time reaches T_1 and T_2, the mobility function switches from f_1 to f_2 and from f_2 to f_3, respectively.

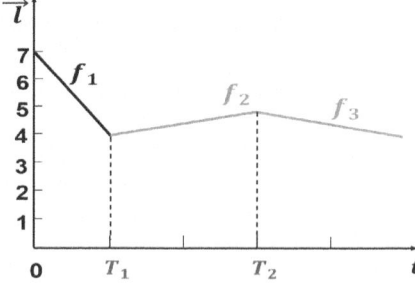

Fig. 2. The mobility model of node n

3.2   Scope Extrusion

In this paper, each name (usually a channel) is restricted to a specific scope, preventing messages sent through a channel from being observed by nodes outside its scope. When this limitation applies to a channel, it is termed channel restriction. Obviously, the notion of scope is the basis for ensuring data security. Nodes within the scope can broadcast the restricted name (usually a channel) as a message to nodes out of the scope, expanding the scope by absorbing nodes receiving this name, namely, via scope extrusion [20]. To explain the notion of scope extrusion in detail, we give the following example in Fig. 3.

Example 2. Initially, the scope of c contains nodes N_1, M_1, and M_2. Only nodes N_1 and N_2 are within the scope of channel c'. N_1 broadcasts channel c' via channel c to nodes outside the scope (i.e., M_1 and M_2). We assume that M_1 and M_2 are both within the communication range of c. Thus, they can receive c' via c successfully. Consequently, they enlarge the scope of c'.

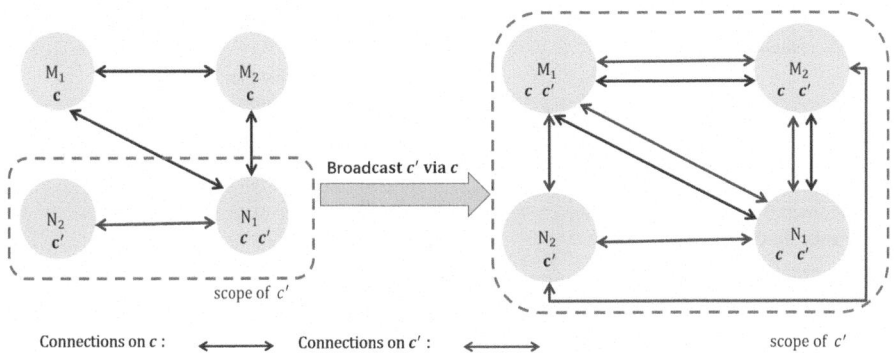

Fig. 3. Scope Extrusion

Scope Graph: To better explore channel restriction and scope extrusion in our denotational approach, we introduce the notion of the scope (global) graph, which is a mapping from a name (usually a channel) to its scope. The scope of a name includes nodes with that name, and can be extended by adding nodes receiving this name via scope extrusion. For a channel, only nodes in its scope set can communicate via it. Mathematically, the scope graph is described as $S = \{na_1 \& \{n_1, \cdots, n_i\}, \cdots, na_v \& \{n_k, \cdots, n_j\}\}$, where $na_1 \& \{n_1, \cdots, n_i\}$ denotes that the scope of name na_1 contains nodes $n_1, \cdots,$ and n_i. In Fig. 3, the scope of c' is extended from $S(c') = \{N_1, N_2\}$ to $S'(c') = \{N_1, N_2, M_1, M_2\}$.

3.3   The SMrCaIT Calculus

Table 1 shows the syntax of SMrCaIT with three expression types: messages for representing IoT network data, processes for modeling node logic, and networks as pools of nodes running in parallel. Due to the page limit, we do not introduce the message layer and the network layer in detail here (see Appendix A for more information).

Table 1. The syntax of SMrCaIT

Message				
	m, m_1	$::=$	$\tilde{n}$	Name
			$\mid \ x$	Variable
			$\mid \ g(m_1, \cdots, m_l)$	Function Application
Process				
	P, Q	$::=$	**nil**	Termination
			$\mid \ P \sqcap Q$	Nondeterministic Choice
			$\mid \ P \, ; Q$	Sequential Composition
			$\mid \ $ **if** $[m = m_1]$ **then** P **else** Q	Conditional
			$\mid \ $ **while** $[m = m_1]$ **do** P	Iteration
			$\mid \ c^{\Delta T}!\langle m \rangle$ **then** P **else** Q	Output
			$\mid \ c^{\Delta T}?\langle x \rangle$ **then** P **else** Q	Input
			$\mid \ s^{\Delta T}?y$ **then** P	Sensor Reading
			$\mid \ a^{\Delta T}!m$ **then** P	Actuator Writing
			$\mid \ P \parallel Q$	Parallel Composition
Network				
	N, N_1	$::=$	0	Empty Network
			$\mid \ _n[\phi \bowtie P]_{T_f}^f$	Node
			$\mid \ (\nu \tilde{n})N$	Restriction
			$\mid \ N \parallel N_1$	Parallel Composition

Process level:

(1) nil means that this process terminates.

(2) $P \sqcap Q$ stands for the nondeterministic choice, which chooses process P or process Q non-deterministically.

(3) $P \, ; Q$ is sequential composition. It first executes process P. After P terminates successfully, process Q starts performing.

(4) if $[m = m_1]$ **then** P **else** Q models the conditional choice construct. If the condition is satisfied (i.e., m is equal to m_1), process P runs; otherwise, process Q executes.

(5) while $[m = m_1]$ **do** P represents the iteration construct.

(6) $c^{\Delta T}!\langle m \rangle$ **then** P **else** Q states that process P obtains control if the output action occurs successfully within T time units. Otherwise, Q starts to work after T time units.

(7) $c^{\Delta T}?(x)$ **then** P **else** Q illustrates that if the process receives a message via channel c within T time units, the following process is P. Otherwise, Q takes control after T time units.

(8) $s^{\Delta T}?y$ **then** P first spends T time units to activate sensor s. Then, a message is read from s and stored in the variable y for access by following process P.

(9) $a^{\Delta T}!m$ **then** P denotes that, after taking T time units to start actuator a, a node writes message m into a. After that, the process P starts executing.

(10) $P \parallel Q$ means that processes P and Q run in parallel.

3.4 Guided Choice

To support our exploration of the algebraic parallel expansion laws, we further enrich SMrCaIT with three types of guarded choices.

- **Instantaneous Guarded Choice:**

$$\|_{i \in I}\{g_i \to N_i\}$$

where $g_i \in \{c!\langle m\rangle @(n,f,T_f), \ c?\langle x\rangle @(n,f,T_f), \ c.[m/x]@((n,f,T_f),(n_1,f_1,T_{f_1})),$
$b_i \& \tau @(n,f,T_f), (vm)c!\langle m\rangle @(n,f,T_f), (vm)c.[m/x]@((n,f,T_f),(n_1,f_1,T_{f_1}))\}.$

- **(1)** $c.[m/x]@((n,f,T_f),(n_1,f_1,T_{f_1}))$ denotes that node n successfully sends m to another node n_1 via channel c, where $[m/x]$ assigns m to the variable x.
- **(2)** $b_i \& \tau @(n,f,T_f)$ shows that node n executes a silent action (i.e., τ) if the Boolean expression b_i is true, where τ does nothing and terminates immediately. $(vc')M$ ensures that communication actions occurring on c' (i.e.., $c'!\langle m\rangle @(n,f,T_f)$ or $c'.[m/x]@((n,f,T_f),(n_1,f_1,T_{f_1})))$ are invisible outside of M. We conceal these actions by replacing them with $true \& \tau @(n,f,T_f)$.

- **Delay Guarded Choice:**

$$\#t \to N$$

The delay guarded choice presents that the subsequent network N starts to execute after delaying t time units.

- **Hybrid Guarded Choice:**

$$\begin{aligned}
&\|_{i \in I}\{g_i \to N_i\} \\
&\oplus \exists t' \in (0 \dots t) \bullet \#t' \to N \\
&\oplus \#t \to N''
\end{aligned}$$

The third type is the hybrid guarded choice, which has three branches combined by the notation $\oplus$, where $\oplus$ denotes the disjointness of timed behaviors.

4 Denotational Semantics

Now, we explore the denotational semantics of SMrCaIT via the UTP framework, involving the semantic model, healthiness conditions, and the denotational semantics for basic commands and parallel composition.

4.1 Semantic Model

For formalizing the denotational semantics for SMrCaIT, we introduce the observation tuple $(time, time', st, st', trc, trc', trs, trs', mf, mf')$ (Fig. 4).

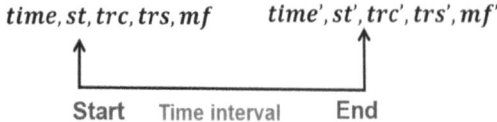

Fig. 4. Observation tuple

(1) *time* and *time'* are the start and end instants of an observation time interval, respectively. Here, ▲ stands for the time interval, where ▲ = *time'* − *time*.

(2) *st* and *st'* are the initial and final execution states of the program, respectively. The state of the program has the following three possibilities.

- *ter* : When a process enters a *ter* state, it terminates successfully. Specifically, "*st* = *ter*" denotes that the previous process terminates successfully, and the current one begins.
- *wait* : When a process awaits communication or the activation of a sensor or actuator, it enters a *wait* state. "*st* = *wait*" indicates the prior process entering a *wait* state. The current process cannot be performed.
- *div* : When a process enters a *div* state, it becomes nonterminating and unpredictable. "*st* = *div*" indicates that the previous process diverged, causing the current process to fail to execute.

(3) We define a pair of variables, namely *trc* and *trc'*. *trc* is the initial communication trace of a process, inherited from its predecessor. *trc'* is the final communication trace that contains the contribution of the current process. A communication trace is a sequence of communication snapshots, and a communication snapshot is a quintuple denoted as (t, idl, S, o, ζ).

- t is the time when the communication action occurs.
- *idl* is a set with node essentials. Each element in *idl* is (n, l), with l being node n's current location.
- S is the current scope graph when the communication action happens.
- o signifies an observation action, as $c.v$ or τ. $c.v$ describes sending message v via channel c. Also, τ is a communication action unrelated to the current node, which occurs in the environment.
- To facilitate trace merging, we use flag ζ to classify observation actions into three types. **(a)** $\zeta = 1$ denotes that the observation action is an output action (i.e., $c!\langle m \rangle$) performed by the current process. **(b)** $\zeta = 2$ indicates an input action $(c?\langle x \rangle)$ done by the current process. **(c)** To ensure orderly trace merging, $\zeta = 0$ signals a communication action occurring in the environment from the view of the current node. This unrelated communication action can be seen as a silent action τ.

(4) Similarly, we establish scope traces to synchronize the (global) scope graph (see page 5), which contains the scope of each name (usually a channel).

trs and trs' to are the initial and final scope traces, respectively. A scope trace is composed of scope snapshots, and a snapshot is a triple having the form (t, S', u).

- t is the time when the scope graph is changed.
- S' stands for the newly contributed scope graph.
- Flag u indicates whether the scope graph is changed by the current process (described as $u = 1$) or by the environment (denoted as $u = 0$).

We give some notations to deal with (communication or scope) traces. To simplify, we use tr and tr' to represent trc and trc', or trs and trs'. $tr' - tr$ is the trace generated by the current process. $tr_1 \frown tr_2$ concatenates traces tr_1 and tr_2. $\mathbf{head}(tr)$ is the first snapshot of the trace tr. $\mathbf{tail}(tr)$ holds the remaining sequence after removing $\mathbf{head}(tr)$. $\mathbf{last}(tr)$ is the last snapshot of tr. Notations are given $\pi_i (i = 1, 2, 3, 4, 5)$ to get the ith element of a snapshot.

(5) $mf = (f, T_f)$ and $mf' = (f', T_{f'})$ are the initial and final mobility function pairs of a node, respectively.

4.2   Healthiness Conditions

We propose some healthiness conditions that every process must satisfy. **H1** forbids trace shortening and time reversing. **H2** indicates the following two requirements. The current process cannot be executed if the previous process enters a *wait* state, keeping values constant. Otherwise, the current process begins. As mentioned previously, $st = div$ denotes that the behavior of the previous process is unpredictable. In this case, the current process never executes, and inherited initial values are unobservable. Thus, each process should satisfy **H3**.

(H1) $P = P \wedge \mathbf{Inv}(trc, trs, time)$,,
    where $\mathbf{Inv}(trc, trs, time) =_{df} trc \preceq trc' \wedge trs \preceq trs' \wedge time \leq time'$,
        and $trc \preceq trc'$ denotes that trace trc is a prefix of trace trc'.
(H2) $P = \prod \lhd st = wait \rhd P$,
    where $P \lhd b \rhd Q =_{df} (b \wedge P) \vee (\neg b \wedge Q)$, and
    $\prod =_{df} (st' = st) \wedge (time' = time) \wedge (trc' = trc) \wedge (trs' = trs) \wedge (mf' = mf)$.
(H3) $P = \mathbf{Inv}(trc, trs, time) \lhd st = div \rhd P$

To describe the denotational semantics for the SMrCaIT calculus, we define the following function $\mathcal{H}(X)$ that satisfies the above three healthiness conditions.

$$\mathcal{H}(X) =_{df} \mathbf{Inv}(trc, trs, time) \lhd st = div \rhd \left(\begin{array}{l} \prod \lhd st = wait \rhd \\ (X \wedge \mathbf{Inv}(trc, trs, time)) \end{array} \right)$$

4.3   Denotational Semantics of Basic Commands

We now study the denotational semantics of basic commands. $\mathbf{beh}(N)$ is used to describe the behavior of a network N, i.e., the denotational semantics of N.

(1) Termination: nil models a termination process. Executing **nil** cannot change the execution state and takes no time (i.e., $\blacktriangle = 0$). However, (communication and scope) traces can be extended by the contributions from the environment (i.e., other processes running in parallel).

$$\mathbf{beh}(_n[\phi \bowtie \mathbf{nil}]_{T_f}^f) =_{df} \mathcal{H} \begin{pmatrix} st' = ter \wedge \blacktriangle = 0 \wedge mf' = mf \wedge trc' = trc^\frown ecom \\ \wedge \pi_4(ecom) \in \tau^* \wedge \pi_5(ecom) \in 0^* \wedge \\ trs' = trs^\frown envir \wedge \pi_3(envir) \in 0^* \end{pmatrix}$$

$trc' = trc^\frown ecom$ and $\pi_5(ecom) \in 0^*$ together denote that the environment can communicate before executing this process. $trs' = trs^\frown envir$ and $\pi_3(envir) \in 0^*$ mean that the environment can change the (global) scope graph prior to performing this process. 0^* is a sequence of several 0s, meaning that the environment can do any number of actions.

(2) Output: We now study the denotational semantics of the output action, which has three branches, illustrated in Fig. 5.

$$\mathbf{beh}(_n[\phi \bowtie c^{\Delta T}!\langle m \rangle \, \mathbf{then} \, P \, \mathbf{else} \, Q]_{T_f}^f) =_{df}$$

$$\begin{pmatrix} \left(\begin{pmatrix} \mathbf{beh}(\mathbf{Mob}(f, T_f) \& \tau@(n, f', T_{f'})); \\ \mathbf{beh}(_n[\phi \bowtie c^{\Delta T}!\langle m \rangle \, \mathbf{then} \, P \, \mathbf{else} \, Q]_{T_{f'}}^{f'}) \end{pmatrix} \vee \quad (a) \\ \mathbf{beh}(c!\langle m \rangle@(n, f, T_f)); \mathbf{beh}(_n[\phi \bowtie P]_{T_f}^f) \quad (b) \end{pmatrix} \vee \quad (2.1) \\ \exists t' \in (0 \dots T) \bullet \mathbf{beh}(\#t'); \\ \left(\begin{pmatrix} \mathbf{beh}(\mathbf{Mob}(f, T_f) \& \tau@(n, f', T_{f'})); \\ \mathbf{beh}(_n[\phi \bowtie c^{\Delta T - t'}!\langle m \rangle \, \mathbf{then} \, P \, \mathbf{else} \, Q]_{T_{f'}}^{f'}) \end{pmatrix} \vee \quad (c) \\ \left(\mathbf{beh}(c!\langle m \rangle@(n, f, T_f)); \mathbf{beh}(_n[\phi \bowtie P]_{T_f}^f) \right) \quad (d) \end{pmatrix} \vee \quad (2.2) \\ \mathbf{beh}(\#T); \begin{pmatrix} \mathbf{beh}(\tau@(n, f', T_{f'})); \mathbf{beh}(_n[\phi \bowtie Q]_{T_{f'}}^{f'}) \quad (e) \\ \lhd \mathbf{Mob}(f, T_f) \rhd \\ \mathbf{beh}(\tau@(n, f, T_f)); \mathbf{beh}(_n[\phi \bowtie Q]_{T_f}^f) \quad (f) \end{pmatrix} \quad (2.3) \end{pmatrix}$$

where $(f', T_{f'}) = \Omega(f(time), time)$ and $T_{f'} > time$.

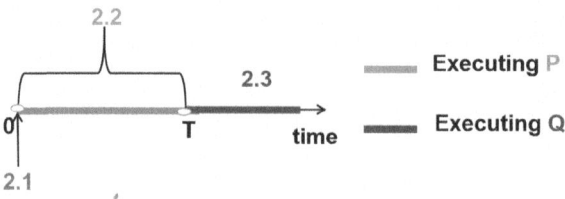

Fig. 5. The behavior of output action

- The first branch (i.e., formula **(2.1)**) shows that at the triggering time, the mobility function is replaced, or the output action occurs.
  (a) In formula **(a)**, $\mathbf{beh}(\mathbf{Mob}(f, T_f)\&\tau@(n, f', T_{f'}))$ denotes that the condition of replacing the mobility function (i.e., $\mathbf{Mob}(f, T_f)$ in page 11) is satisfied at the beginning, so that the mobility function f is replaced with f'. This replacement is seen as a silent action. After that, the process continues under the control of the new mobility function pair $(f', T_{f'})$.
  (b) In formula **(b)**, $\mathbf{beh}(c!\langle m \rangle@(n, f, T_f))$ depicts the behavior of the output command, showing that node n broadcasts a message m via channel c at the activeness time, where the current mobility function pair of n is (f, T_f). The following behavior is $\mathbf{beh}(_n[\phi \bowtie P]_{T_f}^f)$.
- In the second branch (i.e., formula **(2.2)**), the replacement of the mobility function or the execution of the output command occurs after t' time units.
- The last branch (i.e., formula **(2.3)**) denotes that this output command does not happen within T time units. After T time units, depending on whether the mobility function f needs to be changed, the following behavior can be described as $\mathbf{beh}(_n[\phi \bowtie Q]_{T_{f'}}^{f'})$ or $\mathbf{beh}(_n[\phi \bowtie Q]_{T_f}^f)$.

$\mathbf{Mob}(f, T_f)$ decides whether to replace a mobility function, which takes the pair (f, T_f) as input and returns a Boolean result. If the current time $time$ is equal to T_f (i.e., $time = T_f$), or f is allowed to be changed arbitrarily (i.e., $T_f = \Diamond$), or the node reaches the boundary under the control of f (i.e., $f(time) \in \mathbf{bd}(A)$), then the current mobility function pair (i.e., (f, T_f)) should be replaced with the new pair (i.e., $(f', T_{f'})$) generated by the mobility model $\Omega(f(time), time)$. Here, $T_{f'} > time$ is used to avoid meaningless substitutions.

$$\mathbf{Mob}(f, T_f) =_{df} \left(T_f = time \vee T_f = \Diamond \vee f(time) \in \mathbf{bd}(A) \right)$$

Next, we explore $\mathbf{beh}(c!\langle m \rangle@(n, f, T_f))$, which is executed instantaneously, so $\blacktriangle = 0$. To record this execution, a communication snapshot $(time', \{(n, f(time'))\}, \pi_2(last(trs')), c.m, 1)$ is added to the end of the trace trc, where $\pi_2(last(trs'))$ is the current scope graph when this output action occurs. Before executing this action, the environment can perform communication actions (described by $ecom$) and change the scope graph (shown by $envir$).

$$\mathbf{beh}(c!\langle m \rangle@(n, f, T_f)) =_{df}$$
$$\mathcal{H} \begin{pmatrix} st' = ter \wedge \blacktriangle = 0 \wedge mf' = mf \wedge trs' = trs^\frown envir \wedge \pi_3(envir) \in 0^* \wedge \\ trc' = trc^\frown ecom^\frown \langle\langle (time', \{(n, f(time'))\}, \pi_2(last(trs')), c.m, 1) \rangle \\ \wedge \pi_4(ecom) \in \tau^* \wedge \pi_5(ecom) \in 0^* \end{pmatrix}$$

$$\mathbf{beh}(\#t) =_{df} \mathcal{H} \begin{pmatrix} \left(\left(st' = wait \wedge \blacktriangle < t \right) \vee \left(st' = ter \wedge \blacktriangle = t \right) \right) \wedge \\ trc' = trc^\frown ecom \wedge \pi_4(ecom) \in \tau^* \wedge \pi_5(ecom) \in 0^* \wedge \\ trs' = trs^\frown envir \wedge \pi_3(envir) \in 0^* \end{pmatrix}$$

(3) Input: Similar to the output command, the denotational semantics of the input action also has three branches (i.e., formulas **(3.1)**, **(3.2)**, and **(3.3)**), where $Type(c)$ represents the type of messages transmitted in channel c.

$$\mathbf{beh}(_n[\phi \bowtie c^{\Delta T}?\langle x\rangle \,\mathbf{then}\, P \,\mathbf{else}\, Q]^f_{T_f}) =_{df}$$

$$
\left(
\begin{array}{l}
\left(
\left(
\begin{array}{l}
\mathbf{beh}(\mathbf{Mob}(f,T_f)\&\tau@(n,f',T_{f'}));\\
\mathbf{beh}(_n[\phi \bowtie c^{\Delta T}?\langle x\rangle \,\mathbf{then}\, P \,\mathbf{else}\, Q]^{f'}_{T_{f'}})
\end{array}
\right) \vee
\right.\\
\left.\;\;\exists m \in Type(c) \bullet \mathbf{beh}(c^{\Delta T}?\langle m\rangle@(n,f,T_f)); \mathbf{beh}(_n[\phi \bowtie P[m/x]]^f_{T_f})\right) \quad \vee \quad (3.1)\\[6pt]
\exists t' \in (0\dots T) \bullet \mathbf{beh}(\#t');\\
\left(
\begin{array}{l}
\mathbf{beh}(\mathbf{Mob}(f,T_f)\&\tau@(n,f',T_{f'}));\\
\mathbf{beh}(_n[\phi \bowtie c^{\Delta T-t'}?\langle x\rangle \,\mathbf{then}\, P \,\mathbf{else}\, Q]^{f'}_{T_{f'}})
\end{array}
\right) \vee \\
\left(
\begin{array}{l}
\exists m \in Type(c) \bullet \mathbf{beh}(c^{\Delta T}?\langle m\rangle@(n,f,T_f));\\
\mathbf{beh}(_n[\phi \bowtie P[m/x]]^f_{T_f})
\end{array}
\right) \quad \vee \qquad\qquad (3.2)\\[6pt]
\mathbf{beh}(\#T);\;
\left(
\begin{array}{l}
\mathbf{beh}(\tau@(n,f',T_{f'})); \mathbf{beh}(_n[\phi \bowtie Q]^{f'}_{T_{f'}})\\
\lhd \mathbf{Mob}(f,T_f)\rhd\\
\mathbf{beh}(\tau@(n,f,T_f)); \mathbf{beh}(_n[\phi \bowtie Q]^f_{T_f})
\end{array}
\right) \qquad\qquad (3.3)
\end{array}
\right)
$$

We explore the behavior of the input statement $\mathbf{beh}(c^{\Delta T}?\langle m\rangle@(n,f,T_f))$. This input action is performed instantaneously. Unlike the output command, the execution of input actions extends not only trc but also trs. In detail, a communication snapshot $(time', \{(n, f(time'))\}, last(trs^\frown envir), c.m, 2)$ is added to the end of trc to record the execution of this input action. Meanwhile, the current node n is absorbed into the scope of m, changing the scope graph. A scope snapshot $(time', S[(S(m)\cup\{n\})/S(m)], 1)$ expands trs, where $S[(S(m)\cup\{n\})/S(m)]$ enlarges the scope of m (i.e., $S(m)$) by absorbing n. To distinguish two new snapshots, we represent them with two shades of gray.

$$\mathbf{beh}(c^{\Delta T}?\langle m\rangle@(n,f,T_f)) =_{df}$$

$$
\mathcal{H}
\left(
\begin{array}{l}
st' = ter \wedge \blacktriangle = 0 \wedge mf' = mf \wedge\\
trc' = trc^\frown ecom^\frown \langle(time', \{(n, f(time'))\}, last(trs^\frown envir), c.m, 2)\rangle \;\wedge\\
\pi_5(ecom) \in 0^* \wedge S = \pi_2(last(trs^\frown envir)) \wedge\\
\pi_3(envir) \in 0^* \wedge trs' = trs^\frown envir^\frown \langle(time', S[(S(m)\cup\{n\})/S(m)], 1)\rangle
\end{array}
\right)
$$

4.4 Parallel Composition

Now, we explore the behavior of two parallel networks, where a network might be a single node or the parallel composition of multiple nodes. The denotational semantics for the parallel composition $N_1 \parallel N_2$ is shown below.

$$\mathbf{beh}(N_1 \parallel N_2) =_{df} \left(\begin{array}{ll} \exists st_1, st_1', st_2, st_2', time_1, time_1', time_2, time_2', \\ \quad trc_1, trc_1', trc_2, trc_2', trs_1, trs_1', trs_2, trs_2' \bullet \\ \quad st_1 = st_2 = st \wedge time_1 = time_2 = time\wedge \\ \quad trc_1 = trc_2 = trc \wedge trs_1 = trs_2 = trs \wedge & (1) \\ \mathbf{beh}(N_1)[st_1, st_1', time_1, time_1', trc_1, trc_1', trs_1, trs_1'/ \\ \quad st, st', time, time', trc, trc', trs, trs'] \wedge & (2) \\ \mathbf{beh}(N_2)[st_2, st_2', time_2, time_2', trc_2, trc_2', trs_2, trs_2'/ \\ \quad st, st', time, time', trc, trc', trs, trs'] \wedge & (3) \\ \mathbf{Merge} & (4) \end{array} \right)$$

Formula (1) denotes that two parallel components have the same initial value of the state, time, and traces. Formulas (2) and (3) display the independent behavior of two components. To conveniently combine the behavior, formulas (2) and (3) first rename their variables. In formula (4), **Merge** is presented to merge states, termination time, and the (communication and scope) traces.

$$\mathbf{Merge} =_{df} \left(\begin{array}{ll} ((st_1' = ter \wedge st_2' = ter) \Rightarrow st' = ter)\wedge \\ ((st_1' = div \vee st_2' = div) \Rightarrow st' = div)\wedge \\ \left(\begin{array}{l} (st_1' = wait \wedge st_2' \neq div)\vee \\ (st_1' \neq div \wedge st_2' = wait) \end{array} \right) \Rightarrow st' = wait) \wedge & \textbf{(a)} \\ time' = max(time_1', time_2') \wedge & \textbf{(b)} \\ \exists u \in (trc_1' - trc_1) \parallel (trc_2' - trc_2) \bullet trc' = trc^\frown u\wedge \\ \exists v \in (trs_1' - trs_1) \parallel (trs_2' - trs_2) \bullet trs' = trs^\frown v & \textbf{(c)} \end{array} \right)$$

Formula (a) signals the final state of this parallel composition, where the priorities of the three types of program states can be expressed as $div > wait > ter$. The formula (b) denotes that the termination time of the parallel composition is the maximum terminal time of N_1 and N_2. The formula (c) merges the traces of two components by using the rules proposed below.

We use tr_1 and tr_2 to stand for the (communication or scope) traces of N_1 and N_2, respectively. Next, we present some rules for merging traces, and only traces of the same type can be merged.

- **(Rule 1)** $\epsilon \parallel \epsilon =_{df} \{\epsilon\}$ • **(Rule 2)** $tr_1 \parallel \epsilon =_{df} \{tr_1\}$
- **(Rule 3)** $tr_1 \parallel tr_2 =_{df} tr_2 \parallel tr_1$
- **(Rule 4)** To merge communication traces (trc_3 and trc_4), we first give some notations to extract elements from their first snapshots (i.e., $\mathbf{head}(trc_3)$ and $\mathbf{head}(trc_4)$). Next, we call the entities corresponding to trc_3 and trc_4 the first and second components, respectively.

$$t_1 = \pi_1(\mathbf{head}(trc_3)), \quad idl_1 = \pi_2(\mathbf{head}(trc_3)), \quad S_1 = \pi_3(\mathbf{head}(trc_3)),$$
$$o_1 = \pi_4(\mathbf{head}(trc_3)), \quad \zeta_1 = \pi_5(\mathbf{head}(trc_3)),$$
$$t_2 = \pi_1(\mathbf{head}(trc_4)), \quad idl_2 = \pi_2(\mathbf{head}(trc_4)), \quad S_2 = \pi_3(\mathbf{head}(trc_4)),$$
$$o_2 = \pi_4(\mathbf{head}(trc_4)), \quad \zeta_2 = \pi_5(\mathbf{head}(trc_4))$$

$$trc_3 \parallel trc_4 =_{df} \left(\left(\left(\left(\left(\left(\begin{array}{c} (T_1 \lhd Com_1 \rhd \emptyset) \\ \lhd \zeta_1 = 1 \rhd \\ (T_2 \lhd Com_2 \rhd \emptyset) \\ \lhd \zeta_1 = 1 \lor \zeta_2 = 1 \rhd T_3 \end{array} \right) \right) \lhd o_1 = o_2 \rhd \emptyset \right) \lhd \zeta_2 \neq 0 \rhd T' \right) \lhd \zeta_1 \neq 0 \rhd \\ (T'' \lhd \zeta_2 \neq 0 \rhd T''') \right) \lhd t_1 = t_2 \rhd \emptyset \right),$$

where,

$$Com_1 =_{df} \left(\begin{array}{c} \exists (n_2, l_2) \in idl_2 \bullet \{(n_1, l_1)\} = idl_1 \land \\ \mathbf{Dis}(l_1, l_2) \leq \mathbf{Rng}(\pi_1(o_1)) \land n_2 \in S_2(\pi_1(o_1)) \end{array} \right),$$

$$Com_2 =_{df} \left(\begin{array}{c} \exists (n_1, l_1) \in idl_1 \bullet \{(n_2, l_2)\} = idl_2 \land \\ \mathbf{Dis}(l_1, l_2) \leq \mathbf{Rng}(\pi_1(o_2)) \land n_1 \in S_1(\pi_1(o_2)) \end{array} \right),$$

$T' =_{df} \mathbf{head}(trc_3)^\frown (\mathbf{tail}(trc_3) \parallel \mathbf{tail}(trc_4))$,

$T'' =_{df} \mathbf{head}(trc_4)^\frown (\mathbf{tail}(trc_3) \parallel \mathbf{tail}(trc_4))$,

$T''' =_{df} \mathbf{head}(trc_3)^\frown (\mathbf{tail}(trc_3) \parallel \mathbf{tail}(trc_4)) \cup \mathbf{head}(trc_4)^\frown (\mathbf{tail}(trc_3) \parallel \mathbf{tail}(trc_4))$,

$T_1 =_{df} \langle (t_1, idl_1, S, o_1, 1) \rangle ^\frown (\mathbf{tail}(trc_3) \parallel \mathbf{tail}(trc_4))$,

$T_2 =_{df} \langle (t_2, idl_2, S, o_2, 1) \rangle ^\frown (\mathbf{tail}(trc_3) \parallel \mathbf{tail}(trc_4))$,

$T_3 =_{df} \langle (t_1, idl_1 \cup idl_2, S, o_1, 2) \rangle ^\frown (\mathbf{tail}(trc_3) \parallel \mathbf{tail}(trc_4))$.

S is the combination of S_1 and S_2, defined as follows.

$$S(c) =_{df} \begin{cases} S_1(c) \cup S_2(c), & \text{if } c \in Chan(S_1) \cap Chan(S_2). \\ S_1(c), & \text{if } c \in Chan(S_1) \land c \notin Chan(S_2). \\ S_2(c), & \text{otherwise.} \end{cases}$$

where c stands for any channel of S_1 and S_2, i.e., $\forall c \in Chan(S_1) \cup Chan(S_2)$. $\mathbf{Dis}(\overrightarrow{l}, \overrightarrow{l_1}) \leq \mathbf{Rng}(c)$ denotes that the distance between $\overrightarrow{l}$ and $\overrightarrow{l_1}$ is within the communication range of channel c. The details of this rule are as follow (Fig. 6).

▲ **Step 1:** $t_1 = t_2$ means that the time recorded in the snapshots of the traces of two parallel components must be the same. We then go to **Step 2** for further exploration. Otherwise, the merged trace is an empty set (i.e., $\emptyset$).
▲ **Step 2:** If $\zeta_1 \neq 0$ is false, o_1 is an unrelated action (occurring in the environment) from the view of the first component. Next, we switch to **Step 3**. Otherwise, we go to **Step 4**.
▲ **Step 3:** If $\zeta_2 \neq 0$ is further invalid, the second entity is also a bystander of the action o_2. We then arbitrarily choose one snapshot (i.e., $\mathbf{head}(trc_3)$ or $\mathbf{head}(trc_4)$) and put it at the end of the merged trace, described as T'''. Otherwise, if $\zeta_1 = 0$ and $\zeta_2 \neq 0$, we extend the merged trace with the snapshot $\mathbf{head}(trc_3)$, shown as T''.
▲ **Step 4:** From **Step 2**, we get that $\zeta_1 \neq 0$ is true, meaning that the first component itself does action o_1. If $\zeta_2 \neq 0$ is further unsatisfied, we enlarge

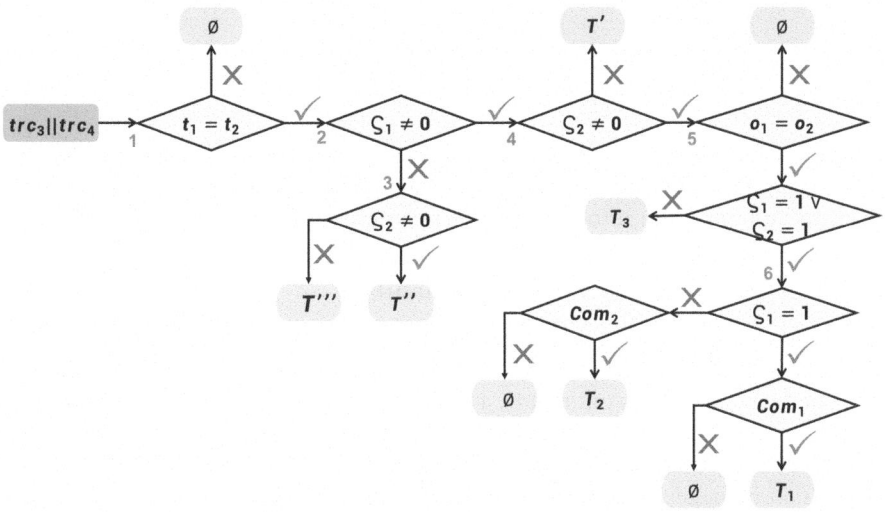

Fig. 6. The explanation of **Rule 4**

the merged trace with **head**(trc_3) as T'. If $\zeta_1 \neq 0 \wedge \zeta_2 \neq 0$ is valid, two components are both participants, further addressed by **Step 5**.

▲ **Step 5:** $o_1 = o_2$ requires that the communication actions recorded in the snapshots of the two components should be the same, if they are both participants (i.e., $\zeta_1 \neq 0 \wedge \zeta_2 \neq 0$). If $\zeta_1 = 1 \vee \zeta_2 = 1$ is further false, two components are both receivers, and then the integrated snapshot $(t_1, idl_1 \cup idl_2, S, o_1, 2)$ is added to the end of the merged trace, detailed as T_3. Otherwise, $\zeta_1 = 1 \vee \zeta_2 = 1$ is true, meaning that one of the two components is the sender, and another one is the receiver, handled by **Step 6**.

▲ **Step 6:** If $\zeta_1 = 1$, the first component is the sender. If the communication condition Com_1 is further satisfied, we extend the merged trace with $(t_1, idl_1, S, o_1, 1)$. Otherwise, the merged trace is an empty set. If $\zeta_1 \neq 1$, the second component is the sender, which can be treated similarly.

- **(Rule 5)** We now merge two nonempty scope traces trs_3 and trs_4, with the following conditions. First, $t_1 = t_2$ and $S_1' = S_2'$ together state that the time and the scope graph recorded in the snapshots of the two scope traces should be the same. In addition, $(u_1 + u_2) <= 1$ requires that any modification of the scope graph by the parallel composition is actually implemented by at most one of its components, not both components together. If the above conditions are satisfied, the snapshot $(t_1, S_1', u_1 + u_2)$ is added to the merged trace. Otherwise, the merged trace is an empty set (i.e., $\emptyset$).

$$t_1 = \pi_1(\mathbf{head}(trs_3)), \quad S_1' = \pi_2(\mathbf{head}(trs_3)), \quad u_1 = \pi_3(\mathbf{head}(trs_3))$$
$$t_2 = \pi_1(\mathbf{head}(trs_4)), \quad S_2' = \pi_2(\mathbf{head}(trs_4)), \quad u_2 = \pi_3(\mathbf{head}(trs_4))$$

$$trs_3 \parallel trs_4 =_{df} \left(\begin{array}{c} \langle(t_1, S_1', u_1 + u_2)\rangle ^\frown (\mathbf{tail}(trs_3) \parallel \mathbf{tail}(trs_4)) \\ \lhd t_1 = t_2 \wedge S_1' = S_2' \wedge (u_1 + u_2) <= 1 \rhd \emptyset \end{array} \right)$$

5   Algebraic Semantics

We present the algebraic laws for the SMrCaIT calculus, especially laws for the parallel composition of two guarded choices. Using these laws, we can convert any SMrCaIT program into a unified form (a guarded choice form).

5.1   Algebraic Laws of Basic Commands

We introduce the algebraic laws of basic commands in the SMrCaIT calculus, employing laws of the output command as an illustration. We omit similar algebraic laws for other commands. For some commands, such as **Output** and **Input**, two distinct algebraic laws exist based on different time intervals, where timers are either 0 or greater than 0. We previously introduced $\mathbf{Mob}(f, T_f)$ (see page 11) to manage mobility function replacements. Here, we use variable *now* to track the current time, which is equivalent to the *time* in $\mathbf{Mob}(f, T_f)$. For instance, if f and T_f are to be substituted at t_0 (initial time), *now* becomes t_0.

- **(Output0)** $_n[\phi \bowtie c^{\Delta 0}!\langle m \rangle \text{ then } P \text{ else } Q]^f_{T_f} =_n [\phi \bowtie Q]^f_{T_f}$

When the timer of the output statement reduces to 0, process Q starts to execute immediately. Law **(Output0)** reflects the case.

- **(Output1)** $_n[\phi \bowtie c^{\Delta T}!\langle m \rangle \text{ then } P \text{ else } Q]^f_{T_f}$

$$= \left(\begin{array}{l} \left(\mathbf{Mob}(f, T_f) \& \tau@(n, f', T_{f'}) \rightarrow_n [\phi \bowtie c^{\Delta T}!\langle m \rangle \text{ then } P \text{ else } Q]^{f'}_{T_{f'}} \right) \\ \| \ (c!\langle m \rangle @(n, f, T_f) \rightarrow_n [\phi \bowtie P]^f_{T_f}) \end{array} \right)$$

$$\oplus \exists t' \in (0 \cdots T) \bullet \#t' \rightarrow \left(\begin{array}{l} \left(\begin{array}{l} \mathbf{Mob}(f, T_f) \& \tau@(n, f', T_{f'}) \rightarrow \\ {}_n[\phi \bowtie c^{\Delta T - t'}!\langle m \rangle \text{ then } P \text{ else } Q]^{f'}_{T_{f'}} \end{array} \right) \\ \| \ (c!\langle m \rangle @(n, f, T_f) \rightarrow_n [\phi \bowtie P]^f_{T_f}) \end{array} \right)$$

$$\oplus \#T \rightarrow \left(\begin{array}{l} \left(\mathbf{Mob}(f, T_f) \& \tau@(n, f', T_{f'}) \rightarrow_n [\phi \bowtie Q]^{f'}_{T_{f'}} \right) \\ \| \ \left(\neg\mathbf{Mob}(f, T_f) \& \tau@(n, f, T_f) \rightarrow_n [\phi \bowtie Q]^f_{T_f} \right) \end{array} \right)$$

where $(f', T_{f'}) = \Omega(f(now), now)$ and $T_{f'} > now$.

(1) At the beginning of this process, the mobility function needs to be replaced, or this output action is executed.

(2) The replacement of the mobility function or this output action occurs after $t'(t' \in (0 \cdots T))$ time units from the activeness time of this process.

(3) During delaying T time units, this output action has not been executed. Two possibilities correspond to whether the mobility function needs to be changed, respectively.

5.2 Algebraic Laws of Parallel Composition

We now study the algebraic laws of parallel composition, focusing on the parallel composition of guarded choices, as shown in Table 2. We explain the detail by taking **Par-4-2** as an example.

Table 2. Parallel composition of two guarded choices

	Instantaneous	Delay	Hybrid
Instantaneous	(Par-4-1), (Par-4-2)	(Par-5)	(Par-6)
Delay		(Par-7)	(Par-8)
Hybrid			(Par-9-1), (Par-9-2)

- **(Par-4-2)** Let $N = N_1 \| N_2$ $\qquad$ $M = M_1 \| M_2$

$$N_1 = \|_{i \in I} \{g_i \to N_i\} \qquad N_2 = \|_{w \in W} \{c_w!\langle m_w\rangle @(n_w, f_w, T_{f_w}) \to N'_w\}$$
$$M_1 = \|_{j \in J} \{h_j \to M_j\} \qquad M_2 = \|_{w \in W} \{c_w?\langle x_w\rangle @(n'_w, f'_w, T_{f'_w}) \to M'_w\}$$

then $N \| M = \|_{i \in I} \{g_i \to N_i \| M\}$

$\qquad \| \|_{j \in J} \{h_i \to N \| M_j\}$

$\qquad \| \|_{w \in W} \{ c_w \cdot [m_w/x_w]@((n_w, f_w, T_{f_w}), (n'_w, f'_w, T_{f'_w})) \to N'_w \| M'_w \}$

(Par-4-2) formalizes the parallel composition having communications between two instantaneous guarded choice components (e.g., N_2 and M_2). Assume that there is no communication between N_1 and M_1, and the communication condition (i.e., $\mathbf{Dis}(f_w(now), f'_w(now)) \leq \mathbf{Rng}(c_w)$) holds, where *now* is the current time when this process is triggered. Then, we can have the algebraic description of $N \| M$ as above. There are three possibilities for the first action of $N \| M$, i.e., g_i, h_j or communication action $c_w.[m_w/x_w]@((n_w, f_w, T_{f_w}), (n'_w, f'_w, T_{f'_w}))$.

5.3 Algebraic Laws of Channel Restriction and Scope Extrusion

Based on the above algebraic laws, we can convert any parallel program without restricted channels into a guarded choice form. We present law **(Par-10)** to implement channel restriction. Further, we give laws **(Par-11)**, **(Par-12)**, and **(Par-13)** to handle scope extrusion.

- **(Par-10)** The notion of channel restriction binds a channel into a specific scope. For example, $(vc)M$ means that communications occurring on c are invisible for nodes outside of M. This law replaces output actions and synchronous communication actions happening on c (i.e., $c!\langle m\rangle @(n, f, T_f)$ and $c.[m/x]@((n, f\ T_f), (n', f', T_{f'})))$ with the silent action (i.e., $true \& \tau @(n, f, T_f)$). Figure 7 shows how this law deals with an output action, where channels w and c are different, and N is a node.

If $M = \|_{i \in I}\{g_i \to M_i\}$, **then** $(vc)M = \|_{i \in I}\{(vc)g_i \to (vc)M_i\}$.
If $M = \#t \to M'$, **then** $(vc)M = \#t \to (vc)M'$.
If $M = \|_{i \in I}\{g_i \to M_i\}$, **then** $(vc)M = \|_{i \in I}\{(vc)g_i \to (vc)M_i\}$,

$$\oplus \#t' \to M' \qquad\qquad \oplus \#t' \to (vc)M'$$

$$\oplus \#t \to M'' \qquad\qquad \oplus \#t \to (vc)M'',$$

where $(vc)g_i = \begin{cases} true\&\tau@(n,f,T_f), & \text{if } g_i \in ComA_c. \\ g_i, & \text{otherwise.} \end{cases}$

$ComA_c =_{df} \{c!\langle m \rangle @(n,f,T_f),\ c.[m/x]@((n,f,T_f),(n',f',T_{f'}))\}.$

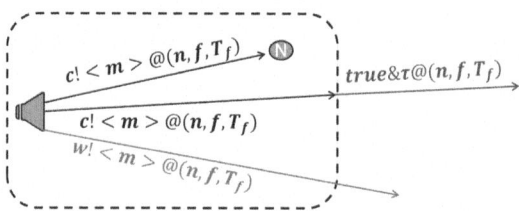

Fig. 7. Scope of c

Next, we introduce algebraic laws for scope extrusion, including. **(Par-11)**, **(Par-12)**, and **(Par-13)**. Law **(Par-11)** is responsible for the extrusion of restricted names. Law **(Par-12)** takes care of communicating restricted names via broadcast channels. Law **(Par-13)** signals the completion of a broadcast session. Due to the page limit, we only give **(Par-12)** as an example here.

- **(Par-11)** If $HF(N) = \boxed{c!\langle \tilde{n} \rangle @(n,f,T_f)} \to HF(N')$ **and** $c \neq \tilde{n}$,

  then $HF((v\tilde{n})N) = \boxed{(v\tilde{n})c!\langle \tilde{n} \rangle @(n,f,T_f)} \to HF(N')$.

- **(Par-12)** If $HF(N) = \boxed{(v\tilde{n})c!\langle \tilde{n} \rangle @(n,f,T_f)} \to HF(N')$

  $HF(N_1) = c?\langle x \rangle @(n',f',T_{f'}) \to HF(N_1')$,

  $\mathbf{Dis}(f(now), f'(now)) \leq \mathbf{Rng}(c)$, **and** $c \neq \tilde{n}$,

  then $HF(N \parallel N_1) = \boxed{(v\tilde{n})c.[\tilde{n}/x]@((n,f,T_f),(n',f',T_{f'}))}$

  $\to HF(N' \parallel N_1')$.

- **(Par-13)** If $HF(N) = \boxed{(v\tilde{m})c!\langle \tilde{m} \rangle @(n,f,T_f)} \to HF(N')$,

  then $HF((vc)N) = \boxed{true\&\tau@(n,f,T_f)} \to HF((vc)(v\tilde{m})N')$.

6   Conclusion and Future Work

This paper explored the denotational and algebraic semantics of SMrCaIT using the UTP approach. Our denotational semantics utilizes communication traces and scope traces to record the occurrence of communication actions with timeouts and the update of the scope of each name, respectively. This allows us to employ the denotational approach for achieving message communication between parallel components and ensure communication security based on channel restrictions and scope extension. In addition, we proposed the algebraic laws for SMrCaIT, particularly for parallel composition, channel restriction, and scope extrusion. With these laws, any SMrCaIT program can be transformed into a unified form (i.e., the guarded choice form).

In the future, we will study the deductive semantics of the SMrCaIT calculus via Hoare Logic [21]. We will further discuss the semantics linking theory of the SMrCaIT calculus and try to implement its semantics in suitable tools like Coq [22], Isabelle/HOL [23], or PVS [24].

Acknowledgements. This work was partially supported by the National Key Research and Development Program of China (No. 2022YFB3305102), the National Natural Science Foundation of China (No. 62032024), the "Digital Silk Road" Shanghai International Joint Lab of Trustworthy Intelligent Software (No. 22510750100), and Shanghai Trusted Industry Internet Software Collaborative Innovation Center.

A   Further Explanation of SMrCaIT

In Sect. 3.3 (page 5), we have given the SMrCaIT calculus and explained its process level. Here, we further introduce its message level and network level.

Message level:

As a successor of the applied pi calculus [12], SMrCaIT allows messages to include not only atomic (or pure) names but also values constructed from names and functions. By embedding names into the value space, SMrCaIT implements the connection between value-passing communications and name-passing communications.

(1) $\tilde{n}$ means that messages can be atomic (or pure) names.
(2) x is a variable, denoting that messages can be values of variables.
(3) Σ is a finite set of function symbols, such as encryption, decryption, pairing, etc. Usually, each function symbol has an arity, except for constant function symbols. Let g range over the functions of Σ, and l match the arity of g. $g(m_1, \cdots, m_l)$ indicates that messages can also be values constructed from messages (e.g., names) and functions.

Network level:

(1) 0 stands for an empty network.

(2) $_n[\phi \bowtie P]^f_{T_f}$ represents an IoT network node (e.g., a vehicle, a phone, or a robot), where n is the node ID, P is the internal process, f and T_f are its mobility function and the timeout of f, respectively. $f(t)$ stands for the current location of node n at time t. Additionally, the physical interface ϕ is a mapping from sensors or actuators to values. For the security of nodes, each physical interface is private to a node. Given a node $_n[\phi \bowtie P]^f_{T_f}$, the sensors in ϕ can be read only by the corresponding internal process P. Similarly, actuators belonging to ϕ can be modified only by P.

(3) $(\nu \tilde{n})N$ means that the name $\tilde{n}$ (e.g., a cryptographic key, a channel, or other secrets) is private to network N, where $(\nu c)N$ means that channel c is bound to N, and it is invisible to nodes outside N.

(4) $N \parallel N_1$ indicates that networks N and N_1 run in parallel.

References

1. Hoare, C.A.R., He, J.: Unifying Theories of Programming. Prentice Hall, London (1998)
2. Dunne, S., Stoddart, B. (eds.): UTP 2006. LNCS, vol. 4010. Springer, Heidelberg (2006). https://doi.org/10.1007/11768173
3. Bowen, J.P., Zhu, H. (eds.): UTP 2016. LNCS, vol. 10134. Springer, Cham (2017). https://doi.org/10.1007/978-3-319-52228-9
4. Liu, Z., Woodcock, J., Zhu, H. (eds.): Theories of Programming and Formal Methods. LNCS, vol. 8051. Springer, Heidelberg (2013). https://doi.org/10.1007/978-3-642-39698-4
5. Rayes, A., Salam, S.: Internet of Things from Hype to Reality. Springer, Cham (2022). https://doi.org/10.1007/978-3-030-90158-5
6. Zhou, H., Liu, B.W., Dong, P.P.: The Technology System Framework of the Internet of Things and Its Application Research in Agriculture. In: Li, D., Chen, Y. (eds.) CCTA 2011. IAICT, vol. 368, pp. 293–300. Springer, Heidelberg (2012). https://doi.org/10.1007/978-3-642-27281-3_35
7. Atzori, L., Iera, A., Morabito, G.: The internet of things: a survey. Comput. Netw. **54**(15), 2787–2805 (2010)
8. Nienhuis, K., Joannou, A., Bauereiss, T.: Rigorous engineering for hardware security: formal modelling and proof in the cheri design and implementation process. In: 2020 IEEE Symposium on Security and Privacy (SP), pp. 1003–1020. IEEE (2020)
9. Lanese, I., Bedogni, L., Di Felice, M.: Internet of things: a process calculus approach. In: Shin, S.Y., Maldonado, J.C. (eds.) Proceedings of the 28th Annual ACM Symposium on Applied Computing, SAC '13, Coimbra, Portugal, March 18-22, 2013, pp. 1339–1346. ACM (2013)
10. Bodei, C., Degano, P., Ferrari, G.-L., Galletta, L.: Where do your IoT ingredients come from? In: Lluch Lafuente, A., Proença, J. (eds.) COORDINATION 2016. LNCS, vol. 9686, pp. 35–50. Springer, Cham (2016). https://doi.org/10.1007/978-3-319-39519-7_3
11. Chen, N., Zhu, H.: A process calculus SMrCaIT for IoT. J. Softw. Evol. Process. **36**(5), e2595 (2024)
12. Abadi, M., Blanchet, B., Fournet, C.: The applied pi calculus: mobile values, new names, and secure communication. J. ACM **65**(1), 1:1–1:41 (2018)

13. Plotkin, G.D.: A structural approach to operational semantics. J. Log. Algebraic Methods Program. **60–61**, 17–139 (2004)
14. Stoy, J.E.: Foundations of denotational semantics. In: Bjøorner, D. (ed.) Abstract Software Specifications. LNCS, vol. 86, pp. 43–99. Springer, Heidelberg (1980). https://doi.org/10.1007/3-540-10007-5_35
15. Hoare, C.A.R., et al.: Laws of programming. Commun. ACM **30**(8), 672–686 (1987)
16. Shi, L., Zhao, Y., Liu, Y., Sun, J., Dong, J.S., Qin, S.: A UTP semantics for communicating processes with shared variables and its formal encoding in PVS. Formal Aspects Comput. **30**(3-4), 351–380 (2018)
17. Watt, D.A.: Programming Language Syntax and Semantics. Prentice Hall International Series in Computer Science. Prentice Hall, Landon (1991)
18. Camp, T., Boleng, J., Davies, V.: A survey of mobility models for ad hoc network research. Wirel. Commun. Mob. Comput. **2**(5), 483–502 (2002)
19. Godskesen, J.C., Nanz, S.: Mobility models and behavioural equivalence for wireless networks. In: Field, J., Vasconcelos, V.T. (eds.) COORDINATION 2009. LNCS, vol. 5521, pp. 106–122. Springer, Heidelberg (2009). https://doi.org/10.1007/978-3-642-02053-7_6
20. Abadi, M., Gordon, A.D.: A calculus for cryptographic protocols: the Spi calculus. Inf. Comput. **148**(1), 1–70 (1999)
21. Hoare, C.A.R.: An axiomatic basis for computer programming. Commun. ACM **12**(10), 576–580 (1969)
22. Huet, G., Kahn, G., Paulin-Mohring, C.: The coq proof assistant a tutorial. Rapport Technique, 178 (1997)
23. Paulson, L.C. (ed.): Isabelle. LNCS, vol. 828. Springer, Heidelberg (1994). https://doi.org/10.1007/BFb0030541
24. Owre, S., Rushby, J.M., Shankar, N.: PVS: A prototype verification system. In: Kapur, D. (ed.) CADE 1992. LNCS, vol. 607, pp. 748–752. Springer, Heidelberg (1992). https://doi.org/10.1007/3-540-55602-8_217

Specifying Fault-Tolerant Mixed-Criticality Scheduling

Alan Burns[1]($\boxtimes$) and Cliff B. Jones[2]

[1] Department of Computer Science, University of York, York, UK
alan.burns@york.ac.uk
[2] School of Computing, Newcastle University, Newcastle upon Tyne, UK

Abstract. This paper extends the ideas behind rely-guarantee conditions to cope with the specification of real-time schedulers that support Fixed Priority (FP) scheduling. The sporadic task model is considered in which tasks with defined minimum periods and worst-case execution times are assigned priorities; the shorter the period the higher the priority. At run-time the task with the highest priority executes preemptively. A Mixed-Criticality approach that partitions work between safety-critical event-triggered (ET) tasks and mission-critical time-triggered (TT) tasks is tackled. Previous work has considered faults arising from jobs executing for longer than expected; this chapter addresses arrival faults—run-time faults may occur when jobs from the same ET task arrive earlier than expected; the required fault-tolerant response is to compensate by executing the TT tasks less frequently. The specification is split over two phases, a Planning phase that confirms that the assumptions concerning the resource needs of the application can be managed on the chosen hardware platform and a run-time Scheduling phase whose specification combines rely-guarantee conditions, state-invariants and predicates to require that progress is made at a sufficient pace to ensure that all deadlines are met in both normal and fault-tolerant modes of operation. The scheduling phase is executed only if the Planning phase succeeds.

Keywords: real-time systems · mixed criticality scheduling · formal specification · rely-guarantee conditions · fault-tolerance

Tribute to Jim Woodcock

As a friend and colleague I have often benefited from the guidance and insight Jim has given me with regard to all things formal (and many things informal as well!). He is clearly an international ambassador for the broad topic of formal methods, and has made many contributions to the development of the art. As important, he has also dedicated considerable time and effort to the application and understanding of the role of formal methods in the broader disciplines of Software Engineering and Computer Science. My work with Jim has convinced me that he is a scholar, an educator, a leader, a researcher and a teacher. I am more than happy to mark his, on-going, achievements with a contribution to this volume. AB.

© The Author(s), under exclusive license to Springer Nature Switzerland AG 2024
S. Foster and A. Sampaio (Eds.): *The Application of Formal Methods*, LNCS 14900, pp. 22–42, 2024.
https://doi.org/10.1007/978-3-031-67114-2_2

1   Introduction

The essence of scheduling is to ensure that jobs (units of work) complete by their deadlines. There are a number of different scheduling approaches that can support real-time mixed-criticality systems. In [JB23], we addressed the EDF (Earliest Deadline First) protocol and focused on recovery from execution time overruns. In the current chapter, we tackle the more widely used Fixed Priority scheduling algorithm and consider recovery from faults that are caused by the environment generating too much work.

With FP (Fixed Priority) scheduling, the application must handle a bounded number of tasks. Each task gives rise to a sequence of jobs. During planning, priorities are assigned to the tasks and the run-time scheduler always executes the current job of the active task with the highest priority.

Jobs are released for execution by one of two mechanisms.

- Time-Triggered jobs are released by the passage of time. They are defined by their *period* and are thus also known as *periodic* tasks.
- The alternative is Event-Triggered jobs. They are released by actions from the system's environment which typically triggers the release of a job by an interrupt. This irregular release pattern leads to these Event-Triggered jobs being known as the outcome of executing *sporadic* tasks.

To bound the load on the system, which is necessary for a system to be able to guarantee that all deadlines are met, sporadic tasks must have a defined maximum rate at which the triggering events are assumed to occur. This is typically specified as a minimum interval between jobs from the same task and is also known as the *period* of the sporadic task.

With time-triggered jobs, the system itself controls their release. Hence, in the absence of a software error in the run-time dispatcher, these jobs will never arrive too early.[1] This is not the case with event-triggered jobs that are triggered from the environment and hence assumptions must be made about their intensity.

To enhance the robustness of schedulers, in 2007 Vestal's [Ves07] proposed that jobs should be distinguished by allocating them different "criticality" levels. If a fault occurs during execution, computation effort can then be allocated to the most critical jobs at the expense of the less critical ones.

Since 2007, a wide range of protocols has been proposed and published [BD17, BD22]. In the current chapter we adopt the elastic task model [BLA98, SZ13, GOH18]: we assume that the event-triggered jobs are all concerned with emergency events that have safety-critical implications. The related tasks have periods defined that reflect assumptions about the maximum intensity of these emergency events. However, the system's designer wants to tolerate safely a fault in the model of the environment that might occasionally cause jobs from the same task to execute closer together than the defined period of the task.

---

[1] But, for uniformity, time-triggered jobs can be viewed as being initiated by a clock interrupt.

The time-triggered jobs are, by comparison, only mission-critical. Their periods reflect optimal, energy efficient, performance but these periods can be extended to a certain degree with no safety implications – just a tolerable degradation of the system's performance.

This model leads to run-time behaviour that is moded: there is a Normal mode and a Fault-Tolerant mode. In the latter, the sporadic tasks are allowed to have shorter periods than in the Normal mode and the periodic tasks have longer periods. To support this model, a run-time scheduler must be derived and the characteristics of the application tested during the planning phase to ensure compliance. This is the focus of the remainder of the chapter.

Plan of Chapter

Section 2 outlines the rely-guarantee ideas and their evolution towards handling the scheduling application; brief notes on the notation used in the current chapter are also included. Section 3 discusses planning in general. The heart of the chapter (Sect. 4) formalises FP scheduling; Sect. 5 connects what is covered here on FP scheduling with our earlier paper on EDF. Some conclusions are drawn in Sect. 6.

2   Background

In an effort to make this chapter self contained, this section sets out background material; the discussion in [JB23] is slightly longer.[2]

2.1   Rely-Guarantee "thinking"

The objective of finding a top-down compositional way of formally developing concurrent programs led to specific decomposition rules in [Jon81] (shorter introductions can be found in [Jon83a, Jon83b]). Briefly the idea is to mirror the way in which pre and post conditions record assumptions and commitments about sequential programs but to extend the approach to concurrency. Given that interfering threads can change a shared state, rely conditions record state changes that a specified component must tolerate; commitments to stay within bounded interference are recorded in guarantee conditions. It is important to understand that execution of operations specified in this way is not atomic: the essence of the rely-guarantee approach is that execution of operations is concurrent and the specifications must define complementary assumptions and commitments about interactions.

The phrase "rely-guarantee thinking" marks a shift in which the systematic thinking about recording assumptions has been applied to systems that include components that are not being "designed"; for example, in [BHJ20]

---

[2] A chapter by Jones in the current volume says more about the background research on rely and guarantee conditions.

rely conditions are used to record assumptions about physical components of a CPS (Cyber-Physical System); extending the recording of tolerated and imposed interference to layers of rely and guarantee conditions is shown in [JB23] to admit the specification of fault tolerant behaviour.

There is no necessity to use the inference rule for parallel composition in the current chapter. It is only necessary to check that the rely assumptions of each component are matched by the commitments recorded in guarantee conditions of its sibling components. Section 5 employs data type invariants to express constraints that apply to multiple rely or guarantee conditions.

The original decision to write rely and guarantee as relations over states is expressively limiting in that it does not offer a way to require progress or "liveness". Although state assertions are normally associated with establishing "safety" properties (for more detail, see [Sch97]), the model in the current chapter has to include an internal clock to specify scheduling and this makes it possible to express the progress requirement in an invariant (see *inv-State* in Sect. 4.4).

2.2   Notes on Notation

This chapter makes some use of the notation associated with VDM [Jon90, ISO96, Daw91]; most of this should present no difficulty to readers familiar with other formal methods such as Z [WD96], Event-B [Abr10] or Alloy [Jac12] but this section reviews specific VDMisms used below.

VDM specifications are strongly typed and use is made of familiar mathematical types such as sets (X-**set**) and sequences (Y^*). Finite constructed functions which are sets of pairs with a many:one restriction are referred to as mappings and the type is defined by:

$$D \xrightarrow{m} R$$

The domain and range of a mapping can be determined by applying the appropriate operator:

$$\mathbf{dom} : (D \xrightarrow{m} R) \to D\text{-}\mathbf{set}$$
$$\mathbf{rng} : (D \xrightarrow{m} R) \to R\text{-}\mathbf{set}$$

Values of mappings can be enumerated:

$$\{2 \mapsto \mathbf{true}, 3 \mapsto \mathbf{true}, 4 \mapsto \mathbf{false}\}$$

or defined implicitly:

$$\{i \mapsto \textit{is-prime}(i) \mid i \in \{2..4\}\}$$

A useful update operator is:

$$\dagger : (D \xrightarrow{m} R) \times (D \xrightarrow{m} R) \to (D \xrightarrow{m} R)$$
$$\{2 \mapsto \mathbf{true}, 3 \mapsto \mathbf{true}, 4 \mapsto \mathbf{false}\} \dagger \{3 \mapsto \mathbf{false}, 5 \mapsto \mathbf{false}\} =$$
$$\{2 \mapsto \mathbf{true}, 3 \mapsto \mathbf{false}, 4 \mapsto \mathbf{false}, 5 \mapsto \mathbf{false}\}$$

An operator that selects only the pairs whose first elements are in the defined set is:

$$\lhd: D\text{-set} \times (D \xrightarrow{m} R) \to (D \xrightarrow{m} R)$$

A simple record type can be defined:

$$Example :: \quad a \; : \; TypeA$$
$$b \; : \; TypeB$$

This declaration implicitly defines the selectors:

$$a: Example \to TypeA$$
$$b: Example \to TypeB$$

and a constructor function:

$$mk\text{-}Example: TypeA \times TypeB \to Example$$

As adopted in programming languages such as ML [HMT88], constructor functions can be written as parameters (more generally, in "left-hand positions") to name the sub-components of an argument of the stated type; for example:

$$fn(mk\text{-}Example(a, b\text{-}name)) \quad \triangleq \quad \cdots a \cdots b\text{-}name \cdots$$

Records are often used to define states and states are changed by VDM "operations" whose definitions list the variables that they can access (their "frame") and whether access is read only (**rd**) or read and write (**wr**).

Operations are defined using pre/post/rely/guarantee clauses which are marked by keywords (e.g. *Job* in Fig. 4).

A useful extension of record type definitions notation is to define data type invariants that are predicates; for example:

$$PrimeStore :: \quad n \; : \; \mathbb{N}$$
$$p \; : \; \mathbb{B}$$

where

$$inv\text{-}PrimeStore(mk\text{-}PrimeStore(n, p)) \quad \triangleq \quad p \Leftrightarrow is\text{-}prime(n)$$

The invariant limits the type so that:

$$mk\text{-}PrimeStore(3, \textbf{true}) \in PrimeStore$$
$$mk\text{-}PrimeStore(3, \textbf{false}) \notin PrimeStore$$
$$mk\text{-}PrimeStore(4, \textbf{true}) \notin PrimeStore$$

3 Formalising Planning and Scheduling

In a recent paper [JB23], we proposed a formal framework to model the joint activities of first planning and then scheduling a real-time cyber physical system:

$$Passage\text{-}of\text{-}Time \; \|$$
$$Planning \; ; \; \{Scheduler \; \| \; Job_1 \; \| \; Job_2 \; \| \; \cdots \; \| \; Job_k\}$$

Recall that –as stated above– the operands of the parallel construct execute concurrently and any "atomic" behaviour of their sub-operations has to be defined in rely-guarantee conditions. In a real-time system the passage of time is always important. It is external to the system and cannot be controlled by the system but imposes challenging constraints on both the Planning and Scheduling phases. As identified in the research on time bands [BH10], the granularity of time that is at issue in the former process is orders of magnitude coarser than during run-time.

The entities that consume resource at run time are referred to as *Jobs*; the overall challenge of scheduling is to ensure that all jobs complete by their deadline. A pre-run-time *Planning* phase is concerned with determining the feasibility of both the resource demands of the jobs and their arrival patterns. The model adopted in this chapter assumes that all jobs have a known worst-case execution time (WCET, or C) and that jobs originating from the same task have a minimal arrival interval (T).

Planning is concerned with choosing (or designing) a specification of the run-time algorithm (*Scheduler*) that controls the execution of jobs and ensures that all deadlines are met. The previous paper [JB23] focussed on EDF (Earliest Deadline First) in which case *Planning* only has to establish that this algorithm will suffice even with the worst-case arrival pattern (*Planning* would abort if EDF cannot be proven to schedule the application load). In the current work, the more industrially common FP (Fixed Priority) scheduling scheme is addressed. Here *Planning* not only checks feasibility but also confirms a set of priorities that are to be used by the run-time *Scheduler*.

As well as the expected run-time behaviour, planning has to consider (hopefully rare) cases where safety-critical jobs arrive at more frequent intervals than is allowed for in the default planning assumptions. In our treatment of EDF [JB23], over-running expected worst-case execution time estimates was treated as a "fault" and resulted in a switch to a fault-tolerant mode being made to ensure that high-criticality tasks were allowed larger budgets to ensure they completed by their deadlines. A similar approach is adopted here to handle overly frequent job arrivals: if safety-critical event-triggered tasks are invoked too frequently, then a mode change occurs that reacts by reducing the frequency of the mission-critical time-triggered tasks.

As noted above the first activity within the planning phase is to develop a specification of the required scheduling behaviour. This specification has two functions:

1. It allows a schedulability test to be developed – this will enable the application's task set to be checked for compliance with the requirements of the scheduling approach.
2. It gives rise to the specification that will be used to develop the actual code of the run-time scheduler.

The test that enables an application to be checked for schedulability must be feasible, for example, have only (low) polynomial-time complexity. Also its implicit assertion – *if the test is passed, and the application behaves according to the constraints employed in the test, then at run-time all deadlines will be satisfied* – must be validated to the required level of assurance. For safety-critical application this implies that the test should be subject to mechanised proof.

For Fixed Priority Scheduling, response-time analysis is the usual method of determining if a collection of tasks and jobs will meet all their deadlines. For mixed-criticality systems, which typically involve more than one mode of operation there are a number of examples of this form of analysis [Ves07, DRRG10, BBD11, BD20, BD14, REC18, SDZZ16]. Unfortunately none of these scheduling schemes have been subject to mechanised proof, however Brandenburg and colleagues have demonstrated [BB20, MBB22, BVB+22] how assumptions, definitions and proofs can be mechanised and verified with the support of the Coq proof assistant. A particular feature of their research is a focus on readable proofs.

It is beyond the scope of the current chapter to derive and verify a schedulability test for the proposed mixed-criticality model. Nevertheless the assumptions on which such a test would be constructed are covered in detail. This includes the resource needs and arrival patterns of the jobs, but also incorporates estimates of key elements of the run-time overheads experienced by the implementation of the scheduler. Two such parameters are ρ, the maximum drift between external time and any internal computer clock, and τ the maximum time between a triggering event occurring at the interface to the system and the resulting job being released for execution.

4   Specifying the Fixed Priority Scheduler

In this section we develop the specification of the fixed-priority scheduler; the constant parameters defining each job are listed in Sect. 4.1. The assumptions concerning job arrivals are covered in Sect. 4.2. Each job, at run-time, has a static priority and the scheduler must always run the active job with the highest priority. The decision taken during Planning to have two modes of operation (Normal and Fault Tolerant) means that jobs have two, mode-specific, priorities (see Sect. 4.3). The parameters that define the dynamic state of the run-time system are introduced in Sect. 4.4; in Sect. 4.5 the relationship between external time and internal clock values is formalised. From these building blocks the specification of the scheduler and its methods can be developed, see Sect. 4.6. The theorem that states the correctness of this specification of scheduling is shown in Sect. 4.7.

4.1   Tasks Define Job Types

Each job has a type and it is assumed that a task handles jobs of the same type. Static information includes assumptions and commitments that are assumed in *Planning*—this data is contained in records:

$$JobType :: K \quad : \{\text{TT}, \text{ET}\}$$
$$D \quad : Duration$$
$$C \quad : Duration$$
$$T_N : Duration$$
$$T_F : Duration$$

where

$$inv\text{-}JobType(mk\text{-}JobType(k, d, c, tn, tf)) \quad \triangleq$$
$$(k = \text{TT} \ \Rightarrow \ tn \leq tf) \wedge (k = \text{ET} \ \Rightarrow \ tf \leq tn)$$

The K field of *JobType* indicates the kind of tasks (and thus their jobs): they are either time-triggered, TT, (also known as Periodic) or event-triggered, ET (also known as Sporadic). The D field of *JobType* contains the relative deadline of the job (the extent of time after the job arrives by which it should complete) and the C field contains the estimate of the maximum resource that will be consumed by the job (typically known as "worst case execution time", WCET). We assume that this value is obtained by measurement and includes the cost of executing the code of any preempting scheduler function.[3]

Finally, the T fields define the period of the time-triggered jobs or the minimum gap between sequential execution of the event-triggered jobs (of the same type). There are two T parameters to reflect the fact that the run-time system can be in one of two modes: in the Normal mode (N), jobs of the same type are separated by the duration T_N; if an event-triggered job arrives early (before T_N has passed, but after T_F) then a run-time mode change occurs to a fault-tolerant mode (F) and the inter-arrival intervals for each of the job types are modified to be defined by the T_F parameter. The modification to task periods is constrained by the invariant *inv-JobType*: event-triggered tasks can have shorter periods in the fault-tolerant mode; but to compensate time-triggered tasks are assigned longer periods. We assume that the relative deadline D remains the same in both modes; an alternative model in which D is also mode-specific would be a straightforward extension.

4.2 Job Arrival Assumptions

Within the *Planning* phase, assumptions are made about the occurrences of the jobs: specifically that there is a minimum interval of time between jobs from the same task. This is slightly complicated by there being two sets of T intervals depending on whether the mode is N or F.

Any specific run-time execution experiences a list of *Times* at which *Jobs* of each task arrive; this can be captured by $TaskId \rightarrow Time^*$; each such list is, of course, strictly monotonically increasing (as the passage of time is assumed to be one-directional). Whether a specific $TaskId \rightarrow Time^*$ respects the T assumptions is defined by the predicate:

---

[3] If the overheads of the scheduler were significant, they would need to be separately accounted for in the schedulability test developed and applied during Planning.

$$respects : \{N, F\} \times (\mathit{TaskId} \rightarrow \mathit{Time}^*) \times (\mathit{TaskId} \xrightarrow{m} \mathit{JobType}) \rightarrow \mathbb{B}$$

$$respects(\mathit{mode}, \mathit{occm}, \mathit{tkm}) \quad \triangleq$$
$$\forall ty \in \mathbf{dom}\ tkm \cdot \forall i \in \{1..(\mathbf{len}\ occm(ty) - 1)\} \cdot$$
$$(\mathit{mode} = N \;\Rightarrow\; tkm(ty).T_N \leq occm(ty)(i+1) - occm(ty)(i)) \wedge$$
$$(\mathit{mode} = F \;\Rightarrow\; tkm(ty).T_F \leq occm(ty)(i+1) - occm(ty)(i))$$

pre dom $occm = \mathbf{dom}\ tkm$

Any particular execution can be viewed as alternating phases in normal (N) or fault-tolerant (F) mode; whether T_N or T_F is used depends on *mode*: But for: $tkm \in (\mathit{TakId} \xrightarrow{m} \mathit{JobType})$, a given instance, say *occurrences* $\in (\mathit{TaskId} \rightarrow \mathit{Time}^*)$ must at least satisfy:

$$respects(F, \mathit{occurrences}, \mathit{tkm})$$

Note that *respects* applies to both time-triggered and event-triggered tasks. However for time-triggered, the Scheduler itself controls their releases and hence they are assured to execute at their specified (mode-specific) rate. For event-triggered, the Scheduler can determine which mode the system should be in, but it must rely on the environment to never generate two occurrences from the same task that are closer together than T_F.

Any specific execution of the *Scheduler* starts in mode N with no active jobs; this can be followed by alternating F/N phases. The move from N to F mode is caused by any ET job arriving before its assumed minimum gap; normal service can be resumed when there are no active jobs which allows the mode to revert from F to N.

As stated above, the *Planning* process has to consider all possible arrival patterns under the assumption that the actual arrivals at run-time *respects* the expected T gaps. Furthermore, the selection between T_N and T_F is governed by the current *mode*.

4.3   Assigning Priorities During Planning

Planning can be viewed as a predicate: in normal mode, given a set of priorities for each job, it establishes that the jobs can be scheduled providing the ET jobs arrive no more often than expected. Additionally, *Planning* must also establish that the alternative priorities chosen for F mode will suffice given the adjusted inter-job arrival times.

It is however more convenient to view *Planning* as a function that yields the priorities:

$$\mathit{Planning}: (\mathit{TaskId} \xrightarrow{m} \mathit{JobType}) \rightarrow (\mathit{TaskId} \xrightarrow{m} \mathit{Priorities})$$

$$\mathit{Priorities} :: \; P_N \; : \; \mathit{Priority}$$
$$P_F \; : \; \mathit{Priority}$$

Values of type *Priority* are represented as integers; with the larger the integer the higher the priority. P_N is the priority of each of the jobs of the task in the Normal node; P_F is the modified value that pertains to the fault-tolerant mode.

4.4   State of Run-Time Model

In our proposed framework, specifications of scheduling algorithms are expressed in terms of a run-time state. The following *State* differs from the one defined and used in [JB23] in the addition of the *LA* field that is needed to record the time of the last arrival of each job type; this is required to define the assumptions concerning the time intervals between job arrivals.

$$
\begin{aligned}
State :: \ t \qquad &: \ ClockValue \\
active \ &: \ JobId \xrightarrow{m} JobInfo \\
used \quad &: \ JobId \xrightarrow{m} Duration \\
run \quad &: \ [JobId] \\
shared \ &: \ Id \xrightarrow{m} Value \\
mode \quad &: \ \{N, F\} \\
LA \quad &: \ TaskId \xrightarrow{m} [ClockValue]
\end{aligned}
$$

Scheduling software needs a way of tracking and measuring time: unfortunately a completely precise measure of *Time* in the world external to the computer cannot be engineered so the t field is shown as containing a *ClockValue*. The relationship between t and external time is made precise in Sect. 4.5.

When a job does start, a *JobInfo* record is added to the *active* map of *State* associated with the new *JobId*. Such records have the following fields:

$$
\begin{aligned}
JobInfo :: \ type \ &: \ TaskId \\
d \quad &: \ ClockValue \\
P \quad &: \ Priority
\end{aligned}
$$

Where the *type* field is set to the *TaskId* of the job; the d field is set to the actual deadline which is computed by adding the value in the D field of *JobType* to the clock value at which the job starts (the current value of the t field in the *State*).

As part of the Planning exercise, priorities are assigned to each job type. There are two distinct values that correspond to the required priorities in the two modes of operation. These are contained in a mapping (*TaskId* $\xrightarrow{m}$ *Priorities*) that is accessible to the run time system but not shown as a field of *State* because the values therein do not change. The P field of *JobInfo* contains the current priority of a job (i.e. either P_N or P_F from *Priorities* must be copied into the P field of *JobInfo*).

As well as the *JobInfo*, it is necessary to track the resource (execution time) that the job has consumed; this is stored in the *used* map in *State*.

The fourth field of *State* records which job (if any) is actually running; a scheduler sets *run* to a *JobId* that is in the domain of *active* to make the corresponding job execute. Note, a VDM optional type ($[T]$) either contains a value of type T or is **nil**.[4]

---

[4] Whether one or more jobs can run at the same time depends on the number of processors; here, only the single processor case is handled. While it is straightforward to change *run* so that it contains a (possibly empty) set of *JobId*s, this change would require addressing a host of other scheduling issues.

Jobs themselves perform actions that affect shared entities (*shared* will at least contain shared variables). The final two fields note the current mode of the system (at time t) and, for each task, the time of the last arrival of a job for that task; this is used to check if a new job arrival from an event-triggered task is too close to the previous one (which would cause a change of mode from N to F).

We now define the invariant of an *FP* run-time scheduler:

$inv\text{-}State : State \rightarrow \mathbb{B}$

$inv\text{-}State(st) \quad \triangle$

      dom $st.used =$ **dom** $st.active \wedge$

      $(st.active = \{\,\} \wedge st.run =$ **nil** $\vee st.run \in$ **dom** $st.active) \wedge$

      $\forall j \in$ **dom** $st.active \cdot$

            $st.active(j).P \leq st.active(st.run).P \wedge$

            $st.t \leq st.active(j).d$

The second conjunct ensures that, if there are active jobs, the *JobId* of the running job is a member of the domain of the *active* map. The quantified conjunct of the *inv-State* predicate records the key *FP* decision that the job with the highest priority is executing and the key scheduling obligation of any real-time system that no job should execute beyond its deadline.

As a consequence of this final conjunct, any system with active jobs must make progress in the sense that they must be granted enough resource: for all jobs to complete before their deadlines, the run-time behaviour cannot stall—this is what is normally classed as a "liveness" issue. Any action must *eventually* occur, as all actions are contained within jobs, and all jobs finish before their deadlines (and progress of time is unstoppable!). The presence of t in the *State* and the fact that it is required to advance (see $\mathcal{T}$ below) results in *inv-State* ensuring progress.

4.5   *Time* vs Computer Clocks

System deadlines relate to the commonly accepted notion of time in the physical world; software cannot detect this directly and can only read the internal clock of the hardware on which it runs. To formalise this [JB23] distinguishes *ClockValues* from *Time*. The objects (Σ) used in the description of scheduling are mathematical functions from a dense *Time* set to the *States* defined above.

Clearly, little can be achieved unless the *ClockValues* consistently approximate *Time* and here a notion from the research on time bands [BH10] is used, $=_\rho$ indicates that two values are equal to within the precision, ρ, of the time band under discussion. The relationship between $\alpha \in Time$ and $t \in ClockValue$ is defined by the predicate $\mathcal{T}$:

$$\mathcal{T} : \Sigma \rightarrow \mathbb{B}$$

$$\mathcal{T}(\sigma) \;\; \triangleq$$
$$(\forall \alpha \in Time \cdot \sigma(\alpha).t =_\rho \alpha) \wedge$$
$$(\forall \alpha_1, \alpha_2 \in Time \cdot \alpha_1 < \alpha_2 \;\Rightarrow\; \sigma(\alpha_1).t \leq \sigma(\alpha_2).t)$$

Furthermore, a run-time scheduler can only ensure that e advances by moving the appropriate *JobId* to *run*. While a job is running, its execution time is advanced in accordance with:

$$\mathcal{E} : \Sigma \rightarrow \mathbb{B}$$

$$\mathcal{E}(\sigma) \;\; \triangleq$$
$$\forall \alpha_1, \alpha_2 \in Time \cdot$$
$$\forall j \in (\mathbf{dom}\, \sigma(\alpha_1).used \cap \mathbf{dom}\, \sigma(\alpha_2).used) \cdot$$
$$((\forall \alpha \mid \alpha_1 \leq \alpha \leq \alpha_2 \cdot j = \sigma(\alpha).run) \;\Rightarrow\;$$
$$\sigma(\alpha_2).used(j) - \sigma(\alpha_1).used(j) =_\rho \alpha_2 - \alpha_1) \wedge$$
$$((\forall \alpha \mid \alpha_1 \leq \alpha \leq \alpha_2 \cdot j \neq \sigma(\alpha).run) \;\Rightarrow\;$$
$$\sigma(\alpha_2).used(j) = \sigma(\alpha_1).used(j))$$

Using the definitions above, Σ with its invariant is:

$$\Sigma = Time \rightarrow State$$

where

$$inv\text{-}\Sigma : \Sigma \rightarrow \mathbb{B}$$

$$inv\text{-}\Sigma(\sigma) \;\; \triangleq \;\; \mathcal{T}(\sigma) \wedge \mathcal{E}(\sigma)$$

It is useful to think of the different time granularities of activity in terms of time bands [BH10]. The real-world notion of *Time* progresses faster than can be recorded in any internal *ClockValue*: $\mathcal{T}$ (and $\mathcal{E}$) induce discrete changes even when the *Scheduler* or the *Jobs* are not changing *States*. The post condition for a *Job* or those for methods of the *Scheduler* (see below) specify coarse changes of *State* but the corresponding rely conditions show that they tolerate changes to the t component—also notice that these operations only have read access to t.

4.6   *Scheduler* Class and Methods

The overall requirements on the *Scheduler* class are given first followed by the specifications of its methods.

In Fig. 1, there is no post condition for *Scheduler* because it is not meant to terminate; *pre-Scheduler* requires that initialisation has established *LA* values so that the first jobs that arrive for each task are judged to be timely. The predicate *rely-Scheduler* expresses two assumptions: no ET can arrive more frequently than its more generous (shorter) interval and all jobs must abide by their WCETs.

Scheduler

ext rd *tkm*　　: $TaskId \xrightarrow{m} JobType$
　　rd *prm*　　: $TaskId \xrightarrow{m} Priorities$
　　rd *t*　　　: $ClockValue$
　　wr *active* : $JobId \xrightarrow{m} JobInfo$
　　wr *used*　: $JobId \xrightarrow{m} Duration$
　　wr *run*　　: $\left[JobId\right]$
　　wr *mode* : $\{N, F\}$
　　wr *LA*　　: $TaskId \xrightarrow{m} ClockValue$
pre $active = \{\} \land$
　　$\forall tid \in \textbf{dom}\ tkm \cdot LA(tid) \leq t - tkm(tid).T_N$
rely $(\forall j \in (\textbf{dom}\ active' - \textbf{dom}\ active) \cdot$
　　　$tkm(active'(j).type) = \text{ET} \Rightarrow$
　　　　　　$t - LA(tkm(active'(j).type) \geq tkm(active'(j).type).T_F)) \land$
　　$\forall j \in \textbf{dom}\ used' \cdot$
　　　$used'(j) \leq tkm(active'(j).type).C$

Fig. 1. Specification of the *Scheduler* class

Notice also that *tkm* and *prm* are used but are not part of *State* because they are constant.

Notice that the constraints in the rely condition are on the primed value of *active* to mark that the property must hold after activity of any other entity.

The *Arrival* operation is split depending on its starting mode (in both cases, the last arrival (LA) must be updated):

– In *Arrival$_N$* (see Fig. 2), the change to mode F is triggered by early arrival of an ET job (one could think of this as *Mode-Down*). In either case, a new *JobInfo* is created for the newly arrived job; when switching to mode F, all of the priorities of the active jobs must be adjusted.
– In *Arrival$_F$* (see Fig. 3), things are actually simpler but notice that *mode* is marked as read only because *Arrival$_F$* cannot change the F mode.

Turning to the obligations on jobs (see Fig. 4); crucially, the guarantee condition of *Job* obliges each job to stay within its estimated worst-case execution time (and the transitive closure requires this to be true on job termination). The undefined *work* predicate in *post-Job* is a reminder that each job has work to do that would result in changes to the shared entities—but specifying the detailed function of individual job types is not of concern here.

Removal of the *JobId* from the domain of *active* is performed by *Completion* and *inv-State* ensures that the *JobId* is also removed from the domain of *used*; because *Completion* has write access to *used*, its guarantee condition notes that it will not affect the *used* entries of any other jobs. There is also an indirect requirement to re-establish *inv-State* by ensuring that the *JobId* of the active job with the next highest priority is moved to *run*.

$Arrival_N$ $(tid:\ TaskId)$

ext rd tkm $\quad:\ TaskId \xrightarrow{m} JobType$
$\quad$**rd** prm $\quad:\ TaskId \xrightarrow{m} Priorities$
$\quad$**rd** t $\qquad:\ ClockValue$
$\quad$**wr** $active\ :\ JobId \xrightarrow{m} JobInfo$
$\quad$**wr** $used$ $\quad:\ JobId \xrightarrow{m} Duration$
$\quad$**wr** run $\quad:\ \left[JobId \right]$
$\quad$**wr** $mode$ $\ :\ \{N, F\}$
$\quad$**wr** LA $\qquad:\ TaskId \xrightarrow{m} ClockValue$

pre $mode = N\ \wedge$
$\quad (tkm(tid).K = \textsc{Tt}\ \Rightarrow\ t =_\rho LA(tid) + tkm(tid).T_N)$

rely $t \le t'$

guar $(\mathbf{dom}\ used) \vartriangleleft used' = used$

post $LA' = LA \dagger \{tid \mapsto t\}\ \wedge$
$\quad (tkm(tid).K = \textsc{Et} \wedge t - LA(tid) \ge tkm(tid).T_N\ \Rightarrow$
$\qquad mode' = N\ \wedge$
$\qquad \exists j \in (JobId - \mathbf{dom}\ active) \cdot$
$\qquad\quad active' = active \cup$
$\qquad\qquad\qquad\qquad \{j \mapsto mk\text{-}JobInfo(tid, tkm(tid).D + t, prm(tid).P_N)\}\ \wedge$
$\qquad\quad used'(j) = 0)\ \wedge$
$\quad (tkm(tid).K = \textsc{Et} \wedge t - LA(tid) < tkm(tid).T_N\ \Rightarrow$
$\qquad mode' = F\ \wedge$
$\qquad \exists j \in (JobId - \mathbf{dom}\ active) \cdot$
$\qquad\quad active' =$
$\qquad\qquad \{k \mapsto mod\text{-}pri(active(k), prm(k).P_F) \mid k \in \mathbf{dom}\ active\} \cup$
$\qquad\qquad \{j \mapsto mk\text{-}JobInfo(tid, tkm(tid).D + t, prm(tid).P_F)\}\ \wedge$
$\qquad\quad used'(j) = 0)$

$mod\text{-}pri : JobInfo \times Priority \to JobInfo$

$mod\text{-}pri(mk\text{-}JobInfo(tid, d, p), p')\ \ \triangleq\ \ mk\text{-}JobInfo(tid, d, p')$

Fig. 2. Specification of the $Arrival_N$ operation and a sub-function

$Arrival_F$ $(tid: TaskId)$

ext rd tkm : $TaskId \xrightarrow{m} JobType$
    rd prm : $TaskId \xrightarrow{m} Priorities$
    rd t : $ClockValue$
    wr $active$: $JobId \xrightarrow{m} JobInfo$
    wr $used$: $JobId \xrightarrow{m} Duration$
    wr run : $\left[JobId \right]$
    rd $mode$: $\{N, F\}$
    wr LA : $TaskId \xrightarrow{m} ClockValue$
pre $mode = F \wedge$
    $(tkm(tid).K = \mathrm{TT} \Rightarrow t =_\rho LA(tid) + tkm(tid).T_F)$
rely $t \leq t'$
guar $(\mathbf{dom}\, used) \lhd used' = used$
post $LA' = LA \dagger \{tid \mapsto t\} \wedge$
    $\exists j \in (JobId - \mathbf{dom}\, active) \cdot$
        $active' = active \cup$
                $\{j \mapsto mk\text{-}JobInfo(tid, tkm(tid).D + t, prm(tid).P_F)\} \wedge$
        $used'(j) = 0$

Fig. 3. Specification of the $Arrival_F$ operation

Job $(id: JobId)$

ext rd tkm : $TaskId \xrightarrow{m} JobType$
    rd t : $ClockValue$
    rd $active$: $JobId \xrightarrow{m} JobInfo$
    rd $used$: $JobId \xrightarrow{m} Duration$
    wr $shared$: $Id \xrightarrow{m} Value$
rely $t \leq t' \leq active'(id).d$
guar $used'(id) \leq tkm(active(id).type).C$
post $work(shared, shared')$

$Completion$ $(id: JobId)$

ext wr $active$: $JobId \xrightarrow{m} JobInfo$
    wr $used$: $JobId \xrightarrow{m} Duration$
    wr run : $\left[JobId \right]$
pre $id = run$
guar $(\mathbf{dom}\, used - \{id\}) \lhd used' = (\mathbf{dom}\, used - \{id\}) \lhd used$
post $active' = \{id\} \lhd\!\!\!- active$

Fig. 4. Specification of the Job and $Completion$ operations

$$ModeUp$$

ext rd $active$: $JobId \xrightarrow{m} JobInfo$
    wr $mode$: $\{N, F\}$
pre $mode = F \wedge active = \{\,\}$
post $mode' = N$

Fig. 5. Specification of the *ModeUp* operation

The switch back to mode Normal which can certainly be made when there are no active jobs is given in Fig. 5.[5] Notice that the need to update any priorities is obviated by $active = \{\,\}$: there are no active jobs!

4.7 The FP Planning Theorem

The overall requirement of the combination of Planning and Scheduling phases is a commitment to ensure that all jobs complete by their deadlines; clearly this is only possible under assumptions. The data for these assumptions is threefold: the expected arrival patterns of ET jobs; the release intervals of TT jobs; and the expected WCETs of all jobs. An outline of the *Planning* operation is given in Fig. 6:

- information about job arrivals (*respects*) is an input to *Planning*—but notice that this predicate is read by the planner—it can only be applied to the run-time events;
- the information about tasks (and thus their jobs) is contained in *tkm*.

The result of *Planning* is to generate *prm* in a way that satisfies the *schedule* predicate. In the FP case, the obvious output of a successful planning phase is two sets of priorities—one for each mode (N/F). But it is helpful to view *Planning* as also creating a verification that, if the derived schedulability test is passed, all of the overall assumptions hold and –in addition– the *Scheduler* employs the priorities as intended, then the *Job* deadlines will be met. This is referred to as "the (FP) planning theorem".

$$Planning\,()\ success\colon \mathbb{B}$$

ext rd tkm : $TaskId \xrightarrow{m} JobType$
    rd $respects$: $\{N, F\} \times TaskId \rightarrow Time^*) \times (TaskId \xrightarrow{m} JobType) \rightarrow \mathbb{B}$
    wr prm : $TaskId \xrightarrow{m} Priorities$
post $success \Rightarrow schedule(tkm, prm')$

Fig. 6. Specification of the *Planning* operation

---

[5] Earlier mode changes would need to be checked carefully in *Planning*.

Moving on to the *Scheduler* itself, its inputs include the priorities computed by *Planning*. Logically, the correctness of the *Scheduler* also relies on the fact that the job arrivals satisfy the *respects* predicate but, since jobs arrive one at a time, this is expressed as a rely condition on the *Scheduler* operation. Similarly, the fact that jobs complete within their WCETs is a rely condition that is matched by a guarantee condition on the *Job* operation.

Given these assumptions and the specifications of the run-time operations requiring that the priorities are handled as required,[6] the planning theorem confirms that the deadlines will be met.

There is one other issue of timing that requires that the *Arrival* operations are invoked within τ of an interrupt requiring a ET job to execute: the scheduler must ensure that the *trigger-all* predicate, given below, is satisfied by the actual arrival pattern, say:

$trigger\text{-}all(occurences, \sigma)$

This implies that whenever a job occurs, a new *JobId* is created for this job and placed within the set of active jobs. To be added to this set it is necessary for one or other version (depending on the mode) of the *Arrival* method to be executed. Moreover, to comply with the timing constraint the job must be active within time τ of its occurrence (and, if this job has a higher priority than any other job within *active*, then *inv-State* ensures it is assigned to *run*) and will then make progress towards its deadline.

$$trigger\text{-}all : (TaskId \rightarrow Time^*) \times \Sigma \rightarrow \mathbb{B}$$

$$trigger\text{-}all(occm, \sigma) \quad \triangle$$
$$\forall tid \in \mathbf{dom} \; occm \cdot trigger\text{-}one(tid, occm(tid), \sigma)$$

$$trigger\text{-}one : TaskId \times Time^* \times \Sigma \rightarrow \mathbb{B}$$

$$trigger\text{-}one(tid, occl, \sigma) \quad \triangle$$
$$\forall i \in \{1..\mathbf{len} \; occl\} \cdot$$
$$\exists \alpha \in \mathbf{dom} \; \sigma, j \in JobId \cdot$$
$$0 < (\alpha - occl(i)) \leq \tau \wedge$$
$$j \notin \mathbf{dom} \; (\sigma(occl(i)).active) \wedge$$
$$j \in \mathbf{dom} \; (\sigma(\alpha).active) \wedge$$
$$(\sigma(\alpha).active)(j).type = tid$$

5   Comparison Between the Current and Previous Models

Our previous paper [JB23] also employed rely-guarantee thinking to specify a real-time scheduling approach; there are two major differences from the model presented above:

---

[6] Notice that *inv-State* also shows the FP requirement that the highest priority job is in *run*. Because of the need to cope with fault tolerance, the scheduler must also switch modes appropriately.

- The basic scheduling protocol was EDF (Earliest Deadline First) rather than FP (Fixed Priority).
- The faults that were tolerated were overruns of execution time budget rather than the early arrival of event-triggered tasks.

Nevertheless the basic specification approach is the same, for example

- Both applications have two levels of criticality: in the earlier paper ([JB23]) these are designated *HI* and *LO* (hence *HI*-crit and *LO*-crit tasks); in the current chapter the *HI*-crit tasks are identified as being Event-Triggered (ET) and the *LO*-crit Time Triggered (TT). The two levels give rise to Normal (N) and Fault Tolerant (F) modes of behaviour.
- A state invariant is used to force progress – all active jobs must complete before their deadline.

Inevitably in this later work, facing new challenges has led to some modifications to the model presented in [JB23], for example

- The entity that records the current execution time of a job, e, is now defined in the *used* field of *State* rather than being a component of *JobInfo*; this make it clear that the Scheduler cannot directly modify its value.
- The method used to define the arrival patterns of jobs originating from the same task is extended to be able to cope with event-triggered (sporadic) tasks.

In this section we briefly consider how the two schemes could be combined. Of course only one scheduling protocol can be employed, so in keeping with the main focus of this chapter we select FP. We stay with two criticality levels (*HI* and *LO*) and cope with a further fault in the model presented above: in addition to event-triggered *HI*-crit jobs arriving too early we also wish to tolerate these *HI*-crit jobs executing for more than their 'normal' execution time limit.

In the current chapter the early arrival of jobs from the same event-triggered task (within T_N) is tolerated by the time triggered tasks having their periods extended from T_N to T_F. In [JB23] a *HI*-crit job executing for more than C_N is tolerated by aborting all *LO*-crit jobs. Although an event-triggered task can have consecutive jobs released within T_N, there is a hard assumption that they will never be released within T_F. Similarly, with all Mixed-Criticality examples, it is assumed that, although a *HI*-crit job can execute for more than C_N, it cannot execute for more than C_F[7].

With the fault-model now incorporating two distinct faults there is a choice as to how to manage the potential fault-tolerant behaviours. This choice must be addressed during Planning as it determines how the MCS will maintain an adequate level of service during periods of system overload. The two main possibilities are, in addition to the normal N mode,

- a single F mode that is switched to if either fault occurs; or

---

[7] Represented by $C+X$ in [JB23].

– two F modes; FT implying that a job has arrived too early for the normal mode, and FC implying that a job has executed beyond what is sanctioned in the normal mode.

With the latter, there is now the need for a further mode that incorporates FT and FC; we denote this as the FTC mode.

These four modes give rise to a number of possible transitions, for example N to FT to FTC. Here the LO-crit time-triggered tasks would first have their periods increased and then they would be abandoned when FTC is entered. However with the alternative sequence of N to FC to FTC, the transition to FC will cause the LO-crit tasks to be abandoned and hence the move to FTC has little consequence other than a possible rearranging of the priorities of the 'early arriving' sporadic tasks.

With both of these three stage transitions the initial step could, of course, be followed by a return to N rather than a further degradation to FTC. Once in FTC the only exit transition is a direct return to N that will occur when there are no active jobs.

The details of this extended specification are not provided here; they are straightforward but would require a significant part of the model presented in [JB23] to be repeated.

6   Conclusions

This chapter has progressed previous work that linked rely-guarantee thinking with the challenges arising from attempts to specify the correct behaviour of fault-tolerant, real-time, cyber-physical systems (CPS). The model examined here utilises Fixed Priority scheduling and supports mixed-criticality applications that consist of safety-critical event-triggered tasks and mission-critical time-triggered tasks. The overall objective of the deployed CPS is that all run-time jobs that arise from these tasks complete by their deadlines. To achieve this objective we have proposed a framework that consists of a *Planning* phase followed by a *Scheduling* phase. The link between these phases is a set of assumptions that define the allowed and expected behaviours of the application's tasks. An assumption that is the main focus in this chapter is that these tasks have a maximum arrival frequency (defined as a minimum time interval between jobs coming from the same task).

The fault class to be tolerated is that –in rare (but not impossible) situations– safety-critical tasks will be triggered too frequently. The compensatory response is to reduce the frequency of the mission-critical tasks and thereby allow the more intense behaviour of the safety-critical task to be managed.

The role of *Planning* is to allocate the priorities to each task and to define the frequencies of the time-triggered tasks in both the normal and fault tolerating modes of operation. *Planning* defines and applies a schedulability test that must be passed if the *Scheduling* phase is to be sanctioned.

Overall the chapter presents a formal specification of a run-time scheduler together with a precise definition of the assumptions applied during planning.

Planned further work includes:

– Writing out a model that combines handling of both faults from exceeding WCET and those that result from premature job arrivals;
– investigating the usefulness of our specifications in the verification or derivation of the implementation.

Acknowledgements. EPSRC's Platform Grant (STRATA) funded the early collaboration of the two current authors and Jones gratefully acknowledges funding from Leverhulme grant RPG-2019-020.
It is a pleasure to thank the anonymous referees for their detailed comments.

References

[Abr10] Abrial, J.-R.: Modeling in Event-B: System and Software Engineering. Cambridge University Press, Cambridge (2010)

[BB20] Bozhko, S., Brandenburg, B.B.: Abstract response-time analysis: a formal foundation for the busy-window principle. In: Proceedings of the 32nd Euromicro Conference on Real-Time Systems (ECRTS 2020), pp. 6.1–6.23 (2020)

[BBD11] Baruah, S.K., Burns, A., Davis, R.I.: Response-time analysis for mixed criticality systems. In: Proceedings IEEE Real-Time Systems Symposium (RTSS), pp. 34–43 (2011)

[BD14] Burns, A., Davis, R.I.: Adaptive mixed criticality scheduling with deferred preemption. In: Proceedings of IEEE Real-Time Systems Symposium (RTSS), pp. 21–30 (2014)

[BD17] Burns, A., Davis, R.I.: A survey of research into mixed criticality systems. ACM Comput. Surv. **50**(6), 1–37 (2017)

[BD20] Burns, A., Davis, R.I.: Schedulability analysis for adaptive mixed criticality systems with arbitrary deadlines and semi-clairvoyance. In: Proceedings of IEEE Real-Time Systems Symposium (RTSS), pp. 12–24 (2020)

[BD22] Burns, A., Davis, R.I.: Mixed criticality systems: a review (13th edition). Technical Report MCC-1(13). https://www-users.cs.york.ac.uk/ab38/review.pdf and the White Rose Repository, Department of Computer Science, University of York, 2022

[BH10] Burns, A., Hayes, I.J.: A time band framework for modelling real-time systems. Real-Time Syst. **45**(1–2), 106–142 (2010)

[BHJ20] Burns, A., Hayes, I.J., Jones, C.B.: Deriving specifications of control programs for cyber physical systems. Comput. J. **63**(5), 774–790 (2020)

[BLA98] Buttazzo, G., Lipari, G., Abeni, L.: Elastic task model for adaptive rate control. In: IEEE Real-Time Systems Symposium, pp. 286–295 (1998)

[BVB+22] Bedarkar, K., Vardishvili, M., Bozhko, S., Maida, M., Brandenburg, B.B.: From intuition to Coq: a case study in verified response-time analysis of FIFO scheduling. In: 2022 IEEE Real-Time Systems Symposium (RTSS), pp. 197–210. IEEE (2022)

[Daw91] Dawes, J.: The VDM-SL Reference Guide. CRC Press, London (1991)

[DRRG10] Dorin, F., Richard, P., Richard, M., Goossens, J.: Schedulability and sensitivity analysis of multiple criticality tasks with fixed-priorities. Real-Time Syst. J. **46**(3), 305–331 (2010)

[GOH18]   Gill, C., Orr, J., Harris, S.: Supporting graceful degradation through elasticity in mixed-criticality federated scheduling. In: Li, J., Guo, Z., (eds.) Proceedings of 6th Workshop on Mixed Criticality Systems (WMC), RTSS, pp. 19–24 (2018)

[HMT88]   Harper, R., Milner, R., Tofte, M.: The definition of standard ML, version 2. Technical Report ECS-LFCS-88-62, LFCS Report Series (1988)

[ISO96]   ISO/IEC. Vienna Development Method - specification language: Part 1. base language. International Standard ISO/IEC 13817-1, ISO/IEC (1996)

[Jac12]   Jackson, D.N.: Software Abstractions: Logic, Language, and Analysis. MIT Press, Cambridge (2012)

[JB23]   Jones, C.B., Burns, A.: Extending rely-guarantee thinking to handle real-time scheduling. Formal Methods Syst. Des. **62**, 119–140 (2023)

[Jon81]   Jones, C.B.: Development Methods for Computer Programs including a Notion of Interference. PhD thesis, Oxford University, 6 1981. Printed as: Programming Research Group, Technical Monograph 25

[Jon83a]   Jones, C.B.: Specification and design of (parallel) programs. In: Proceedings of IFIP'83, pp. 321–332. North-Holland (1983)

[Jon83b]   Jones, C.B.: Tentative steps toward a development method for interfering programs. Trans. Program. Lang. Syst. **5**(4), 596–619 (1983)

[Jon90]   Jones, C.B..: Systematic Software Development Using VDM. Prentice Hall International, Second Edition, Hoboken (1990)

[MBB22]   Maida, M., Bozhko, S., Brandenburg, B.B.: Foundational response-time analysis as explainable evidence of timeliness. In: 34th Euromicro Conference on Real-Time Systems (ECRTS 2022). Schloss Dagstuhl-Leibniz-Zentrum für Informatik (2022)

[REC18]   Ramanathan, S., Easwaran, A., Cho, H.: Multi-rate fluid scheduling of mixed-criticality systems on multiprocessors. Real-Time Syst. **54**, 247–277 (2018)

[Sch97]   Schneider, F.B.: On Concurrent Programming. Texts in Computer Science. Springer-Verlag (1997). https://doi.org/10.1007/978-1-4612-1830-2

[SDZZ16]   Su, H., Deng, P., Zhu, D., Zhu, Q.: Fixed-priority dual-rate mixed-criticality systems: schedulability analysis and performance optimization. In: Proceedings of Embedded and Real-Time Computing Systems and Applications (RTCSA), pp. 59–68. IEEE (2016)

[SZ13]   Su, H., Zhu, D.: An elastic mixed-criticality task model and its scheduling algorithm. In: Proceedings of the Conference on Design, Automation and Test in Europe, DATE, pp. 147–152 (2013)

[Ves07]   Vestal, S.: Preemptive scheduling of multi-criticality systems with varying degrees of execution time assurance. In: Proceedings of Real-Time Systems Symposium (RTSS), pp. 239–243 (2007)

[WD96]   Woodcock, J., Davies, J.: Using Z: Specification. Refinement and Proof, Prentice Hall International (1996)

Clarifying Assumptions

Cliff B. Jones$^{(\boxtimes)}$

School of Computing, Newcastle University, Newcastle upon Tyne, UK
cliff.jones@ncl.ac.uk

Abstract. The correctness of a program can only be judged with respect to a specification; clarifying and recording the assumptions about the context in which a program is to be used is a crucial part of such a specification. Programs that either employ concurrent threads or execute concurrently in a changing environment experience interference; recording assumptions about interference needs something more expressive than pre/post condition specifications. This chapter evaluates the effectiveness of rely-guarantee conditions for documenting tolerable and induced interference. An important message is that it is sometimes easier and clearer to begin by studying an overall system rather than seeking to describe details of low-level internal devices (which might be viewed as "implementation patterns").

Keywords: formal methods · concurrency · interference · data races · synchronisation · rely-guarantee conditions · fault-tolerance

Tribute to Jim Woodcock

It is a pleasure to contribute to this volume that marks Jim's retirement from the University of York—he is both a long-standing friend and a major figure in the field of formal methods. In addition to his fundamental insights, what is inspiring in Jim's contributions is his search for relevance of formalism to (software) engineering. His insistence on applicable formalism can be seen in his work as editor-in-chief of the journal *Formal Aspects of Computing*. In electing Jim as a Fellow, the *Royal Academy of Engineering* also recognised the relevance of his work to practical challenges. An example that relates to the material in this chapter is that he led the first industrial use [WD88] of rely-guarantee ideas whilst he was employed in GEC. I am confident that Jim will continue to inspire and challenge us from new locations and I look forward to many future interactions.

1 Introduction

The risks of making assumptions are evident in everyday life; the danger is magnified where assumptions are not explicitly identified. Computer programs are executed by a dumb servant that does not ask "did you really mean …?":

© The Author(s), under exclusive license to Springer Nature Switzerland AG 2024
S. Foster and A. Sampaio (Eds.): *The Application of Formal Methods*, LNCS 14900, pp. 43–70, 2024.
https://doi.org/10.1007/978-3-031-67114-2_3

unrecorded assumptions made by the developer of a program can result in it being unsafe to use. Furthermore, such undocumented assumptions can be exploited by malign agents in security attacks (the late Roger Needham reserved the pointed noun "miscreants" for such attackers). This chapter argues for the importance of finding ways to clarify assumptions about software and to record them in a way which clarifies them for potential users and anyone who subsequently modifies the software.

The idea of augmenting the familiar concept of pre and post condition specifications with rely and guarantee conditions is described below in Sect. 2.3. The approach was originally conceived as a way to facilitate top-down development of shared-variable concurrent programs or –even if they were not developed that way– to provide understandable documentation of such software. A key challenge that the rely-guarantee approach had to overcome was finding a way of offering "compositionality" in the presence of interference. After the initial success of the approach in [Jon81], it was shown that rely conditions could be useful to record assumptions about external system components; in Cyber-Physical systems (CPS) these external components were often physical devices. This emphasised further the importance of "clarifying assumptions".

The current chapter benefits from some work on recording historical developments in the research on concurrency but here the aim is to identify deeper issues and to offer a critical assessment of the rely-guarantee approach; this includes identifying some open questions (which also aims to clarify (meta) assumptions).

1.1   Verification of Sequential Programs

The papers by Bob Floyd [Flo67] and Tony Hoare [Hoa69] are justifiably seen as providing foundation stones of research on the verification of sequential programs.[1] The reader is assumed to be familiar with the approach of writing "Hoare-triples" as judgements $\{P\}\ S\ \{Q\}$ meaning that a program text S achieves post condition Q providing execution begins in a state satisfying pre condition P.[2]

There have been some unproductive debates around the phrase "proving programs correct" which the current author has no interest in fuelling. The following points reflect the current author's view

- Even underlying the more measured statement of showing that "programs satisfy their specifications", there are important assumptions such as that the semantics embodied in the compiler matches that assumed by the programmer, issues of "clean termination" [Sit74, CH79] and, with concurrency, "fairness" [Fra86, vGH15].
- Just as static typing can avoid certain sorts of programming slips ever reaching execution, using inference rules to reason about constructs in programs can ensure that classes of run-time failures cannot occur.

---

[1] For more historical context and impact see [Jon03, Pri20].

[2] Questions about termination and whether using post conditions that are predicates of only the final state are touched on below.

– It should at least be accepted that the Floyd-Hoare approach provides a way of removing important classes of errors in software.

———

The "fault-error-failure" trichotomy from [ALRL04] is useful in thinking about software. A failure in the development process can give rise to a fault in a program—but such a fault may never be encountered; execution of an incorrect program can result in a state that is in error but even this might not become visible as a failure of the program to meet its specification. Only when the error state results in a visible failure would it have an impact on its environment. And there the pattern can repeat itself: the failure of the software might be identified (and potentially tolerated) as a fault in a wider system. As is made clear in [ALRL04], being precise about the perimeter of the system under discussion is crucial for any proper analysis of failure.

The admittedly important topic of arriving at a specification that captures the real requirements for a system is not addressed in this chapter; writing and contemplating a (formal) specification might help focus on system capabilities but is not a guarantee of appropriateness.

1.2 Development Methods

The Floyd-Hoare approach initially provided a way to reason about an extant program text—in Floyd's paper the program was represented in a flowchart — Hoare used a more conventional program text. But in both cases, verification is *post facto* in the sense that the program is assumed to exist before verification reasoning commences. This begs the question of how programmers are to create programs; if they are of any size, programs are likely to contain errors and the verification step can identify errors only late in the development process—which is unlikely to constitute a cost-effective procedure.

Hoare made the crucial step in [Hoa71] to employ his "axioms" in a design process; this involves reading the inference rules about program constructs from the conclusion to the hypotheses rather than in the more conventional order. For example, Hoare's rule for verifying assertions about while statements,

$$\boxed{\text{while}} \ \frac{\{P \wedge b\} \ S \ \{P\}}{\{P\} \ \textbf{while} \ b \ \textbf{do} \ S \ \textbf{od} \ \{P \wedge \neg b\}}$$

might be read top to bottom as a way of justifying a judgement about a repetitive construct from a proven judgement about the body of the loop (S). To invert the reading order, it is useful to employ a rule for weakening specifications,

$$\boxed{\text{weaken}} \ \frac{\{P\} \ S \ \{Q\} \qquad P' \Rightarrow P \qquad Q \Rightarrow Q'}{\{P'\} \ S \ \{Q'\}}$$

which leads to a more natural design rule where the post condition of the conclusion is not assumed to have been conveniently couched in a particular format $(P \wedge \neg b)$; a "top-down" rule for decomposing a task specified by P/Q is:

$$\text{while}_{TD} \quad \frac{\begin{array}{c} \{P1\} \ S \ \{Q1\} \\ P \wedge b \ \Rightarrow \ P1 \\ Q1 \wedge \neg b \ \Rightarrow \ Q \end{array}}{\{P\} \ \textbf{while} \ b \ \textbf{do} \ S \ \textbf{od} \ \{Q\}}$$

Here it is easy to see how the given P/Q specification can be viewed as a design task that can be decomposed to a specification for a sub-component S.

Redundancy is a prime tool for enhancing dependability; *post facto* verification can offer that staple but may not be cost-effective if applied late; stepwise verification in the design process provides the redundancy in a step-by-step check—a design step can be verified in terms of specifications for yet-to-be-developed components; those components can subsequently be tackled with their isolated specifications as the sole criteria of their acceptability. Such a formal design process can be thought of as proceeding "top down" from the abstract specification to the detailed code that satisfies that specification. Undertaken carefully such a process can be thought of as "posit and prove": the designer's intuition of a plausible decomposition of a large task into smaller challenges is checked by proof and any mistakes identified and resolved before more work is based on them. Avoiding the waste of "scrap and rework" is precisely why formal methods can be cost-effective.

Even where steps are made without proof –but are perhaps subject to formal design reviews– the resulting design rationale preserves vital insight for subsequent modifications.

In contrast to this top-down approach, a development which creates entire programs and only after they are executable attempts either proof or some form of model checking can be termed "bottom up" in the sense that abstractions of the functionality of the code have to be rediscovered.

These terms might sound judgemental but actually both processes have a part to play in development. Faced with "legacy code", there is little alternative to adopting a bottom-up approach. It is also true that useful tools can be constructed that can detect classes of faults in extant software. Fortunately there is a symbiosis in that top-down thinking can identify useful abstractions that can inform the construction of bottom-up tools. In the other direction, adding assertions to a program can help a model-checking tool avoid reporting "false-positives".

1.3   Concurrency

The efficacy of the Floyd-Hoare ideas to provide a top-down development approach relies on "compositionality": the inference rule given above for while constructs relies on the specification of the loop body—not on any detail of its implementation—the developer of that body need not know anything about the context into which its code will be placed.

The prime property of concurrency is "interference": the state of one thread can be changed by other sibling or contextual code—the progress of one thread can depend on signals from another. It is precisely this interference that makes it challenging to find compositional methods for the design of concurrent software. (The very title of [dRdBH+01] is "Concurrency Verification: Introduction to Compositional and Noncompositional Methods" which pinpoints the issue.)

It might again be suspected that there is negative intent in the choice of the word "interference" and Edsger Dijkstra chose the adjective "cooperating" in the title ("Cooperating sequential processes") of one of his early contributions to the research on concurrency [Dij65]. It is certainly true that careful use of signalling progress between threads has the feeling of cooperation and, as discussed in Sect. 3.4, often controls the interference on states; but the setting and testing of, say, semaphores clearly influences inter-thread progress so this chapter uses the term "interference" for any such cross thread influence.

1.4   Structure of Chapter

The remainder of this chapter is divided as follows: Sect. 2 reviews both the challenge of –and approaches to– reasoning about concurrency and shared-variable interference; that section concludes with the original proposal to employ rely-guarantee conditions and Sect. 3 summarises some further applications and extensions of that idea; Sect. 4 outlines current research aimed at coping with synchronisation issues. Brief conclusions are offered in Sect. 5.

2   Reasoning About Interference on States

This section builds up to the "rely-guarantee" approach whose inception dates back to publications in the 1980 s. The challenge to which this research was responding was precisely that of offering a compositional development approach for shared-variable concurrency. As indicated in Sect. 2.3 below, an inference rule can be given that provides conditions under which a specified function can be decomposed into specified threads whose execution can be shown to achieve the requirements of the major function. Crucially, for a large class of applications, such rules do support a posit-and-prove approach to design.

At its most basic, the message is that assumptions must be thought about and recorded if compositionality is to be achieved; for concurrent software, such assumptions have to encompass interference. That (over) simplified message becomes useful only with a way of reasoning about interference and Sect. 2.3 provides an existence proof of such inference rules. Before coming to that, the background to the rely-guarantee research is sketched in Sect. 2.1; early non-compositional approaches are briefly reviewed in Sect. 2.2; related issues of compositional development of data structures are covered in Sect. 2.4 while Sect. 2.5 reviews the sometimes contentious topic of ghost variables.

2.1   Background to Rely-Guarantee Research

It is worth considering the context of any research avenue. Prior to the attack on concurrency, the current author spent two multi-year spells at the IBM Laboratory in Vienna. During the first, he proposed [JL71] a move from Peter Lucas' "twin machine" proofs [Luc68] to what later became known as "retrieve functions". (Which Robin Milner identified as homomorphisms in [Mil71].) Between the two spells in Vienna, work in IBM's UK Lab built on Floyd's ideas but employed post conditions that were relations between initial and final states;[3] this included –in [Jon73, §3.5]– recognising that conventional relational composition was not rich enough to define the composition of the semantics of two statements. (The second spell in Vienna focussed on language description methods and, other than giving rise to the acronym "VDM", is of less relevance here.)

Prompted by the wrk on development methods for sequential programs, it is unsurprising that top-down thinking was key to the objectives when seeking a way of reasoning about concurrency. Not only were post conditions predicates of two states, there was also a ("satisfiability") requirement that a pre condition is given and that termination was required for all states satisfying the pre condition. This prompted a natural ordering relation for satisfaction: pre conditions could be widened and the non-determinism in post conditions could be narrowed— always maintaining the requirement of satisfiability. Technically, the satisfiability proof obligation is:[4]

$$\forall \sigma \in \Sigma \cdot pre(\sigma) \;\Rightarrow\; \exists \sigma' \in \Sigma \cdot post(\sigma, \sigma')$$

It was not difficult to show that sequential programming constructs were monotone with respect to the satisfaction ordering. There was an additional bonus with using relational post conditions: it becomes straightforward to establish loop termination by requiring that the body of a loop observes a well-founded relation.[5] Thus "total correctness" was built into the relational rules.

———

For large specifications, presenting them as triples such as those used in Sect. 1.2 above is impractical and VDM specifications are usually laid out as named "operations" using keywords to identify the pre and post conditions; also the names and types of variables to which an operation has access are identified together with a note of whether **wr**ite or only **r**ead permission is granted.

---

[3] It is at least plausible that the adoption by Hoare and others of post conditions of the final state alone derived from Floyd's decision to write assertions as flowchart annotations.

[4] In fact, satisfiability was normally discharged by constructing (the next step of) an implementation. (This issue becomes important in Sect. 2.3 with concurrency.).

[5] Furthermore, it is useful to distinguish between left and right composition of the loop relation with that of the body of the loop—they match different ways of programming loops—see [Jon80].

Specifications of yet-to-be-designed components were written within code in [Jon80] as a way of providing a structured development record. (The two-dimensional layout of operations made this less compact than Carroll Morgan's "refinement calculus" [Mor90]. It is perhaps worth adding a note of caution here: Strachey was obviously right in maintaining that it is easier to manipulate a formula that fits on one line than something that spans many lines—but specifications of large systems are unlikely to fit on one line and computing research cannot define its range of interest by an arbitrary length constraint.)

Another feature of [Jon80] was the importance attached to data abstraction and reification—this topic is picked up in Sect. 2.4 below. This material on the program development aspects of "VDM" was taught during the late 1970s in many IBM internal courses and it was this that led to [Jon80].

2.2   Verification (*Post Facto*) of concurrent programs

The 1970s saw a linked series of research contributions on the verification of concurrent programs. Just as Floyd and Hoare had started with *post facto* verification, the insights from Ed Ashcroft, Zohar Manna and Susan Owicki were thought out in terms of verifying programs that had already been designed. (This string of contributions is covered in more detail in [Jon23] but is worth sketching here because it sets the context of the results in Sect. 2.3.)

The joint paper by Ashcroft and Manna [AM71] shows how a program that employs concurrent threads can be translated into a non-deterministic program with equivalent semantics. Both the starting point and the resultant program are represented as flowcharts. The translation is illustrated on several examples but there is not a completely general algorithm. The obvious weakness of the approach is that the expansion can result in a huge non-deterministic program but the underlying observation that concurrent threads give rise to non-deterministic merges is basic and does reduce the challenge of proving results about concurrency to an already solved problem.

Ed Ashcroft moved from Stanford to Waterloo University in Canada where he tackled in [Ash75] the precipitate and worrying expansion of the earlier joint work: he introduced the idea of indexing the state assertions (familiar from Floyd and Manna's proposals) by "control states". One way of thinking about control states is to view them as expressions of placing fingers to point to the next statements in each thread that could be executed. While it is true that Ashcroft had potentially to consider as many non-deterministic alternatives as were explicitly constructed in the Ashcroft-Manna proposal, it was much easier in Ashcroft's new approach to see where different choices could be merged because there would be no interference.

Although no direct citation link to later research on temporal logic has been found, it is interesting that Ashcroft's introduction of control states establishes the utility of indexing state assertions; his reasoning about programs without the need to position assertions on the program text foreshadows work on temporal logics.

The approach presented in Owicki's thesis [Owi75][6] is much the most influential of this sequence of proposals for *post facto* verification of concurrent programs. (There is a clear and shorter outline in a paper [OG76] co-authored with Gries who was her PhD supervisor.) In essence, Owicki proposes verification of concurrent programs in two phases:

1. initially each thread is viewed as a sequential program and standard Hoare-like proofs are constructed for each thread as though they are to be executed in isolation;
2. after these proofs are constructed (and, strictly, there needs to be an assertion between every statement), a check is made to see whether any step in the correctness argument of a thread can be interfered with by the execution of any statement in another thread.

It is clear that all of these approaches are non-compositional in the sense that the first step is to write the concurrent program. Furthermore, any faults detected when concurrency is eventually faced can result in having to start again with construction. Their lack of compositionality is exactly the distinction explored in [dRdBH+01].

———

Owicki provides a short but illuminating example (*FINDP*) of employing two concurrent threads to search an array of values to find the least index of an element that satisfies some property; if the threads divide the overall task by considering odd/even index values, it is obviously beneficial for the threads to interfere by tracking each other's progress. In [Jon23], *FINDP* is used to reflect on how the two earlier approaches might have fared had the example been known at their publication date. This shows a stronger link between Ashcroft's solo [Ash75] work and Owicki than one might conclude from just reading their papers: admittedly capitalising on some of the predicates that are used in the Owicki proof, Ashcroft's control states link neatly to the points where Owicki has to consider interference in the sequential proofs.

More revealing is the attempt to produce a proof of *FINDP* in the style of the yet earlier [AM71] paper. Because both threads in *FINDP* are written as loops, it betrays the fact that Ashcroft and Manna did not provide a completely general expansion algorithm to their sought-after non-deterministic program and, had they done so, the resultant program would have been unmanageably huge and opaque.

Intriguingly, there is a way to represent a non-deterministic version of *FINDP* but as observed in both [AH22, Chap 8] and [Jon23] this employs Dijkstra's "guarded commands" which were only published in [Dij75]. It is interesting to get under the skin of this achievement: guarded commands can be used to ape something quite close to Ashcroft's "control states".

---

[6] Owicki had access to –and cites– an early draft of Ashcroft's solo paper.

In addition to the question of (non-)compositionality, there are two reservations about the above sequence of three contributions that are worth noting:

- they do not cope with programs that contain nested concurrency;
- more subtly, they all have a hostage to fortune with identifying the granularity of interference: in all three of [AM71, Ash75, Owi75] assignment statements (and expressions in conditional and while statements) are assumed to execute atomically. Thinking about the sequence of machine-level instructions that might result from even $x \leftarrow x + 1$ makes clear that this assumption is unwarranted.[7]

2.3   Recovering Compositionality

In the sense that unhappiness with the lack of a compositional rule for introducing concurrency was a spur, there is a link from Owicki's contribution to the research on rely-guarantee conditions. (There is correspondence between the two authors from early in Jones' Oxford doctoral research and there were interactions at meetings of IFIP's WG 2.3.)

What is obvious with hindsight is that it was necessary to find a convenient way of specifying interference to achieve a compositional inference rule that would facilitate top-down development of concurrent programs. This begs the question of how best to specify interference. In the extreme, the full contextual code has most information; but what is needed is a way to say less so that a top-down compositional design is practicable. The proposal in [Jon81] is, for concurrent components, to add relational rely and guarantee conditions to specifications with pre and post conditions.

It was perhaps fortunate that Jones' earlier work had used relational post conditions since this offered at least a plausible form of assertion to discuss shared-variable interference. Rely conditions are written as relations on states and they express what interference a thread must tolerate. Guarantee conditions are also relations and constrain what (state to state) interference a thread is allowed to generate. The diagram in Fig. 1 indicates a sequence of states ($\sigma_n \in \Sigma$) together with the roles of the four predicates.

It is useful to bear in mind the distinction between assumptions and commitments: both pre and rely conditions can be thought of as permissions to the developer to assume that any deployed context of their code will be bounded; in contrast, guarantee conditions are similar to post conditions in that they have to be adhered to by the running code. Showing that a module can be safely deployed requires establishing –preferably by proof– that the context matches the assumptions.

---

[7] There is a non-solution to this problem (which is wrongly associated with John Reynolds' name): whilst it is true that, if any assignment refers to only one shared variable, the issue appears to be resolved it should be obvious that using a local temporary variable such as t in $t \leftarrow x; \; x \leftarrow t + 1$ only exposes rather than resolves the problem that interference can give rise to non-deterministic behaviour. John Reynolds disowned the so-called "Reynolds' rule" on more than one occasion.

A sequence of states:

showing:

- the pre condition being true of any initial state σ_0 can be assumed by a developer;
- a developer must accept that the state can change during execution but such changes (e.g. σ_i and σ_{i+1}) can be assumed to be bounded by the rely condition which functions like a post condition of any interfering state transition;
- execution of the created code must satisfy the post condition which is a relation between the initial state σ_0 and final state σ_f;
- any state changes during execution of the created code are also bounded — for example, the transition by the code of the specified component from σ_j to σ_{j+1} must satisfy the guarantee condition.

Fig. 1. Rely-guarantee conditions

Both rely and guarantee conditions are reflexive and transitive because there is the possibility of zero or many steps of interference. (This issue could have been handled differently but the convention has proved convenient.)

Simple examples of rely conditions might state that the value of a variable changes monotonically; more interesting than $i \leq i'$ might be uses on sets of values such as $s' \subseteq s$. Rely conditions can also be conditional on Boolean switch values as in $sw \Rightarrow x' = x$ and changes to the value of the switch itself can be subject to assumptions. The simplest rely conditions can record assumptions that avoid "data races" by stating that variables cannot be changed. There is however another way of marking such restrictions in VDM operation specifications and that is to record the "frame" of an operation: the variables to which the operation has access and whether only read access is allowed or both read and write access.

A compact way of presenting judgements for rely-guarantee specifications is:

$$\{P, R\} \, S \, \{G, Q\}$$

Using this format, a rule for decomposing a specification into concurrent threads can be written:

$$\boxed{\| \text{-} I_c} \quad \frac{\{P_1, R \vee G_2\} \, S_1 \, \{G_1, Q_1\}}{\{P_1 \wedge P_2, R\} \, S_1 \, \| \, S_2 \, \{G_1 \vee G_2, Q_1 \wedge Q_2\}}$$

(Actually, a slightly stronger conclusion can add the transitive closure of disjunction of the rely condition R and guarantee conditions of the component.)

Just as Sect. 1.2, it is more useful for top-down development to add appropriate weakening rules and present the top-down inference rule as:

$$\| \text{-}I_{TD} \quad \frac{\begin{array}{l} \{P_1, R_1 \vee G_2\}\ S_1\ \{G_1, Q_1\} \\ \{P_2, R_2 \vee G_1\}\ S_2\ \{G_2, Q_2\} \\ P \ \Rightarrow\ P_1 \vee P_2 \\ R \ \Rightarrow\ R_1 \vee R_2 \\ G_1 \wedge G_2\ \Rightarrow\ G \\ Q_1 \wedge Q_2 \wedge (R \vee G_1 \vee G_2)^*\ \Rightarrow\ Q \end{array}}{\{P, R\}\ S_1\ \|\ S_2\ \{G, Q\}}$$

The rule above handles asymmetric processes such as occur –for example– in concurrent garbage collection [JY19] or Simpson's "four slot" implementation of "Asynchronous Communication Methods" [JH16].

A simpler rule can be stated for symmetric processes:

$$sym\text{-}\| \text{-}I_{TD} \quad \frac{\begin{array}{l} \{P, R \vee \bigvee_i G_i\}\ S_i\ \{G_i, Q_i\} \\ \bigvee_i G_i\ \Rightarrow\ G \\ \bigwedge_i Q_i \wedge (R \vee \bigvee_i G_i)^*\ \Rightarrow\ Q \end{array}}{\{P, R\}\ \|_i\ S_i\ \{G, Q\}}$$

This version of the rule copes with examples such as the use of concurrent processes to remove composite numbers in the "Sieve of Eratosthenes"; it also suffices for a rely-guarantee development of the above-mentioned *FINDP* example from Owicki's thesis. (Both examples are used in [HJ18] to illustrate the algebraic presentation of rely-guarantee that is discussed in Sect. 4.1 below.)

Because it is the subject of further comparisons below, it is useful to note that Tony Hoare looked at disjoint parallelism in his attempts to extend his axiomatic method of [Hoa69] to successively more features of programming languages: in [Hoa72] he states an inference rule that provides a simple way of combining results about separate threads providing they have no variables in common:

$$\| \text{-}I_{disj} \quad \frac{\begin{array}{l} \{P_1\}\ S_1\ \{Q_1\} \\ \{P_2\}\ S_2\ \{Q_2\} \end{array}}{\{P_1 \wedge P_2\}\ S_1\ \|\ S_2\ \{Q_1 \wedge Q_2\}}$$

The seductive simplicity of this rule –which shows immediately that parallel composition does not depend on the order of execution of the two constituent threads– is a useful reference point for other approaches to concurrency when interference has to be faced. Comparing $\| \text{-}I_c$ with $\| \text{-}I_{disj}$ it is clear how rely and guarantee conditions have to match in order for interference to be acceptable.

———

Three technical desiderata are achieved by the rely-guarantee rules above:

– they do work for nested concurrency (this is essential for a top-down development approach);

– they do not fix a level of thread switching granularity such as assuming that assignment statements are executed atomically;
– their soundness with respect to underlying model-based semantics has been established (see Sect. 3.2 below).

An additional testament to the usefulness of top-down development using rely-guarantee rules comes from a development of the Fischer-Galler [GF64] algorithm for what is commonly referred to as the "union-find" problem. When investigating a concurrent "clean up" algorithm for their clever tree representation, it was initially assumed that some locking would be needed but the development in [Jon81] shows that concurrent processes can squash trees whilst the main functions (*Equate*/*Test*) are executing concurrently. (This algorithm is again addressed in [CJ00].)

Furthermore rely-guarantee thinking does provide intuitive support even when development is not completely formal: thinking about interference and making a record of what extent thereof a program is expected to tolerate is a useful discipline; leaving behind some record of the assumptions being made in a development step can steer subsequent maintenance effort away from disastrous precipices.

Several further points can be made from experience with developments using rely-guarantee conditions.

– The compact notation for judgements used in the proof rules above is rarely appropriate for realistic specifications; two-dimensional layouts of specifications with keywords are more readable.
– A notion of "dynamic invariant" was used already in [Jon81]. These relations between the initial state and any state that can arise after transitions from any thread can be useful in thinking out a design.
– Slightly different, is the idea termed "evolution invariants" in [CJ00] which is essentially the union of rely and guarantee conditions from all threads.

There is one issue that distinguishes the rely-guarantee approach from, for instance, Abrial's Event-B [Abr10] proposal. In methods which assume that specified units –be they called "events", "actions", "operations" or whatever– are executed atomically, something like rely-guarantee thinking can only be simulated by breaking high level steps into their atomic components. This does not match the top-down design idea achieved with rely-guarantee specifications where interference is accepted for specified components.

2.4   Data Abstraction/Reification

As is hinted at the end of Sect. 2.1, data abstraction and reification was recognised as an important aspect of sequential program specification and development in [Jon80]—in fact, [Jon86] made the provocative step of moving this material ahead of the far more familiar rules for operation decomposition. The evolution of Jones' recognition of the importance of employing data abstraction to facilitate concise and clear specifications dates back to [Jon70] mentioned above and was further investigated in [Jon72]. Especially with concurrency, the process of design via layers of abstraction of data is a powerful tool that supports a designer's intuition and can be usefully employed even in settings which do not insist on full formality.

It is thus not surprising that many of the early examples of developments using rely-guarantee concepts also deployed data abstraction. The symbiosis of these strands of research was, however, only made explicit in [Jon07]. Even with sequential programs, choosing apposite abstract objects can make it possible to postpone design decisions and thus separate verification issues; this advantage is often magnified with the top-down development of concurrent programs.

One small but indicative example of data abstraction and concurrency can be seen in a development of the simple *FINDP* example discussed in Sect. 2.2 above. If the concurrent processes that are searching respectively the odd/even indexes of the array are to record the fact that they have found an element of the array with the desired property, one possibility is to modify a shared variable—say t. Although this might offer a clear description at one level of abstraction, it would create a potential data race which needs to be reconsidered for the final code. Of course, one option would be to employ a lock and have both threads mediate their access to t using this device but this would have a negative impact on the performance of a design that is aimed at efficiency. A much neater solution is to reify t to two variables –say ot/et– where the two processes have write access only to their own variable but read access to the variable of the other process; the current top value can be accessed by using $min(ot, et)$ in each process—with no need for a lock. This resolves the data race. (Of course, suitable rely and matching guarantee conditions are stated for ot and et.)

A more profound data abstraction was utilised in [JH16] which addresses the development of Simpson's "four slot" implementation. The challenge of "Asynchronous Communications Mechanisms" (ACMs) is that neither the sender nor the receiver process should ever be held up waiting for a lock—furthermore, the reader process must see the most recently completed write. It is immediately obvious that a single buffer cannot support this behaviour and only a little more thought ought convince the reader that two cells will not suffice to provide this degree of asynchrony. But prematurely fixing on four cells has two disadvantages: it closes off the designer's search options (Bornat explores the use of three slots in [BA13]) and it fails to throw any light on the reasoning behind Simpson's design choice to use four slots.

In [JH16] an intermediate abstraction of a mapping from some arbitrary index set (X) to the communicated values is used. On this representation, it is possible to sort out the avoidance of races on the indexes and identify exactly which is the freshest completed write. A further step of data reification can then be shown to satisfy the necessary properties with four slots.

Another reason why the cited development of the four slot implementation of ACMs is informative is the observation that Peter O'Hearn makes in [O'H07] about Concurrent Separation Logic (CSL) being tailored to race-free programs whereas –he claims– the rely-guarantee approach fits better with "racy" programs. Avoiding races on the same slot index is the essence of Simpson's ingenious solution and the above cited development identifies exactly the way in which the four-slot idea achieves this. In contrast, the CSL development in [WW10] is less informative and actually stops short of showing that freshness is achieved.

It is however worth noting a warning: a mistaken choice of the level of data abstraction can make it difficult to satisfy the rely conditions. One example (which can be rescued) serves to indicate the potential trap: a concurrent program for the sieve of Eratosthenes for ascertaining primes (up to some maximum value) can be neatly described in terms of sets of natural numbers and the monotonic reduction of the set of candidate numbers looks to be a reasonable rely condition. However, choosing to represent set membership in terms of bits stored in machine-length words means that the equivalent of removing one element from a set hits exactly the same problem that shows $i \leftarrow i + 1$ should not be assumed to be executed atomically. This issue is resolved in [HJM23] by judicious use of a "compare and swap" instruction. (Level of abstraction issues can be further complicated by data type invariants.)

Despite this warning, it is clear from many examples that thoughtful use of abstract data in specifications and reification in development are again massive aids to understandable design records for concurrent programs.

2.5   Ghost Variables

Many examples of verifications of concurrent programs employ "ghost variables" (also referred to as "auxiliary variables"); the idea is that local variables can be added to a thread to simplify reasoning about its potential interactions with contextual code.

It is worth sounding a note of caution about the overuse of ghost variables. To some extent, this warning derives from experience in a different aspect of formal development. Peter Lucas showed in [Luc68] that the early VDL descriptions of programming languages could be used to verify compiling algorithms by constructing "twin machines" that included the entire states of two models (that of the abstract specification and that of the implementation); showing that the combined model preserved what would now be called a "data type invariant" established the formal relationship. In [Jon70] capital was made out of the fact that a good specification should be "more abstract than" any implementation and this was the start of the VDM notions of "retrieve functions" etc.[8]

---

[8] What happens when a specification has to have redundancy to express non-determinacy that can be removed in an implementation is exemplified in [Mar85] and carefully worked out in [Nip86].

The reservation about employing ghost variables in the verification of concurrent programs is that there is no obvious precise definition as to when they are being over used. In particular, such variables can record intimate details of the flow of control in one thread and, if the specification of another thread uses these variables, any semblance of compositionality is destroyed.

An admittedly imprecise test for the use of ghost variables is that they should only be tolerated when the binding between the thinking in the design of the threads is too intimate for a realistic separation. One example of this is with "on-the-fly garbage collection" [JY19] where the mutator code has to tango with the collector concept.

2.6 Using a Fiction of Atomicity

This section might appear to constitute a digression from the rely-guarantee theme but it describes an approach that connects to the future plans discussed in Sect. 4.2. The research sometimes termed "atomicity refinement" did in fact constitute a digression and it was one prompted by an unease that having four clauses to specify any operation could become cumbersome. (Benefiting from hindsight it is clear that judicious use of frame definitions can radically reduce this problem.)

The crux of the idea is to use a "fiction of atomicity" as a design abstraction [Jon96]; it will often prove necessary to "split (software) atoms safely" in subsequent development steps [Jon07]; the relevant proof obligation is to show that observational equivalence is preserved. It should be clear that this is an attempt to provide a top-down development method that has strong links with (bottom-up) verification via "linearisability" [HW90].

It is important to distinguish the general call for atomicity refinement from the specific existence proof in [Jon93] where a small object-oriented language was used to provide a precise interface for the observational equivalence arguments; the correctness argument of the required equivalences was based on a π-calculus [SW01] semantics. (Davide Sangiorgi published formal bi-simulation proofs of the equivalences in [San99].)

3 Developments of "rely-guarantee thinking"

The original publications on rely-guarantee did not immediately attract a lot of attention but the proposals have subsequently spawned significant research avenues. This section describes some of the ideas that go beyond the inference rules given in Sect. 2.3 and might be described as "R-G thinking".[9]

In [Din02], Juergen Dingel proposes a refinement calculus (compare [Mor90]) that is based on rely-guarantee ideas (Dingel's thesis –from which the long journal paper is derived– was supervised by Steve Brookes at CMU).

---

[9] So as to avoid encumbering this chapter with yet more references, the interested reader is referred to [§10.2] [HJM23] for a fuller list of consequent publications.

A notable characteristic of the most productive of the follow-on research is that it has often been driven by practical applications. For example, papers with Ken Pierce led to an extension of the notation that made it possible to reason about all "possible values" that might occur during a period of computation. The need for this was found when developing in [JP11] an implementation of Simpson's four-slot algorithm. It was subsequently realised that the possible-values concept could be used to record in [JH16] a simple and clear specification for Asynchronous Communication Mechanisms. (See also [HBDJ13].)

Research on synchronisation by Ketil Stølen and others is discussed in Sect. 3.4 below.

3.1   Assumptions About External Components

Moving beyond using rely-guarantee thinking as an approach to the decomposition of specifications into yet-to-be-designed components, it is also possible to use rely conditions to record assumptions about system components that are given rather than being under the control of the designer; such components might be physical sub-systems or even human actors.[10] Using a simple sluice gate example, [BHJ20] illustrates how an overall system specification of a cyber-physical system can be used as a starting point to derive a specification for a control system under assumptions about both the physical components and their connections via sensors and actuators. This is an example of it being easier to understand the specification of an overall system than it is to jump into implementation details of control systems too early.

A further development of these ideas is to use layers of rely and guarantee conditions to cope with degrees of fault tolerance: strong assumptions can be made and paired with commitments to desired behaviour but these can be supplemented with weaker sets of assumptions paired with behaviour that at least offers a reduced –but defined– level of service. A recent publication on this approach [JB23] tackles real-time scheduling.[11]

It is important to review all aspects of a specification when making a deployment decision: of course, post conditions must fit the needs of the intended environment but it is equally important to review all of the assumptions that are recorded in both rely and pre conditions.

3.2   Semantics and Tool Support

Inference rules such as those in Sect. 2.3 need to be shown to be sound with respect to a model-based semantics. The early attempt in [Jon81] used a Baroque

---

[10] The first use of this idea was firmly problem based. During a consultancy activity we were introduced to an "Inherently safe reactor protection system" [SW89]: the design certainly had many interesting fault-tolerant features but the assumptions about which failures would be covered were not fully listed. This prompted the idea of using rely conditions for fault-tolerance.

[11] The joint chapter with Alan Burns in the current volume applies this approach to Fixed-Priority schedulers.

operational semantics that was written prior to the publication of Gordon Plotkin's "SOS" [Plo81]; the use of VDL was far less clear! In [Pre01], Leonor Prensa-Nieto used Isabelle [NPW09] to prove the soundness of both Owicki's approach and a set of rely-guarantee rules. Perhaps because the former approach fails to cope with nested parallelism and also assumes that assignment statements are executed atomically, Prensa-Nieto carried over both restrictions. Both limitations are lifted in the SOS model used in [CJ07, Col08].

Further tool support has been developed including that described in [MD17] and [BRS+00] with the latter work based on KIV [STE+14] offering an interesting link to Ben Moszkowski's "Interval Temporal Logic" [Mos86].

More recent semantic models are discussed in Sect. 4.1 along with comments on their Isabelle implementation.

3.3   Related Research

Research on Concurrent Separation Logic (CSL) [O'H07] is extensive[12] and has led to tool support that is used in industry (see for example [DFLO19]). It is Important to note that the main focus of Reynolds' original "separation logic" (see [Rey02]) and CSL is to tackle dynamically managed heap storage.

There are in fact many variants of (concurrent) separation logics (see [Par10])—what is written here focusses on the essence of CSL. A key contribution of CSL is a rule for reasoning about the parallel combination of two statements:

$$\boxed{\| \text{-} CSL} \quad \frac{\{P1\}\ S_1\ \{Q1\}}{\{P1 * P2\}\ S_1 \parallel S_2\ \{Q1 * Q2\}}$$

This rule is deceptively like that from Hoare's [Hoa72] (shown in Sect. 2.3 as $\| \text{-} I_{disj}$) but with the profound difference that the separating conjunction operator $(*)$ which is used in $\| \text{-} CSL$ can be applied only if its operands refer to distinct heap addresses.

It is certainly the case that many intricate low-level concurrent programs use dynamically allocated memory addresses and the correctness of such programs can depend on avoiding data races by reasoning about the exchange of ownership of specific addresses between threads. As such, CSL researchers might appear to have distinct goals from those working on rely-guarantee reasoning. However "RGSep" [VP07, Vaf07] and "SAGL" [FFS07] are explicit combinations of CSL and rely-guarantee verification (the second of which was followed by "Local rely-guarantee reasoning" [Fen09] and Hongjin Liang's "Refinement verification" [Lia14]). Furthermore, "Deny-guarantee" ideas are set out in [DFPV09].

Interaction with CSL researchers has exhibited both friendly rivalry and productive exchanges. Interesting examples include Richard Bornat and colleagues' challenge to the Jones-Pierce publications on specifications and developments of

---

[12] An insider historical account of the evolution of CSL ideas can be found in [BO16].

Simpson's four-slot approach to ACMs: [BA10] uses RGSep whereas [BA13] uses a combination of a "linearisation" approach with rely-guarantee ideas.

A rather different approach to designing programs that use heap storage is to adopt a top-down view of separation. An investigation prompted by studying CSL examples shows how separation can be viewed as an abstraction in developments and subsequent reification can be tackled so as to show that the use of the heap addresses maintain the required separation. The line of thinking is that variables in a specification are by default assumed to be distinct; a design which works on separate variables can in some cases be reified to a representation in heap storage that preserves the required avoidance of overlap. Rather than focus on rules for reasoning about the low-level detail of address ownership, data structures that are linked by pointers are checked to preserve just the level of separation on which a designer has relied. Two examples are presented in [JY15] and it would be interesting to apply the same approach to other CSL material. This provides a further example of it being easier to focus on the specification of wide systems rather than their detailed implementation.

3.4   Tackling Synchronisation

Because reasoning is still concerned with threads influencing one another, the term "interference" can also be applied to inter-process synchronisation. It is however clear that Dijkstra's term of "cooperation" might look to be a better fit to synchronisation. In fact, synchronisation is frequently used precisely to control interference on state changes—in for example using critical sections to avoid data races.

Issues of synchronisation were not handled by the original rely-guarantee conditions because of the limited expressiveness of relations about interfering state changes. Other than the position that any implementation should terminate (for any valid starting state satisfying the pre condition) there was initially no way of reasoning about progress. It is possible to introduce "ghost variables" that artificially extend the expressiveness of state assertions but a more assertional approach to progress arguments should facilitate clearer reasoning.

Separate research by Ketil Stølen [Stø90, Stø91] and Xu Qiwen [Xu92] proposed the addition of a fifth predicate to specifications: in Stølen's proposal, a **wait** condition defines states in which a process can fail to progress. This makes it possible to argue about deadlock. His approach achieves relative completeness by employing auxiliary variables.

A choice has then to made between reasoning about detailed interaction between all threads or exploring the consequences of doggedly insisting that –under stated assumptions– any component should terminate. This option is discussed further in Sect. 4.2 but it should be clear that the expressive limitations of the original rely-guarantee proposals must be addressed by recording some form of assumptions about the environment of each process.

One argument against the position that "everything must terminate" is that the "satisfiability" test for a specification becomes problematic. But in fact, even for simple pre/post condition specifications of sequential programs, satisfiability is normally an intuitive test rather than a formal proof and it is ultimately discharged by designing an implementation that does satisfy a specification.

———————

There is of course extensive separate research on synchronisation including:

- programming language constructs—[Ast23] offers a historical trace from the challenge of building operating systems (aka "monitors") to the programming language concept of "monitors".
- Petri Nets—see for example [Rei13]
- process algebras—see for example [BW90]—including the tasteful embedding in "Circus" [WC02]
- Temporal Logics—see for example [Sch97]

4   Further Abstractions

Although "rely-guarantee thinking" has been shown to be effective in a variety of application areas, this argues the case for further research rather than closing down the topic.

Three desiderata influence the choice of possible directions:

- supporting a "posit-and-prove" mode of development points to the need for some form of top-down decomposition rules;
- (linked to this) formal rules that can be interpreted as intuitive prompts make it practical to graduate the actual level of formality used;
- the possibility of underpinning development ideas with tool support is clearly important whether it be mechanising user-guided transformations or the generation of proof obligations.

This section considers two complementary avenues of abstraction that, it is hoped, will supplement the effectiveness of the original rely-guarantee ideas.

4.1   Algebraic Presentation

At least back to [HHJ+87], it was recognised that searching for, and recording, equivalences between program texts was one approach to providing semantics for language constructs. This avenue has been assiduously pursued by Tony Hoare and a thorough survey of the research is available in [Str21].

Ian Hayes was one of the authors of [HHJ+87] and –together with colleagues– has applied this algebraic approach to find abstract presentations of the rely-guarantee approach to concurrency. The advantages of algebraic approaches include the identification of properties that are general; for example, early rely-guarantee developments distribute rely and/or guarantee conditions over sequential and parallel decomposition without a formal proof that this was justified, whereas such distributive laws are explicitly justified in [HJM23]. Perhaps more tellingly, algebraic approaches can often support general proofs that can then be specialised to multiple situations.

A further bonus of algebraic approaches is that they offer a route to theorem proving support and the research at Queensland University is available as Isabelle theories from the *Archive of Formal Proofs* (see also [AGS14] and [MD17]).

It is interesting to trace the steps of abstraction from the specific inference rules shown in Sect. 2.3.

- In [HJC14], it was shown that rely and guarantee conditions can be handled by commands that restrict behaviour. For example, a guarantee command written as **guar**$g \bullet c$ allows only the behaviours of the command c whose atomic steps also satisfy g. Similarly, code for c that aborts if the environment makes a transition that is not in accord with r satisfies a rely command **rely**$r \bullet c$. The technical report makes use of a refinement calculus (see [Mor90]) presentation that is more compact than the keyword layout.
- In [CHM17] extensive use is made of "Aczel traces" to provide a semantics and clauses of a specification are combined with a "weak conjunction operator"; this makes the algebraic structure more visible than in earlier presentations.
- A move from a weak specification command to a strong version is made in [HJM23] in order to handle total (rather than partial) correctness. Considerable attention is given to progress arguments and, matching Leslie Lamport's TLA+ (Temporal Logic of Actions) [Lam02], the need for temporal operators is kept to a minimum.

Alastair Armstrong's thesis [Arm16] also gives an algebraic treatment of rely-guarantee ideas.

4.2   Implementation Patterns

This section explores a direction for the use of abstraction in development that –although different from the algebraic ideas in the preceding section– is complementary to that research. The point of departure is to favour starting any development with an overall system specification and to postpone reasoning about implementations that employ detailed synchronisation constructs.

From a top-down view, synchronisation constructs are likely to be used to achieve a design decision. For example, two threads that share a one-place buffer might be a *Producer* and a *Consumer*; performance can be gained by the computation to generate a value in *Producer* being executed concurrently with *Consumer* processing the previous value. Coding this with two locks for *buffer-full/buffer-empty* is a simple implementation pattern but it is actually achieving exactly the semantic effect of producing a value followed by processing that value; furthermore, it is trivial to see that the work portions of *Producer* and *Consumer* can overlap safely providing they have disjoint frames. An implementation pattern in this case would avoid detailed reasoning about the locks.

Another common pattern whose need can be identified by comparing rely and guarantee conditions is "mutual exclusion". For example, two operations

O_1/O_2 might have differing rely and guarantee conditions and, if they are to be used sequentially in one thread that executes concurrently with another thread, it could be necessary to control which of O_1/O_2 are executing at the same time as a specified portion of the other thread.

A further pattern which might look more elaborate actually exhibits greater separation. Two threads can share access to a queue that is used to pass values from one thread to the other; one thread is essentially piping values to the other and in the majority of cases there is likely to be no other shared data. Whilst it is true that the synchronisation on empty and full queues requires some care at the low-level, the concept of piping is a known implementation pattern and the concept of "(safely) splitting software atoms" discussed in Sect. 2.6 can be applied. The fact that there are clever algorithms for managing shared access to queues should not complicate the reasoning at the system level.

Generalising the points above, the proposal is that, starting from the general idea that synchronisation orchestrates periods of restricted interference, it feels worth exploring how many (or few) patterns of concurrent combinations are required.

Another area where coping with the most general case can be argued to complicate reasoning even in simpler instances is termination. Non-termination is, of course, an issue without concurrency—it arises with sequential programs. What concurrency adds is that progress can depend on actions external to the thread under consideration. Recognising this makes it clear that the issue is how to record assumptions about external activity and the case is made above that such assumptions should not say too much about the context.

A portion of code that loops forever is dangerous and must be deployed with the utmost care; in the vast majority of useful programs a way of terminating their execution is included. Of course, a micro-computer that is being poured into cement to monitor a building will have an outer loop of the form **while true do** $\cdots$ **od** but this can again be viewed as a "design pattern". If the position is adopted that the vast majority of portions of code about which one wishes to reason should terminate under stated assumptions (pre and rely conditions), some issues of providing semantics for infinite computations can be localised. This does need a semantic model but taking the most complicated case of non-termination as a default leads to complications in reasoning about "magic" or "miracles".

An abstraction of design patterns would need to be underpinned by a semantics and it is thus hoped that the idea is symbiotic with the algebraic abstractions outlined in Sect. 4.1. The aim would be to add design patterns to other top-down approaches; the patterns themselves should be determined by looking at overall applications rather than from low-level implementation tricks.

5   Conclusions

The success of rely-guarantee thinking to date must in part be due to having picked a tractable way to express interference. Although deciding to express rely and guarantee conditions as relations over states was clearly restrictive, these assertions have been shown to be effective in providing top-down developments of a variety of programs that admit shared-variable interference.

The most glaring lacuna of the original proposal was its inability to deal with progress arguments. Overcoming this gap should not walk back into the trap of having to provide excessive assumptions about the environment into which yet-to-be-developed components will fit. Evidence from attempts so far indicates that useful descriptions of what enables a component to make progress can be made abstract enough to avoid over-proscribing contexts. One lucky outcome of the paper in this volume coauthored with Alan Burns was that the presence of a "clock" in the state admits a way of expressing progress in terms of a data-type invariant. (Other interesting developments in that paper are the use of data-type invariants as a form of "meta" rely-guarantee condition and the way in which the first phase establishes the conditions under which the second phase satisfies its specification.)

Returning to the title of the current chapter, it is of course meant to encourage work on clarifying and documenting assumptions about the expected use of computer systems; but the alternative of reading the "clarifying" as an adjective is meant as a reminder that any notational or conceptual tools used to record assumptions should indeed enhance clarity.

Experiments on large specifications are difficult (and not easy to publish) but a focus on small intricate programming tricks may not be the best way to develop approaches that will be applicable to larger applications. It is also worth repeating that experience suggests that it can be clearer to start with a specification of an overall system rather than focus on intriguing –but intricate– components. Abstraction really is our only tool in taming complicated artefacts.

Acknowledgements. Recent research on the core concurrency material has benefited from the collaboration with Ian Hayes and his colleagues Rob Colvin and Larissa Meinicke; over a longer timescale, there have been many rewarding collaborations cited in Sect. 3 and [§10.2] [HJM23]. Coming back to the dedicatee of this paper, I hope that collaboration with Jim Woodcock and Ana Cavalcanti on their RoboStar activities will yield future challenges for rely-guarantee thinking.

Interest in recording the history of formal methods was enhanced by working with Troy Astarte. The author is grateful for the helpful input from referees.

My research was funded by an EPSRC Platform Grant (STRATA) and support from the Leverhulme Trust (RPG-2019-020).

References

[Abr10] Abrial, J.-R.: The Event-B Book. Cambridge University Press, Cambridge, UK (2010)

[AGS14] Armstrong, A., Gomes, V.B.F., Struth, G.: Algebraic principles for rely-guarantee style concurrency verification tools. In: Jones, C., Pihlajasaari, P., Sun, J. (eds.) FM 2014: Formal Methods, pp. 78–93. Springer International Publishing, Cham (2014). https://doi.org/10.1007/978-3-319-06410-9_6

[AH22] Apt, K.R., Hoare, T., editors. Edsger Wybe Dijkstra: his Life, Work and Legacy. ACM (2022)

[ALRL04] Avizienis, A., Laprie, J.-C., Randell, B., Landwehr, C.: Basic concepts and taxonomy of dependable and secure computing. IEEE Trans. Dependable Secure Comput. **1**(1), 11–33 (2004)

[AM71] Ashcroft, E.A., Manna, Z.: Formalization of properties of parallel programs. In: Meltzer, B., Michie, D., editors, Machine Intelligence, vol. 6, pp. 17–41. Edinburgh University Press (1971)

[Arm16] Armstrong, A.: Formal Analysis of Concurrent Programs. PhD thesis, University of Sheffield (2016)

[Ash75] Ashcroft. E.A.: Proving assertions about parallel programs. J. Comput. Syst. Sci. **10**(1), 110–135 (1975)

[Ast23] Astarte, T.K.: From monitors to monitors: an early history of concurrency primitives. Minds and Machines (2023)

[BA10] Bornat, R., Amjad, H.: Inter-process buffers in separation logic with rely-guarantee. Formal Aspects Comput. **22**(6), 735–772 (2010)

[BA13] Bornat, R., Amjad, H.: Explanation of two non-blocking shared-variable communication algorithms. Formal Aspects Comput. **25**(6), 893–931 (2013)

[BHJ20] Burns, A., Hayes, I.J., Jones, C.B.: Deriving specifications of control programs for cyber physical systems. Comput. J. **63**(5), 774–790 (2020)

[BLX23] Bowen, J.P., Li, Q., Xu, Q. (eds.): Theories of Programming and Formal Methods. LNCS, vol. 14080. Springer, Cham (2023). https://doi.org/10.1007/978-3-031-40436-8

[BO16] Brookes, S., O'Hearn, P.W.: Concurrent separation logic. ACM SIGLOG News **3**(3), 47–65 (2016)

[BRS+00] Balser, M., Reif, W., Schellhorn, G., Stenzel, K., Thums, A.: Formal system development with KIV. In: Maibaum, T. (ed.) Fundamental Approaches to Software Engineering, pp. 363–366. Springer, Berlin, Heidelberg (2000). https://doi.org/10.1007/3-540-46428-X_25

[BW90] Baeten, J.C.M., Weijland, W.P.: Process Algebra. Cambridge Tracts in Theoretical Computer Science. Cambridge University Press (1990)

[CH79] Coleman, D., Hughes, J.W.: The clean termination of Pascal programs. Acta Informatica **11**(3), 195–210 (1979)

[CHM17] Colvin, R.J., Hayes, I.J., Meinicke, L.A.: Designing a semantic model for a wide-spectrum language with concurrency. Formal Aspects Comput. **29**(5), 853–875 (2017)

[CJ00] Collette, P., Jones, C.B.: Enhancing the tractability of rely/guarantee specifications in the development of interfering operations. In Gordon Plotkin, Colin Stirling, and Mads Tofte, editors, Proof, Language and Interaction, chapter 10, pp. 277–307. MIT Press (2000)

[CJ07]   Coleman, J.W., Jones, C.B.: A structural proof of the soundness of rely/guarantee rules. J. Log. Comput. **17**(4), 807–841 (2007)

[Col08]   Coleman, J.W.: Constructing a tractable reasoning framework upon a fine-grained structural operational semantics. PhD thesis, Newcastle University School of Computer Science (2008)

[DFLO19]   Distefano, D., Fähndrich, M., Logozzo, F., O'Hearn, P.W.: Scaling static analyses at Facebook. Commun. ACM **62**(8), 62–70 (2019)

[DFPV09]   Dodds, M., Feng, X., Parkinson, M., Vafeiadis, V.: Deny-guarantee reasoning. In: Castagna, G. (ed.) Programming Languages and Systems. Lecture Notes in Computer Science, vol. 5502, pp. 363–377. Springer, Berlin / Heidelberg (2009). https://doi.org/10.1007/978-3-642-00590-9_26

[Dij65]   Dijkstra, E.W.: Cooperating sequential processes (1965)

[Dij75]   Dijkstra, E.W.: Guarded commands, non-determinacy, and formal languages. Commun. ACM **18**(8) (1975)

[Din02]   Dingel, J.: A refinement calculus for shared-variable parallel and distributed programming. Formal Aspects Comput. **14**, 123–197 (2002)

[dRdBH+01] de Roever, W.P., et al.: Concurrency Verification: Introduction to Compositional and Noncompositional Methods. Cambridge Tracts in Theoretical Computer Science. Cambridge University Press (2001)

[Fen09]   Feng, X.: Local rely-guarantee reasoning. In: Proceedings of the 36th annual ACM SIGPLAN-SIGACT Symposium on Principles of Programming Languages, POPL '09, pp. 315–327, New York, NY, USA (2009)

[FFS07]   Feng, X., Ferreira, R., Shao, Z.: On the relationship between concurrent separation logic and assume-guarantee reasoning. In: De Nicola, R. (ed.) Programming Languages and Systems, pp. 173–188. Springer, Berlin, Heidelberg (2007). https://doi.org/10.1007/978-3-540-71316-6_13

[Flo67]   Floyd, R.W.: Assigning meanings to programs. In: Schwartz, J.T., editor, Mathematical Aspects of Computer Science, Proceedings of Symposia in Applied Mathematics vol. 9, pp. 19–32. American Mathematical Society (1967)

[Fra86]   Francez, N.: Fairness. Monographs in Computer Science. Springer-Verlag, New York (1986). https://doi.org/10.1007/978-1-4612-4886-6

[GF64]   Galler, B.A., Fischer, M.J.: An improved equivalence algorithm. Commun. ACM **7**(5), 301–303 (1964)

[HBDJ13]   Hayes, I.J., Burns, A., Dongol, B., Jones, C.B.: Comparing degrees of non-deterministim in expression evaluation. Comput. J. **56**(6), 741–755 (2013)

[HHJ+87]   Hoare, C.A.R., et al.: Laws of programming. Communications of the ACM **30**(8), 672–687 (1987). see Corrigenda in Communications of the ACM **30**(9), 770

[HJ18]   Hayes, I.J., Jones, C.B.: A guide to rely/guarantee thinking. In: Bowen, J.P., Liu, Z., Zhang, Z. (eds.) SETSS 2017. LNCS, vol. 11174, pp. 1–38. Springer, Cham (2018). https://doi.org/10.1007/978-3-030-02928-9_1

[HJC14]   Hayes, I.J., Jones, C.B., Colvin, R.J.: Laws and semantics for rely-guarantee refinement. Technical Report CS-TR-1425, Newcastle University (2014)

[HJM23]   Hayes, I.J., Jones, C.B., Meinicke, L.A.: Specifying and reasoning about shared-variable concurrency. In: Bowen et al. [BLX23], pp. 110–135 (2023)

[Hoa69]   Hoare, C.A.R.: An axiomatic basis for computer programming. Commun. ACM **12**(10), 576–580 (1969)

[Hoa71] Hoare, C.A.R.: Proof of a program: FIND. Commun. ACM **14**(1), 39–45 (1971)

[Hoa72] Hoare, C.A.R.: Towards a theory of parallel programming. In: Hoare, C.A.R., Perrott, R.H., editors, Operating System Techniques, pp. 61–71. Academic Press, New York, 1972. Proceedings of a Seminar at Queen's University, Belfast, August–September (1971)

[HW90] Herlihy, M., Wing, J.M.: Linearizability: a correctness condition for concurrent objects. ACM Trans. Program. Lang. Syst. **12**(3), 463–492 (1990)

[JB23] Jones, C.B., Burns, A.: Extending rely-guarantee thinking to handle realtime scheduling. Formal Methods Syst. Design **62**(1–3), 119–140 (2024). https://doi.org/10.1007/s10703-023-00441-y

[JH16] Jones, C.B., Hayes, I.J.: Possible values: exploring a concept for concurrency. J. Logical Algebraic Methods Program. **85**(5), 972–984 (2016)

[JL71] Jones, C.B., Lucas, P.: Proving correctness of implementation techniques. In: Engeler, E. (ed.) Symposium on Semantics of Algorithmic Languages, pp. 178–211. Springer, Berlin, Heidelberg (1971). https://doi.org/10.1007/BFb0059698

[Jon70] Jones, C.B.: A technique for showing that two functions preserve a relation between their domains. Technical Report LR 25.3.067, IBM Laboratory, Vienna (1970)

[Jon72] Jones, C.B.: Formal development of correct algorithms: an example based on Earley's recogniser. In: SIGPLAN Notices, vol. 7, no. 1, pp. 150–169. ACM (1972)

[Jon73] Jones, C.B.: Formal development of programs. Technical Report 12.117, IBM Laboratory Hursley, 6 (1973)

[Jon80] Jones, C.B.: Software Development: A Rigorous Approach. Prentice Hall International, Englewood Cliffs, N.J., USA (1980)

[Jon81] Jones, C.B.: Development Methods for Computer Programs including a Notion of Interference. PhD thesis, Oxford University, 6. Printed as: Programming Research Group, Technical Monograph 25 (1981)

[Jon86] Jones, C.B.: Systematic Software Development Using VDM. Prentice Hall International (1986)

[Jon93] Jones, C.B.: Constraining interference in an object-based design method. In: Gaudel, M.-C., Jouannaud, J.-P. (eds.) TAPSOFT'93: Theory and Practice of Software Development, pp. 136–150. Springer, Berlin, Heidelberg (1993). https://doi.org/10.1007/3-540-56610-4_61

[Jon96] Jones, C.B.: Accommodating interference in the formal design of concurrent object-based programs. Formal Methods Syst. Design **8**(2), 105–122 (1996)

[Jon03] Jones, C.B.: The early search for tractable ways of reasoning about programs. IEEE Ann. Hist. Comput. **25**(2), 26–49 (2003)

[Jon07] Jones, C.B.: Splitting atoms safely. Theoret. Comput. Sci. **375**(1–3), 109–119 (2007)

[Jon23] Jones, C.B.: Three early formal approaches to the verification of concurrent programs. Minds Mach. **34**, 73–92 (2023). https://doi.org/10.1007/s11023-023-09621-5

[JP11] Jones, C.B., Pierce, K.G.: Elucidating concurrent algorithms via layers of abstraction and reification. Formal Aspects Comput. **23**(3), 289–306 (2011)

[JY15]   Jones, C.B., Yatapanage, N.: Reasoning about separation using abstraction and reification. In: Calinescu, R., Rumpe, B. (eds.) Software Engineering and Formal Methods: 13th International Conference, SEFM 2015, York, UK, September 7-11, 2015. Proceedings, pp. 3–19. Springer International Publishing, Cham (2015). https://doi.org/10.1007/978-3-319-22969-0_1

[JY19]   Jones, C.B., Yatapanage, N.: Investigating the limits of rely/guarantee relations based on a concurrent garbage collector example. Formal Aspects Comput. **31**(3), 353–374 (2019). on-line April (2018)

[Lam02] Lamport, L.: Specifying systems: the TLA+ language and tools for hardware and software engineers. Addison-Wesley Longman Publishing Co., Inc, USA (2002)

[Lia14] Liang, H.: Refinement Verification of Concurrent Programs and Its Applications. PhD thesis, USTC, China (2014)

[Luc68] Lucas, P.: Two constructive realisations of the block concept and their equivalence. Technical Report TR 25.085, IBM Laboratory Vienna (1968)

[Mar85] Marshall, L.S.: A formal specification of line representations on graphics devices. In: Ehrig, H., Floyd, C., Nivat, M., Thatcher, J. (eds.) Formal Methods and Software Development, pp. 129–147. Springer, Berlin, Heidelberg (1985). https://doi.org/10.1007/3-540-15199-0_9

[MD17]   Dias, D.M.: Mechanising an algebraic rely-guarantee refinement calculus. PhD thesis, Newcastle University (2017)

[Mil71] Milner, R.: An algebraic definition of simulation between programs. Technical Report CS-205, Computer Science Department, Stanford University (1971)

[Mor90] Morgan, C.: Programming from Specifications. Prentice Hall (1990)

[Mos86] Moszkowski, B.C.: Executing Temporal Logic Programs. Cambridge University Press (1986)

[Nip86] Nipkow, T.: Non-deterministic data types: models and implementations. Acta Informatica **22**(6), 629–661 (1986)

[NPW09] Nipkow, T., Wenzel, M., Paulson, L.C. (eds.): Isabelle/HOL. LNCS, vol. 2283. Springer, Heidelberg (2002). https://doi.org/10.1007/3-540-45949-9

[OG76]   Owicki, S.S., Gries, D.: An axiomatic proof technique for parallel programs I. Acta Informatica **6**, 319–340 (1976)

[O'H07] O'Hearn, P.W.: Resources, concurrency and local reasoning. Theor. Comput. Sci. **375**(1-3), 271–307 (2007)

[Owi75] Owicki, S.S.: Axiomatic Proof Techniques for Parallel Programs. PhD thesis, Department of Computer Science, Cornell University. Published as technical report 75–251 (1975)

[Par10] Parkinson, M.: The next 700 separation logics. In: Leavens, G., O'Hearn, P., Rajamani, S. (eds.) Verified Software: Theories. Tools, Experiments, volume 6217 of Lecture Notes in Computer Science, pp. 169–182. Springer, Berlin / Heidelberg (2010). https://doi.org/10.1007/978-3-642-15057-9_12

[Plo81] Plotkin, G.D.: A structural approach to operational semantics. Technical Report DAIMI FN-19, Aarhus University (1981)

[Pre01] Nieto, L.P.: Verification of Parallel Programs with the Owicki-Gries and Rely-Guarantee Methods in Isabelle/HOL. PhD thesis, Institut für Informatic der Technischen Universität München (2001)

[Pri20]   Priestley, M.: Flow diagrams, assertions, and formal methods. In: Sekerinski, E., et al. (eds.) FM 2019. LNCS, vol. 12233, pp. 15–34. Springer, Cham (2020). https://doi.org/10.1007/978-3-030-54997-8_1

[Rei13]   Reisig, W.: Understanding Petri Nets: Modeling Techniques, Analysis Methods. Springer-Verlag, Case Studies (2013). https://doi.org/10.1007/978-3-642-33278-4

[Rey02]   Reynolds, J.C.: Separation logic: a logic for shared mutable data structures. In: Proceedings of 17th LICS, pp. 55–74. IEEE (2002)

[San99]   Sangiorgi, D.: Typed π-calculus at work: a correctness proof of Jones's parallelisation transformation on concurrent objects. Theory Pract. Object Syst. **5**(1), 25–34 (1999)

[Sch97]   Schneider, F.B.: On Concurrent Programming. Springer, New York, NY (1997). https://doi.org/10.1007/978-1-4612-1830-2

[Sit74]   Sites, R.L.: Proving that Computer Programs Terminate Cleanly. PhD thesis, Computer Science Department, Stanford University. Printed as STAN-CS-74-418 (1974)

[STE+14] Schellhorn, G., Tofan, B., Ernst, G., Pfähler, J., Reif, W.: RGITL: a temporal logic framework for compositional reasoning about interleaved programs. Ann. Math. Artif. Intell. **71**(1–3), 131–174 (2014)

[Stø90]   Stølen, K.: Development of parallel programs on shared data-structures. PhD thesis, Manchester University. Published as technical report UMCS-91-1-1 (1990). https://breibakk.no/kst/PhD-thesis.htm

[Stø91]   Stølen, K.: A method for the development of totally correct shared-state parallel programs. In: Baeten, J.C.M., Groote, J.F. (eds.) CONCUR '91, pp. 510–525. Springer, Berlin, Heidelberg (1991). https://doi.org/10.1007/3-540-54430-5_110

[Str21]   Struth, G.: Trimming the hedges: an algebra to tame concurrency. In: Jones, C.B., Misra, J., editors, Theories of Programming: the Life and Works of Tony Hoare, chapter 14. ACM (2021)

[SW89]   Smith, I.C., Wall, D.N.: Programmable electronic systems for reactor safety. Atom, (395) (1989)

[SW01]   Sangiorgi, D., Walker, D.: The π-Calculus: A Theory of Mobile Processes. Cambridge University Press, Cambridge, United Kingdom (2001)

[Vaf07]   Vafeiadis, V.: Modular Fine-Grained Concurrency Verification. PhD thesis, University of Cambridge (2007)

[vGH15]   van Glabbeek, R., Höfner, P.: Progress, fairness and justness in process algebra. arXiv preprint of ACM Surveys article arXiv:1501.03268 (2015)

[VP07]   Vafeiadis, V., Parkinson, M.: A marriage of rely/guarantee and separation logic. In: Caires, L., Vasconcelos, V.T. (eds.) CONCUR 2007. LNCS, vol. 4703, pp. 256–271. Springer, Heidelberg (2007). https://doi.org/10.1007/978-3-540-74407-8_18

[WC02]   Woodcock, J., Cavalcanti, A.: The semantics of circus. In: Bert, D., Bowen, J.P., Henson, M.C., Robinson, K. (eds.) ZB 2002. LNCS, vol. 2272, pp. 184–203. Springer, Heidelberg (2002). https://doi.org/10.1007/3-540-45648-1_10

[WD88]   Woodcock, J.C.P., Dickinson, B.: Using VDM with rely and guarantee-conditions. In: Bloomfield, R.E., Marshall, L.S., Jones, R.B. (eds.) VDM 1988. LNCS, vol. 328, pp. 434–458. Springer, Heidelberg (1988). https://doi.org/10.1007/3-540-50214-9_27

[WW10] Wang, S., Wang, X.: Proving Simpson's four-slot algorithm using owner-ship transfer. In: VERIFY Workshop, Edinburgh (2010)

[Xu92] Xu, Q.: A theory of state-based parallel programming. PhD thesis, Oxford University Computing Laboratory (1992)

PCSP# Denotational Semantics
with an Application in Sports Analytics

Zhaoyu Liu[1]([✉]), Murong Ma[1], Kan Jiang[1], Zhe Hou[2], Ling Shi[3],
and Jin Song Dong[1]

[1] National University of Singapore, Singapore, Singapore
`e0253678@u.nus.edu`
[2] Griffith University, Nathan, Australia
[3] Nanyang Technological University, Singapore, Singapore

Abstract. The chapter introduces probabilistic CSP# (PCSP#) as a formal language for modeling probabilistic systems, emphasizing its foundational role in concurrent and parallel computation. PCSP# is an extension of communicating sequential programs (CSP#) that enables the modeling of probabilistic behaviors and uncertainties in system designs. We provide the formal syntax and denotational semantics for PCSP# based on the UTP framework. We also introduce the Process Analysis Toolkit (PAT) as a formal modeling and verification tool for complex concurrent and probabilistic systems, particularly focusing on its extension CSP# and its variant, PCSP#. The chapter explores the applications of PCSP# in sports analytics, specifically in modeling tennis matches. It demonstrates how PCSP# can be used to analyze match outcomes, develop strategies, and provide training recommendations based on past match data. Experimental results from historical data in the past decade show that formal methods applied to sports analytics yield high-performance and accurate models that are explainable and suitable for strategy and training recommendations.

Keywords: Denotational Semantics · System Modeling · Probabilistic Model Checking · Sports Analytics

Dedication:
During his undergraduate studies, Prof. Jin Song Dong (the last author of this chapter), the leader of the NUS Formal Methods group, studied Jim's book, "Software Engineering Mathematics" [60], where Jin Song encountered the Z notation [63] and was deeply impressed by its precision and coherence. Jim's prolific contributions, reflected in both papers and presentations, left a lasting imprint on Jin Song's research endeavors. Their first encounter occurred in 1996 at the FME conference in Oxford, marking the commencement of numerous

© The Author(s), under exclusive license to Springer Nature Switzerland AG 2024
S. Foster and A. Sampaio (Eds.): *The Application of Formal Methods*, LNCS 14900, pp. 71–102, 2024.
https://doi.org/10.1007/978-3-031-67114-2_4

*subsequent meetings across various
international locales. Jim consistently ranks
as a top candidate for keynote addresses at
major conferences organized by Jin Song, a
testament to the enduring impact of his
insights. Furthermore, Jin Song holds dear
the cherished moments spent with Jim and
their family during their early gatherings in
Singapore. Jin Song and his team would
like to dedicate this chapter to honor the
occasion of Jim's retirement from the
University of York in September 2024.*

1   Introduction

Communicating Sequential Processes (CSP) [16] is a formal language for describing patterns of interaction in concurrent systems. Developed by Tony Hoare in the late 1970 s, CSP serves as a foundational model for studying concurrent and parallel computation. The language provides a rigorous framework for specifying the behavior of concurrent processes, emphasizing communication and synchronization between them.

In CSP, concurrent processes are represented as independent entities that communicate by sending and receiving messages over channels. These channels serve as communication pathways, enabling processes to exchange information and coordinate their activities. The language allows for the definition of complex systems by composing simpler processes and specifying their interactions through communication events. Key concepts in CSP include process behavior, communication primitives, and synchronization mechanisms. Processes in CSP exhibit sequential behavior, executing a series of steps in a defined order, while communication primitives such as channel input and output operations facilitate message passing between processes. Synchronization mechanisms, such as synchronization barriers and process synchronization, ensure that processes coordinate their activities in a coherent manner.

CSP has found applications in various domains, including concurrent programming, distributed systems, and formal verification. Its formal semantics enable a rigorous analysis of system properties, such as deadlock freedom, liveliness, and safety [38]. Additionally, CSP has inspired the development of other concurrency models and programming languages [35,44], contributing to the advancement of concurrent computing theory and practice.

A prominent application of CSP is the Process Analysis Toolkit (PAT) [51], which is a comprehensive software tool designed for the formal modeling, analysis, and verification of concurrent systems. PAT provides a user-friendly environment for specifying and analyzing complex systems using formal methods. PAT supports various formal modeling languages, including CSP, allowing users to describe concurrent systems as sets of interacting processes. These processes communicate and synchronize their actions through channels, enabling the modeling of intricate systems with concurrency and communication patterns.

PAT has been widely used in academia and industry for the formal verification of concurrent systems, including communication protocols, distributed systems, and hardware designs. Its user-friendly interface and powerful analysis capabilities make it a valuable tool for researchers, engineers, and developers working in the field of concurrent and distributed computing. Notably, PAT extends the CSP language with C# to make the modeling task user-friendly for programmers, resulting in communicating sequential programs (CSP#) [49]. Moreover, PAT has various modules that extend CSP# further to variants such as Stateful Timed CSP# [50] and probabilistic CSP# (PCSP#) [52]. This chapter focuses on the latter and its applications.

PCSP# allows users to specify probabilistic behaviors and uncertainties in system designs. It enables the representation of systems that exhibit stochastic or non-deterministic behaviors, such as probabilistic transitions, uncertain actions, and random events. This probabilistic extension enhances the expressiveness of CSP#, enabling the modeling of a wider range of real-world systems, including stochastic processes, randomized algorithms, and probabilistic protocols. The key features include probabilistic transitions, uncertain actions, and random events. PCSP# is widely used in probabilistic systems modeling, reliability analysis, fault tolerance analysis, security analysis, performance evaluation, and so on. This chapter demonstrates its application from a new angle: sports analytics. We show how PCSP# is used to model a tennis match, considering a variety of actions in the game and how they transit to each other. The probabilities are mined from past match data. Such a model enables in-depth analysis of the tennis match, including match outcome prediction, strategy analysis, and training recommendations.

In what follows we will describe the syntax and semantics of PCSP#, and then we will give a detailed case study on tennis analytics. Similar techniques can be easily applied to other racket sports.

2 The Probabilistic CSP# Language (PCSP#)

A PCSP# model comprises definitions of constants, shared variables, channels, and processes. The process is an extension of CSP# with probabilistic multichoice. Its main syntax is defined as follows.

$$
\begin{aligned}
P, P_i, Q ::= \; &Stop \mid Skip & &- \text{primitives} \\
\mid \; &a \to P & &- \text{event prefixing} \\
\mid \; &ch!exp \to P & &- \text{channel output} \\
\mid \; &ch?m \to Proc(m) & &- \text{channel input} \\
\mid \; &e\{prog\} \to P & &- \text{data operation prefix} \\
\mid \; &[b]P & &- \text{state guard} \\
\mid \; &P \,\square\, Q \mid P \sqcap Q & &- \text{choices} \\
\mid \; &P \; ; \; Q & &- \text{sequence} \\
\mid \; &P \setminus X_1 & &- \text{hiding} \\
\mid \; &P \parallel_{(X_1, X_2)} Q \mid P \parallel\mid_{X_2} Q & &- \text{parallel/interleaving} \\
\mid \; &N \mid \mu N \cdot P & &- \text{recursion} \\
\mid \; &\mathbf{pcase}\{pr_0 : P_0; \; pr_1 : P_1; \; \cdots ; & &\quad\; probabilistic \\
&pr_k : P_k\} & &\quad\; multi - choices
\end{aligned}
$$

where P, P_i, Q range over processes, a is an action name, exp is an arithmetic expression, m is a bound variable, e is the name of a non-communicating event denoting sequential program $prog$ which updates global shared variables, b is a Boolean expression, X_1 is a set of actions, X_2 is a set of synchronous channel inputs and outputs, N is an identifier, and pr_i is a positive integer to express the probability weight. The syntax of program $prog$ can be referred to [43].

Process $Stop$ communicates nothing and process $Skip$ terminates successfully. Process $a \to P$ engages in action a first and then behaves as process P. Synchronous channels communicate through handshaking. Specifically, a process $ch!exp \to P$ which is ready to perform an output through ch will be enabled if another process $ch?m \to Proc(m)$ is ready to receive input through the same channel ch simultaneously, and *vice versa*. The expression exp in $ch!exp$ is evaluated atomically with the occurrence of the output. Process $e\{prog\} \to P$ generates an event e, executes $prog$ *atomically*, and after that process behaves as P. Note that global shared variables are updated in the atomic execution of the program $prog$. Process $[b]P$ waits until condition b becomes *true* and then behaves as P. The condition checking is conducted atomically with the occurrence of the first event or state transition in P. Two choices are supported, i.e., $P \,\square\, Q$ for external choice, and $P \sqcap Q$ for internal choice. Sequential composition $P \; ; \; Q$ behaves as P until P terminates and then behaves as Q. Process $P \setminus X_1$ hides all occurrences of events in X_1. In process $P \parallel_{(X_1, X_2)} Q$, P and Q run in parallel and communicate through multi-part event synchronization (i.e., common events in X_1 and synchronous channels in X_2). In contrast, in process $P \parallel\mid_{X_2} Q$, P and Q run independently (except for communications through synchronous channels in X_2). Lastly, in probabilistic multi-choices process $\mathbf{pcase}\{pr_0 : P_0; \; pr_1 : P_1; \; \cdots ; \; pr_k : P_k\}$, with probability $\frac{pr_i}{pr_0 + pr_1 + \cdots pr_k}$, the process behaves as P_i.

3   The Denotational Semantics for PCSP#

The Unifying Theories of Programming (UTP) [17] offers a mathematical framework to describe and analyze programs across various paradigms, such as imperative, concurrent and so on. For each programming paradigm, a program is modeled as a relation between its initial and subsequent (intermediate or final) states. Relations are represented as predicates over observational variables to capture all aspects of program behaviours.

In the UTP framework, theories of programming paradigms contain three essential elements: *alphabet, signature* and *healthiness conditions*. The *alphabet* is a set of observational variables that can be used to record external observations of the program behaviour. These variables include both inputs to and outputs from the program. Variables of initial observations are undashed, representing the state before program execution, and variables of subsequent observations are dashed, representing the state after execution. The *signature* defines the syntax of the rules to represent the elements of a theory. The *healthiness conditions* are a selection of laws identifying valid predicates that characterise a theory. A healthiness condition is associated with observational variables in the alphabet. It is defined by an idempotent function on predicates. A healthy program represented by predicate P satisfies healthiness condition ϕ if it is a fixed point of ϕ: $P = \phi(P)$.

3.1   Semantic Model

To address the challenge of designing an appropriate semantic model which can cover different paradigms like communications, shared variables and probabilistic choices for the denotational semantics of PCSP#, we blend probability with communication events and states containing shared variables. We introduce *mixed* traces to record the interactions of processes with the global environment and its associated probability.

Observational Variables. The following variables are introduced in the alphabet of observations of PCSP# process behaviours. Some of them (i.e., ok, ok', $wait$, $wait'$, ref, and ref') are similar to those in the denotational semantics of CSP# [42]. The key difference is that probabilities are recorded in the traces in PCSP#.

- tr, tr': $\mathsf{seq}((\mathsf{S} \times \mathsf{S}^{\perp} \times \mathsf{PROB}) \cup (\mathsf{S} \times \mathsf{E} \times \mathsf{PROB}))$ record a finite sequence of observations on the interaction of the processes with the global environment. It is a 3-tuple consisting of pre-state, event/post-state and associated probability.
  - S is the set of all possible mappings (states), and a state $s : \mathsf{VAR} \to \mathsf{int}$ is a total function which maps global shared variables names from VAR into values of integer int. Notice that the types of variable values and channel messages are integer in our proposed semantics.

- E is the set of all possible events, including actions, channel inputs or outputs, synchronous channel communications and event τ_p which indicates the probabilistic choice selection.
- PROB is the set of probabilities with the range of $[0..1]$.
- $S \times S^\perp \times PROB$ is the set of 3-tuples, where each tuple consists of a pre-state recording the initial variable values before the observation, a post-state recording the final values after the observation, and its associated probability. $S^\perp \triangleq S \cup \{\perp\}$ represents all states, where the improper state $\perp$ indicates non-termination.
- $S \times E \times PROB$ denotes a set of occurring events under the pre-states with corresponding probabilities. The reason of recording the pre-state is that the value of the expression which may contain shared variables in a channel output shall be evaluated under this state. Additionally, we record the probability for the occurrence of the event.

Healthiness Conditions. In PCSP#, processes satisfy the following healthiness conditions.

$\mathbf{H}_p = \mathbf{R1} \circ \mathbf{R2} \circ \mathbf{R3} \circ \mathbf{CSP1} \circ \mathbf{CSP2}$

R1 ensures that a process can only extend the record and never change the past history of the observations.

$\mathbf{R1}(P) = P \wedge tr \le tr'$

R2 restricts that the execution of a process is independent of the history before its activation.

$\mathbf{R2}(P(tr, tr')) = \sqcap_s P(s, s \frown (tr' - tr))$

R3 characterises that a process cannot start if its predecessor has not finished, or otherwise, the values of all observational variables are unchanged.

$\mathbf{R3}(P) = II \triangleleft wait \triangleright P$

where $P \triangleleft b \triangleright Q \triangleq b \wedge P \vee \neg b \wedge Q$ and $II \triangleq (\neg ok \wedge tr \le tr') \vee (ok' \wedge tr' = tr \wedge wait' = wait \wedge ref' = ref)$.

CSP1 captures that when a process is in a divergent state, it can only arbitrarily extend the trace.

$\mathbf{CSP1}(P) = (\neg ok \wedge tr \le tr') \vee P$

CSP2 states that if an observation of a process is valid when ok' is false, then the observation should also be valid when ok' is true.

$\mathbf{CSP2}(P) = P \ ; \ ((ok \Rightarrow ok') \wedge tr' = tr \wedge wait' = wait \wedge ref' = ref)$

Although PCSP# satisfies the same healthiness conditions of CSP#, observational variables tr, tr' in our semantic model record additional information for probability. We adopt the same names for the idempotent functions used in CSP# for consistency.

3.2   Semantics of Processes

We first illustrate our semantic definitions of core processes: event prefixing, synchronous channel output/input, data operation prefixing, probabilistic multi-choices, and parallel composition. These process operators are frequently used to specify complex probabilistic systems involving channel-based communications, shared variables, and probabilistic behaviour. We further present the semantics of other process operators and refinement at the end.

Event Prefixing. Process $a \to P$ engages in action a first and afterwards behaves as process P. Action a occurs instantaneously, and may require simultaneous participation by more than one processes, which is captured when the process is in a waiting state $\neg wait'$, it cannot refuse this action a (represented by predicate $a \notin ref'$). When the action a is performed, the trace is augmented by the observation (represented by the predicate $tr' = tr ^\frown \langle (s, a, 1) \rangle$), where the probability of action a occurring is recorded as 1, reflecting the absence of probabilistic choices in the selection.

$$a \to P \mathrel{\widehat{=}} \mathbf{H}_p \left(ok' \wedge \left(\begin{array}{l} a \notin ref' \wedge tr' = tr \\ \triangleleft wait' \triangleright \\ \exists\, s \in \mathsf{S} \cdot tr' = tr ^\frown \langle (s, a, 1) \rangle \end{array} \right) \right) ; P$$

Synchronous Channel Output/input. PCSP# allows messages to be sent or received synchronously through channels. In the pairwise synchronisation, a synchronous channel communication $ch.exp$ can take place only if an output $ch!exp$ is enabled and a corresponding input $ch?m$ is also ready. There are two possible behaviours: when a process is waiting to communicate on channel ch (represented by $\neg wait'$), it cannot refuse any channel input over ch provided by the environment to perform a channel communication (represented by $ch? \notin ref'$) for channel output process or any channel output provided by the environment (represented by $ch! \notin ref'$) for channel input process; or a process sends the output/receives a message through ch and terminates without divergence. Note that probability recorded in the trace is 1 and the definition of semantics function $\mathcal{A}$ for arithmetic expressions can be referred to [43].

$$ch!exp \to P \mathrel{\widehat{=}} \mathbf{H}_p \left(ok' \wedge \left(\begin{array}{l} ch? \notin ref' \wedge tr' = tr \\ \triangleleft wait' \triangleright \\ \exists\, s \in \mathsf{S} \cdot tr' = tr ^\frown \langle (s, ch!\mathcal{A}[\![exp]\!](s), 1) \rangle \end{array} \right) \right) ; P$$

$$ch?m \to Proc(m) \mathrel{\widehat{=}}$$
$$\exists\, v \in \mathsf{int} \cdot \left(\mathbf{H}_p \left(ok' \wedge \left(\begin{array}{l} ch! \notin ref' \wedge tr' = tr \\ \triangleleft wait' \triangleright \\ \exists\, s \in \mathsf{S} \cdot tr' = tr ^\frown \langle (s, ch?v, 1) \rangle \end{array} \right) \right) ; Proc(v) \right)$$

Data Operation Prefixing. In process $e\{prog\} \to P$, the sequential program *prog* is executed atomically and its observation is the updates on shared variables after the execution of all programs. If the program does not terminate (represented by $(s, \bot) \in \mathcal{C}[\![prog]\!]$), then the process enters a waiting state, and its trace is extended with the record of non-termination. On the other hand, if the evaluation succeeds and terminates, then the process terminates and the state transition is recorded in the trace. In both cases, the probability is recorded as 1 in the extended trace. Function $\mathcal{C}$ defines the semantics of the sequential programs which can be referred to [43]. Note that the non-communicating event e is not recorded in the trace since such an event would not synchronise with other events and it is a label to denote the data operation.

$$e\{prog\} \rightarrow P \ \widehat{=}$$

$$\mathbf{H}_p \left(ok' \wedge \exists\, s \in \mathsf{S} \cdot \left(\begin{array}{l} wait' \wedge tr' = tr \ \frown \langle(s, \bot, 1)\rangle \\ \lhd(s, \bot) \in \mathcal{C}[\![prog]\!] \rhd \\ \neg wait' \wedge \exists\, s' \in \mathsf{S} \cdot (tr' = tr \ \frown \langle(s, s', 1)\rangle \\ \wedge (s, s') \in \mathcal{C}[\![prog]\!]) \end{array} \right) \right) ; \ P$$

Probabilistic Multi-choices. In process **pcase**$\{pr_0 : P_0;\ pr_1 : P_1;\ \cdots;\ pr_k : P_k\}$, if **pcase** is activated, then it transmits to a process via event τ_p with a corresponding probability. Event τ_p denotes the probabilistic choice selection which will not synchronize with other events. The semantics covers all cases of reaching the successive states following different probability weights. For example, after the execution, the process moves into process P_0 with the probability $\frac{pr_0}{pr}$. In this case, the trace is extended with the tuple $(s, \tau_p, \frac{pr_0}{pr})$. Note that $pr = \sum_{i=0}^{k} pr_i$ is the sum of all the probability weights.

$$\mathbf{pcase}\{pr_0 : P_0;\ pr_1 : P_1;\ \cdots;\ pr_k : P_k\} \ \widehat{=}$$

$$\bigvee_{i \in \{0..k\}} \left(\mathbf{H}_p \left(ok' \wedge \left(\begin{array}{l} tr' = tr \\ \lhd wait' \rhd \\ \exists\, s \in \dot{\mathsf{S}} \cdot tr' = tr \ \frown \langle(s, \tau_p, \frac{pr_i}{pr})\rangle \end{array} \right) \right) ; \ P_i \right)$$

Parallel Composition. Probabilistic multi-choices process executes independently when running in parallel with other processes. Thus, the semantics definition of parallel composition $P \parallel_{(X_1, X_2)} Q$ in PCSP# is similar to that in CSP#. The trace execution covers three aspects: (1) common actions of P and Q require simultaneous participation, (2) synchronous channel output in one process occurs simultaneously with the corresponding channel input in the other process, and (3) other kinds of events occur independently. Note that set X_1 contains common actions and set X_2 covers all synchronous channel inputs and outputs.

$$P \parallel_{(X_1, X_2)} Q \mathrel{\widehat{=}}$$

$$\mathbf{H}_p \begin{pmatrix} \exists\, 0.ok, 0.wait, \\ 0.ref, 0.tr, \\ 1.ok, 1.wait, \\ 1.ref, 1.tr \end{pmatrix} \cdot \begin{pmatrix} P[0.ok, 0.wait, 0.ref, 0.tr/ok', wait', ref', tr'] \wedge \\ Q[1.ok, 1.wait, 1.ref, 1.tr/ok', wait', ref', tr'] \wedge \\ M(X_1, X_2) \end{pmatrix} $$

$$\text{where } M(X_1, X_2) \mathrel{\widehat{=}} \begin{pmatrix} (ok' = 0.ok \wedge 1.ok) \wedge \\ (wait' = 0.wait \vee 1.wait) \wedge \\ (ref' = (0.ref \cap 1.ref \cap X_2) \cup ((0.ref \cup 1.ref) \cap X_1) \\ \cup ((0.ref \cap 1.ref) - X_1 - X_2)) \\ (tr' - tr \in (0.tr - tr \parallel_{X_1} 1.tr - tr)) \end{pmatrix}$$

The merge predicate $M(X_1, X_2)$ encapsulates four types of behaviours in a parallel composition. Firstly, the composition diverges if either process diverges (expressed as $ok' = 0.ok \wedge 1.ok$). Secondly, the composition terminates if both processes terminate ($wait' = 0.wait \vee 1.wait$). Thirdly, the composition handles synchronous channel outputs/inputs that are refused by both processes ($0.ref \cap 1.ref \cap X_2$), all actions in the set X_1 that are refused by both processes ($(0.ref \cup 1.ref) \cap X_1$), and events not in the set X_1 and X_2 but refused by both processes ($(0.ref \cap 1.ref) - X_1 - X_2$). Lastly, the trace of the composition belongs to the set of traces produced by the *trace synchronisation* function $\parallel_{X_1}$ as elaborated below.

Function $\parallel_{X_1}$ models how to merge two individual traces into a set of all possible traces; there are five cases covering both traces are empty, one of the trace is empty and both traces are non-empty. In the following definitions, s_1, s_1', s_2, s_2' are representative elements of variable states with termination, a, a_1, a_2 are representative elements of actions, ch is a representative element of channel names, τ_p is the event denoting the probabilistic choice selection, v, v_1, and v_2 are values with integer type, and p_1 and p_2 are probabilities with range of $[0..1]$.

- Firstly, function $\parallel_{X_1}$ is symmetric, i.e., $t_1 \parallel_{X_1} t_2 = t_2 \parallel_{X_1} t_1$.
- The first case (**case-1**) covers two scenarios, (1) if both input traces are empty, the result is a set of an empty sequence; (2) if only one input trace is empty, the result is determined based on the first observation of that non-empty trace: if that observation is an action in the set X_1 which requires synchronisation, then the result is a set containing only an empty sequence, or otherwise, the first observation is recorded in the merged trace.

case-1

$1°\ \langle\rangle \parallel_{X_1} \langle\rangle = \{\langle\rangle\}$

$2°\ (\langle (s_1, h, p_1) \rangle \frown t) \parallel_{X_1} \langle\rangle = \begin{cases} \{\langle\rangle\} & \text{if } h \in X_1 \\ \{\langle (s_1, h, p_1) \rangle \frown l \mid l \in (t \parallel_{X_1} \langle\rangle)\} & \text{otherwise} \end{cases}$

where $h \in \{a, ch?v, ch!v, ch.v, \tau_p, s_1', \bot\}$

- The second case (**case-2**) covers a communication is over a synchronous channel. There are two aspects, (1) if the first observations of two input traces match (see Definition 1 below), then a synchronisation may occur (denoted by the set $\mathcal{G}_1$) or at this moment a synchronisation does not occur (denoted by the set $\mathcal{G}_2$); (2) otherwise, either channel communication executes. Function $\mathsf{match_p}$ returns *true* if channel input and output from two processes respectively are enabled under the same pre-state with the same value.

Definition 1 (Match). *Given two 3-tuples* $tp_1 = (s_1, h_1, p_1)$ *and* $tp_2 = (s_2, h_2, p_2)$, *where* $h_1 \in \{ch?v_1, ch!v_1, ch.v_1\}$, $h_2 \in \{ch?v_2, ch!v_2, ch.v_2\}$, *we say that they are matched if* $s_1 = s_2$, $\{h_1, h_2\} = \{ch?v_1, ch!v_2\}$, *and* $v_1 = v_2$ *are satisfied, denoted as* $\mathsf{match_p}(tp_1, tp_2)$.

case-2 $\langle(s_1, h_1, p_1)\rangle ^\frown t_1 \|_{X_1} \langle(s_2, h_2, p_2)\rangle ^\frown t_2 =$

$$\begin{cases} \mathcal{G}_1 \cup \mathcal{G}_2 & \text{if } \mathsf{match_p}((s_1, h_1, p_1), (s_2, h_2, p_2)) \\ \mathcal{G}_2 & \text{otherwise} \end{cases}$$

where $h_1 \in \{ch?v_1, ch!v_1, ch.v_1\}$, $h_2 \in \{ch?v_2, ch!v_2, ch.v_2\}$, $\mathcal{G}_1 \hat{=} \{\langle(s_1, ch.v,$ $p_1 \times p_2)\rangle ^\frown l \mid l \in t_1 \|_{X_1} t_2\}$, *and* $\mathcal{G}_2 \hat{=} \{\langle(s_1, h_1, p_1)\rangle ^\frown l \mid l \in t_1 \|_{X_1} \langle(s_2, h_2, p_2)\rangle$ $^\frown t_2\} \cup \{\langle(s_2, h_2, p_2)\rangle ^\frown l \mid l \in \langle(s_1, h_1, p_1)\rangle ^\frown t_1 \|_{X_1} t_2\}$.

- The third case (**case-3**) considers the synchronisation of two actions (a_1 and a_2). There are four scenarios with respect to the initial states (s_1 and s_2) and actions from the first observations of two traces: (1) if both actions are in the set X_1 but different or actions under different pre-states, then the result is a set containing only an empty sequence; (2) if actions from X_1 are the same and under the same pre-state, then a synchronisation occurs; (3) if one of the actions is not in X_1, the execution of the action is postponed to occur; and (4) if both actions are not in X_1, then either action can occur.

case-3 $\langle(s_1, a_1, p_1)\rangle ^\frown t_1 \|_{X_1} \langle(s_2, a_2, p_2)\rangle ^\frown t_2 =$

$$\begin{cases} \{\langle\rangle\} & \begin{array}{l} a_1, a_2 \in X_1 \wedge \\ (a_1 \neq a_2 \vee s_1 \neq s_2) \end{array} \\[2ex] \{\langle(s_1, a_1, p_1 \times p_2)\rangle ^\frown l \mid l \in t_1 \|_{X_1} t_2\} & \begin{array}{l} a_1, a_2 \in X_1 \\ \wedge a_1 = a_2 \wedge s_1 = s_2 \end{array} \\[2ex] \{\langle(s_2, a_2, p_2)\rangle ^\frown l \mid l \in \langle(s_1, a_1, p_1)\rangle ^\frown t_1 \|_{X_1} t_2\} & a_1 \in X_1 \wedge a_2 \notin X_1 \\[1ex] \{\langle(s_1, a_1, p_1)\rangle ^\frown l \mid l \in t_1 \|_{X_1} \langle(s_2, a_2, p_2)\rangle ^\frown t_2\} & \\ \cup & a_1 \notin X_1 \wedge a_2 \notin X_1 \\ \{\langle(s_2, a_2, p_2)\rangle ^\frown l \mid l \in \langle(s_1, a_1, p_1)\rangle ^\frown t_1 \|_{X_1} t_2\} & \end{cases}$$

- The fourth case (**case-4**) deals with the situation that the first observation of one input trace is in a waiting state (captured by $\bot$). This waiting state arises because the evaluation of the sequential program does not terminate. There are three scenarios for consideration: (1) if both observations are in waiting states, the result is a set of either observation, (2) if the other first observation is an action requiring the synchronisation ($h \in X_1$), the result contains the waiting observation only, (3) or otherwise, either observation from two processes occurs.

case-4

$1^\circ \langle (s_1, \bot, p_1) \rangle \parallel_{X_1} \langle (s_2, \bot, p_2) \rangle = \{ \langle (s_1, \bot, p_1) \rangle, \langle (s_2, \bot, p_2) \rangle \}$

$2^\circ \langle (s_1, \bot, p_1) \rangle \parallel_{X_1} \langle (s_2, h, p_2) \rangle \frown t =$

$$\begin{cases} \{ \langle (s_1, \bot, p_1) \rangle \} & \text{if } h \in X_1 \\ \{ \langle (s_1, \bot, p_1) \rangle \} \cup \{ \langle (s_2, h, p_2) \rangle \frown l \mid l \in \langle (s_1, \bot, p_1) \rangle \parallel_{X_1} t \} & \text{otherwise} \end{cases}$$

where $h \in \{ a, ch?v, ch!v, ch.v, \tau_p, s_2' \}$

- The last case (**case-5**) defines the case when the first observation of one trace is an action a, a post-state s_1', or a τ_p event, and the other is a channel input $ch?v$, output $ch!v$, communication $ch.v$, a τ_p event, or a post-state s_2'. The merged observation depends on the action a in set X_1 or not, (1) if so, then its occurrence is postponed ($\mathcal{G}_3$), (2) or otherwise, either observation from two processes occurs ($\mathcal{G}_3 \cup \mathcal{G}_4$).

case-5 $\langle (s_1, h_1, p_1) \rangle \frown t_1 \parallel_{X_1} \langle (s_2, h_2, p_2) \rangle \frown t_2 = \begin{cases} \mathcal{G}_3 & \text{if } h_1 \in X_1 \\ \mathcal{G}_3 \cup \mathcal{G}_4 & \text{otherwise} \end{cases}$

where $h_1 \in \{ a, \tau_p, s_1' \}$, $h_2 \in \{ ch?v, ch!v, ch.v, \tau_p, s_2' \}$, $\mathcal{G}_3 \mathrel{\widehat{=}} \{ \langle (s_2, h_2, p_2) \rangle \frown l \mid l \in \langle (s_1, h_1, p_1) \rangle \frown t_1 \parallel_{X_1} t_2 \}$, and $\mathcal{G}_4 \mathrel{\widehat{=}} \{ \langle (s_1, h_1, p_1) \rangle \frown l \mid l \in t_1 \parallel_{X_1} \langle (s_2, h_2, p_2) \rangle \frown t_2 \}$.

Other Processes and Refinement. The semantics of other processes are the same as those counterparts in the CSP# model [43] except state guard ($[b]P$). For process $[b]P$, Boolean expression b is evaluated simultaneously with the occurrence of the first event of process P. Like CSP#, in some situations, the process P behaves like *Skip*. Thus, no state could be observed to judge the truth of condition b. To address this, we construct process $\widehat{P}$ from P by adding a stuttering step.

$$[b]P \mathrel{\widehat{=}} \widehat{P} \lhd (\mathcal{B}(b)(\pi_1(head(tr' - tr))) \wedge tr < tr') \rhd Stop$$

$$\widehat{P} \mathrel{\widehat{=}} P \wedge tr < tr' \vee P(tr, tr) \wedge \exists s \in \mathsf{S} \cdot tr' - tr = \langle (s, s, 1) \rangle$$

Refinement is a powerful technique for developing software systems that are correct by construction. In the UTP theory, it is expressed as an implementation satisfying a specification.

Definition 2 (Refinement). *Let P and Q be predicates for PCSP# processes with the same shared variable state space, the refinement $P \sqsupseteq Q$ holds iff $[P \Rightarrow Q]$.*

In the above definition, universal quantification implication means that for all observational variables, $\forall ok, ok', wait, wait', ref, ref', tr, tr' \cdot P \Rightarrow Q$ holds. In our current definition, the refinement ordering is strong; every observation that satisfies P must also satisfy Q. It requires that the associated probability in every observation of the trace shall be the same. The discussion on the probability comparison in the definition of refinement will be our future work.

4   Sports Analytics Using Probabilistic Model Checking

Sports analytics refers to the utilization of data science, artificial intelligence (AI), psychology, and Internet of Things (IoT) devices to enhance sports performance, strategic planning, and decision-making processes. It involves the collection, processing, and interpretation of data from various sources such as video recordings and scouting reports. This data aids in assessing both individual player and team performances [7], mitigating the risk of injuries [24], and assisting coaches in making well-informed decisions during both gameplay and training sessions. In this study, we employ Probabilistic Model Checking (PMC), a technique commonly employed in reliability analysis for intricate safety systems. We explain how this methodology can be adapted to sports strategy analytics, thereby augmenting the likelihood of achieving victory by considering the reliability of a player's specific sub-skill sets.

4.1   Overview

This section takes tennis as a paradigmatic example; however, our methodology has the potential for generalization across other racket sports, like table tennis and badminton, as well as team-based sports such as soccer, basketball, and American football. In tennis, an individual's overall probability of winning is typically contingent upon the reliability of their constituent skills, such as serving, returning, forehand, and backhand [8, 25]. Furthermore, players may exhibit varied playing styles in response to different opponents. Our approach involves the modeling of tennis matches utilizing Markov Decision Processes (MDP) incorporating shot-by-shot actions, thus encapsulating intricate behaviors, including non-deterministic occurrences like coin tosses to determine the serving player and strategic choices such as body serves. The model leverages diverse match-related information, including player archetypes and potential actions, with probability distributions and success rates of these actions derived from historical data. Using the MDP model, we perform probabilistic reasoning for in-depth strategic analysis, such as deep strategy analytics for performance enhancement, facilitated by the PAT model checker [51]. Although there is existing work on modeling tennis using MDP [53], our method, to the best of our knowledge, is the first to apply PMC for analytical purposes in this domain.

   To rigorously evaluate the efficacy of our proposed strategies, we employ the MDP model to predict match outcomes and analyze alterations in winning probabilities ensuing from the implementation of different strategies. Our predictions are validated using data sourced from professional tennis matches (ATP and WTA) spanning the last decade. Furthermore, we execute experiments to directly compare our suggested strategies with actual strategic adaptations observed in past match data. The empirical findings demonstrate a strong correlation between the majority of our recommended strategies and the strategic adjustments applied by elite players, resulting in notable enhancements in their win rates.

4.2 The Proposed Approach

In this section, we introduce our methodology for tennis strategy analytics. The overview of our approach is given in Fig. 1. Initially, data is collected from online repositories, and video analytics methodologies are employed to enable automated data fusion. Subsequently, we model a tennis match as a MDP, thereby enabling the simulation of matches involving any player pairing. The developed

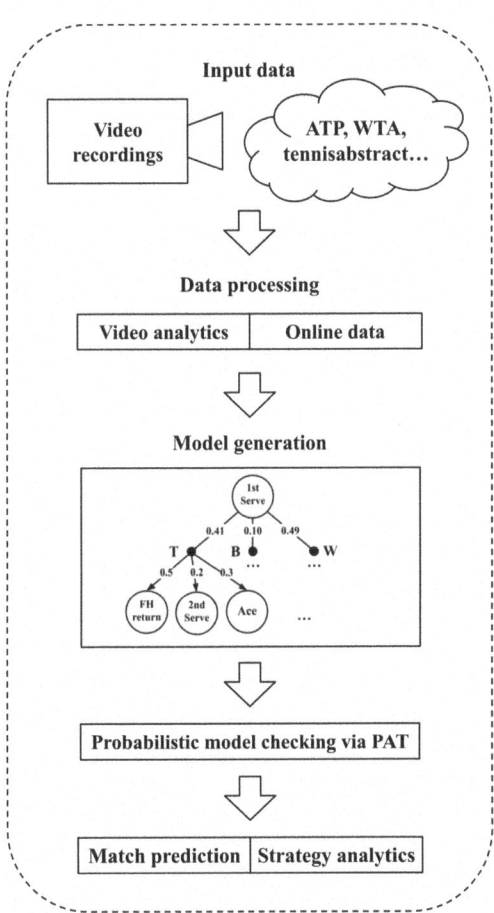

Fig. 1. The system pipeline of our approach.

MDP model is instantiated in the PCSP# language and facilitates the prediction of match outcomes and the execution of strategy analytics via probabilistic model checking.

4.3   Data Mining

The dataset utilized in our investigation comprises comprehensive shot-by-shot descriptions for both players, crucial for constructing tennis models. To acquire this data, information is gathered from various sources.

– *Online data source.* Initially, our dataset is sourced from tennisabstract.com, an online repository that aggregates and annotates over 10,000 ATP and WTA matches dating back to 1959, encompassing comprehensive match data. Below illustrates an instance of a shot-by-shot record for a single point:

```
1st serve wide; forehand return crosscourt;
backhand crosscourt; forehand down the middle;
forehand inside-out; forehand crosscourt;
backhand crosscourt; forehand crosscourt;
backhand down the line; backhand forced error.
```

We have developed a C# program to autonomously retrieve the matches of interest and extract data from the specified website. Furthermore, we have crafted a parser to extract related data, compute corresponding probabilities for individual sub-skills, and seamlessly integrate the outcomes into our pipeline as input parameters for the PCSP# model. Additionally, the program can automatically invoke the PAT console, which will launch the toolkit and output the desired results.
– *Video analytics.* In addition to data sourced from online repositories, there remains a dearth of detailed shot-by-shot information for many matches. To augment data coverage and cater to athletes at all levels, including college and junior players, we have devised a transformer-based seq2seq model capable of accurately recognizing intricate action sequences from fast-paced videos. Taking video clips as input, the model outputs detailed shot-by-shot data (e.g., serve to T → backhand cross-court → forehand down the line, etc.). Notably, this model can be trained end-to-end on a single GPU.
Moreover, recent advancements in Large Language Models (LLMs) have expanded their capabilities to perform multi-modal inference, enabling textual, visual, and auditory inputs. Specifically, GPT-4 exhibits proficiency in analyzing video content by processing image sequences. Initial evaluations on sports datasets showcase GPT-4's adeptness in various video comprehension tasks, such as sports genre classification, contextual understanding, and action identification, albeit with certain limitations in fine-grained classification and temporal analysis.

4.4   Modeling Tennis in MDP

The task of modeling tennis matches is intricate, necessitating a delicate balance between precision and efficiency. An optimal model must accurately reflect the dynamic conditions of matches while also maintaining an appropriate level of abstraction to facilitate explainability and efficient analysis. Our modeling approach adeptly addresses these requirements by giving an expressive representation coupled with analytical capabilities.

In this section, our emphasis lies on singles tennis matches, wherein two players are denoted as $P1$ and $P2$. To predict the match outcome, we examine the winning probability within a *simplified* tiebreak game, modeled as a representation of the entire match. In a simplified tiebreak game, victory is attained by the player who first accumulates 7 points. In this example, 7–6 still counts as a win. Our analysis operates under the premise that the player with the highest likelihood of triumphing in the tiebreak game also possesses a superior probability of clinching the entire match. This abstraction improves computational performance when using PAT.

We model a tennis match using MDP, incorporating insights derived from expert knowledge in tennis. States and actions within the model are described using tennis-specific terminology to facilitate understanding by players and coaches. The model integrates diverse factors including court positioning (deuce court, middle court, or ad court), player characteristics (right-handed or left-handed), and various shot types. The ingredients of the MDP are outlined below.

State Space. A state within the model corresponds to the instance when a player performs a shot. These states are grouped into four distinct categories: serve, return, stroke, and termination states. Serve states have four types: first serve in the deuce court, second serve in the deuce court (if the initial serve is unsuccessful), first serve in the ad court, and second serve in the ad court (if the first serve is unsuccessful). Return states denote the action of returning a serve and are classified into four types: forehand return of a serve from the deuce court, backhand return of a serve from the deuce court, forehand return of a serve from the ad court, and backhand return of a serve from the ad court. Stroke states include actions executed within the deuce court, middle court, and ad court. Termination states signal the completion of the tiebreak game. Possible termination state outcomes include scores such as 7–1 (a win for $P1$), 5–7 (a win for $P2$), and 7–6 (a win for $P1$).

Action Space. For each state s, a player has a range of potential actions depending on their positioning on the court and handedness. In total, there are 16 actions available, comprising:

– First/Second serve to T, Body (B), Wide (W);
– Fore/Backhand (FH/BH): cross-court (CC), down the line (DL), down the middle (DM), inside-out (IO), inside-in (II).

Transition Function. The transition function, denoted as $P : S \times A \times S \rightarrow [0, 1]$, quantifies the probability of transitioning to a new state given a state-action

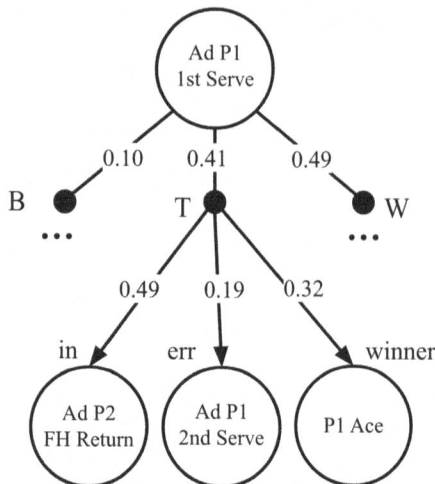

Fig. 2. A partial MDP model demonstrating a serve.

pair. Each state-action pairing can result in one of three possible outcomes: **in** (indicating that the action succeeds without immediately resulting in a point), **winner** (denoting that the action directly leads to winning a point), or **error** (signifying that the action fails). In the event of a **winner** or **error**, the process advances to a new state for the subsequent serve, with a point awarded to the rally winner. Upon either player accumulating 7 points, the process transitions to the termination state. Conversely, if the action outcome is **in**, the process progresses to a non-termination state depending on the current state and action undertaken.

Policy. The policy π denotes the probability distribution across all possible actions for each state, expressed as $\pi(a \mid s) = Pr(A = a \mid S = s)$. It characterizes how players select various actions within each state. For instance, a serving policy might allocate 60% probability to serving to T, 30% to W, and 10% to B.

The policy and transition probabilities for the MDP are derived from relevant historical data between two players (will be discussed in Sect. 4.7). The likelihood of a player selecting action a from a given state s (i.e., the policy) is determined by

$$Pr(a \mid s) = \frac{N(s, a)}{N(s)}.$$

The transition probability, indicating the likelihood of transitioning to the subsequent state s' after executing action a from state s, is computed by

$$Pr(s' \mid s, a) = \frac{N(s, a, s')}{N(s, a)},$$

where $N(s)$ represents the frequency of a player's visits to state s, $N(s, a)$ is the number of times a player has executed action a in state s, and $N(s, a, s')$ is

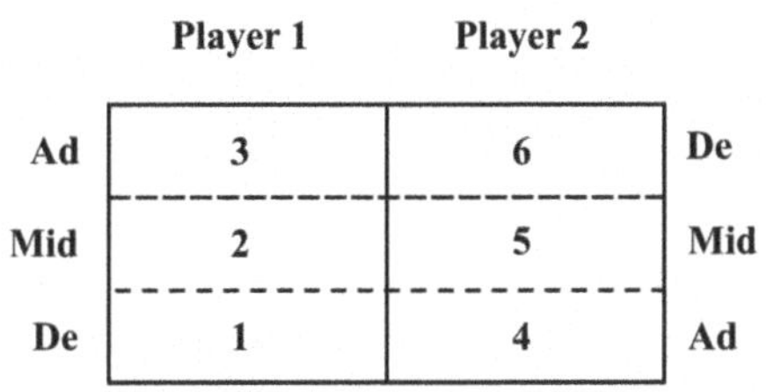

	Player 1	Player 2	
Ad	3	6	De
Mid	2	5	Mid
De	1	4	Ad

Fig. 3. A 6 region tennis court with ball position variables 1–6. Variable 0 indicates a winner, and 9 indicates an error.

the number of times when a player has taken action a from state s, resulting in state s'.

4.5   Implementation in PCSP#

We demonstrate the application of the developed MDP model in the PCSP# language through an example of a tiebreaker game played between two right-handed players. The tennis court is partitioned into 6 regions, as depicted in Fig. 3, where the labels *de*, *mid*, and *ad* denote the deuce court, middle court, and ad court, respectively.

Model for Serve. Each player has the option to serve from either their deuce court or ad court, with a second serve opportunity available if the first attempt is unsuccessful. The ensuing example depicts a right-handed player executing their initial serve from the ad court, mirroring the process depicted in Fig. 2.

$$Ad\_P1Serve = pcase\ \{$$
$$20 : Serve T\_in\{ball = 5\} \rightarrow Ad\_P2\_FHR$$
$$8 : Serve T\_winner\{ball = 0\} \rightarrow Ace\{score1 + +;$$
$$if\ (score1 == 7)\ \{won == P1\}\} \rightarrow NextPt$$
$$13 : Serve T\_err\{ball = 9\} \rightarrow Ad\_P1Serve\_2nd$$
$$25 : Serve W\_in\{ball = 4\} \rightarrow Ad\_P2\_BHR$$
$$5 : Serve W\_winner\{ball = 0\} \rightarrow Ace\{score1 + +;$$
$$if\ (score1 == 7)\ \{won = P1\}\} \rightarrow NextPt$$
$$19 : Serve W\_err\{ball = 9\} \rightarrow Ad\_P1Serve\_2nd$$
$$7 : ServeB\_in\{ball = 4\} \rightarrow (Ad\_P2\_FHR\ []\ Ad\_P2\_BHR)$$
$$0 : ServeB\_winner\{ball = 0\} \rightarrow Ace\{score1 + +;$$
$$if\ (score1 == 7)\ \{won = P1\}\} \rightarrow NextPt$$
$$3 : ServeB\_err\{ball = 9\} \rightarrow Ad\_P1Serve\_2nd\ \}\ ;$$

To associate actions with their corresponding probabilities during serving, the aforementioned process employs the PCSP# probabilistic choice operator "pcase". There exist three available actions: (1) 41% serve to the T (*ServeT*), (2) 49% serve wide (*ServeW*), and (3) 10% serve to the body (*ServeB*). Each action entails three potential outcomes: *in*, *winner*, or *err*. Taking the action *ServeT* as an example, player $P1$ possesses a 20% probability of successfully hitting the ball in without directly scoring a point (modeled by event *ServeT_in*, with the ball variable set to 5), with their opponent responding by returning a forehand shot from the ad court (modeled by process *Ad_P2_FHR*). There is a 13% chance of failing the initial *ServeT* (modeled by *ServeT_err*, with the ball variable set to 9), necessitating a second serve, depicted by the process *Ad_P1Serve_2nd*. Additionally, there is an 8% probability of directly scoring a point (modeled by *ServeT_winner*, with the ball variable set to 0), resulting in an increment to player $P1$'s score (score1++). If $P1$ attains 7 points, the *won* variable is updated to $P1$; otherwise, the process transitions to *NextPt* for the subsequent serve or the conclusion of the game.

Model for Return. A player has the option to return a serve from the deuce or ad court using either a forehand or backhand shot. For instance, the process *Ad_P2_BHR* describes how player $P2$ executes a backhand return against player $P1$'s wide serve from the ad court.

$$Ad\_P2\_BHR = pcase \ \{$$
$$24 : BH\_CrossCourt\_in\{ball = 3\} \rightarrow P1\_ad\_stroke$$
$$21 : BH\_DownLine\_in\{ball = 1\} \rightarrow P1\_de\_stroke$$
$$36 : BH\_DownMid\_in\{ball = 2\} \rightarrow P1\_mid\_stroke$$
$$4 : Ad\_BHR\_winner\{ball = 0\} \rightarrow Winner\{score2 + + ;$$
$$if \ (score2 == 7) \ \{won = P2\}\} \rightarrow NextPt$$
$$15 : Ad\_BHR\_err\{ball = 9\} \rightarrow \{score1 + + ;$$
$$if \ (score1 == 7) \ \{won = P1\}\} \rightarrow NextPt \ \} ;$$

When player $P1$ serves from their ad court, player $P2$ may opt to return backhand cross-court (*BH_CrossCourt*), backhand down the line (*BH_DownLine*), or backhand down the middle (*BH_DownMid*), each with different probabilities. Processes *P1_de_stroke*, *P1_ad_stroke*, and *P1_mid_stroke* represent player $P1$'s stroke from the deuce, ad, and middle courts, respectively. To simplify the model, all potential winning shots (or errors) are amalgamated into a single event denoted as *Ad_BHR_winner* (or *Ad_BHR_err*). If player $P2$ returns with a winning shot, they score directly (i.e., score2++); conversely, if they commit an error, player $P1$ gains one point (i.e., score1++).

Model for Stroke. Each player has a stroke process for each court position (deuce, ad, or middle court). The process for each court incorporates strokes executed with both forehand and backhand techniques, as well as scenarios involving winning shots and errors. The following exemplifies player $P1$'s stroke from the deuce court.

$$P1\_de\_stroke = pcase \{$$
$$40 : FH\_CrossCourt\_in\{ball = 6\} \rightarrow P2\_de\_stroke$$
$$11 : FH\_DownLine\_in\{ball = 4\} \rightarrow P2\_ad\_stroke$$
$$23 : FH\_DownMid\_in\{ball = 5\} \rightarrow P2\_mid\_stroke$$
$$0 : BH\_InsideOut\_in\{ball = 6\} \rightarrow P2\_de\_stroke$$
$$2 : BH\_InsideIn\_in\{ball = 4\} \rightarrow P2\_ad\_stroke$$
$$1 : BH\_DownMid\_in\{ball = 5\} \rightarrow P2\_mid\_stroke$$
$$9 : de\_stroke\_winner\{ball = 0\} \rightarrow Winner\{score1 + + \,;$$
$$if \ (score1 == 7) \ \{won = P1\}\} \rightarrow NextPt$$
$$14 : de\_stroke\_err\{ball = 9\} \rightarrow \{score2 + + \,;$$
$$if \ (score2 == 7) \ \{won = P2\}\} \rightarrow NextPt \ \} \,;$$

Predict Winning Probability. To predict the probability of a player winning, we establish a predicate designating the target player as the victor of the tiebreaker game (i.e., the first to accumulate 7 points), and subsequently find a state that meets the criteria using probabilistic reach ability analysis. For instance, the below assertion describes the property of player $P1$ emerging victorious in the game.

$$\# \ define \ player1Win \ won \ == \ player1;$$
$$\# \ assert \ TieBreakGame \ reaches \ player1Win \ with \ prob;$$

4.6   Strategy Recommendations

Through PAT's capability to check the ramifications of alterations to the probability distribution of actions, we can propose strategies aimed at enhancing a player's likelihood of winning, drawing on sensitivity analysis derived from probabilistic model checking. Two primary categories of strategies can be discerned, as outlined in Algorithm 1.

Pre-match Strategy. The first category of strategy pertains to intricate tactics concerning play patterns. This category is inherently linked to the probability distributions of actions. For instance, one might opt to shift 10% of T serves to W serves against a specific opponent if historical data indicates that the opponent struggles with returning W serves. Since coaching is prohibited during a tennis match, we denote this first type of strategy as "pre-match strategy", as it can be directly implemented by a player prior to the commencement of the match without altering the ability (i.e., reliability/success rate) of their sub-skills. The details of this strategy are outlined in Algorithm 1, wherein optimal actions to increase are identified for each state (e.g., player $P1$ should utilize more forehand cross-court shots in the deuce court against player $P2$).

Training Strategy. The second category of strategy aims to enhance the success rates of specific shot types through targeted training. This strategy is termed "training strategy". It may not be immediately applicable just before a match, as a player cannot instantaneously improve a skill. For instance, prior to facing Nadal, renowned for his potent forehand, Federer might concentrate on refining his backhand down-the-line shots in the ad court to reduce errors by 2%. Such a strategy not only elevates Federer's success rate with his backhand but also diminishes the threat posed by Nadal's forehand, as the down-the-line shot directs play to Nadal's backhand side.

4.7 Evaluation

We employed the PAT model checker to realize our model and conducted experiments on real-world professional tennis matches to evaluate the effectiveness of our strategy analytics methodology. Specifically, our experiments were devised to address the following research questions:

Algorithm 1: Computing the optimal strategy.

Input: current state s, policy π, percentage change $\delta\%$
Result: a_{best} (the best action to increase in state s)
// Δ_{max} is the maximum increase in winning chance
1   $\Delta_{max} \leftarrow -\infty$; $a_{best} \leftarrow None$;
2   **for** $a \in \pi(s)$ **do**
3   **if** *pre-match strategy* **then**
      // pre-match strategy
      // add action a's percentage by $\delta\%$
4       $Pr(a \mid s) \leftarrow Pr(a \mid s) + \delta\%$;
5   **for** $a' \in \pi(s) \setminus [a]$ **do**
6        $\mid$ $Pr(a' \mid s) \leftarrow Pr(a' \mid s) - \frac{\delta\%}{|\pi(s)|}$;
7   **else**
      // training strategy
      // reduce action a's error by $\delta\%$
8       $Pr(in \mid s, a) \leftarrow Pr(in \mid s, a) + \delta\%$;
9       $Pr(err \mid s, a) \leftarrow Pr(err \mid s, a) - \delta\%$;
    // compute the increase in winning chance
10    $\Delta p_{win} \leftarrow$ increase in winning chance;
    // update the best action to increase
11   **if** $\Delta p_{win} > \Delta_{max}$ **then**
12     $\mid$ $\Delta_{max} = \Delta p_{win}$; $a_{best} = a$;

RQ1: How accurate is the model in predicting players' winning chances when playing against different opponents?

RQ2: Does our model provide effective pre-match and training strategies to increase players' winning chances?

RQ3: What new insights a player/coach can get from our strategy recommendations?

RQ1: Winning Chance Prediction Accuracy. To predict one's probability of winning against a specific opponent, our framework offers the flexibility to extract data from pertinent matches occurring prior to the date of the target match. For example, let us consider predicting a match between players $P1$ and $P2$, each with Elo rankings $e1$ and $e2$, respectively. To acquire data for $P1$, we gather information from matches involving $P1$ and opponents akin to $P2$ during the preceding two years. Here, "akin" denotes opponents sharing (1) the same handedness as $P2$, and (2) Elo rankings falling within the range of $[e2 - \delta_{elo}, e2 + \delta_{elo}]$, where $\delta_{elo} \in \mathbb{N}$. A similar approach is adopted to gather data for player $P2$. Once the relevant matches have been selected from historical records, we can construct the MDP model and predict the outcome of the match. Typically, the processing time for each match is approximately 1 s.

We utilize the bookmakers' odds[1] as our reference point, as it currently represents the state-of-the-art approach in the domain. Previous investigations have not consistently outperformed the predictions made by bookmakers over an extended period. This is primarily attributed to the valuable information typically possessed by bookmakers, including weather conditions, recent player performances, injury reports, and insider insights, which are often challenging to access. Nevertheless, we demonstrate that our predictions yield positive returns when compared to the bookmakers' odds through betting simulations spanning the past decade using a python program. Furthermore, we conduct a comparative analysis of our methodology against existing tennis prediction models documented in the literature.

Betting Simulation. In our experiment, we apply a well-established betting strategy — Kelly criterion [54], which is given as

$$f = k \times (p - \frac{1-p}{b}) \tag{1}$$

where p represents the predicted probability of winning the bet, b signifies the payout resulting from a successful bet, k denotes the Kelly multiplier for risk management, and f denotes the fraction of the current bankroll to be wagered (with betting being avoided when $f < 0$). To assess profitability, we compute the return on investment (ROI) and the annualized return on investment (annualized ROI) [36]. The initial bankroll is initialised at \$10,000.

We investigate different constraints regarding the range of Elo ranking differences, denoted as $\delta_{elo} \in [50, 200]$, during the selection of related historical matches. When δ_{elo} assumes a smaller value, the chosen matches exhibit higher quality, albeit potentially limited in quantity. Conversely, with an increase in δ_{elo}, a larger pool of matches is included, albeit they may possess less direct relevance to the target matches.

---

[1] http://www.tennis-data.co.uk/.

We designate the Kelly multiplier as $k = 0.1$ for the purpose of long-term betting strategies. Additionally, our betting approach concentrates exclusively on matches that entail a minimum of 4 relevant historical matchups for each player, ensuring prediction accuracy. The outcomes of the betting simulations are depicted in Table 1. Examination of the table reveals that models with $\delta_{elo} = 50$ and 100 yield long-term profits, with annualized ROIs of 7.49% and 14.98%, respectively. However, a further elevation in δ_{elo} leads to negative profitability. This occurs because, although a larger number of matches become available for betting, the selected historical matchups exhibit decreased relevance to the target players. Consequently, a value of $\delta_{elo} = 100$ emerges as the optimal point for performance. This experiment underscores the exceptional predictive performance of our model in determining the winning probability of tennis matches.

Comparison with Existing Methods. A reliable winning probability prediction model should support well-calibrated estimations that closely align with real-world outcomes. Notably, predictions indicating a 70%-30% chance or 95%-5% chance of winning significantly impact performance analytics, despite both scenarios predicting the same winner. Traditional metrics such as accuracy and log-loss do not adequately capture the true winning probabilities. To address this limitation, we assess the models' predictions using the expected calibration error (ECE) [12]. The ECE quantifies the disparity between predicted probabilities and observed outcomes. For instance, if player $P1$ is predicted to have a winning probability of 40% against player $P2$, we gather all matches where the predicted winning chance hovers around 40% and ascertain whether approximately 40% of those matches indeed resulted in victory for player $P1$.

Formally, we partition the predicted winning probabilities into M bins and calculate the average discrepancy between the predicted and observed outcomes.

Table 1. Betting results over the past 10 years.

δ_{elo} ($\pm$)	# of bets	Profits	ROI	Annualized ROI
50	461	$10,592	105.92%	7.49%
100	1,388	$30,385	**303.85%**	**14.98%**
150	2,177	−$8,194	−81.94%	−15.73%
200	2,871	−$8,471	−84.71%	−17.12%

Table 2. ECE scores for different methods.

Method	ECE
Point-based [18]	0.0973
Paired comparison [32]	0.0317
Bookmakers	0.0207
Our method	**0.0099**

This calculation is weighted by the number of examples in each bin. The ECE is computed as follows:

$$ECE = \sum_{m=1}^{M} \frac{\mid B_m \mid}{N} \mid acc(B_m) - conf(B_m) \mid \qquad (2)$$

where B_m is the mth bin, $\mid B_m \mid$ is the size of the bin, N is the number of samples, $acc(B_m)$ is the proportion of positives in bin B_m, and $conf(B_m)$ is the average predicted probability in bin B_m. In our experiment, we use $M = 5$.

We evaluate the performance of our model with $\delta_{elo} = 100$ against other established match outcome prediction models, which include a point-based method [18], a paired comparison method [32], and bookmakers. As illustrated in Table 2, our model exhibits the best performance with the lowest ECE of 0.0099.

Our model demonstrates accurate prediction of players' winning probabilities, validated through betting simulations spanning the last decade, achieving an annualized ROI of 14.98%. Furthermore, our model surpasses existing prediction models, exhibiting the lowest ECE.

Table 3. The system recommends actions for enhancement compared to the actual strategy adjustments made by players. "Win%" indicates the likelihood of winning. "Align_P" represents the proportion of our pre-match suggestions that align with players' actual strategy adjustments. "Align_T" indicates the fraction of our training recommendations that align with players' actual sub-skill enhancements.

Player	Opponent	Turning-point year	Win% before year	Win% after year	Align_P	Align_T
Federer R.	Nadal R.	2017	20.0%	83.3%	9/11	8/11
Nadal R.	Djokovic N.	2017	26.1%	60.0%	7/11	8/11
Wawrinka S.	Djokovic N	2016	28.6%	50.0%	8/11	7/11
Murray A.	Nadal R.	2015	14.3%	50.0%	10/11	8/11
Thiem D.	Nadal R.	2018	16.7%	57.1%	6/11	6/11
Medvedev D.	Zverev A.	2020	25.0%	83.3%	6/11	7/11
Zverev A.	Tsitsipas S.	2021	20.0%	50.0%	8/11	7/11
Thiem D.	Djokovic N.	2018	25.0%	60.0%	9/11	6/11
Djokovic N.	Tsitsipas S.	2020	50.0%	100.0%	9/11	8/11
Zverev A.	Nadal R.	2020	20.0%	66.7%	6/11	8/11
Federer R.	Murray A.	2014	40.0%	100.0%	6/11	9/11
Djokovic N.	Medvedev D.	2021	50.0%	100.0%	9/11	7/11
Zverev A.	Federer R.	2018	33.3%	66.7%	8/11	9/11
Thiem D.	Federer R.	2019	50.0%	100.0%	7/11	10/11
Djokovic N.	Murray A.	2014	58.3%	82.4%	7/11	7/11
Cilic M.	Djokovic N.	2016	0.0%	33.3%	8/11	8/11
Rublev A.	Medvedev D.	2021	0.0%	50.0%	7/11	10/11

RQ2: Tennis Strategy Effectiveness. Our system empowers users to assess the impact of different pre-match or training strategies on their performance, facilitating the identification of optimal approaches for improvement. However, assessing the real-world efficacy of these strategies poses challenges, as asking professional players to modify their playing styles or skill levels for observation is impractical. Therefore, we evaluate the effectiveness of these strategies based on insights gleaned from historical data.

For example, consider the dataset comprising 16 documented matches between Roger Federer and Rafael Nadal from 2011 to 2022. Prior to 2017, Federer won only 2 out of 10 matches, yielding a 20% winning rate. However, post-2017, his winning rate surged to 83% after securing victories in 5 out of 6 matches. Notably, upon analyzing Federer's actions and the reliability of his sub-skills, noticeable differences are evident before and after 2017. To ascertain whether this improvement stems from strategic alterations, we constructed two MDP models based on historical data-one before 2017 and the other after. Employing Probabilistic Model Checking, we computed Federer's winning rate, yielding results of 35.7% and 53.2%, respectively, aligning with the actual outcomes.

Moreover, we aim to investigate whether our system can aid players in pinpointing pre-match and training strategies to attain optimized enhancements in the future. Our objective is to evaluate the following:

- For pre-match strategy, identify the best action to increase in each state by modifying **probability distributions**.
- For training strategy, identify the best action to improve/train on in each state by modifying **success rates**.
- Check whether the player has indeed increased/improved on the identified actions later on.

For instance, utilizing data predating 2017, our system suggests that Federer's optimal pre-match maneuver against Nadal involves employing the "forehand cross-court" strategy when returning the ball at the deuce court. Post-2017 data corroborates that Federer did indeed execute more forehand cross-court returns. Concerning training strategies, leveraging data from before 2017, our approach suggests that Federer's most advantageous improvement opportunity in the "ad court stroke" scenario entails employing the "backhand down the line" tactic toward Nadal's backhand side. Subsequent to 2017, data indicates that Federer did, in fact, enhance this sub-skill, achieving an increased success rate.

We implemented the aforementioned approach across all 11 states for both pre-match and training strategies. The outcomes revealed that: (1) concerning pre-match strategies, 9 out of 11 optimal actions identified by our method corresponded with Federer's actual adjustments; and (2) for training strategies, 8 out of 11 recommended enhancement actions were in concordance with Federer's actual improvements, specifically in terms of elevating action success rates.

To further corroborate our methodology, we curated additional instances akin to Federer's matchups against Nadal and subjected them to the same validation procedure. These instances adhere to a pattern wherein a player exhibits a notable surge in win rate against a specific opponent subsequent to a certain temporal threshold (e.g., the year 2017). We leveraged data predating this threshold to formulate recommendations and utilized post-threshold data to verify our suggestions. Table 3 synthesizes the empirical findings, revealing that the majority of recommendations delineated by our system align with players' actual strategy adjustments and enhancements. Hence, we conlude that our strategy analytics approach is both rational and efficacious.

The strategies posited by our model demonstrate effectiveness as they closely correspond with real-world strategy adaptations made by elite players, resulting in substantial enhancements when facing specific opponents, as evidenced by historical data.

Table 4. Different pre-match and training strategies at each state.

Player	Opponent	De_Serve	Ad_Serve	De_FHR	Ad_FHR	De_BHR	Ad_BHR	De_Stroke	Mid_Stroke	Ad_Stroke
Pre-match Strategy										
Nadal R.	Djokovic N.	W	W	CC	DL	CC	IO	FH_IO	FH_IO	BH_IO
Wawrinka S.	Djokovic N.	W	T	CC	II	IO	DL	BH_II	BH_IO	FH_IO
Thiem D.	Djokovic N.	T	W	CC	CC	IO	CC	FH_CC	BH_IO	FH_II
Cilic M.	Djokovic N.	T	B	DL	CC	DM	DL	FH_CC	FH_IO	BH_DL
Zverev A.	Tsitsipas S.	B	T	CC	CC	CC	CC	FH_DL	FH_CC	FH_II
Zverev A.	Nadal R.	T	W	DL	IO	CC	CC	FH_CC	FH_IO	FH_DM
Zverev A.	Federer R.	T	T	CC	DM	II	DM	FH_DL	FH_CC	BH_DL
Training Strategy										
Thiem D.	Nadal R.	T	W	CC	II	IO	DL	FH_CC	FH_CC	FH_II
Thiem D.	Djokovic N.	T	W	CC	CC	IO	DL	FH_CC	FH_CC	BH_DL
Thiem D.	Federer R.	W	T	DL	II	DM	CC	FH_DL	FH_IO	BH_CC

RQ3: New Insights for Players and Coaches. It may be contended that our recommendations significantly coincide with the practices already employed by professional athletes. Nonetheless, these invaluable insights may not be readily available to players lacking equivalent levels of coaching staff and resources. Our objective is to democratize high-caliber strategy analysis for the wider tennis community. In this section, we will delve further into the insights engendered by our system and illustrate how players and coaches can derive benefits from them.

Our system is capable of generating opponent-specific strategy recommendations tailored to various player matchups. Table 4 showcases examples of our pre-match and training strategy suggestions. It's important to emphasize that we present only the most effective strategy in some states, which corresponds to the action yielding the highest gains when increasing the probability distributions or success rates by 2%. Our strategy recommendations demonstrate significant diversity across different matchups. For example, we propose distinct pre-match strategies for Zverev against different opponents, such as employing more forehand cross-court (FH_CC) against Nadal and forehand down the line (FH_DL) against Federer in the De_Stroke state. Moreover, when different players face the same opponent, our system suggests Wawrinka to increase his forehand inside-out (FH_IO) and Cilic to enhance his backhand down the line (BH_DL) at Ad_Stroke when playing against Djokovic.

At times, our method can propose "unusual" or novel strategy suggestions that players or coaches may not have considered. For example, through analyzing matches between Roger Federer and Andy Murray before 2014, our system indicates that Federer's most effective pre-match strategy was to employ more backhand down the line shots towards Murray's forehand, contrary to the common belief that attacking the opponent's backhand side is more effective. Interestingly, after 2014, Federer did not lose any match against Murray and indeed increased his usage of backhand down the line shots by 4.8%. Given our model's ability to accurately predict match outcomes, we can provide formal verification that our suggested strategies have the potential to enhance players' winning chances in theory.

Moreover, even if players or coaches are aware of the specific sub-skills requiring refinement, they may lack precise guidance on the adjustments or improvements needed to maximize their winning probabilities effectively. Our system is able to compute exact figures for these enhancements. One potential application is to aid players in tailoring their training regimes more efficiently. For instance, if two players are both instructed to enhance their forehand down the line, but the anticipated impacts on their winning probabilities vary (for instance, by reducing the error rate of forehand down the line by 2%, one player's winning probability may increase by 4%, while the other's may increase by 8%), the second player should allocate a larger proportion of their training regimen to this skill, assuming a fixed training duration.

Overall, our model offers insightful strategy recommendations that surpass conventional knowledge. These strategies demonstrate significant diversity across various matchups and can be rigorously validated. Furthermore, we can provide players with tailored training regimens to enhance their performance efficiently and effectively.

5   Related Work

5.1   Integration and Evolution of Formal Specification Languages in System Modeling and Verification

TCOZ, proposed by Mahony and Dong [27–29], integrates Object-Z [45] and Timed CSP [6], and share similar language design style with Circus [3,40,61] by Woodcock et al. Following the TCOZ language design, CSP# substitutes Object-Z with C# programming language for tractable model checking, leading to the development of PAT which incorporates multiple CSP# variants [2,9,33,46–48,50,51].

UTP, developed by Hoare and He, unites various programming theories using a common mathematical framework aimed at formal specification and verification. This framework supports multiple paradigms including sequential, object-oriented, concurrent, and real-time programming [4,10,13,14,14,17,26,31,34,35, 37,41,43,58].

Miyazawa et al. formalize RoboChart, a notation for real-time robot systems using CSP and tock-CSP within the UTP framework. Other contributions include defining probabilistic semantics for RoboChart and integrating probabilistic choice in its state machines [4,5,30,39,62,64].

He et al. and Bresciani et al. discuss extensions to Dijkstra's guarded commands and UTP to incorporate probabilistic choice, enhancing the modeling of randomized algorithms and probabilistic properties. Zhu et al. provide foundational denotational semantics for a probabilistic timed shared-variable language, though it may lack in addressing event-driven aspects typical in probabilistic CSP# models [1,15,65].

5.2   Sports Analytics in Racket Sports

This section focuses on the literature on sports analytics in racket sports, which has not been extensively explored. Racket sports, including tennis, table tennis, and badminton, typically involve two players hitting a ball across a net on a court. Previous works have employed computer vision techniques to track players and the ball in broadcast videos [19,20]. Other studies have aimed to predict the next shot location based on the current context and historical data [57] or action recognition [23].

In the field of sports strategy analytics, there have been some notable works. Terroba et al. [53] presented an MDP-based framework using Monte Carlo tree search to find optimal policies. However, this work did not formally verify the effectiveness of the proposed policies and only tested with a limited amount of data. Other works such as Wei et al. [59] and Wang et al. [56] focused on evaluating individual actions by determining the expected probability of winning a rally, taking into consideration the context such as player locations, movement speeds, and ball speed. Wang et al. [55] also evaluated actions by categorizing table tennis shots as "good" or "bad" based on expert knowledge and evaluated actions based on video clips. These works provide deeper insights into games and evaluate individual action based on how it affects the rally's outcome while taking the context (e.g., player locations and movement speeds, the speed of the incoming ball) into account. However, the evaluation results are difficult for players to memorize or apply.

There has been extensive research in the area of professional tennis match outcome prediction. Kovalchik [21] classified prediction models into three categories: regression-based, point-based, and paired comparison. These models have been compared with bookmaker odds [22]. Regression-based models aim to find features that are highly correlated with match outcomes and predict winning probabilities using regression algorithms [11]. Point-based methods estimate the probability of winning a match by first estimating the probability of winning a single point and then using Markov chains to compute the probability of winning the entire match [18]. Paired comparison methods aggregate past matches between players to determine their relative strength rankings and forecast future match results [32]. The FiveThirtyEight Elo variant is one of the most popular paired comparison methods and has been widely used in media.

However, these existing methods primarily concentrate on predicting match outcomes and lack the capability to perform comprehensive strategy analysis. In contrast, our approach not only accurately predicts match results, but also provides insightful analysis of players' strategies.

6   Conclusion

PCSP# enables the specification of probabilistic behaviors and uncertainties in system designs, expanding the expressiveness of CSP to model a broader range of real-world systems. Its features, including probabilistic transitions, uncertain actions, and random events, have found applications in various domains such as probabilistic systems modeling, reliability analysis, fault tolerance analysis, security analysis, and performance evaluation. This chapter has demonstrated a novel application of PCSP# in sports analytics through the PAT model checker, specifically in modeling tennis matches. By leveraging past match data, PCSP# facilitates detailed analysis of match outcomes, strategy assessment, and training recommendations. Moving forward, the continued development and adoption of PCSP# and similar formal modeling techniques hold great potential for advancing sports analytics and enhancing the understanding and optimization of complex systems in various domains.

References

1. Bresciani, R., Butterfield, A.: Towards a UTP-style framework to deal with probabilities. Technical Report TCD-CS-2011-09, FMG, Trinity College Dublin, Ireland (2011)
2. Bride, H., et al.: N-PAT: a nested model-checker: (System Description). In: Peltier, N., Sofronie-Stokkermans, V. (eds.) Automated Reasoning: 10th International Joint Conference, IJCAR 2020, Paris, France, July 1–4, 2020, Proceedings, Part II, pp. 369–377. Springer International Publishing, Cham (2020). https://doi.org/10.1007/978-3-030-51054-1_22
3. Cavalcanti, A., Sampaio, A., Woodcock, J.: Refinement of actions in circus. In: Derrick, J., Boiten, E.A., Woodcock, J., von Wright, J. (eds.) BCS FACS Refinement Workshop 2002, Refine 2002, Satellite Event of FLoC 2002, Copenhagen, Denmark, July 20-21, 2002. Electronic Notes in Theoretical Computer Science, vol. 70, pp. 132–162. Elsevier (2002). https://doi.org/10.1016/S1571-0661(05)80489-X
4. Cavalcanti, A., Woodcock, J.: A Tutorial Introduction to CSP in Unifying Theories of Programming. In: Cavalcanti, A., Sampaio, A., Woodcock, J. (eds.) Refinement Techniques in Software Engineering, pp. 220–268. Springer, Berlin, Heidelberg (2006). https://doi.org/10.1007/11889229_6
5. Conserva Filho, M.S., Marinho, R., Mota, A., Woodcock, J.: Analysing RoboChart with Probabilities. In: Massoni, T., Mousavi, M.R. (eds.) Formal Methods: Foundations and Applications: 21st Brazilian Symposium, SBMF 2018, Salvador, Brazil, November 26–30, 2018, Proceedings, pp. 198–214. Springer International Publishing, Cham (2018). https://doi.org/10.1007/978-3-030-03044-5_13

6. Davies, J.: Specification and proof in real-time CSP. Cambridge University Press (1993)
7. Dong, J.S., et al.: Sports analytics using probabilistic model checking and deep learning. In: 2023 27th International Conference on Engineering of Complex Computer Systems (ICECCS), pp. 7–11. IEEE (2023)
8. Dong, J.S., Shi, L., Jiang, K., Sun, J., et al.: Sports strategy analytics using probabilistic reasoning. In: 20th International Conference on Engineering of Complex Computer Systems, ICECCS 2015, pp. 182–185. IEEE (2015)
9. Fernando, D., Dong, N., Jégourel, C., Dong, J.S.: Verification of Nash-equilibrium for probabilistic BAR systems. In: 21st International Conference on Engineering of Complex Computer Systems, ICECCS 2016, pp. 53–62. IEEE Computer Society (2016)
10. Foster, S., Thiele, B., Cavalcanti, A., Woodcock, J.: Towards a UTP semantics for modelica. In: Bowen, J.P., Zhu, H. (eds.) Unifying Theories of Programming, pp. 44–64. Springer International Publishing, Cham (2017). https://doi.org/10.1007/978-3-319-52228-9_3
11. Gu, W., Saaty, T.L.: Predicting the outcome of a tennis tournament: based on both data and judgments. J. Syst. Sci. Syst. Eng. **28**(3), 317–343 (2019)
12. Guo, C., Pleiss, G., Sun, Y., Weinberger, K.Q.: On calibration of modern neural networks. In: International Conference on Machine Learning, pp. 1321–1330. PMLR (2017)
13. Jifeng, H.: UTP semantics for web services. In: Davies, J., Gibbons, J. (eds.) IFM 2007. LNCS, vol. 4591, pp. 353–372. Springer, Heidelberg (2007). https://doi.org/10.1007/978-3-540-73210-5_19
14. He, J., Li, X., Liu, Z.: rCOS: a refinement calculus of object systems. Theor. Comput. Sci. **365**(1–2), 109–142 (2006)
15. He, J., Seidel, K., McIver, A.: Probabilistic models for the guarded command language. Sci. Comput. Program. **28**, 171–192 (1999)
16. Hoare, C.: Communicating Sequential Processes. Prentice-Hall (1985)
17. Hoare, C., He, J.: Unifying Theories of Programming. Prentice-Hall (1998)
18. Ingram, M.: A point-based Bayesian hierarchical model to predict the outcome of tennis matches. J. Quantit. Anal. Sports **15**(4), 313–325 (2019)
19. Jiang, K., Izadi, M., Liu, Z., Dong, J.S.: Deep learning application in broadcast tennis video annotation. In: 2020 25th International Conference on Engineering of Complex Computer Systems (ICECCS), pp. 53–62. IEEE (2020)
20. Jiang, K., Li, J., Liu, Z., Dong, C.: Court detection using masked perspective fields network. In: 2023 IEEE 28th Pacific Rim International Symposium on Dependable Computing (PRDC), pp. 342–345. IEEE (2023)
21. Kovalchik, S.A.: Searching for the goat of tennis win prediction. J. Quantit. Anal. Sports **12**(3), 127–138 (2016)
22. Leitner, C., Zeileis, A., Hornik, K.: Is federer stronger in a tournamentwithout nadal? an evaluation of odds and seedings for wimbledon 2009. Austrian J. Stat. **38**(4), 277–286 (2009)
23. Liu, Z., Guo, J., Wang, M., Wang, R., Jiang, K., Dong, J.S.: Recognizing a sequence of events from tennis video clips: addressing timestep identification and subtle class differences. In: 2023 IEEE 28th Pacific Rim International Symposium on Dependable Computing (PRDC), pp. 337–341. IEEE (2023)
24. Liu, Z., Jiang, K., Dong, J.S.: Sports injury prediction in professional tennis. In: 2023 IEEE 28th Pacific Rim International Symposium on Dependable Computing (PRDC), pp. 304–308. IEEE (2023)

25. Liu, Z., Jiang, K., Hou, Z., Lin, Y., Dong, J.S.: Insight analysis for tennis strategy and tactics. In: 2023 IEEE International Conference on Data Mining (ICDM), pp. 1169–1174. IEEE (2023)
26. Liu, Z.: Linking formal methods in software development: a reflection on the development of rCOS. In: Bowen, J.P., Li, Q., Xu, Q. (eds.) Theories of Programming and Formal Methods: Essays Dedicated to Jifeng He on the Occasion of His 80th Birthday, pp. 52–84. Springer Nature Switzerland, Cham (2023). https://doi.org/10.1007/978-3-031-40436-8_3
27. Mahony, B., Dong, J.S.: Blending Object-Z and Timed CSP: an introduction to TCOZ. In: Proceedings of the 20th International Conference on Software Engineering, pp. 95–104 (1998)
28. Mahony, B., Dong, J.S.: Timed communicating object Z. IEEE Trans. Software Eng. **26**(2), 150–177 (2000)
29. Mahony, B., Dong, J.S.: Overview of the semantics of TCOZ. In: Araki, K., Galloway, A., Taguchi, K. (eds.) IFM'99, pp. 66–85. Springer, London (1999). https://doi.org/10.1007/978-1-4471-0851-1_5
30. Miyazawa, A., Ribeiro, P., Li, W., Cavalcanti, A., Timmis, J., Woodcock, J.: RoboChart: modelling and verification of the functional behaviour of robotic applications. Softw. Syst. Model. **18**, 3097–3149 (2019). https://doi.org/10.1007/s10270-018-00710-z
31. Morgan, C., McIver, A., Seidel, K., Sanders, J.W.: Refinement-oriented probability for CSP. Formal Aspects Comput. **8**(6), 617–647 (1996)
32. Morris, B., Bialik, C., Boice, J.: How we're forecasting the 2016 us open. https://fivethirtyeight.com/features/how-were-forecasting-the-2016-us-open/. Search in (2016)
33. Nguyen, T.K., Sun, J., Liu, Y., Dong, J.S.: Symbolic model-checking of stateful timed CSP using BDD and digitization. In: Aoki, T., Taguchi, K. (eds.) Formal Methods and Software Engineering, pp. 398–413. Springer, Berlin, Heidelberg (2012). https://doi.org/10.1007/978-3-642-34281-3_28
34. Oliveira, M., Cavalcanti, A., Woodcock, J.: A denotational semantics for circus. Electron. Notes Theor. Comput. Sci. **187**, 107–123 (2007)
35. Oliveira, M., Cavalcanti, A., Woodcock, J.: A UTP semantics for circus. Formal Aspects Comput. **21**(1–2), 3–32 (2009)
36. Phillips, J.J.: Measuring return on investment, vol. 2. American Society for Training and Development (1994)
37. Qin, S., Dong, J.S., Chin, W.-N.: A semantic foundation for TCOZ in unifying theories of programming. In: Araki, K., Gnesi, S., Mandrioli, D. (eds.) FME 2003: Formal Methods: International Symposium of Formal Methods Europe, Pisa, Italy, September 8-14, 2003. Proceedings, pp. 321–340. Springer, Berlin, Heidelberg (2003). https://doi.org/10.1007/978-3-540-45236-2_19
38. Roscoe, A.W.: The Theory and Practice of Concurrency. Prentice Hall (1997)
39. Roscoe, A.: Understanding Concurrent Systems, 1st edn. Springer-Verlag, Berlin, Heidelberg (2010). https://doi.org/10.1007/978-1-84882-258-0
40. Sampaio, A., Woodcock, J., Cavalcanti, A.: Refinement in circus. In: Eriksson, L.-H., Lindsay, P.A. (eds.) FME 2002:Formal Methods—Getting IT Right: International Symposium of Formal Methods Europe Copenhagen, Denmark, July 22–24, 2002 Proceedings, pp. 451–470. Springer, Berlin, Heidelberg (2002). https://doi.org/10.1007/3-540-45614-7_26
41. Sherif, A., Cavalcanti, A., Jifeng, H., Sampaio, A.: A process algebraic framework for specification and validation of real-time systems. Form. Asp. Comput. **22**(2), 153–191 (2010)

42. Shi, L., Zhao, Y., Liu, Y., Sun, J., Dong, J.S., Qin, S.: A UTP semantics for communicating processes with shared variables. In: Groves, L., Sun, J. (eds.) Formal Methods and Software Engineering, pp. 215–230. Springer, Berlin, Heidelberg (2013). https://doi.org/10.1007/978-3-642-41202-8_15

43. Shi, L., Zhao, Y., Liu, Y., Sun, J., Dong, J.S., Qin, S.: A UTP semantics for communicating processes with shared variables and its formal encoding in PVS. Form. Asp. Comput. **30**(3–4), 351–380 (2018)

44. Smith, G.: A semantic integration of object-Z and CSP for the specification of concurrent systems. In: Fitzgerald, J., Jones, C.B., Lucas, P. (eds.) FME '97: Industrial Applications and Strengthened Foundations of Formal Methods: 4th International Symposium of Formal Methods Europe Graz, Austria, September 15–19, 1997 Proceedings, pp. 62–81. Springer, Berlin, Heidelberg (1997). https://doi.org/10.1007/3-540-63533-5_4

45. Smith, G.: The Object-Z specification language. Kluwer Academic Publishers (2000)

46. Song, S., Hao, J., Liu, Y., Sun, J., Leung, H., Dong, J.S.: Analyzing multi-agent systems with probabilistic model checking approach. In: 34th International Conference on Software Engineering, ICSE 2012, pp. 1337–1340. IEEE Computer Society (2012)

47. Song, S., Sun, J., Liu, Y., Dong, J.S.: A model checker for hierarchical probabilistic real-time systems. In: Madhusudan, P., Seshia, S.A. (eds.) CAV 2012. LNCS, vol. 7358, pp. 705–711. Springer, Heidelberg (2012). https://doi.org/10.1007/978-3-642-31424-7_53

48. Sun, J., Liu, Y., Dong, J.S.: Model checking CSP revisited: introducing a process analysis toolkit. In: Margaria, T., Steffen, B. (eds.) ISoLA 2008. CCIS, vol. 17, pp. 307–322. Springer, Heidelberg (2008). https://doi.org/10.1007/978-3-540-88479-8_22

49. Sun, J., Liu, Y., Dong, J.S., Chen, C.: Integrating specification and programs for system modeling and verification. In: The 3rd IEEE International Symposium on Theoretical Aspects of Software Engineering (TASE'09), pp. 127–135. IEEE Computer Society (2009)

50. Sun, J., Liu, Y., Dong, J.S., Liu, Y., Shi, L., André, E.: Modeling and verifying hierarchical real-time systems using stateful timed CSP. ACM Trans. Softw. Eng. Methodol. **22**(1), 3:1–3:29 (2013)

51. Sun, J., Liu, Y., Dong, J.S., Pang, J.: PAT: towards flexible verification under fairness. In: Bouajjani, A., Maler, O. (eds.) CAV 2009. LNCS, vol. 5643, pp. 709–714. Springer, Heidelberg (2009). https://doi.org/10.1007/978-3-642-02658-4_59

52. Sun, J., Song, S., Liu, Y.: Model checking hierarchical probabilistic systems. In: Dong, J.S., Zhu, H. (eds.) ICFEM 2010. LNCS, vol. 6447, pp. 388–403. Springer, Heidelberg (2010). https://doi.org/10.1007/978-3-642-16901-4_26

53. Terroba, A., Kosters, W., Varona, J., Manresa-Yee, C.S.: Finding optimal strategies in tennis from video sequences. Int. J. Pattern Recogn. Artif. Intell. **27**(06), 1355010 (2013)

54. Thorp, E.O.: Portfolio choice and the Kelly criterion. In: Stochastic Optimization Models in Finance, pp. 599–619. Elsevier (1975)

55. Wang, J., et al.: Tac-Valuer: knowledge-based stroke evaluation in table tennis. In: Proceedings of the 27th ACM SIGKDD Conference on Knowledge Discovery & Data Mining, pp. 3688–3696 (2021)

56. Wang, W.Y., Chan, T.F., Yang, H.K., Wang, C.C., Fan, Y.C., Peng, W.C.: Exploring the long short-term dependencies to infer shot influence in badminton matches.

In: 2021 IEEE International Conference on Data Mining (ICDM), pp. 1397–1402. IEEE (2021)

57. Wang, W.Y., Shuai, H.H., Chang, K.S., Peng, W.C.: ShuttleNet: position-aware fusion of rally progress and player styles for stroke forecasting in badminton. In: Proceedings of the AAAI Conference on Artificial Intelligence, vol. 36, pp. 4219–4227 (2022)

58. Wei, K., Woodcock, J., Burns, A.: Timed Circus: timed CSP with the miracle. In: 16th IEEE International Conference on Engineering of Complex Computer Systems, ICECCS 2011, pp. 55–64. IEEE Computer Society (2011)

59. Wei, X., Lucey, P., Morgan, S., Reid, M., Sridharan, S.: The thin edge of the wedge: accurately predicting shot outcomes in tennis using style and context priors. In: Proceedings of the 10th Annual MIT Sloan Sport Anal Conference, Boston, MA, USA, pp. 1–11 (2016)

60. Woodcock, J.: Software Engineering Mathematics. CRC Press (1988)

61. Woodcock, J., Cavalcanti, A.: The semantics of circus. In: Bert, D., Bowen, J.P., Henson, M.C., Robinson, K. (eds.) ZB 2002:Formal Specification and Development in Z and B, pp. 184–203. Springer, Berlin, Heidelberg (2002). https://doi.org/10.1007/3-540-45648-1_10

62. Woodcock, J., Cavalcanti, A., Foster, S., Mota, A., Ye, K.: Probabilistic semantics for RoboChart: a weakest completion approach. In: Ribeiro, P., Sampaio, A. (eds.) Unifying Theories of Programming: 7th International Symposium, UTP 2019, Dedicated to Tony Hoare on the Occasion of His 85th Birthday, Porto, Portugal, October 8, 2019, Proceedings, pp. 80–105. Springer International Publishing, Cham (2019). https://doi.org/10.1007/978-3-030-31038-7_5

63. Woodcock, J., Davies, J.: Using Z: Specification, Refinement, and Proof. Prentice-Hall Inc, USA (1996)

64. Ye, K., Cavalcanti, A., Foster, S., Miyazawa, A., Woodcock, J.: Probabilistic modelling and verification using RoboChart and PRISM. Softw. Syst. Model. **21**(2), 667–716 (2022)

65. Zhu, H., Sanders, J.W., He, J., Qin, S.: Denotational semantics for a probabilistic timed shared-variable language. In: Wolff, B., Gaudel, M.-C., Feliachi, A. (eds.) Unifying Theories of Programming, pp. 224–247. Springer, Berlin, Heidelberg (2013). https://doi.org/10.1007/978-3-642-35705-3_11

Towards the Composition of Digital Twins

Peter Gorm Larsen[1]([✉])(iD), Prasad Talasila[1](iD), and John Fitzgerald[2](iD)

[1] DIGIT, Department of Electrical and Computer Engineering, Aarhus University,
Aarhus, Denmark
{pgl,prasad.talasila}@ece.au.dk
[2] School of Computing, Newcastle University, Newcastle upon Tyne, UK
john.fitzgerald@ncl.ac.uk

Abstract. This paper describes challenges in the composition of cyber-physical systems enabled by digital twins. Digital twins link virtual models with the real systems that they represent, adding value to these models throughout the system's life. As we come to rely on federations of systems, there is good reason to be interested in the composition of both models and twins. A practical example demonstrates the composition of twins of two robots, building on a "Digital Twin as a Service" platform. In considering how this field may develop, we highlight the influence of business and commercial factors, such as the need to deal with the diverse interests of their stakeholders, that are expected to have a significant technical impact.

Keywords: System of Systems · Cyber-Physical Systems · Digital Twins · Model-based Systems Engineering · Model Composition

1 Dedication

This paper describes a small step in a journey of collaboration and friendship that began in the 1990s when Peter Gorm Larsen (PGL) and Jim Woodcock were leading the semantic definitions of the VDM and Z specification languages respectively. Indeed, PGL recalls the two going together to Pittsburgh to present their work to the ASCII Committee. In 1993, Jim chaired the first Formal Methods Europe (FME) conference in Odense at which PGL was the organising chair. Maintaining a working relationship through FME, which was chaired by Peter Lucas and then John Fitzgerald (JSF), there was a series of successful research projects funded by the European Commission. Collaboration was renewed in the COMPASS project coordinated by JSF, meeting the challenges of Systems-of-Systems (SoS) engineering – a subject that has strong resonances in this paper. Later, the journey continued beyond discrete systems in the INTO-CPS project led by PGL, creating a well-founded tool chain for systematic development of Cyber-Physical Systems (CPSs). In several of these projects, we developed a pattern in which Jim would lead on semantics, JSF on methods, and PGL on tools. Recently we have collaborated with Jim in the Digital Twins for Cyber-Physical Systems (DiT4CPS) project focussing on the systematic engineering of digital twins for CPSs, in which Jim has shone light into the darker areas of

© The Author(s), under exclusive license to Springer Nature Switzerland AG 2024
S. Foster and A. Sampaio (Eds.): *The Application of Formal Methods*, LNCS 14900, pp. 103–122, 2024.
https://doi.org/10.1007/978-3-031-67114-2_5

the semantic foundations of these ever more important systems, focussing on tolerances, uncertainties and probabilistic approaches.

Through our decades of collaboration, Jim's work on formal approaches, their application and composition, has had a profound and long-lasting impact. It is a pleasure to contribute to this collection as a small token of thanks for the many lessons that we have learned from him, as much as for the pleasure of his comradeship.

2   Introduction

Digital Twins (DTs) are virtual representations of real-world systems. They add value to those real-world systems by giving stakeholders the ability to use digital technology to visualise and analyse system states and dynamics, detect performance degradation and undertake predictive "what if ...?" studies, among many other things. However, a DT is more than a just a model; it operates concurrently with its real-world counterpart, sometimes known as its Physical Twin (PT), with which it communicates over a digital infrastructure. It thereby bridges the gap between a system "as designed", "as built" and "as used". A DT should not unduly diminish the value of the PT itself. Consequently, the DT engineering challenge is that of creating and maintaining a *DT-enabled system* composed of the DT, the PT and the communications connecting them. Ensuring the dependability of such a cyber-physical composite of concurrent processes is an interesting and important challenge [6].

As DTs are developed for an ever-wider range of domains, including manufacturing, infrastructure and the built environment, the importance of federating or composing DT-enabled systems also grows. For example, a materials supplier and a chemical manufacturer may wish to compose the DTs of their processes in order to provide a new DT of the two systems working in a "pipeline" architecture in order to see the combined properties that emerge from their collaboration. Such a composition task presents a challenge for DT engineering research, which must provide effective, well-founded methods and tools that work with existing heterogeneous DTs that can be, to a greater or lesser degree, independently owned and managed, echoing features of SoS engineering [22].

In this paper, we present open challenges for DT composition with the aid of a proof-of-concept composition of DTs of robots in a flexible manufacturing cell, using a *Digital Twin as a Service (DTaaS)* platform. Section 3 sets the scene by considering CPSs, DTs and SoSs. We then review the forms of DT composition that may need to be supported (Sect. 4). We describe the implementation of the DTaaS platform in Sect. 5 and discuss our "flex cell" example in Sect. 6. Finally, Sect. 7 identifies directions for future work towards establishing a well-founded discipline for the composition of DTs and DT-enabled systems.

3   Background

We first consider the scope of DTs of CPSs in Sect. 3.1 and briefly introduce SoS concepts in Sect. 3.2.

3.1 Cyber-Physical Systems, Digital Twins and DT-Enabled Systems

Our work aims to provide techniques and tools that can be applied within systems engineering processes from concept definition to system maintenance and disposal [15]. Our systems of interest are *cyber-physical* in character. A CPS is an engineered system composed of diverse computational and physical processes that interact with one another and with their environment (Figure 1). In practice, a CPS model is likely to be built out of models of discrete and continuous processes, each of which is expressed in a notation appropriate to the phenomena it describes. For example, the description of a manufacturing plant as a CPS may have models of mechanics expressed as systems of differential equations over dense time, and models of network behaviour described in discrete-event formalisms.

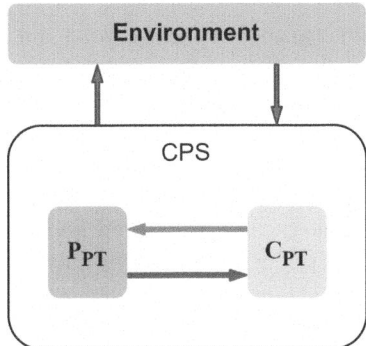

Fig. 1. Elements of a CPS and its interaction with its environment (from [7]).

Note that, although we use the term *"Physical Twin"*, a PT is likely to be a CPS with computational, physical and human elements. For example, depending on its purpose, the DT of a production line might have the physical machinery in scope, as well as the current throughput rates of machines, the shift scheduling of the human operators, and the digital system that does the scheduling.

As yet, there is no common definition of the DT concept. In some sources, any digital model qualifies as a DT, but Tekinerdogan and Verdouw provide a more nuanced characterisation that focuses on the levels of automation present in the operational relationship between the PT and DT [30]. As summarised in Fig. 2, one can think of a digital model of a physical object as a representation that may be used to inspire and specify the manual design and subsequent evolution of the physical object, and which may be manually updated as the physical object evolves. Where the digital-to-physical flow can be automated, the focus is on the model *generating* the physical object. A digital representation that is automatically kept up to date with the evolution of its physical counterpart is referred to as a *Digital Shadow (DS)* and the DT term is reserved for DSs that

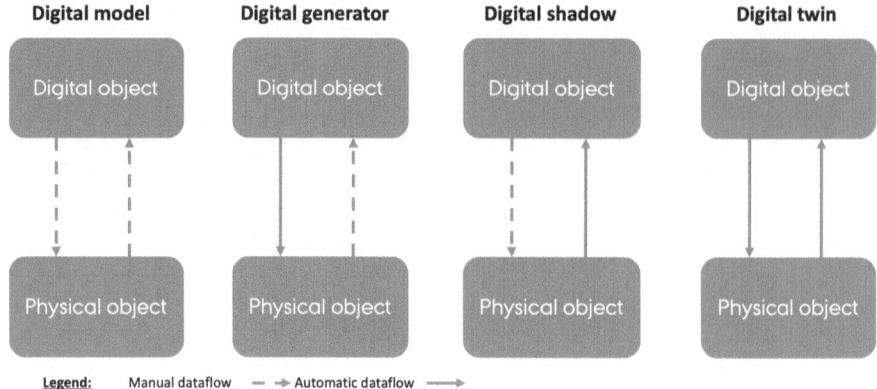

Fig. 2. Identified relationships between digital object and physical object (after [30]).

may also influence the PT through an automated data flow. The majority of applications that we see currently qualify as DSs. However, the divide between a DT and a DS is not clear-cut; in many cases it is essential to engage with human users, a feature that raises challenges in the composition of DTs.

At a simple level, a DT is composed of data, models, and services that use them (Fig. 3). The data are drawn from the PT and environment via sensor and communications technology, and are stored and managed by the DT. The models describe aspects of the PT and potentially its environment, and are themselves managed by the DT as they evolve or are updated. DT services are built on these models and data to add value, for example by tuning models on the basis of live data, identifying potential failures before they arise, or supporting visualisation. Some services will interact directly with stakeholders in the DT-enabled system while others may be enablers, performing analyses that are used by the stakeholder-facing services.

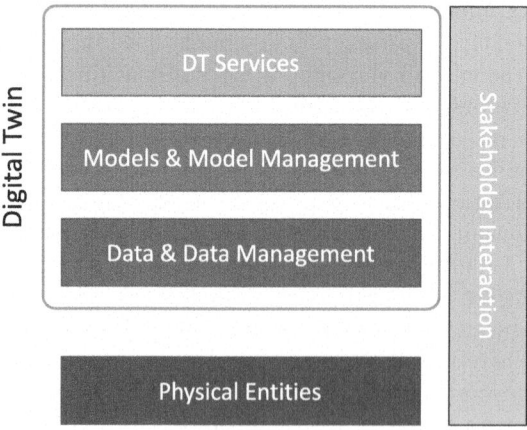

Fig. 3. Elements of a DT (data, models, and services) organised as "layers".

The needs of the stakeholders will result in technical requirements on the models, data and services within the DT. Oakes et al. have suggested that these will relate to relevance, verifiability, substitutability, and fidelity [23]. Verification of the models within the DT is likely to relate to the preservation of these properties as the PT and its environment evolve.

We will use the term *DT-enabled system* to refer to the composition of the DT, PT and their communications channels. Our goal is to enable the composition of DT-enabled systems. Basic "top-level" stakeholder-facing services may enable visualisation of the state, history and trajectory of the PT, and these may be relatively straightforward to combine as we scale up from individual DT-enabled systems to compositions. More advanced services such as those supporting prediction of the consequences of events in the PT may need to return results faster than real-time, and their composition would naturally present greater challenges.

3.2 System of Systems

Composing DT-enabled systems can be viewed as a "System of Systems" (SoS) Engineering activity. The term "System of Systems" has been in use since the 1950 s to describe systems that are composed of independent constituent systems which act jointly towards a common goal [22]. Four categories of SoSs are identified by the US Department of Defense [25]:

Directed: The SoS is built to fulfil specific purposes. Constituent systems have the ability to operate independently, but are managed to satisfy a concrete purpose. This category is typically easy to deal with from a DT perspective since it is mainly coordinated from one organisation.

Collaborative: The constituent systems are not compelled to follow a central management, but voluntarily participate in a collaboration to fulfil the overall goal. In order to get DTs combined in this case it is essential to form an ecosystem of different contributing organisations.

Acknowledged: The SoS recognises a common purpose and goal while the constituent systems retain independent control and objectives. Evolution of the common purpose is based on collaboration between the SoS and the constituent systems. In this case DTs are combined in an ad-hoc manner.

Virtual: The SoS is without either managerial control or a common purpose. This makes the behaviour and the fulfilled goals highly emergent, but also entails that the exact means and structures producing the system functionality are difficult to discern and distinguish. From a DT perspective composition of DTs is also established in an ad-hoc manner.

Three of these categories were originally defined by Maier [18], while the "Acknowledged" type was later proposed by Dahmann and Baldwin [5].

The Horizon 2020 project COMPASS [9] sought to develop a well-founded model-based approach for the engineering of SoSs. Within the project, Woodcock and colleagues developed the COMPASS Modelling Language (CML) [31] which enables the description of compositions of constituent systems in a contractual style [20,33]. A CML model defines types, functions, channels, and processes. The type system of CML is taken directly from VDM and includes support for numeric types, finite sequence, sets and mappings, as well as records, all of which can be further constrained through type invariants. Functions are pure mathematical mappings between inputs and outputs, which can be specified explicitly via λ-calculus, or implicitly using pre- and post-conditions. In general we adopt the syntax of VDM-SL [8] for the functional and imperative parts of the language, whilst using Circus-style syntax [32] for the concurrent and reactive parts. Circus is a composition of Communicating Sequential Processes (CSP) [13,14] and Z [34].

Other formalisms may be brought to bear on the challenge of DT compositions. For example, when considering mobility a formalism such as the π-calculus [21,27] is relevant. However, some features that are relevant to the DT composition problem, such as the description of data ownership and services, are not so well supported as first class concepts in current formalisms, and so in practice may have to be described informally in accompanying text.

4   Composing DT-Enabled Systems

We consider three forms of composition problem. The simplest is one in which there no relevant connection between the PTs, so that they form a *fleet* of individual systems (discussed in Sect. 4.1). The second scenario is when the PTs actually interact or interfere with each other in the physical world so that the composition of the DTs must take connections between the PTs into account (discussed in Sect. 4.2). Finally, we consider PTs that collaborate in some fashion, with the potential to change their composition dynamically and with some level of autonomy. The need for the corresponding DTs to reflect this leads to a more complex kind of composition that we discuss further in Sect. 4.3.

4.1   A Fleet of Digital Twins

Our inspiration for this type of composition comes from ("smart") products that offer optional digital services alongside the product. There are numerous examples of this – from headphones to toothbrushes – where the product-specific DS or DT will typically reside as an application on a user's smartphone. The owner of the product (the individual PT) will be able to get data from their own DT, but the producer of the product will gather the data from all the DT-enabled product instances. This can be considered as a fleet of DT-enabled systems that help the producer to learn about usage and performance of the products, for example by deploying machine learning on data gathered from the fleet as a whole. Such information can be used both to update the software of existing products and influence the design of future products for the market.

As an example, consider a fleet of "smart" sports watches developed and marketed by a manufacturer for wearers. Such watches offer some functionality to their wearers, but the manufacturer may maintain DTs of them in order to offer enhanced services and gain insights how the watches are actually performing and being used.

We may think of the watches as CPSs that are each PTs. Each watch includes sensors that gather data about the performance of the physical parts of the watch (e.g., battery performance) and its environment, namely the human wearer. The data is stored locally on the watch. Functionality in the watch converts the gathered data to forms that can be visualised on the watch's small display showing, for example, number of steps taken or heart rate over a period. In some cases the owner explicitly provides state change information to the watch (e.g., when starting an activity such as a timed run), whereas in other cases the watch may conduct its own state change estimations (e.g., when the owner falls asleep).

In our example, the manufacturer also supplies the owners with a smartphone application that can transfer the data stored locally to a cloud solution. This means that the owner decides when data is uploaded, so the streaming of data to this DT is not continuous but instead appears in intermittent bursts. This limits the kinds of predictive functionality available from the DT. Instead, much of the DT's added value may be in visualising data over a longer period. This is rather like having an edge device that is used to transfer the data to the cloud sporadically. Communications from the DT to the PT are likely to be limited to software updates pushed to the watch.

In a case like this, we might think of a PT in the following form:

$$PT = (C_{PT} \parallel_{\{sensors,actuator\}} P_{PT}) \parallel_{\{sensors\}} Env$$

where $\parallel_{\{sensors\}}$ is similar to the CSP parallel composition operator where the *sensors* subscript indicates the "channels" that are used between the adjacent processes, C_{PT} represents the cyber-elements from the PT, P_{PT} represents the physical elements from the PT, and *Env* represents the environment in which the PT operates.

In our smart watch example, the capabilities offered by the DT to the PT's user are limited because it lacks a comprehensive model of the PT's environment (the wearer). It is mainly offers a visualisation service, e.g. different kinds of dashboards. In order to offer a near real-time DT capability, for example for prediction of performance, it would be necessary to have a much richer (and potentially computationally demanding) model of the PT and its environment. Gathered data about, for example, the PT's performance or dependability, of primary interest to the manufacturer, could continue to be analysed and displayed to the DT users, however.

From a fleet perspective, the collective DT can be considered as:

$$DT_{fleet} = \parallel\mid (PT_n, DT_n, Env_n)$$

where $\parallel\mid$ is similar to the CSP interleaving operator. The composition of the DTs and PTs in this case is very simple because the individual PTs are truly independent. From a fleet perspective the only potential challenge is fully keeping track of the version of the software in each of the PTs. In general, updating this remotely needs to be carried out when the individual PT is in a safe state. In this particular example the human user will be involved in the decision, and thus it is clear that this is ensured by the user and in this case there is nothing critical being monitored. From a visibility perspective, it is also important that owners of PTs can only see data from their own PT. This is probably typical for products that can be considered as business-to-consumer where individuals are interested in purchasing products that are able to provide this kind of digital services on top of the actual physical product.

4.2   A Hierarchy of Digital Twins

A significantly more challenging case is one in which we have a hierarchy of DTs that are independently owned and operated in a directed SoS. Here the composition of the corresponding PTs needs to be reflected in the composition of the DTs. In the cases where the different DTs are owned and/or operated by different legal entities there may be interoperability challenges. There is then a need to form an ecosystem in which the different organisations involved strike mutually beneficial deals combining DTs for the greater good. However, there will typically be one organisation that will lead such a directed SoS, typically the main top-level supplier or owner of the CPS in question. Assuming such an arrangement can be reached, the challenge is to provide sufficient configuration information about the way the PTs are coupled to the DTs to enable the composition.

Examples of this type of SoS-based DT structure arise in the built environment. For example, a large building will involve many elements such as building management systems, the heating and ventilation systems, water and power supplies that may each have their own DTs. In order to achieve globally optimised properties such as energy consumption or systems reliability, it is necessary to provide a well-founded integration of these DT-enabled systems which have complex physical interactions. Such an integration or federation requires common semantic foundations such as the Industry Foundation Classes (IFC) standard supporting Building Information Modelling (BIM). Even here, this requires unique identification of the individual PTs to be present to ensure consistency between models "as designed" and "as built" (as is often the case today). Without this, significant manual effort is required to ensure that the DTs are aware of the true connections between the PTs. In addition, there is reason to include or integrate models of the local environmental conditions.

At a naïvely simple level, this kind of situation might be expressed in the following form:

$$DT_{hierarchy} = (PT_n \parallel_{\{sensors, actuators\}} DT_n(configuration\ of\ PTs) \parallel Env_n)$$

where the "*configuration of PTs*" is shared between the different DTs. However, it is much more complicated than this because communications between the PTs and DTs may follow different protocols, making interoperability is key to success. There also needs to be common agreement on meanings, formats and units. Thus, in order to establish dependable DTs in each hierarchy there is a need for standardisation by independent organisations or by a leading participant in the SoS.

In an SoS setting with many constituent DT-enabled systems, each potentially separately owned and managed, we would expect to see a more heterogeneous collection of communications protocols than in the fleet considered above. For example, different forms of data correction, compensation, compression or encryption might be used. Consequently, the newly composed hierarchy has to meet the challenge of delivering known levels of dependability in this context.

4.3 Collaboration Between Digital Twins

The most challenging kind of composition of DT is when there is a desire for collaboration between the owners/operators of DT-enabled systems in a non-directed SoS (typically an acknowledged or collaborative SoS) in which it is necessary to find mutually beneficial arrangements for stakeholders. The need for communication standards is imperative. As an example, the recent developments for the smart home ecosystem with Thread[1] and Matter[2] is an interesting initiative since it is led by a number of the tech giants, and so may move more rapidly than some standardisation efforts.

In terms of composition, the situation here could look similar that of Sect. 4.2, but with the additional complication that some of the "channels" may be hidden for potential competitors in the ecosystem for business reasons. So, in addition to the interoperability challenges mentioned above, the willingness to share information may vary among the participants. An additional complexity comes from the fact that alliances between organisations may vary over time. This creates a clear need to consider how to express the contractual terms governing the technical relationships between DT-enabled systems in the long term.

5   Realising Composition of DT-Enabled Systems

We have so far considered DT composition at only a rather abstract level. How might it play out in practice? We have developed a Digital Twin as a Service (DTaaS) software platform as a collaborative environment for users to create, use and share DTs [29][3]. In this section, we describe the platform's foundations (Section 5.1) and implementation (Section 5.2) of this platform and consider how it might in practice support the fleet, hierarchy and collaborative forms of DT composition (Sect. 5.3 and Sect. 5.4).

---

[1] https://en.wikipedia.org/wiki/Thread_(network_protocol).

[2] https://en.wikipedia.org/wiki/Matter_(standard).

[3] https://github.com/INTO-CPS-Association/DTaaS.

5.1   Building DTs from Reusable Components

Giving potential users the opportunity to create DTs from reusable components is one way of lowering the threshold to DT adoption. One proven way to approach component re-use is through the use of object-orientation, and in our setting this requires the identification of domain-specific entities. As a starting point, it has been previously identified that data, models, tools and services can be useful non-overlapping entities in the DT space [1,3,28]. Figure 4 shows a class diagram outlining the relationship between these entities.

In a DT-enabled system, data forms the crucial link between a PT and its DT. Data comes from either the environment (Env) or the PT, both of which change dynamically. However, having repeatable and reproducible operating conditions at the level of Env and PT is essential to the development of DT. The mocks (both Env and PT) attempt to capture such conditions and act as base scenarios under which a DT must always fulfil its requirements. The conditions can be captured in two ways. The first is experimental measurements which produce a trace of operating conditions at both Env and PT. The traces can then be put under a data component to be used later for creation and use of DTs. Another way is to use simplified mathematical equations of Env and PT that can produce quasi-experimental measurements. These equations act as generators producing the trace of experimental measurements. The generated traces are the only option available in the early stages of PT and DT development especially when experimental traces are not available.

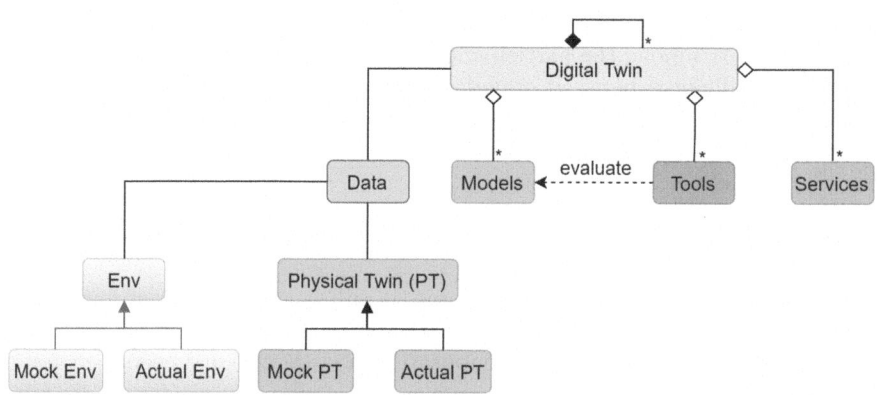

Fig. 4. Class diagram representation of DT composition for implementation in DT platforms.

The models represent abstractions of the PT relevant to the DT's purpose and desired predictive power. These abstractions could be domain-specific engineering, data-driven or lifecycle assessment models [2]. A DT may have multiple PT models to address different user requirements. Thus a DT must be composable from multiple models. The models are not often executable as stand-alone

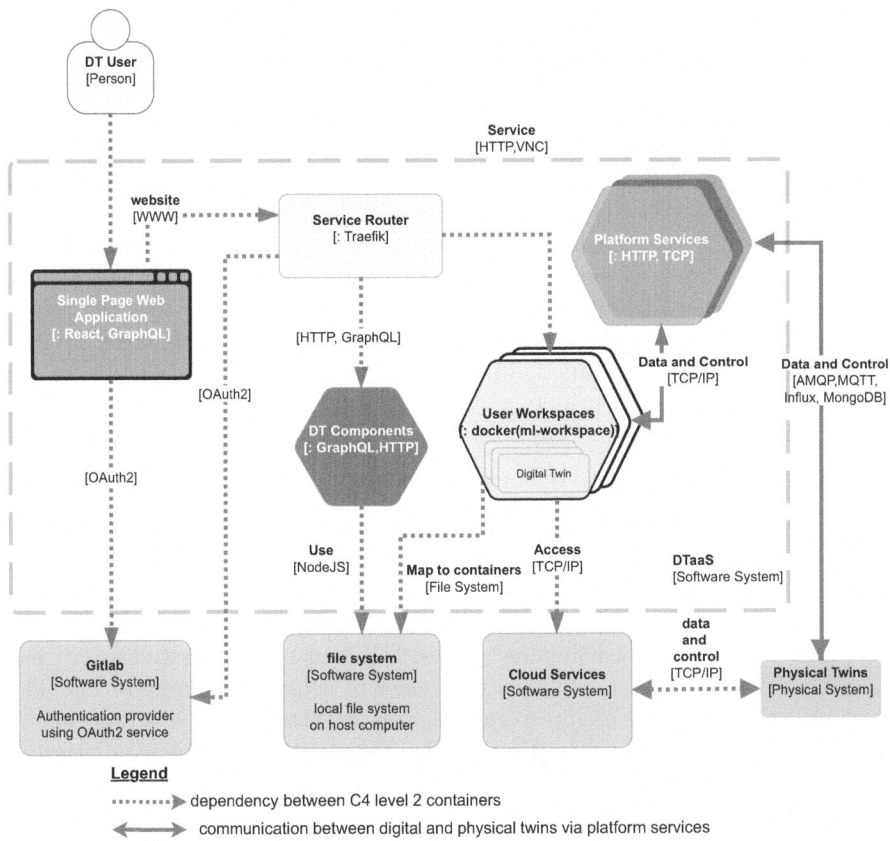

Fig. 5. System architecture of the Digital Twin as a Service software platform.

entities. They require execution or evaluation tools running in a specific execution environment. For example, finite element models cannot be evaluated in a symbolic logic-rooted execution tool. Thus, there is often a dependence between the model used and the matching tool used. The management of different DT components can be distributed on the World-Wide Web, even among different organisations [19]. In addition, a DT often provides services to either users or other software systems [24]. These services deliver value required of the DTs and can either be provided by integrating existing external or using dedicated internal services.

The construction of DTs for a set of related PTs can be specified as a distinct class. Each DT class will include DT components as a set of class properties tied together with meaningful class-level behaviours. Instead of specifying DT classes in any general purpose programming language, the DT user community has relied on the use of Domain Specific Languages (DSLs)[4,5]. A DT class defined in a DSL can still have properties and behaviours. However, the popular DSLs take the approach of specifying the structure of DTs without any links to other DT components mentioned above. This structural approach is suitable for adopting the information-schema of a software system onto DTs. However the rich nuances of DT domain entities are not captured in these information-schema centric approaches. Also the advantage of behavioural specification in a DT class is not possible using such approaches. There have also been efforts to use Development & Operations (DevOps) and configuration languages such as Ansible[6] to specify DTs. The advantage of such an approach is the ability to execute DTs on a distributed compute infrastructure. These configuration languages are also good at dynamic reconfiguration of infrastructure. Thus dynamic changes in the structure of DTs become feasible.

5.2   The Digital Twin as a Service Platform

DTs can be created within the DTaaS using reusable DT components already available on the platform. Users can execute their own DTs within DTaaS with an optional integration of external services, and can share ready-to-use DTs with other users. It is also possible for the owner of a DT to offer a DT as a service (hence the platform's name). Thus, DTs can become first-class citizens inside the DTaaS platform and thus it is easier to define their composition. The Fig. 5 shows a simplified architectural diagram of DTaaS. This diagram follows the conventions of C4 model[7]. Each of the hexagons is a sub-system referred to as container in C4 model. The dependence between containers is indicated with a dotted arrow which points from the container towards the container it is dependent upon.

The DTaaS is a distributed software system designed using microservice architectural principles. Users interact with DTaaS as a web application. The service router provides integration of all the services with the web application. The required authorisation to services is provided via the OAuth2 protocol[8]. The *DT Components* service is responsible for providing access to the reusable DT components (Sect. 5.1) stored in the file system. The DTaaS provides dedicated workspace environments for users. These workspaces have integrated software development tools such as Jupyter Lab, VS Code, and git using which software developers can create DT components. The workspaces also provide a graphical desktop environment in which the engineering models like finite element models, co-simulation models [11], reduced order models can be developed using engineering software tools such as OpenModelica[9] and Matlab[10]. The DT users often

---

[4] https://github.com/Azure/opendigitaltwins-dtdl.

[5] https://www.eclipse.org/basyx/.

[6] https://www.ansible.com/.

[7] https://c4model.com/.

[8] https://oauth.net/2/.

[9] https://openmodelica.org/.

[10] https://se.mathworks.com/products/matlab.html.

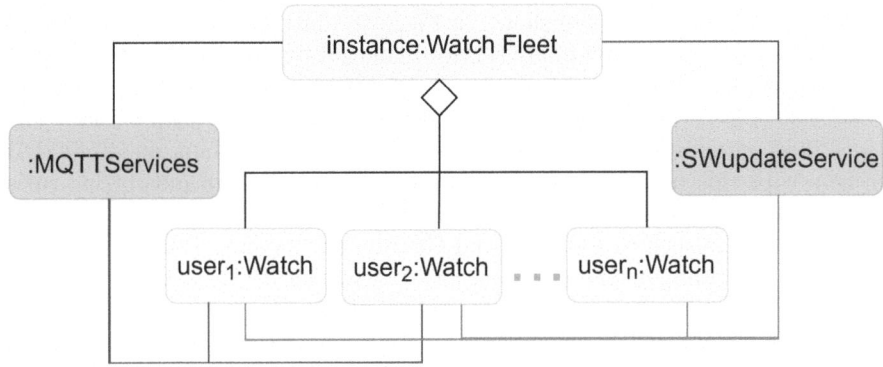

Fig. 6. An object diagram linking the fleet of sports watches to unique watches worn by customers. The fleet object can also be linked to unique watches via two services, namely MQTTService and SWUpdateService.

rely on visualisation components to aid with the interaction and decision-making processes. The workspaces of DTaaS allow execution of robotic visualisation software (e.g., URSim) and 3D interactive components (e.g., Unity projects). The user workspaces have direct access to the Internet and external cloud services. The DTs executing on cloud services can be integrated with the DTs running inside user workspaces. Such a feature provides support for collaborative DTs.

The DTaaS has native integration of MongoDB and InfluxDB databases. Both these services enable data storage for both PT and DT. In addition, the Eclipse MQTT and RabbitMQ (AMQP) services provide bidirectional communication between PT and DT.

5.3 Support for a Fleet and Hierarchy of Digital Twins

Section 4.1 details the concepts underpinning a fleet of DTs, which we realise as a collective DT that provides additional value on top of multiple DTs created from the same DT class. Figure 6 shows one possible object diagram for a fleet of sports watches described in Sect. 4.1. The DT objects of unique watches are aggregated into DT object for a fleet. In this case, the DT objects of watches have to provide two interfaces – one for customer watches and one for DT fleet object. Here, the DT fleet object can potentially get direct access to DT objects of watches. This might not always be preferable from a privacy perspective. One approach to mitigating the privacy problem is to separate the services exposed by a DT object into two interfaces. The fleet object can receive privacy-aware, user approved information from a first interface while the customers receive their completion information via the second interface. The DTaaS does not currently have support for DTs of fleets. But the architecture of DTaaS can be extended to provide such support.

It is also possible to remove direct aggregation and only link the DT fleet object with DTs of watches via multiple service Application Programming Interfaces (APIs). Two services are shown in Fig. 6 to illustrate this possibility. The first service is the software update service managed by fleet object. The second service is MQTT which can be used to send the data from customer watches to the fleet object. This kind of data exchange is supported within DTaaS. The generic fleet integration of monitoring services such as Grafana and InfluxDB can help with this task. Such services support specification of monitoring rules for one or more DTs. The segregation and aggregation of DTs is possible using custom languages such as Flux [16] and Grafana dashboards [12].

Section 4.2 highlights the potential for of hierarchical DTs. The DTaaS supports hierarchical twins using class properties. Within the context of DTaaS, a DT is also a reusable entity enabling its creation using other DTs. A hierarchical DT can be created using DTs of different types. The result is similar to a diagram shown in Fig. 6 except for the fact that the DTs aggregated are of different types. The integration of third-party DT frameworks supporting hierarchical DTs [4,17] is another proven way to support hierarchy of DTs within DTaaS. However, integration is only possible if third-party frameworks provide well-established API with scope for mapping the reusable DT components approach of the DTaaS to their platforms. One such example is Eclipse Hono[11]. This framework provides API to communicate with PTs over many network protocols. Thus Hono can be used for PT and DT communication with DTs being managed inside the DTaaS.

The DT Manager framework [17] supports hierarchical DTs and can be run within a user workspace. Similarly, commercial DT frameworks such as Amazon Web Services IoT Greengrass, Microsoft Azure DTs and Eclipse Ditto-Hono-Vorto can be connected with DTs running inside DTaaS. Each of these third-party frameworks supports hierarchical DTs and integration of DTaaS with them enhances the features provided to users of DTaaS.

5.4   Support for Collaboration Between Digital Twins

Whether dealing with intra-organisation DTs where there may ne relatively high levels of collaboration or with less tightly coupled inter-organisation DTs, standard protocols are required for coherent operation. These protocols for PTs can be standard operating procedures of an enterprise. The corresponding protocols for DTs are specified in terms of service interfaces – the APIs. The APIs can be either DT-specific or dependent on the services integrated with a DT. In the case of DTaaS, there is the possibility of integrating both services provided by the DTaaS platform and also use a service as a component during the construction of a DT class. The DTs running in user workspaces have access to cloud services and the Internet. If DTs belonging to external organisation(s) have APIs, these APIs can be wrapped in code libraries and published as DT components in DTaaS. Users can then construct DTs which will have integration with external DTs.

The potential for building DTs from reusable components has been discussed in Sect. 5.1. One class of the reusable components are DTs themselves. A DT can

---

[11] https://eclipse.dev/hono/.

be defined and configured to consist of other DTs. In such a case, the management of the composed DT is the responsibility of the composing DT. It benefits from the services provided by the composed DT and it can also have the possibility of integrating more DT assets with an existing DT to provide additional services However, architectures supporting collaboration between different parties such that DTs included in the composition can only be seen/accessed by their owners have not yet been explored in depth.

6   The Flex Cell Use Case

In this section, we consider a proof-of-concept composition of DTs that has been implemented using commercial robots in the Digital Transformation lab at Aarhus University (AU). These robots are used for research in DTs, semantic and skill-based software development. The example is based on a "flex cell" intended to introduce programmability and flexibility into the manufacturing operations done at a workstation. The flex cell (shown in Fig. 7) has two robots, namely a UR5e and a Kuka LBR iiwa 7 [10]. A DT of this flex cell has been instantiated successfully inside DTaaS, and linked with the flex cell PT.

The two robots have been manufactured by independent companies with different software and hardware interfaces, but need to be programmed to perform collaborative tasks on the workstation while following the safety constraints which need to be programmed into the robots. Any movement commands sent to the robots need to be coordinated to complete required tasks and also checked against the safety constraints.

Neither the robot models nor the flex cell come with Internet connectivity. However bidirectional connectivity between PTs and DTs is a prerequisite for the development of DTs. In our example system, a localised IoT gateway has been developed to provide a network interface to the robots. A RaspberryPi computer has been programmed to serve as an IoT gateway interface between the robots, the DTaaS platform and the Internet. The gateway supports connectivity with RabbitMQ and MQTT protocols. RabbitMQ is a robust publish-subscribe protocol, while MQTT protocol is typically used for data exchange. Both these protocols are used for exchange of data and control commands between DT and PT. The DTaaS hosts RabbitMQ and MQTT brokers as platform services which are available to all DTs running within DTaaS and to the linked PTs. Both these platform services are used by the flex cell PT and DT for communication.

Although intended to be part of one flex cell, the two robots have independent control and data and robotic arms. Hence it is best to deal with these two as having two independent DTs. The flex cell DT needs to compose DTs of both robots thus giving rise to a simple system of systems/hierarchical DT composition. Since AU has produced both of the DTs involved and they are open to the integrating level, we see this as an example of hierarchical DT composition. If the DTs were produced by the separate robot manufacturers for example, potentially with IP-constrained interfaces, this would be more like a collaborative composition.

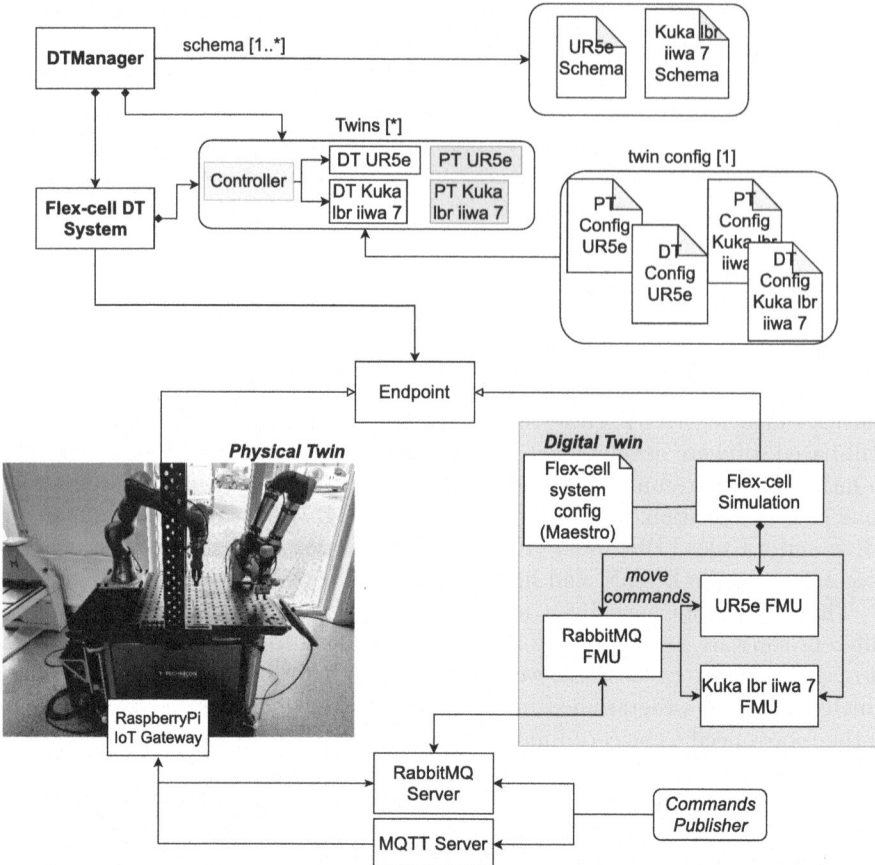

Fig. 7. Flex cell PT and its DT. There is a possibility of selecting between real and mock PT with mock PT running inside DTaaS (from [10,17]).

The robot DTs and flex cell DT are managed by the DTManager framework [10,17]. The DT Manager creates one DT System for each DT in a directed SoS setting. It is a directed SoS because a DT is created for both robots, but it would be a collaborative SoS if the two manufacturers had developed their own DTs and shared those with their users. The DT Manager configures each DT as per its respective schema which contains a set of properties, models and behaviours that the DT needs to have. The schema is flexible and can be based on the context in which a DT is to be used. Each robot has three different models. One tool is used for performing co-simulation at system of systems level. The DT schema specifies the model to be used. The DT config and DT schema together integrates the data, models and services needed for each of the robots DTs and the flex cell.

The DT Manager creates a flex cell DT, the required DTs for the two robots and then hands over management of these to the overall flex cell DT system. This system then takes over the responsibility of running the DT as per the DT configuration. The DT system creates DT and PT objects for each robot with the help of configuration provided for each of them. The PT objects are proxies for storing the state of flex cell PT. This stored state is used for checking potential discrepancy between the state of PT and DT. In addition, there is a SoS DT configuration which is shown within the DT block of Fig. 7. There is a bidirectional connectivity between PTs and DTs using RabbitMQ protocol. This protocol access configuration is also a part of hierarchical DT configuration.

Figure 7 shows *commands publisher* which sends robot movement commands that are utilised by both the PT and DT. These commands are sent using MQTT and RabbitMQ protocols. The PT receives commands using both the protocols, the DT receives them using RabbitMQ protocol.

Bidirectional communication between the DT and PT happens over a network, typically the Internet. Consequently, issues such as intermittence, unpredictable delays, and commercial network policies influence PT-DT interactions. One approach to managing such issues might be to develop distributed DTs that include "lightweight" DTs running near PT and more resource-intensive, sophisticated DTs running in the cloud [26]. Since the DT assets of robot and flex cell are available for reuse, multiple users can instantiate distinct DTs for the same flex cell PT. These DTs can have different configurations yielding different insights.

7   Concluding Remarks

The composition of DT-enabled systems is likely to arise in different contexts, but it is worth noting that there are significant and interesting challenges associated with such compositions. In this paper we have touched on several of these challenges and discussed both the conceptual aspects and practical aspects of how the compositions can be realised today. There is no doubt that in order for DTs to be composed and deliver the value envisaged there are many challenges that must be overcome. In order to enable composition of DTs we would propose several strands of research:

Standardised DT interfaces: As described from Sect. 4.2 onwards, interoperability between DTs requires standardisation of DT interfaces at semantic levels. In the research conducted for notations such as CML the interoperability is purely ensured at the modelling level but in DT-enabled systems, data and services also matter. For the models included inside a DT different levels of abstraction may be used and thus the validity frame for each of them should also be formalised, such that users can see if they would be applicable for the intended use.

Collaborative DTs: Since DTs can have different purposes, they can support different desirable functionalities. When we compose DTs it is essential that their purposes also are aligned. If, for example, one DT supports predictive maintenance when another supports autonomy for the PT then the composition of such different DTs need to be aligned if they can collaborate dependably. There is no doubt that there can be conflicts between stakeholders that must be resolved if such collaborate DTs are to become reality. When DTs are treated as first class citizens in a DTaaS platform, it would probably also be beneficial if the services provided by each DT also would be clear to potential users.

Making DTs open (enough) to stakeholders: One of the main obstacles to successful composition of DTs is the balance between effective sharing and the protection of Intellectual Property (IP) among the owners of constituent DT-enabled systems. Thus, it is essential to be able to support protection of IP in a dependable, confidence-inspiring way. This represents as much of a challenge for non-technical business negotiation and risk management as it does for technical information security. While existing collaboration platforms where access to files are strictly controlled by access rights may provide initial solutions, they are only valuable if the parties involved in a collaboration can understand and make use of them.

Acknowledgements. We are grateful to the Poul Due Jensen Foundation for supporting the establishment of a Centre for Digital Twin Technology at Aarhus University, advancing the principles, tools and applications of DT Engineering. We are grateful to our numerous collaborators at Aarhus and Newcastle, and to the anonymous reviewers for valuable feedback on the original version of this paper.

References

1. Abburu, S., Berre, A.J., Jacoby, M., Roman, D., Stojanovic, L., Stojanovic, N.: Cognitwin–hybrid and cognitive digital twins for the process industry. In: 2020 IEEE International Conference on Engineering, Technology and Innovation (ICE/ITMC), pp. 1–8. IEEE (2020)
2. et al, V.Z.: Industrial digitalization in the Industry 4.0 era: classification, reuse and authoring of digital models on digital twin platforms. Array, p. 100176 (2022). https://doi.org/10.1016/j.array.2022.100176
3. Autiosalo, J., Vepsäläinen, J., Viitala, R., Tammi, K.: A feature-based framework for structuring industrial digital twins. IEEE Access **8**, 1193–1208 (2019)
4. Convent, L., Hungerecker, S., Leucker, M., Scheffel, T., Schmitz, M., Thoma, D.: TeSSLa: temporal stream-based specification language. In: Massoni, T., Mousavi, M.R. (eds.) Formal Methods: Foundations and Applications: 21st Brazilian Symposium, SBMF 2018, Salvador, Brazil, November 26–30, 2018, Proceedings, pp. 144–162. Springer International Publishing, Cham (2018). https://doi.org/10.1007/978-3-030-03044-5_10
5. Dahmann, J., Baldwin, K.: Understanding the current state of US defense systems of systems and the implications for systems engineering. In: IEEE Systems Conference. IEEE (2008)
6. Feng, H., Gomes, C., Thule, C., Lausdahl, K., Iosifidis, A., Larsen, P.G.: Introduction to digital twin engineering. In: Proceedings of the 2021 Annual Modeling

and Simulation Conference. IEEE, Virtual Conference (2021). https://doi.org/10.23919/ANNSIM52504.2021.9552135

7. Fitzgerald, J., Gomes, C., Larsen, P.G. (eds.): The Engineering of Digital Twins. Springer (2024)

8. Fitzgerald, J., Larsen, P.G.: Modelling Systems – Practical Tools and Techniques in Software Development. Cambridge University Press, The Edinburgh Building, Cambridge CB2 2RU, UK, Second Edn. (2009). https://doi.org/10.1017/CBO9780511626975, ISBN 0-521-62348-0

9. Fitzgerald, J., Larsen, P.G., Woodcock, J.: Modelling and analysis technology for systems of systems engineering: research challenges. In: INCOSE. Rome, Italy (2012)

10. Gil, S., Mikkelsen, P.H., Tola, D., Schou, C., Larsen, P.G.: A modeling approach for composed digital twins in cooperative systems. In: 2023 IEEE 28th International Conference on Emerging Technologies and Factory Automation (ETFA), pp. 1–8. IEEE (2023). https://doi.org/10.1109/ETFA54631.2023.10275601

11. Gomes, C., Thule, C., Broman, D., Larsen, P.G., Vangheluwe, H.: Co-simulation: a survey. ACM Comput. Surv. **51**(3), 49:1–49:33 (2018)

12. Grafana Labs:https://grafana.com/grafana/dashboards/ (2024), Grafana Dashboards

13. Hoare, C.: Communicating sequential processes. Commun. ACM **21**(8) (1978). https://doi.org/10.1145/359576.359585

14. Hoare, T.: Communication Sequential Processes. Prentice-Hall International, Englewood Cliffs, New Jersey 07632 (1985)

15. IEEE: International Standard ISO/IEC/IEEE 15288:2023(en), Systems and software engineering — System life cycle processes. ISO/IEC and IEEE Computer Society (2023)

16. InfluxData: https://docs.influxdata.com/flux/v0/ (2024). Flux Query Language Documentation

17. Lehner, D., Gil, S., Mikkelsen, P.H., Larsen, P.G., Wimmer, M.: An architectural extension for digital twin platforms to leverage behavioral models. In: 2023 IEEE 19th International Conference on Automation Science and Engineering (CASE), pp. 1–8 (2023). https://doi.org/10.1109/CASE56687.2023.10260417

18. Maier, M.W.: Architecting principles for systems-of-systems. In: Sixth International Symposium of the International Council on Systems Engineering. INCOSE (1996)

19. Mathworks Inc.: https://se.mathworks.com/products/thingspeak.html (2024). ThingSpeak for IoT Projects

20. Meyer, B.: Applying design by contract. IEEE Comput. **25**(10), 40–51 (1992)

21. Milner, R.: Communicating and Mobile Systems: the π-Calculus. Cambridge University Press (1999)

22. Nielsen, C.B., Larsen, P.G., Fitzgerald, J., Woodcock, J., Peleska, J.: Model-based engineering of systems of systems. ACM Comput. Surv. **48**(2) (2015). http://dl.acm.org/citation.cfm?id=2794381

23. Oakes, B.J., et al.: Examining model qualities and their impact on digital twins. In: 2023 Annual Modeling and Simulation Conference (ANNSIM), pp. 220–232. IEEE (2023)

24. Oakes, B.J., et al.: A digital twin description framework and its mapping to asset administration shell. In: Pires, L.F., Hammoudi, S., Seidewitz, E. (eds.) Model-Driven Engineering and Software Development: 9th International Conference, MODELSWARD 2021, Virtual Event, February 8–10, 2021, and 10th International

Conference, MODELSWARD 2022, Virtual Event, February 6–8, 2022, Revised Selected Papers, pp. 1–24. Springer Nature Switzerland, Cham (2023). https://doi.org/10.1007/978-3-031-38821-7_1

25. OUSD(AT&L), DoD: Systems and Software Engineering. Systems Engineering Guide for Systems of Systems. Tech. Rep. Version 1.0., Office of the Deputy Under Secretary of Defense for Acquisition and Technology, Department of Defense, Washington DC (2008)

26. Picone, M., Mamei, M., Zambonelli, F.: A flexible and modular architecture for edge digital twin: implementation and evaluation. ACM Trans. Internet Things **4**(1), 1–32 (2023)

27. Robin Milner, J.P., Walker, D.: A calculus of mobile processes Part I. Tech. Rep. ECS-LFCS-89-85, Department of Computer Science-University of Edinburgh, The King's Building, Edinburgh EH9 3JZ (1989)

28. Talasila, P., Craciunean, D.C., Bogdan-Constantin, P., Larsen, P.G., Zamfirescu, C., Scovill, A.: Comparison between the hubcap and digitbrain platforms for model-based design and evaluation of digital twins. In: Cerone, A., Gomes, C., Palmieri, M. (eds.) Proceedings of the 5th Workshop on Formal Co-Simulation of Cyber-Physical Systems. CoSim CPS (2021)

29. Talasila, P., Gomes, C., Mikkelsen, P.H., Arboleda, S.G., Kamburjan, E., Larsen, P.G.: Digital Twin as a Service (DTaaS): a platform for digital twin developers and users. In: 2023 IEEE Smart World Congress (SWC), pp. 1–8 (2023). https://doi.org/10.1109/SWC57546.2023.10448890

30. Tekinerdogan, B., Verdouw, C.: Systems architecture design pattern catalog for developing digital twins. Sensors **20**(18) (2020). https://doi.org/10.3390/s20185103

31. Woodcock, J., Cavalcanti, A., Fitzgerald, J., Larsen, P., Miyazawa, A., Perry, S.: Features of CML: a formal modelling language for systems of systems. In: Proceedings of the 7th International Conference on System of System Engineering. IEEE (2012). https://doi.org/10.1109/SYSoSE.2012.6384144

32. Woodcock, J., Cavalcanti, A.: The semantics of circus. In: Proceedings of the 2nd International Conference of B and Z Users on Formal Specification and Development in Z and B, pp. 184–203. ZB '02, Springer-Verlag, London, UK, UK (2002)

33. Woodcock, J., Cavalcanti, A., Fitzgerald, J., Foster, S., Larsen, P.G.: Contracts in CML. In: Margaria, T., Steffen, B. (eds.) Leveraging Applications of Formal Methods, Verification and Validation. Specialized Techniques and Applications, pp. 54–73. Springer, Berlin, Heidelberg (2014). https://doi.org/10.1007/978-3-662-45231-8_5

34. Woodcock, J., Davies, J.: Using Z – Specification, Refinement, and Proof. Prentice Hall International Series in Computer Science (1996)

Formal Modelling of Peercoin
and Proof-of-Stake Protocols

Kent Leeding, Steve Schneider$^{(\boxtimes)}$ ⓘ, and Helen Treharne ⓘ

Surrey Centre for Cyber Security, University of Surrey, Guildford, UK
s.schneider@surrey.ac.uk

Abstract. The Blockchain approach to Distributed Ledger Technology aims for a decentralised approach to the writing of information onto a digital Ledger, an append-only sequence of blocks. Different blockchain protocols provide a variety of mechanisms for achieving consensus on selecting the agent to add the next block. Consensus is important to ensure agreement across the different agents maintaining their own record of the state of the blockchain and updates on it. Proof-of-stake protocols use the amount of 'stake' agents hold in the blockchain to determine who should produce the next block, so that agents with greater commitment produce more of the blocks. This is a technology where the practice sometimes runs ahead of the theory: a number of implementations have been developed, however the protocols are complex and not always underpinned by analysis. This chapter explores an approach to formal modelling of such protocols using the PRISM model-checker, and their analysis with respect to some fairness properties expected of proof-of-stake protocols, also captured within PRISM, and in the presence of particular attacks on fairness. The approach is exemplified on the Peercoin protocol where the analysis reveals some vulnerabilities.

Keywords: Formal Modelling · PRISM · Proof-of-stake · Peercoin

Dedication: *This chapter is dedicated to Jim Woodcock on the occasion of his retirement, in recognition of his leadership throughout his career in the development and application of Formal Methods across many domains. Schneider and Treharne have had the privilege to know him for several decades and we have always appreciated the clarity and elegance of his work, and enjoyed working with him. Jim is an exceptional communicator, both as a speaker and in writing, with a passion for ensuring his audience understands the insights behind intricate technical arguments. This chapter takes the formal approach exemplified by Jim's work, aiming to obtain understanding of a complex*

© The Author(s), under exclusive license to Springer Nature Switzerland AG 2024
S. Foster and A. Sampaio (Eds.): *The Application of Formal Methods*, LNCS 14900, pp. 123–143, 2024.
https://doi.org/10.1007/978-3-031-67114-2_6

*protocol by developing a formal model and
specification, and using these to extract
insight through formal analysis.*

1   Introduction

A blockchain is an implementation of a distributed ledger that manages its content as a sequence of blocks replicated by multiple parties, with each block containing entries on the ledger [20]. A blockchain protocol describes the steps and interactions to be taken by participating agents to maintain an accurate account of the replicated shared data. The *permissionless* approach allows arbitrary agents (potentially unknown and untrusted) to participate in a blockchain protocol contributing to the blockchain infrastructure. Protocols need to be designed to ensure that such a network of contributing agents, even when working towards their own selfish interests, form a consensus on the data being appended to the chain. In a well-designed protocol this data then becomes immutable and finalised. A recent survey of blockchain protocols [19] covers a range of consensus mechanisms across different approaches to blockchain.

The permissionless blockchain was pioneered by Satoshi Nakamoto with the release of the Bitcoin design [14] and subsequent implementation in 2008. Bitcoin, a combination of many well-understood mechanisms, was a first-of-its-kind blockchain protocol. A core element of the Bitcoin design is the inclusion of the proof-of-work mechanism, originally introduced in Hashcash [1]. The proof-of-work mechanism incorporates the need to expend energy in the form of computational resources to provide security to the protocol by limiting the influence any individual participant can exert on the overall network. Specifically, proof-of-work is used to elect agents to propose a block to append to the chain, with the work performed then being used to help form a consensus on the proposed state of the chain. The chain is progressed only when work is performed and this progress can only be undone by alternative progress, which requires greater work. An honest majority assumption and a reward structure that incentivises honest behaviour and disadvantages dishonest behaviour yields a secure and tamper-proof append-only ledger. However, in practice proof-of-work consumes substantial energy resource and raises questions about its sustainability.

The concept of *proof-of-stake* is an alternative to proof-of-work, which uses the stake owned by agents as the basis for electing a block proposer, rather than the computational resource requirements of proof-of-work. This has become a popular protocol choice compared to the well-established proof-of-work design, requiring far less energy to maintain the blockchain ledger. Many proof-of-stake designs have now been proposed and implemented, though few have been formally analysed. There are many design approaches, which fall under two design categories; eventual consensus, seen in designs such as Peercoin [10] and Ouroboros [9], and block-wise Byzantine agreement, seen in designs such as Algorand [2] and Tendermint [12]. These two categories require a $>\frac{1}{2}$ and $>\frac{2}{3}$ honest majority respectively which, if broken, could allow adversaries to attack and control aspects of the ledger. This could be in the form of liveness attacks, such as forcing the network into deadlock states and halting the progress [17], and safety violations, such as forcing reorganisations to alternative chain histories [3] and performing double-spending [7].

When participating in these protocols, an important aspect is for agents to receive rewards (benefits) proportional to the resource they provided. These are often in the form of *coins* recorded on the ledger so that the total number of coins owned by each participant is on the record and transparent. This is considered a matter of fairness [8] and is particularly important for proof-of-stake protocols since agents are generally rewarded with additional stake used to participate. A disproportionate reward mechanism could disrupt the distribution of stake, leading to a rich-get-richer effect [5]. We need to be confident that such reward mechanisms do not allow adversaries to perform strategies to maximise the rewards gained from participation, shifting the ratio of stake in their favour, potentially breaking honest majority assumptions over long periods.

In this chapter we formalise three desirable fairness properties:

- Resource Proportional Elections. Agents are selected to propose blocks proportionally to their stake ratio. Note that proposed blocks might not be chosen to be finalised (added to the main chain) due to contention between proposed blocks.
- Resource Proportional Block Finalisations. An agent should have blocks finalised proportionally to their stake ratio (i.e., subsequent to resolving contention between proposed blocks).
- Resource Proportional Rewards. The explicit rewards (newly minted coins and collection of fees) gained by agents are proportional to their stake ratio.

Additionally, we introduce a notion of robustness against the following two well-known adversarial strategies:

1. Sybil strategy [4]. An adversary purposely splits their stake among multiple entities, so the total amount of stake is shared across a number of identities all under the control of one agent.
2. Pooling strategy [16]. A single or coalition of adversaries pool their stake into a single entity in order to gain a collective advantage.

These two strategies are complementary. The first is concerned with gaining an advantage through splitting stake across multiple identities. The second is concerned with gaining an advantage through combining stakes of different agents into stake all under the name of a single entity. These are the two primary ways the stake of protocol participants can be manipulated, so we describe these as adversarial strategies. It is desirable for a proof-of-stake protocol to provide no advantage to adversaries employing either of these two strategies, and this is what we will be analysing for.

A protocol is robust against a strategy if adversarial agents following the strategy perform no better than if they had behaved honestly.

The Peercoin protocol was initially described in a whitepaper [10]. It included design decisions introduced to encourage stability of Peercoin and encourage participation. We focus particularly on two such design decisions. The first is motivated by the aim that Peercoin should be resistant to manipulation from agents with a majority stake through control of contiguous blocks. This motivates the introduction of a delay to the re-use of stake once it has been used to elect an agent, to offset the tendency for a large stake to dominate the selection of agents. The second design decision is motivated by the desire to encourage agents to retain their stake, for stability of the stake distribution: hence Peercoin includes in its design that the longer an agent holds stake (up to some maximum duration) the greater the probability that it will enable that agent to be elected.

In this chapter we use formal modelling to analyse an abstraction of the Peercoin protocol with respect to fairness. For this work we use the probabilistic model checker PRISM [11] to formally model an abstraction of the first proof-of-stake protocol design, Peercoin, as proposed in the 2012 whitepaper [10]. For this we describe the Peercoin protocol in terms of probabilistic guarded commands using the PRISM input language, and a property specification used to calculate, from the model, agents' expected performance in elections, block finalisations and rewards. The model is analysed over different initial stake distributions to investigate how agents perform with various stake ratios. Three models are built and analysed: where all participants are honest; where there is a Sybil attack (i.e., where the adversary follows a Sybil strategy); and where there is a pooling attack (i.e., where an adversary follows a pooling strategy).

We find that the Peercoin protocol is susceptible to the Sybil attack strategy, in which an agent splits their stake and acts as multiple agents each with smaller stake. We see that this strategy allows agents to have disproportionately more blocks finalised than is reflected by their stake. This arises as a result of Peercoin's age requirement imposed on stake, a separate design decision within Peercoin to prevent participants with large stake from proposing sequences of consecutive blocks.

This chapter is structured as follows: Sect. 2 introduces the Peercoin algorithm; Sect. 3 introduces the modelling tool PRISM and describes key aspects of the formal model of Peercoin and formalisations of the fairness requirements; Sect. 4 describes and interprets the results of the PRISM analysis; and Sect. 5 makes some concluding remarks.

2   Peercoin

Peercoin (PPC, PPCoin) [10,15,21], initially proposed in 2012, was the first blockchain protocol that introduced an element of proof-of-stake. Proof-of-stake relies on a coin distribution for agent selection—without coins, the protocol lacks a selection pool.

The Peercoin protocol is comprised of both proof-of-work and proof-of-stake mechanisms. Initially, difficulty metrics were set that allowed for blocks to be produced only through proof-of-work, which seeds the initial coin distribution. In proof-of-work, miners race to solve cryptographic hash puzzles for block rewards, which are then traded between agents in the system. Over time, a distribution of coins is formed which permits the use of proof-of-stake. The proof-of-stake threshold is decreased to allow the creation of proof-of-stake blocks, forming a blockchain comprised of both proof-of-work and proof-of-stake blocks. The difficulty of proof-of-work blocks is increased, so that blocks produced through proof-of-work become infeasible, tending towards a proof-of-stake only protocol.

Agents are elected to propose blocks based on the stake they own in the protocol. This removes the computational work required to find solutions to the cryptographic hash puzzles used in proof-of-work protocols such as Bitcoin [14] and the original Ethereum [18] among others. Agents check if they are selected in any particular time period by performing a single computation for every eligible Unspent Transaction Output (UTxO) they own (i.e. a measure of the coins they have received but not yet spent), corresponding to the stake that they possess.

2.1 Peercoin Protocol

A proof-of-stake block is produced when a valid *coinstake* transaction is included in a valid candidate block. A valid coinstake transaction is formed of a stake *kernel* which meets a hash target similar to cryptographic hash puzzles found in proof-of-work designs. In proof-of-work designs, participants called *miners*, race to find solutions to these puzzles. Miners hash the blockheader of their candidate block combined with a value which is a proposed solution, until the hash is below the current target value. This is sometimes described as a hash value that contains a specific number of leading zeros, determined by the puzzle difficulty.

In proof-of-stake, the stake kernel is a collection of data that includes pre-computed chain information that changes irregularly, a timestamp, and a single UTxO that is used to produce the solution.

The Peercoin protocol also uses a concept called *coinage* inspired by the age of the coin, which is simply the value of a UTxO (number of coins) to a participant multiplied by the time that has elapsed since the UTxO was created, known as the holding period.

$$utxo.age = time - utxo.time \qquad (1)$$

$$coinage = utxo.value \times utxo.age \qquad (2)$$

The coinage value is calculated and verified by each participant, as it depends solely on the value of a UTxO, the age at which this was created, and the current time. Both the value and age of an output are contained in the transaction, which is recorded in each agent's ledger.

An agent may have several separate UTxOs, each representing a single value. The sum of all UTxO values is then the agent's overall stake. A UTxO used in a coinstake transaction as an input, becomes spent, 'consuming' the coinage and creating a new UTxO with $utxo.time = time$ so that $utxo.age = 0$.

A participant performs the following computation on each eligible UTxO they hold to determine if they are selected to propose the next block as a result of holding that UTxO:

$$hash(kernel, utxo) < modifier \times utxo.value \times min(utxo.age, maxAge) \qquad (3)$$

Algorithm 1. Peercoin Protocol for each Participant

1: *wallet* ← *utxos*   ▷ Wallet is formed of the set of total UTxOs.
2: *time* ← *current_time*
3: **while** *true* **do**
4:     *kernel* ← {*stake_modifier, time*}
5:     **for** *utxo* **in** *wallet* **do**   ▷ Check every UTxO in wallet.
6:         *utxo.age* ← *time* − *utxo.time*
7:         **if** *utxo.age* ≥ *minAge* **then**   ▷ Age requirement.
8:             *hk* ← *hash*(*kernel, utxo*)
9:             **if** *hk* ≤ *modifier* × *utxo.value* × *min*(*utxo.age, maxAge*) **then**
                                                                    ▷ Elected.
10:                 *utxo.time* ← *time*   ▷ New UTxO produced at current time.
11:                 *break*   ▷ Exit for loop on produced block.
12:             **end if**
13:         **end if**
14:     **end for**
15:     *time* ← *time* + 16
16: **end while**

Note that the age used for the computation of the selection is capped at $maxAge$. This computation is illustrated in Algorithm 1.

This algorithm describes the election step for each participant. A kernel hash is calculated for each UTxO they own during the current time until they calculate a solution (valid hash). If the participant calculates a valid hash, the UTxO used to produce this is consumed with a new UTxO produced at the current time. Following this search through the wallet, *time* is incremented by 16 seconds representing the start of the next period where the process repeats.

The parameter *modifier*, inversely proportional to the *difficulty* setting, is tuned by the network to control the rate of block production. The hash target of the stake kernel is influenced linearly by the coinage of the UTxO being consumed and is described as being a target per unit coinage consumed. The hash function here is playing the role of a pseudo-random number generator. Therefore, the greater the coinage being consumed the higher the probability of meeting the conditions for being selected. For example, if one agent has double the coinage of another then it has double the probability of being selected to produce a block.

This computation is similar to the hash puzzles in proof-of-work, however here a participant is not seeking to solve a puzzle but rather calculating a single hash for each UTxO they own, once per defined time interval (by incrementing the timestamp input in the kernel). Since this is achievable with modest computational resources, this neutralises the computational demands of typical proof-of-work protocols, since increased computational resource does not increase the likelihood to meet the condition to mine a block.

Peercoin also introduces a minimum age requirement of 30 days for a UTxO to be eligible for use in the election process.

$$hash(kernel, utxo) \leq modifier \times utxo.value$$
$$\times min(utxo.age, maxAge) \times [utxo.age \geq 30days] \quad (4)$$

Peercoin introduces constant adjustments to the difficulty giving the hash target value to combat sudden changes to the network's block production rate.

In the case of multiple agents being selected at the same time to produce a block (e.g., if multiple agents hit their hash target in the same time period), the agent with the highest consumed coinage is chosen by the network as the main chain. This is analogous to the approach taken in proof-of-work protocols, in which chains with the highest work performed are chosen, here replacing that work with consumed coinage. The design of Peercoin introduces the consumption of coinage and the delay before UTxOs are eligible in order to counter the possibility of majority attacks (where agents with a majority of the coins can manipulate the chain through dominating the selection of blocks), since agents are forced to delay after producing a block before they can produce their next block.

Participants are rewarded when they produce a block through block rewards, where newly minted coins are added to the UTxO used in the coinstake transaction. A base amount of Peercoin tokens are minted per unit of coinage consumed.

3 Formal Modelling

Although the requirements of the Peercoin protocol can be understood informally, it is not always obvious whether they are met by a proposed protocol, and some more rigorous means are required to justify claims about such requirements made for protocols.

Formal modelling enables protocols to be analysed with respect to particular requirements. A model-checking approach allows a formal model of a protocol to be explored by a tool in order to understand its run-time behaviour with respect to particular requirements. Such an approach requires that

1. the protocol should be described in a particular formal language to enable exploration,
2. the requirements should also be expressible in a formal way that can be managed within the tool, and
3. the protocol description can be analysed and evaluated with respect to the requirements.

Formal modelling requires abstraction to keep the model-checking manageable (in the face of potential state-space explosion) while retaining the key elements of the protocol. A model should be as simple as possible but no simpler[1], meaning

---
[1] Words attributed to Einstein.

that it should keep sufficient detail so that the important behaviours are retained, but should not be unnecessarily detailed.

In the case of Peercoin there is a probabilistic element to the modelling of the protocol since agent election is a probabilistic process dependent on the distribution of coinage. It is this aspect that makes PRISM [11] a natural choice of tool for this analysis. The above requirements can be captured formally within the PRISM tool, either expressed as properties within probabilistic computational tree logic (PCTL) [6] or expressed as desired results of analysis, enabling analysis of the protocol with respect to these requirements.

Extracts of these models are described here, with the line numbers used reflecting those in the description of the models found in [13]. Our abstract model (as simple as possible) will contain three agents, a small delay for which a UTxO is not eligible, and a static stake. We also assume that the network is fully connected and synchronised, so that information known to an agent is known to all agents at the beginning of the next step. These abstractions maintain sufficient detail to explore the behaviour of the protocol with respect to the desirable properties, and are already sufficient to identify where the protocol does not behave in accordance with the requirements. The complete PRISM model and property descriptions are available in a GitHub repository [13]. We give extracts below to explain the key aspects of the model and analysis.

3.1   A Brief Introduction to PRISM

The PRISM tool [11] is a probabilistic symbolic model-checker: it supports analysis of systems made up of concurrent agents that include probabilistic behaviour.

PRISM describes component processes through the language of guarded commands with probabilities. A guarded command has a label, a guard which describes when the command is enabled and can fire, and a selection of actions with probabilities: if the command is selected then action $action\_i$ is executed with probability $prob\_i$. Listing 1.1 shows the format of a guarded command in PRISM. The probabilities in a guarded command must sum to 1. The action is described in terms of a relation between the values of the variables before the action and after it (with the values after expressed with primed variables), e.g. $n' = n + 3$ states that the action increases the value of n by 3.

```
[label] guards -> prob_1 : action_1 + ... + prob_n : action_n;
```

Listing 1.1. A guarded command with probabilities

A model of an agent contains a collection of guarded commands. A guarded command is *enabled* in a state if its guard is true in that state. When that agent executes a guarded command then one of the command's actions is selected according to its probability, and the state update expressed by the action is performed.

A PRISM model consists of a collection of agents. Multiple agents can have labels in common for their guarded commands. Concurrency is realised through agents' synchronisation on labels: if multiple agents have a command with the same label then all agents synchronise on their labelled command. The label is only enabled if it is enabled for all of the agents involved, i.e., all the guards must be true together.

An execution of the model consists of a sequence of steps, where each step consists of selection of an enabled label, and each participating agent performs its state update for its associated guarded command. If several labels are enabled in a particular state, then any of them can be selected with equal probability.

Model-checking in PRISM allows particular requirements on executions of a model to be evaluated. It enables PCTL assertions to be checked for the model. It also supports instrumentation of the models so that aspects of executions can be tracked through the mechanism of *rewards*. PRISM also supports calculation of expectations of particular outcomes expressed in terms of rewards. These will be exemplified below as we model Peercoin and analyse the model.

3.2 Modelling the Protocol

The model gives an initial distribution of stake. We model a system with three agents, and initialise the agent set as each owning a particular fraction of the total staked coins. For example Listing 1.2 shows a distribution of one third of the stake to each agent:

```
4  // Stake ratio distribution
5  const double r1 = 1/3;
6  const double r2 = 1/3;
7  const double r3 = 1/3;
```

Listing 1.2. Stake distribution.

In our analysis we will consider a range of different distributions of initial stake in order to explore the behaviour of the protocol across different balances of stake.

We also fix small values for the minimum and maximum age for a UTxO, and an overall limit on age to keep the state space finite and manageable.

```
12  // Stake age parameters
13  const int minAge = 3;
14  const int maxAge = 9;
15  const int ageLimit = 36;
```

Listing 1.3. Minimum and maximum age and age limit.

Agents repeatedly cycle through the block mining protocol steps. We explain the modelling of Agent 1 below; Agents 2 and 3 are entirely similar.

The first step, labelled [election], (Lines 64–66, Listing 1.5) is to check (if eligible) whether agents have a solution to the hash computation. This is abstracted as a probabilistic choice, with probability given by the formula p which is proportional to a combination of stake r and age min(age + age_update, maxAge)/maxAge as described for Peercoin above. This abstraction is suitable as we take the output from the hash function as our source of (pseudo-)randomness.

```
20  // Agent 1 probability of being elected to produce a block
21  formula p = r1 * min(age1+age_update,maxAge)/(maxAge);
```

Listing 1.4. Agent 1 probability of successful election.

If it does have a solution on this cycle (Line 64), which represents an agent being selected to propose a block, then *selected*1 is set to the value 1. All three agents synchronise on [election] and each sets their own selected variable if elected.

The second step (Lines 69–72) is to resolve any contention if multiple agents have been selected, choosing a winner from among the set of selected agents, and resetting the winner's *age* variable. All agents synchronise on all [consensus] labels and so a choice will be made between all those which have been selected and have the largest coinage. The consensus action labels are followed by a number, [consensus1], [consensus2], and [consensus3], indicating which agent is selected. If multiple agents are valid choices (i.e., two or more agents have been elected and have the same, largest coinage), then a choice is made between these commands with equal probability. The formula *maxCoinage* calculates which block was produced with the highest coinage from the current produced blocks. This is the mechanism Peercoin uses to resolve contention between elected agents. If their coinage is also the same then a probabilistic choice will be made between the winners as a tie-breaker.

The third step is [reset], in which the age parameter for the winning agent, keeping track of time since the last win, is reset to 0.

```
55  // Module process for agent 1
56  module agent1
57
58      // Agents local variables
59      age1 : [0..ageLimit] init minAge-1;
60      selected1 : [0..1] init 0;
61      winner1 : [0..1] init 0;
62
63      // Solution search - local election
64      [election]  eligible -> p:(selected1'=1)&(age1'=min(age1+age_update,ageLimit))
65                            + 1-p:(age1'=min(age1+age_update,ageLimit));
66      [election] !eligible -> (age1'=age1+age_update);
67
68      // Highest coinage selection rule
69      [consensus1] selected1=1&(r1*age1)=maxCoinage -> (selected1'=0)&(winner1'=1);
70      [consensus2] selected2=1&(r2*age2)=maxCoinage -> (selected1'=0);
71      [consensus3] selected3=1&(r3*age3)=maxCoinage -> (selected1'=0);
72      [consensus0] selected_agents=0 -> (selected1'=0);
73
74      // Reset to prepare for next sub-slot
75      [reset] winner1=1 -> (winner1'=0)&(age1'=0);
76      [reset] winner1=0 -> true;
77
78  endmodule
```

Listing 1.5. Agent module.

The variables selected and winner will be used to formulate the properties we want to analyse, using the reward mechanism to track how often an agent wins (and hence produced a block) through an execution.

We can also model adversarial attacks, specifically Sybil attacks and pooling attacks.

A general Sybil attack occurs when a single agent splits their stake across multiple identities all under their control. We consider an abstraction where agent 2 with stake $r2$ splits into two identities, splitting their stake into $r2a$

and $r2b$ by a ratio between 0 and 1. Our analysis can then explore the effect of different splits, and consider the combined gains as against the alternative gains of agent 2 alone.

```
9  // How agent 2 will split their stake between the new accounts
10 const double split;  // (0,1)
11
12 // New agents stake ratios
13 const double r2a=r2*split;
14 const double r2b=r2-r2a;
```

Listing 1.6. Sybil strategy: two new agent distribution.

Conversely the pooling strategy combines the stakes $r2$ and $r3$ of agents 2 and 3 into a single stake $r4$ under control of a single agent 4.

```
9  // New agent stake ratio
10 const double r4=r2+r3;
```

Listing 1.7. Pooling strategy: pooled agent.

3.3 Desirable Properties

From the point of view of fairness in proof-of-stake, we are primarily interested in understanding an agent's performance in being elected, producing blocks and gaining rewards. An agent producing blocks and gaining rewards proportionally to the stake they control is not only fair but underpins a protocol's long term stability. A deviation from proportionality could undermine the assumptions which proof-of-stake protocol security relies upon. A protocol that holds an honest majority assumption, but exhibits a disproportionate block production or reward mechanism, could break this assumption in implementation over time.

We capture the above concerns in PRISM using reward structures in the model, which applies rewards (or equivalently costs i.e., negative rewards) to specific states and/or transitions as captured by a predicate. A reward structure consists of a name, a predicate, and a function on the state evaluating to an integer. For example, the reward structure in Lines 164–166 in Listing 1.8 defines that if a step in the model describes moving to a state which has agents selected to propose blocks, captured by the predicate `selected_agents > 0` (only possible after a command with the `election` action label), then a reward value equal to the number of selected agents, i.e. the value `selected_agents` is given to that state. This tracks the total number of selections.

PRISM provides a mechanism for capturing expected rewards over an execution. The R operator applies to a particular named reward over executions up to a particular length. In abstract terms, `R{"reward1"}=?[C<=T]` is the expected value of the reward variable `reward1` over all executions of length T, given that `reward1` is updated on every step for which its predicate is true. For a given model, PRISM is able to calculate this expected value.

Using the R operator in the property specification, we can calculate the expected total reward (ETS) given to an execution of the model of length T (Eq. 6). In this case, this describes the expected total number of successful elections (across all agents) during the execution. A reward structure is described similarly for a single agent (here chosen as agent A_3) (Lines 158–160, Listing 1.8) to calculate the expected successful elections for that particular agent (EAS, Eq. 5). Reward structures are similarly defined for the agents and total blocks produced (Eqs. 10 and 11) and rewards gained (Eqs. 15 and 16).

```
156  // Reward value of 1 applied to any state
157  // in which agent 3 was selected to produce blocks
158  rewards "agent_elected"
159      selected3 = 1 : 1;
160  endrewards
161
162  // Reward value of [1..n] applied to any state
163  // in which agents were selected to produce blocks
164  rewards "total_elected"
165      selected_agents > 0 : selected_agents;
166  endrewards
```

Listing 1.8. Reward structure examples.

Resource Proportional Elections

Maintaining a fair election is fundamental to a decentralised blockchain protocol. Those selected to produce blocks partake in the vital role of progressing the ledger, with full control of inclusion, exclusion, and ordering of transactions. An election mechanism is considered fair if agents are selected to produce blocks proportionally to the stake they control.

A protocol has resource proportional elections if, over a sufficiently long time, agents are expected to be selected as leaders proportional to the stake they controlled during that period. This can be calculated in the model by dividing the agent's expected successful elections by the total successful elections observed in executions of particular lengths (Eq. 7) and comparing the result with the agent's stake ratio (Eq. 8). These are captured using the R property operator, calculating the cumulative reward for all possible executions of length T. The predicate RP_e (Eq. 9) states what the fairness property is with respect to fair elections: that the proportion of elections for an agent should match their proportion r_i of the overall stake (as defined in Listing 1.2). This equality is exact in the property definition but variations allowing tolerance within some margin can also be expressed.

$$EAS := \text{R}\{\text{"agent\_elected"}\}=?\,[\text{C<=T}] \qquad (5)$$

$$ETS := \text{R}\{\text{"total\_elected"}\}=?\,[\text{C<=T}] \qquad (6)$$

$$\text{Proportion of Elections} := EAS/ETS \qquad (7)$$

$$\text{Elections Proportion over Stake} := \text{Proportion of Elections}/r_i \qquad (8)$$

$$RP_e := \text{Elections Proportion over Stake} = 1 \qquad (9)$$

Resource Proportional Block Finalisations

Being a block producer is usually, as is the case for Peercoin, a pre-requisite of gaining explicit rewards or stake. Additionally the agent in charge of producing a block has full control of the data being included in the chain. It is important that agents do not have undue influence or control over the production of blocks, as this would open the protocol up to attacks, including potential double spending [7]. If agents are expected to produce blocks disproportionately to their stake ratio, this would suggest that there may be strategies that allow agents to perform better in the protocol than their peers.

A protocol has resource proportional block finalisation if, over a sufficiently long time, agents are expected to have their blocks finalised in proportion to the fraction of stake they controlled during that period. Being selected does not necessarily translate into having a block finalised. At times, multiple agents may be selected and a consensus must be made as to who from this set is chosen to produce the block. This is calculated in the model by dividing the agent's expected finalised blocks by the total finalised blocks observed in executions of particular lengths (Eq. 12) and comparing the result with the agent's stake ratio (Eq. 13). The predicate RP_b states what the fairness property is with respect to fair block finalisations: that the proportion of blocks finalised for an agent should match their proportion r_i of the overall stake (as defined in Listing 1.2).

$$EAB := \texttt{R\{"agent\_blocks"\}=?[C<=T]} \quad (10)$$
$$ETB := \texttt{R\{"total\_blocks"\}=?[C<=T]} \quad (11)$$
$$\text{Proportion of Blocks} := EAB/ETB \quad (12)$$
$$\text{Blocks Proportion over Stake} := \text{Proportion of Blocks}/r_i \quad (13)$$
$$RP_b := \text{Blocks Proportion over Stake} = 1 \quad (14)$$

Resource Proportional Rewards

Block proposers typically gain an explicit reward once their blocks are finalised, usually in the form of newly minted coins and/or a collection of fees. This reward is typically added to the agent's stake, updating the stake distribution, which is then used to seed future election cycles. It is important that the ratios described by the distribution of stake is not disrupted by the reward function over long periods, and that agents maintain the same probability of producing blocks over time. Disproportionate reward functions may lead to a rich-get-richer effect, potentially shifting stake ratios in favour of small agent sets, breaking honest majority assumptions.

A protocol has resource proportional rewards if, over a sufficiently long time, agents are expected to gain a ratio of the rewards equal to the ratio of stake they controlled during that period. This is calculated in the model by dividing the agent's expected rewards by the total rewards observed in executions (of particular lengths) (Eq. 17) and comparing the result with the agent's stake ratio (Eq. 18). The predicate RP_r states what the fairness property is with respect to fair rewards: that the proportion of rewards gained by an agent should match their proportion r_i of the overall stake (as defined in Listing 1.2).

$$EAR := \text{R}\{\texttt{"agent\_rewards"}\}=?\,[\texttt{C<=T}] \quad (15)$$
$$ETR := \text{R}\{\texttt{"total\_rewards"}\}=?\,[\texttt{C<=T}] \quad (16)$$
$$\text{Proportion of Rewards} := EAR/ETR \quad (17)$$
$$\text{Rewards Proportion over Stake} := \text{Proportion of Rewards}/r_i \quad (18)$$
$$RP_r := \text{Rewards Proportion over Stake} = 1 \quad (19)$$

Analysis

The Peercoin protocol can be analysed in PRISM with respect to each of these fairness requirements to evaluate whether it meets each of RP_b, RP_e and RP_r.

In addition, the protocol can be evaluated with respect to the attacks described above. We use a model that includes the Sybil attack (where one agent has two identities) and one that includes the Pooling attack (where two agents operate collectively under a single identity). In each case the expected proportions over stake, of Elections, Blocks or Rewards, can be compared with those obtained in the case with honest agents, to see if the adversarial behaviour provides any advantage over the honest case.

4   Results and Analysis

We analyse each model (honest, Sybil, and pooling) against the desirable properties discussed in Sect. 3.3. For this, we explore execution paths of length $T = 300$ steps. This represents a chain segment of $[0..100]$ possible blocks since at most a single block is produced during each 3-step cycle in the model (`election`, `consensus`, and `reset`). Agent sets of size $n = 3$ are analysed with a range of initial distributions. We consider the outcomes for an honest agent with initial stake ranging from 0.05 to 0.9, where the other two agents' initial stakes are such that the total three stakes sum to 1.

Resource Proportional Elections: RP_e

The results from the property formula described by Eq. 7 are displayed in Fig. 1a. PRISM determines the expected Proportion of Elections for each of the initial stake proportions r_i along the x-axis. The stacked range of possible values for each r_i corresponds to the different distributions of stake of the remaining two agents.

The agent's proportion of elections clearly deviates from the resource proportional property, indicated by the line $y = x$. The results indicate that an agent with stake ratios $r_i < 0.35$ performs better, and with stake ratio $r_i > 0.4$ performs worse than the property requires. This is also displayed in Fig. 1b, showing the results for the property formula described in Eq. 8. These results describe the agent's performance compared to directly proportional as a multiple of their stake ratio, with the resource proportional result described by the line $y = 1$. For example we see that in our model agents with small stake ratios $r_i < 0.2$ are elected over 1.5 times more often than if elections were resource proportional.

These results lead to a closer inspection of the protocol, which identifies that this arises from the age requirement that forces agents to wait for a minimum amount of time after election before being re-elected. Agents with high stake ratios are more likely to be selected and chosen as block proposer which consumes their coinage, forcing them into spending longer periods waiting to become eligible again, when their high proportion of stake would otherwise have led to an expectation of another election sooner. Hence agents with a very large proportion of the stake are disadvantaged by the age requirement, and underperform relative to their stake. This means that agents with smaller stake will conversely do better than their stake would justify in the presence of other agents with substantial stake. This is what is shown in Fig. 1.

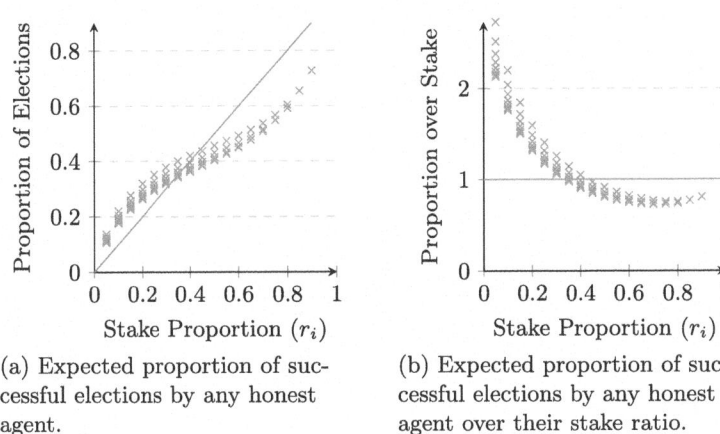

(a) Expected proportion of successful elections by any honest agent.

(b) Expected proportion of successful elections by any honest agent over their stake ratio.

Fig. 1. Honest agents expected election results.

Resource Proportional Blocks: RP_b

Results described by Figs. 2a and 2b show results similar to those in Fig. 1. The differences are most visible when r_i is close to 1. Agents with small stake ratios perform better, and large stake ratios perform worse than resource proportional. Here however, the results are not quite as pronounced. Closer inspection identifies that this is because of the rule selecting the UTxO with highest coinage in cases of election contention, meaning agents with largest stake are disproportionately likely to be chosen. These results are therefore pulled slightly toward proportional ($y = x$ and $y = 1$) in Figs. 2a and 2b, respectively).

We have identified from this analysis that the Peercoin abstraction does not behave fairly: it does not observe resource proportional elections or block

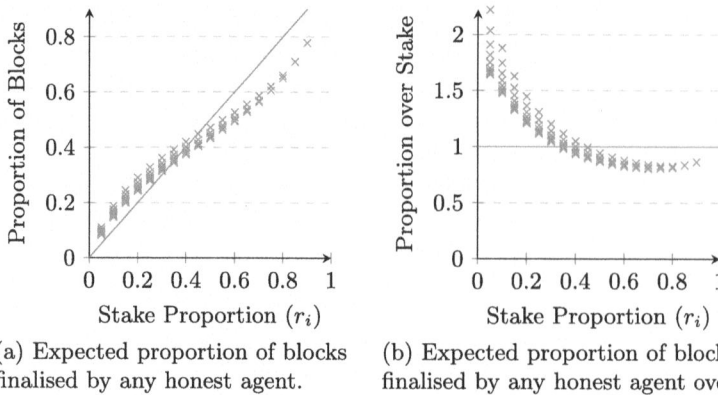

(a) Expected proportion of blocks finalised by any honest agent.

(b) Expected proportion of blocks finalised by any honest agent over their stake ratio.

Fig. 2. Honest agents expected block finalisation results.

finalisations. We see that an agent, even when acting honestly, can over perform when starting with a small stake, or under perform when starting with a large stake.

Resource Proportional Rewards: RP_r

The expected proportion of rewards gained by any honest agent, shown in Fig. 3a forms a line very close to $y = x$ suggesting an almost resource proportional result. However we see that agents with small stake ratios $r_i < 0.2$ gain lower rewards than would be considered fair.

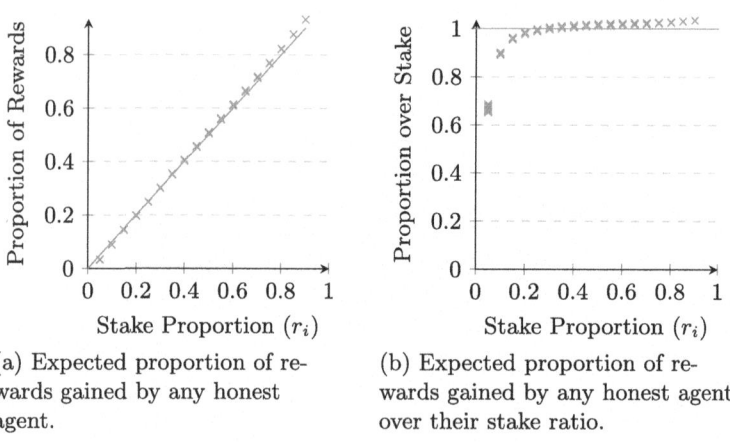

(a) Expected proportion of rewards gained by any honest agent.

(b) Expected proportion of rewards gained by any honest agent over their stake ratio.

Fig. 3. Honest agents expected rewards gained.

At a surface level this is a surprising outcome given the previous results on elections and block finalisations in which agents with smaller stake appear to do better. This reward mechanism appears to be very close to being fair apart from for agents with a very low proportion of stake. This arises because the Peercoin reward mechanism is a function on coinage: the longer it takes for an agent to produce a block, the greater the reward they gain from doing so, proportionally to that time. Hence the delays that are imposed following successful production of a block do not impact on the rewards eventually obtained as they are evened out by the increased rewards due to greater coinage.

However in the model we set a maximum age which imposes a cap on the amount of time that can be incorporated into the reward. If the expected time for an agent to be elected goes beyond that maximum age, then the reward obtained will not reflect the time spent waiting to be elected, and so the reward will be less than the fair amount. This situation arises for agents with very small stake, since the time they can expect to wait to be elected is inversely proportional to their proportion of stake. Agents with a larger stake can expect to be elected before they reach the maximum age, so their expected reward is not capped in the same way. This is indeed what is reflected in Fig. 3.

The simplicity and small parameters of the model means that this result is more pronounced than in the real implementation, but even in the implementation of Peercoin there is an age limit (one year) after which the reward no longer increases. What we see in Fig. 3 is the result of agents with lower stake ratios reaching and exceeding that age limit before successfully producing blocks. When the age limit is increased in the model, agents become less likely to reach and exceed this limit, which would result in data points becoming bounded more closely around the line $y = 1$.

Resistance to Attack

The analysis above considered Peercoin in the context of honest participants. We now consider its performance in the presence of adversarial agents who may not follow the Peercoin protocol and instead seek to gain an advantage through behaving counter to the requirements of the protocol.

Robustness to Sybil. Our abstract model of a Sybil adversary consists of $n = 2$ agents with agent A_2 splitting their stake between two new agents A_{2a} and A_{2b}, making $n = 3$ total acting agents. We investigate a range of ratios for the split into two of the Sybil agent's stake. The results described in Fig. 4 show the Sybil agents expected proportion of successful elections, blocks finalised, and rewards gained over their stake. These are displayed alongside the case in which agent A_2 is performing the protocol honestly (i.e., not splitting the stake).

We see that the agent performs strictly better in successful elections and block finalisations over all stake ratios by adopting the Sybil strategy. The maximum stake ratio that results in performing better than resource proportional is increased from ≤ 0.5 to ≤ 0.6. However, the agent performs worse than the honest

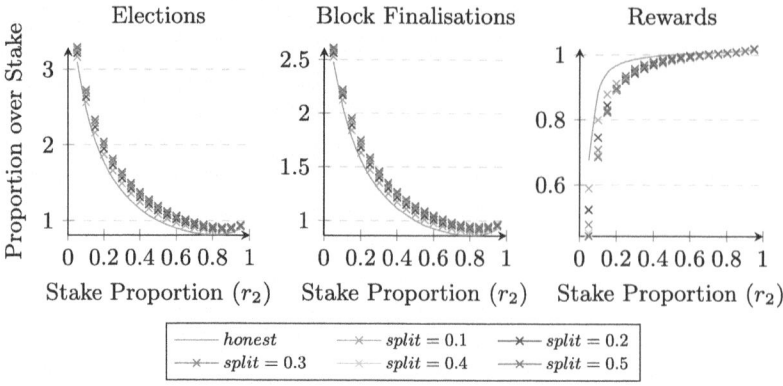

Fig. 4. Sybil agents expected proportion of successful elections, block finalisations and rewards gained over their stake ratio.

strategy in gaining rewards for all stake ratios, and this is seen most prominently at lower stake ratios.

These results arise for the following reasons: by splitting their stake ratio between two identities, agents maintain an almost identical probability of being selected and producing blocks whilst only risking the consumption of coinage from part of their stake rather than the whole. This results in an agent's continued participation with the remaining part of their stake, while other agents who do not split their stake are forced to wait for their entire stake to reach the minimum age after they have produced a block. To maximise the gain in expected successful elections and block finalisations, an agent could split their stake such that each new agent is expected to reach the maximum age before producing a block.

Conversely, the Sybil strategy performing agent obtains a reduction of explicit rewards. Since the reward function depends on the coinage consumed, splitting the stake between multiple agents reduces the expected reward per agent. This is due to each agent having an increased probability of reaching and exceeding the age limit before producing a block, limiting the reward gained and losing reward expectation in the way that we see in Fig. 3. Hence a Sybil strategy will be attractive to an adversary who wishes to increase their influence over the content of the blocks: they can increase the proportion of blocks they can produce, even though their expected reward will be decreased.

Robustness to Pooling. The pooling model observes $n = 3$ agents with agents A_2 and A_3 purposely pooling their stake into a single agent A_4, making $n = 2$ total acting agents. The results described in Fig. 5 show the pooled agents expected proportion of successful elections, blocks finalised, and rewards gained over their stake. These are displayed alongside the combined case in which agents A_2 and A_3 are performing the protocol separately and honestly.

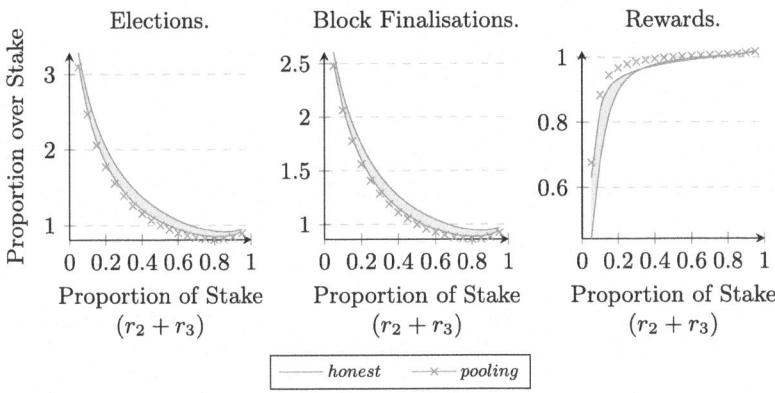

Fig. 5. Pooling agents expected proportion of successful elections, block finalisations and rewards gained over their stake ratio.

As we might expect, the results for the pooling strategy are the converse to the results for the Sybil strategy. The pooled agent performs slightly worse in successful elections and block finalisations than the worse case scenario of agents A_2 and A_3 performing honestly for all stake ratios. However, the agent is able to gain more rewards than agents A_2 and A_3 were able to gain acting honestly. These results are expected since an adversary that pools their stake into a single agent will have that stakes coinage consumed quicker, resulting in spending longer periods waiting to become eligible.

Rewards gained are increased since the agents have a decreased probability of reaching and exceeding the age limit imposed by the model. The reward per successful block produced is therefore less likely to be bound by this limit.

5   Conclusions

In this chapter we showed how formal modelling and analysis provided fresh insight into the behaviour of the Peercoin protocol, and how it can be vulnerable to attack. Specifically, we formally modelled an abstraction of the protocol and showed that two particular design decisions within it—(1) a minimum age requirement imposed on stake to prevent agents from producing chains of blocks, and (2) a maximum age requirement on use of stake to determine its owner's election—are responsible for the protocol failing to hold desirable fairness properties. We show through modelling how an agent's ability to produce blocks or gain rewards can be enhanced further by applying a Sybil or pooling strategy respectively. Although at first glance an age requirement and a consumption of this age may seem to slow attackers' abilities in producing blocks, which is the reasoning behind the rule, the reality is not quite so simple. An agent that performs a Sybil attack strategy performs significantly better in producing blocks than those acting honestly, leading to lower initial stake requirements on attacks. Additionally, if splitting stake is beneficial to participants then this will incentivise agents to do such splitting, leading to blockchain bloat. Improved robustness to these strategies and an increase in fairness can be obtained by the removal of the delay for stake eligibility following its use in producing a block. This can be confirmed by analysing the model with `minAge = 1`.

In this chapter we have considered two static attacker strategies, Sybil and pooling, but more dynamic attack strategies could also be modelled within PRISM, for example an adversary who is able to switch between Sybil and pooling. The Peercoin protocol could be analysed in such a context for the same properties as we have explored in this chapter.

In addition to the specific analysis on Peercoin, the approach is applicable to other proof-of-stake protocols and provides a general approach for considering such protocols.

It captures fairness requirements, and provides a means for investigating protocols in the face of Sybil and pooling attacks. We have seen how the functionality provided by PRISM enables such analysis to be carried out. This gives another illustration of the power and utility of abstraction and formal analysis.

Acknowledgements. This work was carried out in the course of Kent Leeding's PhD, supported by HM Government.

Disclosure of Interests. None of the authors has any competing interests in respect of this work.

References

1. Back, A.: Hashcash-a denial of service counter-measure (2002). http://www.hashcash.org/papers/hashcash.pdf. Accessed 20 Mar 2024
2. Chen, J., Micali, S.: Algorand. arXiv preprint arXiv:1607.01341, abs/1607.01341 (2016)
3. Deirmentzoglou, E., Papakyriakopoulos, G., Patsakis, C.: A survey on long-range attacks for proof of stake protocols. IEEE Access **7**, 28712–28725 (2019)
4. Douceur, J.R.: The sybil attack. In: Druschel, P., Kaashoek, F., Rowstron, A. (eds.) IPTPS 2002. LNCS, vol. 2429, pp. 251–260. Springer, Heidelberg (2002). https://doi.org/10.1007/3-540-45748-8_24
5. Fanti, G., Kogan, L., Oh, S., Ruan, K., Viswanath, P., Wang, G.: Compounding of wealth in proof-of-stake cryptocurrencies. In: Goldberg, I., Moore, T. (eds.) FC 2019. LNCS, vol. 11598, pp. 42–61. Springer, Cham (2019). https://doi.org/10.1007/978-3-030-32101-7_3
6. Hansson, H., Jonsson, B.: A logic for reasoning about time and reliability. Formal Aspects Comput. **6**(5), 512–535 (1994)
7. Hoepman, J.-H.: Distributed double spending prevention. CoRR, abs/0802.0832 (2008)
8. Huang, Y., Tang, J., Cong, Q., Lim, A., Xu, J.: Do the rich get richer? Fairness analysis for blockchain incentives. CoRR, abs/2103.14713 (2021)
9. Kiayias, A., Russell, A., David, B., Oliynykov, R.: Ouroboros: a provably secure proof-of-stake blockchain protocol. In: Katz, J., Shacham, H. (eds.) CRYPTO 2017. LNCS, vol. 10401, pp. 357–388. Springer, Cham (2017). https://doi.org/10.1007/978-3-319-63688-7_12

10. King, S., Nadal, S.: Ppcoin: peer-to-peer crypto-currency with proof-of-stake. Peer-coin whitepaper (2012). https://decred.org/research/king2012.pdf. Accessed 20 Mar 2024
11. Kwiatkowska, M., Norman, G., Parker, D.: PRISM: probabilistic symbolic model checker. In: Field, T., Harrison, P.G., Bradley, J., Harder, U. (eds.) TOOLS 2002. LNCS, vol. 2324, pp. 200–204. Springer, Heidelberg (2002). https://doi.org/10.1007/3-540-46029-2_13
12. Kwon, J.: Tendermint: consensus without mining, draft v0.6 (2014). https://tendermint.com/static/docs/tendermint.pdf. Accessed 20 Mar 2024
13. Leeding, K.: Peercoin-prism model github repository (2024). https://github.com/kaleeding/Peercoin-PRISM-Models. Accessed 20 Mar 2024
14. Nakamoto, S.: Bitcoin: a peer-to-peer electronic cash system (2008). https://bitcoin.org/bitcoin.pdf. Accessed 20 Mar 2024
15. Peercoin Foundation. Peercoin: The sustainable cryptocoin (2024). https://www.peercoin.net/university/#/9-peercoin-proof-of-stake-consensus. Accessed 20 Mar 2024
16. Rosenfeld, M.: Analysis of bitcoin pooled mining reward systems. CoRR, abs/1112.4980 (2011)
17. Thin, W.Y.M.M., Dong, N., Bai, G., Dong, J.S.: Formal analysis of a proof-of-stake blockchain. In: 2018 23rd International Conference on Engineering of Complex Computer Systems (ICECCS). IEEE (2018)
18. Wood, G.: Ethereum: a secure decentralised generalised transaction ledger, EIP-150 revision (2014). https://gavwood.com/paper.pdf. Accessed 20 Mar 2024
19. Jie, X., Wang, C., Jia, X.: A survey of blockchain consensus protocols. ACM Comput. Surv. **55**(13s), 1–35 (2023)
20. Yaga, D., Mell, P., Roby, N., Scarfone, K.: Blockchain technology overview. CoRR, abs/1906.11078 (2019)
21. Zhao, W., Yang, S., Luo, X., Zhou, J.: On peercoin proof of stake for blockchain consensus. In: 2021 The 3rd International Conference on Blockchain Technology, ICBCT 2021 (2021)

On the Unification of Conformance Notions

Jan Peleska[✉] [ID], Wen-ling Huang[ID], and Robert Sachtleben[ID]

Department of Mathematics and Computer Science, University of Bremen,
Bibliothekstrasse 1, 28359 Bremen, Germany
{peleska,huang,rob_sac}@uni-bremen.de

Abstract. Most artefacts in software and system development - from software code to behavioural models - rely on conformance relations as the most important means to cope with the ever-growing complexity of today's cyber-physical systems. There exists, however, a multitude of such relations, depending on the modelling formalisms used, from refinement relations in the CSP process algebra, via Galois connections used for abstract interpretation, to several variants of equivalence and reduction relations to be applied in finite state machine modelling. Though all intended to reduce complexity without losing essential properties, these different notions of conformance are by no means equivalent. This is because they serve different purposes and use different rules for the degrees of freedom to be allowed in a conforming artefact. The Unifying Theories of Programming provide a universal notion of conformance (called 'refinement' in UTP) that is based on the very basic logical requirement that the refining artefact should in some sense imply the refined artefact – possibly after hiding some observables without relevance. In this chapter, we use conformance relations that are popular in the field of finite state machines to investigate whether different important conformance notions can really be subsumed as special cases of this very liberal UTP refinement concept.

Keywords: Conformance · Equivalence · Refinement · Reduction · UTP

Dedication:
This work is dedicated to Jim Woodcock on the occasion of his retirement. Dear Jim, your infectious enthusiasm for precise thinking and mathematical rigour and your sense of duty for developing high-quality systems influenced our own scientific careers, as well as our diligence when dealing with industrial applications far more than you can imagine!

Wen-ling Huang has been funded by the German Federal Ministry for Economic Affairs and Energy (BMWi), Grant Agreement 20X1908E.

S. Foster and A. Sampaio (Eds.): *The Application of Formal Methods*, LNCS 14900, pp. 144–171, 2024.
https://doi.org/10.1007/978-3-031-67114-2_7

1   Introduction

1.1   Background and Objectives

Conformance relations are essential for modelling, developing, and verifying complex systems. Depending on the underlying formalism, however, a multitude of these relations – typically more than one per formalism – have been proposed, and all of them differ, sometimes in a fairly subtle way. To name just a few of them, the Z notation[1] comes with a refinement calculus for data and operations that is similar, but by no means identical to refinement in VDM [18] or in B [1], though these formalisms address similar target systems. Refinement in CSP [12,27] differs from observation congruence in CCS [20]. For finite state machines (Mealy machines) alone, five conformance relations are used in the literature [17], and there are still some situations where none of them are completely adequate, as will be pointed out in this chapter.

It is therefore desirable to represent different modelling formalisms and their conformance relations in a general framework where their properties can be investigated, compared, and potentially improved and unified. The obvious choice for such an undertaking are the Unifying Theories of Programming (UTP) [13,32,33]. UTP comes with a very basic, and therefore highly flexible, refinement concept based on logical implication, and it has been successfully used to encode an impressive variety of other formalisms with their specific conformance relations as UTP theories, both for the purpose of comparisons between formalisms and for unified, tool supported verification approaches [2,6–8]

The main objective of this chapter is to present an analysis of the conformance relations used for finite state machines (FSMs). FSMs are very popular in the field of protocol specification and model-based testing, in particular with testing methods allowing us to *prove* that implementations conform to their reference model under certain hypotheses [5,31]. More complex implementations under test require more expressive modelling formalisms [14,23,25]. FSMs, however, still remain important for model-based testing, since more expressive representations can frequently be abstracted to FSMs. Moreover, guarantees about the test strength of test suites for these representations can be obtained by translating FSM test suites into test suites of the more expressive domain [15,16].

We present the FSM conformance relations first in a set-theoretic context that is typically used in the model-based testing communities. This material is then transformed into a UTP theory for further analysis.

1.2   Main Contributions

We present a critical analysis of the existing FSM conformance relations and explain why they still have certain deficits in practically relevant situations. Based on this assessment, two novel unifying conformance relations are presented, one for different notions of equivalence, and the other for notions of

---

[1] https://www.iso.org/standard/21573.html.

refinement (called 'reduction' in the FSM context). A UTP theory for FSMs with these conformance relations is elaborated, and it is shown that the new relations, while unifying all the existing ones, give rise to practically relevant new conformance concepts that are applicable in the same theory framework.

1.3   Overview

In the first part of Sect. 2, we review standard concepts of well-known conformance relations between finite state machines. In the second part of this section, a critical analysis of these conformance relations indicates that both an improvement and a unification of these relations seems advisable. This results in a new definition of the so-called *universal quasi-equivalence* relation and the universal reduction relation advocated by the authors. In Sect. 3, a novel UTP theory for finite state machines with universal reduction as its core refinement relation is presented. The merits of the UTP theory in comparison to more conventional set-based representations and arguments about finite state machines are discussed. The chapter ends in Sect. 4 with a conclusion.

Throughout the text, we refer to related work where appropriate. While most of the chapter is self-contained, we assume that readers are familiar with the foundations of UTP.

2   Finite State Machines and Conformance Relations

2.1   Definition of Finite State Machines

A *finite state machine (FSM)* (also called Mealy machine) is a tuple $M = (S, s_0, R, \Sigma_I, \Sigma_O)$ with finite state space S, initial state $s_0 \in S$, finite input and output alphabets Σ_I, Σ_O, and transition relation $R \subseteq S \times \Sigma_I \times \Sigma_O \times S$. Intuitively speaking, a tuple (s_1, x, y, s_2) is an element of R, if M, when in state s_1, can transit to state s_2 if an input x is given. In this case, input x triggers output y. The typical graphical representation of FSMs uses directed graphs with labelled edges: the graph nodes are given by the states $s \in S$. The graph's labelled edges $s_1 \xrightarrow{x/y} s_2$ are given by the elements $(s_1, x, y, s_2) \in R$ of the FSM's transition relation. Examples are given in Sect. 3 below.

It is often practical to represent transition relations $R \subseteq S \times \Sigma_I \times \Sigma_O \times S$ as set-valued total functions

$$\underline{R} : (S \times \Sigma_I) \longrightarrow \mathbb{P}(\Sigma_O \times S); \quad (s, x) \mapsto \{(y, u) \mid (s, x, y, u) \in R\}.$$

With this definition, an FSM M is called *completely specified* if and only if $|\underline{R}(s, x)| > 0$ for all pairs (s, x) of states and inputs. If M is not completely specified, it is called *partially defined*. M is *deterministic* if and only if $|\underline{R}(s, x)| \leq 1$ for all state and input pairs (s, x). This means that partially defined FSMs can still be deterministic. As soon as $|\underline{R}(s, x)| > 1$ for at least one state/input pair, M is called *nondeterministic*.

The *language* $L(s_1)$ of a state $s_1 \in S$ is the set of all finite input/output sequences $(x_1, y_1) \ldots (x_k, y_k) \in (\Sigma_I \times \Sigma_O)^*$ that can be created by applying an input sequence $x_1 \ldots x_k$ to state s_1. More formally, $(x_1, y_1) \ldots (x_k, y_k) \in L(s_1)$ if and only if

$$\exists s_2, \ldots, s_{k+1} \in S \, . \, \forall i = 1, \ldots, k \, . \, (s_i, x_i, y_i, s_{i+1}) \in R.$$

Note that this definition of $L(s_1)$ implies prefix-closure, as is to be expected for the description of any process behaviour where past actions "cannot be undone". The language of FSM M is identical to the language of its initial state, $L(M) = L(s_0)$.

An FSM M is *observable* if for every pair of transitions

$$(s_1, x, y, s_2), (s_1, x, y', s_2') \in R$$

emanating from the same state s_1, the target state is uniquely determined by the input/output pair. More formally,

$$\big((s_1, x, y, s_2), (s_1, x, y', s_2') \in R \wedge y = y'\big) \Rightarrow (s_2 = s_2').$$

Deterministic FSMs are automatically observable. For a given input sequence $\overline{x} \in \Sigma_I^*$, the target state reached under $\overline{x}$ is uniquely determined. For observable nondeterministic FSMs, the state reached under a trace $tr \in L(M)$ is uniquely determined. For any state $s \in S$ and trace $tr \in L(s)$, the target state reached from s under tr is denoted by s-**after**-tr.

In the remainder of this chapter, we assume every FSM to be observable, since there exist algorithms transforming non-observable FSMs into observable ones without changing the language [19, Appendix II].

2.2   FSM Conformance Relations

The "classical" conformance relations between an FSM M_1 serving as reference model and another FSM M_2 over the same input/output alphabet serving as implementation are

EQ0 *Language equivalence*: $L(M_2) = L(M_1)$.
RED0 *Reduction*: $L(M_2) \subseteq L(M_1)$.

The following theorem hints at the fact that *"interesting things happen only in presence of nondeterminism and/or partial specification"*.

Theorem 1. *For completely specified, deterministic FSMs reduction is equivalent to language equivalence.*

Proof. Trivially, if *arbitrary* FSMs M_2 and M_1 are language-equivalent, then M_2 is a reduction of M_1 and vice versa, since $L(M_2) = L(M_1)$ implies $L(M_2) \subseteq L(M_1)$ and $L(M_1) \subseteq L(M_2)$. Conversely, suppose that $L(M_2) \subseteq L(M_1)$ for completely specified, deterministic FSMs M_2, M_1. Suppose further that there exists and input/output trace $tr \in L(M_1) \setminus L(M_2)$. Then tr cannot be empty, since the empty trace is contained in the language of every FSM: it reaches the initial state. We can partition this trace into $tr = tr_1.(x, y).tr_2$ (tr_1 and tr_2 may be empty), such that $tr_1 \in L(M_2)$, but $tr_1.(x, y) \notin L(M_2)$.

Since M_1, M_2 are deterministic the states s_1 and s_2 reached by tr_1 in M_1 and M_2, respectively, are uniquely determined. According to our assumption, $(x, y) \in L(s_1)$, but $(x, y) \notin L(s_2)$. Since M_2 is completely specified, there must exist another output $z \neq y$, such that $(x, z) \in L(s_2)$, and, consequently, $tr.(x, z) \in L(M_2)$. However, since M_1 is deterministic and $(x, y) \in L(s_1)$ we conclude that $(x, z) \notin L(s_1)$, and thus $tr.(x, z) \notin L(M_1)$. This contradicts the assumption that M_2 is a reduction of M_1 and completes the proof.   □

If both M_1 and M_2 are completely specified, but M_1 is nondeterministic, true reduction exists and can be interpreted – just as many refinement notions of other modelling formalisms – in the way that *"M_2 is less nondeterministic than M_1, because some design choices have been made in M_2 whose potential alternatives were expressed in M_1 by nondeterministic (internal) choice."* Just as guaranteed, for example, by CSP trace refinement, reduction preserves all safety properties expressed over traces that are fulfilled by the reference model M_1. Since M_2 is completely specified, it also performs "useful things" according to the reference model, since every input sequence $\overline{x} \in \Sigma_I^*$ can be executed on M_2 and produces outputs conforming to the behaviour of M_1.

This intuitive and appealing interpretability of reduction is no longer applicable if we allow for partially specified reference models M_1 and implementations M_2. In the extreme case, the empty FSM producing only the empty trace ε is a reduction of M_1 which guarantees full safety by doing nothing at all. In M_1-states where no outgoing transition exists for a certain input, it has to be decided what the implementation should do in the corresponding state. This question has been widely discussed in the literature, and the following options for interpreting undefined state/input pairs in a reference model are considered as acceptable and useful [10, 11, 24, 29].

U1 The unspecified input $x \in \Sigma_I$ in a given state $s \in S$ is just a shorthand for the fact that x has no effect in state s. This could simply be represented by a self-loop $s \xrightarrow{x/-} s$, using the special symbol $- \in \Sigma_O$ denoting *"no output"* for event-based interfaces or *"no output change"* for state-based interfaces. This interpretation is used, for example, in UML state machines [21].

U2 Alternatively, the unspecified input can be a shorthand for the fact that x is not allowed in the current state, and provision of x will lead to an exception leading into an error state. This could be modelled by a transition $s \xrightarrow{x/\texttt{error}} s_{\texttt{error}}$, where $s_{\texttt{error}}$ is an additional error state and $\texttt{error} \in \Sigma_O$ a specific error message.

U3 The unspecified input can represent deliberate under-specification in the sense that *"provision of x in state s leads to a behaviour to be specified in another reference model."* This interpretation is used, for example, in the ioco-relation suggested by Tretmans [4] for model-based testing against

Input/Output transition systems. The interpretation is especially useful in the context of scenario-based specifications. These are applied in situations where a comprehensive reference model for the expected behaviour of an implementation cannot be created, due to complexity reasons. The unspecified (s, x)-pair in a scenario model indicates that it triggers another scenario that should be specified elsewhere in the scenario library [9, 22].

U4 The unspecified input can represent a situation where providing x is physically or logically impossible for the environment. In graphical user interfaces (GUI), for example, certain buttons are not always visible, so *"input x via mouse-click on button B"* is disabled in certain states of the GUI. This interpretation and its analysis in model-based testing has been investigated by Sachtleben et al. [29]. It is quite effective when testing GUIs or technical systems where inputs can be disabled for mechanical reasons (like a card read slot in an ATM where a card has already been inserted). Logically impossible inputs occur, for example, when FSMs are used for the purpose of predicate abstraction. This is explained in Example 1 below.

There is a general agreement in the communities using FSMs that the unspecified state/input pairs induced by short-hand notations **U1** and **U2** do not "deserve" novel refinement concepts: the FSMs can simply be extended to result in completely specified FSMs reflecting the intended behaviour. Our FSM tool support library libfsmtest [3], for example, allows to set flags during FSM instantiation where partial FSM models can be provided and automatically completed according to interpretation **U1** and **U2**, respectively.

Observe that Interpretation **U4** in this list cannot be simply represented by refusing x in the CSP-sense: graphical user interfaces never refuse an input in the way that users are blocked in the process of providing x. Instead, every input that is visible in a GUI state can be provided by means of mouse-clicks or keyboard inputs, and every invisible GUI element can never lead to any interaction (refused, ignored, etc.), because *"it is just not there"*. The following example illustrates the need for interpretation **U4** when using FSMs for predicate abstraction.

Example 1. Consider the task theTask() shown in C programming style in Listing 1. It reads inputs from shared (global) variable x and writes outputs to shared variable y. The inputs are provided by another task. It can be assumed that x remains unchanged during the processing loop.[2] Likewise, the outputs are processed by a further task not shown here. Task theTask() sets output y to one if internal variable m has a positive value, otherwise y is set to zero. This is performed once per processing loop, after m has been updated. Variable m is decremented whenever input x changes from a value that is greater than m to a value less or equal to m. Note that this is not possible if m is less than zero, since x is of type unsigned int. Variable m is incremented whenever input x changes from a value that is less or equal to one to a value greater than one, provided that m is less or equal to zero. Thus m always stay in range $\{-1, 0, 1\}$.

---

[2] The code to ensure this is not shown in Listing 1. Typically, this is achieved by using mutual exclusion mechanisms like strict alternation or Peterson's algorithm [30].

To verify temporal properties like

Prop 1. *If in a sequence of inputs, condition* x ≤ m *changes from* false *to* true[3] *infinitely often, the output* y *also changes from one to zero infinitely often*

it is useful to abstract the concrete program to an FSM whose inputs and outputs represent logical conditions. For the current example, such an FSM and its alphabets is shown in Fig. 1. Machine M_{abs} is not completely specified. In state s_0, input b is unspecified since its occurrence has no effect because m is greater than zero. Therefore, interpretation **U1** is appropriate for state/input pair (s_0, b). In state s_2, input a is unspecified because condition x ≤ m can never become true in this state. Thus interpretation **U4** is appropriate for (s_2, a). Note that the task providing inputs on x is never blocked, since it writes to a shared variable. Therefore, an interpretation by means of refusals blocking the occurrence of a is unsuitable.

With M_{abs} at hand, it is easy to verify that property **Prop 1** specified above does not hold, since the infinite repetition of transition sequence

$$s_0 \xrightarrow{a/w} s_1 \xrightarrow{b/w} s_0$$

contains infinitely many a-inputs but never switches y from one to zero.   □

Listing 1. Task theTask() discussed in Example 1.

```
1  unsigned int x;
2  unsigned int y;
3  void theTask(void) {
4      int m = 1;
5      unsigned int xOld = x;
6      do {
7        if ( x <= m && xOld > m ) m = m − 1;
8        if ( x > 1 && xOld <= 1 && m <= 0 ) m = m + 1;
9        y = ( m >= 0 ) ? 1 : 0;
10       xOld = x;
11     }
12 }
```

---

[3] The change of a predicate from false to true is associated with a so-called *change event*, as used, for example, in UML state machines [21].

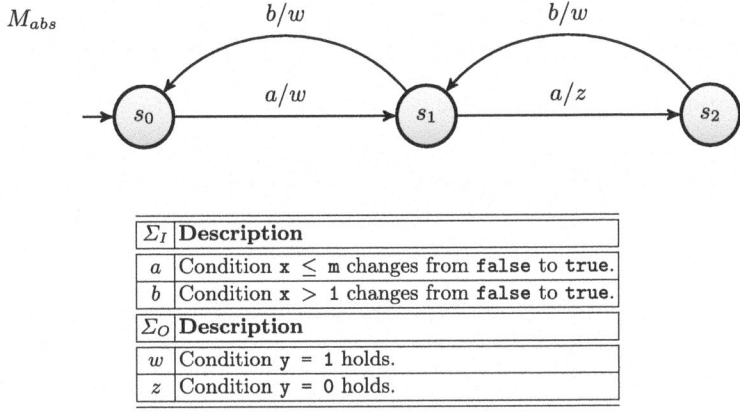

Σ_I	Description
a	Condition x $\leq$ m changes from false to true.
b	Condition x $>$ 1 changes from false to true.
Σ_O	**Description**
w	Condition y = 1 holds.
z	Condition y = 0 holds.

Fig. 1. FSM abstracting theTask(), as discussed in Example 1.

Interpretations **U3**, **U4**, however, have inspired two more equivalence relations and associated reduction definitions. To facilitate these definitions, the following notation is introduced for any FSM M. For $s \in S$ and $x \in \Sigma_I$ define

$$\mathbf{out}_M(s, x) = \{y \in \Sigma_O \mid \exists u \in S \centerdot (s, x, y, u) \in R\}, \qquad (1)$$

so $\mathbf{out}_M(s, x)$ denotes the set of all outputs that can be expected from FSM M when providing input x in state s. For deterministic FSMs M, the set $\mathbf{out}_M(s, x)$ contains zero or one elements. For a trace $tr \in L(M)$, we use abbreviation $\mathbf{out}_M(tr, x) = \mathbf{out}_M(s_0\text{-}\underline{\text{after}}\text{-}tr, x)$.

Interpretation **U3** has lead to the concepts quasi-equivalence and quasi-reduction.

EQ3 *Quasi-equivalence*, as introduced by Hierons [10,11][4], states the following conditions for M_2 to be quasi-equivalent to M_1. (1) After having run through any trace $tr \in L(M_2) \cap L(M_1)$, any input x specified for M_1 must also be specified for M_2. This input must lead to the same outputs in both machines, that is, $\mathbf{out}_{M_2}(tr, x) = \mathbf{out}_{M_1}(tr, x)$. (2) If input x' is not specified for M_1 after such a trace tr ($\mathbf{out}_{M_1}(tr, x') = \varnothing$), M_2 may produce any output for x' and then behave like an arbitrary sub-FSM. According to this definition, quasi-equivalence is reflexive and transitive, but not symmetric.

RED3 *Quasi-reduction* [10,11] requires that implementation M_2, after having run through a trace $tr \in L(M_2) \cap L(M_1)$ that is possible for the reference model as well, is defined for every input x that is defined for the reference model. The outputs associated with x in M_2 must also be "allowed" in the reference model, so every $tr.(x, y) \in L(M_2)$ must be a trace of M_1, or equivalently, $\mathbf{out}_{M_2}(tr, x) \subseteq \mathbf{out}_{M_1}(tr, x)$. For inputs x'

---

[4] A slightly different definition has been proposed by Petrenko et al. [26].

where no behaviour has been specified in M_1 after having run through tr, M_2 may exhibit the behaviour of an arbitrary FSM.

Interpretation **U4** has inspired the concept of strong reduction [29].

RED4 FSM M_2 is a *strong reduction* of M_1 if and only if M_2 is a "conventional" reduction of M_1 $(L(M_2) \subseteq L(M_1))$ and, after having run through any trace $tr \in L(M_2)$ (which is automatically also a trace of M_1), the set of specified inputs for M_2 equals the set of specified inputs for M_1.

Though the conformance relations described above look fairly heterogeneous, Huang and Sachtleben [17,28] have shown that they can be derived from a general, surprisingly intuitive, concept: each of these relations r can be re-defined by introducing a suitable relation $H_r \subseteq \mathbb{P}(\Sigma_O) \times \mathbb{P}(\Sigma_O)$ and setting

$$M_2 \ r \ M_1 \text{ iff } \forall tr \in L(M_2) \cap L(M_1); x \in \Sigma_I \centerdot (\mathbf{out}_{M_2}(tr,x), \mathbf{out}_{M_1}(tr,x)) \in H_r.$$

For language-equivalence **EQ0**, for example, define

$$H_{\mathbf{EQ0}} = \{(A,A) \mid A \subseteq \Sigma_O\}.$$

For quasi-reduction **RED3**, define

$$H_{\mathbf{RED3}} = \{(A,B) \mid A \neq \varnothing \wedge A \subseteq B \subseteq \Sigma_O\} \cup \{(C,\varnothing) \mid C \subseteq \Sigma_O\}.$$

The other conformance relations defined above can be expressed in this style as well [17]. Moreover, Huang and Sachtleben have demonstrated that there are several other relations $H_{r'} \subseteq \mathbb{P}(\Sigma_O) \times \mathbb{P}(\Sigma_O)$ leading to conformance relations r' that are certainly useful, but have not been discussed in the literature so far.

2.3   Critical Assessment of FSM Conformance Relations

Dealing with different conformance relations is quite common in many modelling formalisms. There is, however, a subtle difference between partially specified FSMs and the associated conformance relations described above and, for example, CSP processes and trace, failures, or failures-divergence refinement [12,27]. As Petrenko et al. [24] pointed out, a partial FSM M_1 is like a template for (an infinite number of) fully specified machines M_2, where the latter are completely specified and implement suitable reactions to the unspecified state/input pairs in M_1, according to the options **U1**,...,**U4** described above. The selection of a conformance relation **EQ3**, **RED3**, **RED4** limits the range of acceptable implementations regarding the interpretation options to be applied for unspecified state/event pairs.

In contrast to that, CSP reference processes P_1 always fully specify the most liberal behaviour of associated implementations. There are no unspecified events e in any process state P_1/tr ("P_1 after having run through trace tr"): e may be nondeterministically refused or accepted, but when accepted, the subsequent acceptable behaviour is well-defined. In the worst case, the behaviour may be chaotic (CHAOS process) or arbitrary "in a good-natured way" (RUN process), but it is still fully specified in P_1, quite different from the template character of partial reference FSMs M_1. Any implementation P_2 fulfilling one of the three CSP conformance relations (=refinement in CSP) always fully preserves or reduces the behaviours admissible according to P_2 in the sense that P_2 executes fewer traces, blocks less, and diverges less than allowed according to P_1. This concept allows for the elegant lattice interpretations for CSP, where each refinement notion is a partial order, and the semantics of recursive processes can be explained as fixed points of monotonic recursion functions.

From our perspective, the FSM conformance relations **EQ3**, **RED3**, **RED4** also have a fundamental weakness: they require that a valid implementation M_2 must treat all unspecified state/input pairs $(s, x) \in S \times \Sigma_I$ of the reference model M_1 in the same way! In the cases of **EQ3** and **RED3**, all the unspecified (s, x) must be kept unspecified or replaced by some explicit behaviour. In case of **RED4**, all the unspecified (s, x) must be kept unspecified, since x is not supposed to happen in state s. From a practical perspective, it is certainly preferable to specify *for every unspecified state/input pair (s, x) of M_1 separately* which interpretation **U1**,…,**U4** has to be chosen in an acceptable implementation.

2.4 Unified Equivalence and Reduction Concepts for FSMs

Elaborating the interpretation that unspecified state/event pairs either cannot happen or should be considered as shorthand notations for certain types of behaviour, we advocate to extend FSM specifications by an *acceptance map* from state/input pairs to interpretations:

$$acc : S \times \Sigma_I \longrightarrow \{\mathtt{A}(\text{ccepted}), \mathtt{I}(\text{gnored}), \mathtt{E}(\text{rror}), \mathtt{U}(\text{nspecified}), \mathtt{D}(\text{isabled})\}. \quad (2)$$

This function is interpreted as follows: (1) $acc(s, x) = \mathtt{A}$ means that there is a transition defined in R, starting with (s, x). (2) $acc(s, x) = \mathtt{I}$ is shorthand for an ignored event, so that a self-loop transition $(s, x, -, s)$ is implicitly added to R (interpretation **U1** in Sect. 2.2). (3) $acc(s, x) = \mathtt{E}$ marks a forbidden input, leading to an error transition (interpretation **U2** in Sect. 2.2). (4) $acc(s, x) = \mathtt{U}$ marks an unspecified input (interpretation **U3** in Sect. 2.2). (5) $acc(s, x) = \mathtt{D}$ marks a disabled input (interpretation **U4** in Sect. 2.2). All functions acc need to fulfil the following consistency condition for all $(s, x) \in S \times \Sigma_I$.

$$acc(s, x) = \mathtt{A} \Leftrightarrow \mathbf{out}(s, x) \neq \varnothing \quad (3)$$

so the accepted state/input pairs are exactly the ones that can be extended to a four-tuple that is a member of the transition relation. This consistency condition implies obviously that $acc(s, x) \in \{\mathtt{I}, \mathtt{E}, \mathtt{U}, \mathtt{D}\}$ if and only if $\mathbf{out}(s, x) = \varnothing$.

We use the following abbreviations for frequently referenced image sets derived from acc.

$$
\begin{aligned}
A(s) &\mathrel{\widehat{=}} \{x \in \Sigma_I \mid acc(s, x) = \mathtt{A}\} \\
I(s) &\mathrel{\widehat{=}} \{x \in \Sigma_I \mid acc(s, x) = \mathtt{I}\} \\
E(s) &\mathrel{\widehat{=}} \{x \in \Sigma_I \mid acc(s, x) = \mathtt{E}\} \\
U(s) &\mathrel{\widehat{=}} \{x \in \Sigma_I \mid acc(s, x) = \mathtt{U}\} \\
D(s) &\mathrel{\widehat{=}} \{x \in \Sigma_I \mid acc(s, x) = \mathtt{D}\}
\end{aligned}
\tag{4}
$$

Moreover, to prohibit partial implementations that are **RED0**-reductions omitting too much functionality, a second function called *options map*

$$
opt : S \longrightarrow \mathbb{P}(\mathbb{P}(\Sigma_I)) \text{ with consistency condition } \forall s \in S \centerdot opt(s) \subseteq \mathbb{P}(A(s)) \tag{5}
$$

is defined: $opt(s)$ defines the options allowed to reduce the accepted inputs of a state s in a standard reduction. If $opt(s) = \mathbb{P}(A(s))$ for all $s \in S$, we get unrestricted reduction **RED0**: an implementation can choose to implement any subset, even the empty set, of $A(s)$ as accepted events in the corresponding implementation state. If $opt(s) = \{A(s)\}$, *every* accepted input of state s needs to be implemented. If $opt(s) = \{A_1, \ldots, A_k\}$ with $A_i \subseteq A(s)$, then the implementation needs to realise reactions to all inputs from exactly one set $A_i \in opt(s)$, while all inputs from $A(s) \setminus A_i$ must be disabled.

Note that opt is considered as a *parameter of the reduction*, to introduce more "subtle" refinements than just language containment as required by **RED0**. The FSM whose state space and acceptance map is associated with opt, say, M_1, is not affected by the options map: in any state s, M_1 always accepts all inputs x satisfying $acc(s, x) \neq \mathtt{D}$.

Since all FSMs are considered to be observable, every reachable state s of an FSM M can be written as $s = s_0\text{-}\underline{\mathtt{after}}\text{-}tr$ for some trace $tr \in L(M)$. Therefore, the abbreviation $acc(tr, x) \mathrel{\widehat{=}} acc(s_0\text{-}\underline{\mathtt{after}}\text{-}tr, x)$ for $(tr, x) \in L(M) \times \Sigma_I$ is well-defined. Likewise, we write $A(tr), I(tr), E(tr), U(tr), D(tr)$, where tr stands for $s_0\text{-}\underline{\mathtt{after}}\text{-}tr$.

An FSM is now equipped with the extended definition

$$
M = (S, s_0, R, \Sigma_I, \Sigma_O, acc),
$$

resolving under-specification with the help of mapping acc. Completely specified FSMs are characterised by[5] $acc(s, \Sigma_I) = \{\mathtt{A}\}$ for all $s \in S$. For partial FSMs, the interpretation of unspecified inputs can now be performed on a per-state basis.

The merits of auxiliary maps acc and opt become visible in the insight that the two equivalence relations and three reduction relations discussed above can really be regarded as instances of *one* equivalence relation and *one* reduction relation, for specific choices of acc and opt. Moreover, the two novel definitions give rise to several new conformance relations that have not yet been discussed

---

[5] We use short-hand notation $acc(s, X) \mathrel{\widehat{=}} \{acc(s, x) \mid x \in X\}$ for set-valued function arguments $X \subseteq \Sigma_I$.

in the literature but are obviously appealing from a practical perspective. These insights complement the results achieved by Huang and Sachtleben [17] who showed on the more abstract level of prefix-closed languages that different conformance notions can be derived from one general concept.

Definition 1 (Universal Quasi-Equivalence EQU).

Given FSMs $M_i = (S_i, s_{i,0}, R_i, \Sigma_I, \Sigma_O, acc_i)$, $i = 1, 2$, where FSM M_1 plays the role of a reference model, and M_2 that of an implementation. We say that M_2 is universally quasi-equivalent to M_1 if and only if the following conditions hold for all traces $tr \in L(M_2) \cap L(M_1)$.

1. $\exists C \subseteq U_1(tr) \boldsymbol{.} A_2(tr) = A_1(tr) \cup C \wedge$
$$\forall x \in A_1(tr) \boldsymbol{.} \mathbf{out}_2(tr, x) = \mathbf{out}_1(tr, x) \wedge$$
$$U_2(tr) = U_1(tr) \setminus C$$
2. $I_2(tr) = I_1(tr)$
3. $E_2(tr) = E_1(tr)$
4. $D_2(tr) = D_1(tr)$

The intuitive interpretation of Definition 2 is as follows. Conditions 2, 3 and 4 simply state that inputs that are ignored, lead to error indications, or are disabled in certain states of the reference model must remain ignored, erroneous, or disabled in the corresponding states of any equivalent FSM model.

The crucial part of Definition 2 is encoded in its first condition which is structured into several conjuncts. The first part of Condition 1 states that, after having performed a trace that is also possible for the implementation, all inputs that are accepted in the reference model are also accepted by the implementation. Moreover, every output associated in the (potentially nondeterministic) reference model with such an input must also be possible for the implementation. But there is an additional degree of freedom for the implementation, which makes the general definition reflexive and transitive, but not symmetric, just as seen in the definition of quasi-equivalence: inputs of a subset C that are unspecified after tr for the reference model (this is indicated by $C \subseteq U_1(tr)$) may be accepted (with resulting arbitrary behaviour) in the implementation. Consequently, the set $U_2(tr)$ of unspecified inputs in the implementation is reduced by the inputs in C that now have become accepted.

The options map opt_2 of the implementation must not allow disabling these novel accepted inputs from C: the decision to accept a previously unspecified input and associate it with a concrete behaviour must not be undone by another refinement. In contrast to that, option sets of accepted inputs that were available in the reference model remain options in the implementation.

Note that universal quasi-equivalence turns into the symmetric equivalence relation **EQ0**, as soon as the reference model has no unspecified events, so that C becomes the empty set.

Definition 2 (Universal Reduction REDU).

Given FSMs $M_i = (S_i, s_{i,0}, R_i, \Sigma_I, \Sigma_O, acc_i)$, $i = 1, 2$, let opt_1 be an options map associated with M_1. We say that M_2 is a universal reduction of M_1 with respect to opt_1 if and only if the following conditions hold for all traces $tr \in L(M_2) \cap L(M_1)$.

1. $\exists B \in opt_1(tr); C \subseteq U_1(tr) \cdot A_2(tr) = B \cup C \wedge$
$$\forall x \in B \cdot \mathbf{out}_2(tr, x) \subseteq \mathbf{out}_1(tr, x) \wedge$$
$$D_2(tr) = D_1(tr) \cup (A_1(tr) \setminus B) \wedge$$
$$U_2(tr) = U_1(tr) \setminus C$$
2. $I_2(tr) = I_1(tr)$
3. $E_2(tr) = E_1(tr)$

The intuition behind Definition 2 is similar to that of universal quasi-equivalence, but now there are more degrees of freedom for the implementation. As in Definition 1, the implementation, after having run through a trace tr that is also in the language of the reference model, may accept unspecified inputs from a set C of the reference model. However, it may also *reduce* the set of accepted inputs by choosing an option $B \in opt_1(tr)$ that is a real subset of the inputs accepted by the reference model. For the accepted inputs of B that are also accepted by the reference model, the implementation may produce a subset of the associated outputs that are possible for the reference model, so the implementation may be more deterministic than the reference model. Accepted inputs of the reference model that are no longer handled due to the choice of options in the implementation become disabled and will remain so in all further reductions, since the sets of disabled events can only made larger in a reduction, never smaller.

As specified in Item 2 and Item 3, universal reduction requires that an implementation ignores the same state/input pairs as the reference model, and the same state/input pairs must result in an error as in the specification. If it is desired that some ignored inputs or inputs leading to errors could be omitted in a reduction, the related state/input pairs need to be associated with new types of "ignore" or "error" outputs, and explicit transitions need to be introduced for them in the reference model, so that they become accepted inputs in the reference model.

Since universal reduction is parameterised by an option map associated with the reference model, the question arises which conditions need to be fulfilled by a *sequence* of options maps to make reduction transitive. This question is answered by the following theorem which we state without proof.

Theorem 2. Let $M_i = (S_i, s_{i,0}, R_i, \Sigma_I, \Sigma_O, acc_i)$, $i = 1, \ldots, \ell$ denote a sequence of FSMs and opt_i, $i = 1, \ldots, \ell - 1$ a sequence of option maps such that

1. opt_i is associated with M_i for $i = 1, \ldots, \ell - 1$, and
2. M_{i+1} is a universal reduction of M_i with respect to opt_i for $i = 1, \ldots, \ell - 1$.

Suppose that the option maps fulfil the following conditions for all $i = 1, \ldots, \ell - 1$ and all traces $tr \in L(M_i) \cap L(M_{i+1})$.

$$\exists B \in opt_i(tr); C \subseteq U_i(tr) \cdot$$
$$\left(A_{i+1}(tr) = B \cup C \wedge opt_{i+1}(tr) = \{B' \cup C \mid B' \subseteq B \wedge B' \in opt_i(tr)\} \right).$$

Then this chain of reductions is transitive in the sense that M_{i+j} is a universal reduction of M_i with respect to opt_i for all $i \in \{1, \ldots, \ell - 1\}$ and $j \geq 1$ with $i + j \in \{2, \ldots, \ell\}$. □

The theorem's requirement for an admissible sequence of option maps ensures that newly accepted inputs from some set $C \subset U_i(tr)$ may never become unspecified again in further reductions $i + j$, $j \geq 1$. However, options that are subsets of $opt_i(tr)$ remain options in reduction $i + 1$.

The following Theorems validates the definition of **REDU** by showing that standard reduction **RED0**, quasi-reduction **RED3**, and strong reduction **RED4** are equivalent to **REDU**, when choosing special variants for the acceptance map and the options map of the reference model.

Theorem 3 (REDU and RED0). *Let $M_i = (S_i, s_{i,0}, R_i, \Sigma_I, \Sigma_O, acc_i)$, $i = 1, 2$ be FSMs, where M_1 has acceptance map*

$$\forall s \in S \cdot acc_1(s, \Sigma_I) \subseteq \{\mathtt{A}, \mathtt{D}\}.$$

Define the options map

$$\forall s \in S \cdot opt_1(s) = \mathbb{P}(A_1(s))$$

*which is associated with M_1. Then, if M_2 is a universal reduction of M_1 with respect to opt_1, M_2 is also a **RED0**-reduction of M_1.*

*Conversely, any FSM $M_2 = (S_2, s_{2,0}, R_2, \Sigma_I, \Sigma_O)$ that is a **RED0**-reduction of M_1 can be associated with an acceptance map acc_2 such that M_2 is a universal reduction of M_1.*

Proof. Assume that M_2 is a **REDU**-reduction of M_1 according to the assumptions of the first part of the theorem. We assume that M_2 is *not* a **RED0**-reduction of M_1 and derive a contradiction. To this end, assume that $tr \in L(M_2) \setminus L(M_1)$, such that $tr = tr_1.(x, y).tr_2$ with $tr_1 \in L(M_2) \cap L(M_1)$ and $tr_1.(x, y) \notin L(M_2) \cap L(M_1)$. Since $L(M_2)$ is prefix-closed, we know that $tr_1.(x, y) \in L(M_2)$.

Case 1. Assume that $acc_1(tr_1, x) = \mathtt{A}$. Since $U_1(tr_1) = \varnothing$ according to the assumptions about acc_1, the input x must be an element of a set $B \in opt_1(tr_1)$ selected according to Condition 1 in Definition 2. Consequently, according to the same condition, $y \in \mathbf{out}_2(tr_1, x) \subseteq \mathbf{out}_1(tr_1, x)$. Thus, $tr_1.(x, y)$ is also an element of $L(M_1)$, a contradiction to the assumption that $tr_1.(x, y) \notin L(M_2) \cap L(M_1)$.

Case 2. Assume that $acc_1(tr_1, x) = \mathtt{D}$. Then, again according to Condition 1 in Definition 2, x must also be an element of $D_2(tr_1)$, a contradiction to the assumption that $tr_1.(x, y) \in L(M_2)$.

Conversely, assume that $L(M_2) \subseteq L(M_1)$ with acc_1 and opt_1 defined according to the assumptions of the theorem. Define an acceptance map for M_2 by

$$\forall (s, x) \in S_2 \times \Sigma_I \cdot acc_2(s, x) \mathrel{\hat{=}} \begin{cases} \mathtt{A} & \text{if} \quad \mathbf{out}_2(s, x) \neq \varnothing \\ \mathtt{D} & \text{otherwise} \end{cases}$$

We show that $M_2 = (S_2, s_{2,0}, R_2, \Sigma_I, \Sigma_O, acc_2)$ is a **REDU**-reduction of M_1 with respect to opt_1. To this end, assume that $tr \in L(M_2) \cap L(M_1) = L(M_2)$. Define $B = A_2(tr)$. Then $B \in opt_1(tr)$, because $opt_1(tr) = \mathbb{P}(A_1(tr))$ and $A_2(tr) \subseteq A_1(tr)$, since M_2 is a **RED0**-reduction of M_1. This also implies for all $x \in A_2(tr)$ that $\mathbf{out}_2(tr, x) \subseteq \mathbf{out}_1(tr, x)$. Moreover, by definition of acc_2 and by the **RED0**-reduction property, it is ensured that $D_2(tr) = D_1(tr) \cup (A_1(tr) \setminus A_2(tr)) = D_1(tr) \cup (A_1(tr) \setminus B)$. This shows that M_2 fulfils Condition 1 of Definition 2. For Condition 2 and Condition 3, there is nothing to prove. Thus M_2 is a **REDU**-reduction of M_1 and completes the proof of the theorem. □

Theorem 4 (REDU and RED3). *Let* $M_i = (S_i, s_{i,0}, R_i, \Sigma_I, \Sigma_O, acc_i, opt_i)$, $i = 1, 2$ *be FSMs, where* M_1 *has acceptance map and options map*

$$\forall s \in S \, . \, acc_1(s, \Sigma_I) \subseteq \{\mathtt{A}, \mathtt{U}\}$$

and

$$\forall s \in S \, . \, opt_1(s) = \{A_1(s)\}.$$

Then, if M_2 *is a universal reduction of* M_1 *with respect to* opt_1, M_2 *is also a* **RED3**-*reduction (quasi-reduction) of* M_1.

Conversely, any FSM $M_2 = (S_2, s_{2,0}, R_2, \Sigma_I, \Sigma_O)$ *that is a* **RED3**-*reduction of* M_1 *can be associated with an acceptance map* acc_2, *such that* M_2 *is a universal reduction of* M_1 *with respect to* opt_1.

Proof. Assume that M_2 is a **REDU**-reduction of M_1 according to the assumptions of the first part of the theorem. Let $tr \in L(M_2) \cap L(M_1)$. Since M_2 is a universal reduction of M_1, Condition 1 of Definition 2 holds. Since $opt_1(tr) = \{A_1(tr)\}$ according to the prerequisites of the theorem, the set B in Condition 1 equals $A_1(tr)$, and there exists $C \subseteq U_1(tr)$, such that $A_2(tr) = B \cup C$. M_2 will not introduce any disabled inputs, since Condition 1 assures $D_2(tr) = D_1(tr) \cup (A_1(tr) \setminus B) = \varnothing$, because $D_1(tr) = \varnothing$ according to the definition of acc_1 and $B = A_1(tr)$. Validity of Condition 1 implies further that

$$\forall x \in A_1(tr) \, . \, \mathbf{out}_2(tr, x) \subseteq \mathbf{out}_1(tr, x),$$

and this is exactly the condition for quasi-reduction.

Conversely, assume that M_2 is a quasi-reduction of M_1. Define

$$\forall (s, x) \in S_2 \times \Sigma_I \, . \, acc_2(s, x) = \begin{cases} \mathtt{A} & \text{if} \quad \exists y \in \Sigma_O \, . \, (x, y) \in L_{M_2}(s) \\ \mathtt{U} & \text{otherwise} \end{cases}$$

Now let $tr \in L(M_2) \cap L(M_1)$. Set $B = A_1(tr) \in opt_1(tr)$ and $C = A_2(tr) \setminus A_1(tr)$ (note that $A_2(tr)$ is a superset of $A_1(tr)$ because every input x defined for M_1 after trace tr must also be defined for M_2, due to the quasi-reduction property). Also, $C \subseteq U_1(tr)$, since all inputs outside $A_1(tr)$ are necessarily contained in $U_1(tr)$, due to the definition of acc_1. Quasi-reduction implies that $\mathbf{out}_2(tr, x) \subseteq \mathbf{out}_1(tr, x)$ for all $x \in B = A_1(tr)$. Moreover, the definition of acc_2 ensures that $U_2(tr) = U_1(tr) \setminus C$. The set $D_2(tr)$ of disabled inputs is empty according to the definition of acc_2. Since $D_1(tr)$ is empty as well and $B = A_1(tr)$, the conjunct $D_2(tr) = D_1(tr) \cup (A_1(tr) \setminus B)$ in Condition 1 of Definition 2 also evaluates to true. Again, Conditions 2 and Condition 3 of Definition 2 do not contribute, since the sets involved are all empty. This shows that M_2 with the above choice of acc_2 induces a universal reduction of M_1 with respect to opt_1 and completes the proof of the theorem. $\qquad\square$

Similarly, it is shown that universal reduction covers strong reduction as a special case.

Theorem 5 (REDU and RED4). *Let $M_i = (S_i, s_{i,0}, R_i, \Sigma_I, \Sigma_O, acc_i)$, $i = 1, 2$ be FSMs, where M_1 has acceptance map*

$$\forall s \in S \centerdot acc_1(s, \Sigma_I) \subseteq \{\mathtt{A}, \mathtt{D}\}.$$

Define an options map associated with M_1 by

$$\forall s \in S \centerdot opt_1(s) = \{A_1(s)\}.$$

Then, if M_2 is a universal reduction of M_1, M_2 is also a **RED4**-*reduction (strong reduction) of M_1 with respect to opt_1.*

Conversely, any FSM $M_2 = (S_2, s_{2,0}, R_2, \Sigma_I, \Sigma_O)$ that is a **RED4**-*reduction of M_1 can be associated with an acceptance map acc_2, such that M_2 is a universal reduction of M_1 with respect to opt_1.* $\qquad\square$

Similarly, the definition of universal quasi-equivalence can be validated to show that it covers **EQ0** and **EQ3** for special choices of acceptance map and options map. Alternative representations of the definitions and theorems above have been proposed by Huang and Sachtleben [17] using only concepts of prefix-closed languages without reference to concrete modelling formalisms like FSMs.

2.5   Option-Preserving Reduction – A Novel Conformance Relation

To give an example how universal reduction **REDU** induces new conformance relations that can be quite helpful from a practical perspective, let us consider the product line modelling case, where one core product is instantiated in different variants. As a concrete case, consider a GUI for a product with different variants, where it is advisable to specify the different GUI instances associated with each product variant in one comprehensive FSM. Suppose, in one system state s, GUI buttons x_i can be used to activate different product functions, but each product variant would only offer a certain subset of these functions. Buttons x_1, x_2, x_3 should be available for variant 1, buttons x_1, x_2 for variant 2, and buttons x_1, x_4, x_5 in variant 3. In the FSM specifying the GUI behaviour for all three variants, state s would specify $acc(s, x_i) = \mathtt{A}$ for $i = 1, \ldots, 5$. The outgoing transitions and subsequent states for each pair (s, x_i) would specify the detailed functionality associated with x_i, so that the state machine model specifies the full behaviour of all variants.

To derive a specific model for, say, variant 3, an options map *opt* is defined, so that $opt_{\text{variant } 3}(s) = \{\{x_1, x_4, x_5\}\}$ (perhaps plus some additional inputs that should always be available in state s). Then every universal reduction of the comprehensive model with option map $opt_{\text{variant } 3}$ will make exactly the buttons x_1, x_4, x_5 available in state s, while buttons x_2, x_3 remain disabled. For the product line, M_1 would be associated with a library of options maps $opt_{\text{variant } i}$, $i = 1, 2, 3, \ldots$.

3   A UTP Theory for FSMs

3.1   FSMs as UTP Processes

Unsurprisingly, the UTP formalisation of FSMs bears some resemblance to the UTP theory of reactive processes [13, Chapter 8]. It is, however, significantly simpler than UTP theories for process algebras like CSP for several reasons.

- There is no concept of divergence, since FSMs do not have τ-transitions or guard-based loops that could run infinitely. Every transition between states terminates immediately when fired.
- The FSM notion of parallel composition does not use concepts like channels and variable values passed from writers to readers. (We consider here only sequential FSMs interacting with their environment.)
- The conventional FSM definition as a tuple $M = (S, s_0, R, \Sigma_I, \Sigma_O)$ allows for a generic FSM representation in UTP, as will be seen below.

The UTP theory $\mathsf{FSM}(\Sigma_I, \Sigma_O)$ is parametrised by the input and output alphabets: any relationship between FSMs of interest will always rely on their input and output alphabets to be identical. The conformance relations for FSMs described above suggest that the following semantic variables should be present in a UTP theory for finite state machines.

1. A trace variable $tr : (\Sigma_I \times \Sigma_O)^*$ and its post-state counterpart tr'.
2. Acceptance variables $X, X' : \mathsf{P}(\Sigma_I)$ specifying the inputs that are accepted in the current FSM state.
3. As for reactive processes, sequential composition of FSM fragments is relevant, so we need variables $wait, wait' : \mathbb{B}$ with the analogous interpretation as for reactive processes:
   - $wait$ is **true** if the preceding process has not yet terminated, since it is still waiting for inputs from the environment.
   - $wait'$ is **true** if the current FSM is waiting for inputs to be provided by the environment.
4. State variables $state, state' : S$ encode the FSM state.
5. Auxiliary variables $any, any' : \mathbb{B}$ are used to indicate whether unspecified behaviour is performed, after an unspecified input x has been provided in some state s $(acc(s, x) = \mathsf{U})$.
6. The acceptance map acc is considered as a constant symbol of the UTP alphabet.

Summarising, the alphabet of UTP theory $\mathtt{FSM}(\Sigma_I, \Sigma_O)$ is

$$\Sigma = \{tr, tr', X, X', wait, wait', state, state', any, any', acc, acc'\} \qquad (6)$$

with the variable types specified above. We need the same healthiness rules as defined for reactive processes.

$$\mathbf{R1}(M) \;\widehat{=}\; M \wedge tr \leq tr'$$
$$\mathbf{R2}(M(tr, tr')) \;\widehat{=}\; M(\langle\,\rangle/tr, (tr' - tr), tr')$$
$$\mathbf{R3}(M) \;\widehat{=}\; I\!I \vartriangleleft wait \vartriangleright M$$
$$\mathbf{R} \;\widehat{=}\; \mathbf{R3} \circ \mathbf{R2} \circ \mathbf{R1}$$

Any valid FSM M must be a fixed point of $\mathbf{R}$, that is, M needs to fulfil $M = \mathbf{R}(M)$.

The *identity process*

$$I\!I \equiv tr' = tr \wedge X' = X \wedge state' = state \wedge wait' = wait \wedge any' = any \qquad (7)$$

is useful to specify that FSM fragments have no effect after termination or while waiting for the previous FSM fragment to terminate.

We interpret FSM states without emanating transitions as "good-natured" termination states. For the latter, the definition

$$\mathtt{TERM} \;\widehat{=}\; \mathbf{R3}\big(X' = \varnothing \wedge tr' = tr \wedge \neg wait' \wedge any' = any\big) \qquad (8)$$

is used. When $\mathtt{TERM}$ is activated and $wait$ is $\mathtt{false}$, the process will no longer accept any input, won't change the trace executed so far, and terminate immediately ($wait' = \mathtt{false}$).

We define further FSM-specific healthiness conditions as follows.

$$\mathbf{F0}(M) \;\widehat{=}\; M \wedge acc' = acc \wedge \big(\forall x \in \Sigma_I \bullet acc(state, x) = \mathtt{A} \Leftrightarrow \mathbf{out}_M(state, x) \neq \varnothing\big)$$
$$\mathbf{F2}(M) \;\widehat{=}\; M \wedge (any \Rightarrow any')$$
$$\mathbf{F3}(M) \;\widehat{=}\; \mathtt{TERM} \vartriangleleft D(state) = \Sigma_I \vartriangleright$$
$$\Big(M \wedge \big((tr' = tr \wedge X' = \Sigma_I \setminus D(state) \wedge$$
$$state' = state \wedge wait' \wedge any' = any) \vee$$
$$(tr < tr' \wedge \mathrm{ignore} \wedge \mathrm{errors} \wedge \mathrm{undef})\big)\Big)$$

$$\mathrm{ignore} \;\widehat{=}\; (\mathrm{last}(tr') = (x, y) \wedge x \in I(state)) \Rightarrow$$
$$(state' = state \wedge y = - \wedge \neg wait' \wedge any' = any)$$

$$\mathrm{errors} \;\widehat{=}\; (\mathrm{last}(tr') = (x, y) \wedge x \in E(state)) \Rightarrow$$
$$((y = \mathtt{error} \wedge \neg wait' \wedge any' = any); \mathtt{TERM})$$

$$\mathrm{undef} \;\widehat{=}\; (\mathrm{last}(tr') = (x, y) \wedge x \in U(state)) \Rightarrow$$
$$\big(y \in \Sigma_O \setminus \{-, \mathtt{error}\} \wedge (\neg wait' \wedge any'); \mathtt{ANY}\big)$$

$$\mathbf{F}(M) \;\widehat{=}\; \mathbf{F2} \circ \mathbf{F1} \circ \mathbf{F0}$$

Healthiness condition **F0** introduces the acceptance map acc as a constant to be used in a UTP representation of a valid FSM. The third conjunct just asserts the consistency condition for these maps specified in Eq. (3), with $\mathbf{out}_M(state, x)$ defined in Eq. (1). Recall that $D(s), I(s), E(s), U(s), A(s)$ are just abbreviations for expressions involving acc, as specified in Eq. (4). These are used in **F1** and in the process specifications below.

Healthiness condition **F1** states that the *any* variable which is set as soon as an FSM engages in an input leading to undefined behaviour can never be unset. This is needed for specifying universal quasi-equivalence and reduction in UTP.

Healthiness condition **F3** specifies all the behavioural boundary conditions to be fulfilled by any well-defined extended FSM, as introduced in Sect. 2.4.

1. Condition $D(state) = \Sigma_I$ identifies the situations where all inputs are disabled in the current FSM state. This leads to immediate termination.
2. All other sub-conditions in **F1** refer to situations where enabled inputs exist. This is specified in the else-branch of the if-construct. The healthiness assertions for these situations are structured into two cases.
   (a) As long as no interaction is offered by the environment (condition $tr' = tr$), an FSM must accept all inputs that are not disabled in the current state; this is expressed by $X' = \Sigma_I \setminus D(state)$. The FSM remains stable in the current state ($state' = state$), and $wait'$ is set to indicate that no progress is possible without an input from the environment. Note that this behaviour is similar to that required for ACP processes (healthiness condition **ACP1** [13, Chapter 8]): whenever some inputs are enabled, the FSM *must* process an input/output pair before being allowed to terminate.
   (b) When an interaction occurs, this is identified by condition $tr < tr'$. Any FSM must handle ignored inputs, erroneous inputs and undefined inputs in the same way. This is expressed by predicates 'ignore', 'errors', 'undef'.
3. Predicate 'ignore' states that inputs to be ignored must always produce the "–" output and keep the FSM in the current state.
4. Predicate 'errors' states that erroneous inputs always lead to the "error" output, followed by termination.
5. Predicate 'undef' states that undefined inputs can be associated with arbitrary outputs but $-, \mathtt{error}$. Then the any' flag is set, and the subsequent behaviour that of an arbitrary FSM, as captured by the UTP process ANY described below.

It is easy to see that $\mathbf{F0}, \mathbf{F1}, \mathbf{F2}$ and thus $\mathbf{F}$ are idempotent.

The process ANY to be defined next is used to indicate that any behaviour—including ignored events, error indications with subsequent termination, "ordinary" termination, or infinite execution of any input/output sequence—is acceptable. To define ANY, we use the definition

$$\mathrm{Part}_4(\Sigma_I) = \{(A, I, E, D) \in \mathbb{P}(\Sigma_I)^4 \mid A \cup I \cup E \cup D = \Sigma_I, \mathrm{disjoint}(A, I, E, D)\}$$

to denote the set of all partitions of Σ_I consisting of four partition elements: all $(A, I, E, D) \in \mathrm{Part}_4(\Sigma_I)$ are pairwise disjoint, and their union covers Σ_I. Since

Σ_I is finite, $\mathrm{Part}_4(\Sigma_I)$ is finite as well, so we can assume an indexed ordering

$$\mathrm{Part}_4(\Sigma_I) = \{(A_1, I_1, E_1, D_1), \ldots, (A_k, I_k, E_k, D_k)\}.$$

The set of partitions induce a set of states

$$S_{\mathrm{any}} = \{1, \ldots, k\}.$$

Moreover, $\mathrm{Part}_4(\Sigma_I)$ induces a well-defined acceptance function

$$acc_{\mathrm{any}} : S_{\mathrm{any}} \times \Sigma_I \longrightarrow \{\mathtt{A}, \mathtt{I}, \mathtt{E}, \mathtt{U}, \mathtt{D}\}; \quad acc_{\mathrm{any}}(i, x) = \begin{cases} \mathtt{A} \text{ iff } x \in A_i \\ \mathtt{I} \text{ iff } x \in I_i \\ \mathtt{E} \text{ iff } x \in E_i \\ \mathtt{D} \text{ iff } x \in D_i \end{cases}$$

With this notation, $\mathtt{ANY}$ can be specified as shown in Listing 2. Process $\mathtt{ANY}$ nondeterministically selects a state in range $1, \ldots, k$ and assigns it to variable *state*. This identifies partition $(A(state), I(state), E(state), D(state)) \in \mathrm{Part}_4(\Sigma_I)$. Then $\mathtt{ANY}$ allows for the most liberal behaviour for this partition element that is consistent with the new FSM interpretation. By applying the healthiness condition **F** to the disjunction in line 6, the special cases covering disabled, ignored, error and undefined inputs are handled. Otherwise, an arbitrary accepted input is associated with any output in line 6, and the next recursion is processed.

Similar to the proof that the sequential composition of two ACP processes again satisfies the ACP healthiness condition [13, p. 200] it is shown that the sequential composition of two processes P_i, $i = 1, 2$ satisfying $P_i = \mathbf{F}(P_i)$ again satisfies $(P_1; P_2) = \mathbf{F}(P_1; P_2)$. This allows to conclude that $\mathtt{ANY}$ fulfils

$$\mathtt{ANY} = (\neg wait' \wedge any' \wedge acc' = acc_{\mathrm{any}}); \mathbf{F} \circ \mathbf{R3}\Big(\mu(\mathtt{ANY}_0) \bullet J(\mathtt{ANY}_0)\Big),$$

so it fulfils the healthiness conditions required for valid FSM representations in UTP. Note that **R1** and **R2** are not referenced anywhere since they are trivially fulfilled.

Listing 2. $\mathtt{ANY}$ process.

```
1  ANY ≙ (¬wait' ∧ any' ∧ acc' = acc_any); R3(μ(ANY₀) • J(ANY₀))

2  --
3  ANY₀ ≙ J(ANY₀)
4  --
5  J(ANY₀) ≙ ((⊓ᵏᵢ₌₁(state := i));
6              F(⊓_{a∈A(state),b∈Σ_O\{−,error}}(tr' = tr ⌢ ⟨(a,b)⟩ ∧ ¬wait'))); ANY₀
```

Listing 3. UTP representation of extended FSM specification.

```
1  --
2  -- UTP specification of an FSM M = (S, s₀, R, Σ_I, Σ_O, acc)
3  --
4  M ≙ (state' = s₀ ∧ ¬wait' ∧ ¬any' ∧ acc' = acc);
5      R3(μ(M_{s₀}, ..., M_{s_n}) • F_{s₀}(M_{s₀}, ..., M_{s_n}))
6      -- start in initial state s₀
7  --
8  -- FSM state specifications as recursive functions over
9  -- higher-order state variables M_s
10 --
11 M_s ≙ F_s(M_{s₀}, ..., M_{s_n}) -- for s = s₀, ..., s_n
12 --
13 -- Mutual recursion functions: F_s(M_{s₀}, ..., M_{s_n})
14 --
15 F_s(M_{s₀}, ..., M_{s_n}) ≙ F( ⊓_{(a,b,u)∈{(x,y,z) | x∈A(s)∧(s,x,y,z)∈R}}
16                            ((tr' = tr ⌢ ⟨(a,b)⟩ ∧ state' = u ∧ ¬wait' ∧ ¬any')); M_{state}
```

The generic representation of any FSM $M = (S, s_0, R, \Sigma_I, \Sigma_O, \underline{acc})$ in UTP is given by a mutually recursive predicate equations as follows. The states $S = \{s_0, \ldots, s_n\}$, the initial state s_0, the transition relation R, and the acceptance map acc specified in Eq. (2) are considered as generic parameters of any FSM representation in UTP. With these parameters, any FSM can be specified as shown in Listing 3.

1. The FSM M is represented as the least fixed point of function F_{s_0} specified by a system of mutually recursive process equations over second-order variables $M_{s_0}, \ldots, M_{s_n}$ (line 4).
2. Every FSM state s and the state's behaviour is encoded by a recursive UTP process denoted by higher-order variable M_s (line 11).
3. The recursion function F_s specifying the behaviour in state M_2 (line 15,16) processes a disjunction over all accepted inputs $x \in A(s)$ according to the transition relation R and sets the post-state accordingly.
4. By applying healthiness condition **F** to this disjunction, the cases where no enabled inputs exist, as well as ignored, erroneous, and undefined inputs are handled.
5. After that, if the process has not terminated due to disabled inputs, the next recursion M_{state} in the post-state reached is processed.

Again, the argument that the sequential composition of processes satisfying the healthiness condition **F** again fulfils **F** is used to show that M indeed satisfies **F** ∘ **R3**.

M_1

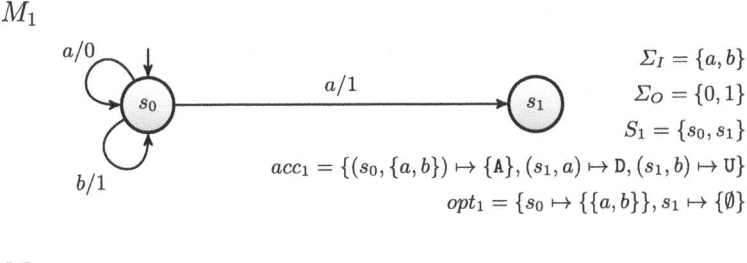

$$\Sigma_I = \{a, b\}$$
$$\Sigma_O = \{0, 1\}$$
$$S_1 = \{s_0, s_1\}$$
$$acc_1 = \{(s_0, \{a, b\}) \mapsto \{A\}, (s_1, a) \mapsto D, (s_1, b) \mapsto U\}$$
$$opt_1 = \{s_0 \mapsto \{\{a, b\}\}, s_1 \mapsto \{\emptyset\}$$

M_2

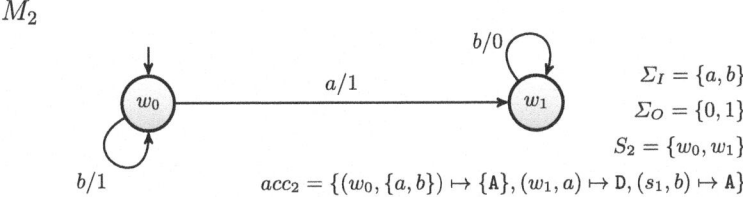

$$\Sigma_I = \{a, b\}$$
$$\Sigma_O = \{0, 1\}$$
$$S_2 = \{w_0, w_1\}$$
$$acc_2 = \{(w_0, \{a, b\}) \mapsto \{A\}, (w_1, a) \mapsto D, (s_1, b) \mapsto A\}$$

Fig. 2. FSMs M_1, M_2 discussed in Example 2.

Example 2. Consider the two FSMs M_1, M_2 depicted in Fig. 2 with their acceptance maps and an option map for M_1. Their UTP representation as systems of mutually recursive equations are shown in Listing 4. In this representation, the healthiness condition **F** has been resolved according to the specific transition relations and acceptance maps of these machines. □

3.2 Universal Quasi-Equivalence and Universal Reduction in UTP

As described by Hoare and Jifeng [13], the most elegant way to describe conformance between UTP processes P (reference model) and Q (refining model) is by showing that Q implies P for all variable valuations (notation $[Q \Rightarrow P]$), possibly after hiding some symbols x of the alphabet without relevance using existential quantification (notation $[(\exists x \bullet Q) \Rightarrow (\exists x \bullet P)]$). Indeed, it has been shown that this works very well for the refinement notions of CSP and similar process algebras [13]. Also in our case of FSMs, it is fairly easy to see that $[(\exists x \bullet M_2) \Rightarrow (\exists x \bullet M_1)]$ implies conventional reduction **RED0**, when hiding a tuple x of all alphabet symbols but tr, tr'.

For universal quasi-equivalence **EQU** and universal reduction **REDU**, however, the situation is slightly more complex: (1) Universal quasi-equivalence is not symmetric, so it cannot be simply expressed by $[(\exists x \bullet M_2) \Rightarrow (\exists x \bullet M_1)]$ and $[(\exists x \bullet M_1) \Rightarrow (\exists x \bullet M_2)]$ for some suitable x. (2) Universal reduction needs to fully preserve ignored events and failure events. Moreover, the sets of disabled events may only grow, while the sets of accepted events in certain states may grow by inputs left unspecified in the reference model and be reduced at the same time with respect to the events accepted in the reference model. Thus there is no simple subset relation between accepted inputs of the implementation and those of the reference model.

Listing 4. UTP representations of FSM M_1 and M_2 from Figure 2.

```
 1  --
 2  -- Specification of M₁
 3  --
```

4 $M_1 \mathrel{\hat=} (state' = s_0 \land \neg wait' \land \neg any' \land acc' = acc_1);$

5 $\qquad \mathbf{R3}\big(\mu(M_{1,s_0}, M_{1,s_1}) \bullet F_{1,s_0}(M_{1,s_0}, M_{1,s_1})\big)$

```
 6  --
```

7 $M_{1,s_0} \mathrel{\hat=} F_{1,s_0}(M_{1,s_0}, M_{1,s_1})$

8 $M_{1,s_1} \mathrel{\hat=} F_{1,s_1}(M_{1,s_0}, M_{1,s_1})$

```
 9  --
```

10 $F_{1,s_0}(M_{1,s_0}, M_{1,s_1}) \mathrel{\hat=} \big(X' = \{a,b\} \land state' = state \land wait' \land any' = any\big) \lhd tr' = tr \rhd$

11 $\qquad\qquad \Big(\big((tr' = tr \frown \langle (a,0) \rangle \land state' = s_0 \land \neg wait' \land \neg any'); \ M_{1,s_0}\big)$

12 $\qquad\qquad \sqcap \big((tr' = tr \frown \langle (b,1) \rangle \land state' = s_0 \land \neg wait' \land \neg any'); \ M_{1,s_0}\big)$

13 $\qquad\qquad \sqcap \big((tr' = tr \frown \langle (a,1) \rangle \land state' = s_1 \land \neg wait' \land \neg any'); \ M_{1,s_1}\big)\Big)$

```
14  --
```

15 $F_{1,s_1}(M_{1,s_0}, M_{1,s_1}) \mathrel{\hat=} \big(X' = \{b\} \land state' = state \land wait' \land any' = any\big) \lhd tr' = tr \rhd$

16 $\qquad\qquad \big(\sqcap_{y \in \{0,1\}}(tr' = tr \frown \langle (b,y) \rangle \land \neg wait' \land any'); \ \mathbf{ANY}\big)$

```
17  --
18  -- Specification of M₂
19  --
```

20 $M_2 \mathrel{\hat=} (state' = w_0 \land \neg wait' \land \neg any' \land acc' = acc_2);$

21 $\qquad \mathbf{R3}\big(\mu(M_{2,w_0}, M_{2,w_1}) \bullet F_{2,w_0}(M_{2,w_0}, M_{2,w_1})\big)$

```
22  --
```

23 $M_{2,w_0} \mathrel{\hat=} F_{2,w_0}(M_{2,w_0}, M_{2,w_1})$

24 $M_{2,w_1} \mathrel{\hat=} F_{2,w_1}(M_{2,w_0}, M_{2,w_1})$

```
25  --
```

26 $F_{2,w_0}(M_{2,w_0}, M_{2,w_1}) \mathrel{\hat=} \big(X' = \{a,b\} \land state' = state \land wait' \land any' = any\big)$

27 $\qquad\qquad \lhd tr' = tr \rhd$

28 $\qquad\qquad \Big(\big((tr' = tr \frown \langle (b,1) \rangle \land state' = w_0 \land \neg wait' \land \neg any'); \ M_{2,w_0}\big)$

29 $\qquad\qquad \sqcap \big((tr' = tr \frown \langle (a,1) \rangle \land state' = w_1 \land \neg wait' \land \neg any'); \ M_{2,w_1}\big)\Big)$

```
30  --
```

31 $F_{2,w_1}(M_{2,w_0}, M_{2,w_1}) \mathrel{\hat=} \big(X' = \{b\} \land state' = state \land wait' \land any' = any\big) \lhd tr' = tr \rhd$

32 $\qquad\qquad \big((tr' = tr \frown \langle (b,0) \rangle \land state' = w_1 \land \neg wait' \land \neg any'); \ M_{2,w_1}\big)$

Fortunately, UTP offers a more general way to specify conformance, using *specifications Spec* instead of the proper reference process and proving $[Q \Rightarrow Spec]$ instead of $[Q \Rightarrow P]$. Of course, *Spec* will refer to the behaviour of the reference model P, but it may contain additional constraints that can be exploited in our case to express the subtleties of **EQU** and **REDU**.

Listing 5. UTP specification for universal quasi-equivalence.

```
1  --
2  -- Universal quasi-equivalence specification is parameterised by
3  -- reference model M₁ = (S₁, s₁,₀, R₁, Σ_I, Σ_O, acc₁) and option map opt₁
4  --
```

$$5 \quad \text{Equ}(M_1) \triangleq \Big(\exists X, X', wait, wait', state, state', any_1, any_1', acc_1, acc_1' \bullet$$

$$6 \qquad\qquad \big(M_1[any_1, any_1', acc_1, acc_1' / any, any', acc, acc'] \wedge \text{EquSpec} \big) \Big)$$

```
7  --
```

$$8 \quad \text{EquSpec} \triangleq (any \Rightarrow any_1) \wedge$$

$$9 \qquad\qquad \Big(\neg any_1 \Rightarrow \big(I(tr) = I_1(tr) \wedge E(tr) = E_1(tr) \wedge D(tr) = D_1(tr) \wedge$$

$$10 \qquad\qquad\qquad (\exists C \subseteq U_1(tr) \bullet A(tr) = A_1(tr) \cup C \wedge$$

$$11 \qquad\qquad\qquad (\forall x \in A_1(tr) \bullet \mathbf{out}(tr, x) = \mathbf{out}_1(tr, x)) \wedge$$

$$12 \qquad\qquad\qquad U(tr) = U_1(tr \setminus C)) \big) \Big)$$

The specification $\text{Equ}(M_1)$ of universal quasi-equivalence is shown in Listing 5. It hides all alphabet symbols but $tr, tr', acc, acc', any, any'$ and consists of the conjunction of the reference FSM M_1 and an extra constraint EquSpec. In M_1, symbols any, any', acc, acc' are renamed by attaching an index 1. This allows to relate the current valuations of these symbols any, any', acc, acc' in the implementation, say, M_2, to the corresponding symbols in the reference FSM. This is done in the conjunct EquSpec.

Constraint EquSpec requires that an implementation may show unspecified behaviour (this is expressed by $any = \mathbf{true}$) only if the reference FSM has entered the ANY process as well (expressed by $any_1 = \mathbf{true}$). Moreover, as long as we are on a trace tr that is still specified by M_1, the conditions of Definition 1 must be fulfilled. Note that I_1, E_1, U_1, D_1 are abbreviations for expressions over the reference model's acceptance map acc_1, as defined in Eq. (4). The symbol $\mathbf{out}_1(tr, x)$ originally defined in Eq. (1), refers to M_1's transition relation R_1, it can be re-written as $\mathbf{out}_1(tr, x) = \{y \mid \exists u \in S_1 \bullet (s_{1,0}\text{-}\underline{\mathbf{after}}\text{-}tr, x, y, u) \in R_1\}$.

It is easy to see that specification $\text{Equ}(M_1)$ encodes the definition of **EQU**, so that the following theorem holds.

Theorem 6. *If*

$$[(\exists X, X', wait, wait', state, state' \bullet M_2) \Rightarrow \text{Equ}(M_1)]$$

then M_2, when interpreted as an FSM, is universally quasi-equivalent to M_1 in the sense of Definition 1. □

The UTP specification $\text{Redu}(M_1, opt_1))$ for universal reduction **REDU** with respect to some option map opt_1 is shown in Listing 6.

Listing 6. UTP specification for universal reduction.

```
1  --
2  -- Universal reduction specification is parameterised by
3  -- reference model M₁ = (S₁, s₁,₀, R₁, Σᵢ, Σₒ, acc₁) and option map opt₁
4  --
```

$$5 \quad \text{Redu}(M_1, opt_1) \mathrel{\widehat{=}} \Big(\exists X, X', wait, wait', state, state', any_1, any_1', acc_1, acc_1' \bullet$$

$$6 \qquad\qquad\qquad \big(M_1[any_1, any_1', acc_1, acc_1'/any, any', acc, acc'] \wedge \text{ReduSpec} \big) \Big)$$

```
7  --
```

$$8 \quad \text{ReduSpec} \mathrel{\widehat{=}} (any \Rightarrow any_1) \wedge$$

$$9 \qquad \Big(\neg any_1 \Rightarrow \big(I(tr) = I_1(tr) \wedge E(tr) = E_1(tr) \wedge$$

$$10 \qquad\qquad (\exists B \in opt_1(tr); C \subseteq U_1(tr) \bullet A(tr) = B \cup C \wedge$$

$$11 \qquad\qquad\qquad (\forall x \in B \bullet \mathbf{out}(tr, x) \subseteq \mathbf{out}_1(tr, x)) \wedge$$

$$12 \qquad\qquad\qquad D(tr) = D_1(tr) \cup (A_1(tr) \setminus B) \wedge$$

$$13 \qquad\qquad\qquad U(tr) = U_1(tr) \setminus C) \big) \Big)$$

It is specified in analogy to $\text{Equ}(M_1)$, and an analogous theorem states that $\text{Redu}(M_1, opt_1)$ encodes universal reduction.

Theorem 7. *If*

$$[(\exists X, X', wait, wait', state, state' \bullet M_2) \Rightarrow \text{Redu}(M_1, opt_1)]$$

then M_2, when interpreted as an FSM, is a universal reduction of M_1 with respect to opt_1 in the sense of Definition 2. □

Example 3. Consider again M_1 and M_2, as shown in Fig. 2 and Listing 4. We wish to show that M_2 is a universal reduction of M_1 with respect to opt_1 defined in Fig. 2. To show that

$$[(\exists X, X', wait, wait', state, state' \bullet M_2) \Rightarrow \text{Redu}(M_1, opt_1))]$$

holds with $\text{Redu}(M_1, opt_1)$ as specified in Listing 6, we proceed as follows. First we observe that *any* never becomes **true** in M_2. Therefore, the first conjunct in constraint **ReduSpec** (line 8 in Listing 6) is always **true**. Next, the sets $I(tr), E(tr)$ in M_2 are always empty, since outputs $-$, **error** are never produced. Analogously, $M_1[any_1, any_1', acc_1, acc_1'/any, any', acc, acc']$ has only empty sets $I_1(tr), E_1(tr)$.

Next, using neutral second order identifiers W, Z,

$$F_{2, w_0}(W, Z) \Rightarrow F_{1, s_0}(W, Z)$$

holds when hiding all symbols of the alphabet but tr and tr'. This is easy to see since $F_{2,w_0}(W, Z)$ consists of two of the three disjuncts used in $F_{1,s_0}(W, Z)$ (lines 11–13 in Listing 4). Moreover,

$$F_{1,s_0}(W, Z) \Rightarrow A_1(tr) = \{a, b\} \wedge D_1(tr) = \varnothing \wedge U_1(tr) = \varnothing$$

and

$$F_{2,w_0}(W, Z) \Rightarrow A(tr) = \{a, b\} \in opt_1(tr) \wedge D(tr) = \varnothing \wedge U(tr) = \varnothing.$$

This shows the validity of `ReduSpec` when M_1 and M_2 are simultaneously in states $F_{1,s_0}(W, Z)$ and $F_{2,w_0}(W, Z)$, respectively. With input/output event $(b, 1)$ both M_1 and M_2 return to $F_{1,s_0}(W, Z)$ and $F_{2,w_0}(W, Z)$, respectively, so `ReduSpec` holds forever on traces repeating $(b, 1)$.

For input/output event $(a, 1)$ the M_1 transits to $F_{1,s_1}(X, Y)$ and M_2 to $F_{2,w_1}(X, Y)$. Here

$$F_{2,w_1}(X, Y) \Rightarrow F_{1,s_1}(X, Y)$$

holds when hiding the irrelevant symbols, because $F_{1,s_1}(X, Y)$ can produce all outputs for input b and $F_{2,w_1}(X, Y)$ only output 0 and $F_{2,w_1}(X, Y) \Rightarrow$ `ANY`.

When entering $F_{1,s_1}(X, Y)$ and $F_{2,w_1}(X, Y)$, respectively, both states have input a disabled, so $D(tr) = D_1(tr)$ and $A_1(tr) = \varnothing$. Thus `ReduSpec` holds. From the next b-input on, any_1 is set to `false`, so there is nothing further to show for `ReduSpec`. This completes our proof sketch to show that M_2 is a universal reduction of M_1 with respect to opt_1.

It is easy to see that M_2 is not universally quasi-equivalent to M_1, since after the initialisations in lines 4 and 19 of Listing 4, the trace tr is empty, $\neg any_1$ holds and $\mathbf{out}_1(\langle\ \rangle, a) = \{0, 1\}$, but $\mathbf{out}(\langle\ \rangle, a) = \{1\}$, as can be derived from the definition of F_{2,w_0} in lines 25–27. This violates constraint `EquSpec` of the specification in Listing 5.   □

4   Conclusion

In this chapter, an analysis of the most popular conformance notions for finite state machines has resulted in two new proposals for unified (quasi-)equivalence and reduction relations. A UTP theory of finite state machines with universal reduction as the core means to compare machine behaviour has been presented. The merits of the UTP encoding in comparison to more conventional representations and proofs about finite state machines have been discussed.

For future work, we intend to elaborate mechanised conformance proofs for finite state machines and universal reduction represented in UTP, using the proof support for UTP in Isabelle/HOL, as provided by Foster, Woodcock, and further authors [7].

References

1. Abrial, J.: The B-Book - Assigning Programs to Meanings. Cambridge University Press, Cambridge (1996). https://doi.org/10.1017/CBO9780511624162
2. Bailey, L., Woodcock, J., Foster, S., Metere, R.: Checking and automating confidentiality theory in Isabelle/UTP. CoRR abs/2310.10658 (2023). https://doi.org/10.48550/arXiv.2310.10658
3. Bergenthal, M., Krafczyk, N., Peleska, J., Sachtleben, R.: libfsmtest - an open source library for FSM-based testing. In: Clark, D., Menéndez, H.D., Cavalli, A.R. (eds.) ICTSS 2021. LNCS, vol. 13045, pp. 3–19. Springer, Cham (2021). https://doi.org/10.1007/978-3-031-04673-5_1
4. van der Bijl, M., Rensink, A., Tretmans, J.: Compositional testing with ioco. In: Petrenko, A., Ulrich, A. (eds.) FATES 2003. LNCS, vol. 2931, pp. 86–100. Springer, Heidelberg (2004). https://doi.org/10.1007/978-3-540-24617-6_7
5. Chow, T.S.: Testing software design modeled by finite-state machines. IEEE Trans. Softw. Eng. **SE-4**(3), 178–186 (1978)
6. Foster, S., Baxter, J., Cavalcanti, A., Miyazawa, A., Woodcock, J.: Automating verification of state machines with reactive designs and Isabelle/UTP. In: Bae, K., Ölveczky, P.C. (eds.) FACS 2018. LNCS, vol. 11222, pp. 137–155. Springer, Cham (2018). https://doi.org/10.1007/978-3-030-02146-7_7
7. Foster, S., Baxter, J., Cavalcanti, A., Woodcock, J., Zeyda, F.: Unifying semantic foundations for automated verification tools in Isabelle/UTP. Sci. Comput. Program. **197**, 102510 (2020). https://doi.org/10.1016/j.scico.2020.102510
8. Foster, S., Thiele, B., Cavalcanti, A., Woodcock, J.: Towards a UTP semantics for Modelica. In: Bowen, J.P., Zhu, H. (eds.) UTP 2016. LNCS, vol. 10134, pp. 44–64. Springer, Cham (2017). https://doi.org/10.1007/978-3-319-52228-9_3
9. Hauer, F., Schmidt, T., Holzmüller, B., Pretschner, A.: Did we test all scenarios for automated and autonomous driving systems? In: 2019 IEEE Intelligent Transportation Systems Conference, ITSC 2019, Auckland, New Zealand, 27–30 October 2019, pp. 2950–2955. IEEE (2019). https://doi.org/10.1109/ITSC.2019.8917326
10. Hierons, R.M.: Testing from partial finite state machines without harmonised traces. IEEE Trans. Software Eng. **43**(11), 1033–1043 (2017). https://doi.org/10.1109/TSE.2017.2652457
11. Hierons, R.M.: FSM quasi-equivalence testing via reduction and observing absences. Sci. Comput. Program. **177**, 1–18 (2019). https://doi.org/10.1016/j.scico.2019.03.004
12. Hoare, C.A.R.: Communicating Sequential Processes. Prentice-Hall Inc., Upper Saddle River (1985)
13. Hoare, C., Jifeng, H.: Unifying Theories of Programming. Prentice-Hall, Hoboken (1998)
14. Huang, W., Krafczyk, N., Peleska, J.: Exhaustive property oriented model-based testing with symbolic finite state machines. Sci. Comput. Program. **231**, 103005 (2024). https://doi.org/10.1016/J.SCICO.2023.103005
15. Huang, W., Peleska, J.: Complete model-based equivalence class testing. Softw. Tools Technol. Transf. **18**(3), 265–283 (2016). https://doi.org/10.1007/s10009-014-0356-8
16. Huang, W., Peleska, J.: Complete model-based equivalence class testing for nondeterministic systems. Formal Aspects Comput. **29**(2), 335–364 (2017). https://doi.org/10.1007/s00165-016-0402-2

17. Huang, W., Sachtleben, R.: Conformance relations between input/output languages. In: Haxthausen, A.E., Huang, W., Roggenbach, M. (eds.) Applicable Formal Methods for Safe Industrial Products. LNCS, vol. 14165, pp. 49–67. Springer, Cham (2023). https://doi.org/10.1007/978-3-031-40132-9_4
18. Jones, C.B.: Systematic Software Development Using V.D.M. Prentice-Hall International Series in Computer Science (1986)
19. Luo, G., von Bochmann, G., Petrenko, A.: Test selection based on communicating nondeterministic finite-state machines using a generalized WP-method. IEEE Trans. Software Eng. **20**(2), 149–162 (1994). http://doi.ieeecomputersociety.org/10.1109/32.265636
20. Milner, R.: Communication and Concurrency. Prentice-Hall Inc., Hoboken (1989)
21. Object Management Group: OMG Unified Modeling Language (OMG UML), version 2.5.1. Technical report, OMG (2017)
22. Peleska, J.: New distribution paradigms for railway interlocking. In: Margaria, T., Steffen, B. (eds.) ISoLA 2020. LNCS, vol. 12478, pp. 434–448. Springer, Cham (2020). https://doi.org/10.1007/978-3-030-61467-6_28
23. Peleska, J., Huang, W., Cavalcanti, A.: Finite complete suites for CSP refinement testing. Sci. Comput. Program. **179**, 1 – 23 (2019). http://www.sciencedirect.com/science/article/pii/S0167642319300620
24. Petrenko, A.: Checking Experiments With Protocol Machines. Protocol Test Systems, IV, Proceedings of the IFIP TC6/WG6.1 Fourth International Workshop on Protocol Test Systems, Leidschendam, The Netherlands, 15–17 October 1991 (1991)
25. Petrenko, A.: Checking experiments for symbolic input/output finite state machines. In: Ninth IEEE International Conference on Software Testing, Verification and Validation Workshops, ICST Workshops 2016, Chicago, IL, USA, 11–15 April 2016, pp. 229–237. IEEE Computer Society (2016). https://doi.org/10.1109/ICSTW.2016.9
26. Petrenko, A., Yevtushenko, N.: Conformance tests as checking experiments for partial nondeterministic FSM. In: Grieskamp, W., Weise, C. (eds.) FATES 2005. LNCS, vol. 3997, pp. 118–133. Springer, Heidelberg (2006). https://doi.org/10.1007/11759744_9
27. Roscoe, A.W.: Understanding Concurrent Systems. Springer, London (2010). https://doi.org/10.1007/978-1-84882-258-0
28. Sachtleben, R.: Conformance relations between input/output languages. Archive of Formal Proofs (2023). https://www.isa-afp.org/entries/IO_Language_Conformance.html
29. Sachtleben, R., Peleska, J.: Effective grey-box testing with partial FSM models. Softw. Test. Verification Reliab. **32**(2) (2022). https://doi.org/10.1002/stvr.1806
30. Tanenbaum, A.S., Bos, H.: Modern Operating Systems, 4th edn. Prentice Hall Press, Hoboken (2014)
31. Vasilevskii, M.P.: Failure diagnosis of automata. Kibernetika (Transl.) **4**, 98–108 (1973)
32. Woodcock, J., Cavalcanti, A., Foster, S., Oliveira, M., Sampaio, A., Zeyda, F.: UTP, circus, and Isabelle. In: Bowen, J.P., Li, Q., Xu, Q. (eds.) Theories of Programming and Formal Methods. LNCS, vol. 14080, pp. 19–51. Springer, Cham (2023). https://doi.org/10.1007/978-3-031-40436-8_2
33. Woodcock, J., Foster, S.: UTP by example: designs. In: Bowen, J.P., Liu, Z., Zhang, Z. (eds.) SETSS 2016. LNCS, vol. 10215, pp. 16–50. Springer, Cham (2017). https://doi.org/10.1007/978-3-319-56841-6_2

Abstracting and Verifying Decentralised Systems in CSP

A. W. Roscoe[1,2,3]([⊠]) [iD], Pedro Antonino[1] [iD], and Jonathan Lawrence[1] [iD]

[1] The Blockhouse Technology Ltd., Oxford, UK
awroscoe@gmail.com, {pedro,jonathan}@tbtl.com
[2] Department of Computer Science, University of Oxford, Oxford, UK
[3] University College Oxford Blockchain Research Centre, Oxford, UK

Abstract. Interest in decentralised systems such as blockchains and network computers has increased in the last few years, with increasing globalisation and distrust of centralised authorities. These systems typically comprise a loosely coupled population of both honest and malevolent (Byzantine) agents, communicating with each other using message passing. A significant issue in the design of decentralised systems is ensuring predictable (i.e. correct) behaviour despite malevolent agents being present. This paper uses CSP to formalise the programming of assemblies of distributed agents to operate as sequential state machines, or *consensus machines*, to achieve predictable outcomes. Such consensus machines may be live (guaranteed to complete, or *total*) or subject to deadlock (fail to complete, or *partial*), depending on the assumed proportion of malign agents in the assembly. An assembly of agents forming a consensus machine can be modelled in CSP in several alternative styles. This paper concentrates on how multiple consensus machines (whose agent sets may intersect) can mimic parallel threads communicating via single-writer shared variables, which may sometimes act as *signals*. Examples included are an application to a blockchain consensus protocol and a mutual exclusion algorithm. The effect of different communication assumptions on the implementation of shared variables is also analysed.

Keywords: Consensus · State machine · Blockchain · Process
algebra · Formal methods

Dedication:

To Jim Woodcock on his retirement. For 40 years, we have worked to make software engineering into a science and to make verification usable by software engineers. There is still more for us to do!

1 Introduction

Making decentralised entities reach a consensus is a well-known topic of research in the area of distributed computing. Many protocols have been devised to

© The Author(s), under exclusive license to Springer Nature Switzerland AG 2024
S. Foster and A. Sampaio (Eds.): *The Application of Formal Methods*, LNCS 14900, pp. 172–202, 2024.
https://doi.org/10.1007/978-3-031-67114-2_8

achieve this goal [8, 21, 22, 26]. Consensus is difficult to achieve if some agents are malicious. This type of agent is often termed *Byzantine* and protocols that can reach an agreement (i.e. a consensus) despite the participation of such agents are said to be *Byzantine-fault tolerant*.

This topic has been revived with the emergence of blockchains. A *blockchain* is a distributed system in which the agents (some of whom are Byzantine) have to agree on its transaction history [24]. These transactions represent actions taken by the system, which modify the system's state. For instance, a transaction can represent the transfer of some underlying currency from one participant in the blockchain to another. These transactions are aggregated into blocks which are then ordered to form a chain of blocks. Blockchains have gained a lot of popularity and are being used in many different domains [4, 6, 34].

This paper explores the concept of a *consensus machine* as a formalism to capture the complex nature of agreement-based systems precisely and clearly; our ultimate motivation is to use this formalism to capture the behaviour of blockchain systems. A consensus machine consists of a distributed set of agents that come together to agree on each (machine) step of the computation they implement. In a way, these distributed agents implement the behaviour of a sequential machine by synchronising, or nearly so, on each step that this sequential machine performs. In our model, consensus machines can also interact with one another via *signals*. A signal is implemented by a set of memory locations controlled by the components of a consensus machine. As with functions, consensus machines may be partial or total. A partial machine can deadlock arbitrarily, whereas a total one is live and will perform all the steps prescribed by the sequential machine it implements.

Using distributed agents to perform a sequential computation may seem odd, but this accounts for the fact that the execution of this computation may include malign agents. The motivation for this type of machine is the following scenario: we have a computation to be performed and a collective of agents, some malign and others benign, the latter being the ones we can trust to execute this computation. The question is, how can we rely on this collective (including its malevolent agents) to perform the computation correctly? Consensus machines are a computational model that aims at implementing Byzantine-fault-tolerant systems. We want to understand how to make decentralised systems predictable, and to build a methodology for programming them to behave like reliable sequential or parallel programs, despite the presence of malevolent agents. Specifically, we want methods to make some specified behaviour the emergent behaviour of a collection of decentralised agents including some malevolent actors.

In this paper, we use consensus machines to implement a *handover* protocol to support blockchain consensus by allowing multi-level consensus mechanisms. In this example, a safe and efficient (but partial) consensus mechanism that malevolent actors can sometimes choose to deadlock can be backed up by one that is live (and total) but less efficient. We analyse this handover example and how it is abstracted into CSP by relying on different communication assumptions. We present both a sequential and a distributed model for the handover protocol, as in [30]; however, the models here and those in that paper are significantly different due to the distinct communication assumptions they make. Even under very weak assumptions, this type of multi-level consensus will normally offer significant improvements in efficiency over a single(-level) live consensus protocol.

We explore the generality of the consensus machine concept by applying it to other contexts, specifically its application to mutual-exclusion algorithms. In such programs, multiple threads may be waiting to access a *critical section* and must coordinate so that at most one thread is in this section at a time. In this paper, we show how such shared-variable programs, in which each location is written by only one thread, have an implementation where each thread is a consensus machine and may include malevolent agents. Mutual exclusion algorithms such as Lamport's Bakery Algorithm and Szymanski's algorithm would be amenable to this technique, and we use the latter as an example.

2   Background

2.1   CSP

CSP (Communicating Sequential Processes) is a formalism used for reasoning about concurrent and distributed systems. These systems and their components are captured as *processes*. In this section, we provide a very brief summary of CSP with a focus on the language constructs we need to make the paper self-contained; see [15, 28, 29] for detailed introductions to CSP.

A CSP process can perform instantaneous events and it can also synchronise with its environment on them; this environment can comprise other processes or some notional external observer. Using these primitives one can model and analyse different patterns of interaction.

The main language constructs that we use in this paper are[1]:

- The processes STOP, and SKIP respectively do nothing, and terminate immediately with the signal ✓. RUN(A) and CHAOS(A) can each perform any sequence of events from A, but while RUN(A) always offers the environment every member of A, CHAOS(A) can non-deterministically choose to offer just those members of A it selects, including none at all.
- a -> P *prefixes* P with the single communication a which belongs to the set Σ of normal visible communications. Similarly [] x : A @ x -> P(x) (replicated external choice) offers a deterministic choice over A and then behaves accordingly.
- CSP has several *choice* operators. P [] Q and P |~| Q respectively offer the environment the first visible events of P and Q, and make an internal decision via τ actions whether to behave like P or Q.
- P \ X (hiding) behaves like P except that all actions in X become (internal and invisible) τs.

---

[1] We use exclusively the machine-readable ASCII version of CSP syntax (CSP_M), rather than the "blackboard" syntax and symbols often used in books and papers.

- P [[R]] (renaming) behaves like P except that whenever P performs an action a, the *renamed* process must perform some b that is related to a under the relation R. R is specified using the CSP_M mapping syntax.
- The CSP_M mapping syntax, [[from <- to | gen]] permits general renaming(s) of one or more events to others. Note the counterintuitive direction of the arrow. The optional generator(s) gen take the form v <- S (defining variable v that ranges over set S), which allows renaming of families of events. Mappings may be one-one (the usual case), many-one or one-many, enabling relational renamings.
- P [| A |] Q is a *parallel* operator under which P and Q act independently except that they have to agree (i.e. synchronise or handshake) on all communications in A. A number of other parallel operators can be defined in terms of this, including P ||| Q = P [|{}|] Q in which no synchronisation happens at all.
- P ; Q (sequential composition) behaves like P until is successfully terminates at which point Q takes over.

CSP has several styles of semantics that can be shown to be appropriately consistent with one another. In this paper, we are concerned with *behavioural* semantics, namely, the meaning, or semantics, of a CSP process is given by the externally visible communications it performs. The best known behavioural models of CSP are based on the following types of observation: *Traces* are sequences of visible communications a process can perform. *Failures* are combinations (s, X) of a finite trace s and a set of actions that the process can refuse in a *stable* state reachable on s. A state is stable if it cannot perform τ. *Divergences* are traces after which the process can perform an infinite uninterrupted sequence of τ actions, in other words diverge. The models are then:

- T in which a process is identified with its set of finite traces;
- F in which it is modelled by its (stable) failures and finite traces;
- FD in which it is modelled by its sets of failures and divergences, both extended by all extensions of divergences: it is *divergence strict*.

2.2   FDR

FDR [9,28,29,33] is a model checker that analyses refinement between finite-state processes defined in CSP. In this paper, we use its latest version: FDR4.[2]

CSP_M is the machine-readable version of CSP, extended with a functional programming language, and is the input language for FDR. It can be used to define complex network of process and data operations succinctly. CSP and FDR have been applied in many domains; a survey of important practical applications can be found in [2]. Perhaps the best-known application is the Security Protocol checker Casper [23] which, given an abstract representation of a cryptographic protocol and some security objectives for it, generates a CSP script which checks to see if the objectives are met. Similarly, compilers have been written from

---

[2] Available at https://cocotec.io/fdr/.

other notations to CSP such as Statecharts [13] and shared-variable programs (see Chaps. 18 and 19 of [29]); in a sense, these applications use CSP to formally capture the semantics of these source notations.

FDR verifies refinements of the form Spec [X= Impl, where Spec is a process representing a specification in one of the standard CSP models X, usually traces, stable failures or failures-divergences. Impl is a CSP representation of the system being verified. To check whether a process Impl satisfies a particular property, Spec is constructed to represent the most general process (in the relevant model) exhibiting the required property.

FDR supports several techniques for tackling the state explosion problem, including hierarchical compression and symmetry reduction [10]. The algorithms underpinning FDR are set out in [9,28,29,31].

3   Stochastic Reasoning

We use a probabilistic model to reason about the participation of malevolent (i.e. Byzantine) agents in a consensus machine. Broadly speaking, we use our model to estimate an upper bound on the number of malevolent agents in a group of agents drawn from a population with a fixed probability of an agent being malevolent. This estimation is probabilistic, namely, the probability of it not being an upper bound (i.e. of there being more malevolent agents than this bound) is chosen to be vanishingly small. This sort of reasoning is also used in the world of finance to deal with risk management: events that happen with a vanishingly small probability are deemed impossible.

In the world of finance and investment, people often talk about 5-σ events, 9-σ events and so on [7]. Here, σ represents the standard deviation of an assumed probability distribution, generally the normal distribution which, thanks to the central limit theorem, is closely approximated by any large collection of independent trials with identical probability, as the number of trials increases. These σ-values each have a precise numerical value that the process being modelled will approximate, provided that the central limit theorem has been applied correctly. See Fig. 1 and Table 1 that illustrate and tabulate these probabilities. There are two versions of each probability, namely, the more usual two-sided version, where the normal distribution takes a value sufficiently far away from the mean on either side – this is the version depicted in the aforementioned figure and table – and the one-sided version, exactly half of this, where we are only interested in the distribution being far away from the mean on one specified side. We will normally be interested in the latter because we are interested in the probability of sufficient things going wrong at once, and do not care if unexpectedly many of them go right.

Financial forecasters and risk assessors frequently mis-apply this style of reasoning [7] because they do not understand the concept of probabilistic independence. Anyone who tells you that a 16-σ event (or similar) has occurred in a financial market has simply misunderstood the underlying mathematics when calculating this chance. The main conclusion is that either the various events

Table 1. Examples of the probability of two-sided k-σ events.

k	prob	k	prob
1	$3.17e^{-1}$	6	$1.97e^{-09}$
2	$4.55e^{-2}$	7	$2.55e^{-12}$
3	$2.69e^{-3}$	8	$1.24e^{-15}$
4	$6.33e^{-05}$	9	$2.25e^{-19}$
5	$5.73e^{-07}$	10	$1.52e^{-23}$

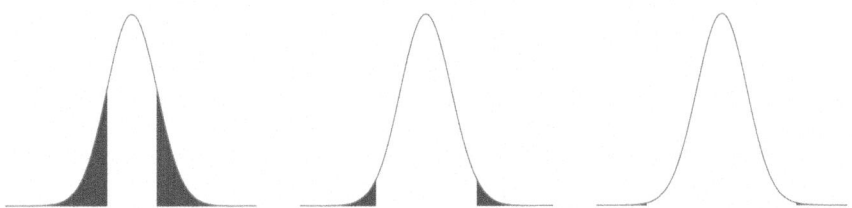

Fig. 1. The areas in red depict the probability for 1-σ, 2-σ and 3-σ events. While the area for 3-σ is barely visible, for 4-σ and onwards, it is not visible at all. (Color figure online)

must really be independent, or the calculations must correctly allow for any failure of independence.

3.1 Judging Impossibility

Suppose we have some system in which a sequence of trials $\langle T_1, \ldots, T_n \rangle$ are performed, where each T_i has a small probability δ_i of failing. In what circumstances is it reasonable simply to assume success because it is so likely that no trial will go wrong? In probabilistic terms, we are seeking to place an upper bound on the chance that any trial T_i fails. Such an upper bound is provided by adding up all the probabilities of failure in the trials that might occur in the sequences of trials up to length n, each under the assumption that all prior trials have succeeded. Let $s(j) = \prod_{i=1}^{j}(1 - \delta_i)$ where $j \geq 1$ and $s(0) = 1$, be the probability of all successes up to (and including) trial j, we can calculate the probability that a trial has failed for a sequence of up to n trials with the following sum.

$$\Delta(n) = \sum_{i=1}^{n} s(n-1) \cdot \delta_i \tag{1}$$

If we pick a value max for n that captures the maximum number of trials of the system's lifetime, we have analysed the probability of failure over this lifetime.

The sum of all δ_i from 1 to n is, therefore, a conservative estimate for $\Delta(n)$; note that $0 \leq s(n-1) \leq 1$. This approximation gets closer to $\Delta(n)$ as the δ_is get smaller; $s(n-1)$ will get closer and closer to 1.

$$\Delta(n) \leq \sum_{i=1}^{n} \delta_i \tag{2}$$

In the case where all the failures look very much the same, or when it is convenient to assume a uniform upper-bound value δ for them all, this just becomes δ multiplied by the maximum number of trials n we are considering.

$$\Delta(n) \leq n \cdot \delta \tag{3}$$

We contrast two scenarios for estimating max. In the first, (malevolent) agents can independently influence the number of trials the system undertakes; so their computational power bounds the number of trials they can perform within some fixed amount of time. In the second, the system regulates the trials it undertakes and agents can only engage on these regulated trials. In these two cases, there is a dichotomy in who regulates (malevolent agents vs system) the frequency of trials during the lifetime of the system. One example of the first case is the Proof-of-Work protocol in a blockchain like Bitcoin [24], whereas Proof-of-Stake protocols [1,17] work more like the second case.

In the first case, the number of possible trials may be huge. It follows that making each sufficiently unlikely to fail that we can disregard the chance of a system failure is a real challenge because we have to bound the activity of potentially evil agents. It would take very careful and conservative analysis to pick a believable max value.

In the second, self-limiting, case it should be relatively straightforward to find a max value that applies for any finite time interval. We will concentrate on that case, noting that in the case where the system is intended to last infinitely its analysis and conditioning could be split into long finite epochs. If we can manage the failure probability in each epoch, then the system designer could choose to make these decrease, so they had a small and finite total sum.

Once we have identified max for a given system lifetime, we can also choose a probability ϵ we allow for the system to fail during this time, but maybe 10^{-9} or 10^{-10}. Thus, we must *engineer the probability* of each individual trial failure δ to be no more than ϵ/max.

3.2   Stochastic Proof

An example property we consider relates to groups of agents that are chosen independently and at random from a single population P. Suppose that everyone agrees that when such a choice is made from P, the probability that each individual agent is malevolent – not committed to follow its expected behaviour – is no more than q. Suppose we get to choose the size N of the groups and a threshold $M < N$. To be precise, the group is the result of N independent choices, and might include repetitions. So the group is a multi-set of agents rather than a set.

Our property is that the group has no more than M malevolent members. This can be computed exactly – on the worst-case assumption that q is the

Table 2. We estimate values of M for examples of N and q and for a fixed δ of 10^{-11}. We use the normal distribution approximation and the 7σ probability (see Table 1) which approximates δ to calculate $M = \mu + 7\sigma$, where $\mu = Nq$ and $\sigma = \sqrt{Nq(1-q)}$.

q\N	25	50	100	200	400	800	1000	1200	1400
0.3	24	38	63	106	185	331	402	472	541
0.2	19	30	48	80	136	240	289	337	385
0.1	14	20	31	50	82	140	167	193	219

actual probability – using the binomial distribution with parameters N and q. And since we will pick N reasonably large, we know we can approximate this closely with the normal distribution with mean $\mu = Nq$ and standard deviation $\sigma = \sqrt{Nq(1-q)}$. It follows that we can choose combinations of N and M, relative to our assumptions about the population, to make this smaller than any chosen trial failure δ – this is what we meant above in talking about engineering a probability.

We can construct a table in which we can compute M – the maximum possible number of malevolent agents picked – as we vary N and q. Table 2 illustrates such a table. Thus, if a decentralised system for which (a) the probability of a malevolent agent being picked actually is q or less, and (b) the choices of the N agents are made independently at random, then the chances of more than M of them being malign is less than δ.

During the life of such a system – in the present paper we are interested in the agents selected to implement a consensus machine – the crucial events are the selection of these groups of agents. A single group V may have many jobs to do but, provided the fact that the number of malevolent agents in V is no more than M guarantees that no non-compliant decision is made, this group only contributes once to *max*.

We rely on the concept of a *stochastic proof* to establish the correctness of consensus machines, that is, in proving properties of our system, we can, and probably do, depend on none of the up to *max* misadventures happening. The sheer unlikelihood of this going wrong means we can actually be certain of the system's good behaviour.

More formally, when we have established that an event will almost surely never happen during the lifetime of a system, a stochastic proof of a property is a conventional proof that assumes that this very unlikely event never happens. The event itself is termed *stochastically impossible*. It is this style of stochastic proof that will explicitly underpin our approach to consensus machines.

In the following, we have chosen N and M in such a way that up to stochastic certainty, we can assume that none of the independently selected groups of N agents chosen have more than M malign members.

4   Consensus Machine

A consensus machine (CM) is implemented by a group of agents that performs some computation by consensus. Each transition of the machine is given by a tuple (S_1, X, S_2) where S_1 is the initial state, X are the inputs, and S_2 the final state. These steps are the product of the agreement between agents. All agents start on the same (shared) initial state S_1, and they have to come together and agree on the inputs X and final state S_2 representing the next step of the machine. This agreement is largely established by voting on what X and S_2 should be for the next step.

The group of agents in a machine is represented by a multi-set D where each agent has a weight denoting the number of votes it possesses in the agreement protocol. This multi-set could be obtained, for instance, by drawing agents independently and randomly from the same population with repetition – say N such agents. Broadly speaking, the agreement protocol tallies the votes of agents, and if they reach a pre-defined threshold T, the machine has come to a consensus on the next step to be taken. We call this set of votes meeting the appropriate threshold a *certificate* for the transition. This level of agreement has to be laid down in the rules and must be sufficiently strong that it is impossible for two contradictory state changes to occur at the same time.

The model we adopt is that all the good agents run identical programs, except for knowledge of their own identity, and that communications between benign agents eventually succeed. We assume that all agents know all the identities in the group. The total number of votes in D is N, and we assume that M or fewer of them belong to malevolent agents. Malevolent agents can deviate from the agreed protocol but not completely arbitrarily. Specifically, they cannot break cryptographic primitives. The benign agents are expected to create cryptographic signatures for the votes they cast. Thus, malevolent agents cannot impersonate the votes of the benevolent agents because they cannot break this primitive. Malevolent agents can, however, cast votes for two different machine transitions for the same step. We also assume that they can collude: they can covertly talk between themselves without revealing these messages to benign agents. The same does not hold for benign agents.

The level of agreement for the agents in this machine must tolerate the misbehaviour of malevolent agents, i.e., it must prevent the machine from agreeing on two distinct transitions even if they deviate from the agreement protocol by, say, voting on two distinct transitions at the same time. A machine is safe if it prevents this sort of behaviour. To illustrate this property, let us say, we have 3 agents, each one with a vote, and $M = 1$ is malevolent, a threshold of $T = 2$ would not be enough. One benign agent could vote for transition (S_1, X, S_2) whereas the other could vote for (S_1, X', S_2'), and the malevolent could vote for both transitions; creating two contradicting certificates. A threshold of $T = 3$ instead would accommodate this sort of misbehaviour. In general, a threshold guaranteeing that more than half of the benign votes in D participate in the agreement would prevent malevolent actors from creating inconsistent certificates.

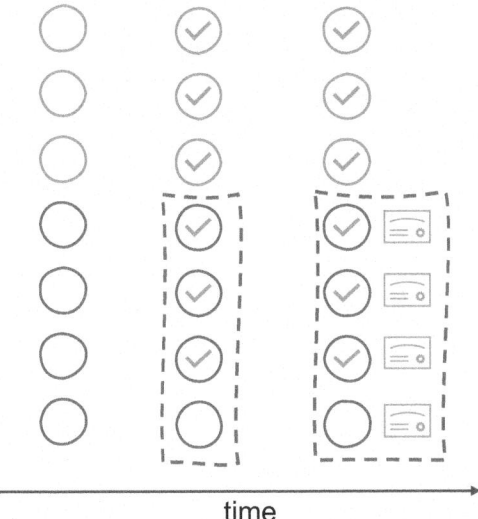

time

Fig. 2. Example of how a certificate can be created covertly. The circles represent the agents in the system: green are benign and red are malevolent. The green ticks represent participation on the agreement, and the little green certificate icons the creation of agreement certificates. The dotted red rectangles denote covert communication among the malign agents. The output of benign agents are visible to all. (Color figure online)

The existing certificates for the machine form a chain which extends a step at a time as agreements are reached; in fact they represent the history of the consensus machine. Each agent in D should keep a record of the certificates it has seen, and it must have transitioned between states as prescribed by this history.

As T members of D must be aware that the machine has reached S_i before they can move to the next state, there is some level of synchrony between agents as the machine's execution progresses. If we demand that a large majority agreement is needed for decisions – something that most situations will require – the agents in D will progress in near synchrony. If an agent becomes aware of a certificate for a transition to a state beyond its one, it can jump forward.

A certificate can be created covertly. This would happen, for instance, if a malign agent uses its own vote (and maybe that of other malign agents) to reach T without divulging its (their) vote. So no one else might ever know it – or the malevolent creator could release it whenever it wants to – for example, to try to confuse any step of the machine. The agreement protocol should prevent this sort of confusion. Figure 2 illustrates the covert creation of a certificate.

There is a real difference between consensus machines where the agreement threshold is greater than the minimum number of benign agents (i.e. $T < N - M$ where $N - M$ gives the minimum number of benign agents), and those where it is less than or equal to this: $T \geq N - M$.

In the first case, the malevolent agents (if the maximum assumed number are present) can certainly indefinitely delay progress, and also can keep a certificate covert for as long as they like or for ever. That is because at least one malevolent agent needs to participate in the agreement, and they can just refuse to do so – or can do so in such a way that only malevolent agents can create a certificate. We call such a consensus machine *partial*, after the common term partial correctness where progress cannot be forced.

In the second case, the benign agents have the numbers to come to an agreement but they must converge to a common value to do so, and that depends on how deterministic they are. Assume we can ensure (a) that benign agents will only endorse a transition when they have sufficient information so as not to be affected by more data, (b) that they eventually converge (i.e. align their data) by some means and (c) are deterministic in their decisions (i.e. given the same information, they choose the same transition). So eventually all benign agents will converge to having the same (local) data which will trigger their (deterministic) decision (i.e. vote) on the same X and S_2 for the next step. Thus, as their numbers allow it $(T \geq N - M)$, a certificate ratifying this transition will be created and will be distributed amongst all agents who are willing to listen. For instance, under these strong determinism assumptions, and the (stochastic) certainty that less than half of the votes in D are malign, if we set the agreement threshold $T = N - M$, it guarantees that a certificate will be created. That is because we now know, by the strong determinism assumptions, that there can be no disagreement between benign agents. Moreover, we also know that though certificates might first appear in malevolent agents, they will eventually be created and seen by all benign agents given that benign agents alone have the number to create a certificate. The presence of fewer malign agents than the threshold prevents them from coming to a decision without the participation of benign nodes and, thus, violating the safety property we expect from consensus machines. Machines where benign agents will eventually reach an agreement without the participation of malevolent ones are termed *total*, because total correctness is the usual term for correctness including progress properties.

There is a really tight requirement for a consensus machine to make progress. We would expect that enough time is allowed for all of D to converge to having the same information from which to deduce and decide on X. There should be opportunities for the members of D to share information, either before or as part of the sharing of their transition choices $(S1, X, S2)$.

We propose two notions of agreement:

A. A threshold T that ensures the participation of at least one benign agent in an agreement provides a *weakly decisive* level of agreement.
B. A threshold T that ensures the participation of more than half of the benign agents in an agreement provides a *strongly decisive* agreement.

The weak form is sufficient in circumstances where two benign agents cannot give separate answers – for instance, in the strong determinism assumptions we describe above. However, to get a clear and unambiguous decision in general we need strongly decisive agreement or else the malevolent members could fabricate

Table 3. We estimate values of M for examples of N and q and for a fixed δ of 10^{-18}. We use the normal distribution approximation and the 8.8σ probability which approximates δ to calculate $M = \mu + 8.8\sigma$, where $\mu = Nq$ and $\sigma = \sqrt{Nq(1-q)}$. Note that $M + 1$ is the threshold for weakly decisive agreement, whereas the threshold for strongly decisive agreement is the average of this value and N. * means that no such M exists.

q\N	25	50	100	200	400	800	1000	1200	1400
0.3	*	44	71	118	201	355	428	500	571
0.2	23	35	56	90	151	260	312	362	412
0.1	16	24	37	58	93	155	184	212	239

certificates for two or more contradictory outcomes. For example, two different versions of the next machine transition might get endorsed. This argument will be familiar from Byzantine agreement.

There are many potential ways in which the multi-set of agents D can be crafted, we consider here the case where D is created by independently choosing N agents, with repetition, from a uniform pool of agents where the probability that a chosen agent be malign is q. We now have an opportunity to engineer probability as explained in Sect. 3: we can find (stochastic) upper bounds M for the number of malevolent agents in D and use it to set T for the desired level of agreement.

The strength of agreement required (i.e. T) will depend on M, which in turn depends on q, N, and the threshold δ for stochastic certainty. Table 3 illustrates some values for M when $\delta = 10^{-18}$ which is about 8.8σ. Note its great similarity to the tables and calculations of the preceding section.

The minimum number of participating agents required for weakly decisive agreement is equal to the maximum possible number of malign agents that could be present in the selected multi-set (within the bounds of stochastic certainty) *plus one*, that is, $T \geq M + 1$, (provided that $M < N$; otherwise the inequality cannot be satisfied).

The minimum number of agents needed for strongly decisive agreement is the same plus half of the (minimum) benign agents, i.e. $T \geq M + 1 + (N - M)/2$, where we use truncated division. These formulas and the values in Table 3 can be used to calculate example values for T for both forms of agreement. For instance, for $N = 200$ and $q = 0.3$, $T = 119$ provides weakly decisive agreement whereas $T = 160$ provides strongly decisive agreement. For $N = 1400$ and $q = 0.1$, we have $T = 240$ for weakly decisive versus $T = 820$ for strongly decisive agreement.

The larger N is, the more headroom for non-agreement or silence there is, but the more effort goes into successful agreement. The aim in any implementation is to get the balance right, which depends on issues such as reliability of agents and communication, and the expected game played by the enemy. Our expectation is that, in almost all cases, malign agents will in fact behave well, allowing large thresholds to be reached. Table 3 shows how much more efficient it can be to rely on large thresholds relative to N.

5   The Handover Protocol

In this section, we demonstrate a first application of consensus machines. The models presented in this section and in the next are available in our repository.[3] We present an example where two separate consensus machines interact to create a sophisticated consensus mechanism, supported by our stochastic reasoning. One machine is partial and efficient whereas the other is less efficient but total, and we rely on a *handover protocol* for the total machine to take over if the partial one deadlocks. Both machines run only for the duration of a single consensus decision process. Each decision requires the instantiation of a new pair of consensus machines.

Let us first examine the partial consensus machine *PM*, where P stands for primary in this protocol. For this machine:

1. The worst that can happen is that no agreement appears, because there are never enough malign agents involved to reach the threshold for a decision without the participation of benign agents.
2. So, if malign agents make improper decisions or decline to give any verdict, there will be no decision at all. *PM* will effectively deadlock.
3. This means we cannot depend on *PM* to make decisions, even when we need one.
4. If this is a crucial decision, then a back-up mechanism is required. We will call this secondary mechanism *SM*, which will often be a consensus machine with a larger set of agents.
5. The effectiveness of this back-up should discourage disruption to *PM*.

Anyone who has studied concurrency is familiar with the phenomenon of deadlock: a set of processes that, unable to agree on any action, can do nothing at all. We have designed the *PM* machine so that it will deadlock without giving a decision unless the agents concerned make a unique and safe decision.

Deadlock is nice and clean. Process algebras like *CSP* give us ways of reasoning about and overcoming deadlock. In terms of process algebra, we would like to combine the primary mechanism *PM*, which is safe but not live because it might behave like deadlock or *STOP*, with a secondary one *SM* that is both safe and live, in the sense that it will always deliver a decision. Ideally, this combination should be equivalent to *PM* when that is not *STOP*, and *SM* if it is.

SM might simply be a suitable form of Byzantine agreement based on a set of agents large enough, given the assumed communication model, to make it live. The intention with this protocol is not that *SM* should be used regularly, rather that its presence should deter the actions by lazy or malevolent agents in *PM* that would trigger it.

In more detail, the objective of the handover protocol is as follows:

1. We start with a safe and efficient primary consensus machine *PM* that is safe but need not be live, and a safe and live secondary consensus machine *SM* that need not be efficient.

---

[3] https://github.com/pedrotbtl/cmachines.

2. The two machines each run its own end of the protocol, and each implements a mechanism to send signals to the other.

3. *PM* starts and *SM* is delayed by its agents running a time-out designed to ensure that *PM* will normally decide by the time that this time-out fires. The time-out does not fire if, by the appointed time, *PM* has made a decision visible to all and signalled this to *SM*. We are assuming, however, that *PM* can deadlock at any time.

4. If *SM* starts it sends a signal to *PM* to stop, but because of the decentralised nature of *PM* and the presence of malign agents, this signal may be too late.

5. Once *SM* starts, it inevitably makes a decision.

6. Consequently, there is the possibility that both *PM* and *SM* announce decisions – a disastrous case would be if they announced different decisions.

7. The handover protocol prevents this by splitting *PM*'s decision announcement into a pre-decision and decision (which will be the same), and having *PM* send *SM* a signal announcing the former's (pre-)decision ω before the actual decision itself is made public.

8. The pre-decision is made as soon as *PM* can reach a valid decision. The pre-decision signal is made as part of the handover protocol.

9. *SM* checks for the signal from *PM* before calculating its own decision. If a signal is present, it simply copies ω. So although *PM* and *SM* may both announce decisions, they are the same.

Our underlying expectation for such a consensus protocol is that malign agents who are present in *PM* will almost certainly decide to behave well, that is, the system will decide on a value by running just the efficient *PM*. If malign agents in *PM* do not behave well, they can only postpone a decision. This delay could be punished with missing out on a financial reward for making *PM* come to a decision. This sort of incentive structure is very common in the domain for which this protocol has been designed to target: blockchains.

In the following, we present two CSP models for our handover protocol. The *sequential model* represents consensus machines *PM* and *SM* as their sequential abstractions. It captures the emergent combined behaviour of their respective distributed sets of agents. The *distributed model*, on the other hand, captures how the collective behaviour of each machine is realised by its set of agents. In other words, the sequential model describes the expected behaviour of the protocol whereas the distributed model illustrates one way of realising this.

5.1 Sequential Model

In the sequential model, *PM* and *SM* are each modelled as a sequential CSP process. Each machine has a location it writes to and these are also depicted by CSP processes. They communicate via these shared storage locations; each of them implement a one-way signal from one machine to the other.

The datatype `Decisions` denotes the possible decision values for our protocol. `storevalsP` and `storevalsS` denote the values that machines *PM* and

SM can, respectively, write to their own location. Note how *PM* can write pre-decision and decision values (i.e. `Predec.v` and `Decided.v`, respectively) whereas *SM* only signals whether it has started. The usage of channels will becomes apparent as we describe the behaviour of our CSP processes.

```
datatype Decisions = V1 | V2

datatype storevalsP = NullP | Predec.Decisions | Decided.Decisions
datatype storevalsS = NullS | Started

channel startreadP, startreadS, endwriteS, endwriteP, timeout
channel startwriteP,readP,readfixP:storevalsP
channel startwriteS,readS,readfixS:storevalsS
channel predecide, decide, decideS: Decisions
```

The storage location for the *PM* machine is defined by the following process. In this process, reads and writes have a start (i.e. denoted by events `startreadP` and `startwriteP.z`) and end (i.e. denoted by events `readP.z` and `endwriteP`) points. The read action has a (mid-)point in which the value to be read is fixed, denoted by event `readfixP.x`. This location does not allow two writes (or two reads) to happen concurrently, but a write and a read can. If the read is fixed then (represented by process `PSrw`), the value to be read can be either the previously written value or the value in the process of being written; this choice is non-deterministic. The `readfix` event is a convenient way of recording that when a read happens the returned value is any value written or overwritten during the period of the read. We term this the decentralised model of locations/variables.

```
PS(x) = startreadP -> PSr(x)
        [] startwriteP?z -> PSw(x,z)

PSr(x) = readfixP.x -> PSf(x,x)
         [] startwriteP?z -> PSrw(x,z)

PSw(x,z) = endwriteP  -> PS(z)
           [] startreadP  -> PSrw(x,z)

PSrw(x,z) = endwriteP -> PSr(z)
            []
            (readfixP.x -> PSwf(x,z,x) |~| readfixP.z -> PSwf(x,z,z))

PSf(x,z) = readP.z -> PS(x)
           [] startwriteP?y ->  PSwf(x,y,z)

PSwf(x,y,z) = readP.z -> PSw(x,y)
              [] endwriteP -> PSf(y,z)
```

The machine *SM* has a location that is defined by process `SS(x)` which behaves exactly like `PS(x)` except that it relies on channels `startreadS`, readfixS, readS, startwriteS and endwriteS, instead of the end-in-P channel counterparts.

The behaviour of the primary machine is given by PM. It first pre-decides on the value V1 (it writes the value to its location), then it probes whether machine *SM* has started. If so, it just deadlocks. If *SM* has not started, it moves on to decide on V1. PMren simply does a renaming of predecide.v and decide.v into their startwriteP counterparts for the purpose of location synchronising.

```
PM = predecide.V1 -> endwrite1 -> startreadS -> readS?state ->
    if state == Started then STOP
    else decide.V1 -> endwrite2 -> STOP

PMren = PM[[predecide.v <- startwriteP.Predec.v,
    decide.v <- startwriteP.Decided.v | v <- Decisions]]
```

The PM process (and hence also the PMren process) always deadlock at the end of each run because the model considers only a single run of the handover protocol. Each distinct consensus decision requires new instances of *PM* and *SM*.

The behaviour of *SM* is given by the following process. Once a time-out is fired, it starts by reading whether *PM* has come to a decision already. If so, it deadlocks as a decision has already come out of *PM* and so it does not need to do anything. If not, it needs to come to a decision. It writes to its location that it has started, and then proceeds to check if *PM* has come to a pre-decision or decision in the meantime. If so, it will just reaffirm this decision. Otherwise, it will come to its own decision on value V2. Note that V1 represents the decision that has been initiated by *PM* (even if *SM* ultimately decides on it) whereas V2 represents a decision that *SM* has come to on its own.

```
SM = timeout -> startreadP ->
    (readP?_:{NullP,Predec.v | v <- Decisions}  ->
        startwriteS.Started -> endwriteS -> startreadP ->
        ((readP.NullP -> decideS.V2 -> STOP)
        []
        ([] v:Decisions @
            (readP.Predec.v -> decideS.v -> STOP
            [] readP.Decided.v -> decideS.v -> STOP))))
```

The behaviour of *PM* and *SM* is given by process CMS. Note that *PM*'s behaviour is put in parallel with CHAOS(Events) as a way to model its ability to deadlock – or fail to offer some of its events – at any moment. The Signals process model the signals of *PM* and *SM*, and System represents the parallel combination of machines and signals.

```
CMS = (PMren[|Events|]CHAOS(Events)) ||| SM

Signals = PS(NullP)||| SS(NullS)
```

```
System = CMS [|{|startwriteP,startwriteS, endwriteP, endwriteS,
    startreadP, startreadS, readP,readS|}|] Signals
```

We use FDR to check that the system is both *safe and live*. Safety means that only a single value is decided on – even if both machines come to a decision, they must be on the same value. We capture the safety requirement by the following assertion in the traces model. The `Safety` specification does not allow two diverging decisions to be made by *SM* and *PM*.

```
DV(v) = RUN({decideS.v, startwriteP.Decided.v})
```

```
ASf = {decideS.v,startwriteP.Decided.v | v <- Decisions}
```

```
Safety = CHAOS(Events) [| ASf |] (DV(V1) [] DV(V2))
```

```
assert Safety [T= System
```

Liveness means that the system must not deadlock before a decision is made. This is captured by the following assertion in the stable-failures model. The specification `DFU(ASf)` can behave arbitrarily but it cannot deadlock before a decision event is performed. After that, it can behave completely arbitrarily.

```
DFU(X) = |~| x:Events @ x ->
    (if member(x,X) then CHAOS(Events) else DFU(X))
```

```
assert DFU(ASf) [F= System
```

5.2   Distributed Model

In order to illustrate how the sequential model can be realised in practice, we create a *distributed model* where each machine is captured by its collection of underlying agents. These agents, then, try to implement their respective roles in the protocol in the presence of Byzantine actors.

Our distributed model is parameterised by the following variables. `PN` (`SN`) denotes the number of agents in machine *PM* (*SM*), and `PNS = {0..PN-1}` (`SNS = {0..SN-1}`) gives the "identities" of the agents. `PG` (`SG`) denotes the number of benign agents in *PM* (*SM*), and `PT` (`ST`) the threshold denoting the number of agent decisions that form a machine decision for *PM* (*SM*). Our analysis is based on the weak communication assumption that we only depend on delivery of messages for liveness, and then only depend on message between benign agents eventually getting through.

The datatype `Decisions` denotes the possible decision by the machine, and `Vals` denotes the values that can be written/signalled by the agents of machine *PM*. The channel `set_predec` is used by *PM* agents to write their (local) pre-decision to their location, whereas `predec` is used by *SM* agents to read the locations of *PM* agents. Similarly, The channel `set_started` is used by *SM* agents to write whether they have started to their location, whereas started is used by *PM* agents to read the locations of *SM* agents. Channels dec_p and dec_s are used by agents from *PM* and *SM*, respectively, to signal their (local) decision. Finally, the channel timeout is used by *SM* agents to capture the firing of a time-out that triggers the start of their behaviour.

```
datatype Decisions = V1 | V2
datatype Vals = Null | Dec.{V1}

channel set_predec : GS.Vals
channel predec : GS.HS.Vals

channel dec_p : GS.Decisions
channel dec_s : HS.Decisions

channel timeout : HS

channel set_started : HS
channel started : GS.HS.Bool
```

The pre-decision locations for agents in *PM* is given by the following process. Each agent g in *PM* controls such a location and it is the only one allowed to write to it. The Null value can be read from this location until the controlling agent writes to it – the agents can only write once to it. Once a value is written, that is the value that will be read subsequently.

```
Predec(g) = set_predec.g?v -> RUN({predec.g.h.v | h <- SNS})
            []
            predec.g?h!Null -> Predec(g)
```

The behaviour of agent g in *PM* is given by the following process. If it does not agree with the machine's pre-decision, it writes Null to its location and stops. If it does agree, it communicates this pre-agreement, by writing Dec.V1 to its location. Then, it goes on to implement its end of the handover protocol. It checks for an appropriate number of non-started agents in *SM*, and then it decides on V1. This check is implemented by process CheckStarted which relies on parameter STT to determine how many non-starting agents in *SM* must be seen before the agent decides. We later discuss how this parameter affects safety and liveness. Note that this check ensures that STT agents in *SM* must see the pre-decision of agent g if it decides.

```
P(g) = set_predec.g.Dec.V1 -> CheckStarted(g,{}); RUN({dec_p.g.V1})
       []
       set_predec.g.Null -> STOP
```

```
CheckStarted(g,NS) =
    started.g?h:diff(SNS,NS)!false ->
        CheckStarted(g,union(NS,{h}))
    []
    started.g?h!true -> CheckStarted(g,NS)
    []
    card(NS) > STT & SKIP
```

The behaviour of agent g of *PM* together with its location is given by the following process. It differentiates between benign and malign agents. A benign agent is given by the expected parallel composition of P and its location Predec whereas a malign agent is given by a chaotic process that can pre-decide and decide on any value, and it can also deadlock.

```
PP(g) =
    if g < PG then
        P(g) [|{|set_predec|}|] Predec(g)
    else
        CHAOS({|predec.g,dec_p.g|})

AlphaPP(g) = {|predec.g,dec_p.g,started.g,set_predec.g|}
```

Agents in *SM* rely on locations to signal whether they have started or not. The location signals that agent h in *SM* has not started until it signals to the location that it has with event set_started.h.

```
    Start(h) = set_started.h -> Started(h)
               []
               started?g!h.false -> Start(h)

    Started(h) = started?g!h.true -> Started(h)
```

Agent h in *SM* is described by the following process. Once the time-out fires, it communicates to its location that it has started. It then checks for enough pre-decisions from agents in *PM* or enough null values. If it reads more than NDT null values, it decides on V2 – this many null values should be a proof that *PM* cannot come to a decision on V1. If it receives more than PDT pre-decisions on V1, it means that it is safe for the agent to decide on V1 – the agent has enough information to believe that *PM* has come to a decision on V1. Note that we have simplified this model with respect to the sequential one by not requiring agents to check for a decision from *SM* before starting. We elaborate on the values for NDT and PDT later.

```
S(h) = timeout.h -> set_started.h -> CheckPredec(h, {}, {})

CheckPredec(h,AS,NS) =
    let US = union(AS,NS) within
```

```
predec?g:diff(PNS,US)!h.Null ->
    CheckPredec(h,AS,union(NS,{g}))
[]
predec?g:diff(PNS,US)!h.Dec.V1 ->
    CheckPredec(h,union(AS,{g}),NS)
[]
card(NS) > NDT & RUN({dec_s.h.V2})
[]
card(AS) > PDT & RUN({dec_s.h.V1})
```

The behaviour of an *SM* agent and its location is given by the following process. Once more, we differentiate between benign and malign agents, with the former being captured by the expected parallel combination of agent plus location, and the latter being captured by a chaotic process that can decide on any value, lie about having started, and even deadlock.

```
SS(h) =
    if h < SG then
        S(h) [|{|set_started|}|] Start(h)
    else
        CHAOS(union({|dec_s.h|},{|started.g.h | g <- PNS |}))

AlphaSS(h) = union({|timeout.h, dec_s.h, set_started.h|},
    {| predec.g.h, started.g.h | g <- PNS |})
```

The system involving the two consensus machines is given by SYSTEM where PPS encompasses the agents and locations of *PM* and SSS those of *SM*. We could also represent the system as a collection of agents and a collection of locations that are ultimately assembled in the same way as for the sequential model. We have decided to combine an agents with its controlled location early in our composition to make use of compression techniques [32]. In this case, compression can be applied to each PP and SS processes.

```
PPS = || g : PNS @ [AlphaPP(g)] PP(g)

SSS = || h : SNS @ [AlphaSS(h)] SS(h)

SYSTEM = PPS [|{|predec,started|}|] SSS
```

Our system does not explicitly represent machine decisions. It only accounts for local decisions made by the agents. The machine decision is a combination of these local decisions. We use the following *watchdog* processes [12] to keep track of the local decisions being made by agents in each machine and emit a machine decision event once enough local agent decisions are seen; we use decision_p to denote that a decision has been made by *PM* and decision_s for *SM*. Decider_p is the watchdog for *PM* and Decider_s is that for *SM*. The system combined with the two watchdog processes is given by process DEC_SYSTEM.

```
channel decision_p
channel decision_s : Decisions

Decider_p(DS) =
    if card(DS) < PT then
        dec_p?g:diff(PNS,DS)!V1 -> Decider_p(union(DS,{g}))
    else
        decision_p -> STOP

Decider_s(V1S,V2S) =
    let US = union(V1S,V2S) within
        if card(V1S) >= ST then
            decision_s.V1 -> STOP
        else if card(V2S) >= ST then
            decision_s.V2 -> STOP
        else
            dec_s?h:diff(SNS,US)!V1 ->
                Decider_s(union(V1S,{h}),V2S)
            []
            dec_s?h:diff(SNS,US)!V2 ->
                Decider_s(V1S, union(V2S,{h}))

DEC_SYSTEM = SYSTEM [|{|dec_p,dec_s|}|]
                (Decider_p({}) ||| Decider_s({},{}))
```

Our safety specification is given as follows. Either *PM* and *SM* both decide on V1, or *SM* decides alone on V2. Our specification assumes that *PM* can only decide on V1 for the sake of simplicity. The proof obligation for our safety property is captured by the assertion below.

```
SAFE = decision_p -> decision_s.V1 -> STOP
    []
      decision_s.V2 -> STOP
      []
      decision_s.V1 -> decision_p -> STOP

assert SAFE [T= DEC_SYSTEM \ diff(Events,{|decision_p, decision_s|})
```

With regard to liveness, we specify that the system must not deadlock before a decision is made, captured by process LIVE. Moreover, for the sake of liveness, we must also assume convergence, namely, that the agents at some point agree on a value to be decided upon. In our model, we only need to require convergence for the agents in *PM*. This convergence is enforced by process CONVERGENCE. We capture our liveness requirement with the assertion below.

```
LIVE =
    |~| ev : Events @ ev ->
```

```
        if member(ev,{|decision_s, decision_p|}) then CHAOS(Events)
        else LIVE

CONVERGENCE =
    RUN({set_predec.g.Dec.V1 | g <- {0..PG-1}})
    |~|
    RUN({set_predec.g.Null | g <- {0..PG-1}})

assert LIVE [F= DEC_SYSTEM [|{|set_predec|}|] CONVERGENCE
```

We check both of these assertions in FDR for some instances of our system. We now turn to the discussion on how to set the parameters of our model so that both safety and liveness properties are achieved. For PT and ST, we ensure that these values encompass more than half of benign agents for the respective machines. For instance, we can have the following definitions, where X/2 is integer division (i.e. returns the quotient of the division). These values would prevent a machine from deciding on two values given that, for that, a benign agent would have to decide on two values at the same time – a contradiction. Any value above these would do too. For liveness, we also need ST <= SG, namely, the benign agents in *SM* must be able to come to a decision without the influence of malign agents.

```
PT = PG/2 + PN - PG + 1
ST = SG/2 + SN - SG + 1
```

For STT, we want to choose a value that prevents *SM* from coming to a decision without being aware of *PM*'s potential decision. That is, we want to choose a value so that any agent deciding on *PM* must have communicated a pre-decision to enough of *SM* agents so that they cannot form a decision. So, requiring STT >= 2*SN - ST - SG is what is necessary for preventing *SM* to come to a decision, but for the sake of liveness, we make STT = SN - 1, namely, we require all agents in *SM* to be aware of *PM* agents pre-decisions. If we require fewer than that, agents in *SM* can be blocked by not seeing enough pre-decision or null values.

For PDT and NDT, the pre-decision and null-value thresholds, we require the following values. The NDT+1-many null values represent a proof that a V1 decision cannot have been created by the agents in *PM*; hence *SM* can decide on V2. Similarly, PDT+1-many V1 values are a proof that a "null" decision could not have been made by *PM*; hence *SM* decide on V1. For the sake of liveness, we must ensure that PDT and NDT are both less than PG so that the benign agents alone in *PM* can make the system progress.

```
PDT = 2*PN - PG - PT
NDT = 2*PN - PG - PT
```

We should point out that the proportion of malign agents in *PM* is typically higher than that of *SM*. This is a consequence of the "level of liveness" of these two machines. While *PM* must be able to handover control to *SM*, *SM* must be able to come to a decision. Broadly speaking, the former requires fewer benign agents than the latter. While *PM* needs more than half of the agents to be benign for that purpose, *SM* requires more than 2/3 to reach a decision. If we use our stochastic reasoning to find the number of agents that we need to draw to create the group of agents implement *PM* and *SM*, we see that *PM* requires a much smaller set of agents in comparison to *SM*; see, for example, Tables 2 and 3 and which Ns are required for 1/2 vs 2/3 proportion of benign agents. That is the main motivation for proposing this protocol. This observation together with incentive structures that will encourage malign agents to act benevolently is the reason why this protocol should be fairly efficient in practice, namely, *PM* (and its fewer agents) should frequently decide on behalf of the entire system. If circumstances allowed us to make stronger communication assumptions about the implementation of the signals, we could choose a significantly smaller *PM* size.

6 Szymanski's Algorithm

Szymanski's algorithm [35] is a mutual exclusion protocol: threads go on to access the critical section in a non-overlapping way. In our model, each thread is a consensus machine. In this section, we only describe sequential CSP models for these machines.

The protocol is modelled on a waiting room with two doors: one leading into it and another one to leave it on the way to the critical section. Each thread controls a variable (i.e. location) that it alone writes to, but that other threads can read from. This variable denotes the state of the thread controlling it – the variable can assume 5 values: 0 means that the thread is outside of the critical section and has no interest to get in, 1 indicates the thread intends to enter the critical section, 2 means that the thread is waiting for other threads in the waiting room, 3 denotes that the thread has entered the waiting room, 4 means that the thread has left the waiting room to enter the critical section. We will explain how the threads coordinate on these values soon.

We use the variable NN to denote the number of threads in our CSP model. PNAMES gives the name of the threads, IVARNAMES the names of the locations (i.e. variables), and IVARVALUES gives the values that the variables can take. The channels writei1 and writei2 are used to start and end a write, respectively. The channels readi1, fix, readi2 are used to start, fix, and end a read, respectively. We use a decomposition of writing and reading similar to that used for the locations in the handover example.

```
THREADS = {1..NN}
datatype PNAMES = P.THREADS
datatype IVARNAMES = IV.THREADS
IVARVALUES = {0..4}
```

```
channel writei1: IVARNAMES.PNAMES.IVARVALUES
channel writei2: IVARNAMES.PNAMES
channel readi1: IVARNAMES.PNAMES
channel readi2: IVARNAMES.PNAMES.IVARVALUES
channel fix: IVARNAMES.IVARVALUES
channel css,cse:PNAMES
```

In this version of a location, its value relative to writes is either settled or not, hence these two states (i.e. Dvari and Dvariw). It has a most recent consensus on what a read of it will show. This consensus, in general, will have been formed after some reads started, and they can return this value, while ones started since need a new fix before they can deliver. So, three parameters are the before and after fix reads, and the most recent fix. There is only ever one read active per thread, and these are distinct from p, the writer. So, a new read can come from any member of the complement of the union of the writer and the current active readers.

```
Comp(p,B,A) = diff(PNAMES,Union({{p},A,B}))

Dvari(v,x,p,BFR,AFR,f) =
    writei1.v.p?y -> Dvariw(v,x,y,p,BFR,AFR,f)
    [] readi1.v?q:Comp(p,AFR,BFR) ->
        Dvari(v,x,p,union({q},BFR),AFR,f)
    [] fix.v.x -> Dvari(v,x,p,{},union(BFR,AFR),x)
    [] readi2.v?q:AFR!f -> Dvari(v,x,p,BFR,diff(AFR,{q}),f)

Dvariw(v,x,y,p,BFR,AFR,f) =
    writei2.v.p -> Dvari(v,y,p,BFR,AFR,f)
    [] readi1.v?q:Comp(p,AFR,BFR) ->
        Dvariw(v,x,y,p,union({q},BFR),AFR,f)
    [] fix.v.x -> Dvariw(v,x,y,p,{},union(BFR,AFR),x)
    [] fix.v.y -> Dvariw(v,y,y,p,{},union(BFR,AFR),y)
    [] readi2.v?q:AFR!f -> Dvariw(v,x,y,p,BFR,diff(AFR,{q}),f)
```

The location controlled by thread n is given by the following process.

```
Var(n) = Dvari(IV.n,0,P.n,{},{},0)\{|fix|}
```

It turns out to be crucial that if the more recent of two live values is fixed as the value of a read then no later fix can yield the earlier one.

The behaviour of thread n is given by process Szym(n). We explain briefly what each of its component processes do, and later we describe and explain their behaviour in detail. The thread initially communicates its intention to enter the critical section; the first WriteI. Then, it waits for all threads to be either outside of the critical section, to have expressed intent to enter the critical section, or to be waiting in the room; Await1. Then, it enters the waiting room; the second WriteI. If any other thread has indicated that they intend to enter the critical section, the thread goes on to wait in the (waiting) room, and it waits there until some other thread leaves the waiting room. If no thread has indicated that they intend to enter the critical section, the thread just moves forward; Cond. Then, it indicates that it is about to enter the critical section; the third WriteI. The thread, then, goes on to wait for all the threads with a lower identifier to finish their critical section operation; Await3. Then, the thread itself enters the critical section; CS. Before leaving the critical section, it waits for the threads with a greater identifier to be either outside of the critical section, to have expressed intent to enter the critical section, or to be about to enter the critical section; Await4. Finally, when this wait is over, it leaves the critical section; the last WriteI.

```
Szym(n) = WriteI(P.n,IV.n,1);
          Await1(n);
          WriteI(P.n,IV.n,3);
          Cond(n);
          WriteI(P.n,IV.n,4);
          Await3(n);
          CS(n);
          Await4(n);
          WriteI(P.n,IV.n,0);
          Szym(n)
```

Intuitively, if two processes are about to enter the critical section (in state 4), they will enter in order from lowest to highest identifier; thanks to Await3. This property ensures their mutually exclusive access to the critical section.

The thread p uses the following process to write x to its location v.

```
WriteI(p,v,x) = writei1.v.p.x -> writei2.v.p -> SKIP
```

The process Await1(i) scans the locations of all the threads looking for values outside of {0,1,2}. If it finds such a value, it scans the locations again. It stops the (re-)scanning when no such value is found.

```
scanvars(i) = <IV.j | j <- <1..NN>, j != i >

Await1(i) = Await1b(i,scanvars(i),{})
Await1b(i,<>,vals) =
    if diff(vals,{0,1,2})=={} then SKIP else Await1(i)
Await1b(i,<v>^vs,vals) = readi1.v.P.i ->
    readi2.v.P.i?x -> Await1b(i,vs,union({x},vals))
```

The process Cond(i) scans the thread locations looking for a value 1. If found, it writes 2 to its controlled location i and moves on to behave like Await2. If not, it terminates.

```
Cond(i) = Cond2(i,scanvars(i),{})
```

```
Cond2(i,<>,vals) = if member(1,vals) then
                      (WriteI(P.i,IV.i,2); Await2(i))
                   else SKIP
Cond2(i,<v>^vs,vals) = readi1.v.P.i ->
   readi2.v.P.i?x -> Cond2(i,vs,union({x},vals))
```

The process `Await2(i)` scans the thread locations looking for a value 4. If found, it terminates. Otherwise, it keeps re-scanning the location until a 4 is found.

```
Await2(i) = Await2b(i,scanvars(i),{})
Await2b(i,<>,vals) =
   if member(4,vals) then SKIP else Await2(i)
Await2b(i,<v>^vs,vals) = readi1.v.P.i ->
   readi2.v.P.i?x -> Await2b(i,vs,union({x},vals))
```

The process `Await3(i)` scans the locations for threads with a smaller identifier than i. If all of them have a value in {0,1}, it terminates. Otherwise, it keeps re-scanning these locations until that is the case.

```
ltvars(i) = <IV.j | j <- <1..i-1>>

Await3(i) = Await3b(i,ltvars(i),{})
Await3b(i,<>,vals) =
   if diff(vals,{0,1})=={} then SKIP else Await3(i)
Await3b(i,<v>^vs,vals) = readi1.v.P.i ->
   readi2.v.P.i?x -> Await3b(i,vs,union({x},vals))
```

The process `Await4(i)` scans the locations for threads with a greater identifier than *i*. If all of them have a value in {0,1,4}, it terminates. Otherwise, it keeps re-scanning these locations until that is the case.

```
gtvars(i) = <IV.j | j <- <i+1..NN>>

Await4(i) = Await4b(i,gtvars(i),{})
Await4b(i,<>,vals) =
   if diff(vals,{0,1,4})=={} then SKIP else Await4(i)
Await4b(i,<v>^vs,vals) = readi1.v.P.i ->
   readi2.v.P.i?x -> Await4b(i,vs,union({x},vals))
```

The process `CS(i)` depicts the critical-section access by thread i.

```
CS(i) = css.P.i -> cse.P.i -> SKIP
```

The threads, variables and system are modelled as follows.

```
Threads = ||| n:{1..NN} @ Szym(n)

Vars = ||| n:{1..NN} @ Var(n)

System = Threads [|{|writei1,writei2,
                    readi1,readi2|}|] Vars
```

For this consensus machine application, we look into another type of safety specification, that is, *mutual exclusion*. We require that no two threads reach their critical section at the same time. This specification is captured by MutexSpec and by the following assertion:

```
MutexSpec = css?x -> cse.x -> MutexSpec

assert MutexSpec [T= System \ diff(Events,{|css,cse|})
```

A traces refinement check performed by FDR (which succeeded) confirms the correctness of the above assertion; hence, the required mutual exclusion property is satisfied. Our model shows how the consensus machine approach, in which each machine behaves analogously to a separate parallel thread, can implement sophisticated concurrent algorithms such as mutual exclusion. This result gives confidence that the approach would apply to other concurrent algorithms with single-writer shared variables.

7 Related Work

Intuitively speaking, consensus machines are an application of the idea of *refinement* for distributed systems. Many languages and verification frameworks are based around the idea of having both a specification and an implementation/realisation of a system, and checking whether the latter *refines* (i.e. satisfies) the former [20,29]; some even advocate for a layered approach to the verification of concurrent programs [14,18]. We look at consensus machines as being specified by their sequential models and implemented/realised by the distributed counterparts. A peculiarity of consensus machines is that they are especially concerned with Byzantine behaviour and how to tolerate it. So, the distributed implementations for consensus machines explicitly take into account malevolence of the underlying agents and how to overcome that.

The Byzantine agreement problem [26] is a classical problem in computer science and many protocols have been designed to solve it under different assumptions [19,21,22,27]. This problem has received renewed interest recently with the advent of blockchains, leading to a number of new protocols that try to achieve consensus in distributed systems [1,3–5,11,17,24,36,37]. The main motivation for the creation of the handover protocol was to integrate it in a Proof-of-Stake style blockchain protocol. Broadly speaking, the role of a blockchain is to periodically and constantly extend its chain of blocks with new valid blocks. Our protocol was designed to be used every time that the blockchain has to choose the next block to be added to its chain. The blockchain agents are selected to implement *PM* and *SM* (and the handover protocol), and decide on the next block to be added.

The way in which the consensus machines interact is closer in nature to how concurrent programs interact in a shared-variable model [16]. Our handover protocol, for instance, is more similar in nature to mutual exclusion than Byzantine agreement protocols [19, 22, 25, 37]. The reason for that is the way in which we model these interactions via signals. In a way, these are like variables that are shared between the consensus machines – this similarity is very apparent in our sequential models. On the other hand, Byzantine agreement protocols are typically designed around the use of the votes to form decisions and of a threshold/quorum to ensure safety. Distributed models will often rely on this sort of protocol to implement the consensus machines themselves like we do here.

8 Conclusions

In [30], we presented a new approach to blockchain consensus and hence realised we needed to formalise how decentralised assemblies of agents make decisions. In the present paper, we have examined this latter topic in more detail and created improved ways of modelling these assemblies in CSP and verifying them with FDR. We have made an explicit distinction between partial and total consensus machines, noting that covert certificates are more of a problem for the former than the latter.

We have made a detailed study of how consensus machines communicate with each other via signals and single-writer shared variables – which are effectively the same thing. We have shown how these signals need to be constructed to reflect underlying assumptions about communications, and how to do this effectively even under weak assumptions.

These improvements have reinforced the effectiveness of the two-level consensus algorithm presented in [30], designed to benefit from occasions when malign agents behave well, but still prevent them from achieving bad (inconsistent) decisions or forking. Essential for this is the handover protocol that we have re-examined here.

The motivation for this two-level consensus, which easily extends to a multi-level one, is to overcome malevolent actors in decision-making. In future work, we hope to develop this to a more general approach to structuring consensus, for example, allowing more general data to be considered if no decision arises from a more restricted set. This would mean that consensus could proceed without agents having to agree on a complex data set.

We have implemented a standard distributed algorithm, namely Szymanski's mutual exclusion, to illustrate how consensus machines can reliably implement both sequential and parallel algorithms in a decentralised context with malevolent actors. We hope this is a useful contribution to software engineering in this context.

References

1. Bentov, I., Gabizon, A., Mizrahi, A.: Cryptocurrencies without proof of work. In: Clark, J., Meiklejohn, S., Ryan, P.Y., Wallach, D., Brenner, M., Rohloff, K. (eds.) Financial Cryptography and Data Security, pp. 142–157. Springer, Heidelberg (2016)
2. Brookes, S.D., Roscoe, A.W.: CSP: a practical process algebra. In: Theories of Programming: The Life and Works of Tony Hoare, 1 edn., pp. 187–222. Association for Computing Machinery, New York (2021). https://doi.org/10.1145/3477355.3477365
3. Buchman, E., Kwon, J., Milosevic, Z.: The latest gossip on BFT consensus. CoRR arXiv:1807.04938 (2018)
4. Buterin, V.: Ethereum: a next-generation smart contract and decentralized application platform (2014). https://ethereum.org/whitepaper/
5. Camenisch, J., Drijvers, M., Hanke, T., Pignolet, Y.A., Shoup, V., Williams, D.: Internet computer consensus. In: Proceedings of the 2022 ACM Symposium on Principles of Distributed Computing, pp. 81–91. PODC 2022. Association for Computing Machinery, New York (2022). https://doi.org/10.1145/3519270.3538430
6. Crosby, M., Pattanayak, P., Verma, S., Kalyanaraman, V., et al.: Blockchain technology: beyond bitcoin. Appl. Innov. **2**(6–10), 71 (2016)
7. Dowd, K., Cotter, J., Humphrey, C., Woods, M.: How unlucky is 25-sigma? J. Portfolio Manage. **34**, 76–80 (2008). https://doi.org/10.3905/jpm.2008.709984
8. Dwork, C., Lynch, N., Stockmeyer, L.: Consensus in the presence of partial synchrony. J. ACM (JACM) **35**(2), 288–323 (1988)
9. Gibson-Robinson, T., Armstrong, P., Boulgakov, A., Roscoe, A.W.: FDR3 — a modern refinement checker for CSP. In: Ábrahám, E., Havelund, K. (eds.) TACAS 2014. LNCS, vol. 8413, pp. 187–201. Springer, Heidelberg (2014). https://doi.org/10.1007/978-3-642-54862-8_13
10. Gibson-Robinson, T., Lowe, G.: Symmetry reduction in CSP model checking. Int. J. Softw. Tools Technol. Transfer **21**(5), 567–605 (2019)
11. Gilad, Y., Hemo, R., Micali, S., Vlachos, G., Zeldovich, N.: Algorand: scaling byzantine agreements for cryptocurrencies. In: Proceedings of the 26th Symposium on Operating Systems Principles, pp. 51–68. SOSP 2017. Association for Computing Machinery, New York (2017).https://doi.org/10.1145/3132747.3132757
12. Goldsmith, M., Moffat, N., Roscoe, B., Whitworth, T., Zakiuddin, I.: Watchdog transformations for property-oriented model-checking. In: FME, pp. 600–616 (2003)
13. Harel, D.: Statecharts: a visual formalism for complex systems. Sci. Comput. Program. **8**(3), 231–274 (1987)
14. Hawblitzel, C., Petrank, E., Qadeer, S., Tasiran, S.: Automated and modular refinement reasoning for concurrent programs. In: Kroening, D., Păsăreanu, C.S. (eds.) Computer Aided Verification, pp. 449–465. Springer, Cham (2015). https://doi.org/10.1007/978-3-319-21668-3_26
15. Hoare, C.A.R.: Communicating Sequential Processes. Prentice Hall (1985)
16. Hopkins, D., Roscoe, A.W.: SVA, a tool for analysing shared-variable programms. In: Proceedings of AVoCS 2007, pp. 177–183 (2007). http://web.comlab.ox.ac.uk/oucl/work/bill.roscoe/publications/119.pdf
17. Kiayias, A., Russell, A., David, B., Oliynykov, R.: Ouroboros: a provably secure proof-of-stake blockchain protocol. In: Katz, J., Shacham, H. (eds.) Advances in Cryptology - CRYPTO 2017, pp. 357–388. Springer, Cham (2017). https://doi.org/10.1007/978-3-319-63688-7_12

18. Kragl, B., Qadeer, S.: Layered concurrent programs. In: Chockler, H., Weissenbacher, G. (eds.) Computer Aided Verification, pp. 79–102. Springer, Cham (2018). https://doi.org/10.1007/978-3-319-96145-3_5

19. Lamport, L.: The part-time parliament. ACM Trans. Comput. Syst. **16**(2), 133–169 (1998). https://doi.org/10.1145/279227.279229

20. Lamport, L.: Specifying Systems: The TLA+ Language and Tools for Hardware and Software Engineers. Addison-Wesley Longman Publishing Co., Inc, USA (2002)

21. Lamport, L., Shostak, R., Pease, M.: The byzantine generals problem. ACM Trans. Program. Lang. Syst. **4**(3), 382–401 (1982). https://doi.org/10.1145/357172.357176

22. Liskov, B.H., Wing, J.M.: A behavioral notion of subtyping. ACM Trans. Program. Lang. Syst. **16**(6), 1811–1841 (1994). https://doi.org/10.1145/197320.197383

23. Lowe, G.: Casper: a compiler for the analysis of security protocols. J. Comput. Secur. **6**(1–2), 53–84 (1998)

24. Nakamoto, S., et al.: Bitcoin: A Peer-to-peer Electronic Cash System (2008)

25. Ongaro, D., Ousterhout, J.: In search of an understandable consensus algorithm. In: Proceedings of the 2014 USENIX Conference on USENIX Annual Technical Conference, pp. 305–320. USENIX ATC 2014, USENIX Association, USA (2014)

26. Pease, M., Shostak, R., Lamport, L.: Reaching agreement in the presence of faults. J. ACM **27**(2), 228–234 (1980). https://doi.org/10.1145/322186.322188

27. Rabin, M.O.: Randomized byzantine generals. In: 24th Annual Symposium on Foundations of Computer Science (sfcs 1983), pp. 403–409 (1983). https://doi.org/10.1109/SFCS.1983.48

28. Roscoe, A.W.: The Theory and Practice of Concurrency. Prentice Hall (1998)

29. Roscoe, A.W.: Understanding Concurrent Systems. Springer (2010). https://doi.org/10.1007/978-1-84882-258-0

30. Roscoe, A.W., Antonino, P., Lawrence, J.: The consensus machine: formalising consensus in the presence of malign agents. In: Bowen, J.P., Li, Q., Xu, Q. (eds.) Theories of Programming and Formal Methods. Lecture Notes in Computer Science, vol. 14080, pp. 136–162. Springer, Cham (2023). https://doi.org/10.1007/978-3-031-40436-8_6

31. Roscoe, A.W., Gardiner, P.H.B., Goldsmith, M.H., Hulance, J.R., Jackson, D.M., Scattergood, J.B.: Hierarchical compression for model-checking CSP or how to check 10^{20} dining philosophers for deadlock. In: Brinksma, E., Cleaveland, W.R., Larsen, K.G., Margaria, T., Steffen, B. (eds.) TACAS 1995. LNCS, vol. 1019, pp. 133–152. Springer, Heidelberg (1995). https://doi.org/10.1007/3-540-60630-0_7

32. Roscoe, A.W., Gardiner, P.H.B., Goldsmith, M., Hulance, J.R., Jackson, D.M., Scattergood, J.B.: Hierarchical compression for model-checking CSP or how to check 10^{20} dining philosophers for deadlock. In: TACAS, pp. 133–152 (1995)

33. Roscoe, A. W.: Model-checking CSP, chap. 21. Prentice Hall (1994). http://www.cs.ox.ac.uk/people/bill.roscoe/publications/50.ps

34. Swan, M.: Blockchain: Blueprint for a New Economy. O'Reilly Media, Inc. (2015)

35. Szymanski, B.K.: A simple solution to lamport's concurrent programming problem with linear wait. In: Proceedings of the 2nd International Conference on Supercomputing, pp. 621–626. ICS 1988. Association for Computing Machinery, New York (1988). https://doi.org/10.1145/55364.55425

36. Wood, G.: Ethereum Yellow Paper. https://ethereum.github.io/yellowpaper/paper.pdf
37. Yin, M., Malkhi, D., Reiter, M.K., Gueta, G.G., Abraham, I.: HotStuff: BFT consensus with linearity and responsiveness. In: Proceedings of the 2019 ACM Symposium on Principles of Distributed Computing, pp. 347–356. PODC 2019. Association for Computing Machinery, New York (2019). https://doi.org/10.1145/3293611.3331591

Towards an Algebra for Unifying Theories of Concurrent Programming (UTCP)

Andrew Butterfield$^{(\boxtimes)}$

Trinity College Dublin, Dublin, Ireland
`butrfeld@tcd.ie`

Abstract. Unifying Theories of Concurrent Programming (UTCP) is a denotational semantics of shared-variable concurrency, expressed using the notation and methodology of Unifying Theories of Programming (UTP). A key feature is that it is compositional, in that the semantics of a composite is described in terms of the semantics of its sub-components. The underlying language used is that which is used to define a Concurrent Kleene Algebra (CKA). This includes the notions of skip, atomic actions, iteration, and non-deterministic, sequential, and parallel composition. This chapter makes progress toward proving that UTCP satisfies the CKA laws. We describe the methodology used, and give proofs for key ideas, as well as proofs and proof-sketches for many of the laws. We also discuss open issues, the most notable being the precise nature of *miracle* in this setting. The chapter finishes with a roadmap of how we might encode well-established UTP concepts such as Designs and Reactive Systems on top of UTCP.

Keywords: Unifying Theories of Concurrent Programming ·
Concurrent Kleene Algebra · Denotational Semantics

1 Introduction

An Appreciation

My first academic encounter with Jim Woodcock was at FME'93 in Odense, when I presented my first Formal Methods paper [4]. I got actively involved with Formal Methods Europe at that point, and attended many of their meetings in subsequent years. I have happy memories of sitting in airport waiting lounges with him on our return journeys, discussing the merits, etc., of various formalisms. This led to a decision, at FM99 in Toulouse, that we would start an active collaboration. We started with the semantics of Handel-C [11,12] which led to many publications in this space. A key turning point was when I spent 6 months on sabbatical with him in 2003, in Kent. Here I was introduced to what has now become my research paradigm of choice: Unifying Theories of Programming (UTP) [17]. This led to work looking at ways to add time-slots [9] to the *Circus* language he worked on with Ana Cavalcanti [26]. Other joint work included: Flash Memory [7]; POSIX Grand Challenge Roadmap [16]; and Heterogenous Semantics [27]. He has always been a good friend and great

S. Foster and A. Sampaio (Eds.): *The Application of Formal Methods*, LNCS 14900, pp. 203–232, 2024.
https://doi.org/10.1007/978-3-031-67114-2_9

inspiration for me over the years. He even played a key role in the more recent direction of my research by pointing me to the Views paper by Dinsdale-Young et. al. [14], which inspired me to go on my current deep dive into shared-variable concurrency. Thank you Jim!

1.1   Introduction to UTCP

Unifying Theories of Concurrent Programming (UTCP) is a denotational semantics of shared-variable concurrency, expressed using the notation and methodology of Unifying Theories of Programming (UTP). This theory was developed out of prior research into lightweight languages for loosely describing business process flows that included non-deterministic choice as a feature [8,23]. A key point was the Views paper by Dinsdale-Young et. al. [14], that introduced the notion of a View as a particular Semigroup and/or Monoid, abstracting state and composition, that characterised generic concurrent behaviour. They demonstrated how a wide range of concurrency reasoning approaches could all be instantiated as Views. These approaches include: Owicki-Gries, Rely-Guarantee, Separation Logic, and various Type systems, among others. The most abstract/general view is based on the same shared-state concurrency language that was used by Hoare and colleagues when they defined Concurrent Kleene Algebra (CKA) [18]. This also coincided with the loosest version of the business process flows language we had been exploring.

The motivation for this work has been to develop a compositional (denotational) semantics for this base language, in UTP, using a homogeneous alphabet where s is the before-state, and s' is the after-state. It turned out that some static observables needed to be added to manage necessary context information in order for this to work [6]. The aim of this chapter is to demonstrate how we might prove that the UTCP semantics satisfies the CKA laws.

1.2   Structure of This Chapter

In Sect. 2 we summarise the language and semantics of UTCP, and present the laws of CKA, using the UTCP notation. Then, in Sect. 3 we describe our overall proof methodology, describing the key concepts needed to construct the correctness arguments. We then showcase proofs of key laws in Sect. 4, going to details of the reasoning. Finally, in Sect. 5 we discuss related work, and then we conclude in Sect. 6.

2   Background

2.1   UTP

The Unifying Theories of Programming framework [17] uses predicate calculus to define before-after relationships over appropriate collections of free observation variables. The before-variables are undashed, while after-variables have dashes.

A simple approach would be to simply observe the values of program variables, in which case the before- and after-*values* of program variable v would be represented by observational variables v and v' respectively. For example, the meaning of an assignment statement might be given as follows:

$$x := e \quad \widehat{=} \quad x' = e \land \nu' = \nu$$

The definition says that, *if* the assignment terminates, then the final value of variable x will be set equal to the value of expression e in the before-state, while the other variables, denoted collectively here by ν, remain unchanged. This leads to a theory of partial correctness for imperative programs.

The theory can be extended to cover total correctness by introducing Boolean observations of program starting (ok) and termination (ok'). In this case, we find that we need a technique that allows us to identify predicates whose interpretation is nonsense, and eliminate them from any semantic theory we might construct. For example, the predicate $\neg ok \land ok'$ describes a situation in which a program has not started, but has terminated.

In UTP we use the concept of healthiness conditions to specify which predicates are meaningful in the context of our theory. For the total correctness theory to work, we need to ensure that all predicates have the form $ok \land P \implies ok' \land Q$, where P and Q do not refer to ok or ok'. This is interpreted as saying, if the program is started and P holds true at the start, then the program will terminate with Q being satisfied at the end.

A standard UTP approach is to define healthy predicates as being fixed-points of suitable idempotent, monotonic predicate transformers. For example, in the total correctness theory, we can define a predicate transformer $\mathbf{H}(P) \widehat{=} ok \implies P$. A predicate D that satisfies $D = (ok \implies D)$ is one that only asserts its behaviour once it is started ($ok = \mathbf{true}$). Our healthiness conditions (Sect. 2.2) are expressed in this fashion.

An important characteristic of both the UTP theories referred to above, is that their predicates are interpreted as a relation between the before-state and after-state of a *complete* program execution. The "standard" treatment of process-algebra concurrency (e.g. ACP,CCS,CSp) in UTP [17, Chps. 7,8], is focused on a model where parallel processes work with their own copy of global variables (if any), and where a merge function is used to merge their values once the parallel construct terminates. The observables include ok, $wait$, tr, and ref.

2.2   UTCP

The Unifying Theory of Concurrent Programming (UTCP) that we developed [6] formalises shared-variable concurrency, also as a relation between before- and after-states. It was derived by adapting Woodcock and Hughes Unifying Theories of Parallel Programming (UTPP) [28], in which statement syntax had labels, and the program state consisted of variable state s, as well as a set ls of labels of currently active statements, where semantics was defined as a relation between ls, s and ls', s'. A statement would only be ready to run when its label was in ls, and once it had run, it would replace its own label (in ls') with the label of the following statement. A key part of our adaptation was adding a label generator g, designed to ensure that all statement labels were unique by construction. We also provided observation variables in and out to denote the starting and ending labels of constructs. The three new variables, g, in, and out, also differ from s and ls in that they did not have dashed counterparts. They are *static* observables. Their role is to manage the relationships between composite commands, and their sub-components. This means that we have a non-homogeneous alphabet $(g, in, out, s, ls, s', ls')$. A key paper in this regard is one by Lamport [22] which we did not encounter until this work was largely done. In it he developed an axiomatic semantics for concurrency, and described some key principles that must hold for such a semantics to work. A key one is being able to talk both about one component in its own right, but also about any use of it as a subcomponent. This aspect is handled by our use of g, in, out.

Here we briefly summarise key UTCP concepts such as labels and their generators, observation variables, atomic actions, healthiness conditions, and semantic definitions. A fuller motivation and discussion can be found in [6].

Labels. In order to manage flow-of-control, we need to be able to identify when every construct starts, is running, and ends. We adopted the idea from [28] that flow of control is managed by an auxiliary variable ls whose value is the set of all labels of constructs that are able to execute. Given some notion of labels ($l \in Lbs$), we introduce a generator ($g \in Gen$) that supports two operations: $new : Gen \to Lbl \times Gen$ that produces a new label and a new generator; while $split : Gen \to Gen \times Gen$ splits a generator into two new ones. In all cases we require that any labels obtained from new generators will not have been obtained previously from any of their parent generators.

To avoid long nested calls of new, $split$ and projections π_1, π_2, we defined the following terse label and generator expression syntax:

$$g \in GVar \qquad \text{The } sole \text{ Generator variable}$$
$$G \in GExp ::= g \mid G_: \mid G_1 \mid G_2$$
$$L \in LExp ::= \ell_G$$

Here $G_:$ denotes the generator left once new has been run on G, with ℓ_G denoting the label so generated: $(\ell_G, G_:) = new(G)$. Expressions G_1 and G_2 denote the two outcomes of applying $split$ to G: $(G_1, G_2) = split(G)$. Effectively we have $\_:$, $\_1$, and $\_2$ as postfix operators acting on generators. We use $labs(G)$ to denote all the labels that G can generate and we require the following laws to hold:

$$labs(G) = \{\ell_G\} \cup labs(G_:) \cup labs(G_1) \cup labs(G_2)$$
$$\ell_G \notin labs(G_:) \cup labs(G_1) \cup labs(G_2)$$

We also require $labs(G_:)$, $labs(G_1)$, and $labs(G_2)$ to be mutually disjoint. This language allows us to take a generated label expression like

$$\pi_1(new(\pi_2(new(\pi_2(split(\pi_2(new(\pi_1(split(g))))))))))).$$

and replace it with $\ell_{g1:2:}$. This notation is compact, and may appear very contrived. However it has one very strong advantage: it makes generators and their labels "relocatable", in much the same way as some program code can be so considered. The variable g can be viewed as a sort of "base", with all of the labels generated from it being relative to that base. We can do this, in one way only, by substituting any generator expression for g. If we replace g with something different, then we "shift" all the associated labels accordingly. If γ and σ range over sequences of :, 1 and 2, then

$$(\ell_{g\gamma})[g\sigma/g] = \ell_{g\sigma\gamma} \tag{1}$$

In effect the substitution "relocates" generator g by running new and $split$ on it as specified by σ, and any labels are in effect generated by this relocated generator using their γ specification. This simple use of substitution gives us a really easy way to compose program fragments in terms of their semantics. This relocation feature is a key aspect identified by Lamport [22].

Observations. The values associated with all (shared) variables are not mentioned individually, but instead are lumped together; and we assume that all actions are labelled and that we can observe the set of labels that are considered to be "active".

$$s, s' : State \tag{2}$$

$$ls, ls' : \mathcal{P}Lbl \tag{3}$$

The role of label-generators is rather different, however. They will be used to generate labels for statements, and we do not want these to change during the lifetime of the program. We will also want to be able to refer in a general way to two key labels associated with any language construct, namely the label (in) that is used to enable the starting of a construct, and the label (out) that is used to signal that the construct has just terminated.

$$in, out : Lbl \tag{4}$$

$$g : Gen \tag{5}$$

These observations are *static*, in that their values do not change during program execution. Instead, these variables record context-sensitive information about how a language construct is situated with respect to its "neighbours", in a way that permits a compositional approach.

This brings us to an important distinction between the usual approach taken by UTP where a program syntax is simply a shorthand notation for its semantics. This "punning" between syntax and semantics largely works for theories of sequential programs or local-state concurrency, mainly because sequences of code lead to simple semantic sequencing. However, in global shared-variable concurrency, code sequences get broken up by interference from parallel execution threads, and there is no longer a simple correspondence between syntactical and semantic sequencing. Here we shall use the notation $P; Q$ to denote *semantic* sequential composition, which means that the execution of P is immediately followed by the execution of Q, without any intervening external interference. It has precisely the standard UTP definition:

$$P; Q \widehat{=} \exists s_m, ls_m \bullet P[s_m, ls_m/s', ls'] \wedge Q[s_m, ls_m/s, ls] \tag{6}$$

The key thing to note is that this definition makes no reference at all to g, *in* or *out*, as these are static observations. We also define state skip (ii) and *semantic* skip (II), the unit for semantic sequential composition, as

$$ii \widehat{=} s' = s$$
$$II \widehat{=} ls' = ls \wedge ii$$

Another important consequence of having to deal with interference, is how we interpret the temporality aspect of s and ls. What precisely differs between an un-dashed variable (s,ls) and the dashed ones (s', ls')? In the basic model of sequential programming, as well as its reformulation using Designs, we interpret s as the value of the state *before* the program runs, and s' as the value *after* the program terminates.

Our move to shared-state concurrency takes a more nuanced view of s'. This is now still interpreted as being the value of the state after the program finished, but is also used to note the state value *during* the run of the program. For UTCP, we have to relax the interpretation for s as well. Now it too can represent the value of state *during* program execution. The only constraint is that the s' observation cannot be from a point in the execution that precedes the s observation. Our semantics admits arbitrary interleaving precisely because it relies on this interpretation.

A special observation *wait* is used in the standard UTP theories of Reactive systems to distinguish between during and after, leading to Foster's concept of Reactive Designs [15]. However, we don't need the *wait* observation because we will use the label-sets (ls, ls') to record that information.

In particular, semantic skip (II) can be interpreted as talking about a single instant in the execution timeline, when nothing can change, or an interval of time in which nothing changes—a so-called "stuttering" step. Stuttering statements are key for concurrency semantics to enable interference to be modelled [2,3,22].

Atomic Actions. An atomic action (a) is simply a global state transformer whose effects, once started, occur immediately and completely, without any external interference. It is a relational predicate that only mentions s and s'. We use the static observables *in* and *out* to explicitly indicate the enabling label (in) for the action, and a disabling, or "done" label (out) for the same action. We use ls and ls' to record the set of enabled labels both before and after the atomic action has run. We can define a predicate that captures the basic behaviour of such "flow-controlled" atomic action:

$$in \in ls \land a \land (ls' = (ls \setminus \{in\}) \cup \{out\}) \tag{7}$$

If in is not in ls, or predicate a is not satisfied by the current value of s, then the semantic predicate reduces to **false**. This denotes an action that is currently not enabled, and is relying on a concurrent action elsewhere to modify ls and/or s. This is analagous to a reactive design when $wait$ is true.

We start by defining the notion of an eXtended basic action, where we explicitly identify the enabling labels (E), those that we remove (R), and those are newly added when done (N):

$$X(E|a|R|N) \mathrel{\widehat{=}} E \subseteq ls \land a \land ls' = (ls \setminus R) \cup N \quad \text{«·X-def·»}$$

A basic action is defined as one where E and R coincide, and is the definition used in the semantics for atomic actions

$$A(E|a|N) \mathrel{\widehat{=}} X(E|a|E|N) \quad \text{«·A-def·»}$$

The reason for the distinction is that basic actions are not closed under semantic sequential composition, whereas extended actions are:

$$
\begin{aligned}
&X(E_1|a|R_1|N_1); X(E_2|b|R_2|N_2) \quad\quad\quad\quad\quad\quad\quad\quad \text{«·X-then-X·»}\\
&= E_2 \cap (R_1 \setminus N_1) = \emptyset \\
&\quad \land X(E_1 \cup (E_2 \setminus N_1) \mid a \,;\, b \mid R_1 \cup R_2 \mid (N_1 \setminus R_2) \cup N_2)
\end{aligned}
$$

The condition $E_2 \cap (R_1 \setminus N_1) = \emptyset$ characterises all those cases were the second X is enabled immediately after the first X terminates (i.e., without any outside interference). The semantic sequential composition of two (extended) basic actions captures the occurrence of both actions in sequence without any intervening interference, known as a *mumbling* step. This means that the first action once enabled, must be able to enable the second one without relying on some external agent. If expression $E_2 \cap (R_1 \setminus N_1)$ is false, this indicates that it is not possible to observe those two actions in sequence, unless some other execution thread manages to add in the missing labels in-between, as an interference step. Again this is seen a key feature in concurrency semantics [2,3,22].

Healthiness. UTCP healthiness is defined to ensure that all atomic actions are in some sense always available to run, should their in label be inserted into ls. In effect we keep them alive by inserting them inside an infinite loop. It is interesting to note that Hoare, in his paper on Unifying Semantics of Concurrent Programming [19, Sec 2.1, p142] states:

> "We will assume that there is an infinite set of possible executions of the command, which can occur in different programs, in different contexts and on different occasions."

Wheels-within-Wheels: Technically we require any healthy UTCP program predicate to be equivalent to a non-deterministic choice of how many times it repeats itself, including zero, using UTP semantic sequential composition.

$$P^0 \cong II \qquad \text{《·seq-0·》}$$
$$P^{i+1} \cong P \,;\, P^i \qquad \text{《·seq-i-plus-1·》}$$
$$\mathbf{WwW}(P) \cong \bigvee_{i \in \mathbb{N}} P^i \qquad \text{《·WWW-as-NDC·》}$$

We note also, that $\mathbf{WwW}$ is monotonic and idempotent.

Label-Set Invariants: In addition, the integrity of the semantics requires that, for any construct, atomic or composite, that *in* and *out* never occupy *ls* at the same time. In addition, for composites, no labels generated by *g* should occupy *ls* when either *in* or *out* are present. We have two kinds of invariants, both of which are concerned with the mutual disjointness, in some sense, of a collection of sets of labels.

We introduce some shorthand notations to avoid excessively long predicates and expressions. We use '|' as a separator between things meant to be disjoint, and commas to list subsets and/or set- elements that should be unioned together. So the fragment $A, b|M, N|x, Y$ is shorthand for the mutual disjointness of $A \cup \{b\}$ and $M \cup N$ and $\{x\} \cup Y$.

To assert mutual set disjointness, we use the following shorthand, where the L_i are label-sets,

$$\{L_1|L_2|\ldots|L_n\} \cong \forall_{i,j \in 1 \ldots n} \bullet i \neq j \implies L_i \cap L_j = \emptyset$$
$$\text{《·short-disj-lbl·》}$$

The first invariant we have, Disjoint Labels (DL) is simply one that asserts, for every construct, that *in*, *out* and the labels of *g* are all different.

$$DL \cong \{in|labs(g)|out\} \quad \text{《·Disjoint-Labels·》}$$

Note that this invariant only refers to the static observation variables. We shall simplify further by stating that in the shorthands presented here that we use just simple *g* to denote $labs(g)$, so DL can be written as $\{in|g|out\}$. Some language constructs strengthen this invariant further.

We also want to assert that certain sets, necessarily mutually disjoint, can never have any of their elements in the global label-set, if any element from one of the other sets is present. Again, we have a shorthand:

$$[L_1|L_2|\ldots|L_n] \cong \forall_{i,j \in 1 \ldots n} \bullet i \neq j \implies (L_i \cap ls \neq \emptyset \implies L_j \cap ls = \emptyset)$$
$$\text{《·short-lbl-exclusive·》}$$

Note here that this is a predicate regarding the contents of *ls*, which is not mentioned explicitly in the shorthand. The second invariant, Label Exclusivity (LE) asserts that any point in time, only elements from of one of *in*, $labs(g)$ or *out* can be present in *ls* (or *ls'*) at any point in time:

$$LE \mathrel{\widehat{=}} [in|g|out] \wedge [in|g|out]' \quad \text{《·Exclusive-Labels·》}$$

Note that $[in|g|out]'$ simply indicates that it refers to ls' rather than ls.

UTCP Healthiness: Every healthy predicate describing a shared-variable concurrent program's behaviour is of the form $\mathbf{WwW}(C)$ for some predicate C and also satisfies DL and LE.

$$\mathbf{W}(P) \mathrel{\widehat{=}} DL \wedge LE \wedge \mathbf{WwW}(P) \quad \text{《·W-def·》}$$

We will discuss key properties of $\mathbf{W}$ when we look at validating the CKA laws (Sect. 3).

Command Semantics. We present the full semantics of atomic commands first, then describe an important classification of expressions and substitutions, before describing the semantics of the four composite command forms.

Atomic Commands. The atomic command $\langle a \rangle$ can be very simply expressed as a basic action with the addition of healthiness conditions:

$$\langle a \rangle \mathrel{\widehat{=}} \mathbf{W}(A(in|a|out))) \quad \text{《·sem:atomic·》}$$

Here we would expect that if LE holds when this action starts, i.e. when $in \in ls$ and it gets to run, that LE' should also hold, with $out \in ls'$. Some actions we will define later will set a to be ii, which means that these actions don't modify s, but instead just focus on changing ls. We refer to these as *control-flow* actions.

Grounded and Sound. Given that we have a distinction between static observations (g, in, out), and dynamic ones (s, s', ls, ls') it is worth extending this distinction to expressions and substitutions. An expression or predicate over observation variables is "ground" if the only variables present are static. The DL healthiness condition is ground, but LE is not, as it refers to ls and ls'. Ground predicates K satisfy some important laws:

$$K \mathbin{;} K = K$$
$$(K \wedge P) \mathbin{;} Q = K \wedge (P \mathbin{;} Q) = P \mathbin{;} (K \wedge Q)$$
$$K \wedge \mathbf{WwW}(P) = \mathbf{WwW}(K \wedge P)$$

A substitution is also deemed "ground", if all the replacement expressions (k) are ground, and the target variables are all static. A ground substitution $[\ldots, k, \ldots / in, g, out]$, herinafter denoted by γ, distributes through semantic sequential composition, both disjoint label-set notations, and $\mathbf{WwW}$. It has no effect on semantic skip.

$$\begin{aligned}
(P \mathbin{;} Q)\gamma &= P\gamma \mathbin{;} Q\gamma & \text{《·seq-gnd-distr·》} \\
\{L_1|\ldots|L_n\}\gamma &= \{L_1\gamma|\ldots|L_n\gamma\} & \text{《·DL-gamma-subst·》} \\
[L_1|\ldots|L_n]\gamma &= [L_1\gamma|\ldots|L_n\gamma] & \text{《·LE-gamma-subst·》} \\
(\mathbf{WwW}(P))\gamma &= \mathbf{WwW}(P\gamma) & \text{《·WwW-gamma-subst·》} \\
II\gamma &= II & \text{《·skip-gamma·》}
\end{aligned}$$

A ground substitution ς, of the form $[I, labs(G), O/in, g, out]$ is *sound* if predicate $\{I|labs(G)|O\}$ holds. Soundness means the substitution cannot transform a predicate satisfying DL and LE into one that does not.

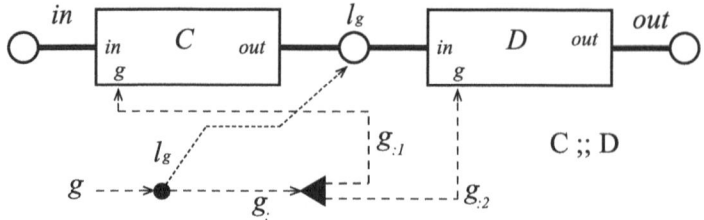

Fig. 1. Label and Generator "plumbing" for $C;;D$.

Composing Actions. The semantics of composite actions basically involves using the generator to produce a suitable number of labels, that are then used in zero or more control-flow actions, of the form $A(E|ii|N)$. The left-over generator is then split as required, and then the components are "connected" into the relevant new labels and generators using sound substitutions. Finally the relevant healthiness conditions are applied. It helps to write all substitutions out in full, in order in, g, then out, so that reading them left-to-right goes with the "flow". It declutters things to then drop the part of the substitution that always reads as $/in, g, out$. So $C[\alpha, \gamma, \omega/in, g, out]$ becomes $C[\alpha, \gamma, \omega]$. This is particularly helpful during calculation.

The semantic definitions are as follows:

$$\mathtt{skip} \hat{=} \langle ii \rangle$$

$$C;;D \hat{=} \mathbf{W}(C[in, g_{:1}, \ell_g] \vee D[\ell_g, g_{:2}, out]) \wedge [in|\ell_g|out]$$

$$C + D \hat{=} \mathbf{W}(\quad A(in|ii|\ell_{g1}) \vee C[\ell_{g1}, g_{1:}, out] \\ \vee A(in|ii|\ell_{g2}) \vee D[\ell_{g2}, g_{2:}, out]\ ) \wedge [in|\ell_{g1}|\ell_{g2}|out]$$

$$C \| D \hat{=} \mathbf{W}(\quad A(in|ii|\ell_{g1}, \ell_{g2}) \\ \vee C[\ell_{g1}, g_{1::}, \ell_{g1:}] \vee D[\ell_{g2}, g_{2::}, \ell_{g2:}] \\ \vee A(\ell_{g1:}, \ell_{g2:}|ii|out)\ ) \wedge [in|(\ell_{g1}|\ell_{g1:}), (\ell_{g2}|\ell_{g2:})|out]$$

$$C^* \hat{=} \mathbf{W}(\quad A(in|ii|\ell_g) \\ \vee A(\ell_g|ii|\ell_{g:}) \vee A(\ell_g|ii|out) \\ \vee C[\ell_{g:}, g_{::}, \ell_g]\ ) \wedge [in|\ell_g|\ell_{g:}|out]$$

First, note that all four composite definitions add further label-set invariants.

We will explain the semantics of some of the above in more detail. For sequential composition, the first component (C) uses the same in label as the construct as a whole, while the second (D) uses that same out label. The generator g is used to generate a label ℓ_g, that replaces out in C and in in D, effectively connecting them. The left-over generator $g_:$ is then split into two, $g_{:1}$ and $g_{:2}$, and these substituted for the g component in C and D respectively (see Fig. 1).

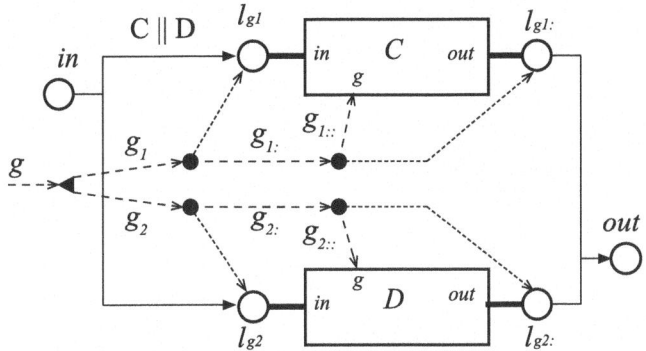

Fig. 2. Label and Generator "plumbing" for $C \parallel D$.

For parallel composition (Fig. 2), we take the generator g and split it to obtain g_1 and g_2. From g_1 we generate two labels ℓ_{g1} and $\ell_{g1:}$, and leftover generator $g_{1::}$. We then use a substitution to replace all references by P to g, in and out with $g_{1::}$, ℓ_{g1} and $\ell_{g1:}$, respectively. We do something similar with g_2 and Q. We also add a top-level control-flow action that is enabled by label in, and adds both ℓ_{g1} and ℓ_{g2} into ls, so enabling both P and Q to start. We then have another control-flow action that waits for both of $\ell_{g1:}$ and $\ell_{g2:}$ to appear in ls, at which point they will be replaced by the top-level out label.

For iteration (Fig. 3), we first perform an apparently vacuous control flow action that removes label in from ls and replaces it with ℓ_g. That enables two actions: one that replaces ℓ_g with out, terminating the iteration; the other switches to label $\ell_{g:}$, which has replaced the in label for the body C. The out label of C is replaced by ℓ_g. It is important to keep the choice regarding terminate/repeat (at ℓ_g) separate from starting an execution of the body (at $\ell_{g:}$).

2.3 Formal Definition of CKA

The concept of Concurrent Kleene Algebra (CKA)was defined in a seminal paper by Hoare and collaborators [18]. This emerged as a result of ongoing work exploring the algebra and laws of shared-variable concurrency. The CKA language covers the same concepts we have in UTCP, namely atomic actions, skip, nondeterminism, sequencing, parallel composition, and iteration. It also includes the infeasible action miracle, and a refinement ordering ($\leq$). It has since become the

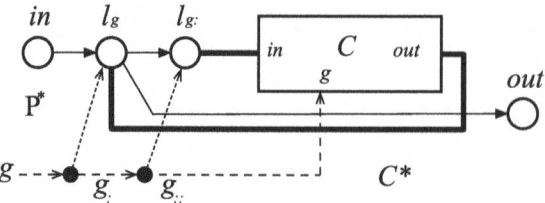

Fig. 3. Label and Generator "plumbing" for C^*.

de-facto algebra for concurrency [18,19,21]. Using our UTCP notation we get the following set of laws, where (C,D,E,F, range over commands):

$$
\begin{aligned}
C + \text{miracle} &= C & &«\!\cdot\text{ndc-unit}\cdot\!» \\
C + C &= C & &«\!\cdot\text{ndc-idem}\cdot\!» \\
C + D &= D + C & &«\!\cdot\text{ndc-symm}\cdot\!» \\
C + (D + E) &= (C + D) + E & &«\!\cdot\text{ndc-assoc}\cdot\!» \\
C \mathbin{;;} \text{skip} &= C & &«\!\cdot\text{seq-r-unit}\cdot\!» \\
\text{skip} \mathbin{;;} C &= C & &«\!\cdot\text{seq-l-unit}\cdot\!» \\
C \mathbin{;;} (D \mathbin{;;} E) &= (C \mathbin{;;} D) \mathbin{;;} E & &«\!\cdot\text{seq-assoc}\cdot\!» \\
C \mathbin{;;} \text{miracle} &= \text{miracle} & &«\!\cdot\text{seq-r-zero}\cdot\!» \\
\text{miracle} \mathbin{;;} C &= \text{miracle} & &«\!\cdot\text{seq-l-zero}\cdot\!» \\
C \mathbin{;;} (D + E) &= C \mathbin{;;} D + C \mathbin{;;} E & &«\!\cdot\text{seq-ndc-distr}\cdot\!» \\
(C + D) \mathbin{;;} E &= C \mathbin{;;} E + D \mathbin{;;} E & &«\!\cdot\text{ndc-seq-distr}\cdot\!» \\
C \parallel D &= D \parallel C & &«\!\cdot\text{par-symm}\cdot\!» \\
C \parallel \text{skip} &= C & &«\!\cdot\text{par-unit}\cdot\!» \\
C \parallel (D \parallel E) &= (C \parallel D) \parallel E & &«\!\cdot\text{par-assoc}\cdot\!» \\
C \parallel \text{miracle} &= \text{miracle} & &«\!\cdot\text{par-zero}\cdot\!» \\
C \parallel (D + E) &= C \parallel D + C \parallel E & &«\!\cdot\text{par-ndc-distr}\cdot\!» \\
\text{skip} + C \mathbin{;;} C^* &= C^* & &«\!\cdot\text{iter-fold}\cdot\!» \\
C + D \mathbin{;;} E \le E &\implies D^* \mathbin{;;} C \le E & &«\!\cdot\text{refine1}\cdot\!» \\
(C \parallel D) \mathbin{;;} (E \parallel F) &\le (C \mathbin{;;} E) \parallel (D \mathbin{;;} F) & &«\!\cdot\text{exchange}\cdot\!»
\end{aligned}
$$

The miracle term, and the ordering in the last two laws ($\le$) are not used in the Views paper. The precise form these take in this theory will be discussed later.

3   Methodology

The general plan for proving UTCP compliance with CKA laws, all of the form $lhs = rhs$, is to expand out their definitions, and then find a suitable mapping on labels between the lhs and rhs. For some laws all we need is to identify a bijection between labels, while some others need a more nuanced approach.

3.1 Composing Atomic Actions

We start by considering the general case of semantic sequential composition of two basic atomic actions:

$$A(E_1|a|N_1); A(E_2|a|N_2)$$

= "Defn. of A"

$$X(E_1|a|E_1|N_1); X(E_2|a|E_2|N_2)$$

= "《·X-then-X·》"

$$E_2 \cap (E_1 \backslash N_1) = \emptyset$$
$$\wedge X(\ E_1 \cup (E_2 \backslash N_1)\ |\ a\ ;\ b\ |\ E_1 \cup E_2\ |\ (N_1 \backslash E_2) \cup N_2\ )\quad 《·\text{A-then-A}·》$$

Note first that this behaviour is not possible if there is an overlap between E_2 and $(E_1 \backslash N_1)$. The latter term denotes labels removed from ls when the first action runs (E_1), that are not added into ls as the action terminates (N_1). If this overlaps with E_2, then at least one enabling label is missing, and so the predicate for the second action evaluates to false, as does the whole composition—basically the first action disables the second, and hence their joint occurrence, *without interference*, can never be observed.

In [6] we described the outcome of expanding out the definition of $\langle a \rangle$, namely $\mathbf{W}(A(in|a|out))$. We find that $\mathbf{WwW}(A(in|a|out)) = II \vee A(in|a|out)$, because $A(in|a|out)^n = \mathbf{false}$ for $n \geq 2$. The first action replaces in by out in ls, disabling any attempt to rerun this action in the absence of outside interference.

$$\langle a \rangle = DL \wedge LE \wedge (II \vee A(in|a|out))$$

With different basic atomic actions we have (assuming $in_1 \neq in_2 \wedge [in_1|out_1] \wedge [in_2|out_2]$):

$$A(in_1|a|out_1); A(in_2|b|out_2)$$

= "《·A-then-A·》"

$$in_2 \cap (in_1 \backslash out_1) = \emptyset$$
$$\wedge X(\ in_1 \cup (in_2 \backslash out_1)\ |\ a\ ;\ b\ |\ in_1 \cup in_2\ |\ (out_1 \backslash in_2) \cup out_2\ )$$

= "simplify, noting assumptions"

$$X(\ in_1 \cup (in_2 \backslash out_1)\ |\ a\ ;\ b\ |\ in_1 \cup in_2\ |\ (out_1 \backslash in_2) \cup out_2\ )$$

This action is enabled if $in_1 \cup (in_2 \backslash out_1)$ is in ls. This can occur in two ways, both of which require in_1 to be present:

1. The first action is intended to enable the second ($out_1 = in_2$, let's call it mid):

$$X(\ in_1 \cup (mid \backslash mid)\ |\ a\ ;\ b\ |\ in_1 \cup mid\ |\ (mid \backslash mid) \cup out_2\ )$$
$$= X(\ in_1\ |\ a\ ;\ b\ |\ in_1 \cup mid\ |\ out_2\ )$$

2. The second action is independently enabled ($out_1 \neq in_2$):

$$X(\ in_1 \cup (in_2 \setminus out_1)\ |\ a\ ;\ b\ |\ in_1 \cup in_2\ |\ (out_1 \setminus in_2) \cup out_2\ )$$
$$= X(\ in_1 \cup in_2\ |\ a\ ;\ b\ |\ in_1 \cup in_2\ |\ out_1 \cup out_2\ )$$

We see here that the result is symmetric in the indices 1 and 2, and indeed we get same outcome if we compose the actions in the opposite order ($A(in_2|b|out_2); A(in_1|a|out_1)$). However, there is also another complication, in that some invariants are more complicated, and can have the effect that $A(in_1|a|out_1)$ in effect disables $A(in_2|b|out_2)$. We designate two atomic actions as *fully independent* if their composition is not disabled by invariants in this way. We will revisit this once we have discussed invariant preservation below.

To sum up, a basic action in our semantics is never run twice without some intervening interference step, as a consequence of the invariants. Two different actions may run back-to-back, if the first enables the second, or they are fully independent and are both currently enabled, in which case they can run back-to-back in either order.

We made use of the DL invariant (in and out are never together in ls) when showing $A(in|a|out)^2 = \textbf{false}$. We also need to prove that atomic actions preserve the invariants. The invariants associated with atomic actions vary, depending on their role — state-change, or control-flow actions. Here are all the atomic actions explicitly mentioned in the semantics, with their additional invariants (beyond the ubiquitous DL and LE):

$$
\begin{aligned}
A(in|a|out) &: [in|out] & A(in|ii|\ell_{g1}) &: [in|\ell_{g1}|\ell_{g2}|out] \\
A(in|ii|\ell_{g2}) &: [in|\ell_{g1}|\ell_{g2}|out] & A(in|ii|\ell_g) &: [in|\ell_g|\ell_{g:}|out] \\
A(\ell_g|ii|\ell_{g:}) &: [in|\ell_g|\ell_{g:}|out] & A(\ell_g|ii|out) &: [in|\ell_g|\ell_{g:}|out] \\
A(in|ii|\ell_{g1}, \ell_{g2}) &: [in|(\ell_{g1}|\ell_{g1:}), (\ell_{g2}|\ell_{g2:})|out] \\
A(\ell_{g1:}, \ell_{g2:}|ii|out) &: [in|(\ell_{g1}|\ell_{g1:}), (\ell_{g2}|\ell_{g2:})|out]
\end{aligned}
$$

For the other actions, note that all labels mentioned in the atomic actions appear in their associated invariant. This means we need only consider the following generic case. If DL and LE with the appropriate substitutions for in and out holds beforehand, then after the corresponding atomic action runs, we find that the corresponding LE' holds:

$$\{E|N\} \wedge [E|N] \wedge A(E|a|N) \implies [E|N]'$$

We assume $\{E|N\} \wedge [E|N]$ and expand it to

$$(E \cap N = \emptyset) \wedge (E \cap ls \neq \emptyset \implies N \cap ls = \emptyset) \wedge (N \cap ls \neq \emptyset \implies E \cap ls = \emptyset)$$

We now evaluate the outcome of running $A(E|a|N)$:

$$A(E|a|N) = E \subseteq ls \wedge a \wedge ls' = (ls \setminus E) \cup N$$

We have two cases. The first is when either $E \not\subseteq ls$ or a is currently **false**, which means the action doesn't run so invariant preservation is vacuously satisfied. The second is when $E \subseteq ls \land a$ is **true**, in which case the invariant $\{E|N\} \land [E|N]$ indicates that no part of N appears in ls. So ls' has all of E removed and all of N added, so we can say that $N \subseteq ls' \land E \cap ls' = \emptyset$.

When might two distinct atomic actions *not* be fully independent? Consider the following simple example:

$\langle a \rangle + \langle b \rangle$

$=$ "Expand semantics of $\langle \rangle$, ignoring II, DL, and LE"

$\quad A(in|a|out) + A(in|b|out)$

$=$ "Semantics of $+$"

$\quad \mathbf{W}(\quad A(in|ii|\ell_{g1}) \lor A(in|a|out)[\ell_{g1}, g_{1:}, out]$
$\quad\quad\quad \lor A(in|ii|\ell_{g2}) \lor A(in|b|out)[\ell_{g2}, g_{2:}, out] \ ) \land [in|\ell_{g1}|\ell_{g2}|out]$

$=$ "Substitution"

$\quad \mathbf{W}(\quad A(in|ii|\ell_{g1}) \lor A(\ell_{g1}|a|out)$
$\quad\quad\quad \lor A(in|ii|\ell_{g2}) \lor A(\ell_{g2}|b|out) \ ) \land [in|\ell_{g1}|\ell_{g2}|out]$

Recall that the sequential composition of $A(in_1|a|out_1); A(in_2|b|out_2)$ is enabled if $in_1 \cup (in_2 \setminus out_1) \subseteq ls$. Now, in our semantics above, $A(in|ii|\ell_{g1})$ and $A(\ell_{g2}|b|out)$ are independent. For $A(in|ii|\ell_{g1}); A(\ell_{g2}|b|out)$ to be enabled, we require:

$$in \cup (\ell_{g2} \setminus \ell_{g1}) \subseteq ls$$
$$= \text{"simplify"}$$
$$in \cup \ell_{g2} \subseteq ls$$

The LE invariant permits this to be true, but the additional invariant ($[in|\ell_{g1}|\ell_{g2}|out]$) forbids this, as only one of in, out, ℓ_{g1}, or ℓ_{g2} can be present in ls at any one time. So this composition is never enabled. The use of invariants in this way in the semantics is absolutely crucial to ensuring that the semantics gives the right outcomes.

Given that we have argued that $A(E|a|N)$ preserves invariants, how do we extend this result to extended actions $X(E|a|R|N)$? First, note that the semantics only defines A actions, and that all the X actions are ultimately the result of the composition of such A actions. But, we know that A actions preserve the invariant, so their composition will, so hence all X actions also preserve the invariants.

3.2 $\mathbf{W}(\ldots)$: The Wash Cycle

The definition of $\mathbf{W}(C)$ expands to a term of the form:

$$GI \land (II \lor C \lor (C; C) \lor (C; C; C) \lor \ldots) \land CI$$

Here GI (General Invariant) is just a shorthand for $DL \wedge LE$, while CI (Composite Invariant) denotes any composition-specific invariant. If C is atomic, then $C;C = \textbf{false}$ by construction and we are left with $II \vee C$, as explained in Sect. 3.1. We need to keep in mind that we have semantic sequential composition here. If C is not atomic, then it is composed of a disjunction of control atomic actions plus one or more sub-components. Each sub-component is itself of the form $(GI \wedge \textbf{WwW}(C_s) \wedge CI_s)\gamma$, where γ is a sound ground substitution. An immediate issue that arises is what does the semantic sequential composition $C;C$ mean precisely, when C is composite. For atomic actions it means that the second instance starts immediately after the first one ends with no other action interfering in between. This doesn't make sense as is for arbitrary composite C that itself may contain many interfering actions. What it does mean is that when the first instance of C terminates, through the running of a action that ends it, that the starting action of the second instance runs immediately. This all seems complicated, but there is a way to get to grips with the outcomes in an intuitive manner.

We start with the case where all the sub-components are themselves atomic, being a mixture of control actions of the form $A(E|ii|N)$, and state actions of the form $A(E|a|N)$. We have $C = A_1 \vee \cdots \vee A_n$, and hence, $\textbf{W}(C)$ expands to:

$$GI \wedge (II \vee (A_1 \vee \cdots \vee A_n) \vee (A_1 \vee \cdots \vee A_n)^2 \vee \ldots) \wedge CI$$

So, we can observe II, and a run of any single action A_i. We will also see runs of the form $A_i; A_j$ where $i \neq j$ and A_i does nothing that disables A_j. We also get similar terms of the form $A_i; A_j; A_k$ where $i \neq j \wedge j \neq k$. With every composite we look at, with only atomic sub-components, we find that there is a finite limit index L, such that $(A_1 \vee \cdots \vee A_n)^L = \textbf{false}$. What we obtain is a disjunction that has every possible feasible sequential *semantic* composition of n actions, where $n \in 0 \ldots L-1$ (remember that $A^0 = II$).

It is instructive to see what these look like. For sequential composition we can observe the execution of the individual actions, as well as their composition (here we use ab (ba) as shorthand for $a;b$ $(b;a)$):

$$\langle a \rangle \;;; \langle b \rangle \qquad \text{《·seq-actions·》}$$
$$A^0 : II \vee$$
$$A^1 : A(in|a|\ell_g) \vee A(\ell_g|b|out) \vee$$
$$A^2 : A(in|ab|out)$$

For non-deterministic choice, we also observe the control actions that implement the non-determinism:

$$\langle a \rangle + \langle b \rangle \qquad \text{《·ndc-actions·》}$$
$$A^0 : II \vee$$
$$A^1 : A(in|ii|\ell_{g1}) \vee A(in|ii|\ell_{g2}) \vee A(\ell_{g1}|a|out) \vee A(\ell_{g2}|b|out) \vee$$
$$A^2 : A(in|a|out) \vee A(in|b|out)$$

Parallelism is more complicated because both branches get enabled:

$\langle a \rangle \parallel \langle b \rangle$ 《·par-actions·》

$A^0 : II \lor$

$A^1 : A(in|ii|\ell_{g1}, \ell_{g2}) \lor A(\ell_{g1}|a|\ell_{g1:}) \lor A(\ell_{g2}|b|\ell_{g2:}) \lor A(\ell_{g1:}, \ell_{g2:}|ii|out) \lor$

$A^2 : A(in|a|\ell_{g1:}, \ell_{g2}) \lor A(in|b|\ell_{g2:}, \ell_{g1}) \lor$
$\quad\quad A(\ell_{g2:}, \ell_{g1}|a|out) \lor A(\ell_{g1:}, \ell_{g2}|b|out) \lor$
$\quad\quad A(\ell_{g1}, \ell_{g2}|ba|\ell_{g1:}, \ell_{g2:}) \lor A(\ell_{g1}, \ell_{g2}|ab|\ell_{g1:}, \ell_{g2:}) \lor$

$A^3 : A(in|ba|\ell_{g1:}, \ell_{g2:}) \lor A(in|ab|\ell_{g1:}, \ell_{g2:}) \lor$
$\quad\quad A(\ell_{g1}, \ell_{g2}|ba|out) \lor A(\ell_{g1}, \ell_{g2}|ab|out) \lor$

$A^4 : A(in|ba|out) \lor A(in|ab|out)$

We note that the full behaviour is made up of 4 actions. The first control action splits in into ℓ_{g1} and ℓ_{g2}, to enable both a and b state actions, which then run independently in either order. A final control action then waits for $\ell_{g1:}$ and $\ell_{g2:}$ to be present, and replaces them with out.

A key feature of all of the above is that there are actions of the form $A(in|\ldots|out)$ that denote a complete sequencing of atomic control and state actions that are enabled by label in, and finish with label out being deposited in ls. Another key point to take away here, is that every composite ultimately gets reduced down to a disjunction of compositions of atomic control and state change actions.

3.3 Atomic Action Flows

We use the term "flow" to describe a feasible sequential composition of atomic control and state actions. A key aspect of flow is that every well-formed command $C(in, g, out)$ has a flow that starts with $in \in ls$, then executes sub-commands using labels drawn from g, and finishes with $out \in ls'$. We call such a flow "complete". The atomic actions in 《·seq-actions·》, 《·ndc-actions·》, and 《·par-actions·》 denote all the possible flows for their respective constructs. The complete flows for $\langle a \rangle \parallel \langle b \rangle$ are $A(in|ab|out)$ and $A(in|ba|out)$. We are interested in complete flows as they are our basis for proving the correctness of the CKA laws w.r.t our semantics.

The labels, and the method for generating them, are key to ensuring that the semantics correctly predicts all and only the possible actions of any given program. But they are a means to an end, and we want to disregard them when discussing program equivalences. We will consider two programs to be equivalent if they have the same collection of complete flows, when actual label values are ignored. We achieve this simply by hiding all label-related observations, leaving only those that involve s and s':

$$flow(C) \,\widehat{=}\, \exists in, g, out, ls, ls' \bullet C$$

Note that the way we define the semantics of C means that the following suffices as a witness to simplify the flow: $ls = \{in\} \land ls' = \{out\}$. When we ignore labels, we end up with a set of sequences of atomic state-changes, hence recovering a set of traces model that is typical of most other concurrency models. If we take the actions from Sect. 3.2 and convert them to flows, we get:

$$flow(\langle a \rangle \;;; \langle b \rangle)$$
$$= \text{``} \langle\!\langle \cdot \text{seq-actions} \cdot \rangle\!\rangle, \; flow\text{''}$$
$$ii \lor a \lor b \lor ab$$
$$\langle a \rangle + \langle b \rangle$$
$$= \text{``} \langle\!\langle \cdot \text{ndc-actions} \cdot \rangle\!\rangle, \; flow, \text{ simplify''}$$
$$ii \lor a \lor b$$
$$\langle a \rangle \parallel \langle b \rangle$$
$$= \text{``} \langle\!\langle \cdot \text{par-actions} \cdot \rangle\!\rangle, \; flow, \text{ simplify''}$$
$$ii \lor a \lor b \lor ba \lor ab$$

It is important to note that the use of $flow$ results in information loss, and in particular, we cannot compose the output of $flow$ in any meaningful way. While the precise values of labels are not important to the overall semantics, the manner in which they are used and *kept distinct* from each other is crucial.

3.4 Composite Flows

So why focus on flows at all? The answer is that, as a concept, they make it much easier to read off the complete flows of a semantic definition. All the flows shown here were discovered/validated during the developments of the UTCP semantics, which involved a lot of tedious check calculations, and led to the development of a predicate "calculator" to make things tractable [5]. For most of that time, the "correct answer" was always self-evident. Consider the part of the definition of parallel composition $C \parallel D$ under the healthiness condition $\mathbf{W}$:

$$A(in|ii|\ell_{g1}, \ell_{g2}) \lor$$
$$C[\ell_{g1}, g_{1::}, \ell_{g1:}] \lor D[\ell_{g2}, g_{2::}, \ell_{g2:}] \lor$$
$$A(\ell_{g1:}, \ell_{g2:}|ii|out)$$

We can read off the flows directly by looking at the begin and end-labels. The first (control) action goes from in to both ℓ_{g1} and ℓ_{g2}. We inductively assume that all the complete flows of $C[\ldots]$ go from ℓ_{g1} to $\ell_{g1:}$, and something similar for $D[\ldots]$. The last (control) action waits for both ℓ_{g1} and ℓ_{g2} and then proceeds to out. We made an inductive assumption above regarding the complete flows of C and D, and the effect of the substitutions applied to them. These substitutions are all sound, which means they map in, out, and the labels generated by g to distinct groups in a consistent manner. This ensure that the flows are not affected.

3.5 Atomic Control Merge

A control action with an out-label that matches the in-label of a command, can be merged with that command, as a result of $\mathbf{W}$'s mixing. A similar situation arises if the action has an in-label that matches the out-label of a command:

$$A(\ell_1|ii|\ell_2); C[\ell_2, g_\sigma, \ell_3] = C[\ell_1, g_\sigma, \ell_3] \quad \ll\text{cntl-l-merge}\gg$$
$$C[\ell_1, g_\sigma, \ell_2]; A(\ell_2|ii|\ell_3) = C[\ell_1, g_\sigma, \ell_3] \quad \ll\text{cntl-r-merge}\gg$$

Intuitively these laws are fairly obvious, as indeed the whole design of the label generation has been to ensure that properties like this hold true.

4   Law Proofs

The approach taken to prove a law of the form $F(C, D) = G(C, D)$, where F and G construct more complex programs using C and D, is to examine the flows of each side and establish a mapping of their labels that show every complete flow in one has a counterpart in the other. When we start to do this we quickly find that the CKA laws fall into two groups:

rearrangements (-symm,-assoc,-distr) These have the same flows, labelled differently, and label bijections suffice for correctness.

collapses (-zero,-unit,-idem) The flows on the more complex side effectively collapse to something just like the flows on the simpler side. This requires an more nuanced observability argument. In particular, all the miracle laws are collapses.

4.1   Proving Rearrangments

The rearrangement laws are:

$$C + D = D + C \qquad \ll\text{ndc-symm}\gg$$
$$C + (D + E) = (C + D) + E \qquad \ll\text{ndc-assoc}\gg$$
$$C \mathbin{;;} (D \mathbin{;;} E) = (C \mathbin{;;} D) \mathbin{;;} E \qquad \ll\text{seq-assoc}\gg$$
$$C \mathbin{;;} (D + E) = C \mathbin{;;} D + C \mathbin{;;} E \qquad \ll\text{seq-ndc-distr}\gg$$
$$(C + D) \mathbin{;;} E = C \mathbin{;;} E + D \mathbin{;;} E \qquad \ll\text{ndc-seq-distr}\gg$$
$$C \,\|\, D = D \,\|\, C \qquad \ll\text{par-symm}\gg$$
$$C \,\|\, (D \,\|\, E) = (C \,\|\, D) \,\|\, E \qquad \ll\text{par-assoc}\gg$$
$$C \,\|\, (D + E) = C \,\|\, D + C \,\|\, E \qquad \ll\text{par-ndc-distr}\gg$$

We will illustrate this technique with the law $\ll\text{seq-ndc-distr}\gg$ regarding the distributivity of ;; through +. The approach has two phases:

1. Expand both sides of the equation using the operator definitions, and then driving all substitution inwards. We also ignore the top-level use of **W**. The LE and DL invariants distribute in through **WwW** so we can invoke them when needed. Steps here involve semantic equivalence and are separated by $=$.

2. Identify the longest runs obtained by doing semantic sequential composition of actions where the output label of one is the same as the input label of another. Steps here generate flows, by a targeted partial expansion of **WwW**, and are separated by $=_\mathbf{w}$. In practice we can identify these directly by careful inspection.

We start with the lefthand side:

$$C \mathbin{;;} (D + E)$$

$=$ "Defn. of $\mathbin{;;}$ — ignoring $\mathbf{W}$ for now."

$$C[in, g_{:1}, \ell_g] \vee (D + E)[\ell_g, g_{:2}, out]$$

$=$ "Defn. of $+$"

$$C[in, g_{:1}, \ell_g] \vee$$
$$\left(\begin{array}{l} A(in|ii|\ell_{g1}) \vee D[\ell_{g1}, g_{1:}, out] \vee \\ A(in|ii|\ell_{g2}) \vee E[\ell_{g2}, g_{2:}, out] \end{array} \right) [\ell_g, g_{:2}, out]$$

$=$ "substitution"

$$C[in, g_{:1}, \ell_g] \vee$$
$$(A(in|ii|\ell_{g1}) \vee D[\ell_{g1}, g_{1:}, out])[\ell_g, g_{:2}, out] \vee$$
$$(A(in|ii|\ell_{g2}) \vee E[\ell_{g2}, g_{2:}, out])[\ell_g, g_{:2}, out]$$

$=$ "substitution"

$$C[in, g_{:1}, \ell_g] \vee$$
$$A(\ell_g|ii|\ell_{g:21}) \vee D[\ell_{g:21}, g_{:21:}, out] \vee$$
$$A(\ell_g|ii|\ell_{g:22}) \vee E[\ell_{g:22}, g_{:22:}, out]$$

Now the righthand side:

$$C \mathbin{;;} D + C \mathbin{;;} E$$

$=$ "defn. $+$"

$$A(in|ii|\ell_{g1}) \vee (C \mathbin{;;} D)[\ell_{g1}, g_{1:}, out] \vee$$
$$A(in|ii|\ell_{g2}) \vee (C \mathbin{;;} E)[\ell_{g2}, g_{2:}, out]$$

$=$ "defn. $\mathbin{;;}$"

$$A(in|ii|\ell_{g1}) \vee (C[in, g_{:1}, \ell_g] \vee D[\ell_g, g_{:2}, out])[\ell_{g1}, g_{1:}, out] \vee$$
$$A(in|ii|\ell_{g2}) \vee (C[in, g_{:1}, \ell_g] \vee E[\ell_g, g_{:2}, out])[\ell_{g2}, g_{2:}, out]$$

$=$ "substitution"

$$A(in|ii|\ell_{g1}) \vee (C[\ell_{g1}, g_{1::1}, \ell_{g1:}] \vee D[\ell_{g1:}, g_{1::2}, out]) \vee$$
$$A(in|ii|\ell_{g2}) \vee (C[\ell_{g2}, g_{2::1}, \ell_{g2:}] \vee E[\ell_{g2:}, g_{2::2}, out])$$

We then read off the flows, starting with label in and ending with label out. On the lefthand side we observe the following: Command C flows from in to ℓ_g. Two independent control actions flow from ℓ_g to either $\ell_{g:21}$ or $\ell_{g:22}$. Command D flows from $\ell_{g:21}$ to out. Command E flows from $\ell_{g:22}$ to out. The end-to-end flows are:

$$C[in, g_{:1}, \ell_g]; A(\ell_g|ii|\ell_{g:21}); D[\ell_{g:21}, g_{:21:}, out]$$
$$C[in, g_{:1}, \ell_g]; A(\ell_g|ii|\ell_{g:22}); E[\ell_{g:22}, g_{:22:}, out]$$

A similar analysis for the righthand side results in:

$$A(in|ii|\ell_{g1}); C[\ell_{g1}, g_{1::1}, \ell_{g1:}]; D[\ell_{g1:}, g_{1::2}, out]$$
$$A(in|ii|\ell_{g2}); C[\ell_{g2}, g_{2::1}, \ell_{g2:}]; E[\ell_{g2:}, g_{2::2}, out]$$

We can immediately see that the lefthand first runs C and then makes the choice, whereas the right starts with the choice and then does the relevant sequence. If we ignore the label information, we see that both sides perform either C followed by D, or C followed by E.

For more rigour, we can apply the control merge laws to the compositions of A and C above to get a lefthand side (using «·cntl-r-merge·»):

$$C[in, g_{:1}, \ell_{g:21}]; D[\ell_{g:21}, g_{:21:}, out]$$
$$C[in, g_{:1}, \ell_{g:22}]; E[\ell_{g:22}, g_{:22:}, out]$$

and righthand side (using «·cntl-l-merge·»):

$$C[in, g_{1::1}, \ell_{g1:}]; D[\ell_{g1:}, g_{1::2}, out]$$
$$C[in, g_{2::1}, \ell_{g2:}]; E[\ell_{g2:}, g_{2::2}, out]$$

So, in both cases, the choice is incorporated in C in some sense. Now we can clearly identify a bijective mapping between the labels on each side:

$$\{in \mapsto in, \ g_{:21} \mapsto g_{1:}, \ g_{:22} \mapsto g_{2:}, \ g_{:21} \mapsto g_{1:}, \ g_{:22} \mapsto g_{2:}, \ out \mapsto out\}$$

4.2 Proving Collapses

The collapsing laws (excluding miracle) are:

$$C + C = C \qquad \text{«·ndc-idem·»}$$
$$C \mathbin{;;} \mathsf{skip} = C \qquad \text{«·seq-r-unit·»}$$
$$\mathsf{skip} \mathbin{;;} C = C \qquad \text{«·seq-l-unit·»}$$
$$C \parallel \mathsf{skip} = C \qquad \text{«·par-unit·»}$$
$$\mathsf{skip} + C \mathbin{;;} C^* = C^* \qquad \text{«·iter-fold·»}$$

We will start with the idempotency of non-determinism «·ndc-idem·». Again we expand both sides. For the righthand side we simply show it with the identity substitution, to make comparison easier.

$LHS \qquad C + C$

$\qquad = \text{"defn +, re-arrange"}$

$\qquad\qquad A(in|ii|\ell_{g1}) \vee C[\ell_{g1}, g_{1:}, out] \ \vee$
$\qquad\qquad A(in|ii|\ell_{g2}) \vee C[\ell_{g2}, g_{2:}, out]$

$\qquad =_{\mathbf{w}} \text{"«·cntl-l-merge·», twice"}$

$\qquad\qquad C[in, g_{1:}, out] \vee C[in, g_{2:}, out]$

$RHS \qquad C$

$\qquad = \text{"id. substitution"}$

$\qquad\qquad C[in, g, out]$

We have the following flows. First the lefthand side:

$$C[in, g_{1:}, out]$$
$$C[in, g_{2:}, out]$$

Next, the righthand side:

$$C[in, g, out]$$

We have the same two labels on all instances, but three different generators. However, these generators have the same pattern of use inside C, so the internal flows will be the same, once we ignore precise label values. Here there is no label bijection as g in the RHS is associated with both $g_{1:}$ and $g_{2:}$ in the LHS. What we can do here is use the idea of a bijection between label-*sets* (here $\{g\} \leftrightarrow \{g_{1:}, g_{2:}\}$). Most of the other collapse laws are very similar.

However, it is worth looking at the iteration fold law. Upto this point we have kept quiet about iteration, limiting ourselves to constructs where the process of expanding $\bigvee_{i \in \mathbb{N}} C^i$ has been shown to terminate for some value $i > 1$. Iteration by its very nature is designed to admit an unbounded degree of unrolling. This naturally raises the question of what happens when we try to expand it.

$$\mathtt{skip} + C \mathbin{;;} C^* = C^* \qquad \text{《·iter-fold·》}$$

We will start with the righthand side (we will need it for the lefthand side in any case).

C^*

$= $ "Defn C^*"

$\quad A(in|ii|\ell_g) \vee A(\ell_g|ii|\ell_{g:}) \vee A(\ell_g|ii|out) \vee C[\ell_{g:}, g_{::}, \ell_g]$

$= $ "∨-idem, rearrange"

$\quad A(in|ii|\ell_g) \vee A(\ell_g|ii|out) \vee$
$\quad A(in|ii|\ell_g) \vee A(\ell_g|ii|\ell_{g:}) \vee C[\ell_{g:}, g_{::}, \ell_g]$

Here we use the ∨-idem law to justify making copies of an action. We stop at this point because, while we have one complete flow from in to out, we also have part of a flow that goes from ℓ_g to ℓ_g via C. This is by design as this is a looping construct. When label $\ell_g \in ls$, there is a choice between exiting, or executing the loop body C. We can summarise all the possible flows as:

$$A(in|ii|\ell_g); (\ A(\ell_g|ii|\ell_{g:}); C[\ell_{g:}, g_{::}, \ell_g]\ )^i ; A(\ell_g|ii|out), \qquad i \in \mathbb{N}$$

Applying 《·cntl-l-merge·》 to the above results in:

$$A(in|ii|\ell_g); (C[\ell_g, g_{::}, \ell_g])^i ; A(\ell_g|ii|out), \qquad i \in \mathbb{N}$$

It might appear that $C[\ell_g, g_{::}, \ell_g]$ might violate some invariants, particularly if C is atomic, so we have $A(\ell_g|a|\ell_g)$. This is not the case—the invariants don't force the contents of ls to change, they just require that certain labels cannot be present in ls at the same time.

Finally, if we assume inductively that any expansion of C has a finite number of actions, then we can say the same for iteration (even if C itself contains an iteration).

We now turn to the lefthand side:

$\mathtt{skip} + C \mathbin{;;} C^*$

$=$ "Defn $+$"

$A(in|ii|\ell_{g1}) \vee \mathtt{skip}[\ell_{g1}, g_{1:}, out] \vee$
$A(in|ii|\ell_{g2}) \vee (C \mathbin{;;} C^*)[\ell_{g2}, g_{2:}, out]$

$=$ "Defn $\mathtt{skip}$ and $;;$"

$A(in|ii|\ell_{g1}) \vee A(in|ii|out)[\ell_{g1}, g_{1:}, out] \vee$
$A(in|ii|\ell_{g2}) \vee$
$(C[in, g_{:1}, \ell_g] \vee C^*[\ell_g, g_{:2}, out])[\ell_{g2}, g_{2:}, out]$

$=$ "substitution"

$A(in|ii|\ell_{g1}) \vee A(\ell_{g1}|ii|out) \vee$
$A(in|ii|\ell_{g2}) \vee$
$C[\ell_{g2}, g_{2::1}, \ell_{g2:}] \vee C^*[\ell_{g2:}, g_{2::2}, out]$

$=$ "Defn. C^*"

$A(in|ii|\ell_{g1}) \vee A(\ell_{g1}|ii|out) \vee$
$A(in|ii|\ell_{g2}) \vee$
$C[\ell_{g2}, g_{2::1}, \ell_{g2:}] \vee$
$(A(in|ii|\ell_g) \vee A(\ell_g|ii|\ell_{g:}) \vee A(\ell_g|ii|out) \vee C[\ell_{g:}, g_{::}, \ell_g])[\ell_{g2:}, g_{2::2}, out]$

$=$ "substitution"

$A(in|ii|\ell_{g1}) \vee A(\ell_{g1}|ii|out) \vee$
$A(in|ii|\ell_{g2}) \vee$
$C[\ell_{g2}, g_{2::1}, \ell_{g2:}] \vee$
$A(\ell_{g2:}|ii|\ell_{g2::2}) \vee A(\ell_{g2::2}|ii|\ell_{g2::2:}) \vee A(\ell_{g2::2}|ii|out) \vee C[\ell_{g2::2:}, g_{2::2::}, \ell_{g2::2}]$

A key feature to note here are two components that are self-loops. One is a control action ($A(\ell_{g2::2}|ii|\ell_{g2::2:})$), while the other involves an instance of C. The first is functionally the same as II, and so is actually harmless as we can always merge it with an action that makes progress. The second ($C[\ell_{g2::2:}, g_{2::2::}, \ell_{g2::2}]$) is the occurrence of C^* on the lefthand side reduced to a self-loop. We can now identify the following complete flows

$A(in|ii|\ell_{g1}); A(\ell_{g1}|ii|out)$

$A(in|ii|\ell_{g2}); C[\ell_{g2}, g_{2::1}, \ell_{g2:}]; A(\ell_{g2:}|ii|\ell_{g2::2}); A(\ell_{g2::2}|ii|out)$

$A(in|ii|\ell_{g2}); C[\ell_{g2}, g_{2::1}, \ell_{g2:}]; A(\ell_{g2:}|ii|\ell_{g2::2}); A(\ell_{g2::2}|ii|\ell_{g2::2:}); A(\ell_{g2::2}|ii|out)$

$A(in|ii|\ell_{g2}); C[\ell_{g2}, g_{2::1}, \ell_{g2:}]; A(\ell_{g2:}|ii|\ell_{g2::2}); C[\ell_{g2::2:}, g_{2::2::}, \ell_{g2::2}]; A(\ell_{g2::2}|ii|out)$

$A(in|ii|\ell_{g2}); C[\ell_{g2}, g_{2::1}, \ell_{g2:}]; A(\ell_{g2:}|ii|\ell_{g2::2}); (C[\ell_{g2::2:}, g_{2::2::}, \ell_{g2::2}])^i ; A(\ell_{g2::2}|ii|out)$

Simplify these by applying control merge liberally:

$A(in|ii|out)$

$C[in, g_{2::1}, out]$

$C[in, g_{2::1}, \ell_{g2::2}]; C[\ell_{g2::2:}, g_{2::2::}, out];$

$C[in, g_{2::1}, \ell_{g2::2}]; C[\ell_{g2::2:}, g_{2::2::}, \ell_{g2::2}]; C[\ell_{g2::2:}, g_{2::2::}, out];$

$C[in, g_{2::1}, \ell_{g2::2}]; C[\ell_{g2::2:}, g_{2::2::}, \ell_{g2::2}]; C[\ell_{g2::2:}, g_{2::2::}, \ell_{g2::2}]; C[\ell_{g2::2:}, g_{2::2::}, out];$

$C[in, g_{2::1}, \ell_{g2::2}]; (C[\ell_{g2::2:}, g_{2::2::}, \ell_{g2::2}])^i ; A(\ell_{g2::2}|ii|out), \quad i \in 4 \ldots$

Applying control merge to the righthand side results in:

$$A(in|ii|out)$$
$$C[in, g_{::}, out]$$
$$C[in, g_{::}, \ell_g]; C[\ell_g, g_{::}, out]$$
$$C[in, g_{::}, \ell_g]; C[\ell_g, g_{::}, \ell_g]; C[\ell_g, g_{::}, out];$$
$$A(in|ii|\ell_g); (C[\ell_g, g_{::}, \ell_g])^i ; A(\ell_g|ii|out) \quad i \in 4 \ldots$$

Here we have the following bijection:

$$\{in \mapsto in , \ell_g \mapsto \ell_{g2::2:} , out \mapsto out\}$$

4.3   Laws Involving **miracle**

The miracle laws are:

$$
\begin{array}{ll}
C + \text{miracle} = C & \langle\!\langle \cdot\text{ndc-unit}\cdot \rangle\!\rangle \\
C \,;; \text{miracle} = \text{miracle} & \langle\!\langle \cdot\text{seq-r-zero}\cdot \rangle\!\rangle \\
\text{miracle} \,;; C = \text{miracle} & \langle\!\langle \cdot\text{seq-l-zero}\cdot \rangle\!\rangle \\
C \,\|\, \text{miracle} = \text{miracle} & \langle\!\langle \cdot\text{par-zero}\cdot \rangle\!\rangle
\end{array}
$$

The real issue here is how to define miracle. The obvious thing to try is that it is simply $\mathbf{W}(\mathbf{false})$, but this simplifies to $DL \wedge LE \wedge II$ We also note that $A(in|\mathbf{false}|out) = \mathbf{false}$, and $\mathbf{W}(\mathbf{false}) = \mathbf{W}(II)$. The issue here is very reminiscent of the end of Chap. 2 of the UTP Book [17, pp55-62], where a semantics for a simple imperative language has been described. However, the loop semantics is problematic, particularly w.r.t the semantics of an infinite loop. The issue is resolved in Chap. 3 of [17] with the concept of Designs, and in particular the new special stability observables ok and ok'. It turns out that the solution for us seems to be to adopt designs at the *atomic action* level. We need to add ok, ok' as observables and to define the actions as designs:

$$A(E|a, B|N) \mathbin{\widehat{=}} E \in ls \wedge a \vdash B \wedge ls' = (ls \setminus E) \cup N$$

We then define miracle as:

$$\mathsf{miracle} \mathbin{\widehat{=}} A(in|\mathbf{true}, \mathbf{false}|out)$$

A simple calculation reduces this to:

$$\mathsf{miracle} = in \in ls \implies \neg ok$$

A sketch of the proof methodology follows, using the «·ndc-unit·» law as an example:

$$C + \mathsf{miracle} = C$$

We expand the LHS:

$LHS \quad C + \mathsf{miracle}$

$= \text{"Defn. of } +\text{"}$

$\qquad A(in|ii|\ell_{g1}) \vee C[\ell_{g1}, g_{1:}, out] \vee$
$\qquad A(in|ii|\ell_{g2}) \vee \mathsf{miracle}[\ell_{g2}, g_{2:}, out]$

$= \text{"expand miracle"}$

$\qquad A(in|ii|\ell_{g1}) \vee C[\ell_{g1}, g_{1:}, out] \vee$
$\qquad A(in|ii|\ell_{g2}) \vee (in \in ls \implies \neg ok)[\ell_{g2}, g_{2:}, out]$

$= \text{"substitution"}$

$\qquad A(in|ii|\ell_{g1}) \vee C[\ell_{g1}, g_{1:}, out] \vee$
$\qquad A(in|ii|\ell_{g2}) \vee (\ell_{g2} \in ls \implies \neg ok)$

The flows we get are:

$$C[in, g_{1:}, out] \vee (in \in ls \implies \neg ok)$$

We can easily show that for any label ℓ:

$$(\ell \in ls \wedge P \vdash Q) \vee (\ell \in ls \implies \neg ok) = (\ell \in ls \wedge P \vdash Q)$$

This means that the miracle term here is absorbed by the actions in C enabled by in.

4.4   Laws Involving Refinement

The refinement laws are:

$$C + D \mathbin{;;} E \le E \implies D^* \mathbin{;;} C \le E \qquad \text{《·refine1·》}$$
$$(C \,\|\, D) \mathbin{;;} (E \,\|\, F) \;\le\; (C \mathbin{;;} E) \,\|\, (D \mathbin{;;} F) \quad \text{《·exchange·》}$$

The interpretation of $lhs \le rhs$ is that it is true if every behaviour in the lhs is also a behaviour in the rhs. For us, each behaviour is a flow, partial or complete, which is defined using disjunctions. We expect that the standard definition of refinement in UTP will work here, so that $lhs \le rhs$ simply becomes $lhs \sqsupseteq rhs$. We leave the verification of these two laws to future work.

5   Related Work

Key work was done on concurrent semantics in the 80 s and 90 s, with a strong focus on fully abstract denotational semantics. Notable work form this period includes that by Stephen Brookes [3] and Frank de Boer and colleagues [2]. Both looked at denotations based on the notion of sets of transition traces, these being sequences of pairs of before-after states. In order to get compositionality the traces of any program fragment had to have arbitrary "stuttering" and "mumbling" state-pairs added to capture the notion of outside interference. Full abstraction meant that the semantics had to identify programs like $skip \mathbin{;;} skip$ with $skip$, while distinguishing between $x := 2$ and $x := 1 \mathbin{;;} x := x + 1$.

The first UTP theory in this area was presented in the UTPP paper by Woodcock and Hughes [28]. This combined guarded commands [13] with the idea of action systems [1], interpreted in UTP as non-deterministic choice over guarded atomic actions, where disabled actions behave like the unit for that choice. This basic lattice-theoretic architecture for the UTPP semantics forms the foundation and inspiration for the UTCP semantics presented here.

More recently, also inspired by [14], the "UTP Views" paper by van Staden [25], starts algebraically, looking at Kleene algebras over languages. Languages here are sets of strings over an alphabet A. He then takes $A = \Sigma \times \Sigma$, which in effect encodes the Brookes model [3]. His semantics fits with the usual UTP approach to concurrency, in that it is based on traces as sequences of some notion of event.

There is however a semantics for shared-variable concurrency that is close in form to the one developed in this chapter. This is the "actions with axioms" approach of Lamport [22]. In this, the semantics of each language construct is given by a set of axioms, that are temporal logic predicates over both program variables, and additional "auxiliary" variables that manage flow of control. The meaning of a composite is given by taking the axioms that describe each of its components, and combining them with appropriate renamings. This requires being able to identify specific sub-components of any given component, and a syntactical method for doing this is described.

The recent work on Reactive Designs/Systems in UTP, by Foster and colleagues [15] is highly relevant to our work with UTCP. Here the observations ok and $wait$ are used to identify *three* phases of the operation of a reactive process: pre-, peri-, and post-condition. A pericondition is what must be true when a process is waiting for external events. Such a reactive design $[P_1 \vdash P_2|P_3]$ is a useful notation for the underlying definition $\mathbf{R}(ok \wedge P_1 \implies (P_2 \lhd wait' \rhd P_3))$. In addition there is a notion of abstract traces, and one possible use for these is to model global mutable state changes. Our work in UTCP is a converse view in a number of senses. We don't need the $wait$ observable because for atomic action $A(E|a|N)$ the normal state is waiting ($wait_E = E \not\subseteq ls$) for something else to populate ls with E. In effect there is a $wait$ predicate tailored for every atomic action. In addition, we have explicit global mutual state, but this could be used to model traces as histories that are only extended.

6   Conclusions

We have presented an argument that supports our thesis that Unifying Theories of Concurrent Programming (UTCP) describes a language that satisfies the laws of Concurrent Kleene Algebra. Parts of the argument are supported by formal proof segments, while other parts are based on careful reasoned arguments and references to hopefully intuitive ideas.

6.1   Future Work

The first key issue for future work is to complete relevant proof methodologies for both miracle and refinement.

We also need to make use of the proof calculator tool support we developed [5] to check our calculations here, and we should note that proving key properties of refinement may also benefit from such support.

The original motivation for UTCP was to follow the lead of the Views paper, and to build methods from that paper, such as Rely-Guarantee [20] on top. However, it now makes more sense to layer Designs, and Reactive systems, including *Circus* on top. One of our longer-term goals is based on being able to give formal semantics to the whole chain of languages we used when using Promela/SPIN to do test generation for the real-time operating system RTEMS [10]. There we identified already existing UTP results we could use with UTCP, such as Sheng's semantics for MDESL [24], or the paper with Woodcock, Foster and myself on Heterogenous Theories [27].

Acknowledgements. This work was supported, in part, by Science Foundation Ireland grants 10/CE/I1855 and 13/RC/2094 to Lero — the Irish Software Engineering Research Centre (www.lero.ie), and by ESA Contract No. 4000125572/18NL/GLC/as, and assistance from RTEMS community.

References

1. Back, R.J.R., Kurki-Suonio, R.: Decentralization of process nets with centralized control. In: Proceedings of the Second Annual ACM SIGACT-SIGOPS Symposium on Principles of Distributed Computing, pp. 131–142. Montreal, Quebec, Canada (1983)
2. de Boer, F.S., Kok, J.N., Palamidessi, C., Rutten, J.J.M.M.: The failure of failures in a paradigm for asynchronous communication. In: Baeten, J.C.M., Groote, J.F. (eds.) CONCUR 1991. LNCS, vol. 527, pp. 111–126. Springer, Heidelberg (1991). https://doi.org/10.1007/3-540-54430-5_84
3. Brookes, S.D.: Full abstraction for a shared-variable parallel language. Inf. Comput. **127**(2), 145–163 (1996). https://doi.org/10.1006/inco.1996.0056
4. Butterfield, A.: A VDM study of fault-tolerant stable storage - towards a computer engineering mathematics. In: Woodcock, J., Larsen, P.G. (eds.) FME 1993: Industrial-Strength Formal Methods, First International Symposium of Formal Methods Europe, Odense, Denmark, April 19-23, 1993, Proceedings. Lecture Notes in Computer Science, vol. 670, pp. 216–234. Springer (1993). https://doi.org/10.1007/BFB0024648
5. Butterfield, A.: UTPCalc — a calculator for UTP predicates. In: Bowen, J.P., Zhu, H. (eds.) UTP 2016. LNCS, vol. 10134, pp. 197–216. Springer, Cham (2017). https://doi.org/10.1007/978-3-319-52228-9_10
6. Butterfield, A.: UTCP: compositional semantics for shared-variable concurrency. In: Cavalheiro, S., Fiadeiro, J. (eds.) SBMF 2017. LNCS, vol. 10623, pp. 253–270. Springer, Cham (2017). https://doi.org/10.1007/978-3-319-70848-5_16
7. Butterfield, A., Freitas, L., Woodcock, J.: Mechanising a formal model of flash memory. Sci. Comput. Program. **74**(4), 219–237 (2009). https://doi.org/10.1016/J.SCICO.2008.09.014
8. Butterfield, A., Mjeda, A., Noll, J.: UTP semantics for shared-state, concurrent, context-sensitive process models. In: 10th International Symposium on Theoretical Aspects of Software Engineering, TASE 2016, Shanghai, China, July 17-19, 2016, pp. 93–100. IEEE Computer Society (2016). https://doi.org/10.1109/TASE.2016.22
9. Butterfield, A., Sherif, A., Woodcock, J.: Slotted-circus. In: Davies, J., Gibbons, J. (eds.) IFM 2007. LNCS, vol. 4591, pp. 75–97. Springer, Heidelberg (2007). https://doi.org/10.1007/978-3-540-73210-5_5
10. Butterfield, A., Tuong, F.: Applying formal verification to an open-source real-time operating system. In: Bowen, J.P., Li, Q., Xu, Q. (eds.) Theories of Programming and Formal Methods - Essays Dedicated to Jifeng He on the Occasion of His 80th Birthday. Lecture Notes in Computer Science, vol. 14080, pp. 348–366. Springer (2023). https://doi.org/10.1007/978-3-031-40436-8_13
11. Butterfield, A., Woodcock, J.: Semantic domains for handel-c. In: Flynn, S., Hurley, T., an Airchinnigh, M.M., Madden, N., McGettrick, M., Schellekens, M.P., Seda, A.K. (eds.) Second Irish Conference on the Mathematical Foundations of Computer Science and Information Technology, MFCSIT 2002, Galway, Ireland, July 18-19, 2002. Electronic Notes in Theoretical Computer Science, vol. 74, pp. 1–20. Elsevier (2002). https://doi.org/10.1016/S1571-0661(04)80762-X
12. Butterfield, A., Woodcock, J.: prialt in handel-c: an operational semantics. Int. J. Softw. Tools Technol. Transf. **7**(3), 248–267 (2005). https://doi.org/10.1007/S10009-004-0181-6

13. Dijkstra, E.W.: A Discipline of Programming. Series in Automatic Computation, Prentice-Hall, Englewood Cliffs, NJ, USA (1976)
14. Dinsdale-Young, T., Birkedal, L., Gardner, P., Parkinson, M.J., Yang, H.: Views: compositional reasoning for concurrent programs. In: Giacobazzi, R., Cousot, R. (eds.) The 40th Annual ACM SIGPLAN-SIGACT Symposium on Principles of Programming Languages, POPL 2013, Rome, Italy - January 23 - 25, 2013, pp. 287–300. ACM (2013)
15. Foster, S., Cavalcanti, A., Canham, S., Woodcock, J., Zeyda, F.: Unifying theories of reactive design contracts. Theor. Comput. Sci. **802**, 105–140 (2020). https://doi.org/10.1016/J.TCS.2019.09.017
16. Freitas, L., Woodcock, J., Butterfield, A.: POSIX and the verification grand challenge: a roadmap. In: 13th International Conference on Engineering of Complex Computer Systems (ICECCS 2008), March 31 2008 - April 3 2008, Belfast, Northern Ireland, pp. 153–162. IEEE Computer Society (2008). https://doi.org/10.1109/ICECCS.2008.35
17. Hoare, C.A.R., He, J.: Unifying Theories of Programming. Prentice-Hall (1998)
18. Hoare, C.A.R.T., Möller, B., Struth, G., Wehrman, I.: Concurrent kleene algebra. In: Bravetti, M., Zavattaro, G. (eds.) CONCUR 2009. LNCS, vol. 5710, pp. 399–414. Springer, Heidelberg (2009). https://doi.org/10.1007/978-3-642-04081-8_27
19. Hoare, T.: Unifying semantics for concurrent programming. In: Coecke, B., Ong, L., Panangaden, P. (eds.) Computation, Logic, Games, and Quantum Foundations. The Many Facets of Samson Abramsky. LNCS, vol. 7860, pp. 139–149. Springer, Heidelberg (2013). https://doi.org/10.1007/978-3-642-38164-5_10
20. Jones, C.B.: Tentative steps toward a development method for interfering programs. TOPLAS **5**(4), 596–619 (1983)
21. Kappé, T., Brunet, P., Silva, A., Zanasi, F.: Concurrent kleene algebra: free model and completeness. In: Ahmed, A. (ed.) ESOP 2018. LNCS, vol. 10801, pp. 856–882. Springer, Cham (2018). https://doi.org/10.1007/978-3-319-89884-1_30
22. Lamport, L.: An axiomatic semantics of concurrent programming languages. In: Apt, K.R. (eds.) Logics and Models of Concurrent Systems. NATO ASI Series, pp. 77–122. Springer Berlin Heidelberg, Berlin, Heidelberg (1985). https://doi.org/10.1007/978-3-642-82453-1_4
23. Mjeda, A., Butterfield, A., Noll, J.: Business process modeling flexibility: a formal interpretation. In: Hammoudi, S., Pires, L.F., Selic, B. (eds.) Proceedings of the 7th International Conference on Model-Driven Engineering and Software Development, MODELSWARD 2019, Prague, Czech Republic, February 20-22, 2019, pp. 465–472. SciTePress (2019). https://doi.org/10.5220/0007577104670474
24. Sheng, F., Zhu, H., He, J., Yang, Z., Bowen, J.P.: Theoretical and practical approaches to the denotational semantics for MDESL based on UTP. Formal Aspects Comput. **32**(2–3), 275–314 (2020). https://doi.org/10.1007/S00165-020-00513-4
25. Staden, S.: Constructing the views framework. In: Naumann, D. (ed.) UTP 2014. LNCS, vol. 8963, pp. 62–83. Springer, Cham (2015). https://doi.org/10.1007/978-3-319-14806-9_4
26. Woodcock, J., Cavalcanti, A.: A concurrent language for refinement. In: Butterfield, A., Strong, G., Pahl, C. (eds.) 5th Irish Workshop on Formal Methods, IWFM 2001, Dublin, Ireland, 16-17 July 2001. Workshops in Computing, BCS (2001), http://ewic.bcs.org/content/ConWebDoc/4146

27. Woodcock, J., Foster, S., Butterfield, A.: Heterogeneous semantics and unifying theories. In: Margaria, T., Steffen, B. (eds.) Leveraging Applications of Formal Methods, Verification and Validation: Foundational Techniques - 7th International Symposium, ISoLA 2016, Imperial, Corfu, Greece, October 10-14, 2016, Proceedings, Part I. Lecture Notes in Computer Science, vol. 9952, pp. 374–394 (2016). https://doi.org/10.1007/978-3-319-47166-2_26
28. Woodcock, J., Hughes, A.: Unifying theories of parallel programming. In: George, C., Miao, H. (eds.) ICFEM 2002. LNCS, vol. 2495, pp. 24–37. Springer, Heidelberg (2002). https://doi.org/10.1007/3-540-36103-0_5

Static Race Detection for Periodic Real-Time Programs with IPCP Locks

Varsha P. Suresh[3]([envelope]) [iD], Rekha Pai[1][iD], Deepak D'Souza[1][iD],
Meenakshi D'Souza[2][iD], and Sujit Kumar Chakrabarti[2][iD]

[1] Indian Institute of Science, Bengaluru, India
deepakd@iisc.ac.in, rekhapai.klm@gmail.com
[2] International Institute of Information Technology Bangalore, Bengaluru, India
{meenakshi,sujitkc}@iiitb.ac.in
[3] Amrita School of Computing, Amrita Vishwa Vidyapeetham, Amritapuri, India
varshaps@am.amrita.edu

Dedication. Many of us authors of this paper have had the pleasure of interacting with Jim over the course of two joint projects that he initiated with us. The first was on the verification of a small real-time operating system called FreeRTOS, sponsored by UKIERI, during 2009–12, and the second was on verification of Simulink models, funded by the Royal Academy of Engineering, during 2016–18. The FreeRTOS project in particular has had a huge influence in my own research work. Apart from learning the basics of deductive refinement-based verification (largely from Jim!) in this project, the FreeRTOS case study turned out to be a rich source of practically-motivated and challenging research problems, ranging from low- and high-level race detection in interrupt-driven programs to the design and verification of a multicore version of FreeRTOS. Solving these problems required us to draw on a range of verification techniques spanning deductive verification, model-checking, and static analysis. The line of work in this paper, namely the analysis of periodic real-time programs, similarly has roots in the projects initiated by Jim.

Deepak D'Souza

Abstract. Periodic real-time programs are an important class of programs popularly used in industrial automation software and embedded applications. They comprise a set of tasks with associated priorities and periodicities, that are executed according to a priority-based preemptive scheduling policy. These programs are essentially multi-threaded programs, and hence suffer from concurrency issues like data races and deadlocks. In our previous work, we gave a sound and fairly precise way to statically detect data races in such programs, using rules that exploit the timing properties of tasks, apart from standard locks-held based rules. The technique, however, handled only non-nested locks with classical locking semantics, while in practice, especially in the automotive sector, such programs often use locks with the immediate priority

---

R. Pai—Working at Indian Institute of Science when this work was done.

© The Author(s), under exclusive license to Springer Nature Switzerland AG 2024
S. Foster and A. Sampaio (Eds.): *The Application of Formal Methods*, LNCS 14900, pp. 233–260, 2024.
https://doi.org/10.1007/978-3-031-67114-2_10

ceiling protocol (IPCP) semantics. In this paper we show how to extend the earlier analysis to programs with (possibly nested) IPCP locks. We implement and evaluate our analysis, and show that it improves on the existing technique, as well as the work of Schwarz et al. which targets a similar class of programs.

Keywords: Real-Time systems · periodic programs · static analysis · data races · response time analysis · priority ceiling protocol

1   Introduction

Periodic real-time programs are a class of programs popularly used in industrial automation systems and embedded system applications. They comprise a set of modules called tasks, each with an associated priority and periodicity. An instance of each task is released at every time instant which is a multiple of its period, and scheduled for execution (typically on a single processor) according to a priority-based preemptive scheduling policy.

These programs are essentially multi-threaded in nature, as the executions of the tasks may interleave with each other, and hence they are prone to concurrency-related issues like data-races and deadlocks. To avoid races and to ensure mutual exclusion while accessing shared structures, tasks may make use of synchronization mechanisms like locks. With standard locks however, there is the problem of priority inversion, wherein a high priority task may have to wait for a lower priority task to complete its critical section (which in turn may be delayed due to preemption by medium priority tasks). Hence the use of priority-inheritance mechanisms like the basic priority-inheritance protocol and ceiling priority inheritance protocols were proposed [19], in which a task essentially "inherits" the priority of higher priority tasks it may block. More specifically, in the basic priority-inheritance protocol, a task τ that holds a lock l inherits the priority of higher priority tasks it blocks (i.e. tasks that are blocked on acquiring l). The ceiling priority-inheritance protocol uses the notion of the *ceiling* priority of a lock l, which is the highest priority of a task that may acquire l. In this protocol, a task is allowed to enter its critical section only if its priority is higher than the ceiling priority of all blocked tasks. In contemporary practice, a variant of these protocols called the "immediate priority ceiling protocol" (or IPCP) is popularly used [17,22], in which a task τ upon taking a lock l, "immediately" inherits the ceiling priority of lock l. On releasing l, the priority of τ is restored to the priority it had just before it acquired the lock. The advantage of priority-inheritance protocols is that one can now bound the blocking time of a task in terms of the execution time of relevant critical sections in lower priority tasks.

In a recent piece of work [20] we had considered the problem of carrying out a May-Happen-in-Parallel (MHP) analysis for periodic programs, with the downstream application of static data-race detection in mind. Essentially, two statements in different threads may "happen in parallel" if they can "interleave" with each other in some execution of the program. The proposed approach gave rules that exploited the priorities and periodicities of tasks to deduce that certain blocks of code in different tasks are "disjoint" (or cannot happen in parallel) in that they cannot overlap in time in any execution of the program. The approach also proposed a way of exploiting platform-specific information (like Worst-Case Execution Time (WCET) of task blocks) to compute the Worst-Case Response Time (WCRT) of tasks (essentially how much time a task takes to complete from the time it is released, taking into account preemption and blocking due to contention for locks), and use it to infer further disjoint-block information.

One drawback of this work was that it only considered programs with *nonnested* locks with *standard* scheduling semantics, limiting the extent to which it could be applied to IPCP programs. In this work we extend the technique to specifically address the class of IPCP programs (including IPCP programs with nested locks). We strengthen the rules from [20] (for instance by dropping assumptions that two tasks do not share a lock). We also show how to compute a precise WCRT for IPCP programs by adapting the analysis of priority-inheritence protocols [3,13,19]. Finally we add a new rule which exploits the IPCP lock semantics.

We have implemented our analysis in a tool called PEPRACER2 as an extension of the tool PEPRACER from [20]. We use our tool to analyse several small IPCP programs from available benchmarks. We show that our analysis compares favourably with the technique of Schwarz et al. [18], which targets IPCP programs (albeit without periodicities, so that tasks are essentially like prioritized interrupts that can occur at any time).

In the next section we present an overview of our technique on an example adapted from one of our benchmarks. IPCP programs and their execution semantics are introduced in Sect. 3. In Sect. 4 we formally define the notions of conflicting accesses and data races. Algorithms for computing safe bounds on WCRT of tasks in IPCP programs are presented in Sect. 6. In Sect. 7 we present the rules for disjointness of tasks and the race detection algorithm for periodic programs. Our experimental evaluation is detailed in Sect. 8, followed by a discussion on related work in Sect. 9.

2 Overview

We provide an overview of our technique with an illustrative example adapted from the "lego_osek" robot controller, based on the OSEK operating system, from [2].

Figure 1 shows an excerpt from this example. The controller's job is to control the motion of the two-wheeled robot to follow a line (that it detects using light sensors) and to detect obstacles along the way (using a sonar sensor) and avoid them by braking and moving to the left. The controller has three tasks TaskDirection, TaskControl, and TaskObstAvoid to regulate robot direction, line-following control and obstacle detection and avoidance respectively. TaskDirection has a high priority of 3 (higher value indicates higher priority) and runs less frequently at 10 ms. TaskControl has mid-level priority (2), and

```
1.  // Shared structures and variables    27. void TaskDirection() {// Per 10, Prio 3 (high)
2.  struct motor right_wheel;             28.   lock(dir_lock);
3.  struct motor left_wheel;              29.   // Direction command from user
4.  struct display lcd;                   30.   dir = get_usr_direction();
5.  struct direction dir;                 31.   unlock(dir_lock);
5.  bool obstacle = 0;                     32. }

6.  void TaskControl() {// Per 9, Prio 2 (med)  33. void TaskObstAvoid() {// Per 8, Prio 1 (low)
7.    int sensor_right, sensor_left;       34.   int sonar_value, sensor_left;
8.    // Read and calibrate sensor values  35.   // Read and calibrate sensor values
9.    sensor_right = get_light_sensor(right);  36.   sonar_value = get_sonar_sensor();
10.   sensor_left = get_light_sensor(left);  37.   sensor_left = get_light_sensor(left);
11.   reset(lcd);                          38.   if (...)
12.   lock(lcd_lock);                      39.     obstacle = 1;
13.   // display sensor values on LCD      40.   else
14.   show_var(lcd, sensor_right, sensor_left);  41.     obstacle = 0;
15.   unlock(lcd_lock);                    42.   lock(lcd_lock);
16.   // Motor control, uses sensor values  43.   reset(lcd);
17.   if (!obstacle) {                     44.   show_var(lcd, sonar_value, sensor_left);
18.     lock(dir_lock);                    45.   unlock(lcd_lock);
19.     temp.dir = dir;                    46.   if (obstacle) { // avoid by moving left
20.     unlock(dir_lock);                  47.     left_wheel.speed = ...;
21.     right_wheel.speed = ...;           48.     left_wheel.brake = 1;
22.     right_wheel.brake = 0;             49.   }
23.     left_wheel.speed = ...;            50. }
24.     left_wheel.brake = 0;
25.   }
26. }
```

Fig. 1. An example Lego-OSEK program adapted from [20]

runs every 9 ms, while `TaskObstAvoid` has the least priority (1) and runs every 8 ms[1].

The tasks access some shared locations, including structures for controlling the robot direction, actuating the left and right wheel motors, an LCD display, and a boolean "obstacle-detected" flag. The `TaskDirection` task gets commands from the user to determine the direction and shares it with the `TaskControl` task after protecting the shared direction variable with the `dir_lock` lock. `TaskControl` reads two light sensor values, does some computation with them, and writes them to the LCD display. The access to the LCD display is protected by acquiring and releasing the `lcd_lock` lock. Finally it sets the local direction variable, computes the new speed and brake values that are then written to the wheel motor structures, after checking that the `obstacle` flag is not set. The `TaskObstAvoid` task reads the sonar and left light sensors, does some computation on them, sets the `obstacle` flag based on these values, and displays them on the LCD (making sure to take a lock on it first). If the `obstacle` flag was set, it goes on to write to the left wheel structure to brake and turn the robot to the left.

This program uses two locks `lcd_lock` and `dir_lock`, which have ceiling priorities 2 and 3 respectively (i.e. the highest priority of tasks that may take the locks are 2 and 3 respectively). Figure 2 shows an execution of the program with the immediate priority ceiling protocol (IPCP) semantics. Consider the execution starting at time 16. `TaskObstAvoid`, the least priority task, is released and

---

[1] This example does not use rate monotonic scheduling.

starts execution. It later acquires the `lcd_lock`. By the IPCP semantics, this task inherits priority 2, the ceiling priority of the lock. At time 18, `TaskControl` with priority 2 is released; however it cannot start execution since `TaskObstAvoid` is executing with the same priority. At time 20, `TaskDirection` with priority 3 is released and pre-empts this task. It completes its execution by time 22 and control switches back to `TaskObstAvoid`, which exits its critical section by time 23 and consequently its priority gets lowered to 1 (its priority before the critical section was entered). The higher priority ready task, `TaskControl`, now starts execution. It finishes by time 31 and the only remaining task, `TaskObstAvoid`, resumes execution. This task finishes by time 32.

We note that there are several conflicting accesses to the shared variables, including lines 14 and 43 to `lcd`, lines 17, 39, 41, and 46 on `obstacle`, lines 19 and 30 on `dir`, and lines 23–24 and 47–48 on `left_wheel`. Apart from some accesses to `lcd` and `dir` which are protected by locks, the other accesses appear to be racy at first glance. For instance, while `TaskObstAvoid` is updating the left wheel structure, it could be preempted by the higher priority `TaskControl` which goes on to write to the same structure. Likewise, while resetting of the `lcd` variable happens in `TaskObstAvoid`, the higher priority `TaskControl` may preempt and proceed to access this variable.

Following [20], the key idea is to exploit the priority, lock semantics, periodicity, and worst-case response times of the tasks, to rule out potential races. Notice that if the ceiling priority of a lock acquired by a low priority task τ_l is higher than the static priority of a high priority task τ_h then τ_h cannot run when control is in the lock block of τ_l. Thus the entire task τ_h cannot interleave with the lock block of τ_l and the accesses in them are non-racy. This is formalised as Rule 7 in Sect. 7. Thus, the unprotected access to `lcd` in `TaskControl` (line 11) is non-racy with the access to the same in `TaskObstAvoid` (line 43). We cannot conclusively say anything about the accesses to the left wheel structure in these tasks, and hence they are listed as potentially racy.

Suppose the periods of `TaskDirection`, `TaskControl`, and `TaskObstAvoid` were changed to 10, 20, and 40 respectively and the locks in `TaskControl` were nested such that the `lcd_lock` was released after line 25. In this new scenario, the low priority `TaskObstAvoid` task is guaranteed to finish its execution before the next instance of the higher priority `TaskControl` task is scheduled. Hence there can be no interleaving of the two tasks. This is formalised as Rule 3 in Sect. 7. We note that the technique in [20] would not be able to infer such facts.

In the following sections, we formalise the computation of worst case response time in the context of nested IPCP locks (see Sect. 6) and propose some rules (like the Rules 3 and 7 mentioned above) that allows us to flag certain conflicting accesses as non racy. The rules can be found in Sect. 7.

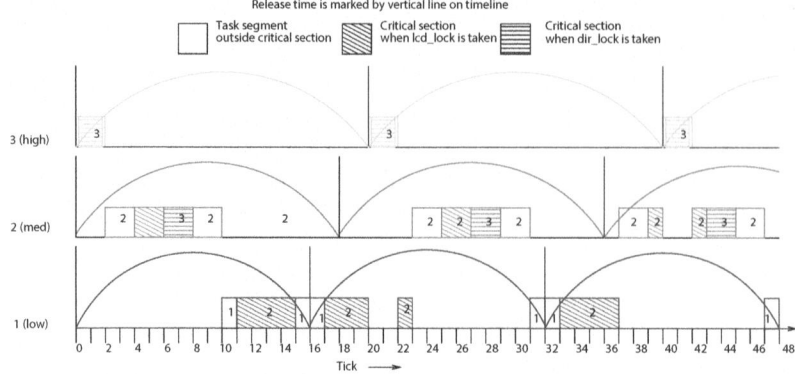

Fig. 2. Example execution of Lego-OSEK example

3   Periodic Programs with IPCP Locks

A *periodic program with IPCP locks* (or *IPCP program* for short) is a finite set of *tasks*. Each task has an associated *function*, *period*, and *priority*. We refer to this priority of a task as its *static* priority. There is a designated *init* task which is the only task that is ready to run initially. The program runs on a *single processor* platform, with tasks sharing the processor according to a certain scheduling semantics. An execution of the program begins with running the function associated with the *init* task, which initializes shared variables. It then makes other tasks ready to run using the `start` command. The *init* task runs only once.

The execution of the tasks is orchestrated by a priority-based preemptive scheduler. As we will see, a task has "dynamic" priority, which is typically its static priority, but which might change to a higher priority based on the locks it acquires. The scheduler selects one of the enabled tasks for execution on a highest-(dynamic)-priority-first basis. A task with period T is enabled (or "released" for execution) every T time units. If there are more than one tasks of the highest priority ready to run, the longest-waiting task is picked for execution.

The task functions operate on a set of shared variables V using assignment statements, and accesses to the shared variables can be synchronized using the `lock-unlock` commands. The set of commands (over a set of variables V) Cmd_V that can be used in an IPCP program are shown in Table 1.

Formally, a *periodic program with IPCP locks* $\mathcal{P}$ is a tuple $(V, L, \mathcal{T})$ where V is a finite set of shared variables, L is a finite set of locks, and $\mathcal{T}$ is a finite set of tasks, including a designated *init* task. A *task* $\tau \in \mathcal{T}$ is a tuple (G_τ, T_τ, p_τ), where G_τ is Control Flow Graph (CFG) representing the task function, T_τ is the period of the task, and p_τ is its priority. The CFG G_τ of task τ is a tuple of the form $(Loc_\tau, I_\tau, ent_\tau, ext_\tau)$, where Loc_τ is the finite set of locations of τ, $I_\tau \subseteq Loc_\tau \times Cmd_V \times Loc_\tau$ is the set of instructions of τ, and $ent_\tau, ext_\tau \in Loc_\tau$ are the entry and exit locations respectively of τ. We denote the set of locations and

Table 1. IPCP Program Commands Cmd_V

Statement	Description
start	Make all tasks ready for execution.
begin	Begins execution of the task.
end	Ends execution of the task.
skip	Do nothing.
$x := e$	Assign the value of expression e to x.
assume(b)	Enabled only if expression b evaluates to $true$; does nothing.
lock(l)	Take lock l.
unlock(l)	Release lock l

instructions in $\mathcal{P}$ by $Loc_{\mathcal{P}} = \bigcup_{\tau \in \mathcal{T}} Loc_\tau$ and $I_{\mathcal{P}} = \bigcup_{\tau \in \mathcal{T}} I_\tau$ respectively, assuming the set of locations to be disjoint across tasks. We will drop the subscripts whenever they are clear from the context.

We will assume that the lock blocks in each task are *well-nested* (in that along any initial path in the CFG of the task each unlock statement corresponds to the last pending lock), and in any complete initial path there are no pending locks at the end.

Locks in L have IPCP scheduling semantics. The *ceiling priority* of a lock l in $\mathcal{P}$, denoted $ceilp_{\mathcal{P}}(l)$, is defined to be the highest priority of a task in $\mathcal{P}$ that may take lock l (i.e. the task contains a lock(l) statement). When a task takes a lock l, the task "inherits" the ceiling priority of l, in the sense that its priority becomes the maximum of its current priority and the ceiling priority of the lock l. Whenever a task releases a lock, its priority reverts to what it was before the lock was taken.

An example IPCP program and the CFG representation of one of its task CheckSensor are shown in Fig. 3. The program has two tasks to control the speed of a robot, apart from the default *init*-task. The CheckSensor task function detects an obstacle based on the touch-sensor input in the *sensor*. An obstacle is detected when the value of the variable sensor is 1. The speed is set to 0 when an obstacle is detected. The MoveLine task function directs the motor to move forward in a line. The CheckSensor is having high priority (value 2) and runs at every 20 time units, while the MoveLine has lower priority (value 1) and runs at every 13 time units. Both tasks access the shared variable *speedAC*. The executions of the program under standard lock semantics and IPCP lock semantics are shown in Fig. 4.

We now define the semantics of an IPCP program $\mathcal{P} = (V, L, \mathcal{T})$ as a labeled transition system $\mathcal{S}_{\mathcal{P}} = \langle S, s_{in}, \Rightarrow \rangle$ where S is the set of states, $s_{in} \in S$ is the initial state, and $\Rightarrow$ is the transition relation, as defined below. In the following, $\mathcal{Q}_{\mathcal{T}}$ denotes the set of possible task priority queues and ϵ_q denotes an empty

(a) Example program   (b) CFG of the `CheckSensor` task

Fig. 3. An example IPCP program and the CFG of one of its tasks

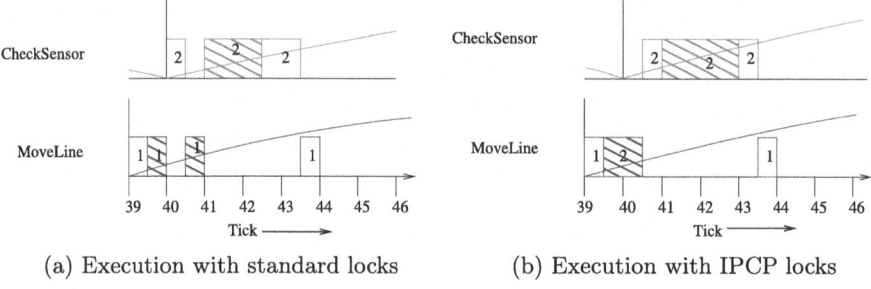

(a) Execution with standard locks   (b) Execution with IPCP locks

Fig. 4. Program Execution

queue. $\mathcal{S}_p$ denotes a stack whose elements are priorities and ϵ_s denotes an empty stack. The map $\mathcal{M}_c : L \to \mathbb{N}$ gives the ceiling priority $ceilp_\mathcal{P}(l)$ for each lock l. We also assume that the tasks have distinct priorities in $P = \{1, \ldots, k\}$ with a higher value indicating higher priority. For an integer expression e, boolean expression b, and an environment ϕ for V, we denote by $\llbracket e \rrbracket_\phi$ the integer value that e evaluates to in ϕ, and $\llbracket b \rrbracket_\phi$ denotes the boolean value that b evaluates to in ϕ. For a function $f : X \to Y$, and elements $x \in X$ and $y \in Y$, we use the notation $f[x \mapsto y]$ to denote the function $f' : X \to Y$ given by $f'(x) = y$, and $f'(z) = f(z)$ for all z different from x.

A state $s \in S$ is a tuple $(\mathcal{R}, \mathcal{W}, \mathcal{A}, \mathcal{B}, pc, \phi, tick, r)$ where

- $\mathcal{R}$ is a priority queue of tasks that are ready to run,
- $\mathcal{W} \subseteq \mathcal{T}$ is the set of tasks that are waiting to be scheduled,
- $\mathcal{A} \in L \rightharpoonup \mathcal{T}$ is a partial map that gives, for each lock, the task that has acquired the lock,
- $\mathcal{B} \in \mathcal{T} \to \mathcal{S}_p$ is a map that gives, for each task, the priority stack. At any given time, the top of a task's stack gives its priority at that time,

- $pc \in \mathcal{T} \rightarrow Loc_\mathcal{P}$ is a map giving the current location of each task,
- $\phi \in V \rightarrow \mathbb{Z}$ is a variable to value map,
- $tick \in \mathbb{N}$ is the time units elapsed since the program started, and
- $r \in \mathcal{T}$ is the currently running task.

The initial state s_{in} is defined to be

$$(\epsilon_q, \mathcal{T} - \{init\}, \emptyset, \lambda\tau.\mathtt{push}(\epsilon_s, p_\tau), \lambda\tau.ent_\tau, \lambda x.0, 0, init),$$

denoting the fact that initially the *init* task is the running task while no other tasks are ready to run and instead are waiting to be scheduled, none of the locks are acquired, the task priority stacks are initialized with the respective static priorities, all the tasks are at their entry locations, all the variables are initialized to zero, and so is the *tick* counter.

We now define the transition relation $\Rightarrow \subseteq S \times I_\mathcal{P} \times S$ as follows. For a state $s = (\mathcal{R}, \mathcal{W}, \mathcal{A}, \mathcal{B}, pc, \phi, tick, r)$, a task τ, and an instruction $\iota = (l, c, l')$ in G_τ, we have $s \Rightarrow_\iota s'$ iff one of the rules given below is satisfied. If for a command c, the conditions on state s specified in the antecedent (the ones mentioned above the line) holds then $s \Rightarrow_\iota s'$ in the consequent (the one below the line) also holds (Fig. 5).

In the START rule, for the start command executed by the *init* task, all the tasks in $\mathcal{W}$ that are waiting to be scheduled are enqueued onto the ready queue $\mathcal{R}$. We now pick the highest priority task, which is at the head of the updated ready queue, to be the next running task. Once the *init* task executes the start command, it plays no role in the rest of the execution.

The rule uses the $\mathtt{ENQ}(Q, S)$ function which when given a priority queue Q of tasks and a set S of tasks, enqueues each task in S onto the queue Q. The function $\mathtt{enq}(Q, s)$ is the standard enqueue function for a priority queue Q. The function $\mathtt{deq}(Q)$ returns the queue with the head element removed. The function $\mathtt{head}(Q)$ when given a priority queue Q of tasks returns the task with the highest priority, which is at the head of Q.

The END rule is defined for the end command to signal completion of the currently running task. Hence the task is inserted into the wait list $\mathcal{W}$. Moreover, the highest priority task in the ready queue $\mathcal{R}$, which is at its head, is removed from $\mathcal{R}$ and made the running task. The rule requires that the ready queue $\mathcal{R}$ be non-empty.

The LOCK rule is defined for the $\mathtt{lock}(m)$ command. If the running task r requests for a lock m which is not acquired by any task (as given by $\mathcal{A}(m) = undef$) then the running task can acquire the lock. It also inherits the lock's ceiling priority which is indicated by pushing this priority on to the task's priority stack for which it uses the standard $\mathtt{push}$ function for stacks. As we will see later in Sect. 5, in IPCP programs a lock requested by a running task will always be available, i.e., the situation $\mathcal{A}(m) = \tau'$ cannot happen. Hence we don't consider this case here.

The UNLOCK rule is defined for the $\mathtt{unlock}(m)$ command. If the running task r requests for the release of the lock m which it was holding then the running task can release the lock. Moreover, its priority goes back to the one it had before

$$\frac{c = \textbf{skip} \quad pc(\tau) = l \quad \tau = r}{s \Rightarrow_\iota (\mathcal{R}, \mathcal{W}, \mathcal{A}, pc[\tau \mapsto l'], \phi, tick, r)} \text{ SKIP}$$

$$\frac{c = \textbf{begin} \quad pc(\tau) = l \quad \tau = r}{s \Rightarrow_\iota (\mathcal{R}, \mathcal{W}, \mathcal{A}, pc[\tau \mapsto l'], \phi, tick, r)} \text{ BEGIN}$$

$$\frac{c = x := e \quad pc(\tau) = l \quad \tau = r}{s \Rightarrow_\iota (\mathcal{R}, \mathcal{W}, \mathcal{A}, pc[\tau \mapsto l'], \phi[x \mapsto [\![e]\!]_\phi], tick, r)} \text{ ASSIGN}$$

$$\frac{c = \textbf{assume}(b) \quad pc(\tau) = l \quad \tau = r \quad [\![b]\!]_\phi = true}{s \Rightarrow_\iota (\mathcal{R}, \mathcal{W}, \mathcal{A}, pc[\tau \mapsto l'], \phi, tick, r)} \text{ ASSUME}$$

$$\frac{c = \textbf{start} \quad pc(\tau) = l \quad \tau = r = init}{s \Rightarrow_\iota (\text{deq}(\text{ENQ}(\mathcal{R}, \mathcal{W} \cup \{r\})), \emptyset, \mathcal{A}, pc[\tau \mapsto l'], \phi, tick, \text{head}(\text{ENQ}(\mathcal{R}, \mathcal{W})))} \text{ START}$$

$$\frac{c = \textbf{end} \quad pc(\tau) = l \quad \tau = r = init \quad \mathcal{R} \neq \epsilon_q}{s \Rightarrow_\iota (\text{deq}(\mathcal{R}), \mathcal{W} \cup \{r\}, \mathcal{A}, pc[\tau \mapsto l'], \phi, tick, \text{head}(\mathcal{R}))} \text{ END}$$

$$\frac{c = \textbf{lock}(m) \quad pc(\tau) = l \quad \tau = r \quad \mathcal{A}(m) = undef}{s \Rightarrow_\iota (\mathcal{R}, \mathcal{W}, \mathcal{A}[m \mapsto r], \text{push}(\mathcal{B}(r), \mathcal{M}_c(m)), pc[\tau \mapsto l'], \phi, tick, r)} \text{ LOCK}$$

$$\frac{\substack{c = \textbf{unlock}(m) \; pc(\tau) = l \; \tau = r \; \mathcal{A}(m) = r \; \text{head}(\mathcal{R}) = \tau' \\ \text{peek}(\mathcal{B}(r), 1) = p_\tau \; \text{top}(\mathcal{B}(\tau')) = p_{\tau'} \; p_\tau \geq p_{\tau'}}}{s \Rightarrow_\iota (\mathcal{R}, \mathcal{W}, \mathcal{A}[m \mapsto undef], \text{pop}(\mathcal{B}(r)), pc[\tau \mapsto l'], \phi, tick, r)} \text{ UNLK}$$

$$\frac{\substack{c = \textbf{unlock}(m) \; pc(\tau) = l \; \tau = r \; \mathcal{A}(m) = r \; \text{head}(\mathcal{R}) = \tau' \\ \text{peek}(\mathcal{B}(r), 1) = p_\tau \; \text{top}(\mathcal{B}(\tau')) = p_{\tau'} \; p_\tau < p_{\tau'}}}{s \Rightarrow_\iota (\text{enq}(\text{deq}(\mathcal{R}), r), \mathcal{W}, \mathcal{A}[m \mapsto undef], \text{pop}(\mathcal{B}(r)), pc[\tau \mapsto l'], \phi, tick, \tau')} \text{ UNLK-S}$$

$$\frac{v = \text{inc}(tick) \quad S = \{\tau' \in \mathcal{W} \mid v \text{ is a multiple of } T_{\tau'}\}}{s \Rightarrow_* (\text{deq}(\text{ENQ}(\mathcal{R}, S \cup \{r\})), \mathcal{W} \setminus S, \mathcal{A}, \mathcal{B}, pc, \phi, v, \text{head}(\text{ENQ}(\mathcal{R}, S \cup \{r\})))} \text{ TICK}$$

Fig. 5. Semantics of IPCP programs

acquiring this lock. In that case, if the previous priority is higher or equal to the highest priority among the ready tasks, then it can continue with the execution. The UNLOCK-S rule defines the case when a context switch is required due to the previous priority being strictly less than the highest priority among the ready tasks. The running task is inserted on to the ready priority queue and the new highest priority task is selected for execution. These rules uses the standard top, peek, and pop functions defined on stacks.

The TICK rule models the handling of a timer interrupt, signalling that a unit of time has elapsed. The *tick* counter is incremented by one, and the tasks in $\mathcal{W}$ whose periods divide the tick count, are moved to the ready queue $\mathcal{R}$. The current running task r is also enqueued onto the ready queue. We now pick the highest priority task in the updated ready queue, which is at its head, as the next task to run.

The SKIP, BEGIN, ASSIGN, and ASSUME rules for the `skip`, `begin`, assignment, and `assume` commands, respectively, are standard.

An *execution* of the program $\mathcal{P}$ is a finite sequence of transitions $\rho = \delta_1, \ldots, \delta_n$ ($n \geq 1$), such that there exists a sequence of states $s_0, \ldots, s_n$ of S, with $s_0 = s_{in}$, and for each i, $\delta_i = (s_{i-1}, \iota_i, s_i)$ for some ι_i and $\delta_i \in \Rightarrow$.

The semantics we have defined so far abstracts away the "real-time" aspect of an IPCP program. We can obtain the real-time semantics of an IPCP program by considering a concrete execution environment which fixes the execution time of each instruction (say in a bounded interval of time), and restricting ourselves to executions where the tick interrupt is driven by a real-time clock and is consistent with the time taken to execute instructions between two ticks. Henceforth we fix such an environment and focus on the induced subset of executions of an IPCP program.

4   Data Races

Let $\mathcal{P} = (V, L, \mathcal{T})$ be an IPCP program. In an execution of $\mathcal{P}$, tasks are executed periodically and hence during the course of execution of $\mathcal{P}$ many instances of a task get executed. Consider two tasks τ_1 and τ_2 in $\mathcal{T}$, and two non-empty paths π and π' in G_{τ_1} and G_{τ_2}, respectively. We say π and π' *may happen in parallel* in $\mathcal{P}$ if there is an execution ρ of $\mathcal{P}$, and instances of τ_1 and τ_2 in ρ which execute along the paths π and π' respectively, in such a way that the paths π and π' interleave (that is, either π' begins after π has begun but not yet ended; or vice-versa).

Following [8,20], we now define when two statements s_1 and s_2 (corresponding, to instructions $\iota_1 = (l_1, c_1, l_1')$ and $\iota_2 = (l_2, c_2, l_2')$) in tasks τ_1 and τ_2, respectively, may happen in parallel. Consider the program $\mathcal{P}'$ obtained from $\mathcal{P}$ by enclosing the statements s_1 and s_2 in `skip` statements. Formally, we obtain $\mathcal{P}'$ by replacing the instruction ι_1 by the instructions $(l_1, \texttt{skip}, m_1)$, (m_1, c_1, m_1'), and $(m_1', \texttt{skip}, l_1')$, where m_1 and m_1' are new locations in Loc_{τ_1}; and similarly for ι_2. Let π_1 be the path $l_1 \overset{\texttt{skip}}{\rightarrow} m_1 \overset{c_1}{\rightarrow} m_1' \overset{\texttt{skip}}{\rightarrow} l_1'$ in $G_{\tau_1'}$, and similarly π_2 in $G_{\tau_2'}$. We now say s_1 and s_2 *may happen in parallel* in $\mathcal{P}$, if the paths π_1 and π_2 may happen in parallel in the program $\mathcal{P}'$.

Two statements are called *conflicting* if they are read/write accesses to the same variable, and at least one of them is a write. We say two statements s_1 and s_2 in $\mathcal{P}$ are involved in a *data race* (or are simply *racy*) if they are conflicting accesses that may happen in parallel. As an example, in the example program of Fig. 3, the accesses to `obstacle` in lines 10 and 20 are conflicting. Without any assumptions on the execution time of these two tasks, these two statements are also racy, since there is an execution of the augmented program in which the skip-blocks around these two statements interleave.

Finally, we define what it means for a "block" of code to happen in parallel with another. A *block* of code in $\mathcal{P}$ is specified by a pair (l, X), where for some task τ in $\mathcal{P}$, l is a location in Loc_τ and $X \subseteq Loc_\tau$ is a subset of locations reachable from l, in task τ. An *initial path* in a block $B = (l, X)$ of a task τ in $\mathcal{P}$, is a non-empty path in G_τ that begins at l and stays within the set of locations X, except possibly for the last location in the path. We say a statement $s = (m, c, m')$ in $\mathcal{P}$ *belongs to* block $B = (l, X)$ if m belongs to the set X. We say two blocks B_1 and B_2 of $\mathcal{P}$ *may happen in parallel* if there are two initial paths π_1 in B_1 and π_2 in B_2, which may happen in parallel with each other. Otherwise, B_1 and B_2 are *disjoint*.

5 Some Properties of IPCP Programs

We now show some properties of IPCP programs that will be useful in computing their worst-case response time in the next section.

We will need the notion of "current ceiling priority" defined in [13]. For an execution of an IPCP program $\mathcal{P}$, we define the *current ceiling priority* of the system at time t to be the highest ceiling priority of the locks that are held at time t, if any are held; and $-\infty$ otherwise. Also, we say a task τ is *blocked* in an execution of $\mathcal{P}$ if at some point in the execution τ is ready to run, but a (statically) lower priority task τ' runs instead. Finally, we say a task τ is *blocked* on a lock l at time t in an execution of $\mathcal{P}$ if τ requests l at time t and the lock is held by a statically lower priority task τ'.

Theorem 1. *Every IPCP progam $\mathcal{P}$ satisfies the following properties:*

- *(Property 1) Once a task begins execution, it cannot be blocked.*
- *(Property 2) There can be no transitive blocking in any execution of $\mathcal{P}$: i.e. a task which blocks another task cannot be blocked in turn by some other task.*
- *(Property 3) A task τ once released may have to wait for at most the duration of one critical section in a lower priority task, before it begins execution.*

Proof. Let us prove the properties one by one.

For Property 1, suppose to the contrary that there was an execution of $\mathcal{P}$ in which a task gets blocked, and let τ be the highest priority such task. Suppose τ begins execution at time t. Let the current ceiling priority at t be p_c.

Case 1: $p_c = -\infty$. This implies that none of the executing tasks are in critical sections, at time t and all the locks are available. Now the only way τ can get blocked is if a lower priority task gets to run before τ completes its execution. But for this to happen, τ has to try to acquire a lock l that is already held. In the current situation, this can only happen if a task τ' of higher static priority than τ preempts it, takes lock l and gets blocked. But this contradicts our assumption that τ was the highest priority task to get blocked in this execution.

Case 2. $p_c \neq -\infty$. This implies that some tasks have taken locks, inherited the respective ceiling priorities (by IPCP semantics) and are in their critical sections at time t. Let the static priority of τ be p. If $p > p_c$, then this implies that τ can start execution at time t and none of the critical sections can block τ at that time. Furthermore, none of the (lower priority) partially run tasks can pre-empt τ till it finishes execution. Thus, all the locks ever required by τ are available throughout and cannot be blocked. If $p \leq p_c$, then by the IPCP semantics there is some task that has inherited the ceiling priority p_c and hence τ cannot start execution.

Thus, the only possibility is that a ready to run task is blocked before it can start execution because a (statically) lower priority task τ' with a higher dynamic priority is running.

Property-2 follows from Property-1, since a task can be blocked only before it starts execution. Such a blocked task cannot block another task.

For Property-3. Let task τ be released at time t and suppose there are n jobs in their critical sections at time t. Let τ_i be an arbitrary task such that it directly blocks τ. The claim is that there can be only one such task.

By IPCP semantics, τ_i immediately inherits a priority at least as high as the static priority of τ when it enters the critical section that blocks τ. This is true till the critical section is exited. Since τ_i immediately inherits such a priority, no task with static priorities between τ and τ_i can be in execution. Since τ_i is chosen arbitrarily, the above is true for τ_i with the lowest static priority that blocks τ. Hence, exactly one job can directly block τ. Moreover, when τ_i exits the blocking critical section, its priority lowers to the one before entering the critical section. Thus, τ pre-empts τ_i and starts execution. Once τ starts execution, no further critical sections in τ_i can block τ by Property-1. Hence only one critical section can directly block τ. By Property-2, τ cannot be blocked indirectly. Hence, τ need to wait for at most the duration of one critical section.   □

6   Computing Response Time

We now discuss the computation of the worst-case response time (WCRT) of an IPCP program.

Consider an IPCP program $\mathcal{P} = (V, L, \mathcal{T})$ satisfying the following assumptions:

- Each task $\tau_i \in \mathcal{T}$ has priority i.
- Each task $\tau_i \in \mathcal{T}$ has a finite number of $lock(l)$-blocks $B^i_{l,1}, \ldots, B^i_{l,n_{l,i}}$, with $n_{l,i} \geq 0$, for each lock variable $l \in L$.
- An upper-bound C_i on the WCET of each task τ_i is known; similarly an upper-bound $C^i_{l,k}$ on the WCET of each block $B^i_{l,k}$ is known.

Equation (1) below tries to capture the WCRT of each task, in a sense made clear in Theorem 2 below. The variables in the equation are the R_i's representing the WCRT of task τ_i, and $C^j_{l,k}$'s representing the WCET of blocks $B^j_{l,k}$.

$$R_i = C_i + \sum_{j>i} (\lceil R_i/T_j \rceil \cdot C_j) + \max_{j<i \wedge 1 \leq k \leq n_{l,j} \wedge ceilp_{\mathcal{P}}(l) \geq i} C_{l,k}^j \qquad (1)$$

Theorem 2. *The least solution to Eq. (1), whenever it exists, is an upper bound on the corresponding WCRT of tasks τ_i.*

Proof. We show that any solution to the equation (1) is an upper bound on the WCRT of the tasks.

Let L_i be a solution to the equation above. To argue that the WCRT of task τ_i is bounded by L_i, consider an execution of an instance of task τ_i where it is made ready at time t. We claim that τ_i must finish its execution before $t + L_i$.

Task τ_i may lose time because of two reasons: (a)It is preempted by higher priority tasks. Like before, this is bounded by $\sum_{j>i}(\lceil L_i/T_j \rceil \cdot C_j)$ (the second term in Eq. (1)). The second reason τ_i may lose time is (b) It is blocked, because some other task τ_j has taken the lock l. Now following the IPCP protocol, a higher static priority task can never block the current task because it will never have a lower dynamic priority with current task. So it must be the case that τ_j is a *lower* priority task than τ_i and ceiling priority of lock block of τ_j is greater than or equal to priority of task τ_i. Suppose τ_i has arrived for execution and it is blocked by the lower priority task τ_j. The blocking happened because the lock block of τ_j, $B_{l,k}^j$ with ceiling priority greater than or equal to priority of the task τ_i was executing. The time taken for blocking will be at most the WCET of the block $B_{l,k}^j$. The other case is block $B_{l,k}^j$ can either have got blocked after acquiring l and before releasing it, this case is ruled out since we don't allow nested locks. The next possibility is $B_{l,k}^j$ was preempted by a still higher priority task τ' with a static priority greater than the ceiling priority of the block. The time for preemption is factored in the calculation of the interference time for the task τ_i, $\sum_{j>i}(\lceil L_i/T_j \rceil \cdot C_j)$.

Once the execution of the lock block completes, the ceiling priority is changed to the static priority of the task τ_j. This is because we are not considering nested locks. So, when τ_i starts execution it cannot be blocked by other low priority tasks. Thus blocking happens only once, thus we take WCET of the lock block in the lower priority tasks which have the maximum value. So, the total time that can be taken away due to τ_i waiting for a lock is bounded by $\max_{j<i \wedge 1 \leq k \leq n_{l,j} \wedge ceilp_{\mathcal{P}}(l) \geq i} C_{l,k}^j$ (corresponding to the third term in Eq. (1)). Thus, there must remain at least C_i amount of time in the interval t to $t + L_i$ for τ_i to execute, and hence it must complete execution before $t + L_i$.   □

Along the lines of [11,20], Algorithm 1 gives an algorithm to compute the least solution to Eq. (1) for an IPCP program, and to thereby (conservatively) check its schedulability.

Algorithm 1: Check Schedulability of IPCP programs

Data: Periodic program $\mathcal{P}$ with locks following IPCP, WCET estimates C_i for
   τ_i and $C_{l,k}^i$ for lock block $B_{l,k}^i$
Result: $\mathcal{P}$ schedulable or not; if schedulable, WCRT estimates for each task
foreach *task* τ_i **do**

> $L_i^{prev} := 0$;
> $L_i := C_i + \max\limits_{j < i \wedge 1 \leq k \leq n_{l,j} \wedge ceilp_{\mathcal{P}}(l) \geq i} C_{l,k}^j$;
> **while** *(L_i does not satisfy Eq. (1) and $L_i < T_i$)* **do**
>> $tmp := L_i$;
>> $L_i := L_i + \sum_{j>i}((\lceil L_i / T_j \rceil - \lceil L_i^{prev} / T_j \rceil) \cdot C_j)$;
>> $L_i^{prev} := tmp$;
>
> **end**
> **if** *(L_i does not satisfy Eq. (1) or $L_i > T_i$)* **then**
>> **return** "Unschedulable";
>
> **end**

end
return "Schedulable", $L_1, \ldots, L_n$;

---

7   Rules of Disjointness

Let $\mathcal{P} = (V, L, \mathcal{T})$ be an IPCP program that has WCRT estimates R_τ for each task τ in $\mathcal{P}$, satisfying $R_\tau \leq T_\tau$ (that is, $\mathcal{P}$ is schedulable). The rules below tell us when two whole task bodies or two blocks within them, are disjoint. These rules sharpen and extend the set of rules from [20]. Figure 6 illustrates Rules 1–5.

– Rule 1 (Same-Priority): *Let τ and τ' be two distinct tasks in $\mathcal{T}$ such that τ and τ' have the same priority (i.e. $p_\tau = p_{\tau'}$). Then τ and τ' are disjoint.*

– Rule 2 (Same-Period): *Let τ and τ' be two distinct tasks in $\mathcal{T}$ such that τ and τ' have the same period (i.e. $T_\tau = T_{\tau'}$). Then τ and τ' are disjoint.*

– Rule 3 (Low-Multiple-of-High): *Let τ_l and τ_h be two tasks in $\mathcal{T}$ such that:*
   • τ_l *has a lower priority than* τ_h; *(i.e. $p_{\tau_l} < p_{\tau_h}$);*
   • *The period of τ_l is a multiple of the period of τ_h (i.e. $T_{\tau_l} = k \cdot T_{\tau_h}$ for some $k \in \mathbb{N}$);*
   • *The WCRT estimate R_{τ_l} of τ_l is at most the period of τ_h (i.e. $R_{\tau_l} \leq T_{\tau_h}$).*
   Then τ_l and τ_h are disjoint.

– Rule 4 (High-Multiple-of-Low): *Let τ_l and τ_h be two tasks in $\mathcal{T}$ such that:*
   • τ_l *has a lower priority than* τ_h; *and*
   • *The period of τ_h is a multiple of the period of τ_l;*

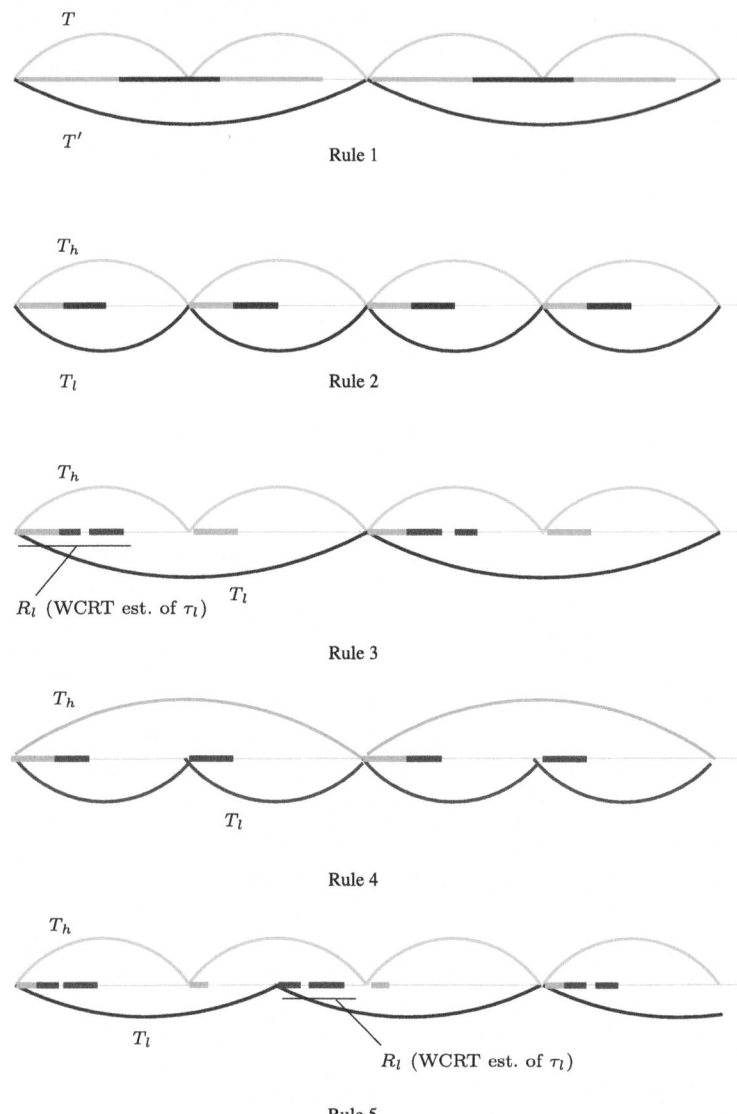

Fig. 6. Illustrating Rules 1–5

Then τ_l and τ_h are disjoint.

– Rule 5 (Low-WCRT): *Let τ_l and τ_h be two tasks in $\mathcal{T}$ such that:*
  - *τ_l has a lower priority than τ_h;*
  - *τ_l and τ_h have periods such that neither is a multiple of the other.*
  - *Let m be the minimum strictly positive value in the set*

$$\{(k \cdot T_{\tau_h}) \mod T_{\tau_l} \mid k \in \mathbb{N}\}.$$

Then the WCRT estimate R_{τ_l} of τ_l is at most m (i.e. $R_{\tau_l} \le m$). Then τ_l and τ_h are disjoint.

- Rule 6 (Lock): *Let B_l and B_l' be two* lock *(l)-*unlock *(l) blocks in distinct tasks τ and τ' respectively. Then B_l and B_l' are disjoint.*

- Rule 7 (Ceiling Priority): *Let τ_l and τ_h be two distinct tasks in $\mathcal{P}$ such that:*
  - τ_l *has a lower priority than τ_h;*
  - *B is a lock block corresponding to a lock m in τ_l, and the ceiling priority of m is greater than or equal to the static priority of τ_h (i.e. $ceilp_{\mathcal{P}}(m) \ge p_{\tau_h}$);*

Then the lock block B in τ_l and the whole task block of τ_h are disjoint (Fig. 7).

Fig. 7. Illustrating Rule 7

We now show that Rules 1–7 are sound.

Theorem 3. *Consider a schedulable IPCP program $\mathcal{P}$. Consider two blocks (task blocks or whole task bodies) which satisfy the premise of any of the Rules 1–7; then the identified blocks are indeed disjoint in $\mathcal{P}$.*

Proof. Let the WCRT estimate for each task τ in $\mathcal{P}$ be R_τ.

Suppose τ and τ' were two tasks in $\mathcal{P}$ satisfying the premise of Rule 1 (that is, they have the same priority). Then τ and τ' can never overlap in their execution instances. Suppose to the contrary, and without loss of generality, that an instance of τ begins execution and subsequently an instance of τ' begins execution before τ has completed. Consider the time point where τ relinquishes the processor for the last time before τ' begins its execution. This point could be because of a preemption by a higher priority process τ''. But once τ'' relinquishes the processor, it will be τ that resumes its execution, which is a contradiction. The only other possibility is that this point was because τ blocked on taking a lock l. But by property 1 of IPCP programs, we know that τ can never block on taking a lock. Hence τ and τ' can never overlap in their execution. The soundness of Rule 2 follows a similar argument.

For Rule 3, suppose the period of τ_l is a multiple of τ_h. Let us say τ_l is made ready at some time t (which must be a multiple of its period T_{τ_l}). Now either t is also a multiple of T_{τ_h}, in which case τ_h will begin execution before τ_l, or τ_h is next scheduled at some time $t' > t$. In the former case, the only reason τ_h may not complete before τ_l gets to execute, is that τ_h is blocked on acquiring a lock. As in earlier arguments, this lock can only have been acquired by a task of static priority *lower* than τ_l. But this is ruled out by the premise of the rule.

In the latter case, by the premise of the rule, $t + R_{\tau_l} \leq t'$. Hence τ_l will complete its execution before τ_h can preempt it at t'.

For Rule 4, suppose T_{τ_h} is a multiple of T_{τ_l}. Consider a time t when τ_l is made ready. If τ_h is not also enabled at t, then by schedulability, τ_l must complete before $t + T_{\tau_l}$, which is before the time τ_h is enabled next. Hence they cannot overlap in this case. If τ_h is also enabled along with τ_l at t, then it must begin execution before τ_l does. The only reason it may not complete before τ_l is allowed to begin execution, is that it is blocked on a acquiring a lock l held by a task of lower priority than τ_l. But this is ruled out by the premise of the rule.

For Rule 5, again consider τ_l and τ_h satisfying the premise of the rule. Let t be a time point where τ_l is made ready. Either t is a multiple of T_{τ_h}, in which case τ_h is also made ready at the same time; or it is not, and arrives at some time t' later than t. The former case is similar to the situation considered in earlier cases, and the instances of τ_l and τ_h cannot overlap. In the latter case, by the premise of the rule, we must have $t + R_{\tau_l} \leq t + m \leq t'$, and hence τ_l would finish its execution by t', and the two tasks cannot overlap. The soundness of Rule 6 is standard.

Finally, suppose τ_l and τ_h are tasks in $\mathcal{P}$ satisfying the premise of Rule 7. Suppose to the contrary that the lock-m block B in τ_l interleaves with τ_h in some execution. Suppose τ_l begins execution of block B first in this interleaved portion of the execution. Then its priority is at least as much as τ_h, and since tasks never block on a lock in IPCP programs, it follows that τ_h cannot begin execution until τ_l releases the lock m. Hence this case is ruled out. The other case is that τ_h begins execution first. Once again τ_h never blocks on a lock (by the property of IPCP programs) and hence the lower priority τ_l can never begin execution until τ_h has finished.   □

7.1   Race Detection Algorithm

We now present an algorithm to detect races in IPCP programs. The algorithm, presented in Algorithm 2, first identifies the set of shared variables accessed in the program and then lists all the conflicting access pairs, which are all assumed to be potentially racy initially. Using the rules in Sect. 7 and the *lockset analysis*, described next, the algorithm then prunes out the pairs of accesses that are guaranteed (by our rules) to be non-racy.

An iterative lockset analysis computes the set of locks held at each statement in a program $\mathcal{P}$. At the program entry, it is assumed that no locks are held. For the lock(l) command, locks held are the set of locks held before this command along with the lock l. For the unlock(l) command, locks held are the set of locks held before this command with the lock l removed. For any other command, the lockset remains the same as held in the previous command. The *join* operation, in this analysis, is the intersection of locksets.

The algorithm uses the notion of "*covers*" which needs further explanation. Let τ_1 and τ_2 be two tasks in a periodic program $\mathcal{P}$ and s_1 and s_2 be two statements in $\mathcal{P}$. We say the pair of tasks (τ_1, τ_2) *covers* the pair of statements (s_1, s_2) if either s_1 is a statement in G_{τ_1} and s_2 is a statement in G_{τ_2} or vice versa (*i.e.* s_1 in G_{τ_2} and s_2 in G_{τ_1}).

Algorithm 2: Race Detection

Data: IPCP program $\mathcal{P}$
Result: List of potential races PR
Identify the set of shared variables V;
Find the list CA of conflicting accesses on V;
$PR := CA$;
Find list DT of disjoint tasks using rules in Sect. 7;
foreach *pair (s_1, s_2) of conflicting accesses in PR* **do**
    if *there is a pair (τ_1, τ_2) of tasks in DT, such that (τ_1, τ_2) covers (s_1, s_2)*
    then
        // (s_1, s_2) are non-racy
        $PR := PR - \{(s_1, s_2)\}$;
    end
end
Perform lockset analysis on each task in $\mathcal{P}$;
foreach *pair (s_1, s_2) of conflicting accesses in PR* **do**
    let L_1 be the lockset at s_1 and L_2 be that at s_2;
    if $L_1 \cap L_2 \neq \emptyset$ **then**
        // (s_1, s_2) are non-racy
        $PR := PR - \{(s_1, s_2)\}$;
    end
end
return PR; // Set of potential races

---

8 Experimental Evaluation

In this section we describe the implementation and evaluation of our race-detection technique. We first describe the implementation of Algorithm 2. We then describe the benchmarks used to evaluate and compare our implementation with other tools.

8.1 Implementation

We implemented Algorithm 2 in the tool PEPRACER2 as an extension of the tool PEPRACER from [20]. A schematic diagram of the tool is shown in Fig. 8. The extension is mainly in the WCRT Analyzer and Rules Checker components. The tool has a preprocessor, which inlines the functions in the input program, a time analyzer which computes WCET of tasks using Heptane [10], and then their

WCRT using Algorithm 1. The CA generator identifies the shared accesses, which are essentially accesses to global variables or shared locations through pointers, in the program, and then lists the conflicting access pairs. The Rules Checker identifies disjoint task pairs using the response times and eliminates conflicting accesses that are non-racy. Rules1-5 described in Sect. 7, are applied on the conflicting accesses to eliminate non-racy pairs. The Lockset Analyzer computes the locks held at each statement in the program and further eliminates the remaining conflicting accesses that are non-racy using Rules 6 and 7. The tool finally displays the potentially racy pairs.

PEPRACER2 is implemented in the OCaml based C Intermediate Language (CIL) static analysis framework [15]. The Inliner step in PEPRACER2 uses the built-in *inline* pass in CIL while the lockset algorithm and Rules Checker are implemented as new passes in CIL.

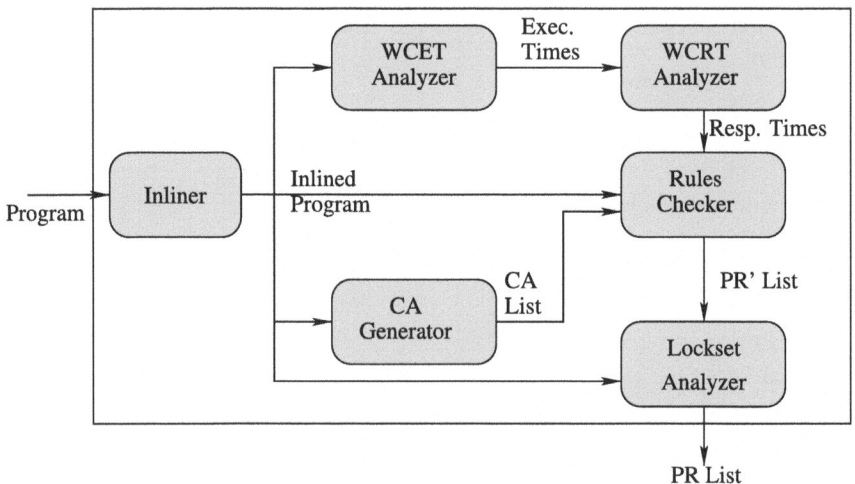

Fig. 8. Schematic of PEPRACER2

Next we describe the WCET Analyzer component. WCET analysis was carried out on the benchmarks using the Heptane [10] tool. Heptane accepts inputs in the form of C programs. To prepare the benchmark programs the following modifications were made to them: All non-C constructs in the benchmarks were translated to suitable C constructs, e.g. TASKs in OSEK programs were converted to correspondingly named functions. All code was merged into a single C file. Some benchmark programs did not have the source for some of their parts. Heptane needs the source code for the entire program being analysed. Hence, all code for which source code was not available was replaced with minimal stubs. Loop bounds were provided using ANNOT_MAXITER as required by Heptane. These loop bounds were computed by manual inspection.

For each benchmark the WCET was separately computed for each of its task entry functions. Heptane supports WCET analysis for ARM and MIPS architectures. Where possible, WCET was run using default settings for both architectures. The difference between the WCET results for both architectures were found to average around 4%, never exceeding 20%. In our analysis we use the values for the ARM architecture.

Some aspects which may lead to our WCET estimates not being conservative are as follows:

1. Stub functions were used for those parts of the code whose source was not available. This accounts for <1% of the total code analysed.
2. Loop bounds were defined using manual inspection.
3. A small number of lines of code had to be masked to prevent Heptane from crashing.

For more accurate WCET analysis, data corresponding to the specific target architecture being considered should be used. Several WCET analysis tools are available [23] both in the commercial and academic domain. The choice of the analysis tool would influence the accuracy of the WCET analysis.

8.2   Benchmarks

We tested the implementation on a few benchmark IPCP programs shown in Table 3. We have used the programs from [20] for experiment evaluation. The programs are from the nxtOSEK benchmark set, lego-osek-master project, ev3OSEK benchmark set, nxt-osek-sumo-master project, AADLib benchmark set [1] and examples in [9] and [14] for evaluation of the tool. The programs in AADLib are configured to run on FreeRTOS while the others are designed to run on the OSEK real time operating system. The program fse_obstacle.c implements a simplified version of a robotic controller which detects obstacles in its proximity while avionics.c specifies the general functions, data interactions, and timing constraints for a hypothetical avionics Mission Control Computer (MCC) system. Biped_robot.c is a sample program for LATTEBOX NXTe/LSC based biped robot. Sumo.c implements a robot which attempts to push its opponent out of a circle. A Bluetooth based radio controlled car is implemented in nxtgt.c. In lego_osek.c a robot detects obstacles and avoids collision by changing angle and speed. Objectfollower.c implements a follower. It goes forward as an object goes forward; when the object stops moving, it stops as well, and follower.c is similar. A two-wheeled self-balancing radio controlled robot is implemented in nxtway_gs.c. Ardupilot.c, taken from [1], is a simple version of the popular autopilot system supporting many vehicle types. sumoR.c and carR.c are racy versions of the programs sumo.c and car.c respectively.

We have annotated the programs with task attributes like periodicity, priority, and WCET time, along with details of locks held. The non-periodic tasks in some of the programs are taken to be tasks with high period. We have inlined the helper functions called in the tasks along with the calls to library functions. This will bring out the accesses to shared structures in the library. For example, the ecrobot library function ecrobot_set_motor_speed, which is called in `lego_osek.c`, accesses the shared `NXT_PORT_A` port. The `GetResource` and `ReleaseResource` functions used to take and release locks, respectively, are taken to be the `lock` and `unlock` command in our analysis.

8.3   Comparison

Table 2. Comparison Results

Program	CAs	PePRacer2		Goblint		Goblint Method
		PRs	Time	PRs	Time	
fse_obstacle	3	0	0.12	3	0.12	3
avionics	51	42	0.13	51	0.20	51
biped_robot	1	0	0.17	1	0.18	1
sumo	146	0	0.31	28	1.89	80
nxtgt	4	0	0.21	4	0.28	4
lego_osek	1320	0	0.12	0	4.21	0
objectfollower	14	0	0.32	11	4.26	14
nxtway_gs	4	0	0.32	4	17.39	4
car	670	0	0.28	4	2.32	404
ardupilot	17	0	0.29	613	9.15	17
test	4	0	0.25	2	0.04	2
follower	1181	0	0.31	0	4.00	1037
sumoR	146	80	0.30	28	1.84	80
carR	670	90	0.29	613	2.30	404

We compare out tool with Goblint [18] and PePRacer [20]. Goblint employs static analyses to detect data races between tasks with differing priority levels. It is based on the methodology of Schwarz et al [18]. The method is designed for embedded real-time systems that use priority-driven preemptive scheduling with task priorities that are dynamically adjusted in accordance with the immediate priority ceiling protocol. The class of programs considered by Schwarz et al. is incomparable to the programs we consider. They essentially analyse IPCP programs without periodicity. Their programs consists of a main task, interrupts, and priority. By"relaxing" the semantics by treating periodic tasks as interrupts, we could still conduct a sound analysis of our IPCP programs using the Goblint tool. Following Goblint's data race detection criteria, a data race happens at a global variable x when program execution hits the variable x at a dynamic priority of j, and x may also be accessed by an interrupt q of static priority greater than j. We compare Goblint with PePRacer2, and the results of the comparison are shown in Table 2. The "Program" column gives the benchmarks

```
...
...
464. static int sizeLCD  ;               513. TASK(TaskMainControlTask){
465. static int areaLCD  ;                    ...
466. static int xLCD  ;                        ...
     ...                                  685. }
     ...
475. TASK(TaskMainAcquisitionTask){      686. TASK(TaskMainDisplayTask){
476.     if ((int )tracking_enabled != 0) {    ...
477.         tmp = send_nxtcam_command(...,...);  ...
478.         tracking_enabled = (S8___0 )tmp;  915. val35 = sizeLCD;
479.     } else {                              ...
         ...                                   ...
         ...                              1037.val38 = areaLCD;
498.         sizeLCD = size;                   ...
499.         areaLCD = area;                   ...
500.         xLCD = x;                    1159.val41 = xLCD;
501      }                                     ...
502      TerminateTask();                      ...
503      return;                         1857.}
504  }
```

Fig. 9. False Negatives in Goblint

used, "CAs" column lists the number of conflicting accesses for a program, the number of potentially racy accesses is listed under "PRs" and the running time of the tool in seconds is given under "Time" for the tools PEPRACER2and Goblint in respective columns. The column "Goblint Method" gives the number of racy accesses as per the race definition in [18].

On running the Goblint tool, we have observed that even for single racy access on a variable, the tool warns about all the accesses on that variable. This results in false positives. Also, Goblint's value set analysis is unsound. This is demonstrated in Fig. 9 which shows an excerpt from "follower.c". In this program, there are three tasks TaskMainAcquisitionTask, TaskMainControlTask, and TaskMainDisplayTask. The shared variables $sizeLCD$, $areaLCD$ and $xLCD$ are accessed in the tasks TaskMainAcquisitionTask and TaskMainDisplayTask. Variable $tracking\_enabled$ which is initially set to non-zero is used in check the condition in line 476. Then the variable is updated at line number 478. Goblint does not reanalyze the task with the updated value because this variable is not shared with other tasks, which would trigger re-evaluation. Hence the lines of code from 479 to 501 are incorrectly considered as dead code. The conflicting accesses at line numbers (498, 915), (499, 1037), and (500,1159) are not considered for analysis. Thus Goblint results in false negatives.

The potentially racy access pairs detected by Goblint is calculated in two ways. First, the warning reported by the tool is considered to calculate the access pairs. This is shown under the column "Goblint" in Table 2. In the second way, we used the data race condition following the definition. As per the definition of data race by Schwarz et al., a pair of conflicting accesses on a variable is racy if the static priority of the first access is greater than the dynamic priority of the second access. We calculated the pairs by applying the data race condition and are shown in column "Goblint [18]" in Table 2. We observed that in lego_osek.c, test.c, and sumoR.c the number of potential races reported by PEPRACER2

```
1. int x;

2. TASK(Task1)              9. TASK(Task2)
3. {                        10. {
4.    x = 5;                11.    x = 10;
5.    GetResource(lcd);     12.    GetResource(lcd);
6.    x = 15;               13.    x = 15;
7.    ReleaseResource(lcd); 14.    ReleaseResource(lcd);
8. }                        15. }
```

Fig. 10. Effectiveness of Rule 7

and Goblint are the same. This is because the accesses resulting in potentially racy access pairs are all protected by resources(or locks). Here, Goblint is also able to detect races. Comparing the results of sumo.c and the racy version of sumo.c, that is sumoR.c we can see that for both programs Goblint is giving same number of potential races. This is because Goblint is only considering priority details to detect data race. But PePRacer2 detects 80 PRs for the sumoR.c and 0 PRs for sumo.c. Similar is the case with car.c and carR.c. Thus our tool was able to detect data races more precisely compared to Goblint.

We also compare our work with PePRacer [20]. The disjoint rules for eliminating non-racy accesses are devised in [20] for periodic programs with standard locks. Also, it does not support nested-locks. The disjoint rules 1, 2, 4 and 6 from [20] are sound for IPCP programs except for WCRT-based rules with nested locks. On running PePRacer and PePRacer2 for the benchmark programs we have observed that the running times of both tools are comparable. Precision in eliminating non-racy accesses is slightly better in PePRacer2. The benchmark programs we used in this study do not have nested locks, so we cannot observe considerable differences in the results. But if we have programs with nested locks, then the WCRT analysis for IPCP programs gives sharper WCRT values. And can perform significantly better in eliminating non-racy conflicting accesses.

8.4 Rule Coverage

Table 3 gives the coverage of the rules (Rules 1–7). Here each rule is independently applied on the conflicting accesses to demonstrate the value of each rule separately. Column "R1" gives the count of CA pairs flagged as non-racy due to Rule 1 only. The case is similar with other columns. Recall that the non-trivial rules like Rules 3–5 use periodicity and/or response time to declare CA pairs as non-racy. A careful analysis of the count for these in Table 3 reveals their usefulness in flagging non-racy pairs. Some pairs are detected by these rules while not covered by the other simpler rules. It is even worthwhile observing that the CA pairs detected as non-racy by Rule 6 (the one based on locks) and by Rule 7 are covered by other rules. The developers can use this information to decide on whether to use expensive constructs like lock-unlock to ensure mutual exclusion when the task periodicity and response time can themselves ensure it.

Table 3. Rule Coverage

Program	CAs	R1	R2	R3	R4	R5	R6	R7
fse_obstacle.c	3	0	0	3	0	0	0	0
avionics.c	51	0	9	-	-	-	0	0
biped_robot.c	1	0	0	0	0	1	1	0
sumo.c	146	35	69	69	69	112	6	10
nxtgt.c	3	0	0	0	3	0	0	0
lego_osek.c	1320	0	0	1320	0	0	1320	1320
objectfollower.c	14	0	0	11	0	3	0	0
nxtway_gs.c	4	0	0	4	0	0	0	0
car.c	670	0	90	133	164	463	117	272
ardupilot.c	17	0	17	17	17	0	0	0
test.c	4	0	0	0	0	0	1	2
follower.c	1179	0	144	144	204	975	4	4
sumoR.c	146	35	69	69	69	35	6	6
carR.c	670	0	0	0	74	463	117	272

To demonstrate the difference in results between R6 and R7 test.c is presented Fig. 10. There are two tasks Task1 and Task2 with priorities 1 and 2 respectively. Conflicting access could not be eliminated by Rules 1–5. We can observe that the number of PRs detected for the program test.c by Rule 6 is 1 and by Rule 7 is 2 in Table 3. Rule 6 detects the conflicting access (6, 13) as disjoint. In addition to (6, 13) one more CA (4, 13) is detected as disjoint by Rule 7. So the number of PRs is 2 in Table 3. This shows the significance of Rule 7 in eliminating a greater number of conflicting accesses even if the rules exploiting periodic details are not applicable.

9   Related Work

Our contribution has two major parts: Computing response times followed by schedulability analysis, and using the same for defining rules for detecting data races statically. We begin with work related to response time computations and analysis of schedulability. Apart from the work of [11,12] that are already mentioned, feasibility analysis for real-time periodic tasks without locks have been studied by Baruah et al. [4] and Pellizzoni and Lipari [16].

In a classical work on real-time systems that use locks, Sha et al. [19] consider a very general setting of priority-based preemptive scheduling, with FCFS among waiting tasks of the same priority, with arbitrarily nested locks, and give sufficient conditions for schedulability of programs under these conditions. They consider programs with the basic priority inheritance and ceiling priority inheritance, and show that such programs have the useful property that the blocking time of a task is bound by the longest WCET of a lock block (critical section) of a lower priority task. This facilitates their analysis and bounds on response time. However they do not consider the immediate priority ceiling protocol, and we show how to extend their analysis to programs with such locks. Audsley et al [3] study schedulability of periodic programs in the presence of aperiodicity and jitter in release times.

Related work on verification of periodic programs can be broadly classi-fied into two categories: Verification of periodic programs using techniques like model checking, symbolic execution etc., and detecting data races in programs for embedded applications similar to periodic programs, using static analysis techniques.

Periodic programs with tasks prioritized in a rate monotonic fashion and com-municating using shared variables, have been verified against safety properties using bounded model checking with different kinds of locks in [5–7]. In the first paper of the papers in this series [6], the authors provide a time-bounded verifica-tion of safety properties where the sequentializations of programs are considered with respect to number of jobs of each task within the time bound. Priority and preemption locks are considered in [6] and the work is extended to include Priority Inheritance Protocol (PIP) locks in [7]. [5] proposes a new sequential composition mechanism to reduce the number of sequentializations and make the bounded verification scalable. However, the verification is bounded to a certain depth, and in general cannot be used to soundly detect all data races.

PLC programs are very similar to our periodic programs and are widely used in embedded safety critical software. Symbolic execution of PLC programs is developed in [9] where the authors convert PLC programs into C programs and use their rate-monotonic, priority-based, preemptive scheduling semantics to reduce the number of inter-leavings considered. The only way to use their symbolic execution to detect data races would be for the developer to introduce a counter for each shared variable and increment/decrement this counter, and then check for violations of assertion that encode a racy accesses to these variables. This technique is unlikely to be scalable.

Static analysis based techniques for detecting data races embedded software kernels and applications have been of recent research interest [8,18,20,21]. As already mentioned, the work this paper is an extension of the race detection framework of [20] to IPCP programs with nested locks. Schwarz et al. [18] pro-vide an algorithm to detect data races in multi-task programs with priority ceiling locks, though without periodicities. Real-time programs with synchro-nization mechanisms including dynamic threads, suspend-resume of scheduler and tasks etc. are considered in [21]. Both these works exploit priorities and locks, but do not consider periodicity and WCRT information like we do, and would lead to less precise results on the class of periodic programs considered in this paper.

10   Conclusion

In this paper we have shown how to extend the approach of Suresh et al. [20] for carrying out a precise may-happen-in-parallel analysis for periodic real-time programs, to a similar class of programs with possibly nested IPCP locks. We show the effectiveness of the analysis in a downstream application of data-race detection for this class of programs.

In future work it would be interesting to see if these ideas can be used to do efficient and precise data-flow analysis for the different classes of periodic real-time programs.

References

1. OpenAADL/AADLib - A library of AADL Components (2011). https://github.com/OpenAADL/AADLib
2. nxtOSEK/JSP: RTOS for Lego MindStorms NXT (2013). http://lejos-osek.sourceforge.net/
3. Audsley, N., Burns, A., Richardson, M., Tindell, K., Wellings, A.: Applying new scheduling theory to static priority preemptive scheduling. Softw. Eng. J. **8**(5), 284–292 (1993)
4. Baruah, S.K., Rosier, L.E., Howell, R.R.: Algorithms and complexity concerning the preemptive scheduling of periodic, real-time tasks on one processor. Real Time Syst. **2**(4), 301–324 (1990)
5. Chaki, S., Gurfinkel, A., Kong, S., Strichman, O.: Compositional sequentialization of periodic programs. In: Giacobazzi, R., Berdine, J., Mastroeni, I. (eds.) VMCAI 2013. LNCS, vol. 7737, pp. 536–554. Springer, Heidelberg (2013). https://doi.org/10.1007/978-3-642-35873-9_31
6. Chaki, S., Gurfinkel, A., Strichman, O.: Time-bounded analysis of real-time systems. In: Proceedings of the Formal Methods in Computer-Aided Design (FMCAD), pp. 72–80. IEEE (2011)
7. Chaki, S., Gurfinkel, A., Strichman, O.: Verifying periodic programs with priority inheritance locks. In: Proceedings of the 13th Formal Methods in Computer-Aided Design (FMCAD), pp. 137–144. IEEE (2013)
8. Chopra, N., Pai, R., D'Souza, D.: Data races and static analysis for interrupt-driven kernels. In: Caires, L. (ed.) ESOP 2019. LNCS, vol. 11423, pp. 697–723. Springer, Cham (2019). https://doi.org/10.1007/978-3-030-17184-1_25
9. Guo, S., Wu, M., Wang, C.: Symbolic execution of programmable logic controller code. In: Proceedings of the 11th Joint Meeting on Foundations of Software Engineering (ESEC/FSE), pp. 326–336. ACM (2017)
10. Hardy, D., Rouxel, B., Puaut, I.: The heptane static worst-case execution time estimation tool. In: Proceedings of the 17th Worst-Case Execution Time Analysis (WCET). OASICS, vol. 57, pp. 8:1–8:12. Schloss Dagstuhl - Leibniz-Zentrum für Informatik (2017)
11. Joseph, M., Pandya, P.: Finding response times in a real-time system. Comput. J. **29**(5), 390–395 (1986)
12. Liu, C.L., Layland, J.W.: Scheduling algorithms for multi-programming in a hard-real-time environment. J. ACM **20**(1), 46–61 (1973)
13. Liu, J.W.S.W.: Real-Time Systems, 1st edn. Prentice Hall PTR, USA (2000)

14. Locke, D., Lucas, L., Goodenough, J.: Generic Avionics Software Specification. Technical report CMU/SEI-90-TR-8 (1990)
15. Necula, G.: CIL – Infrastructure for C Program Analysis and Transformation (v. 1.3.7) (2002). http://people.eecs.berkeley.edu/~necula/cil/
16. Pellizzoni, R., Lipari, G.: Feasibility analysis of real-time periodic tasks with offsets. Real Time Syst. **30**(1–2), 105–128 (2005)
17. Rajkumar, R.: Synchronization in Real-Time Systems: A Priority Inheritance Approach. International Series in Engineering and Computer Science. Springer, New York (1991). https://doi.org/10.1007/978-1-4615-4000-7
18. Schwarz, M.D., Seidl, H., Vojdani, V., Lammich, P., Müller-Olm, M.: Static analysis of interrupt-driven programs synchronized via the priority ceiling protocol. In: Proceedings of the 38th ACM SIGPLAN-SIGACT POPL, pp. 93–104. ACM (2011)
19. Sha, L., Rajkumar, R., Lehoczky, J.P.: Priority inheritance protocols: an approach to real-time synchronization. IEEE Trans. Comput. **39**(9), 1175–1185 (1990)
20. Suresh, V.P., Pai, R., D'Souza, D., D'Souza, M., Chakrabarti, S.K.: Static race detection for periodic programs. In: Sergey, I. (eds.) Programming Languages and Systems, ESOP 2022. LNCS, vol. 13240, pp. 290–316. Springer, Cham (2022). https://doi.org/10.1007/978-3-030-99336-8_11
21. Tulsyan, R., Pai, R., D'Souza, D.: Static race detection for RTOS applications. In: Proceedings of the (FSTTCS). LIPIcs, vol. 182, pp. 57:1–57:20. Schloss Dagstuhl - Leibniz-Zentrum für Informatik (2020)
22. Wellings, A.J., Burns, A., dos Santos, O.M., Brosgol, B.M.: Integrating priority inheritance algorithms in the real-time specification for Java. In: Proceedings of the Tenth IEEE International Symposium on Object and Component-oriented Real-Time Distributed Computing, ISORC 2007, pp. 115–123. IEEE Computer Society (2007)
23. Wilhelm, R., et al.: The worst-case execution-time problem – overview of methods and survey of tools. ACM Trans. Embed. Comput. Syst. **7**(3), 36:1–36:53 (2008)

A Tour Through the Programming Choices: Semantics and Applications

Pedro Ribeiro[1]✉ , Kangfeng Ye[1]✉ , Frank Zeyda[2] ,
and Alvaro Miyazawa[1]

[1] Department of Computer Science, University of York, York YO10 5GH, UK
{pedro.ribeiro,kangfeng.ye,alvaro.miyazawa}@york.ac.uk
[2] Zapopan, Mexico
https://www.linkedin.com/in/frank-zeyda/

Abstract. The discipline of programming, as Edsger Dijkstra would call it, has provided a formal basis for the study of programs where choices are not necessarily deterministic. That is, despite reservations from pioneers, like Tony Hoare, about the inclusion of nondeterministic behaviour in a program. For over 65 years, nondeterminism has played an important role in modelling and reasoning about programs. Moreover, there are at least two major flavours: *angelic* and *demonic*. Further programming choices, such as preferential and probabilistic, have been proposed to capture other important phenomena, for example, in the context of cyber-physical systems, distributed systems, and cryptography. In this chapter, we provide a critical account of these programming choices and their semantics, and discuss their applications. Our account focuses mainly on denotational semantics, and in particular relational models, as is fitting in honour of Jim Woodcock. We discuss approaches based on, or inspired by, weakest preconditions semantics and alphabetised relations, as found in the Unifying Theories of Programming (UTP). They are at the core of the semantics of notations such as Z and *Circus*, and extensions to deal with time and probabilities. Some of the ideas discussed here have been developed in close collaboration with Jim.

Keywords: programming · semantics · choice · relations · refinement · UTP

Acronyms

ACP	Algebra of Communicating Processes
API	Application Programming Interface
AST	Almost Sure Termination
CCS	Calculus of Communicating Systems
CPS	Cyber-Physical System
CSP	Communicating Sequential Processes

F. Zeyda—Independent Researcher.

© The Author(s), under exclusive license to Springer Nature Switzerland AG 2024
S. Foster and A. Sampaio (Eds.): *The Application of Formal Methods*, LNCS 14900, pp. 261–305, 2024.
https://doi.org/10.1007/978-3-031-67114-2_11

cwp	Conjugate Weakest Precondition
FDC	Free Distributive Completion
FMI	Functional Mock-up Interface
FMU	Functional Mock-up Unit
GCL	Guarded Command Language
MA	Master Algorithm
MDP	Markov Decision Process
PPP	Probabilistic Predicative Programming
ProbURel	Probabilistic Unifying Relations
PV	Prospective Value
RW	Random Walk
(S)SRW	(Symmetric) Simple Random Walk
SU	Simulation Unit
UTP	Unifying Theories of Programming
wp	Weakest Precondition
wpe	A wp theory but built on top of three-valued logic
WPE	Weakest Pre-Expectation
ZFC	Zermelo-Fraenkel set theory with axiom of choice

1   Dedication

The authors met Jim Woodcock at York in the early 2000s. Pedro first heard about the UTP as an MEng student when he had the privilege to attend Jim's lectures on the topic in the Summer of 2010. Kangfeng's academic career began from when he came to study for his PhD at York in 2012 under Jim's supervision. While his industry background was in embedded systems, Jim taught him a lot about formal methods. He then worked closely with Jim on probabilistic semantics and verification in various RoboStar projects. Alvaro first heard of Jim's work during his undergraduate degree when he read Jim's excellent book "Using Z: Specification, Refinement, and Proof", which boosted his interest in formal methods. Since then, he had the pleasure of attending several talks by Jim. Frank first met Jim at ZB 2002 and also later at the first symposium on Unifying Theories of Programming that he helped to organise in 2006. He was so taken by Jim's enthusiasm and didactic talent to explain difficult topics in intuitive and accessible ways that he did not think twice when offered the opportunity to work in Jim's research group at York after completing his PhD.

The authors have greatly benefited from Jim's inspiration and mentorship. Thank you, Jim!

2   Introduction

The mathematical rigour advocated by programming pioneers, like Dijkstra and Hoare, has greatly influenced how modern software engineering is approached. In [174] Woodcock et al. provide one of the most comprehensive reviews on the application of formal methods in industry. In recent years, household names such as Amazon, Facebook, and Microsoft, have quietly propelled formal methods to the forefront of their software engineering processes. In the domain of robotics and autonomous systems, however, their wider adoption is more challenging [57]. The mix of concerns, including discrete, continuous, timed and probabilistic phenomena, requires a reconciliation of formalisms for holistic system reasoning.

The unification of formalisms and their semantics has been at the forefront of much of Woodcock's research agenda [170], leveraging the pioneering work of Hoare and He [79] on the alphabetised relational calculus. In the UTP, programs, or relations, are specified via predicates where refinement gives rise to a lattice. It is convenient to model recursion, via fixed points, and *demonic* nondeterminism via the greatest lower bound. However, the latter is but one kind of nondeterministic choice, with other interpretations possible to model backtracking algorithms [45], namely as found in monotonic predicate transformers [8].

Similarly, probabilistic programs, widely used to model randomisation algorithms using probabilistic choice to simplify algorithms and improve performance, can be captured in both relational models [64,66,92] and predicate transformers [103,115]. Whether or not nondeterministic choice is supported and how it interacts with probabilistic choice is the most significant difference between different probabilistic models. A systematic account of predicate transformers is given by McIver and Morgan [102] for sequential and probabilistic programs. Here, in contrast, we are also interested in the study of choices for process calculi.

A somewhat lesser known and semantically more elusive notion of choice is that of *preference*. We think of the preferential choice $S \gg T$ as a kin of nondeterminism $S \sqcap T$ that prefers its first program S, provided that such turns out to be feasible[1]. While there exist several semantic investigations into preferential and prioritised choice , it can be shown that our notion of preference with its desired algebraic properties cannot be formally described using standard predicate transformers. In [186] we show how a theory of expression transforms can capture the meaning of preference in terms of the *prospective value* of a given computation. This approach opens the doors for a whole new program model outside wp: that of preferential computations.

---

[1] Feasible has a mathematical meaning here that we will elaborate on in Sect. 3.3.

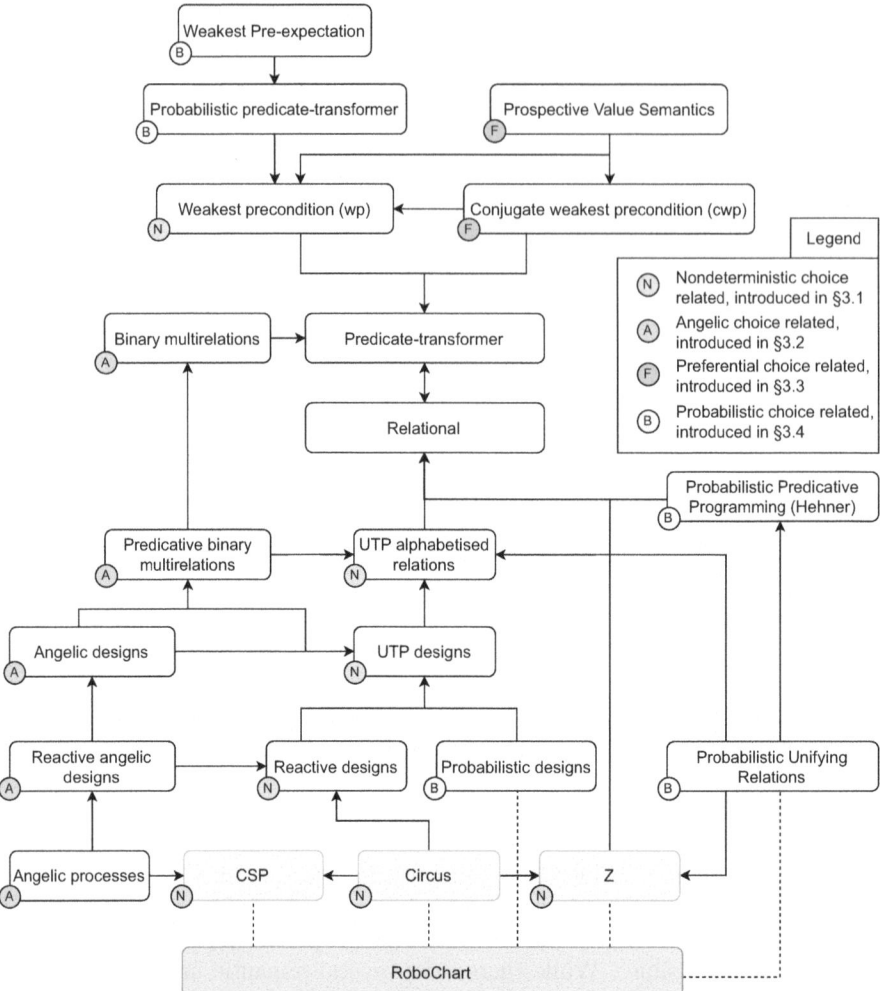

Fig. 1. Hierarchical structure of theories and formal notations, where arrows loosely indicate theory dependencies and influences. RoboChart, a notation for design of robotics software discussed in this chapter, has process-algebraic and probabilistic semantics.

In Fig. 1 we provide an overview of all the semantic models we consider in our discussion, and how they loosely relate to, or have influenced, each other. The top-half concerns predicate transformers, whereas the bottom-half concerns (multi)relational models. At the bottom, we highlight in purple RoboChart [110], a domain-specific notation for formal modelling of robotic controllers, considered as an application in Sect. 4.2, and in light-yellow the formal notations that underpin RoboChart. Solid arrows denote dependencies between theories, while dotted lines indicate the theories on which RoboChart directly depends.

This chapter's aim is to study and contrast different key notions of programming choices: *demonic, angelic, external, preferential* and *probabilistic*, and their fundamental properties. This includes discussions of how these choices may be characterised in different semantic models. We also sketch how they can be used to model different phenomena relevant to cyber-physical systems. In particular, we propose a novel process algebraic model for a co-simulation master algorithm, discuss the role *angelic* choice could play in the design of robotic controllers, and consider the modelling of random walkers using *probabilistic* choice.

In the spirit of some variants of modern literature, readers are not required to read the paper from start to finish but skip and jump to sections that mostly spark their interest, guided by Fig. 1. The key notions of choice, namely *nondeterministic, angelic, preferential,* and *probabilistic* have each a dedicated subsection in Sect. 3, and we strove to make these sections self-contained.

The chapter is structured as follows. In Sect. 3, we provide an account of the examined programming choices, namely by discussing semantic models suitable for characterising choices in sequential programs and process calculi. Then, in Sect. 4, we sketch their novel applications. Finally, we conclude in Sect. 5.

3 Programming Choices

In this section, we address nondeterministic, angelic, preferential and probabilistic choices and discuss their semantics in the context of a variety of semantic frameworks, including UTP and the wp-calculus. While Fig. 1 gave us the big picture of the relationships between programming choices and semantic models, here we shall delve deeper into the intuitive understanding of these choices, and if and how they can be expressed in various semantic models and frameworks.

3.1 Nondeterministic Choice

The ability to write programs that can lead to different executions when started from the same state did not feature in the early theories of computation. Pioneers [36,87], including Turing [160], focused their attention on deterministic machines [3,4], perhaps with good reservations as Dijkstra later quoted Hoare's observation that:

> "A system which permits user programs to become non-deterministic presents dreadful problems to the maintenance engineer: it is not a 'facility' to be lightly granted." [39, p. 12]

Nondeterminism, however, is at the core of computer science, crucial in accounting for uncontrollable phenomena, and particularly elegant for capturing many computational paradigms. It is perhaps not so surprising then, that Rabin and Scott [134] considered nondeterministic automata. In that setting, nondeterminism does not confer extra expressiveness as the power set construction shows, but it can be advantageous in the number of states required. Similarly, context-free grammars allow for nondeterminism in rule application [30]. Importantly, in those models, language acceptance merely requires reaching an accepting state.

Imperative. The earliest use of nondeterminism in a program is due to McCarthy [101], who proposed an ambiguity operator $amb(x, y)$ that nondeterministically returns the values of defined expressions x or y. This would be used to define "computably ambiguous functions" and influence dialects [1,184] of Lisp.

In a different vain, Floyd [45] proposed a nondeterministic assignment that allows for an elegant characterisation of computations that would otherwise require explicit backtracking, such as the eight-queens problem. Novel contributions included the annotation of failure and success points in a program.

Dijkstra would eventually embrace nondeterminism in his language of guarded commands [40] (GCL) after overcoming a "considerable mental resistance" [39, p. 12]. The semantics of commands is given using the wp calculus, where $wp(S, R)$ defines for a post-condition R and command S, the weakest pre-condition that must be satisfied in order for execution of S to terminate and establish R. Importantly, Dijkstra would observe the "Law of the Excluded Miracle", by requiring that $wp(S, F) = F$, and consider conjunctive, rather than arbitrary, predicate transformers. Thus, in that context it is impossible to entertain a program that achieves either outcome as long as one is individually achievable. Consider the program $P = x := 1 \sqcap x := 2$ that has a choice ($\sqcap$) between assigning ($:=$) the value 1 or 2 to a variable x, then we have that $wp(P, \{x = 1 \lor x = 2\})$ is achievable from any state, yet both $wp(P, \{x = 1\})$ and $wp(P, \{x = 2\})$ have *infeasible* preconditions. In that setting, choice is *demonic* following Dijkstra's allegory of a "daemon [that] decides quite arbitrarily" [38, p. 7].

The notion of *demonic* nondeterminism is in stark contrast with Floyd's choice points, that, by analogy, take the *angelic* view. While the treatment of both notions within a single framework is explored further in the next section, they played important roles in the refinement calculus of Back [8], Morgan [112] and Morris [117]. In particular, the adoption of the 'Miracle' would allow the definition of complete lattices. Woodcock would not only write a tutorial on this topic [167], but also discuss how to apply refinement in Z [166]. Such ideas would later be applied in the formalisation of the Mondex smart card, which achieved ITSEC Level E6 [31,175], but not before Woodcock found that Z proof rules were incomplete as elegantly detailed in [152]. This led to the development of backward refinement rules. The Mondex would be one of the first projects to be tackled in the Grand Challenge in Verified Software [84] initiated by Hoare. Freitas and Woodcock would later mechanise their proofs using Z/EVES [52].

Process Calculi. When Hoare proposed Communicating Sequential Processes (CSP), he adopted Dijkstra's GCL as the "sole means of introducing and controlling nondeterminism" [77]. This seminal work spurred an interest in the study of the semantics of CSP, some of which we cover in further detail. Importantly, in contrast with CCS [108] and ACP [13], CSP has a theory for refinement.

One of the earliest denotational models for CSP was proposed by Francez et al. [51] based on *history trees*, where two types of determinism are explicitly distinguished: local, where a process can decide which value to communicate, and global, that depends on the interaction with other processes. This distinction would later lead to the consideration of two distinct choice operators over processes: internal choice ($\sqcap$), that decides irrespective of interaction with the environment; and external choice ($\square$) that allows a process' environment to choose. An example from [51] is recast using these operators and a typed channel e:

Example 3.1. $P = (a \rightarrow e?x \rightarrow Skip \square a \rightarrow e!0 \rightarrow Skip) \, [\![\, \{e\}\,]\!]\, e!1 \rightarrow Skip$

$$Q = (e?x \rightarrow Skip \square e!0 \rightarrow Skip) \, [\![\, \{e\}\,]\!]\, e!1 \rightarrow Skip$$

Here, process P is defined by a parallel composition ($[\![\ldots]\!]$) of two processes synchronising on channel e, but where event a can happen independently. The left hand-side process has a choice ($\square$) between a prefixing ($\rightarrow$) on event a, followed by an input ($e?x$) on e and terminating ($Skip$), or, similarly, after a communicating the value 0 via e, and then also terminating. The right hand-side process, however, can only agree on the value 1 being communicated ($e!1$) via e. We observe that in this case the external choice is actually nondeterministic, as the algebraic laws can show [143], and so P can enter in deadlock. In contrast, process Q does not deadlock, given that the choice can always be resolved.

In [78] Hoare considered a denotational model based on *traces*, that is, the sequences of events a process can perform, restricted to deterministic processes. Traces, however, are inadequate for distinguishing internal and external choice and for preserving liveness, for example, by having deadlock as the maximally refined process. Addressing this, a *failures* semantics would later be considered by Brookes et al. [16], where in addition to traces, the events refused at the end of every trace are also recorded. Related, De Nicola and Hennesy [123] would identify that failures refinement coincides with *must*-testing in CCS.

Refinement in the *failures* semantics, defined simply by (reverse) subset inclusion, similarly to *traces*, gives rise to a partial order where deadlock is no longer the maximally refined process. Instead, however, a process that can only perform a sequence of internal events is maximally refined. Such behaviour can easily be introduced in CSP via hiding ($\backslash$) the event of a guarded recursion. For example, if we let $R = a \rightarrow R$ and then consider $S = R \backslash \{a\}$, then S would have no stable *failures*, and hence would be maximal in the refinement order. To overcome this, Roscoe et al. [143] would propose the *failures-divergences* semantic model, where S is considered to be divergent, that is, the bottom in the refinement order, given that it cannot provide any guarantees on its behaviour.

UTP. Total correctness, as found in wp, would be recast as a theory of designs [171] in the Unifying Theories of Programming (UTP) of Hoare and He [79], a framework of alphabetised relations, in the style of Hehner's predicative programming approach [65], proposed as a sound basis for studying several programming paradigms. Although only published in book form in 1998, the UTP would play a central role in Woodcock's contributions [173] in the following decades.

In the UTP, theories are characterised by three components: an alphabet, that defines the variables considered in a relation; a signature; and a set of healthiness conditions, usually defined by monotonic and idempotent functions over predicates whose fixed points define the valid predicates of a theory. The refinement order is defined by the universally quantified reverse implication of predicates, and gives rise to a complete lattice with *false* as the top element, allowing no observations, and *true* as the bottom, allowing any observation. Importantly, *demonic* nondeterminism is captured via the greatest lower bound.

Designs. As observed by Hoare and He, relations are unsuitable, on their own, to define a model of total correctness, and so the theory of designs employs an auxiliary variable ok' that records whether a program has terminated, and similarly an undashed version, ok, records whether the current program has started. The simplest design is therefore $ok \Rightarrow ok'$, equivalently stated using Hoare and He's turnstile notation as $true \vdash true$, that when started terminates successfully: its pre- and postcondition are both *true*. The above form rules out explicit non-termination ($\neg\, ok'$) or the ability to state anything about program variables before a program starts ($\neg\, ok$). This is captured by two healthiness conditions **H1** and **H2** [79,171]. Another two optional conditions are considered: **H3**, that rules out designs that can make final observations without terminating; and **H4**, that rules out miraculous designs. **H3**-healthy designs correspond to (conjunctive) predicate transformers [25], while miracles allow the specification of *assumptions* and play an important role [169] in theories that we discuss next.

Reactive Designs. Amongst the process calculi studied in the UTP, Hoare and He would propose a recast of CSP [23,79] via a theory of reactive processes that considers auxiliary variables tr, that records the trace of events, and $wait$, that records whether a process is waiting for an interaction with its environment. The key result is that the semantics of CSP processes can be defined as the image of designs through the application of the healthiness condition **R** for reactive processes, that is, using pre- and postconditions. For example, $\mathbf{R}(true \vdash wait' \wedge tr' = tr)$ deadlocks by stating that the process waits and keeps the trace unchanged. Importantly, reactive designs don't satisfy **H3**, as there can be intermediate interactions irrespective of termination in the reactive paradigm. Canham and Woodcock [20] would refer to a postcondition where $wait'$ is *true* as the *peri*condition, emphasising the intermediate nature. Foster et al. [47] would provide a systematic account of all three pre-/peri-/post-conditions of reactive contracts in their Isabelle/UTP [46,50] mechanisation.

Circus. The combination of state-based formalisms and process calculi has received much attention [18,44,144,151]. *Circus* is a combination of Z and CSP, incorporating Dijkstra's guarded commands and Morgan's specification statement, with a UTP semantics [127] given via reactive designs. It targets refinement [22] and has been exploited in the context of industrial and safety-critical applications [126,168]. Woodcock and others would consider extensions of *Circus* to cater for other phenomena, such as time, by exploiting its UTP semantics.

One of the earliest works on *Circus Time* is that of Adnan and He [149,150]. The semantics is given via reactive designs using a model of *failures* within a sequence of discrete time units. A similar structure would be exploited for slotted-*Circus* by Butterfield et al. [19], that can be captured via a generalisation [139] of Foster et al.'s trace algebra [48]. Importantly, reactive miracles would allow Wei et al. [164] to capture deadlines, by pruning periconditions once a deadline has been reached, thus making interactions urgent. Refinements that meet their deadlines more tightly than specified are non-urgent, in the same way that a design is non-miraculous in an environment that meets its assumptions.

3.2   Angelic Choice

Amongst the pioneers [30,146], Floyd [45] is perhaps first in employing nondeterminism as a specification mechanism abstracting away from implementation details of backtracking algorithms. This view would be used by Cook [32] to characterise the class of NP problems. The use of both *angelic* and *demonic* nondeterminism (alternation) would be considered for Turing machines in [27].

Imperative. The earliest use of the term *angelic* seems to be due to Broy and Wirsing [17], who studied four types of nondeterminism via algebraic data types. However, they refer to *unbounded nondeterminism* as *angelic*, and *demonic* as backtracking [90], in contrast to recent works. *Angelic* choice has found use in: parsing [70], modelling of game-like scenarios [8], proof tactics [99,125], constraint [82] and logic programming [91], and in conformance relations [21].

Hesselink [71] would propose a subsumption of the GCL to cope with the semantics of recursion. As Dijkstra points out [41], Hesselink would further study its operational semantics [74] and consider an extension with angelic choice [72]. Dijkstra's work [41] on reasoning about UNITY [28] via arbitrary monotonic predicate transformers also considers both *demonic* and *angelic* choices.

Refinement Calculus. Back and von Wright [8] extensively studied sublattices, where choice can be *angelic* or *demonic*. The lattice of monotonic predicate transformers is the most important, where *angelic* choice and *demonic* choice are duals in the lattice. Related, *angelic* choice has also been used by Gardiner and Morgan [54] to formalise logical variables, which is central to their calculational data-refinement approach, for example, by allowing the postcondition of a specification statement to refer to the initial value of program variables. Ward and Hayes [163] would emphasise in their work, that the angelic choice of the refinement calculus can "look ahead" and avoid aborting, if at all possible.

Multirelations. In theories of total correctness, such as in Z and VDM [85], it is natural to model computations via relations. However, as observed by Rewitzky and Brink [138], and later Back and von Wright [8], relations can only capture one type of nondeterminism, either *angelic* or *demonic*, but not both. Instead, binary multirelations [100,137], that is, relations between a state and a set of states, can be used to model both: the set can be understood to model *angelic* or *demonic* choices, while the relation models the dual, respectively. As observed by Hesselink [73] multirelations are equivalent to one of the constructions of the Free Distributive Completion (FDC) of the state space, originally studied by Morris [118]. More recently, Furusawa et al. [53] have extensively studied multirelations to provide an algebraic account of concurrent dynamic logic [129].

Process Calculi. As mentioned, in the UTP, *demonic* nondeterminism is captured by the greatest lower bound of the lattice. Because it is a theory of relations, it cannot capture both forms of nondeterminism, as established by Cavalcanti et al. [25] who show that, in general, UTP relations are isomorphic to conjunctive predicate transformers. They also consider a predicative encoding of upward-closed binary multirelations, as non-homogeneous alphabetised relations, that is shown isomorphic to arbitrary monotonic predicate transformers. Importantly, it is a theory of designs that satisfies **H3**, and so it is inadequate to give a treatment of *angelic* choice for reactive designs and process calculi.

Ribeiro and Cavalcanti [142] would study this problem further. First, they generalised the predicative encoding of binary multirelations to consider non-**H3** *angelic* designs, and showed that theory to be isomorphic to an extended notion of upward-closed binary multirelations where the target type includes the option of non-termination [141]. Secondly, they used that encoding to study the operators of CSP, recast in a theory of reactive angelic designs [140], and their interplay with *angelic* choice. In that theory, angelic choice can avoid immediate divergence, by satisfying the following law: $(Stop \sqcup Skip)$; $Chaos = Stop$ where $\sqcup$ is *angelic* choice, defined as the least upper bound of the lattice, and ; is sequential composition. That is, the angel can choose to deadlock ($Stop$), rather than diverge ($Chaos$). However, interactions cannot be eliminated in the same way, even if they could to lead to a divergence, as can be seen from the example:

Example 3.2. $(a \rightarrow Skip) \sqcup (b \rightarrow Chaos) = (a \rightarrow Skip) \sqcup (b \rightarrow Choice)$

where a and b are different events. Here, the divergence is avoided by behaving as the most nondeterministic process that does not diverge ($Choice$).

As it turns out, the standard healthiness conditions of reactive processes insist on extension of traces (i.e. no backtracking), and thus disallow any pruning of interactions that could lead to divergence. Instead, [142] considers a theory of angelic processes that does not insist on trace extension. In that context, the following law holds: $a \rightarrow Chaos \sqcup b \rightarrow Skip = b \rightarrow Skip$. That is, the prefixing on a can be eliminated, given that it would lead to a divergence. In that theory, imposition of the standard healthiness conditions, can be used to scope the level of 'backtracking' similarly to a cut operator.

Related, Tyrrell et al. [161] have proposed an axiomatization of CSP, where external choice is referred to as angelic, but where deadlock is indistinguishable from divergence. Roscoe [143] has considered an alternative to external choice via operational combinator semantics of CSP, where, however, the possibility of divergence has no effect on 'backtracking'.

3.3   Preferential Choice

In comparison to other forms of choice discussed in this chapter, preferential choice is a slightly odd companion: it is asymmetric, non-monotonic, and cannot be expressed in the theory of predicate transformers. Intuitively, a preferential choice $S \gg T$ behaves like S as long as S and its continuation is feasible, meaning non-miraculous. It only behaves like T if selection of S results in a miracle further down the line. To illustrate this, we consider the computation:

$$(x := 1 \gg x := 2) \, ; \, U$$

Assuming we have $\mathbf{fis}(U) \equiv \mathsf{true}^2$, meaning that U is feasible from all initial states[3], S behaves similar to $x := 1$ and thus in a deterministic fashion.

However, let us assume U becomes infeasible in a state where $x = 1$. The guarded computation $x \neq 1 \longrightarrow \mathbf{skip}$ precisely exhibits such behaviour. Then, we have that

$$(x := 1 \gg x := 2) \, ; \, x \neq 1 \longrightarrow \mathbf{skip}$$

becomes equivalent to $x := 2$. This behaviour of choosing the second alternative when the first one leads to infeasibility is reminiscent of (standard) nondeterministic choice $S \sqcap T$ and holds there too. We are likewise entitled to refine the second operand T of a preferential choice to obtain a refinement of the entire construct, hence preference shares some semantic properties and traits with nondeterminism. However, things get hairy when we are trying to refine the first operand, which is where monotonicity unfortunately breaks down.

To illustrate this, let us consider the computation:

$$(x := 1 \gg x := 2) \, ; \, (x = 1 \mathbin{\vert} \mathbf{skip})$$

where $x = 1 \mathbin{\vert} \mathbf{skip}$ is a preconditioned program (Floyd assertion) that behaves like $\mathbf{skip}$ when $x = 1$, and otherwise $\mathbf{aborts}$ (does not terminate). We first observe that since the continuation $x = 1 \mathbin{\vert} \mathbf{skip}$ is everywhere feasible, preference always chooses its first program $x := 1$ and the entire computation boils down to $x := 1$, provided that no infeasibility is encountered later on. (For the sake of simplicity, and without limiting generality, we assume the latter is the case.) Note that this is different from nondeterminism, since we can prove that

$$(x := 1 \sqcap x := 2) \, ; \, (x = 1 \mathbin{\vert} \mathbf{skip})$$

is indeed equivalent to $\mathbf{abort}$.

Let us now refine $x := 1$ in $x := 1 \gg x := 2$ by $\mathbf{magic}$— the computation that is everywhere infeasible and thus the top of the refinement lattice of programs. As we already observed, the preference operator, just like nondeterministic choice,

---

[2] Strictly, it is enough to show that $x = 1 \Rightarrow \mathbf{fis}(U)$ universally holds.

[3] In the UTP theory of designs, this is equivalent to saying that healthiness condition **H4** holds for S.

cannot choose a miracle; hence, we have that **magic** $\gg x := 2$ must be equivalent to $x := 2$. However, the composition

$$x := 2 \; ; \; (x = 1 \mid \mathbf{skip})$$

can be shown to be **abort** (the bottom of the lattice). And **abort** is clearly not a refinement of $x := 1$ or, indeed, any other computation apart from itself. This exemplifies that preference is not monotonic in its first operand, given our standard intuitive notion of refinement.

It is moreover easy to see that $x := 1 \gg x := 2$ cannot be the same as $x := 2 \gg x := 1$, hence preference, unlike nondeterminism, is not commutative. A question that remains is whether we can express its semantics at all in the theory of wp predicate transformers, similar to other constructs of the guarded command language of Dijkstra [40]. Sadly, the answer is no, and to illustrate this let us recognise that both $x := 1$ and $x := 1 \gg x := 2$ ought be able to establish exactly the same postconditions Q, meaning that wp$(x := 1, Q)$ and wp$(x := 1 \gg x := 2, Q)$ are expected to be logically equivalent; but they are nevertheless algebraically distinct since they can be distinguished by a context $U \mathbin{\hat=} x \ne 1 \longrightarrow \mathbf{skip}$. That is $x := 1 \; ; \; U$ is **magic** whereas $x := 1 \gg x := 2 \; ; \; U$ is $x := 2$. The closest we get to preferential choice in a wp semantics is Nelson's biased choices, described in [122].

$$S \boxplus T =_{\mathbf{df}} S \sqcap \neg \; \mathbf{fis}(S) \longrightarrow T$$

Unfortunately, this definition does not precisely capture our intuitive semantics of preference, since it is not sensitive to the continuation. For example, $x := 1 \boxplus x := 2$ evaluates to $x := 1 \sqcap \mathbf{fis}(x := 1) \longrightarrow x := 2$ which simplifies to just $x := 1 \sqcap x := 2$, since assignment is universally feasible. In other words,

$$x := 1 \boxplus x := 2 \; ; \; (x = 1 \mid \mathbf{skip})$$

yields **abort** and not **skip**, as we would expect for preference. This makes biased choice less useful as a specification and implementation construct to capture preference. What we expect (see [43] for a discussion) is that preferential choice is sandwiched between nondeterministic choice and biased choice, pertaining to the following refinement relationship in a suitable semantics.

$$S \sqcap T \; \sqsubseteq \; S \gg T \; \sqsubseteq \; S \boxplus T$$

The endpoints of this refinement, we can express in wp semantics, but the middle point $(S \gg T)$ not so. This raises the questions in what semantic framework the $S \gg T$ construct may be expressible. We answered this question in [43]: instead of using a semantics that is based on predicate transformers wp(S, Q), we us a semantics based on expression transformers $S \diamond E$.

Intuitively, expression transformers capture the value of an expression E after execution of some computation S. Due to the fact that S may be non-deterministic, miraculous or abortive, we require a more powerful language of expressions that, in effect, associates expressions with sets of possible outcomes.

Those sets may be empty (capturing the result of executing **magic**) or yield a special distinct value $\bot$ that denotes the outcome of the computation **abort**.

A bespoke mathematical structure to describe $S \diamond E$ turns out to be Hehner's notion of a *bunch* and the underlying bunch theory [68,69]. Bunch theory defines many properties that we expect, by default, to hold in a theory of expression transforms, and has already been used by Morris and Bunkenburg as a vehicle to develop their theory of term transformers [120]. We extended bunch theory in [153,186] to account for the improper bunch $\bot$, and thereby managed to give a model to the GCL in a semantics based on prospective values (pv semantics) that is fully isomorphic to conjunction computations, albeit not appropriate to capture angelic nondeterminism[4].

Not discussing our prospective-value semantics of the GCL in full detail, here is the definitional axiom for the preferential choice operator:

$$(S \gg T) \diamond E \ =_{\mathbf{df}} \ (S \diamond E) , (S \diamond E) = \mathbf{null} \to T \diamond E$$

To dissect the above notation, the comma corresponds to bunch union, and the short right arrow is a guarded form of bunch that evaluates to the empty bunch **null** when the guard is false. The predicate $S \diamond E = \mathbf{null}$ is a way to compute continuation-aware feasibility of S. We note that the continuation is captured by the expression E; we can see this more clearly by considering the expression transformer law for sequence[5]:

$$(S \,;\, T) \diamond E \ =_{\mathbf{df}} \ S \diamond (T \diamond E) \ = \ S \diamond F \quad \text{where} \quad F \mathrel{\widehat{=}} T \diamond E$$

where we can think of T as the continuation of S whose effect is captured by the expression F. So expression transformers together with improper[6] bunch theory provide a suitable abstraction and mathematical framework to formally capture preference, examine its algebraic properties, and prove various kinds of useful laws. (While we do not have space to indulge into this discussion here, details can be found in various papers [43,153,155].)

Bunch theory has sometimes been criticised on the grounds that its consistency is not apparent and thus cannot be taken for granted. Morris and Bunkenburg tried to alleviate this concern already in their publication [119] by providing a set-theoretic model. A more recent article by Stoddart et al. [153] addresses this problem too. Lastly, one might interject that bunch theory is as fundamental as set theory, and therefore may not require a model—just as we usually accept the axioms of ZFC set theory without further ado.

---

[4] Doing so may not be beyond the possibilities of a 'bunchy' semantics, but may require us to distinguish between different kinds of bunches: those that capture sets of demonic outcomes, and those that capture sets of angelic outcomes.

[5] In earlier publications, reviewers sometimes question whether the right hand of the axiom ought not be $T \diamond (S \diamond E)$. We reassure the reader that the law is indeed correct in the form given here, and refer to [185] for additional intuitive justifications.

[6] By this, we refer to Hehner's bunch theory, augmented with an improper (bottom) bunch $\bot$ for every type.

We share Jim Woodcock's curiosity and interest in examining the formalisation of theories of programming in various semantic frameworks and domains. While bunch theory gives us an elegant and concise formal model, it does make sense to explore preference in other semantic frameworks as well; and we shall comment on this in the subsequent paragraphs.

Preference in wp. We already explained that a model of preference in conventional wp semantics is beset with difficulties and most likely unrealizable. However, there is a way to express preference and, more generally, the semantics of what we call preferential computations in a wp theory that uses three-valued logic. More specifically, Gödel logic [6] enables us to distinguish several degrees of truth and is a precursor of fuzzy logic. How can this be useful here?

Let us take inspiration again from the pv expression transformer semantics. Whether a computation S and its continuation is feasible can be dynamically evaluated within the bunch logic via $(S \diamond E) \neq$ **null**; namely, the bunch of values that E may take after executing S is non-empty. In other words, there is at least one behaviour that gives us a prospective value for E. This enables us to effectively check whether the execution of S succeeded or otherwise has failed due to infeasibility. It is a crucial bit of additional information that considers the continuation being captured implicitly in E.

The logical expression $\text{wp}(S, Q)$ does not offer such a test: if, for some initial state, it yields true we have established Q but we don't know how: both $\text{wp}(x := 1, x = 1)$ and $\text{wp}(\textbf{magic}, x = 1)$ evaluate to true where the first one establishes $x = 1$ through a proper terminating behaviour, whereas the second one establishes $x = 1$ vacuously by a miracle. This distinction is lost in the term true; however, we can reintroduce it in a three-valued logic: true now means establishing the postcondition via non-miraculous behaviour, and supertrue means establishing it miraculously. We this have three truth values: false, true and supertrue. They are order in the way that we have enumerated them. We recall that in Gödel logic, such ordering determines the result of logical operators.

At this point, we ask the reader for a leap of faith. While it is out of scope for this publication to go into the details of such a wp theory built on top of a suitable three-valued logic, we note that we have developed a complete mechanisation[7] in Isabelle/HOL already to show that (a) such a theory can be defined, (b) that it supports the definition of all GCL operators including angelic choice, and (c) that it preserves all conventional laws of refinement if restricting ourselves to the core GCL operators. We call this theory a wpe semantics of guarded commands.

We moreover discovered that there is a neat Galois connection between monotonic wp and preferential wpe computations by approximating preference with nondeterminism, and that the resulting laws of this Galois connection can be used to recover a restricted form of compositional refinement in the absence of monotonicity of program operators with respect to refinement *in general*. The

---

[7] Unfortunately, we have not published this material yet but envisage to do so in the near future, via a separate publication and/or technical report.

lose of monotonicity is a lamentable downside of our theory of preference, but we could show that if preference is only introduced in the final step of refinement, we are entitled to replace any nondeterministic choice $S \sqcap T$ by a preferential choice $S \gg T$, irrespective of the absence of general monotonicity laws.

For computations that do *not* involve preference, our mechanised theory shows that refinement has precisely the same meaning as in the standard wp semantics of monotonic computations. Last but not least, we note that the work in [43] goes further by introducing a notion of feasibility-preserving refinement $S \sqsubseteq^* T$ which strengthen conventional refinement $S \sqsubseteq T$ with the caveat $\mathbf{fis}(S) \Rightarrow \mathbf{fis}(T)$ that provides a more useful basis for using (partial) miracles in implementations for backtracking algorithm implementations. Again, this causes monotonicity to break down: here, for sequential composition in the first operand. Nonetheless, the abovementioned replacement of $S \sqcap T$ by $S \gg T$ remains valid, even in this stronger refinement regime.

Preference in UTP. Modelling preference in UTP is more challenging. While nondeterminism is naturally represented in UTP by predicates over before and after states, such as $x' = x - 1 \vee x' = x + 1$, preference (just like probability) gives rise to another structural dimension within the semantic space, with entanglement and closure properties between nondeterministic and preferential behaviours that have to be understood and made precise via healthiness conditions. A sensible strategy is to index computations with a natural number, i.e., by adding an auxiliary variable idx in order to impose an explicit order on behaviours. E.g., $x := 1 \gg x := 2$ in the UTP theory of relations could be modelled as $idx = 1 \wedge x' = 1 \vee idx = 2 \wedge x' = 2$. More accurately, the idx variable would need to be suitably typed in order to tabulate all choices made "along the way", and we would also need a variable idx' to propagate the (updated) value of idx through sequential compositions, similar to the tr and tr' variables in reactive computations. A notable open question is whether this will turn out sufficient for a compositional definition of sequential composition, and what the underlying healthiness conditions ought be. To account for unbounded nondeterminism[8], we would most likely have to move to some larger index type.

A denotational semantics may express preferential computations as sequences of functions (for deterministic programs) or relations (for nondeterminstic programs). Again, we have not developed such a model yet or identified any validity or closure constraints on the underlying mathematical structure. A UTP theory may likely enable us to easily derive a clean denotational model, since UTP typically encodes mathematical structures in a predicative manner, so the gap is inherently small between these approaches.

It is again not the ambition of this chapter to develop such a UTP theory, and the reason we mention it is that we believe it could be just the thing that Jim Woodcock may be excited about, with all the wonderful work he has done in

---

[8] Unbounded nondeterminism is a misnomer: often, we mean infinite albeit *bounded* nondeterminism, i.e., by some transfinite ordinal.

producing novel theories of computation in UTP and pushing the UTP approach to and beyond its perceived limits. We flag this as a future work.

Application of Preference. So far, we confined our discussion mostly the semantic aspects of preference and the ability to mathematically describe it. A fair question is "What can it actually be used for?". And "Is it worth the trouble?". We believe there are a number of applications that still need to be explored, but one of them is to verify the implementation of heuristics in guiding backtracking search. While demonic nondeterminism is often used to express implementor's choice, it is also well understood that nondeterminism exhibits backtracking[9] when combined with guarded computations. In this context, we think of nondeterministic choice as providing the possible moves (or steps) of an algorithmic search problem. An infeasible guard thus triggers backtracking from a dead end during search exploration.

The simple semantics of nondeterminism and guarded commands in wp promises a proof-economic technique to verify computations that make use of guards and choice in the way we hinted above, e.g. to solve puzzles like the Eight Queens or Knight's Tour problem, or similar. The downside is that we have no control of the order in which choices are attempted. And implementing choice as preference is a refinement that resides outside the scope of formal reasoning. Preferential choice, as a semantic operator, lifts it into the realm of formal verification and thereby opens up the possibility of verifying algorithms that use preference as an implementation operator (which most algorithms do).

We concede that this deployment of choice and guards is not the only way to specify search procedures in formal languages: a dual method is to use angelic rather than demonic choice, and use **abort** as a means to trigger backtracking. This approach comes with its own issues: whether a computation fails to terminate and thus behaves like **abort** may be difficult to detect in practice[10], and, semantically, we may need to do so in a sufficiently expressive target language that supports iteration and recursion. Lastly, we may not require demonic or angelic choice either, and use a standard iterative or recursive sequential implementation instead to explore the search space via a stack.

Another application of preference relates to the example of a co-simulation master algorithm (MA) discussed later in Sect. 4.1. Though this is not further developed in this chapter, we believe that preference can be used to model a trial-and-error loop of the MA to steps a set of FMUs with step sizes that become progressively smaller, until all FMUs succeed to concurrently perform the simulation step. In order to reject a (too large) step size, an FMU can use a programming guard $FMU_i \,\hat{=}\, stepsize \leq maxstep_i \longrightarrow FMU_{beh}$. And the exploration of step sizes at the MA modelling level could be realised by a preferential choice as follows:

$$(stepsize := 4 \gg stepsize := 2 \gg stepsize := 1) \; ; \; (FMU_1 \parallel FMU_2 \parallel \cdots)$$

---

[9] More accurately, reversibility as all state is implicitly restored during backtracking.

[10] Note that **abort** is semantically equivalant to a non-terminating computation such as **while** *true* **do skip** .

where FMU_i correspond to a model of the computation carried out by the Functional Mockup Units and the above parallel composition is a suitable version of parallel-by-merge, assuming that FMUs only modify their local disjoint states.

Summary of Preference. We conclude our mini exposition of preferential choice by observing that, despite its elusiveness to a simple semantic treatment, it turns out to be an operator that we believe has significant use in both specifications and implementations. We are hoping to publish further work in the near future that presents a wp(e) semantic model for preferential computations that has been fully formalised in Isabelle/HOL, with key laws and the aforementioned Galois connection being defined and verified. Development of a UTP model is a more long-term goal and we hope we sparked Jim's interest in this as well.

3.4   Probabilistic Choice

Probabilistic algorithms [121] are algorithms that can make random choice at some points. They have been widely applied in many areas such as distributed systems (e.g. Rabin's mutual exclusion with bounded waiting [133], Aspnes et al.'s fast randomized consensus [5]), security and cryptography (public key protocols [42]), sorting (e.g. Hoare's randomized QuickSort [75]), number theory (e.g. Rabin's probabilistic primality testing algorithm [132]), data structuring (e.g. randomized hashing scheme [121]), and robotics (e.g. localisation, mapping, and planning [158]) to simplify algorithms and improve performance. These algorithms are classified as either *Las Vegas* (they always give correct results but the running time varies) or *Monte Carlo* (there is a small probability that they may give wrong results, but the running time is fixed).

To program probabilistic algorithms, conventional non-probabilistic programs are extended with a capability to model randomness, usually using a discrete probabilistic choice construct $(P \oplus_r Q)$ [67,104] or a random number generator $(rand)$ [34,66,92] sampling from the uniform distribution over a set (either finite or infinite for discrete or continuous distributions). To capture high-level specifications for probabilistic programs or analyse them in the abstract level, nondeterministic choice is also introduced in probabilistic programming, such as $pGCL$ [104,114], in which both nondeterministic choice $(P \sqcap Q)$ and probabilistic choice are present.

The semantics for conventional programs such as weakest precondition [40], Hoare logic [76], and predicative programming [65] are boolean functions over state space. They can reason about these programs qualitatively, but not quantitatively which is natural in probabilistic programs. These semantics have been extended to deal with probabilistic programs. We mainly discuss the relational semantics and the predicate-transformer semantics for imperative sequential probabilistic programs, and briefly review probabilistic process algebras.

Imperative - Relational Semantics. In Kozen's seminal papers [92,93], nondeterministic choice in conventional programs is replaced with probabilistic choice and boolean functions are generalised to real-valued functions over state spaces to give the semantics for probabilistic programs as partial measurable functions on a measurable space and continuous linear operators on a Banach space.

The pGCL has relational and predicate-transformer semantics by He, Morgan, and McIver [64]. The relational semantics extends the theory of designs for standard non-probabilistic programs in UTP to *probabilistic designs*. In the relational model, any probabilistic choice refines nondeterministic choice. Actually, the semantics of nondeterministic choice of two programs P and Q is the nondeterministic choice of the probabilistic choices of the embeddings of P and Q in all possible ways (all possible weights from 0 to 1 inclusive). The relational model embeds standard UTP designs in probabilistic designs through the weakest prespecification [80], a generalisation of wp from conditions (specified in only initial observation variables v) to relations (in both initial and final observation variables v and v'). In probabilistic designs, distributions are captured in a probability distribution function *prob* of type $S \rightarrow [0,1]$ over the observation state space S and $\sum_{s \in S} prob(s) = 1$. Different from Kozen's semantics and the Weakest Pre-Expectation (WPE) [104, 115] where probabilistic programs are real-valued functions over state space, the probabilistic programs in the relational model are probabilistic (non-homogeneous) designs relating initial observation state space S and final probabilistic state space on *prob*.

Woodcock [172] became interested in this relational semantics when he considered the probabilistic semantics for RoboChart [110] because of its UTP semantics and algebraic properties which are suitable for reasoning and automation in Isabelle/UTP. He formalised the semantics of the relational model and the proof that the semantic embedding is a homomorphism on the structure of standard programs, probabilistic choice, nondeterministic choice, and sequential composition. He also found interesting details like a law requiring a side condition [172] of the H3 healthiness condition [79, 171] and the lifting law for sequential composition requiring finite state space [179]. The formalisation resulted in the mechanisation of probabilistic designs in Isabelle/UTP [46] by Ye, Woodcock, and Foster [179].

A uniform distribution algorithm modelled in RoboChart using a binary probabilistic choice is proved in [179]. Ye, Woodcock, and Foster [179] found that the most difficult part in proving probabilistic programs using probabilistic designs is the supplement of a witness Q for the existential quantification in [179, Definition 8.2] used in sequential composition of two probabilistic designs in [179, Theorem 8.4]. This is due to a fact that probability distributions are encoded in the variable *prob* which is inside relations. In this view, *probabilistic programs are relational in terms of probability distributions over state space*, and so relations or predicates deal with distributions. To address this challenge, Woodcock and Ye started to look at other approaches with different views of probabilistic programs. They should also be suitable for the mechanisation in Isabelle/UTP.

Hehner's Probabilistic Predicative Programming (PPP) [66, 67] takes another view. PPP generalises boolean functions for predicative programming to real-valued functions. In PPP, *conditional* and *joint* probability are modelled through sequential and parallel composition. One unique feature of the language is its capability to model both epistemic uncertainty (due to the lack of knowledge of information) using the subjective Bayesian approach and aleatoric uncertainty (due to the natural randomness of physical processes). In PPP, *programs are probabilistic (real-valued functions) and relations are over state space*, and so relations only deal with usual state space, not distributions over state space like the relational semantics. This interested Woodcock because the relations over usual state space can be formalised using UTP's alphabetised relations, and so PPP can be mechanised in Isabelle/UTP.

There are, however, several obstacles to the broader adoption of Hehner's work, such as informal syntax and semantics, and simple semantics for probabilistic loops but that is difficult to mechanise. For these reasons, Woodcock introduced an Iverson bracket notation $[\![P]\!]$ [182] (of type $S \to \mathbb{R}$), which maps a predicate P (of type $S \to \mathbb{B}$) into real numbers. This also separates relations from arithmetic. Woodcock replaced PPP's relations with UTP's alphabetised relations, which allows UTP theories on relations and their mechanisation in Isabelle/UTP reused.

Ye, Woodcock, and Foster [182] formalised the syntax and semantics of this new probabilistic framework, called *Probabilistic Unifying Relations* (ProbURel), and introduced the constructive semantics for probabilistic loops using Kleene's fixed-point theorem and the unique fixed-point theorem to simplify the reasoning about probabilistic loops. ProbURel is mechanised in Isabelle/UTP, leveraging the recent mechanisation of the Z mathematical toolkit[11] in Isabelle/UTP by Foster and Woodcock.

PPP does not include nondeterminism. In [66], Hehner discussed informally an approach to reason about nondeterministic choice. Nondeterministic choice is equivalent to an existentially quantified deterministic choice.

$$P \sqcap Q = \exists\, b : \mathbb{B} \bullet \textbf{if } b \textbf{ then } P \textbf{ else } Q$$

Each nondeterministic choice is replaced by such a quantified conditional choice with a new fresh quantifier variable b. The strategy is to move all quantifiers outwards. Based on this definition, nondeterministic choice after a probabilistic choice, such as $P \oplus_r Q; P \sqcap Q$, is oblivious (that is, making a choice without looking at the current (or past) state).

Similarly to PPP, ProbURel does not support nondeterministic choice and continuous distributions. Woodcock and Ye are interested in extending ProbURel in these aspects.

Imperative - Predicate-Transformer Semantics. He, Morgan, and McIver's predicate-transformer semantics [64] for pGCL uses the same weakest prespecification [80] technique to inject standard predicates in Dijkstra's predicate-transformer semantics (the weakest pre-condition) [40] into probabilistic predicates. Based on this injection, probabilistic predicate transformer is an

---

[11] https://github.com/isabelle-utp/Z_Toolkit.

embedding of standard predicate transformer. However, for the constructs that are not standard, such as probabilistic choice, an additional healthiness condition *continuity* is imposed on the probabilistic transformer. Monotonicity and "scaling" can be derived from continuity. They showed the embedding preserves program structure. Interestingly, the embedding of demonic non-deterministic choice (conjunction in standard predicate transformer) becomes *minimum* for probabilistic transformer. The key healthiness condition for this transformer semantics is sublinearity [105].

McIver and Morgan gave WPE or expectation transformer semantics [104, 115] to pGCL. In WPE, the real-valued functions or expressions over state space are called expectations (indeed random variables). So a probabilistic program maps a post-expectation (postE) to a pre-expectation (preE). Indeed, its WPE semantics defines the greatest preE (gp) for a postE: $preE = gp(P, [postE])$ where the square bracket $[\_]$ converts a boolean-valued predicate to an arithmetic value, especially $[true] = 1$ and $[false] = 0$. The semantics for probabilistic choice are the standard weighted average of pre-expectations of its all alternatives. The semantics for nondeterministic choice, however, are the *smaller* pre-expectation (that is, the demonic behaviour against the greatest pre-expectation) in the pre-expectations of its two alternatives. We show below an example of gp for a probabilistic choice.

$$gp(x := x + 1 \oplus_{(2/3)} x := x - 1, [x \geq 0])$$
$$= (1/3) * [x + 1 \geq 0] + (2/3) * [x - 1 \geq 0]$$
$$= (1/3) * [x \geq -1] + (2/3) * [x \geq 1]$$
$$= (1/3) * [x = -1 \lor x = 0] + [x \geq 1]$$

It means that in order for the program to establish $x \geq 0$, the probability of x being -1 or 0 (or $x \geq 1$, or $x < -1$) in its initial state is at least $1/3$ (or 1, or 0). McIver and Morgan [106] also developed refinement for probabilistic programs (pGCL) to ensure correctness by construction.

McIver and Morgan [102] extended expectation transformer from finite state spaces to infinite state spaces, and constructed deterministic, demonic, demonic and angelic probabilistic transformers sequentially (characterised by transformer properties linearity, sublinearity, semi-sublinearity respectively), as Back and von Wright [7] did for non-probabilistic transformers (characterised by transformer properties disjunctivity and conjunctivity, conjunctivity, monotonicity respectively). [102, Fig. 9] illustrates the transformer structure.

WPE attracted the interest of many. Kaminski [88] developed an advanced weakest precondition calculus. McIver et al. [107] presented additional proof rules for loops and loop termination. Further three advancements: expected runtimes, conditioning [128], and mixed-sign expectations were developed and presented in Kaminski's PhD thesis. Schröer et al. [145] developed a deductive verification infrastructure for discrete probabilistic programs to use SMT solvers to verify programs automatically. Batz et al. [11] proposed an approach to use inductive synthesis to find loop invariants for probabilistic programs from templates. Batz et al. [10] used deductive verification technique [145] to synthesise nondeterministic probabilistic programs to find memoryless and deterministic strategies.

Stoddart and Zeyda et al. [153,154] proposed a guarded command language that is able to model nondeterministic choice, preferential choice, and probabilistic choice. The semantics of the language is based on wp and conjugate weakest precondition (cwp), and interpreted in bunch theory [69], instead of set theory. They use $S \diamond E$ to denote the prospective values of an expression E after the execution of a program S. A basic law is developed to link prospective values to cwp. The PV semantics is shown to represent backtracking and the implementation of backtracking via reversible computing [185]. Their semantics for probabilistic choice is a weighted choice of a bunch of three terms, which takes into account the interaction of probabilistic with nondeterministic choice, and the feasibility/continuation and abortion behaviour of probabilistic choice.

In addition to Kozen's, relational, and predicate transformer semantics, many other semantics for imperative probabilistic programming exist. Dahlqvist et al.'s simple imperative probabilistic language [34] uses two constructs, $coin()$ and $rand()$, to introduce discrete and continuous uniform distributions, and both operational and denotational semantics are presented. Hoare logic has also been used to reason about probabilistic programs [9,26,37,135,136].

Probabilistic Process Algebras. Woodcock's interest in probabilistic programming is not restricted to sequential imperative programs. Indeed, he is interested in probabilistic programming based on CSP and *Circus*, and UTP in general, and how it can be used to give semantics to RoboChart. We review different probabilistic models in process algebras, particularly in (1) how to model probability, (2) how to interact with their environment, and (3) how probabilistic choice interacts with nondeterministic choice. Then we discuss the approach that RoboChart uses for probabilistic modelling.

Hansson's *alternating model* [62] distinguishes between nondeterministic and probabilistic choice. Either a nondeterministic choice or a probabilistic choice can be made in each state of this model, and the order of availability of these choices is strictly alternating between a nondeterministic and a probabilistic choice.

In Segala and Lynch's *probabilistic automata* [147], transitions are labelled with probability values. The transition relation is a *steps* function which maps source states to probability distributions over (action, target state) pairs. Actions can be external, modelling interactions with the environment through events, or internal, modelling computation steps through internal events τ. In probabilistic automata, a distribution from a source state may contain more than one action. If all distributions in a probabilistic automaton contain only one action, this automaton is called *simple*. Otherwise, it is called *general*. If from each source state, there is at most one step (or one distribution) enabled, this automaton is called *fully probabilistic*.

Van Glabbeek et al. [162]'s *reactive*, *generative*, and *stratified* models are the different ways to interpret probabilities [98] in processes. Multiple actions can be offered by a process to its environment, but the environment is allowed to choose only one in the reactive model or some in the generative and stratified models. After actions are chosen by the environment, the process makes an internal transition based on the current state and (1) the probability distribution associated with the action in the reactive model, or (2) the globally (or locally) redistributed probability distribution for chosen actions in the generative (or the stratified) model. The reactive model corresponds to the simple probabilistic automaton model without internal nondeterministic choice involving the same actions, in that both allow external nondeterministic choice between different actions (that is, multiple transitions with different external actions from the same state). Interestingly, zero probabilities are permitted in the stratified model to model process priorities.

There are many probability extensions based on: CSP [55,58,94,97,113, 116,124,148,157], CCS [56,61,162,183], and ACP [2], probabilistic transition systems [15,86,96], and automata [63,176]. We particularly review CSP-based extensions because CSP supports refinement and has its semantics in UTP.

Seidel [148] proposed two semantics models for probabilistic CSP: the independent model with external and internal choice and the conditional model without internal choice and hiding.

Lowe [97] presented two languages as refinements of Timed CSP [35,143]: a fully deterministic model (DTCSP) with a notion of priority (the prioritized model) and a probabilistic model (PDTCSP) extended from DTCSP. The two models feature biased external choice, parallel composition, and interleaving. They have no internal nondeterministic choice though PDTCSP has a (internal) probabilistic choice.

Gómez et al.'s probabilistic variant [58] of CSP has no internal nondeterministic choice but has two versions of probabilistic choice: one generative and one reactive to replace internal and external choice in CSP. Similarly, Núñez et al.'s PPA [124] has similar two versions of probabilistic choice.

Morgan and McIver et al.'s PCSP [113,116] uses Jones's general construction to extend CSP with probabilistic choice. In PCSP, probabilistic choice distributes through all other operators, including external choice and internal choice. But internal choice is not idempotent in PCSP. Morgan [113] linked probabilistic action systems (written in pGCL with expectation transformer semantics) and probabilistic CSP, gave traces, failures, and divergences from the probabilistic CSP to the probabilistic action systems.

Mislove's [109] proposed an approach to consider the family of probability convex sets in three possible power domains: lower, upper, and convex to provide a probabilistic extension of CSP (Morgan's PCSP) with both nondeterminism choice and probabilistic choice, importantly, all the laws for them are valid, including the idempotent law for nondeterministic choice.

Georgievska and Andova [55] presented a probabilistic extension of CSP which preserves the distributivity laws and the idempotent law for internal nondeterministic choice, via restricted schedulers. This extension supports internal nondeterministic choice, external choice, probabilistic choice, and parallel composition with hiding.

Sun et al. [157] proposed PCSP#, a probability extension of CSP# which combines high-level modelling operators with low-level procedural codes. The semantics of PCSP# is Markov Decision Processes (MDPs) [130]. The verification of PCSP# programs is supported by the Process Analysis Toolkit (PAT) [156].

Semantics for RoboChart. Because RoboChart's standard semantics is based on CSP and tock-CSP [12], Woodcock showed interest in probabilistic extensions of CSP, discussed previously, to give RoboChart a probabilistic semantics. However, the main issue is the lack of tool support. For this reason, inspired by Jansen et al.'s P-statecharts [83], Woodcock and Ye et al. [178] gave RoboChart a semantics based on the PRISM language [95]. RoboChart adopts the same alternation as [62] between nondeterministic and probabilistic choice, but a probabilistic choice is made only within a transition originating from a nondeterministic state. The PRISM semantics for RoboChart, however, is subject to the state space explosion problem, as discussed in [181] by Ye and Woodcock. Because of these challenges, Woodcock is also interested in the UTP semantics for probabilistic process algebras and its mechanisation in Isabelle/UTP to verify them using theorem proving. However, there are some important questions left to be answered, such as "Out of the existing and possible extensions of CSP to cover probability, which one should be adopted?", "should probability be encoded in traces, or should traces be probabilistic?", etc.

In [180], Ye et al. gave RoboChart operational semantics based on the mechanised CSP and *Circus* [49] in Isabelle/UTP using interaction trees (ITrees) [177], and used priority-based hiding and renaming operators to resolve nondeterminism. Ye, Woodcock, and Foster are interested in extending CSP and *Circus* with probabilistic choice to have sound animation for probabilistic RoboChart models.

4 Applications

In this section, we explore the application of the various choice operators to co-simulation, the semantics of RoboChart, and the modelling of random walks.

4.1 Co-simulation for Cyber-Physical Systems

Simulation techniques are widely adopted in the development of cyber-physical systems (CPS). Typically, their components may be developed using different techniques. To simulate a complete system, co-simulation can be used where components are encapsulated as simulation units (SUs) and a master algorithm orchestrates the simulation by exchanging values between SUs at sample times.

Co-simulation has advantages, in that stakeholders can protect their intellectual property by conforming to an API, such as FMI [14]. However, the master algorithm needs to handle SUs that may reject a simulation step if the chosen

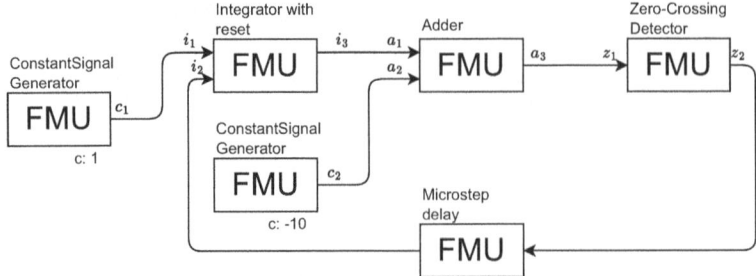

Fig. 2. Example of FMI setup with 6 connected FMUs.

time step is too large. Backtracking algorithms have been proposed [33] that can perform step revision. An example of using FMI is reproduced [33] in Fig. 2, consisting of 6 connected SUs, known as FMUs: constant signal generators, one integrator, an adder, a microstep delay, and a zero-crossing detector (ZCD).

The verification of co-simulation algorithms is a topic that Woodcock and his collaborators approached in [60], where they consider an UPPAAL encoding, however, the step revision procedure is modelled explicitly. The question is whether a formal specification can be constructed using abstract choice operators.

Process Algebraic Model. In what follows, we sketch a process algebraic specification for execution of SUs in FMI with step revision using the *Circus* notation. It is loosely based on the architecture in [24] and follows the constraints of [60]. The communications between SUs are modelled using the following channels:

$$Value ::= absent \mid value\langle\!\langle\mathbb{R}\rangle\!\rangle \qquad \textbf{channel } get : OUTPUT \times Value$$
$$\textbf{channel } doStep : SU \times \mathbb{T} \times \mathbb{T} \qquad \textbf{channel } set : INPUT \times Value$$

get to obtain the output of a SU, and *set* to provide an input, respectively, and *doStep* to step the simulation of a SU. *OUTPUT* and *INPUT* are types labeling the inputs and outputs of each SU, so that the connections between SUs can be modelled, and *Value* is the type of values admissible for communications, a real value or *absent*. *doStep* contains three values, the first drawn from *SU*, a set of SU identifiers, the second is the requested step size, and the third the actual step size accepted, over a time domain $\mathbb{T}$. We observe that according to the FMI2 standard it is possible that a SU may not report an accepted step size at all, and just yield an error. In this model, we omit this detail without loss of generality.

Connections. Input and output labels are associated with SUs via total functions while the connections between them are defined by a total surjection L from

$INPUT$ to $OUTPUT$. From L, we define a process $Exchange$ that captures the valid interactions for FMUs, via synchronisation on get, set and $doStep$.

$$\textbf{process } Exchange \;\widehat{=}\; \vert\vert\vert\; x : L \bullet SetC(first(x), second(x))$$

It is defined by an iterated interleaving over pairs x, drawn from L, of processes $SetC$, omitted here and parameterised by input and output labels, that define when an output is available given its dependency on an input, and whether a SU has been stepped forward in time, following the criteria defined in [60].

Then, given a process algebraic model of all SUs, captured by a process of the same name and whose definition we omit here, we can capture all possible interactions, by taking into account their connections, via a parallel composition with $Exchange$ synchronising on $doStep$, get and set, defined as follows.

$$\textbf{process } SUExchange \;\widehat{=}\; SUs \;[\![\, \{\!|\, doStep, get, set \,|\!\} \,]\!]\; Exchange$$

This process captures all possible simulations, including those that may not step through by the requested step size. A valid simulation is therefore defined by

$$\textbf{process } Simulation \;\widehat{=}\; SUExchange \;[\![\, \{\!|\, doStep \,|\!\} \,]\!]\; ChooseStep$$

where $ChooseStep$ captures the valid steps, that is, where $doStep$ is observed with requested and accepted simulation step sizes that are the same. We consider an approach where angelic choice is used to choose a step size, before a prefixing on $doStep.u.t_r.t_a$, for every SU u. This is sketched in the following $Circus$ process.

$$
\begin{aligned}
&\textbf{process } AngelicStep \;\widehat{=}\; \textbf{begin state } S == [h : \mathbb{T}_1] \\
&\quad DoStep \;\widehat{=}\; su : SU \bullet doStep!su!h?t \rightarrow \{h = t\} \\
&\quad Step \;\widehat{=}\; \vert\vert\vert\; su : SU \bullet DoStep(su) \\
&\quad Main \;\widehat{=}\; h : \textbf{guess}(\mathbb{T}_1) \;;\; Step \;;\; Main \\
&\bullet\; Main \\
&\textbf{end}
\end{aligned}
$$

It has a state variable h and its behaviour is defined by the $Main$ action, that angelically **guess**es a step size h from a finite domain $\mathbb{T}_1$, and then behaves as $Step$ followed by the recursion. $Step$ is defined by the iterated interleaving over su, drawn from the set SUs, of actions $DoStep(su)$. Each action has a prefixing on $doStep!su!h?t$, that uses the chosen step h and is prepared to synchronise on any accepted size t, and afterwards there is an assertion ($\{h = t\}$). If it fails, then the action aborts, including up to the point in $Main$ where h was chosen. While this captures all valid step sizes, it does not require h to be maximal.

Maximum Angelic Step. To address the shortcomings of the previous solution, we consider a modified version of the $AngelicStep$ using both angelic and demonic choice. We assume that a SU that accepts a step size h may also accept a step size h', such that $h' \leq h$. Intuitively, to determine the maximum admitted step size, we need "to experiment" with stepping a SU with values above and below an angelically chosen maximum step size, such that step sizes less than or equal to the maximum succeed, but values above do not. Crucially, failed experiments should be pruned from the model. We frame this in a game-like way as follows.

process *MaxAngelicStep* $\widehat{=}$ **begin state** $S == [h : \mathbb{T}_1;\ real : \mathbb{B}]$
$\quad$ *DoStep* $\widehat{=}$ $su : SU \bullet ([real = \textbf{True}]\ ;\ Stop)$
$\qquad\qquad\qquad\qquad \square\ doStep!su!h?t \to \{real = \textbf{True} \Leftrightarrow h = t\}$
$\quad$ *Step* $\widehat{=}$ $\Big|\Big|\Big|\ su : SU \bullet DoStep(su)$
$\quad$ *Main* $\widehat{=}$ $h : \textbf{guess}(\mathbb{T}_1);$
$\qquad\qquad h, real : [true, (h' \le h \land real' = \textbf{True}) \lor (h' > h \land real' = \textbf{False})];$
$\qquad\qquad Step\ ;\ [real = \textbf{True}]\ ;\ Main$
$\bullet$ *Main*
end

Differently from before, *MaxAngelicStep* has an additional boolean variable *real*, that is used to differentiate between an actual stepping, so it is **True**, and otherwise when an "experiment" with a larger step size is conducted it is **False**.

As before, the *Main* action begins by **guess**ing the step size h. Afterwards, we have a specification statement, whereby the value of h is demonically changed, such that, for lower values the variable *real* is **True**, and for higher values it is **False**. This is followed by a composition with a revised *Step* action and an assumption ($[real = \textbf{True}]$), followed by the recursion. In *DoStep* there is now an external choice between two processes: the first has an assumption that *real* is **True**, in which case it behaves as *Stop*, and otherwise is miraculous; the second has a prefix on *doStep* followed by an assertion that requires *real* to be **True** if, and only if, the step succeeds with value h. We consider all possible cases:

1. $real = \textbf{True} \land h \ne t$: the assertion fails as before, and so the process *Step* aborts given that h is not an admissible step size;
2. $real = \textbf{True} \land h = t$: the assertion succeeds and so do both assumptions, so h is an admissible step size;
3. $real = \textbf{False} \land h \ne t$: the assertion succeeds, but both assumptions fail. Therefore the external choice becomes equal to $\top \square\ doStep \to ...$, where $\top$ is miracle, which prunes waiting behaviours from the process, that is, the pericondition. When this behaviour is propagated to *Main*, as *Step*, its composition with the subsequent assumption $[real = \textbf{True}]$ ensures that overall that behaviour is pruned, given that a failed assumption is miraculous.
4. $real = \textbf{False} \land h = t$: both the assertion and the assumptions fail. This corresponds to an experiment for which a larger step size is admissible, but because of the failed assertions and assumptions the behaviour is also pruned.

The above is but a sketch of a specification for a master algorithm with step revision. Further work is required to establish the laws that would allow introducing the specific mechanisms for step revision in a refinement.

4.2   RoboChart

RoboChart [110] is a diagrammatic modelling language designed to support the specification of robotic software in terms of reactive state machines. These state machines can be combined in parallel to form controllers, which can be composed in parallel to describe the overall software. State machines are formed of transitions, states, and junctions. Transitions represent changes in a system's configuration; they connect two nodes (states and junctions), can be triggered by events and guarded by conditions, and can cause actions to be executed.

States model stable decision points, that is, configurations of the software in which the machine is allowed, potentially indefinitely, to wait for a particular input. Junctions, on the other hand, are not stable; they allow for decisions to be made but do not allow the system to wait indefinitely.

The semantics of RoboChart is defined in terms of *Circus*/CSP processes and supports formal analysis via model-checking and theorem proving. Several well-formedness conditions are necessary to adequately specify the semantics of RoboChart models. Of particular interest is the requirement that the guards of transitions leaving the same junction form a cover (the disjunction of the guards is true). This requirement guarantees that if a junction is reached, there is always one transition whose guard is true, and the system does not get stuck.

There are a number of reasons why this well-formedness condition might be inconvenient. For example, the particular path taken to a junction could guarantee that one of the outgoing transitions is always enabled. Alternatively, a modeller may wish to have simpler models (fewer transitions) and rely on an interpretation in which a transition from a state is only taken if there is a path to another state in which all the transitions are enabled.

Angelic choice discussed in Sect. 3.2 is a suitable alternative to specify the semantics of RoboChart models, in which the well-formedness condition above is relaxed and where the previously discussed interpretation is adopted. The standard semantics of transitions leaving a state can be specified as the external choice of the events that trigger the transitions. In order to adapt this semantics, we must first replace the external choice (in the selection of transitions) with angelic choice and adopt the theory described in [142]. Finally, we must also encode the omitted guards as Chaos. This guarantees that if a junction is reached in which none of the guards of the outgoing transitions is true, the process would backtrack, and an alternative path would be taken.

While such an approach has the potential for more succinct diagrams, it presents practical and theoretical challenges for verification due to the lack of tool support around angelic choice and the extra complexity in analysing the possible paths. The standard semantics balances specification power and automation, with a well-formedness condition that, while not amenable to static analysis, can be checked locally using automated theorem provers.

4.3   Random Walks

Grimmett and Welsh [59] defined various random walks (RW). A RW is *simple* if at each time step it can move only to its next (or neighbouring) positions randomly in one of the lattice directions. A *symmetric* RW has the equal probability for each direction. Otherwise, it is *asymmetric*.

According to Pólya's recurrence theorem [131], a symmetric random walk is recurrent (the probability of revisiting its starting point is 1) only if it is one- or two-dimensional. This simple random walk does not terminate. For this reason, researchers [29, 81, 89, 103, 107] in probabilistic programming and verification are more interested in a variant of the one-dimensional simple random walk (SRW). It is also the Gambler's Ruin Problem with an absorbing barrier at 0. We can model it as a probabilistic program below.

$$x := m; \text{ while}(x > 0)\{x := x - 1 \oplus_p x := x + 1\} \qquad \text{(PSRW)}$$

where x is an integer variable, m denotes the starting position and $m > 0$, and p is the probability of decreasing x by 1.

Grimmett and Welsh [59] proved the termination probability for SRW is $(p/q)^m$ if $q > p$ where $q = 1 - p$, and 1 otherwise. This program is proved to have its termination probability equal to 1 (that is, almost-sure termination (AST)) if p is equal to $1/2$ (so symmetric, as SSRW), according to [29, 81, 103, 107], using the invariant and variant reasoning technique for probabilistic loops. McIver et al. [107] and Chatterjee et al. [29]'s variant rules for loops are based on *supermartingale* [165], a sequence of random variables (RVs) for which the expected value of the current random variable is larger than or equal to that of the subsequent random variable. Moosbrugger et al. [111] developed the tool Amber to automatically prove the one-dimensional SSRW is AST. Furthermore, McIver et al. [107] proved the two-dimensional SSRW terminates almost-surely. Kaminski [89] proposed a wp-style reasoning for bounded expected runtimes and proved the expected runtime of SSRW is infinite.

These studies show the verification of AST for probabilistic loop programs. They, however, have not inferred the exact value of probabilities (either distribution or sub-distribution depending on p and m) and expected runtimes in terms of steps or iterations, or have not automated the inference, which are important for the evaluation of the correctness and performance of probabilistic algorithms (both Las Vegas and Monte Carlo). ProbURel [182] uses a unique (Kleene's) fixed-point theorem to give the semantics to probabilistic loops, which makes it able to infer the exact value of probabilities and expected runtimes. The most difficult part using this theorem is to construct a fixed point fp, or the invariant for the loop. As shown in [182], the exact value of probabilities and expected runtimes of two loop examples (flip a coin till a heads and throw a pair of dices till they have the same outcome) are proved and mechanised in Isabelle/UTP.

Here, we sketch a strategy for the exact inference (to explicitly represent the probability distribution or sub-distribution of PSRW in terms of iterations, parametric in m and p) of this SRW using mathematics and then use probabilistic programming to give the semantics by constructing a fixed point or invariant for the loop in PSRW. Mathematical calculation is not used in programming but is used for comparison.

Mathematics. We define X_i (where $i \in \mathbb{N}$) for the ith toss of the coin or the ith step of the moves, and

$$\mathbb{P}\{X_i = 1\} = q \qquad \mathbb{P}\{X_i = -1\} = p$$

where both p and q are non-negative real numbers and $p + q = 1$.

We use S_n^m to denote the current position of the walker (when starting at position m) after n time steps, so $S_n^m = m + \sum_{i=0}^{n} X_i$. Then the minimum number of time steps the walker reaches 0 from m is defined below.

$$\sigma_0(m) = min(\{n : \mathbb{N}|S_n^m = 0\})$$

So $\sigma_0(1)$ is the minimum number of time steps the walker reaches 0 from 1. We omit the subscript 0 here for simplicity. What we are interested in is the distribution in terms of $\sigma(m)$ or the number of iterations in the PSRW program.

From m, to reach the position 0, the walker needs to reach $m-1$ first, then $m-2$ etc. We note that X_i is independent and the distribution of the walker reaching $m-1$ from m is exactly the same as reaching 0 from 1. We can treat $\sigma(m)$ as the summation of m copies of $\sigma(1)$. Therefore, $\sigma(m) = \sum_{i=1}^{m} \sigma(1)$. So our question is to find out the distribution in terms of the discrete random variable $\sigma(1)$: $\mathbb{P}\{\sigma(1) = n\}$, denoted as $\varphi(n)$. The probability generation function [59] of $\sigma(1)$ is

$$G_{\sigma(1)}(z) = \mathbb{E}\left(z^{\sigma(1)}\right) = \sum_{n=0}^{\infty} \mathbb{P}\{\sigma(1) = n\}z^n = \sum_{n=0}^{\infty} \varphi(n)z^n \qquad \text{(G1)}$$

Then according to the theorem [59] that the generation function for the sum of independent random variables is the product of those for each independent random variable,

$$G_{\sigma(m)}(z) = G_{\sum_{i=0}^{m} \sigma(1)}(z) = \left(G_{\sigma(1)}\right)^m = \left(\sum_{n=0}^{\infty} \varphi(n)z^n\right)^m \qquad \text{(Gm)}$$

So our question now is to determine $\varphi(n)$. First, we can get $\mathbb{E}(z^{\sigma(1)})$ by solving an equation which is formed by conditioning the first move of the walker, as described in [159]. The result is shown below.

$$G_{\sigma(1)}(z) = \mathbb{E}(z^{\sigma(1)}) = \frac{1 - \sqrt{1 - 4pqz^2}}{2qz} \qquad \text{(G1r)}$$

The sum of probabilities is just the generation function when $z = 1$, so

$$G_{\sigma(1)}(1) = \frac{1 - \sqrt{1 - 4pq}}{2q} = \begin{cases} p/q & \text{if } p < q \\ 1 & \text{if } p \geq q \end{cases}$$

SRW for $m = 1$ (that is, $\sigma(1)$) is AST only when $p \geq q$. The Taylor expansion of (G1r) gives the power series below.

$$\frac{1 - \sqrt{1 - 4pqz^2}}{2qz} = \sum_{n=1}^{\infty} \frac{(2n-3)!!2^{n-1}}{n!} p^n q^{n-1} z^{2n-1}$$

where !! denotes the double factorial. Particularly, $(-1)!! = 1$. We use $a(i)$ to denote the coefficient in the power series for z^i, and so

$$a(2n - 1) = \frac{(2n-3)!!2^{n-1}}{n!} p^n q^{n-1}$$

We note that the corresponding $a(2 * n)$ to z^{2n} is 0. Let $i = 2n - 1$, so $n = \frac{i+1}{2}$.

$$a(i) = \frac{(i-2)!!2^{\frac{i-1}{2}}}{(\frac{i+1}{2})!} p^{\frac{i+1}{2}} q^{\frac{i-1}{2}}$$

We can rewrite this power series as follows using the Iverson bracket notation defined in [182].

$$\sum_{n=1}^{\infty} a(2n-1)z^{2n-1} = \sum_{n=0}^{\infty} [\![n\%2 = 1]\!] a(n) z^n \qquad \text{(G1pgf)}$$

where $[\![n\%2 = 1]\!]$ is 0 for all n that is even. According to (G1), now $\varphi(n) = [\![n\%2 = 1]\!] a(n)$. Now we expand the mth power in (Gm),

$$\left(\sum_{n=0}^{\infty} \varphi(n)z^n \right)^m = \sum_{n=0}^{\infty} \left(\overbrace{\underbrace{\sum_{i_1=0}^{n} \sum_{i_2=0}^{i_1} \cdots \sum_{i_{m-1}=0}^{i_{m-2}}}_{m-1} \varphi(n - i_1)\varphi(i_1 - i_2)\ldots\varphi(i_{m-1})}^{\mu(m,n)} \right) z^n$$

Finally, $\mu(m, n)$ above gives the probability of SRW reaching 0 after exact n steps, when starting from m.

Probabilistic Programming. To reason about expected runtimes, as shown in [182], an additional variable t of type natural numbers is introduced in PSRW to count the iterations.

$$x := m; t := 0; \text{ while}(x > 0)\{x := x - 1 \oplus_p x := x + 1; t := t + 1\} \quad \text{(TPSRW)}$$

Unlike the other two verified loop examples (flip a coin and throw a pair of dices) in [182] whose every experiment or iteration is independent of the previous iterations, TPSRW's each iteration is related to all previous iterations because the value of x is updated in each step. For this reason, its loop invariant or the fixed point does not share the same pattern: $p_f^{(n-1)} * p_s$ where p_f (or p_s) is the probability of non-termination (or termination) for each experiment.

However, we observe that $\mu(m, n) = p*\mu(m-1, n-1)+q*\mu(m+1, n-1)$,[12] that is, the termination from m in n steps is only through two alternative ways: move to the left (with probability p) and then terminate from $m-1$ in $n-1$ steps, or move to the right (with probability q) and then terminate from $m+1$ in $n-1$ steps. This observation helps us to define the fixed point of the loop.

$$Ht \mathrel{\widehat{=}} [\![\neg x > 0]\!] * [\![x' = x]\!] * [\![t' = t]\!] + [\![x > 0]\!] * [\![x' = 0]\!]*$$
$$\left(\begin{array}{l} [\![t' - t \geq x]\!] * [\![((t' - t) - x)\%2 = 0]\!] * \mu(x - 1, t' - t - 1) * p+ \\ [\![t' - t \geq x + 2]\!] * [\![((t' - t) - (x + 2))\%2 = 0]\!] * \mu(x + 1, t' - t - 1) * q \end{array} \right)$$

which means if the initial value of x is not larger than 0, the loop behaves like skip (unchanged variables). Otherwise, the loop terminates (that is, when the final value of x is 0, $x' = 0$) through two possible initial steps: x decreased by 1 with probability p or increased by 1 with probability q, corresponding to two operands of the addition in the parenthesis. In the first case, x is equal to 0 only after more than x steps ($t'-t \geq x$) and the number ($t'-t$) of steps must be even (or odd) if x is even (or odd), as encoded in $((t' - t) - x)\%2 = 0$. In the second case, x is equal to 0 only after more than $x+2$ steps ($t' - t \geq x + 2$) because the first step moves away from 0 and the number ($t' - t$) of steps must be even (or odd) if $x + 2$ is even (or odd), as encoded in $((t' - t) - (x + 2))\%2 = 0$.

We have proved that Ht is a fixed point. And the proof is omitted here for brevity. The proof, however, has not been mechanised in Isabelle/UTP. This is part of the future work Ye and Woodcock are interested in.

As shown above, finding the distributions of probabilistic loops and proving their semantics is non-trivial, even for this simple program—PSRW. In ProbU-Rel, Ye et al. [182] developed a constructive semantics for probabilistic loops using Kleene's fixed-point theorem. This can be used to approximate semantics for loops in practice based on iterations. We explain the algorithm as follows.

A loop characterisation function is defined below where P is the loop body.

$$\mathcal{F}(b, P, X) \mathrel{\widehat{=}} \textbf{if } b \textbf{ then } (P \mathbin{;_p} X) \textbf{ else } \mathbb{II}_p$$

According to the theorems [182] about the least fixed point (lfp) and greatest fixed point by construction, lfp and gfp can be constructed using the iteration $\mathcal{F}^n(b, P, \bot)$ from the bottom and the iteration $\mathcal{F}^n(b, P, \top)$ from the top of the complete lattice. Additionally, $\mathcal{F}^n(b, P, \bot)$ is an increasing chain and $\mathcal{F}^n(b, P, \top)$ is an decreasing chain. The unique fixed point theorem shows that if, for all states, the difference $\mathcal{F}^n(b, P, \top) - \mathcal{F}^n(b, P, \bot)$ between the two iterations tends to 0 when n approaches ∞, then the iterations coincide. Using the iterations to determine lfp and gfp, in general, are not decidable because the difference might never be 0 for any n (though its limit might be 0). However, if we bound the difference as $\varepsilon > 0$, there always exists a n such that, for all states, $\mathcal{F}^n(b, P, \top) -$

---

[12] This equation equips us another way to calculate the distribution $\mu(m, n)$ of SRW through recursive functions.

$\mathcal{F}^n (b, P, \bot) < \varepsilon$. Then $\mathcal{F}^n (b, P, \top)$ is an approximation of lfp and $\mathcal{F}^n (b, P, \top)$ is an approximation of gfp though they bias. Then this bounded approximation is decidable. For PSRW, the algorithm is shown below.

(1) choose a small ε, such as $1e - 9$;
(2) compute a n such that the differences for all states are less than ε;
(3) compute $\mathcal{F}^i (b, P, \bot)$ for i from 0 to n; these are the termination probabilities in terms of the number of steps (i), that is, the probability distribution of PSRW up to n steps.

We note that in the approximated distribution, the probabilities for 0 to n steps are exact and only the probabilities after $n+1$ are cut off (that is, all zero).

This approach could address the difficulty of finding and proving the distribution in practice. We plan to also investigate this further in the future.

5 Conclusions

In this chapter, we have taken a *tour* through the programming choices available across state- and process-based paradigms. Nondeterminism plays a fundamental role and traces its roots to the early theories of computation, where it can be viewed as *demonic* or *angelic*. Semantically, the predicate transformer view is perhaps simpler than the (multi)relational one, yet it's pleasing that the choices are duals in the respective lattices induced by refinement. The applications sketched in Sects. 4.1 and 4.2 highlight the need for further work in this area, not least the mechanisation of the theory [142] in Isabelle/UTP [46] and the exploration of refinement laws. Extensions of that theory to calculi covering time [21], perhaps via a relational account of *tock*-CSP [12], and other aspects are also future work. A related question is whether Foster's interaction trees [49] could be extended to give an operational account to both choices, thus paving the way for sound animation, an important bridge for engaging with practitioners.

Preferential choice forces us to step outside the realm of wp predicate transformers, while having an elegant and easy to define model in prospective-value (pv) expression transformers. The core logic of a theory of prospective values that is able to account for both nondeterminism and nontermination requires *improper bunch theory* (a self-flattening set theory with a $\bot$ value for every type) as an integral part, i.e., to model the outcome of computations. Preferential computations forfeit monotonicity, e.g., in the first operand of $S \gg T$, but a restricted form of compositional refinement can be recovered via a Galois connection between wp and pv computations. This enables us to safely replace $S \sqcap T$ in specification by $S \gg T$ in implementations, and thereby formally justify the introduction of heuristics when exploring search spaces.

As hinted in Sect. 3.3, we managed to define and mechanise a suitable model for preference and preferential computations in a wp calculus that builds on top of a three-value logic—an instance of Gödel-Dummett logic—and managed to verify the existence of the abovementioned Galois connection between plain monotonic computations in wp semantics and preferential computations. We expect this work to be published in the near future.

Probabilistic choice can be seen as a refinement of nondeterministic choice because it provides more specific information (probabilities) about how the choice can be made. The semantics of probabilistic choice with the presence of nondeterministic choice are very different in the relational model and the predicate transformer for imperative programs, and in process algebras. The review of probabilistic choice in Sect. 3.4 and its application presented in Sect. 4.3 reveal the need for further work (1) in the extension of ProbURel to support nondeterministic choice and concurrency, (2) in the practical tool support for approximating probabilistic loops using ProbURel in addition to theorem proving for exact verification, and (3) in the extension of ITrees-based CSP and *Circus* [49,180] to support probabilistic choice for the sound animation of probabilistic programs with nondeterministic choice resolved by priorities.

In summary, the type of programming choice that is most suitable very much depends on our modelling needs. In some cases, several types of choices are even feasible to adopt: e.g., backtracking can be modelled by both demonic and angelic choice, using either **magic** or **abort** as a special program to trigger backtracking. The deeper connections between choices at a semantic level are a fascinating area of fundamental research, and the combination of several notions of choice in a single universal theory remains a key challenge for unification.

Acknowledgments. The work on FMI benefited from discussions with Claudio Gomes, Simon Hansen, Jaco van de Pol and Jim Woodcock. EPSRC projects RoboCalc (EP/M025756/1), RoboTest (EP/R025479/1), and CyPhyAssure (EP/S001190/1) funded the work discussed here related to RoboChart.

References

1. Abelson, H., Sussman, G.J.: Structure and Interpretation of Computer Programs, 2nd Edition. MIT Press (1996)
2. Andova, S.: Probabilistic process algebra. Ph.D. thesis, Mathematics and Computer Science, Technische Universiteit Eindhoven (2002). https://doi.org/10.6100/IR561343
3. Apt, K.R., Olderog, E.: Nondeterminism and guarded commands. In: Apt, K.R., Hoare, T. (eds.) Edsger Wybe Dijkstra: His Life, Work, and Legacy, vol. 45, pp. 169–204. ACM/Morgan & Claypool (2022). https://doi.org/10.1145/3544585.3544595
4. Armoni, M., Ben-Ari, M.: The concept of nondeterminism: its development and implications for teaching. ACM SIGCSE Bull. **41**(2), 141–160 (2009). https://doi.org/10.1145/1595453.1595495
5. Aspnes, J., Herlihy, M.: Fast randomized consensus using shared memory. J. Algorithms **11**(3), 441–461 (1990). https://doi.org/10.1016/0196-6774(90)90021-6
6. Baaz, M., Preining, N., Zach, R.: First-order Gödel logics. Ann. Pure Appl. Logic **147**(1), 23–47 (2007). https://doi.org/10.1016/j.apal.2007.03.001
7. Back, R.J.R., von Wright, J.: Duality in specification languages: a lattice-theoretical approach. Acta Informatica **27**(7), 583–625 (1990). https://doi.org/10.1007/bf00259469

8. Back, R., von Wright, J.: Refinement Calculus - A Systematic Introduction. Graduate Texts in Computer Science. Springer, Heidelberg (1998). https://doi.org/10.1007/978-1-4612-1674-2

9. Barthe, G., Grégoire, B., Zanella Béguelin, S.: Formal certification of code-based cryptographic proofs. In: Proceedings of the 36th Annual ACM SIGPLAN-SIGACT Symposium on Principles of Programming Languages, POPL 2009, pp. 90–101. Association for Computing Machinery, New York (2009). https://doi.org/10.1145/1480881.1480894

10. Batz, K., Biskup, T.J., Katoen, J.P., Winkler, T.: Programmatic strategy synthesis: resolving nondeterminism in probabilistic programs. Proc. ACM Program. Lang. 8(POPL), 2792–2820 (2024). https://doi.org/10.1145/3632935

11. Batz, K., Chen, M., Junges, S., Kaminski, B.L., Katoen, JP., Matheja, C.: Probabilistic program verification via inductive synthesis of inductive invariants. In: Sankaranarayanan, S., Sharygina, N. (eds.) Tools and Algorithms for the Construction and Analysis of Systems, TACAS 2023. LNCS, vol. 13994, pp. 410–429. Springer, Cham (2023). https://doi.org/10.1007/978-3-031-30820-8_25

12. Baxter, J., Ribeiro, P., Cavalcanti, A.: Sound reasoning in tock-CSP. Acta Informatica 59, 125–162 (2021). https://doi.org/10.1007/s00236-020-00394-3

13. Bergstra, J.A., Klop, J.W.: Algebra of communicating processes with abstraction. Theor. Comput. Sci. 37, 77–121 (1985). https://doi.org/10.1016/0304-3975(85)90088-X

14. Blochwitz, T., et al.: Functional mockup interface 2.0: the standard for tool independent exchange of simulation models. In: 9th International Modelica Conference, pp. 173–184. The Modelica Association (2012). https://doi.org/10.3384/ecp12076173

15. Bloom, B., Meyer, A.R.: A remark on bisimulation between probabilistic processes. In: Meyer, A.R., Taitslin, M.A. (eds.) Logic at Botik '89. LNCS, pp. 26–40. Springer, Heidelberg (1989). https://doi.org/10.1007/3-540-51237-3_4

16. Brookes, S.D., Hoare, C.A.R., Roscoe, A.W.: A theory of communicating sequential processes. J. ACM 31(3), 560–599 (1984). https://doi.org/10.1145/828.833

17. Broy, M., Wirsing, M.: On the algebraic specification of nondeterministic programming languages. In: Astesiano, E., Böhm, C. (eds.) CAAP '81, Trees in Algebra and Programming, 6th Colloquium, Genoa, Italy, 5–7 March 1981, Proceedings. LNCS, vol. 112, pp. 162–179. Springer, Heidelberg (1981). https://doi.org/10.1007/3-540-10828-9_61

18. Butler, M.J., Leuschel, M.: Combining CSP and B for specification and property verification. In: Fitzgerald, J.S., Hayes, I.J., Tarlecki, A. (eds.) FM 2005: Formal Methods, International Symposium of Formal Methods Europe, Newcastle, 18–22 UK, July 2005, Proceedings. LNCS, vol. 3582, pp. 221–236. Springer, Heidelberg (2005). https://doi.org/10.1007/11526841_16

19. Butterfield, A., Sherif, A., Woodcock, J.: Slotted-circus. In: Davies, J., Gibbons, J. (eds.) 6th International Conference on Integrated Formal Methods, IFM 2007, Oxford, UK, 2–5 July 2007, Proceedings. LNCS, vol. 4591, pp. 75–97. Springer, Heidelberg (2007). https://doi.org/10.1007/978-3-540-73210-5_5

20. Canham, S., Woodcock, J.: Three approaches to timed external choice in UTP. In: Naumann, D.A. (ed.) 5th International Symposium on Unifying Theories of Programming, UTP 2014, Singapore, 13 May 2014, Revised Selected Papers. LNCS, vol. 8963, pp. 1–20. Springer, Heidelberg (2014). https://doi.org/10.1007/978-3-319-14806-9_1

21. Cavalcanti, A., Mota, A., Woodcock, J.: Simulink timed models for program verification. In: Liu, Z., Woodcock, J., Zhu, H. (eds.) Theories of Programming and Formal Methods - Essays Dedicated to Jifeng He on the Occasion of His 70th Birthday. LNCS, vol. 8051, pp. 82–99. Springer, Heidelberg (2013). https://doi.org/10.1007/978-3-642-39698-4_6

22. Cavalcanti, A., Sampaio, A., Woodcock, J.: A refinement strategy for circus. Formal Aspects Comput. **15**(2–3), 146–181 (2003). https://doi.org/10.1007/S00165-003-0006-5

23. Cavalcanti, A., Woodcock, J.: A tutorial introduction to CSP in *Unifying Theories of Programming*. In: Cavalcanti, A., Sampaio, A., Woodcock, J. (eds.) Refinement Techniques in Software Engineering, First Pernambuco Summer School on Software Engineering, PSSE 2004, Recife, Brazil, 23 November–5 December 2004, Revised Lectures. LNCS, vol. 3167, pp. 220–268. Springer, Heidelberg (2004). https://doi.org/10.1007/11889229_6

24. Cavalcanti, A., Woodcock, J., Amálio, N.: Behavioural models for FMI co-simulations. In: Sampaio, A., Wang, F. (eds.) Proceedings of the 13th International Colloquium on Theoretical Aspects of Computing, ICTAC 2016, Taipei, Taiwan, ROC, 24–31 October 2016. LNCS, vol. 9965, pp. 255–273 (2016). https://doi.org/10.1007/978-3-319-46750-4_15

25. Cavalcanti, A., Woodcock, J., Dunne, S.: Angelic nondeterminism in the unifying theories of programming. Formal Aspects Comput. **18**(3), 288–307 (2006). https://doi.org/10.1007/S00165-006-0001-8

26. Chadha, R., Cruz-Filipe, L., Mateus, P., Sernadas, A.: Reasoning about probabilistic sequential programs. Theor. Comput. Sci. **379**(1–2), 142–165 (2007). https://doi.org/10.1016/j.tcs.2007.02.040

27. Chandra, A.K., Kozen, D., Stockmeyer, L.J.: Alternation. J. ACM **28**(1), 114–133 (1981). https://doi.org/10.1145/322234.322243

28. Chandy, K.M., Misra, J.: Parallel Program Design - A Foundation. Addison-Wesley (1989)

29. Chatterjee, K., Fu, H., Novotný, P.: Termination Analysis of Probabilistic Programs with Martingales, pp. 221-258. Cambridge University Press (2020). https://doi.org/10.1017/9781108770750

30. Chomsky, N.: Context-free grammars and pushdown storage. MIT Res. Lab. Electron. Quart. Prog. Rep. **65**, 187–194 (1962)

31. Commission of the European Communities: Information technology security evaluation criteria. (ITSEC), Preliminary harmonised criteria (1991)

32. Cook, S.A.: The complexity of theorem-proving procedures. In: Harrison, M.A., Banerji, R.B., Ullman, J.D. (eds.) Proceedings of the 3rd Annual ACM Symposium on Theory of Computing, 3–5 May 1971, Shaker Heights, Ohio, USA, pp. 151–158. ACM (1971). https://doi.org/10.1145/800157.805047

33. Cremona, F., Lohstroh, M., Broman, D., Natale, M.D., Lee, E.A., Tripakis, S.: Step revision in hybrid co-simulation with FMI. In: 2016 ACM/IEEE International Conference on Formal Methods and Models for System Design, MEMOCODE 2016, Kanpur, India, 18–20 November 2016, pp. 173–183. IEEE (2016). https://doi.org/10.1109/MEMCOD.2016.7797762

34. Dahlqvist, F., Silva, A., Kozen, D.: Semantics of probabilistic programming: a gentle introduction. In: Barthe, G., Katoen, J.P., Silva, A. (eds.) Foundations of Probabilistic Programming, pp. 1–42. Cambridge University Press (2020). https://doi.org/10.1017/9781108770750.002

35. Davies, J., Schneider, S.: A brief history of Timed CSP. Theoret. Comput. Sci. **138**(2), 243–271 (1995). https://doi.org/10.1016/0304-3975(94)00169-j

36. Davis, M.D.: Computability and Unsolvability. McGraw-Hill Series in Information Processing and Computers, McGraw-Hill (1958)
37. den Hartog, J., De Vink, E.: Verifying Probabilistic Programs Using a Hoare like Logic. Int. J. Found. Comput. Sci. **13**(3), 315–340 (2002). https://doi.org/10.1142/S012905410200114X, imported from DIES
38. Dijkstra, E.W.: Correctness concerns and, among other things, why they are resented, November 1974. Invited paper, to be presented at the International Conference on Reliable Software, Los Angeles, 21–23 April 1975; circulated privately. http://www.cs.utexas.edu/users/EWD/ewd04xx/EWD450.PDF
39. Dijkstra, E.W.: Guarded commands, non-determinacy and a calculus for the derivation of programs, June 1974. See EWD:EWD472; circulated privately. http://www.cs.utexas.edu/users/EWD/ewd04xx/EWD418.PDF
40. Dijkstra, E.: A Discipline of Programming. Prentice-Hall Series in Automa, Prentice-Hall (1976)
41. Dijkstra, R.M.: DUALITY: a simple formalism for the analysis of UNITY. Formal Aspects Comput. **7**(4), 353–388 (1995). https://doi.org/10.1007/BF01211214
42. Dolev, D., Yao, A.: On the security of public key protocols. IEEE Trans. Inf. Theor. **29**(2), 198–208 (1983). https://doi.org/10.1109/TIT.1983.1056650
43. Dunne, S., Ferreira, J.F., Mendes, A., Ritchie, C., Stoddart, B., Zeyda, F.: bGSL: an imperative language for specification and refinement of backtracking programs. J. Logical Algebraic Meth. Program. **130**, 100811 (2023). https://doi.org/10.1016/j.jlamp.2022.100811
44. Fischer, C.: How to combine Z with a process algebra. In: Bowen, J.P., Fett, A., Hinchey, M.G. (eds.) The Z Formal Specification Notation, ZUM '98, pp. 5–23. Springer, Heidelberg (1998). https://doi.org/10.1007/978-3-540-49676-2_2
45. Floyd, R.W.: Nondeterministic algorithms. J. ACM **14**(4), 636–644 (1967). https://doi.org/10.1145/321420.321422
46. Foster, S., Baxter, J., Cavalcanti, A., Woodcock, J., Zeyda, F.: Unifying semantic foundations for automated verification tools in Isabelle/UTP. Sci. Comput. Program. **197**, 102510 (2020). https://doi.org/10.1016/j.scico.2020.102510
47. Foster, S., Cavalcanti, A., Canham, S., Woodcock, J., Zeyda, F.: Unifying theories of reactive design contracts. Theor. Comput. Sci. **802**, 105–140 (2020). https://doi.org/10.1016/J.TCS.2019.09.017
48. Foster, S., Cavalcanti, A., Woodcock, J., Zeyda, F.: Unifying theories of time with generalised reactive processes. Inf. Process. Lett. **135**, 47–52 (2018). https://doi.org/10.1016/J.IPL.2018.02.017
49. Foster, S., Hur, C., Woodcock, J.: Formally verified simulations of state-rich processes using interaction trees in Isabelle/HOL. In: Haddad, S., Varacca, D. (eds.) 32nd International Conference on Concurrency Theory, CONCUR 2021, 24–27 August 2021, Virtual Conference. LIPIcs, vol. 203, pp. 20:1–20:18. Schloss Dagstuhl - Leibniz-Zentrum für Informatik (2021). https://doi.org/10.4230/LIPICS.CONCUR.2021.20
50. Foster, S., Zeyda, F., Nemouchi, Y., Ribeiro, P., Wolff, B.: Isabelle/UTP: mechanised theory engineering for unifying theories of programming. Arch. Formal Proofs **2019** (2019). https://www.isa-afp.org/entries/UTP.html
51. Francez, N., Hoare, C.A.R., Lehmann, D.J., de Roever, W.P.: Semantics of nondeterminism, concurrency, and communication. J. Comput. Syst. Sci. **19**(3), 290–308 (1979). https://doi.org/10.1016/0022-0000(79)90006-0
52. Freitas, L., Woodcock, J.: Mechanising Mondex with Z/Eves. Formal Aspects Comput. **20**(1), 117–139 (2008). https://doi.org/10.1007/S00165-007-0059-Y

53. Furusawa, H., Struth, G.: Taming multirelations. ACM Trans. Comput. Log. **17**(4), 28 (2016). https://doi.org/10.1145/2964907

54. Gardiner, P.H.B., Morgan, C.: Data refinement of predicate transformers. Theor. Comput. Sci. **87**(1), 143–162 (1991). https://doi.org/10.1016/0304-3975(91)90029-2

55. Georgievska, S., Andova, S.: Probabilistic CSP: preserving the laws via restricted schedulers. In: Schmitt, J.B. (ed.) Measurement, Modelling, and Evaluation of Computing Systems and Dependability and Fault Tolerance, pp. 136–150. Springer, Heidelberg (2012). https://doi.org/10.1007/978-3-642-28540-0_10

56. Giacalone, A., Jou, C., Smolka, S.A.: Algebraic reasoning for probabilistic concurrent systems. In: Broy, M., Jones, C.B. (eds.) Programming concepts and methods: Proceedings of the IFIP Working Group 2.2, 2.3 Working Conference on Programming Concepts and Methods, Sea of Galilee, Israel, 2–5 April 1990, pp. 443–458. North-Holland (1990)

57. Gleirscher, M., Foster, S., Woodcock, J.: New opportunities for integrated formal methods. ACM Comput. Surv. **52**(6), 117:1–117:36 (2020). https://doi.org/10.1145/3357231

58. Gómez, F.C., de Frutos Escrig, D., Ruiz, V.V.: A sound and complete proof system for probabilistic processes. In: Bertran, M., Rus, T. (eds.) Transformation-Based Reactive Systems Development, pp. 340–352. Springer, Heidelberg (1997). https://doi.org/10.1007/3-540-63010-4_23

59. Grimmett, G., Welsh, D.: Probability: An Introduction. Oxford University Press, Clarendon Press (1986)

60. Hansen, S.T., Gomes, C., Palmieri, M., Thule, C., van de Pol, J., Woodcock, J.: Verification of co-simulation algorithms subject to algebraic loops and adaptive steps. In: Lluch-Lafuente, A., Mavridou, A. (eds.) Proceedings of the 26th International Conference on Formal Methods for Industrial Critical Systems, FMICS 2021, Paris, France, 24–26 August 2021. LNCS, vol. 12863, pp. 3–20. Springer, Heidelberg (2021). https://doi.org/10.1007/978-3-030-85248-1_1

61. Hansson, H., Jonsson, B.: A calculus for communicating systems with time and probabilities. In: 1990 Proceedings of the 11th Real-Time Systems Symposium, pp. 278–287 (1990). https://doi.org/10.1109/REAL.1990.128759

62. Hansson, H.: Time and Probabilities in Formal Design of Distributed Systems. Ph.D. thesis, Department of Computer Systems, Uppsala University (1991)

63. Hartmanns, A., Hermanns, H.: In the quantitative automata zoo. Sci. Comput. Program. **112**, 3–23 (2015). Fundamentals of Software Engineering (selected papers of FSEN 2013). https://doi.org/10.1016/j.scico.2015.08.009

64. He, J., Morgan, C., McIver, A.: Deriving probabilistic semantics via the 'weakest completion'. In: Davies, J., Schulte, W., Barnett, M. (eds.) Formal Methods and Software Engineering, pp. 131–145. Springer, Heidelberg (2004). https://doi.org/10.1007/978-3-540-30482-1_17

65. Hehner, E.C.R.: Predicative programming part I. Commun. ACM **27**(2), 134–143 (1984). https://doi.org/10.1145/69610.357988

66. Hehner, E.C.R.: Probabilistic predicative programming. In: Kozen, D., Shankland, C. (eds.) Proceedings of the 7th International Conference on Mathematics of Program Construction, MPC 2004, Stirling, Scotland, UK, 12–14 July 2004. LNCS, vol. 3125, pp. 169–185. Springer, Heidelberg (2004). https://doi.org/10.1007/978-3-540-27764-4_10

67. Hehner, E.C.R.: A probability perspective. Formal Aspects Comput. **23**(4), 391–419 (2011). https://doi.org/10.1007/s00165-010-0157-0

68. Hehner, E.C.R.: A Practical Theory of Programming, 1st edn. (2024-1-14 edition). Springer, Heidelberg (2024). https://doi.org/10.1007/978-1-4419-8596-5
69. Hehner, E.C.: Bunch theory: a simple set theory for computer science. Inf. Process. Lett. **12**(1), 26–30 (1981). https://doi.org/10.1016/0020-0190(81)90071-5
70. Hesselink, W.H.: LR-parsing derived. Sci. Comput. Program. **19**(2), 171–196 (1992). https://doi.org/10.1016/0167-6423(92)90007-X
71. Hesselink, W.H.: Programs, Recursion and Unbounded Choice. Cambridge University Press (1992)
72. Hesselink, W.H.: Nondeterminacy and recursion via stacks and games. Theor. Comput. Sci. **124**(2), 273–295 (1994). https://doi.org/10.1016/0304-3975(92)00016-K
73. Hesselink, W.H.: Alternating states for dual nondeterminism in imperative programming. Theor. Comput. Sci. **411**(22–24), 2317–2330 (2010). https://doi.org/10.1016/J.TCS.2010.03.016
74. Hesselink, W.H., Reinds, R.: Temporal preconditions of recursive procedures. In: de Bakker, J.W., de Roever, W.P., Rozenberg, G. (eds.) Proceedings of the Sematics: Foundations and Applications, REX Workshop, Beekbergen, The Netherlands, 1–4 June 1992. LNCS, vol. 666, pp. 236–260. Springer, Heidelberg (1992). https://doi.org/10.1007/3-540-56596-5_36
75. Hoare, C.A.R.: Algorithm 64: quicksort. Commun. ACM **4**(7), 321 (1961). https://doi.org/10.1145/366622.366644
76. Hoare, C.A.R.: An axiomatic basis for computer programming. Commun. ACM **12**(10), 576–580 (1969). https://doi.org/10.1145/363235.363259
77. Hoare, C.A.R.: Communicating sequential processes. Commun. ACM **21**(8), 666–677 (1978). https://doi.org/10.1145/359576.359585
78. Hoare, C.A.R.: A model for communicating sequential processes. In: McKeag, R.M., Macnaghten, A.M. (eds.) On the Construction of Programs, pp. 229–254. Cambridge University Press (1980)
79. Hoare, C.A.R., He, J.: Unifying Theories of Programming. Prentice-Hall (1998)
80. Hoare, C., He, J.: The weakest prespecification. Inf. Process. Lett. **24**(2), 127–132 (1987). https://doi.org/10.1016/0020-0190(87)90106-2
81. Hurd, J.: Formal verification of probabilistic algorithms. Technical report, UCAM-CL-TR-566, University of Cambridge, Computer Laboratory, May 2003. https://doi.org/10.48456/tr-566
82. Jagadeesan, R., Shanbhogue, V., Saraswat, V.: Angelic non-determinism in concurrent constraint programming. Technical report, Xerox Park (1991)
83. Jansen, D.N., Hermanns, H., Katoen, J.P.: A probabilistic extension of UML statecharts. In: Formal Techniques in Real-Time and Fault-Tolerant Systems. LNCS, vol. 2469, pp. 355–374. Springer, Heidelberg (2002). https://doi.org/10.1007/3-540-45739-9_21
84. Jones, C.B., O'Hearn, P.W., Woodcock, J.: Verified software: a grand challenge. Computer **39**(4), 93–95 (2006). https://doi.org/10.1109/MC.2006.145
85. Jones, C.B.: Systematic software development using VDM. Prentice Hall International Series in Computer Science. Prentice Hall (1986)
86. Jonsson, B., Yi, W., Larsen, K.G.: Probabilistic extensions of process algebras**this chapter is dedicated to the fond memory of Linda Christoff, Chap. 11. In: Bergstra, J., Ponse, A., Smolka, S. (eds.) Handbook of Process Algebra, pp. 685–710. Elsevier Science, Amsterdam (2001). https://doi.org/10.1016/B978-044482830-9/50029-1
87. Rogers, H.: Theory of Recursive Functions and Effective Computability (Reprint from 1967). MIT Press (1987)

88. Kaminski, B.L.: Advanced weakest precondition calculi for probabilistic programs. Ph.D. thesis, RWTH Aachen University, Germany (2019). http://publications. rwth-aachen.de/record/755408

89. Kaminski, B.L., Katoen, J.P., Matheja, C., Olmedo, F.: Weakest precondition reasoning for expected runtimes of randomized algorithms. J. ACM **65**(5) (2018). https://doi.org/10.1145/3208102

90. Kennaway, R., Hoare, C.A.R.: A theory of nondeterminism. In: de Bakker, J.W., van Leeuwen, J. (eds.) Proceedings of the Automata, Languages and Programming, 7th Colloquium, Noordweijkerhout, The Netherlands, 14–18 July 1980. LNCS, vol. 85, pp. 338–350. Springer, Heidelberg (1980). https://doi.org/10.1007/3-540-10003-2_82

91. Kok, J.N.: On Logic Programming and the Refinement Calculus: Semantics Based Program Transformations. Technical report RUU-CS-90-39, Utrecht University, December 1990

92. Kozen, D.: Semantics of probabilistic programs. J. Comput. Syst. Sci. **22**(3), 328–350 (1981). https://doi.org/10.1016/0022-0000(81)90036-2

93. Kozen, D.: A probabilistic PDL. J. Comput. Syst. Sci. **30**(2), 162–178 (1985). https://doi.org/10.1016/0022-0000(85)90012-1

94. Kwiatkowska, M., Norman, G.: A fully abstract metric-space denotational semantics for reactive probabilistic processes. Electron. Notes Theoret. Comput. Sci. **13**, 182 (1998). Comprox III, Third Workshop on Computation and Approximation. https://doi.org/10.1016/S1571-0661(05)80222-1

95. Kwiatkowska, M.Z., Norman, G., Parker, D.: PRISM 4.0: verification of probabilistic real-time systems. In: Gopalakrishnan, G., Qadeer, S. (eds.) Proceedings of the 23rd International Conference on Computer Aided Verification, CAV 2011, Snowbird, UT, USA, 14–20 July 2011. LNCS, vol. 6806, pp. 585–591. Springer, Heidelberg (2011). https://doi.org/10.1007/978-3-642-22110-1_47

96. Larsen, K.G., Skou, A.: Bisimulation through probabilistic testing. Inf. Comput. **94**(1), 1–28 (1991). https://doi.org/10.1016/0890-5401(91)90030-6

97. Lowe, G.: Probabilistic and prioritized models of timed CSP. Theoret. Comput. Sci. **138**(2), 315–352 (1995). Meeting on the mathematical foundation of programing semantics https://doi.org/10.1016/0304-3975(94)00171-E

98. López, N., Núñez, M.: An overview of probabilistic process algebras and their equivalences. In: Baier, C., Haverkort, B.R., Hermanns, H., Katoen, J.P., Siegle, M. (eds.) Validation of Stochastic Systems. LNCS, vol. 2925, pp. 89–123. Springer, Heidelberg (2004). https://doi.org/10.1007/978-3-540-24611-4_3

99. Martin, A.P., Gardiner, P.H.B., Woodcock, J.: A tactic calculus-abridged version. Formal Aspects Comput. **8**(4), 479–489 (1996). https://doi.org/10.1007/BF01213535

100. Martin, C.E., Curtis, S.A., Rewitzky, I.: Modelling nondeterminism. In: Kozen, D., Shankland, C. (eds.) Proceedings of the 7th International Conference on Mathematics of Program Construction, MPC 2004, Stirling, Scotland, UK, 12–14 July 2004. LNCS, vol. 3125, pp. 228–251. Springer, Heidelberg (2004). https://doi.org/10.1007/978-3-540-27764-4_13

101. McCarthy, J.: A basis for a mathematical theory of computation, preliminary report. In: Bauer, W.F. (ed.) Papers Presented at the 1961 Western Joint IRE-AIEE-ACM Computer Conference, IRE-AIEE-ACM 1961 (Western), Los Angeles, California, USA, 9–11 May 1961, pp. 225–238. ACM (1961). https://doi.org/10.1145/1460690.1460715

102. McIver, A., Morgan, C.: Demonic, angelic and unbounded probabilistic choices in sequential programs. Acta Informatica **37**(4–5), 329–354 (2001). https://doi.org/10.1007/s002360000046
103. McIver, A., Morgan, C.: Abstraction, Refinement and Proof for Probabilistic Systems. Monographs in Computer Science, Springer (2005). https://doi.org/10.1007/b138392
104. McIver, A., Morgan, C.: Introduction to *pGCL*: its logic and its model. In: Abstraction, Refinement and Proof for Probabilistic Systems, pp. 3–36. Springer, New York (2005). https://doi.org/10.1007/0-387-27006-X_1
105. McIver, A., Morgan, C.: Abstraction, Refinement and Proof for Probabilistic Systems, chap. Introduction to pGCL, pp. 3–35. Monographs in Computer Science, Springer (2005). https://doi.org/10.1007/b138392
106. McIver, A., Morgan, C.: Correctness by construction for probabilistic programs. In: Margaria, T., Steffen, B. (eds.) Leveraging Applications of Formal Methods, Verification and Validation: Verification Principles - Proceedings of the 9th International Symposium on Leveraging Applications of Formal Methods, ISoLA 2020, Rhodes, Greece, 20–30 October 2020. LNCS, Part I, vol. 12476, pp. 216–239. Springer, Heidelberg (2020). https://doi.org/10.1007/978-3-030-61362-4_12
107. McIver, A., Morgan, C., Kaminski, B.L., Katoen, J.P.: A new proof rule for almost-sure termination. Proc. ACM Program. Lang. **2**(POPL) (2017). https://doi.org/10.1145/3158121
108. Milner, R.: A Calculus of Communicating Systems. LNCS, vol. 92. Springer, Heidelberg (1980). https://doi.org/10.1007/3-540-10235-3
109. Mislove, M.: Nondeterminism and probabilistic choice: obeying the laws. In: Palamidessi, C. (eds.) Concurrency Theory. CONCUR 2000. LNCS, pp. 350–365. Springer, Heidelberg (2000). https://doi.org/10.1007/3-540-44618-4_26
110. Miyazawa, A., Ribeiro, P., Li, W., Cavalcanti, A., Timmis, J., Woodcock, J.: RoboChart: modelling and verification of the functional behaviour of robotic applications. Softw. Syst. Model. **18**(5), 3097–3149 (2019). https://doi.org/10.1007/s10270-018-00710-z
111. Moosbrugger, M., Bartocci, E., Katoen, J., Kovács, L.: The probabilistic termination tool amber. In: Huisman, M., Pasareanu, C.S., Zhan, N. (eds.) Proceedings of the 24th International Symposium on Formal Methods, FM 2021, Virtual Event, 20–26 November 2021. LNCS, vol. 13047, pp. 667–675. Springer, Heidelberg (2021). https://doi.org/10.1007/978-3-030-90870-6_36
112. Morgan, C.: Programming from Specifications. Prentice Hall International Series in Computer Science, Prentice Hall (1990)
113. Morgan, C.: Of probabilistic wp and CSP—and compositionality. In: Abdallah, A.E., Jones, C.B., Sanders, J.W. (eds.) Communicating Sequential Processes. The First 25 Years: Symposium on the Occasion of 25 Years of CSP, London, UK, 7–8 July 2004. Revised Invited Papers, pp. 220–241. Springer, Heidelberg (2005). https://doi.org/10.1007/11423348_12
114. Morgan, C., McIver, A.: pGCL: formal reasoning for random algorithms. S. Afr. Comput. J. **22**, 14–27 (1999). http://hdl.handle.net/10500/24296
115. Morgan, C., McIver, A., Seidel, K.: Probabilistic predicate transformers. ACM Trans. Program. Lang. Syst. (TOPLAS) **18**(3), 325–353 (1996). https://doi.org/10.1145/229542.229547
116. Morgan, C., McIver, A., Seidel, K., Sanders, J.W.: Refinement-oriented probability for CSP. Form. Asp. Comput. **8**(6), 617–647 (1996). https://doi.org/10.1007/BF01213492

117. Morris, J.M.: A theoretical basis for stepwise refinement and the programming calculus. Sci. Comput. Program. **9**(3), 287–306 (1987). https://doi.org/10.1016/0167-6423(87)90011-6

118. Morris, J.M.: Augmenting types with unbounded demonic and angelic nondeterminacy. In: Kozen, D., Shankland, C. (eds.) Proceedings of the 7th International Conference on Mathematics of Program Construction, MPC 2004, Stirling, Scotland, UK, 12–14 July 2004. LNCS, vol. 3125, pp. 274–288. Springer, Heidelberg (2004). https://doi.org/10.1007/978-3-540-27764-4_15

119. Morris, J.M., Bunkenburg, A.: A theory of bunches. Acta Informatica **37**(8), 541–561 (2001). https://doi.org/10.1007/PL00013316

120. Morris, J.M., Bunkenburg, A., Tyrrell, M.: Term transformers: a new approach to state. ACM Trans. Program. Lang. Syst. **31**(4) (2009). https://doi.org/10.1145/1516507.1516511

121. Motwani, R., Raghavan, P.: Randomized Algorithms. Cambridge University Press (1995)

122. Nelson, G.: A generalization of Dijkstra's calculus. ACM Trans. Program. Lang. Syst. **11**(4), 517–561 (1989). https://doi.org/10.1145/69558.69559

123. Nicola, R.D., Hennessy, M.: Testing equivalences for processes. Theor. Comput. Sci. **34**, 83–133 (1984). https://doi.org/10.1016/0304-3975(84)90113-0

124. Núñez, M., de Frutos, D., Llana, L.: Acceptance trees for probabilistic processes. In: Lee, I., Smolka, S.A. (eds.) Concurrency Theory, CONCUR 1995, pp. 249–263. Springer, Heidelberg (1995). https://doi.org/10.1007/3-540-60218-6_18

125. Oliveira, M., Cavalcanti, A., Woodcock, J.: ArcAngel: a tactic language for refinement. Formal Aspects Comput. **15**(1), 28–47 (2003). https://doi.org/10.1007/S00165-003-0003-8

126. Oliveira, M., Cavalcanti, A., Woodcock, J.: Formal development of industrial-scale systems in Circus. Innov. Syst. Softw. Eng. **1**(2), 125–146 (2005). https://doi.org/10.1007/S11334-005-0014-0

127. Oliveira, M., Cavalcanti, A., Woodcock, J.: A UTP semantics for circus. Formal Aspects Comput. **21**(1–2), 3–32 (2009). https://doi.org/10.1007/S00165-007-0052-5

128. Olmedo, F., Gretz, F., Jansen, N., Kaminski, B.L., Katoen, J.P., Mciver, A.: Conditioning in probabilistic programming. ACM Trans. Program. Lang. Syst. **40**(1), 1–50 (2018). https://doi.org/10.1145/3156018

129. Peleg, D.: Concurrent dynamic logic. J. ACM **34**(2), 450–479 (1987). https://doi.org/10.1145/23005.23008

130. Puterman, M.L.: Markov Decision Processes: Discrete Stochastic Dynamic Programming, 1st edn. Wiley, USA (1994)

131. Pólya, G.: Über eine aufgabe der wahrscheinlichkeitsrechnung betreffend die irrfahrt im straßennetz. Math. Ann. **84**(1–2), 149–160 (1921). https://doi.org/10.1007/bf01458701

132. Rabin, M.O.: Probabilistic algorithm for testing primality. J. Number Theor. **12**(1), 128–138 (1980). https://doi.org/10.1016/0022-314x(80)90084-0

133. Rabin, M.O.: N-process mutual exclusion with bounded waiting by $4 \cdot \log2$ n-valued shared variable. J. Comput. Syst. Sci. **25**(1), 66–75 (1982). https://doi.org/10.1016/0022-0000(82)90010-1

134. Rabin, M.O., Scott, D.S.: Finite automata and their decision problems. IBM J. Res. Dev. **3**(2), 114–125 (1959). https://doi.org/10.1147/RD.32.0114

135. Ramshaw, L.H.: Formalizing the analysis of algorithms. Ph.D. thesis, Stanford University, Stanford, CA, USA (1979). aAI8001994

136. Rand, R., Zdancewic, S.: VPHL: a verified partial-correctness logic for probabilistic programs. In: Ghica, D.R. (ed.) The 31st Conference on the Mathematical Foundations of Programming Semantics, MFPS 2015. Electronic Notes in Theoretical Computer Science, Nijmegen, The Netherlands, 22–25 June 2015, vol. 319, pp. 351–367. Elsevier (2015). https://doi.org/10.1016/j.entcs.2015.12.021

137. Rewitzky, I.: Binary multirelations. In: de Swart, H.C.M., Orlowska, E., Schmidt, G., Roubens, M. (eds.) Theory and Applications of Relational Structures as Knowledge Instruments, COST Action 274, TARSKI, Revised Papers. LNCS, vol. 2929, pp. 256–271. Springer, Heidelberg (2003). https://doi.org/10.1007/978-3-540-24615-2_12

138. Rewitzky, I., Brink, C.: Predicate transformers as power operations. Formal Aspects Comput. **7**(2), 169–182 (1995). https://doi.org/10.1007/BF01211604

139. Ribeiro, P.: A unary semigroup trace algebra. In: Fahrenberg, U., Jipsen, P., Winter, M. (eds.) Proceedings of the 18th International Conference on Relational and Algebraic Methods in Computer Science, RAMiCS 2020. LNCS, Palaiseau, France, 8–11 April 2020, vol. 12062, pp. 270–285. Springer, Heidelberg (2020). https://doi.org/10.1007/978-3-030-43520-2_17

140. Ribeiro, P., Cavalcanti, A.: Angelicism in the theory of reactive processes. In: Naumann, D.A. (ed.) 5th International Symposium on Unifying Theories of Programming, UTP 2014, Revised Selected Papers. LNCS, Singapore, 13 May 2014, vol. 8963, pp. 42–61. Springer, Heidelberg (2014). https://doi.org/10.1007/978-3-319-14806-9_3

141. Ribeiro, P., Cavalcanti, A.: UTP designs for binary multirelations. In: Ciobanu, G., Méry, D. (eds.) Proceedings of the 11th International Colloquium on Theoretical Aspects of Computing, ICTAC 2014. LNCS, 17–19 September 2014, Bucharest, Romania, vol. 8687, pp. 388–405. Springer, Heidelberg (2014). https://doi.org/10.1007/978-3-319-10882-7_23

142. Ribeiro, P., Cavalcanti, A.: Angelic processes for CSP via the UTP. Theor. Comput. Sci. **756**, 19–63 (2019). https://doi.org/10.1016/J.TCS.2018.10.008

143. Roscoe, A.W.: Understanding Concurrent Systems. Texts in Computer Science. Springer, London (2011). https://doi.org/10.1007/978-1-84882-258-0

144. Schneider, S.A., Treharne, H.: Communicating B machines. In: Bert, D., Bowen, J.P., Henson, M.C., Robinson, K. (eds.) Formal Specification and Development in Z and B, ZB 2002, Proceedings of the 2nd International Conference of B and Z Users. LNCS, Grenoble, France, 23–25 January 2002, vol. 2272, pp. 416–435. Springer, Heidelberg (2002). https://doi.org/10.1007/3-540-45648-1_22

145. Schröer, P., Batz, K., Kaminski, B.L., Katoen, J.P., Matheja, C.: A deductive verification infrastructure for probabilistic programs. Proc. ACM Program. Lang. **7**(OOPSLA2), 2052–2082 (2023). https://doi.org/10.1145/3622870

146. Schützenberger, M.P.: On context-free languages and push-down automata. Inf. Control **6**(3), 246–264 (1963). https://doi.org/10.1016/S0019-9958(63)90306-1

147. Segala, R., Lynch, N.: Probabilistic simulations for probabilistic processes. Nordic J. Comput. **2**(2), 250–273 (1995)

148. Seidel, K.: Probabilistic communicating processes. Theoret. Comput. Sci. **152**(2), 219–249 (1995). https://doi.org/10.1016/0304-3975(94)00286-0

149. Sherif, A., He, J.: Towards a time model for circus. In: George, C., Miao, H. (eds.) Proceedings of the 4th International Conference on Formal Engineering Methods of Formal Methods and Software Engineering, ICFEM 2002. LNCS, Shanghai, China, 21–25 October 2002, vol. 2495, pp. 613–624. Springer, Heidelberg (2002). https://doi.org/10.1007/3-540-36103-0_62

150. Sherif, A., He, J., Cavalcanti, A., Sampaio, A.: A framework for specification and validation of real-time systems using *Circus* actions. In: Liu, Z., Araki, K. (eds.) First International Colloquium on Theoretical Aspects of Computing, ICTAC 2004, Revised Selected Papers. LNCS, Guiyang, China, 20–24 September 2004, vol. 3407, pp. 478–493. Springer, Heidelberg (2004). https://doi.org/10.1007/978-3-540-31862-0_34

151. Smith, G., Derrick, J.: Specification, refinement and verification of concurrent systems-an integration of object-z and CSP. Formal Meth. Syst. Des. **18**(3), 249–284 (2001). https://doi.org/10.1023/A:1011269103179

152. Stepney, S., Cooper, D., Woodcock, J.: More powerful Z data refinement: pushing the state of the art in industrial refinement. In: Bowen, J.P., Fett, A., Hinchey, M.G. (eds.) The Z Formal Specification Notation, Proceedings of the 11th International Conference of Z Users, ZUM '98, Berlin, Germany, 24–26 September 1998. LNCS, vol. 1493, pp. 284–307. Springer, Heidelberg (1998). https://doi.org/10.1007/978-3-540-49676-2_20

153. Stoddart, B., Dunne, S., Mu, C., Zeyda, F.: Bunch theory: axioms, logic, applications and model. J. Logical Algebraic Meth. Program. **140**, 100977 (2024). https://doi.org/10.1016/j.jlamp.2024.100977

154. Stoddart, B., Zeyda, F.: A unification of probabilistic choice within a design-based model of reversible computation. Formal Aspects Comput. **25**(1), 107–131 (2013). https://doi.org/10.1007/s00165-007-0048-1

155. Stoddart, B., Zeyda, F., Dunne, S.: Preference and non-deterministic choice. In: Cavalcanti, A., Deharbe, D., Gaudel, MC., Woodcock, J. (eds.) Theoretical Aspects of Computing, ICTAC 2010. LNCS, September 2010, vol. 6255, pp. 137–152. Springer, Heidelberg (2010). https://doi.org/10.1007/11415787_12

156. Sun, J., Liu, Y., Dong, J.S., Pang, J.: PAT: towards flexible verification under fairness. In: Bouajjani, A., Maler, O. (eds.) Computer Aided Verification, CAV 2009. LNCS, pp. 709–714. Springer, Heidelberg (2009). https://doi.org/10.1007/978-3-642-02658-4_59

157. Sun, J., Song, S., Liu, Y.: Model checking hierarchical probabilistic systems. In: Dong, J.S., Zhu, H. (eds.) Formal Methods and Software Engineering, ICFEM 2010. LNCS, pp. 388–403. Springer, Heidelberg (2010). https://doi.org/10.1007/978-3-642-16901-4_26

158. Thrun, S., Burgard, W., Fox, D.: Probabilistic Robotics. Intelligent Robotics and Autonomous Agents. The MIT Press (2005)

159. Tracy, C.A.: Lecture note in First Passage of a One-Dimensional Random Walker (2020). http://www.math.ucdavis.edu/~tracy/courses/math135A/UsefullCourseMaterial/firstPassage.pdf

160. Turing, A.M.: On computable numbers, with an application to the entscheidungsproblem. Proc. Lond. Math. Soc. **s2-42**(1), 230–265 (1937). https://doi.org/10.1112/PLMS/S2-42.1.230

161. Tyrrell, M., Morris, J.M., Butterfield, A., Hughes, A.: A lattice-theoretic model for an algebra of communicating sequential processes. In: Barkaoui, K., Cavalcanti, A., Cerone, A. (eds.) Proceedings of the Third International Colloquium on Theoretical Aspects of Computing, ICTAC 2006. LNCS, Tunis, Tunisia, 20–24 November 2006, vol. 4281, pp. 123–137. Springer, Heidelberg (2006). https://doi.org/10.1007/11921240_9

162. Vanglabbeek, R., Smolka, S., Steffen, B.: Reactive, generative, and stratified models of probabilistic processes. Inf. Comput. **121**(1), 59–80 (1995). https://doi.org/10.1006/inco.1995.1123

163. Ward, N., Hayes, I.: Applications of angelic nondeterminism. In: Australian Software Engineering Conference 1991: Engineering Safe Software; Proceedings, pp. 391–404. Australian Computer Society, Sydney, N.S.W. (1991). https://doi.org/10.3316/informit.553249589811640

164. Wei, K., Woodcock, J., Burns, A.: A timed model of circus with the reactive design miracle. In: Fiadeiro, J.L., Gnesi, S., Maggiolo-Schettini, A. (eds.) 8th IEEE International Conference on Software Engineering and Formal Methods, SEFM 2010, Pisa, Italy, 13–18 September 2010, pp. 315–319. IEEE Computer Society (2010). https://doi.org/10.1109/SEFM.2010.40

165. Williams, D.: Probability with Martingales. Cambridge University Press (1991)

166. Woodcock, J.: An introduction to refinement in Z. In: Prehn, S., Toetenel, W.J. (eds.) Formal Software Development, 4th International Symposium of VDM Europe, VDM '91, Proceedings. LNCS, Noordwijkerhout, The Netherlands, 21–25 October 1991, Volume 2: Tutorials, vol. 552, pp. 96–117. Springer, Heidelberg (1991). https://doi.org/10.1007/BFb0019996

167. Woodcock, J.: A tutorial on the refinement calculus. In: Prehn, S., Toetenel, W.J. (eds.) Formal Software Development, 4th International Symposium of VDM Europe, VDM '91, Proceedings, Volume 2: Tutorials. LNCS, Noordwijkerhout, The Netherlands, 21–25 October 1991, vol. 552, pp. 79–140. Springer, Heidelberg (1991). https://doi.org/10.1007/BFB0019996

168. Woodcock, J.: Using circus for safety-critical applications. In: Cavalcanti, A., Machado, P.D.L. (eds.) Proceedings of the 6th Brazilian Workshop on Formal Methods, WMF 2003. Electronic Notes in Theoretical Computer Science, Campina Grande, Brazil, 12–14 October 2003, vol. 95, pp. 3–22. Elsevier (2003). https://doi.org/10.1016/J.ENTCS.2004.04.003

169. Woodcock, J.: The miracle of reactive programming. In: Butterfield, A. (ed.) Second International Symposium on Unifying Theories of Programming, UTP 2008, Revised Selected Papers. LNCS, Dublin, Ireland, 8–10 September 2008, vol. 5713, pp. 202–217. Springer, Heidelberg (2008). https://doi.org/10.1007/978-3-642-14521-6_12

170. Woodcock, J.: Engineering UToPiA - formal semantics for CML. In: Jones, C.B., Pihlajasaari, P., Sun, J. (eds.) Proceedings of the 19th International Symposium on Formal Methods, FM 2014, Singapore, 12–16 May 2014. LNCS, vol. 8442, pp. 22–41. Springer, Heidelberg (2014). https://doi.org/10.1007/978-3-319-06410-9_3

171. Woodcock, J., Cavalcanti, A.: A tutorial introduction to designs in unifying theories of programming. In: Boiten, E.A., Derrick, J., Smith, G. (eds.) Proceedings of the 4th International Conference on Integrated Formal Methods, IFM 2004. LNCS, Canterbury, UK, 4–7 April 2004, vol. 2999, pp. 40–66. Springer, Heidelberg (2004). https://doi.org/10.1007/978-3-540-24756-2_4

172. Woodcock, J., Cavalcanti, A., Foster, S., Mota, A., Ye, K.: Probabilistic semantics for RoboChart. In: Ribeiro, P., Sampaio, A. (eds.) Unifying Theories of Programming, pp. 80–105. Springer, Cham (2019). https://doi.org/10.1007/978-3-030-31038-7_5

173. Woodcock, J., Cavalcanti, A., Foster, S., Oliveira, M., Sampaio, A., Zeyda, F.: UTP, Circus, and Isabelle. In: Bowen, J.P., Li, Q., Xu, Q. (eds.) Theories of Programming and Formal Methods - Essays Dedicated to Jifeng He on the Occasion of His 80th Birthday. LNCS, vol. 14080, pp. 19–51. Springer, Heidelberg (2023). https://doi.org/10.1007/978-3-031-40436-8_2

174. Woodcock, J., Larsen, P.G., Bicarregui, J., Fitzgerald, J.S.: Formal methods: practice and experience. ACM Comput. Surv. **41**(4), 19:1–19:36 (2009). https://doi.org/10.1145/1592434.1592436

175. Woodcock, J., Stepney, S., Cooper, D., Clark, J.A., Jacob, J.: The certification of the Mondex electronic purse to ITSEC level E6. Formal Aspects Comput. **20**(1), 5–19 (2008). https://doi.org/10.1007/S00165-007-0060-5

176. Wu, S., Smolka, S.A., Stark, E.W.: Composition and behaviors of probabilistic i/o automata. Theoret. Comput. Sci. **176**(1), 1–38 (1997). https://doi.org/10.1016/S0304-3975(97)00056-X

177. Xia, L.y., et al: Interaction trees: representing recursive and impure programs in coq. Proc. ACM Program. Lang. **4**(POPL) (2019). https://doi.org/10.1145/3371119

178. Ye, K., Cavalcanti, A., Foster, S., Miyazawa, A., Woodcock, J.: Probabilistic modelling and verification using RoboChart and PRISM. Softw. Syst. Model. **21**(2), 667–716 (2022). https://doi.org/10.1007/s10270-021-00916-8

179. Ye, K., Foster, S., Woodcock, J.: Automated reasoning for probabilistic sequential programs with theorem proving. In: Fahrenberg, U., Gehrke, M., Santocanale, L., Winter, M. (eds.) Relational and Algebraic Methods in Computer Science, pp. 465–482. Springer, Cham (2021). https://doi.org/10.1007/978-3-030-88701-8_28

180. Ye, K., Foster, S., Woodcock, J.: Formally verified animation for RoboChart using interaction trees. J. Logical Algebraic Meth. Program. **137**, 100940 (2024). https://doi.org/10.1016/j.jlamp.2023.100940

181. Ye, K., Woodcock, J.: RoboCertProb: property specification for probabilistic RoboChart models (2024). https://arxiv.org/abs/2403.08136

182. Ye, K., Woodcock, J., Foster, S.: Probabilistic relations for modelling epistemic and aleatoric uncertainty: semantics and automated reasoning with theorem proving. CoRR **abs/2303.09692** (2023). https://doi.org/10.48550/ARXIV.2303.09692

183. Yi, W., Larsen, K.G.: Testing probabilistic and nondeterministic processes. In: Proceedings of the IFIP TC6/WG6.1 Twelfth International Symposium on Protocol Specification, Testing and Verification XII, pp. 47-61. North-Holland Publishing Co., NLD (1992)

184. Zabih, R., McAllester, D.A., Chapman, D.: Non-deterministic Lisp with dependency-directed backtracking. In: Forbus, K.D., Shrobe, H.E. (eds.) Proceedings of the 6th National Conference on Artificial Intelligence, Seattle, WA, USA, July 1987, pp. 59–65. Morgan Kaufmann (1987). http://www.aaai.org/Library/AAAI/1987/aaai87-011.php

185. Zeyda, F.: Reversible Computations in B. Ph.D. thesis, University of Teesside, Middlesbrough, Tees Valley, TS1 3BX, UK, July 2007

186. Zeyda, F., Stoddart, B., Dunne, S.: A prospective-value semantics for the GSL. In: Treharne, H., King, S., Henson, M., Schneider, S. (eds.) Formal Specification and Development in Z and B, ZB 2005. LNCS, April 2005, vol. 3455, pp. 187–202. Springer, Heidelberg (2005). https://doi.org/10.1007/11415787_12

I Kaptured the System

Colin O'Halloran[✉], William Simmonds, and Nick Tudor

D-RisQ Ltd., Malvern, UK
coh@drisq.com

Abstract. Software Engineers work from High Level Software Requirements, but these are derived from System Requirements Allocated to Software that are articulated by System Engineers. There are often mismatches between these two artefacts because of the use of informal natural language that uses inconsistent terminology leading to ambiguity and information that is incomplete, which leads to miscommunication between System and Software Engineers. This chapter presents the development of System Requirements Allocated to Software in a template-based language with a formal underpinning using a tool called System Kapture®. The requirements are taken from the natural language description of the Steam Boiler challenge problem presented by Jean-Raymond Abrial in the mid-1990s. Guidance on a method for developing the requirements is given along with opportunities for their formal analysis and the context of their use to verify High Level Software Requirements, Simulink® and Stateflow® models and code generated from those models.

Keywords: System Requirements · High Level Software Requirements · model checking

---

Dedication Jim taught the first author, Colin O'Halloran, aspects of the Z language in 1986 as part of a two-week industrial course given by the Programming Research Group at Oxford. Around the same time Jim also taught aspects of the CSP process algebra on a course sponsored by GCHQ's Communications Electronics Security Group (that has now evolved into the NCSC). Since then both Z and CSP have been central to the above authors' research. In particular Z was used in the development of verification technology that was used to independently formally verify Eurofighter Typhoon's flight and engine control software. An outcome of the Typhoon verification work was a treatment in Circus that is underpinned by the UTP research carried out by Jim and his colleagues. The team at D-RisQ and previously in QinetiQ have benefitted greatly from collaborations with Jim and his colleagues over many years. Finally, a hallmark of Jim's career is his ability to make the complex accessible through clarity and elegance of thought. The work discussed in this chapter attempts to bring the same clarity to the area of requirements and is underpinned by the process algebra of CSP.

© The Author(s), under exclusive license to Springer Nature Switzerland AG 2024
S. Foster and A. Sampaio (Eds.): *The Application of Formal Methods*, LNCS 14900, pp. 306–328, 2024.
https://doi.org/10.1007/978-3-031-67114-2_12

1   Introduction

Many errors in software-based systems arises from an error in what the software should achieve, i.e. the requirements. Human review of requirements expressed in informal language helps to detect and correct requirements errors, but this becomes progressively more difficult as the number of requirements increases. There is also the inevitability of requirements change, along with death and tax. Reasons for why developing and maintaining requirements becomes more difficult include: inconsistent use of names; the ambiguity of informal language; and the sheer number of requirements that need to be simultaneously held in a person's mind. Another problem is that ill-considered requirements can make them expensive to verify, or even unverifiable.

There are potentially a number of tiers of requirements e.g., customer requirements, interface requirements etc. In this chapter the focus is on System Requirements, in the context of verification of high level software requirements, software design (or software low level requirements), and software source code.

System requirements enable (amongst other things) communication, development tracking and validation purposes throughout a systems engineering project. When these system requirements are translated so that software engineers can use them, there is an opportunity for errors to be inadvertently introduced. The software process may use models, and indeed, even at the system level models may be used. In either case, there always has to be a set of requirements that describe what is needed. There are a number of reasons why this should be the case. For example, all stakeholders should be able to accessibly understand what the system and software is required to do. This includes not just the developers, but also those that have to develop the validation (systems) and verification (software) cases as well as, crucially, certifiers.

System level requirements allocated to software are also needed by the original developer of the requirements for maintenance. It is almost inevitable that requirements will change, at some time after a project has started, sometimes after it has been delivered and modifications are needed. This might mean that the original developer has moved on, so having them written in a robust, unambiguous, consistent manner saves significant time and cost therefore increasing productivity. Requirements errors are most expensive to address when they manifest themselves during testing or even deployment [1].

This chapter is focused on expressing system level requirements that enable system developers to describe in English what they want the system and software to do. The approach is to use a syntax that enables unambiguous, consistent and verifiable requirements to be written that can be formally analyzed and are accessible to human review, in particular by certification representatives. A tool to support these objectives is essential and crucially embodies a requirements standard that must be present to support certification, see Sect. 5.1.2 of [2]. Such a tool, called System Kapture®, has been developed by D-RisQ Ltd to support the verification objectives of [3]. The Formal Methods approach adopted by D-RisQ is to hide formality so that there is no need to learn all about Formal Methods in order to be able to use System Kapture®, or complementary tools. The Steam Boiler challenge problem [4] is used to illustrate the approach and elicit steps to develop System requirements. System Kapture® has been used within D-RisQ to record system requirements allocated to software for digital tethering of an uncrewed autonomous vehicle and a medical device, but for commercial confidentiality cannot be used here to discuss System Kapture®.

System Kapture® does not solve the problem of requirements elicitation and it is biased to reactive control systems, but we believe that a tool like System Kapture® is necessary for the cost-effective development of critical systems. A wider discussion of the general area of requirements engineering can be found in [5].

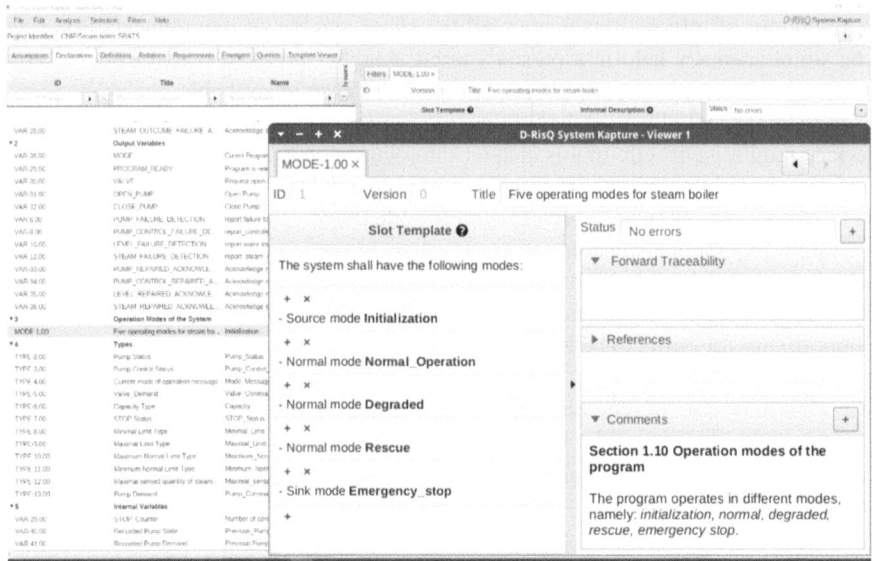

Fig. 1. An example of the System modes template

2 An Overview of System Kapture

2.1 The Purpose of System Kapture

System Kapture® is a tool for recording and checking system requirements. These are expressed using a number of templates having fixed text and variable text slots. Requirements are recorded by instantiating templates and filling in the variable text slots with expressions written in the formal slot language. System Kapture® was designed to allow requirements to be recorded in the first instance at a very abstract level with some things left underspecified. Detail may be added later at the discretion of the user or deferred to the next tier of requirements known as high level software requirements.

2.2 Core Concepts

Some of the core System Kapture® concepts are described sufficiently for an appreciation of the guidelines and example given later.

Modes. In System Kapture® there is a requirement template for declaring the modes of the system. A mode is a binary state of system which is either active (or entered) or inactive (exited) at any particular time. The system may have any number of its modes active at any time, including none or all of them.

Figure 1 shows the Steam Boiler modes declared using the mode template. The *Initialization* mode is specified as a source mode that the system is required to be active from the start. The modes *Normal_Operation*, *Degraded* and *Rescue* are specified as normal modes, which means that in principle they become active or inactive any number of times. The mode *Emergency_Stop* is specified as a sink mode which means once that mode becomes active, it never subsequently become inactive.

Variables. These are the named variable items of data that are expected to be used by the system and referred to by requirements. Variables are declared using the variable template as illustrated in Fig. 2.

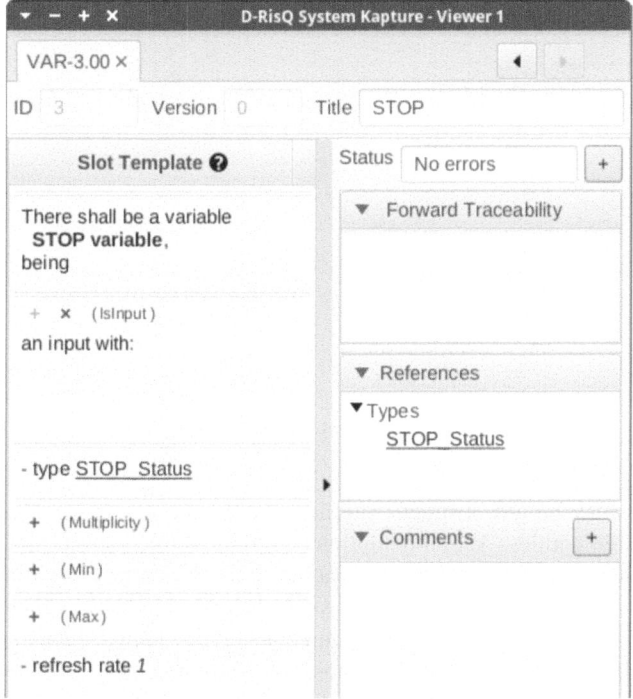

Fig. 2. An example of the variable template

A variable is declared to be either an input, an output or internal. An input variable represents an input parameter to the system from its environment. An output variable represents data intended to be communicated to the system's environment. An internal variable represents data that the system manipulates internally, for example to record state, but is not intended for output. System Kapture® makes no assumptions as to how variables are implemented in practice, that being regarded as a concern of the high level software requirements. The variables could be signals, or shared data or communications across a channel.

Actions and Propositions. It is reasonable to expect that any system requirement to be implemented by software will ultimately amount to a statement specifying that certain actions/functions are to be performed by the system, either unconditionally or conditionally on some state of the system or previous occurrence of other actions. These common notions of action and condition are formalized in System Kapture® as follows. Actions are discrete, of finite duration and uninterruptible; they are declared using the action template as illustrated in Fig. 3.

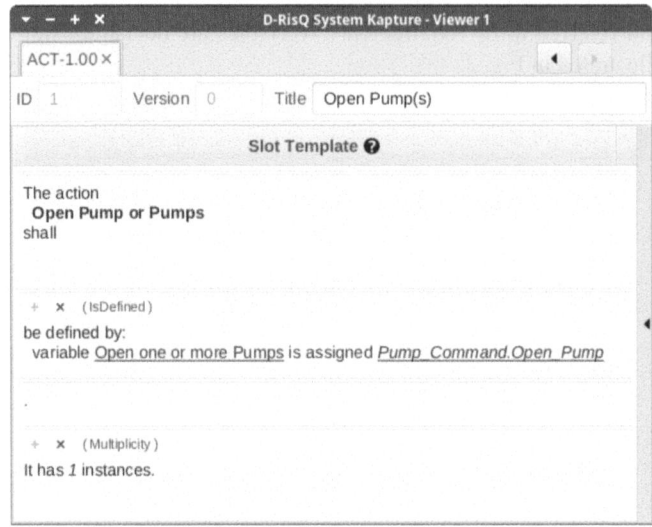

Fig. 3. An example of the action template

An action may be left abstract. Alternatively, an action can be defined in terms of other declared entities. Action definitions are limited to certain forms and include, notably, assignment to internal and output variables and the starting or ending of declared processes. The example shown in Fig. 3 assigns the output variable "Open one or more Pumps" the value *Open_Pump* from the enumerated type *Pump_Command*. Once it has been declared, an action, whether it be abstract or defined, may be referred to by its name in requirements. When generating a formal model of the system, any occurrence of a non-abstract action in a requirement is replaced by its definition.

System Kapture® propositions are statements concerning the state of the system or the environment. At any particular time step, a proposition can evaluate to true, false, or unknown, denoting that it is not known whether it is true or false. In System Kapture®, a logical operation involving an unknown value always returns an unknown value. For the remainder of this chapter, we shall only be interested in propositions that evaluate to true or false. Propositions are declared and defined through the proposition template illustrated in Fig. 4.

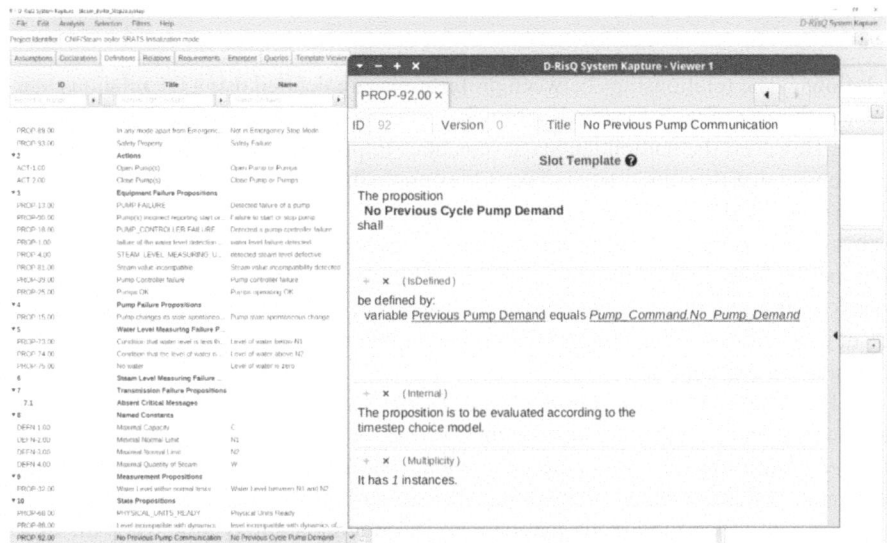

Fig. 4. An example of the proposition template

Propositions are used to construct the conditions and guards in conditional requirements. Like actions, a proposition may be left abstract or be given a definition in terms of other propositions and variables. When a formal model of the system is generated, a non-abstract proposition is replaced by its definition. Each abstract proposition is evaluated according to one of three possible models of evaluation that the user specifies, as follows.

In the single choice model, the first time a proposition is evaluated it may freely evaluate to either true or false. Thereafter, for the remainder of the run of the system, it will always evaluate to the same value. This is useful, for example, for propositions concerning configuration management parameters if they are known to be invariant for any particular run of the system, e.g. "system has been started in maintenance mode".

In the timestep choice model, which is the default model, in each timestep that the proposition is evaluated, it may freely evaluate to either true or false in a consistent manner. Thus, for any given timestep and for any particular requirement, multiple references to the proposition in that requirement will evaluate to the same value.

In the free choice model, the proposition may freely evaluate to true or false at any time. This is the least constraining of the three models.

A proposition may also be declared in each of the three evaluation models as internal, meaning that it represents a statement whose truth or falsity at any time can be determined from information that is internal to the system. If a proposition is not declared as internal, then it is dependent on the environment and currently must be an abstract proposition. In the relation template, abstract propositions impose a limit on expressing constraints on the interaction of the system and its environment. The reason for this limitation is that if a proposition is not abstract then it becomes difficult to check for consistency between propositions, for non-trivial systems.

Relations. The relationships between propositions are defined using the relations template, as shown in Fig. 5. System Kapture® attaches no semantics to the names of propositions. However, the natural language semantics implied by the names of propositions may convey that they are related. Take for example the two propositions "*speed is less than 30 mph*" and "*speed is greater than or equal to 30 mph*". These are clearly intended to always evaluate to the local negation of each other. Such relationships between propositions may be formally enforced by using one of the relation templates. These include relations for enforcing implication, mutual exclusion and logical negation relations among sets of propositions. Depending on their use, relations can be thought of as either formal constraints or assumptions.

In Fig. 5 the proposition "*Level of water is zero*" is an abstract proposition about the environment, but it could have been defined directly in terms of the input variable "*Level of water*". Unfortunately, this opens up a technical difficulty of establishing consistency, in general, between defined propositions that we currently avoid. Instead, the abstract proposition is defined indirectly using the relations template to be true when the input variable is zero. It is separately defined to be false, in REL-3.00, if the input variable is any other non-zero value.

Adding these constraints along with REL-1.00 forces the behavior of the system in its environment to exclude the input variable "*Level of water*" being zero if the pumps are operating without failure. These constraints are necessary to avoid a false positive counterexample of steam being generated when there is no water while water is being pumped in.

Processes. A process is a representation of a series of actions that are executed consecutively by the system, some of them perhaps conditionally. Processes are potentially repeated multiple times during the run of the system. Example processes include collision avoidance procedures carried out by the systems onboard an autonomous vehicle whenever the vehicle is in danger of colliding with an obstacle, or a process which regularly undertakes a series of system validity checks.

A process may be left abstract, which means that the only events it generates in the model of the system are the events representing its starting and ending. In this case the process acts as a kind of placeholder for a series of actions yet to be defined. The starting and ending of a process are types of action, and these will occur as specified in the definition of the process. Once a process has been declared, requirements may be specified as pertaining to that process. Those requirements will then only be "executed" when the process is running.

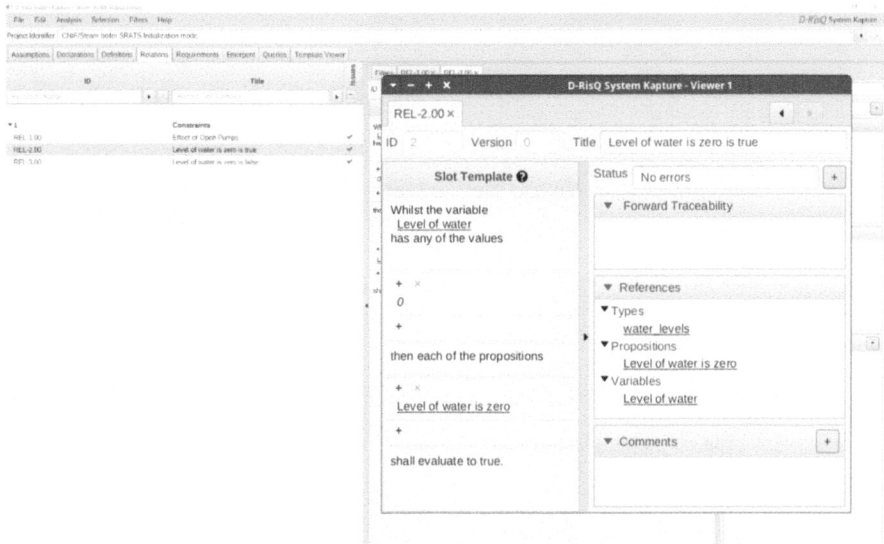

Fig. 5. Defining an abstract proposition indirectly

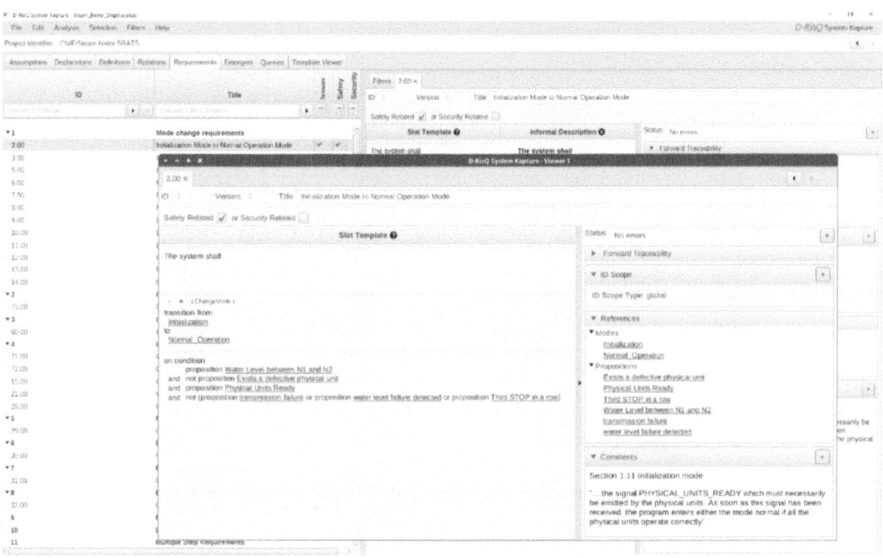

Fig. 6. Mode transition from Initialization to Normal_Operation

Periods. Periods are used to represent periods of specific activity within each run of the system. Unlike processes, periods will typically occur only a few times, perhaps only once, in any run of the system. Common examples of periods are those for starting up or shutting down. Once declared, requirements may be specified as pertaining to the period, meaning that they will only be "executed" when the period is active.

```
template_instance_rid_var_3_p_0_e =
  let
    Type = "variable"
    Id = caesar_id."rid_var_3_p_0_e"
    Slot("Variable") =
      str_."STOP variable"
    Slot("IsInput") = True
    Slot("Type") =
      type."STOP_Status"
    Slot("RefreshRate") =
      int.1
    Slot( _ ) = unspecified
  within
    makeTemplate(Type, Id, Slot)
```

Fig. 7. A template instance for the variable *"STOP variable"*

```
template_instance_rid_req_2_p_0_e =
  let
    Type = "mode change"
    Id = caesar_id."rid_req_2_p_0_e"
    Slot("ChangeMode") = True
    Slot("SourceModeName") =
      mode."Initialization"
    Slot("TargetModeName") =
      mode."Normal_Operation"

    Slot("Condition") =
      and_.(proposition."Water Level between N1 and N2",
      and_.(complement.proposition."Exists a defective physical unit",
      and_.(proposition."Physical Units Ready",
            complement.(or_.(proposition."transmission failure",
                        or_.(proposition."water level failure detected",
                             proposition."Third STOP in a row"))))))
    Slot("Periods") =
      always_implemented
    Slot("Processes") =
      set_.{}
    Slot( _ ) = unspecified
  within
    makeTemplate(Type, Id, Slot)
```

Fig. 8. Template instance of mode transition requirement of Fig. 6

2.3 Underlying Semantics

The declarations, definitions, relations and requirements entered into System Kapture®
are subjected to an initial check that they are well-formed and then data is generated
for each template entered. For example, the declaration of the input variable *"STOP
variable"* using the variable declaration template (previously shown in Fig. 2) gives the
machine readable CSP definition shown in Fig. 7.

The template instance for a requirement for a mode transition from *Initialization* to *Normal_Operation* mode (previously shown in Fig. 6) is shown in Fig. 8. All of the data generated from System Kapture® is included as part of a CSP representation split over a number of files of the intended behaviour of the "execution" of requirements. The CSP representation consists of over six thousand lines of machine readable CSP, so just a snippet of the underlying CSP for scheduling all the requirements entered is shown in Fig. 9.

```
SCHEDULER(<>,_,_) =
    new_timestep ->
    end_of_input_phase ->
    in_period?all_entered_periods ->
    processes_in_progress?procs_in_progress:Set(all_non_immediate_cited_processes) ->
    SCHEDULER(
        direct_and_emergent_reqs_ordered
        ^
        proc_req_ids,
        all_entered_periods,
        procs_in_progress
    )
SCHEDULER(<req_id>^X,all_entered_periods,procs_in_progress) =
    IMPL_PROCESS(req_id)(all_entered_periods,procs_in_progress);
    SCHEDULER(X,all_entered_periods,procs_in_progress)

aSCHEDULER =
    Union({
        ALL_IMPL_ALPHABETS,
        Union({IMPL_ALPHABET(id)|id<-set(proc_req_ids)}),
        {|new_timestep,end_of_input_phase|},
        {in_period.X|X<-Set(all_cited_periods)},
        {processes_in_progress.X|X<-Set(all_non_immediate_cited_processes)}
    })
```

Fig. 9. Scheduling requirements within a round

Informally the CSP sets all possible values for input variables to be explored by FDR in an input phase. It then evaluates defined periods and processes that have been entered into System Kapture®; there are none in the Steam Boiler example. The CSP model then evaluates each requirement in a fixed order based upon abstract propositions used and the input values from the input phase. Once this has been completed a new timestep event occurs, which denotes the completion of a round and the cycle begins again.

Unsurprisingly the state space that FDR explores grows quickly, therefore the input values need to be limited by abstraction. For example, the level of the water is abstracted to 8 values denoting relevant intervals. Such abstractions are refined at the next level down of high level software requirements represented in D-RisQ's Kapture® tool. The refinement of each requirement from System Kapture® to Kapture® can be separately verified.

3 Kapturing a System

There are no definitive rules for expressing system requirements: the style depends on many factors including an organization's specific software development policy, and the nature of the system in question. However, there are some general guidelines which we can recommend be followed when using System Kapture® to record system requirements.

The guidelines cover multiple iterations of the requirements that potentially are successively refined and detail added. The aim is to deliver requirements that:

- are clear and unambiguous;
- cover all the main functions that the system is required to do and not do;
- are relatively abstract, steering clear of software implementation details that are not the concern of system requirements;
- record what is needed to be known to implement the requirements in practice.

3.1 An Iteration of the System Requirements

Step 1. A natural place to start with System Requirements is to identify the discrete modes of the system and transitions between those modes. The declaration of the 5 modes for the Steam Boiler problem is illustrated in Fig. 1. Specifying transition requirements for the Steam Boiler is shown in Fig. 6. The transition is conditional on 3 propositions that are stated in the informal specification in [4], plus a negated disjunction that excludes a transition to the *Emergency_Stop* mode.

For the first step the propositions can all be specified as abstract, later steps can elaborate how these propositions are defined based on additional information in [4]. For example, the proposition *Water Level between N1 and N2* used as one of the conditions for a transition from the mode *Initialization* to *Normal_Operation*, is elaborated in a later iteration to *variable "Level of water" is at least &N1 and variable "Level of water" is at most &N2* where *&N1* and *&N2* denote named constants and *"Level of water"* is a declared input variable. If there any modes which are obviously source or sink modes, such as *Initialization* and *Emergency_Stop* respectively then declare them as such.

Model checking suffers from state-space explosion but at this abstract stage potential divide and conquer approaches can be identified to address the issue. At the system level a natural way to do this is to verify that the different system modes are mutually exclusive, allowing verification of system safety properties to be performed separately for each mode.

Accordingly, the emergent property for the mutual exclusiveness of the system modes of the Steam Boiler was checked. The model check returned a counterexample which led to the transition conditions being tightened. The counterexample resulted in additions to the transition conditions between modes to produce mutually exclusive transitions. Opportunities for model checking and performance are further discussed in Sect. 4.

Step 2. Another natural step is to identify inputs and outputs to a system and declare any types that they have. Following on from the formal analysis mentioned in step 1, output variables should be declared first and used within relevant propositions. Formal

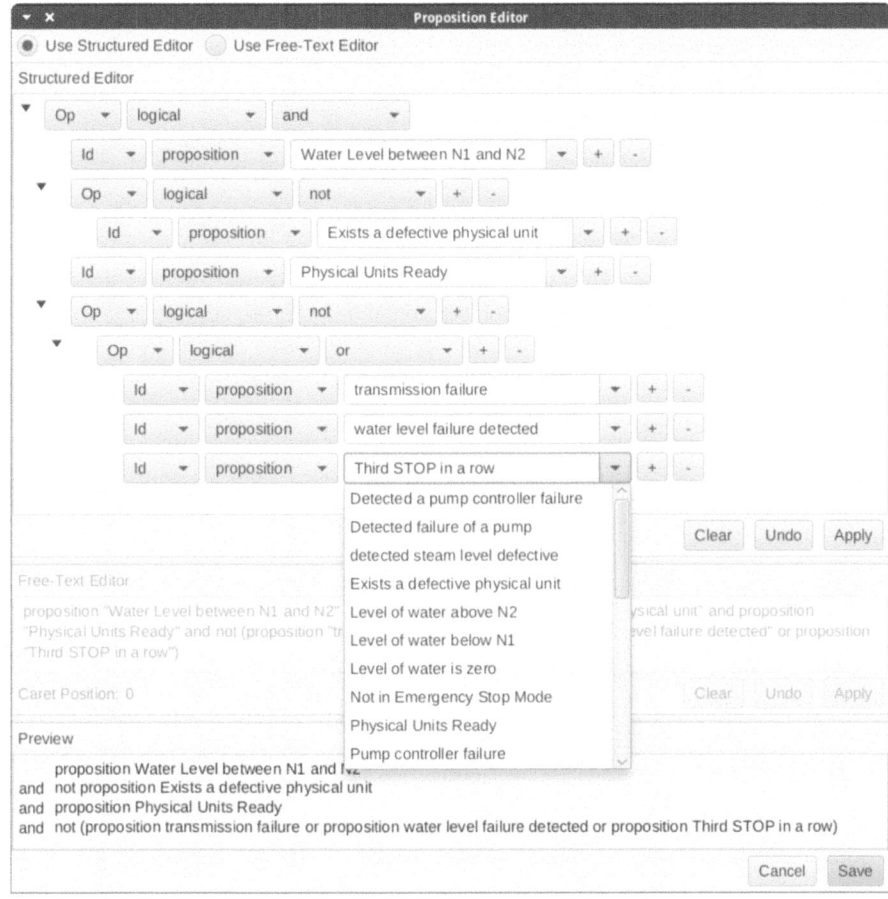

Fig. 10. Structure editor with list of available declared variables

checks can then be extended to include expected outputs without necessarily causing a state-space explosion.

An advantage of declaring variables is that, when using the structured editor, they become available to peruse and select which is a productivity boost, as illustrated in Fig. 10. As familiarity with the expression language grows, the free-text editor can also be used; switching between the two supports productivity as well.

The declaration of input and output variables also has the advantage of allowing the tool to flag up warnings that a variable has not been used anywhere. For example, in Fig. 11 the variable *"Steam boiler waiting message received"* has a yellow triangle to denote that the input variable has not been used anywhere. A decision can then be made whether this acknowledgement is used to specify further requirements at the system level or to defer to the high level software requirements. In general, these warnings help identify missing requirements either through their direct use, or indirectly via their use in Actions or Propositions referenced by a system requirement. Similarly, if an Action or Proposition is not used, a warning will be displayed.

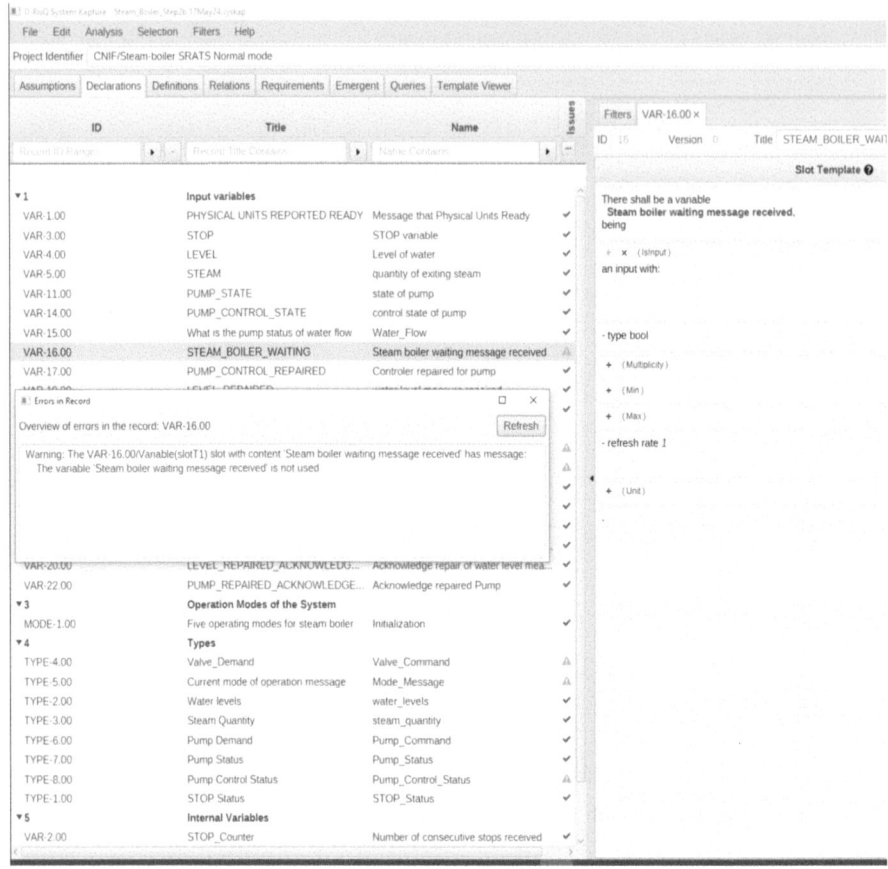

Fig. 11. Example of a warning that a declared variable is not used

The declaration of internal variables will usually arise when information about a previous state is needed. For example, the failure of a pump controller is indicated in [4] by the statement *"The program detects that the unit changes its state spontaneously"*. In order to detect a spontaneous change, a record from the previous timestep needs to be kept of both the state of the pump and of whether it was demanded to change. This leads to the creation of two internal variables *"Previous_Pump_State"* and *"Previous Pump Demand"*.

Step 3. The declaration of input, output and internal variables at Step 2 provides a basis for defining propositions and requirements for each mode. The system requirements that pertain to the intended behaviour of the Steam Boiler in *Initialization* mode is shown in Fig. 12.

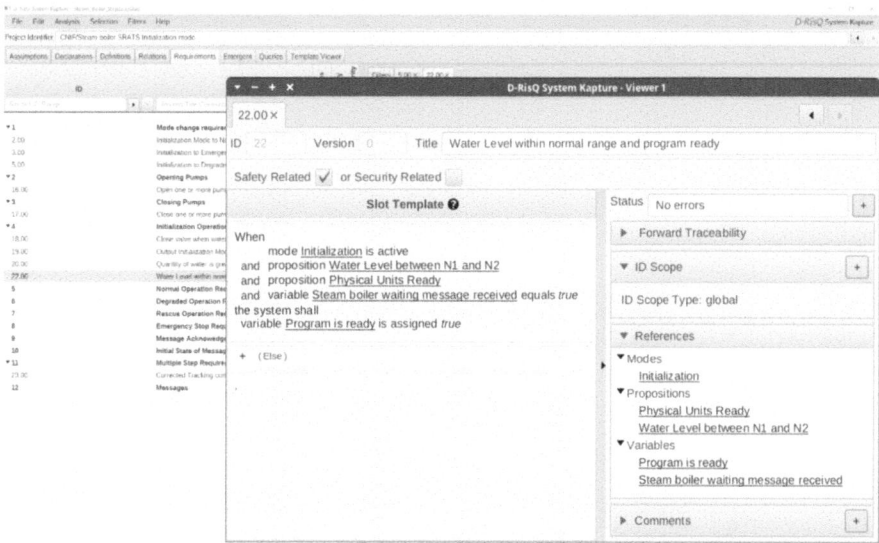

Fig. 12. Requirements pertinent to *Initialization* mode

Similarly, the system requirements that pertain to the intended behaviour of the Steam Boiler in *Normal_Operation* mode is shown in Fig. 13. All the transition requirements into and out of *Normal_Operation* mode are specified along with the intended operation of the Steam Boiler in this mode. The requirements for opening and closing pumps are common to all modes, apart from emergency stop, because they are predicated on the sensed level of water no matter whichever of those nodes are active.

Separate System Kapture® files can be projected out by filtering non-applicable requirements for each mode created and exporting to a System Kapture® file. The exported file can then be verified separately against system safety properties. Since it had previously been established in step 1 that the modes were mutually exclusive and that the transition conditions were unchanged, it was sound to perform the verification for each mode separately. It will often be the case that there will be sets of system requirements that are independent of each other, along with requirements that are shared, and these are often grouped together under modes.

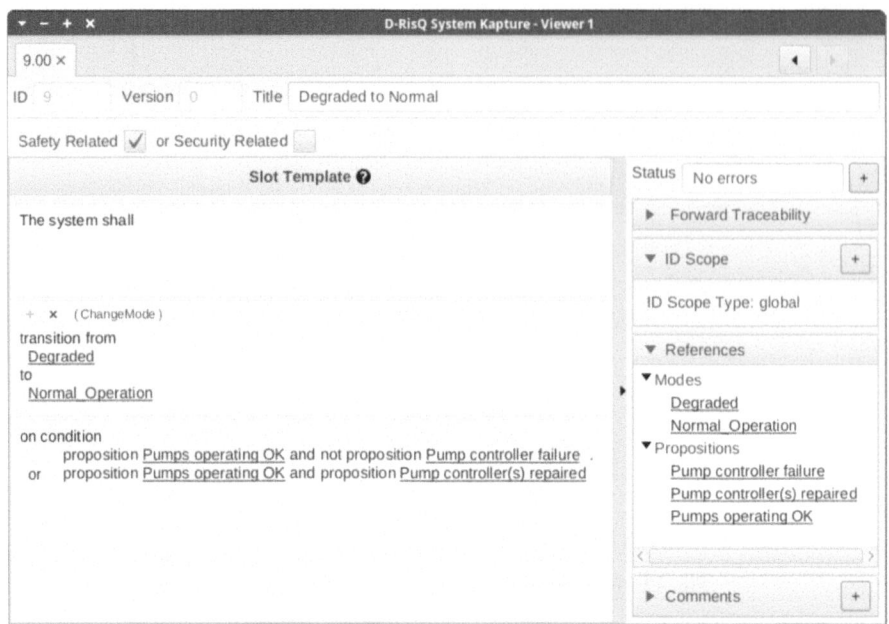

Fig. 13. Requirements pertinent to *Normal_Operation* mode

Step 4. Once all modes have been addressed and verified, all the requirements can be merged together in a single System Kapture® file. Before that occurs the elaboration and refinement of System Kapture® requirements can be expressed incrementally as early as step 3 as high level software requirements in D-RisQ's Kapture® tool as shown in Fig. 14.

The Kapture® requirement for transition from *Initialization* to *Normal_Operation* is similar to the System Kapture® requirement, except that the start and end of the round is explicitly mentioned. The defined propositions of System Kapture® become abbreviations for expression that evaluate to true or false. The abstract propositions become signals with a Boolean type that can be elaborated with complex calculations, such as estimating the level of the water based on incomplete information. Elaboration also occurs through the use of multiple Kapture® requirements to "implement" a single System Kapture® requirement. For example, requirements of the control of individual pumps can be introduced in Kapture® and then essentially collected together as a disjunction to provide a link to the System Kapture® requirement of opening, or closing, one or more pumps. The individual Kapture® requirements can then be individually realized in a Simulink®/Stateflow® model. The Kapture® requirements become the specification for a Simulink®/Stateflow® implementation that can be verified using D-RisQ's Modelworks® tool. Formal support to verify Kapture® requirements against System Kapture® requirements has been developed, but not completely automated at present.

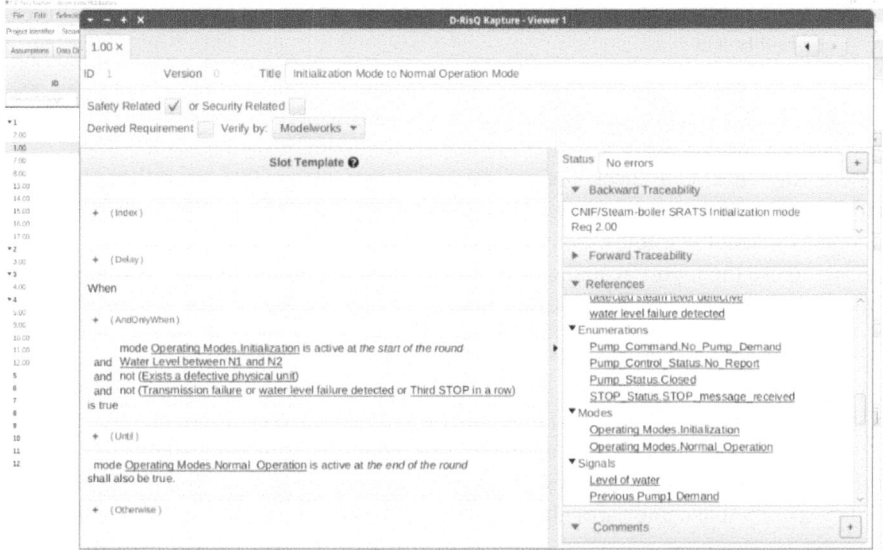

Fig. 14. An incremental record of high level software requirements

4 Analysis of System Requirements

System Kapture® is able to perform a number of stand-alone or self-contained checks and queries on the model of the system that it constructs from the direct requirements, definitions and relations provided by the user. As previously discussed it currently generates data that is fed into an abstract parameterized model in the machine-readable process algebra of CSP [6]. The data plus the model can then be model checked for various properties discussed in this section using the explicit-state model-checker FDR4 [7].

The underlying formalism enables well-formedness and type correctness of the requirements to be checked, but in the near future we wish to conduct these checks by System Kapture® before the generation of the CSP.

The use of an explicit-state model-checker does risk the state explosion problem, however the experience we have gained using System Kapture® indicates that the compilation of the CSP representation in FDR is relatively quick. For example, the full set of requirements with all variables and pumps compiles in a few minutes. The relatively fast compilation means that elastic computing resources can be used to scale the analysis of requirements. For example, D-RisQ has used Amazon's Elastic Compute Cloud (Amazon EC2) with 20 nodes, each node connected by a high bandwidth network, with each node consisting of 32 cores each with 0.25 Tb of RAM as local working memory. The cost of using Amazon EC2 was at the time less than £50 carrying out a state exploration of 20 billion states taking 22 min. Experiments described in [8] reports a refinement check with 10^{12} states was completed in less than 3 h. Despite these impressive results D-RisQ has plans to move to a different representation for more efficient verification checks to scale requirements analysis on ubiquitous machines, such as laptops.

The checks and queries carried out by FDR using CSP generated by System Kapture®
are described below.

4.1   Absence of Errors and Warnings

System Kapture® can check for behaviours of the system that are either obviously
erroneous should they occur, or which may not be errors but which are at least anomalous
enough to warrant warnings. Should an error or warning be raised, the onus is then on
the user to use the report generated by System Kapture® to modify the requirements to
remove that error or discharge the warning.

Errors. The errors, which System Kapture can identify, include:

- An attempt was made to exit a mode that was declared to be a sink mode.
- An attempt was made to read an uninitialized internal or output variable.
- In some behaviours of the system the requirements lead to a contradiction in that
  they specify that some particular mode should be both exited and entered in the same
  round.
- A variable can exceed its stated limits.
- An output variable has not been written when it is required to occur.

When the Steam Boiler requirements were analysed for errors, a failure was reported.
The failure was due to a simultaneous entry into *Normal_Operation* mode and exit
from *Normal_Operation* mode. The report showed that on the second round of a run
a transition from *Degraded* to *Normal_Operation* mode was allowed, but a transition
from *Degraded* to *Rescue* mode was also allowed. In the next round transitions from
Normal_ Operation back to *Degraded* mode and from *Rescue* to *Normal_Operation*
was allowed, hence the simultaneous entry and exit report.

Part of the problem stems from interpreting the description in Sect. 1.13 from [4] of
the behaviour of the system in Degraded mode.

> *"Once all the units which were defective have been repaired, the program comes
> back to normal mode."*

as

The system shall transition from *Degraded* to *Normal_Operation* on condition
(proposition *"Pump operating OK"* or proposition *"Pump controller repaired"*) and
interpreting

> *"As soon as the program sees that the water level measuring unit has a failure,
> the program goes into mode rescue."*

as

The system shall transition from *Degraded* to *Rescue* on condition proposition
"water level failure detected".

These two transition requirements should be mutually exclusive. The other part of the
problem is that the transition conditions for *Normal_Operation* back to *Degraded* mode

and from *Rescue* to *Normal_Operation* should also be mutually exclusive. Adding more detail to the transition conditions to ensure mutual exclusion solved these problems.

Warnings. The warnings, which System Kapture can identify, include:

- An attempt was made to start a defined process when it is already in progress.
- There was an unused write to an internal variable, i.e. in some particular round the variable was written to twice without there being an intermediate read.
- In some behaviours of the system the conditions in a case statement are not exhaustive when no default case has been specified.

4.2 System Always Progresses and Rounds Complete in Bounded Time

There are two checks which combine to verify that the system can always progress and that each timestep is concluded in a bounded period of time. These checks serve as both healthiness checks that the model of the system has been correctly constructed, and that to a certain extent, the requirements are consistent. One or both of these checks may fail in cases where errors and warnings have not been addressed by the user.

4.3 Queries

Queries are a means by which the user can specify certain types of bespoke check.

Currently the form of queries are limited to a basic check that a given action can occur, or that some proposition may become true in at least one behaviour of the system. This differs from the eventuality check described in 4.4 above, in that the action or proposition is not required to happen in all runs of the system, only that it can happen in at least one run.

It is intended to substantially extend the set of queries in future to check for more complex patterns of behaviour. One such future query might be to the effect that some given action can only occur if some condition has been met previously, or that it will occur if the condition has been met. In this way the queries might build up to a library in which use-cases can be formulated and exercised.

For the Steam Boiler example, a check was formulated to the effect that if some given failure was to occur then the system would enter the *Emergency_Stop* mode before the end of the round if was not already in that mode when the failure occurred. The failures considered were:

1. *"water level failure detected"*
2. *"steam measure failure"*
3. *"transmission failure"*
4. *"Pump unit control failure"*

The results of the checks were:

1. It fails in the *"water level failure detected"* case because it is only required to transition to *Emergency_Stop* on occurrence of a *"water level failure detected"* if it is in *Initialization* mode. In other modes it is not required to do so on occurrence of this failure.

2. It fails in the *"steam measure failure"* case because it is only required to transition to *Emergency_Stop* on occurrence of a *"steam measure failure"* if it is in *Rescue* mode. In other modes it is not required to do so on occurrence of this failure.
3. It passes in the *"transmission failure"* case.
4. It fails in the *"Pump unit control failure"* case because it is only required to transition to *Emergency_Stop* on occurrence of a *"Pump unit control failure"* if it is in *Rescue* mode. In other modes it is not required to do so on occurrence of this failure.

The checks are consistent with what is expected. Not all failures lead to *Emergency_Stop*. *Degraded* and *Rescue* are modes that try to cope with some failure. A subsequent failure of certain units in these modes (that already are dealing with a failure) would be expected to transition to *Emergency_Stop* because too much has gone wrong. A consistent statement in [4] is that if there is ever a transmission failure then the mode *Emergency_Stop* should be entered and as a sink mode no transition out of it is possible.

4.4 No Violation of Emergent Requirements

The emergent requirements are requirements that are not directly implementable by software, but are rather properties of the system that are expected to hold, or emerge, as a result of the implementation of the direct requirements. There are four classes of emergent requirement, namely:

- Always requirements, used to specify invariant properties of the system, i.e. that some given proposition about the system state always holds in all runs of the system.
- Eventually requirements, used to specify that some given action will eventually occur at least once, or that some given proposition will eventually become true at least once.
- Mode Set requirements, used to specify that certain given mode combinations always hold, e.g. that a certain subset of the modes are mutually exclusive in that no two can be active at the same time.
- Never requirements, used to specify safety properties, i.e. that some given action will never occur in any run of the system, or that some given proposition will never become true.

The checks are to the effect that all emergent requirements hold.

In the case of the Steam Boiler a system safety property that "in *Initialization* mode the system must never have no water and at the same time steam generated" was entered as an emergent requirement. System Kapture detected that this property fails under the circumstance that all the water pumps failed. The safety property was strengthened to:

"mode *Initialization* is active and variable *"quantity of exiting steam"* is greater than 0 and proposition *"Level of water is zero"* equals true and proposition *"Pumps operating OK"*

and this passed the verification check, however this raised another question.

A mode transition from *Initialization* mode to *Degraded* mode is possible if one of the physical units is defective, therefore the question arises as to why the transition didn't occur, if it had occurred the safety property in the mode *Initialization* would not have been violated.

Inspecting the condition for a transition reveals that as well as one of the physical units being defective, the water level must be between the nominal levels. There is therefore a gap in the requirements that were stated in the informal specification of [4].

There is no requirement about what the system should do in the case when all pumps fail after the input message of "all physical units ready", just as the water level dips below the lower nominal level, while in Initialization mode. This issue shows the value of being able to exhaustively check all behaviours that the system requirements allow in order to analyse whether they completely cover the intended system behaviour.

In the analysis of the requirements for each mode the time taken consists of two phases, a compilation phase and an exploration phase. The compilation phase does not benefit from parallelisation and is the bottleneck. As discussed earlier and reported in [8], the second phase of exploration can increase linearly in the number of cores the exploration is distributed over. The increase in cores increases the parallelization.

In order to get a sense of the size of the problem a deadlock analysis was performed. If the model is deadlock-free then the whole model must have been explored and also provides assurance of consistency in the requirements. The models each took a few seconds to compile; the biggest model took just under two minutes to explore on a laptop with four cores.

5 Conclusions

The template approach to expressing system level requirements enables system developers to describe in English what they want the system and software to do. Of course, like a word processor this doesn't prevent rubbish from being written. However, like a word processor there is analogous support for "spell checking and grammar". Unlike a word processor there is a formal semantic basis to "test" the requirements which is distinct from conventional software development when this is done with executable software when it is the most expensive to change. The use of System Kapture® is distinct from the other solutions to the Steam Boiler problem published in [9] because it hides formality in order to make the requirement statements accessible to regulators and their representatives.

System Kapture® is still under development and important improvements needed are: the introduction of type checking before a formal model is generated; more expressive verification checks; and most importantly, a better way of communicating to a user why a verification has failed.

There will still be limitations to a tool like System Kapture® used on its own, especially when considering physical dynamics that are in the domain of System Control Engineers. Such dynamics are continuous and are described using differential equations. Reasoning about differential equations is certainly possible [10], but not currently within the current capability of System Kapture®. However, the real problem is validating dynamic control and the best way of doing that is through simulation with a digital model of the physical world because it is a natural way for a human to assess validity. After simulation is the potentially expensive use of test rigs and experimentation.

The value of System Kapture® is in the context of other tools that link System Requirements Allocated To Software with tool boxes from The MathWorks that includes Simulink®/Stateflow®. Models in Simulink®/Stateflow® can be simulated with a model of the real world, called a Plant model. It is at this point that continuous system dynamics are discretized and validated against high level software requirements and relevant system requirements. The linkage between System Kapture® and the other verification tools for such a model-based development process is shown in an agile-like development process diagram in Fig. 15.

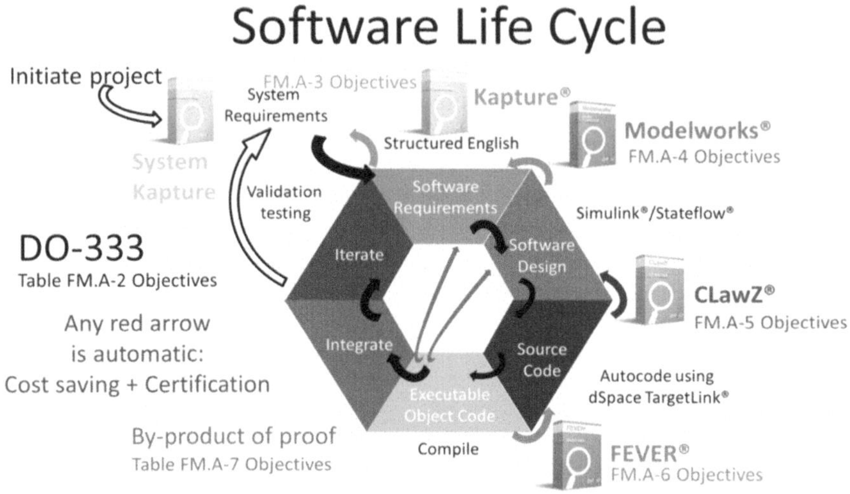

Fig. 15. System Kapture in the context of tools to meet verification objectives of DO-333

The processes in which these tools are to be used must provide evidence to support certification activities, in this case supporting compliance to DO-178C/ED-12C, more specifically the 'Formal Methods Supplement to DO-178C/ED-12C'; referred to as DO-333/ED-216. Undesirable behaviour detected by validation testing must be due to shortcomings in the requirements rather than errors introduced into the software. The automation that is introduced means that validation can be done quickly and re-development to accommodate requirements change due to validation test failures done even faster.

The verification tools have a focus on avoidance of error insertion through the compliance to standards. This starts with system software requirements and System Kapture® and then for high level software requirements, Kapture®, both of which encapsulate a "Requirements Standard" at the appropriate level. As requirements are a human process there is no tool that can say whether the requirements are the right requirements for the task, but there are built-in automated analyses that can be used to assist in ensuring that they are unambiguous, complete, consistent, etc.; they are verifiable because of the underpinning formal representation. Having then developed a design in Simulink®/Stateflow®, Modelworks® [11] (shown in Fig. 15) automatically checks that the design satisfies the high level software requirements (or shows where there is a non-compliance). Before this proof can be undertaken, the design has to be checked for compliance to 'Design Standards' using a Model Advisor script supplied by D-RisQ. The next few steps are largely automatic in that the dSpace Targetlink auto-coder [12] produces C code which is checked for compliance to the predictable and verifiable C-flat semantic subset of C (essential a coding standard) and then CLawZ® [13, 14] automatically proves that the code satisfies the design.

System Kapture® is being used by D-RisQ on its projects, for example currently D-RisQ and ScubaTx [15] are pioneering the use of these tools in the development of cutting-edge software for a revolutionary medical device designed for the extended preservation of organs during transportation.

Acknowledgments. The current development of System Kapture® was funded by Innovate UK through The National Aerospace Technology Exploitation Programme. Thanks go to Karen Stephenson and Nick Moffat for many helpful detailed comments and help with the screenshots. Many thanks to the reviewers whose comments we have tried to address.

Disclosure of Interests. The authors have an interest in the commercial success of the tools described above. The tools under various stages of development but are available free for academic use.

References

1. Lions, J.-L., et al.: European Space Agency Board of Inquiry report into the first flight failure of Ariane 5 1996. http://www.ima.umn.edu/~arnold/disasters/ariane5rep.html
2. RTCA DO-178C/EUROCAE ED-12C Software Considerations in Airborne Systems and Equipment Certification, January 2012
3. RTCA DO-333/EUROCAE ED-216 Formal Methods Supplement to DO-178C/ED-12C and DO-278A/ED-109A, January 2012
4. Abrial, J-R.: Steam-boiler control specification problem. In: Abrial, J-R., Borger, E., Langmaack, H. (eds.) Formal Methods for Industrial Applications 1996. LNCS State-of-the-Art Survey, pp. 500–509. Springer, Heidelberg (1996). https://doi.org/10.1007/BFb0027252
5. Meyer, B.: Handbook of Requirements and Business Analysis. Springer International Publishing, Cham (2022). https://doi.org/10.1007/978-3-031-06739-6
6. Roscoe, A.W.: The Theory and Practice of Concurrency. Prentice Hall (1997)
7. Gibson-Robinson, T., Armstrong, P., Boulgakov, A., Roscoe, A.W.: FDR3: a parallel refinement checker for CSP. Int. J. Softw. Tools Technol. Transf. **18**(2), 149–167 (2015)
8. Gibson-Robinson, T., Roscoe, A.W.: FDR into The Cloud. In: Welch, P.H., et al. (eds.) Communicating Process Architectures 2014. Open Channel Publishing Ltd. (2014)
9. Abrial, J-R., Borger, E., Langmaack, H. (eds.): Formal Methods for Industrial Applications 1996, LNCS State-of-the-Art Survey, pp. 500–509. Springer, Heidelberg (1996). https://doi.org/10.1007/BFb0027227
10. Foster, S., Munive, J.J.H., Struth, G.: Differential Hoare logics and refinement calculi for hybrid systems with Isabelle/HOL. In: 18th International Conference on Relational and Algebraic Methods in Computer Science, RAMiCS 2020. LNCS 12062. Springer, Heidelberg (2020). https://doi.org/10.1007/978-3-030-43520-2_11

11. Botham, J., et al.: PICASSOS–Practical applications of automated formal methods to safety related automotive systems. SAE Technical Paper. http://papers.sae.org/2017-01-0063/

12. TargetLink   webpage.   https://www.dspace.com/en/pub/home/products/sw/pcgs/targetlink.cfm

13. O'Halloran, C.: Automated Verification of auto-code from Simulink. Autom. Softw. Eng. **20**(2), 237–264 (2013)

14. O'Halloran, C.: Nose-gear velocity–a challenge problem for software safety. In: Australian System Safety Conference (ASSC 2014), held in Melbourne, 28–30 May (2014)

15. ScubaTx homepage. https://www.scubatx.com

Proving B with Atelier B

Thierry Lecomte[(✉)]

CLEARSY, Aix en Provence, France
thierry.lecomte@clearsy.com

Abstract. The article focuses on the continuous improvement of Atelier B's automatic proof capabilities since its industrialisation in the 90s. The evolution of Atelier B addressed challenges in proof obligations generation and optimisation, adapting to new languages like Event-B and incorporating newer formats for easier analysis and third-party prover connections. Significant developments include enhancing the proof system to handle complex proof obligations efficiently and integrating external provers for improved proof capabilities. The article also showcases B's industrial applications in critical sectors, emphasising the method's importance in safety-critical software development and the ongoing efforts to facilitate proof activities and integrate AI for better proof automation.

Keywords: Formal proof · Safety critical · B

Dedication:
The author collaborated with Jim Woodcock over several research projects, together with Peter Larsen. FmeRail was an opportunity to meet for the first time and "battle" over railway case studies that showcased our favourite formal methods, in London for the announcement of the Paris Meteor automatic metro[1] secured with B, in Toulouse for the successful FM'99 conference, for the development of cyber-physical systems with the INTO-CPS project, in Shonan for the green tea ceremony, rosé wine tasting in the port of Cassis. Many fond memories, um amor compartilhado pelo Brasil, thank you for taking this formal journey together.

1 Introduction

Mathematical proof is at the heart of the B method. It's both a strength, because software is better validated than with tests, and a weakness, because it's an

---

[1] Inaugurated in December 1998.

S. Foster and A. Sampaio (Eds.): *The Application of Formal Methods*, LNCS 14900, pp. 329–345, 2024.
https://doi.org/10.1007/978-3-031-67114-2_13

activity that requires special skills, more rarely available among a company's workforce. Since Atelier B was industrialised in the 90 s, it has undergone continuous improvement, with a focus on its automatic proof capabilities. As the mathematical proof of B models is specific, the improvements made have themselves been specific. This article presents the salient aspects of this work, carried out in an industrial context. It does not present any scientific studies with other provers or similar tools, as the technical and scientific choices were strongly constrained from the beginning. The remainder of this paper is organised as follows. Section 1 briefly introduces the B method. Section 2 presents the characteristics and constraints associated to the B proof obligations. Section 3 describes the proof system, its architecture and its requirements. The rationale of using B for industrial applications is presented in Sect. 4. Section 5 describes the adaptation of the proof system over almost 3 decades, before concluding.

2   Introduction to the B Method

B [1] is a method for specifying, designing, and coding software systems. It covers central aspects of the software life cycle (Fig. 1): the writing of the technical specification, the design by successive refinement steps and model decomposition (layered architecture), and the source code generation.

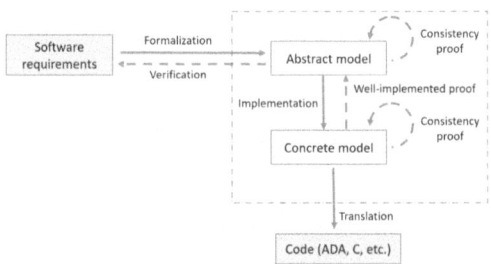

Fig. 1. A typical B development cycle, from requirements to code.

B is also a modelling language that is used for both specification, refinement (Fig. 2), and implementation (Fig. 3). It relies on substitution calculus, first order logic and set theory. All modelling activities are covered by mathematical proof that finally ensures that the software system is correct.

B is structured with modules and refinements. A module is used to break down a large software into smaller parts. A module has a specification (called a machine) where both a static and a dynamic description of the requirements are formalised. It defines a mathematical model of the subsystem concerned:

- an abstract description of its state space and possible initial states,
- an abstract description of operations to query or modify the state.

This model establishes the external interface for that module: every implementation will conform to this specification. Conformance is assured by proof during the formal development process. A module specification is refined. It is re-expressed with more information: adding some requirements, refining abstract notions with more concrete notions, getting to implementable code level. Data refinement consists in introducing new variables to represent the state variables for the refined component, with their gluing invariant[2]. Algorithmic refinement consists in transforming the operations for the refined component. A refinement may also be refined. The final refinement of a refinement column is called the implementation, it contains only B0-compliant models[3]. In a component (machine, refinement, or implementation), sets, constants, and variables define the state space while the invariants define the static properties for its state variables. The initialisation phase (for the state variables) and the operations (for querying or modifying the state) define the way variables are modified. From these, proof obligations are computed such as: the static properties are consistent, they are established by the initialisation, and they are preserved by all the operations.

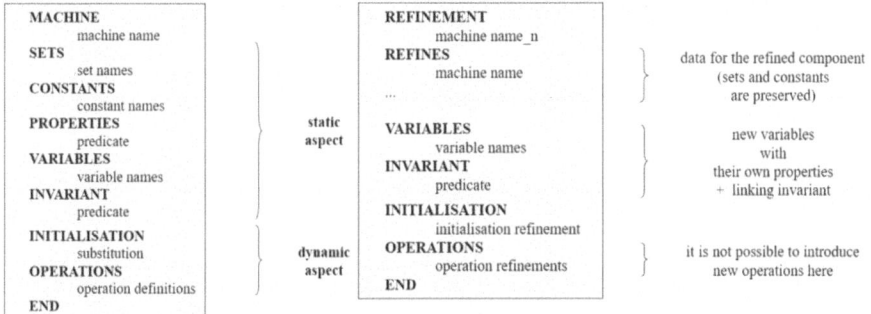

Fig. 2. Structure of MACHINE and REFINEMENT components.

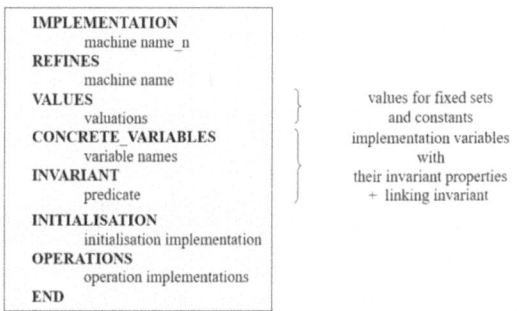

Fig. 3. Structure of IMPLEMENTATION component.

---

[2] A B refinement is composed of an abstract and a concrete a labeled transition system (LTS) related by a gluing invariant. The gluing invariant is a binary predicate over the states of the abstract LTS and the states of the concrete one.

[3] B0 is a subset of the B language, where OPERATIONS are deterministic and data types are restricted. Its syntax is close to any structured language.

Finally a B project is a set of linked B modules. Each module is formed of components: an abstract machine (its specification), possibly some refinements and an implementation[4]. The principal dependencies links between modules are IMPORTS links (forming a modular decomposition tree[5]) and SEES links (read only transversal visibility[6]). Sub-projects may be grouped into libraries. A software developed in B may integrate or may be integrated with traditionally developed code.

3   Atelier B Proof Obligations

3.1   Characteristics and Constraints

Proof obligations (PO) are central to the B verification schema [8]. They are computed from B models (see Fig. 4) to cover several aspects: correctness, overflow, and well-definedness.

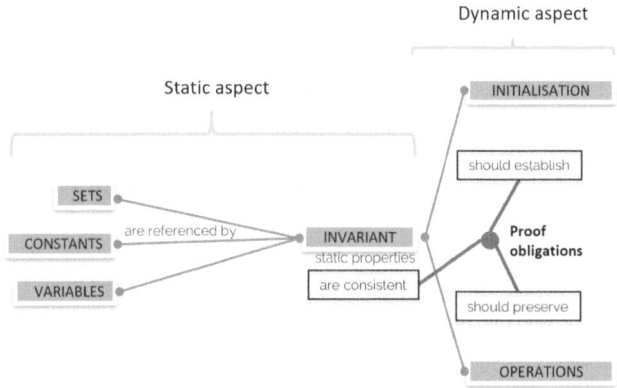

Fig. 4. Proof obligations are linked with model clauses.

The first proof obligation generator developed in the 90 s contained many hard-coded optimisations, which made it difficult to understand how it worked, to optimize the generator, and to modify the B language. Atelier B historically also used custom data formats and specific programming languages. These formats have lasted for several decades because redesigning the formats and the

---

[4] Most components are made of one machine and one implementation. In some cases where the proof is too difficult to handle (the proof obligations are too complex), intermediate refinements (algorithm or data) are introduced to reduce this complexity. Four intermediate refinements may be considered as a maximum.

[5] B is a top-down approach. Models are decomposed into smaller ones.

[6] Read-only components can be seen by components which are not on the same branch of the decomposition tree.

programs would have been too costly. Specific programming languages (like a in-house Prolog-like language) have made it more difficult to convince engineers to work on this software.

In any case, once the first industrial project has been completed, Atelier B was obliged to keep the proof obligation process constant to avoid any proof regression. Any modification in the proof obligations shape, naming, or order would have had a dramatic impact on the effort (i.e. cost) required to maintain B projects proved over the years. The proof obligations are named after the B clauses to which they apply. Mathematical demonstrations are associated with the proof obligations of a clause. Heuristics allow us to continue to associate these demonstrations correctly with the proof obligations, when refactoring the B model for which we do not want to lose the interactive proof work already carried out.

3.2 Evolution

The invention of Event-B in the 2000s required to develop a new proof obligation generator, supporting both B and Event-B languages. The PO file format was left unchanged, but the core of the generator was split into 2 parts: the generation engine itself developed in C++ and the theoretical proof obligations expressed in XSLT [14] that could be modified on the fly without requiring to recompile the engine. Adding Event-B support as well as REAL and FLOAT numbers [5] to Atelier B was greatly eased by this decomposition.

More recent developments provide alternative tools using XML based formats to facilitate the study of B proof obligations and the connection to third party provers. In particular, the proof obligation format pog is a XML-based format for proof obligations. Its definition is provided as an XML Schema Definition. This definition is documented through annotations directly available in the source file. Xsltproc then generates an HTML version of the documentation.

Finally, this new design has made it possible to add a traceability mechanism that enables proof obligations to be associated with models in an immediate and precise manner. This has made it possible to add to the integrated B model editor a colouring of the text indicating its automatic rate of proof as well as the remainder to be proven.

4 Atelier B Proof System

When Atelier B was built, there was no prover capable of handling proof obligations that mixed set theory and arithmetic, and that could contain thousands or even tens of thousands of hypotheses. In addition, the processing time had to be a maximum of ten seconds on average for each proof obligation. This section presents the proof system that was developed for this purpose.

4.1 Automatic Proof

The Automatic Prover PR was developed from scratch. It is made of two distinct parts: a loader and a solver.

Loader. It is designed to minimise PO loading/unloading in memory: PO could have many hypotheses, so unloading all hypotheses from memory when moving to the next PO is not optimal. The hypotheses are grouped into packets, corresponding to the different clauses of a B model. PR unloads from computer memory only those hypotheses that are no longer used and keeps the others. PO file format was structured accordingly.

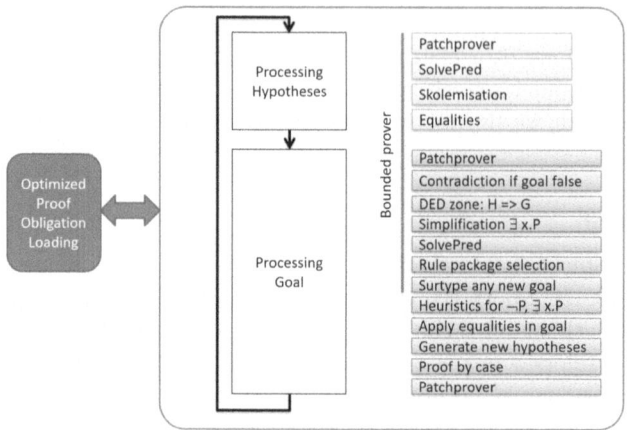

Fig. 5. Structure of PR.

Solver. It generates new hypotheses and transforms the goal in order to obtain ⊤ (represented with the predefined symbol *btrue*). If the solver is successful, the proof obligation is considered proved. If not, the proof obligation remains unproved. A B project is valid only when 100% PO are proved. The solver (Fig. 5) is itself composed of:

- an hypothesis processor, generating new hypotheses but not modifying (replacing) existing ones. Heuristics are applied to either combine or instantiate existing hypotheses, usually in relation with the goal to prove.
- a goal processor, simplifying the current goal by adding local hypotheses derived from existing ones, or by replacing the current goal by one or several sub-goals. Simplification and addition of hypotheses are performed by proof mechanisms. Goal transformation (simplification, decomposition) results from the application of mathematical proof rules. These rules are either part of the prover rules database or are developed by users and specific to each project.

The two processors are executed in sequence: the goal is simplified while new hypotheses are generated. We then hope that the hypotheses generated will trigger rules that will ultimately demonstrate the goal.

Proof Mechanisms. The solver, actionable through the parameter *force*, ranging from 0 to 3, contains 35 mechanisms[7]. They were designed, improved then selected by engineers from different companies, based on experiments on several B projects representing a total of 3000 POs. The selection was made based on both the automatic proof percentage and the complexity/difficulty to prove remaining POs. These mechanisms are assembled in two configurations to form respectively:

- The bounded prover, corresponding to the force 0, comes with limited complexity mechanisms. It is the most efficient prover configuration, used first during automatic proof, usually able to demonstrate 70% of the proof obligations, with a mean execution time of 10 s.
- The unbounded prover includes heuristics that could generate infinite execution. Force 1 is an extension of force 0 prover where new hypotheses are more simplified by applying a stronger normalisation. Force 2 extends force 1 by generating more derived hypotheses. Force 3 extends force 2 by attempting proof by cases. These 3 forces usually increase automatic proof performance by 1 or 2% each.

The hypothesis processor is identical for both bounded and unbounded provers. There is another version of the Automatic Prover called MonoLemma ML. It comes without the optimised loader, to demonstrate a single proof obligation. ML is used to power the Rodin platform as "Atelier B provers" plug-in[8].

4.2   Extending the Prover

The automatic prover builds a proof tree. Its root is the initial goal to be proved. The descendants correspond to the result of simplifications made to the goal by applying the rule base. The leaves correspond to existing hypotheses or axioms (trivially verifiable predicates such as $0 \leq 1$ or TRUE: BOOL). When one of the leaves cannot be demonstrated because it is neither a hypothesis nor an axiom, the prover stops. Interaction with the user then begins, seeking to improve proof performance. Proof helpers available to the user are the addition of user defined rules, a proof-oriented script language, the definition of proof tactics and their selective execution, the conservation of demonstrations when the models change drastically, and graphical display of proof information elements. Interaction is not seen as a one-time action but as an investment in reducing the proof activity on the rest of the project, especially for similar proof obligations.

---

[7] The structure of the prover, the mathematical rules database, the mechanisms constituting both bounded and unbounded provers, and their parameters were designed, defined, and optimised based on the B models developed by the company Matra from 1993 until 1998. Hence the proof performances were not guaranteed when symbols and predicates used are quite different from those in Meteor models. To improve automatic proof percentage, complementary mathematical rule databases need to designed to address specific symbols or patterns.

[8] https://wiki.event-b.org/index.php/Rodin_Platform_Releases.

Addition of User Defined Rules. Three kinds of rules can be added to Atelier B:

- backward rules transforming a goal into 0 or more sub-goals,
- rewriting rules working on expressions and predicates,
- forward rules generating new hypotheses, triggered when the Modus Ponens is activated.

Apart from the Atelier B rules database, user defined rules may be added at component or at project level (PatchProver). The PatchProver is central to the proof performance: it has to be set up gradually based on previous completed projects and managed with a source-code management system. It constitutes the palette that each user has to know well. The addition of user rules in proof component files is only permitted if no (combination of) rules is available in the PatchProver. All rules have to be validated before being used in a project, at least with a manual demonstration.

Proof-Oriented Script Language. It contains more than 30 commands allowing to modify the proof tree or to collect information about it[9]. These commands are able to activate the bounded and unbounded provers, the processing of hypotheses for any force. They are also able to add hypothesis, initiate a proof by cases, trigger the Modus Ponens, start the Predicate Prover or simplify a goal with the Set Solver, and execute an external prover. To avoid long waiting times, some commands are associated with deadlines - the execution of these commands will not last longer than this delay that is a parameter of the command. Similarly, for provers that work better with a limited number of proof obligations, it is possible to specify that only typing hypotheses or hypotheses having a symbol in common with the goal are selected for the proof.

Definition of Proof Tactics and Their Selective Execution. Proof-oriented commands can be saved as demonstration. These are the demonstrations that are replayed often to ensure that the project is still provable. These demonstrations are supposed to be as generic as possible, to be applied on other similar proof obligations. In the interactive prover, when at least one PO has been demonstrated, the user is asked if these demonstrations could be saved in the User Pass, a specific part of the component proof files that only contains proof tactics (generic demonstrations). These demonstrations can be tried on the remaining proof obligations of the current component. These tactics are ordered: the first one is tried on all unproved POs, the other ones on the remaining POs once the previous tactic has been applied. Naturally the most generic, efficient tactics have to be in the first places while the more specific and longest to execute have to positioned further down the list. In addition, it is possible to use filters to make the selection even more precise, by specifying the name of the operation and/or the form of the goal.

---

[9] See https://b-method.gitbook.io/training-resources-for-atelier-b/ for more details.

4.3   Validation

From 1993 to 1998, the Automatic Prover was reverse-engineered, documented, tested, and extended to be ready for RATP qualification. It was made available to the Community and presented at the occasion of B-User Group meetings. The mathematical rules database was published to enable academic research [3]. Proof mechanisms were validated in conformance with software development best practices: documentation peer review, source code inspection, and requirement-based test-bench. Mathematical rules database (2700+ rules) validation was decomposed in two activities: automatic proof with the Predicate Prover PP, and manual proof for the rules not proved or not handled by PP.

Automatic Proof. The Predicate Prover PP was developed specifically to auto-mate this error-prone activity. PP [2] is based on semantic tableau proof system. The 116 inference rules are described by conditional rewrite rules and their application is controlled by strategies (case-split, instantiation of quantified predicates, etc.). The specification of PP was made public to encourage formal research [6,7]. Its specification was also peer reviewed and traceability with source code was established. Its validation consisted in developing an automaton able to replay the demonstration[10] to obtain a contradiction. Then PP has been included into a professional tool including checkers and translator, to specifically support industrial projects. PP is efficient when the number of hypotheses is low, which is the case for mathematical rule validation. The use of PP for proof of OP requires hypothesis filtering to maintain its proof performance.

Manual Proof. The mathematical rules that are not handled or proved by PP had to be verified manually. A form had to be filled with the source code of the rule, its manual translation into mathematical predicate, the verification of its correct typing and the absence of name collision between identifiers and quantified variables. Then a mathematical demonstration with no imposed format had to be provided. Each form was reviewed by a panel of about ten people from five different companies. The remarks made had to be taken into account by the author of the form and then the rule had to be reviewed again, as long as remarks remained. Finally a third party company was in charge on reviewing all forms and to evaluate if the demonstrations were convincing. The validation was completed when all manual demonstrations were deemed to be convincing. The forms and the evaluation report were added to the validation file.

The validation of the rules was a long process, which lasted much longer than the five years of Atelier B Meteor's development. Some errors were detected after 1998. Where possible, the rule was corrected and industry users were invited to re-prove their projects. Most of the time, the rules were "almost correct". Often a restriction on the application domain was missing. It was also detected that some rules were duplicated: as the validation of rules is unitary, this fact remained

---

[10] A sequence of inference rules, with the instantiation value of related quantified variables if any.

undetected for some time. Circumventing the problem required to replace the duplicated rule by a non-applicable rule[11].

During the development of PP, a first attempt to verify the rules database occurred in 1995. The tool handled 1535 rules, the other rules were not processed because of functional limitations (sequences not supported, several guards not yet translated). 59 were detected false, 55 were corrected and verified by PP successfully, 4 were removed because they were wrong (or too specific). A dedicated proof tool with GUI was designed and integrated to Atelier B to provide a systematic verification framework. Finally a few tens of rules have been corrected since 1998. Their detection is often due to incorrect models proved successfully. Backward analysis allows to locate the origin of the error, if it is a rule. If the cause is a faulty mechanism, then the analysis is our responsibility, as the code of the mechanisms is not accessible through the tool, unlike the mathematical rules.

5   B Industrial Applications

B's preferred field of application remains the railway sector, which strongly recommends (standard EN50128) the use of formal methods for the software development of SIL3 or SIL4 critical functions. B is used for safety-related automatic signalling systems for automatic metros. If the figures provided by Alstom and Siemens are aggregated, B would be used for around 30% of CBTC-type[12] automatic metros.

For the first application on line 14 of the Paris metro, the ATP (Automatic Train Protection) function represented 86 kloc of B models, representing 110 kloc of Ada code. This function triggers emergency braking when a danger is detected, in conjunction with speed supervision. This software is typical of the applications that can be developed with B: it is a cyclical, non-parallelised application that acquires inputs, performs calculations and sets outputs. Its main property is that it stops the train if the conditions for train movement are no longer met. Contrary to what one might think, this property is not the absence of collision, as rail transport safety is distributed across several systems on board the train and on the tracks. The train knows the topology of the track on which it is travelling (rails, signals, points, speed limits). Its position is estimated using beacons, odometer and GNSS signals. To determine the train's ability to keep moving forward, we use graph traversal algorithms (to find out where the train is), numerical calculations using integers to calculate kinetic energy, and Boolean equations to determine the triggering of the emergency braking. SIL3 and SIL4 applications require special hardware architectures, in particular the need to duplicate calculations and process the result by vote to ensure the good health of the execution machine. A difference in behavior then implies a switch to fallback mode and immediate shutdown of the train. In the same way, software

---

[11] It was not possible to delete it as it would have modified the order (the name) of the rules, that can be called by their index during interactive proof.
[12] Radio-based train control.

functions must be diversified to avoid the same design error being executed at the same time on 2 ECUs without being detected. As a general rule, based on the same software specification, 2 versions of the same software are developed by two independent teams using different technologies, to avoid common modes. The probability of the 2 software versions producing the same safety-related misbehaviour at the same time is therefore negligible[13].

With Atelier B, only one model needs to be developed. Then two code generators, developed once and for all by two independent teams with different technologies or principles, produce the two required instances of the software. This approach enables us to achieve very significant savings with a single software development, with B. In addition, at the time of certification, since unit and integration tests are replaced by exhaustive mathematical proof, there is no problem justifying software testing.

For the Paris metro, lines 1, 4, 13, and 14 currently have critical functions developed with B. With the Olympic Games and the Grand Paris Express project, lines 15, 16, 17 and 18 will also have such functions by 2030. Other applications linked to the SIL4 CLEARSY Safety Platform use B and Atelier B to develop critical SIL3 and SIL4 certified functions, for metro landing door control, localisation and communication. Last but not least, experiments are currently taking place outside the rail sector for autonomous mobility applications on land and at sea, within different regulatory frameworks. The results of these experiments may well lead to changes in industrial practices and associated standards.

6   Adaptation over Years

To enable greater deployment of B and Atelier B, it is necessary to facilitate the proof activity by maximising the automatic proof rate. To ensure improved proof performance and thus lower development costs, extending interactive proof commands and adding rules packages have reduced scope because the limitations of the proof kernel PR remain. So improvements were sought through features implemented externally, i.e. coupling with third-party provers and using AI for easing interactive proof. Below are listed the main contributions to the proof kernel.

ProB. In the early 2000's, formal data validation started to become more widespread in the railways [10]. In particular, the ProB model-checker was first demonstrated during the EU project DEPLOY [13]. After some optimisations, ProB was able to fully handle large size metro data and validation rules, resulting in the generation of one B machine per validation rule and instantiated with the data related to this rule. To date, the biggest B machine generated for data validation and analysed by ProB contains 10 Mloc. With Atelier B 4.3, ProB

---

[13] Systematic failures during design and random failures during execution are handled with this diversity and redundancy.

was added as an interactive command [12]. Its behaviour is similar to the predicate prover: it does not modify the goal, only trying to demonstrate it. It comes with a time limit (maximum duration) and the possibility to reduce the number of hypotheses by selecting those having one symbol in common with the goal. PRoB allows better handling of arithmetic goals and case-based proofs on reduced domains.

Zenon, iProver, and Alt-Ergo. BWare [9] (2012–2016) was an industrial research project aimed at providing a mechanised framework to support the automated verification of proof obligations. The adopted methodology consists in building a generic verification platform relying on different automated theorem provers, such as first order provers and SMT solvers. This generic platform is built upon the Why3 platform for deductive program verification. The considered first order provers are Zenon and iProver Modulo, while we opted for the Alt-Ergo SMT solver. In this framework, B proof obligations are translated by a specific tool into Why3 files, which are compatible with a Why3 encoding of the B set theory. From these files, Why3 can produce (by means of appropriate drivers) the proof obligations for the automated theorem provers, using the TPTP format for Zenon and iProver Modulo, and a native format for Alt-Ergo. This translation together with the encoding of the B set theory aims to generate valid statements that are appropriate for the automated theorem provers, i.e. whose proofs can be found by these provers. Finally, once proofs have been found by these tools, some of these provers can generate proof objects to be verified by proof checkers. This is the case of Zenon, which can produce proof objects for Coq and Dedukti, and iProver Modulo, which can also produce proof objects for Dedukti. An initial bench of 13,000 proof obligations, issued from several industrial projects, was constituted to evaluate the BWare platform. Atelier B PR prover was able to demonstrate 85% of them, Alt-Ergo 58%, iProver Modulo 19%, and Zenon less than 1%. As can be observed, the first order provers encounter difficulties, which can be explained by the fact that these provers do not know the B set theory. At the end of the project, Alt-Ergo was able to demonstrate 98% of the PO, Zenon 95%, and iProver 28%. We also completed the set of provers: CVC4 was able to demonstrate 94% of the PO, Z3 84%, Vampire 78%, and E 61%. It appears that the project and the supply of POs has improved the performance of some provers. In the case of Alt-Ergo, the remaining POs are existential and require human intelligence to prove (Fig. 6).

Alt-Ergo. LCHIP [11] (2016–2020) was an industrial project aimed at developing a safety computer programmed with B and with enhanced proof capabilities. Alt-Ergo prover was selected from the excellent results obtained during the project BWare. One possibility for improvement was to specialise the production of the Why3 to exploit Alt-Ergo strong points. However the input B models, issued from the safety library, were quite different (lower level modelling) with more arithmetic and bit-wise Boolean functions. In the meantime, Why3 and its programming language WhyML have evolved enough to prevent reusing Why3 generator developed during BWare. Finally the 5000 PO generated from the safety

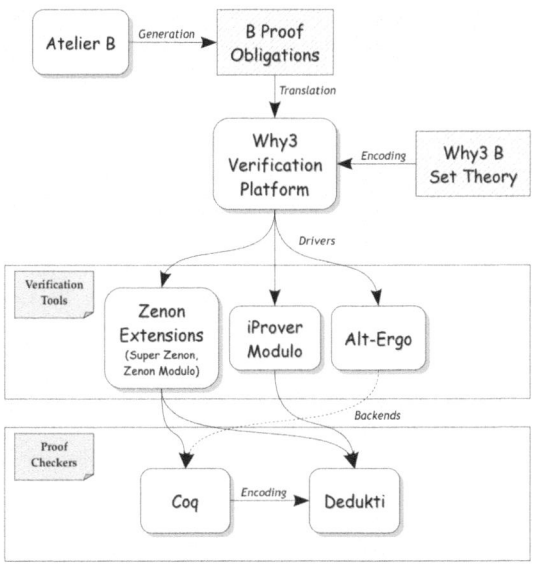

Fig. 6. The BWare Platform for the Automated Verification of B Proof Obligations.

library models were translated into SMT-LIB format and proved with 3 provers: Alt-Ergo proved 56% of the PO, CVC4 54%, and Z3 31%. The results are disappointing, but illustrate the difficulty to develop a universal prover/solver and to maintain a toolchain over the time.

Proof Drudges. DISCONT (2017–2021) aims to provide efficient and easy to use refinement and proof-based techniques and tools that scale to complex systems and offer more convenient and automatic proof platforms centred around B and Event-B, with Atelier B. Iapa [4] is an extension of Atelier B aiming at both integrating additional proof engines and offering hypotheses selection facilities to the user. The iapa tool is invoked within Atelier B on a given component, once the proof obligations of that component have been generated and from the XML-based file. Navigating through these proof obligations is a first core functionality available in iapa. Iapa comes with 6 commands for selecting hypotheses and identifiers[14], in order to limit the number of hypotheses used to prove a goal. Iapa then calls third-party provers through Why3 interface. Finally iapa offers the possibility to take into account proof obligations that are only proved by more than one external prover[15], and thus to improve automatic proof percentage.

---

[14] Identifiers are used to select hypotheses - typing hypotheses and hypotheses containing this identifier.

[15] The probability that two tools developed independently show the same faulty behaviour on the same false proof obligation is neglected.

SMT and SAT Solvers. BLaSST (2022–2026) is a research project aimed at bridging combinatorial and symbolic techniques in automatic theorem proving. The current approach to encoding POs arising from B models in SMT solvers is based on rewriting set-theoretical expressions into pure first-order logic with a primitive binary predicate representing set membership. With this approach, the structure of the original formula gets lost and it introduces many quantifiers that are difficult for solvers to handle. Instead, BLaSST will enhance the solvers to handle a richer input language based on fragments of higher-order logic. In this way, sets and relations can be represented by their characteristic predicates, and the solver can exploit the structure of the original formula, flattening it only when necessary. In particular, we will explore specific strategies for handling higher-order terms that arise from expressions of the B language. The two techniques described previously will be combined in order to embed in a solver with a highly expressive input language the power to reason combinationally. Specifically, we expect that SMT solvers will be able to recognize variables for which a finite set of a priori known values can be relevant and propagate these values in the sense of SAT solving. Similar techniques are used today for reasoning efficiently about bit vectors in SMT solving, and we intend to lift them to POs arising from B models. Second, we will explore to which extent it is possible to generalize the production of counter-examples and abductive reasoning beyond SAT-based encodings. The challenge here is to find useful compromises: there is no hope for fully general techniques and some of the theoretical bases are conflicting.

Dedukti. ICSPA (2022–2026) is a research project aimed at enabling sharing and reusing proofs and theories coming from other proof systems for both B/Event-B and TLA+. The logical framework λΠ-calculus modulo theory, implemented in the system Dedukti, allows to express any formal proof system. We propose to use Dedukti as a unique backend for both B/Event-B and TLA+, where proofs can be verified. This will not only provide confidence in the proofs obtained, but also enable interoperability between proofs, which goes hand in hand with interoperability of models, which we are also aiming for in this project. Importing theories from Dedukti will provide users of B/Event-B and TLA+ with access to their mutual formal library, which has been impossible until now although they are both set-theory oriented.

AI for Easing Proof Process. AIDOART (2021–2024) is a research project aimed at to providing a model-based framework to more efficiently support the continuous software and system engineering of CPSs and CPSoS via AI-augmentation. Our main goal is to develop a module within the Interactive prover that can learn interactive theorem proving from the developer and adapt it to unsolved proofs of the system. Such a module is also expected to provide hints based on PO inspection, rules database survey, and analysis of existing PO demonstration for the project. In this respect, examples of railways systems written in B, with complete specifications and thousands of proofs, are going to be used to train machine learning infrastructure. Unsupervised and supervised learning phases are expected to provide automatic demonstration. Another phase will address the commands with parameters and possibly the reuse/generation of mathematical rules.

Model Editor with Proof Information. Atelier B contains a model editor merging model and proof (Fig. 7) by displaying the number of proof obligations associated to any line of a B model, its current proof status (fully proved or not) and the body of the related proof obligations.

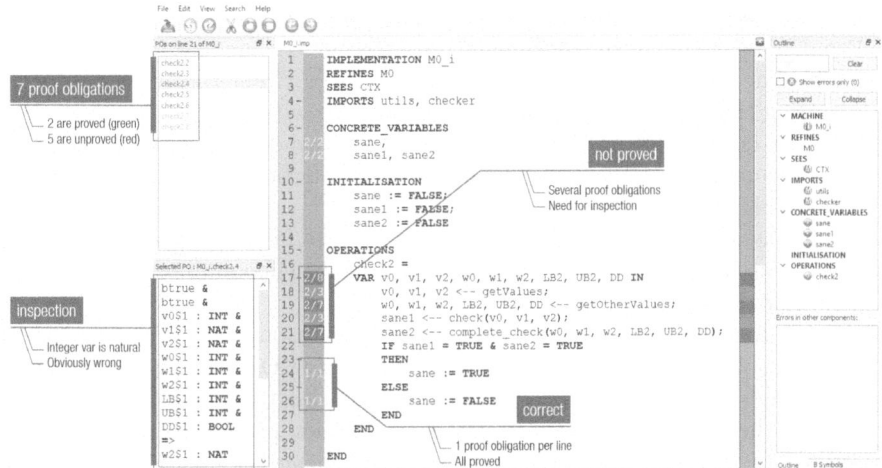

Fig. 7. Atelier B model editor showing proof status.

Proof Obligation Data Set to Experiment with Third-Party Provers. Apero[16] (Atelier B oPEn ResOurces) is a repository providing resources collected during the last decades, for software component development using the B method and for system modelling using Event-B. Proof obligations are anonymous (identifiers are replaced by random ones). They are issued from industry projects involving a large range of human modellers and providing some diversity some diversity in the style. Most of the B operators appear in the POs. All proof obligations are considered true as they were demonstrated automatically or interactively for these projects. As such, they provide a solid basis for the evaluation of provers.

7   Conclusion and Perspectives

This article presents the development and improvement cycle of the Atelier B prover over the last 30 years. This tool was designed and developed within an

---

[16] https://github.com/CLEARSY/apero.

industrial framework with a regulatory objective of certifiability. Regular scientific work has validated certain aspects. However, the impossibility of correcting the proof kernel made it necessary to connect and use third-party proof tools. The increase in processor performance allowed the automatic demonstration timing requirement (10 s meantime) to be met. Research projects managed to increase automatic proof rate from 75% to 98% on some specific kind of modelling. The combination of tools with the same positive result has improved their level of confidence and allowed their use in industrial setting. However a number of challenges remain:

- Proof obligations requiring human intelligence to complete - for example, finding the correct valuation of an existential one. Event-B solve the issue by requiring this value to be part of the model as a witness.
- Merging demonstrations when the modelling is modified. Keeping interactive demonstrations associated to a given PO is difficult, especially when the model is highly refactored.
- Finding counter examples. Trying to demonstrate false proof obligations is a loss. Identifying false proof obligations by exhibiting counter examples would help models to converge quicker.
- Helping to add easing modelling assertions. Assertions appear as hypotheses in proof obligations and could help to demonstrate POs. Suggesting assertions while modelling would also help to converge quicker towards a correct model.
- Stating the equivalence between 2 proof obligation generators. The development of two different tools, with different implementations and optimisations, leads to two different sets of POs that are not trivial to compare as both the hypotheses and goals could have different shapes.

Acknowledgements. The work and results described in this article were partly funded by:
- ECSEL JU under the framework H2020. as part of the project AIDOaRt (AI-augmented automation supporting modelling, coding, testing, monitoring and continuous development in Cyber-Physical Systems).
- ANR under the framework "appel à projets générique 2020". as part of the project ICSPA (Interoperable and Confident Set-based Proof Assistants).

References

1. Abrial, J.: The B-book - assigning programs to meanings. Cambridge University Press (2005)
2. Abrial, JR., Cansell, D.: Click'n prove: interactive proofs within set theory. In: Basin, D., Wolff, B. (eds.) Theorem Proving in Higher Order Logics, TPHOLs 2003. LNCS, vol. 2758, pp. 1–24. Springer, Heidelberg (2003). https://doi.org/10.1007/10930755_1
3. Berkani, K., Dubois, C., Faivre, A., Falampin, J.: Validation des règles de base de l'atelier b. Technique et Science Informatiques **23**, 855–878 (2004)
4. Burdy, L., Deharbe, D., Prun, E.: Interfacing automatic proof agents in Atelier B: introducing "iapa". Electron. Proc. Theoret. Comput. Sci. **240**, 82–90 (2017)

5. Burdy, L., Dufour, J.L., Lecomte, T.: The B method takes up floating-point numbers (2011)
6. Cirstea, H., Kirchner, C.: Theorem proving using computational systems: the case of the B predicate prover, April 2000
7. Cirstea, H., Kirchner, C.: Using rewriting and strategies for describing the B predicate prover, January 2001
8. CLEARSY: Proof Obligations Reference Manual 3.7
9. Delahaye, D., Dubois, C., Marché, C., Mentré, D.: The BWare project: building a proof platform for the automated verification of B proof obligations. In: Ait Ameur, Y., Schewe, KD. (eds.) Abstract State Machines, Alloy, B, TLA, VDM, and Z, ABZ 2014. LNCS, vol. 8477, pp. 290–293. Springer, Heidelberg (2014). https://doi.org/10.1007/978-3-662-43652-3_26
10. Hansen, D., Schneider, D., Leuschel, M.: Using B and ProB for data validation projects. In: Butler, M.J., Schewe, K., Mashkoor, A., Biró, M. (eds.) Abstract State Machines, Alloy, B, TLA, VDM, and Z - 5th International Conference, ABZ 2016. LNCS, Linz, Austria, 23–27 May 2016, vol. 9675, pp. 167–182. Springer, Heidelberg (2016). https://doi.org/10.1007/978-3-319-33600-8_10
11. Lecomte, T., et al.: Low cost high integrity platform. In: 10th European Congress on Embedded Real Time Systems, ERTS 2020, Toulouse, France, January 2020. https://hal.archives-ouvertes.fr/hal-02446132
12. Leuschel, M., Butler, M.: ProB: a model checker for B. In: Araki, K., Gnesi, S., Mandrioli, D. (eds.) FME 2003: Formal Methods. LNCS, pp. 855–874. Springer, Heidelberg (2003)
13. Romanovsky, A.: After and outside DEPLOY: the deploy ecosystem, pp. 197–202, July 2013
14. Wikipedia contributors: XSLT—Wikipedia, the free encyclopedia (2023). https://en.wikipedia.org/wiki/XSLT

Semantics Formalisation – Modelling and Proving Strategies Using Event-B Versus Theories

Thai Son Hoang[1]([✉]) [iD], Colin Snook[1] [iD], Karla Vanessa Morris Wright[3] [iD],
Laurent Voisin[2] [iD], and Michael Butler[1] [iD]

[1] ECS, University of Southampton, Southampton SO17 1BJ, UK
{t.s.hoang,cfs,m.j.butler}@soton.ac.uk
[2] Systerel, 1115 rue René Descartes, 13100 Aix-en-Provence, France
laurent.voisin@systerel.fr
[3] Sandia National Laboratories, 7011 East Avenue Livermore, California 94550, USA
knmorri@sandia.gov

Abstract. The Event-B modelling language has been used to formalise the semantics of other modelling languages such as Time Mobility (TiMo) or State Chart XML (SCXML). Typically, the syntactical elements of the languages are captured as Event-B contexts while the semantical elements are formalised in Event-B machines. An alternative for capturing a modelling language's semantics is to use the Theory plug-in of the Rodin platform to build algebraic datatypes capturing the syntactical elements of the language and operators to represent the various semantical aspects of the language. We take a closer look at the design of the proof rules supporting the datatypes and operators for reasoning and suggest improvements for the Theory plug-in. We use SCXML as an example modelling language for formalisation to compare the two approaches in terms of modelling and proving efforts.

Keywords: Statecharts · SCXML · Event-B · Theory plugin · Semantics formalisation

Dedication:
Jim Woodcock has made a range of important research contributions to formal methods, including semantics and practice of refinement, semantics of concurrency, and integration of state-based and process-oriented methods. He has provided insights into different styles of semantics for formal systems, in particular through his work on Unified Theories of Programming (UTP) and on semantics of Circus (which combines CSP and Z) and

© The Author(s), under exclusive license to Springer Nature Switzerland AG 2024
S. Foster and A. Sampaio (Eds.): *The Application of Formal Methods*, LNCS 14900, pp. 346–374, 2024.
https://doi.org/10.1007/978-3-031-67114-2_14

RoboChart (based on state charts). Our paper is close in spirit to Jim's work on semantics and semantic styles as we explore two approaches to semantics of SCXML, a state machine modelling language.

1   Introduction

Previously, Event-B [1] has been used to formalise the semantics of modelling languages such as Time Mobility (TiMo) [5] or State Chart eXtensible Markup Language (SCXML) [17]. Essentially, the semantics of the languages are captured as discrete transition systems represented by the Event-B models. An advantage of this approach is that the generic properties of the semantics can be captured as invariants of the Event-B models while the syntactical constraints are expressed as axioms, to ensure the correctness of the semantics. Recent work on the Theory plug-in for Rodin [10] enabled the formalisation of the Event-B method within the EB4EB framework [13] which is an Event-B-based modelling framework for manipulating Event-B features using meta-modelling concepts.

Our motivation for this paper is to explore the use of the Theory plugin for capturing the semantics of other modelling languages. In particular, we explore the advantages and disadvantages of two Event-B modelling styles:

- Approach 1: using standard Event-B constructs (i.e., contexts and machines) in an axiomatic style, and
- Approach 2: using the Theory plugin's theories in an algebraic style.

Since the Theory plugin supports polymorphic data types with operators and associated proof rules, it has the potential to improve structuring, and hence clarity, of models, as well as ease and reuse of proofs. We will use SCXML as the example of a language to be modelled. In [9], we reported work in progress on this comparison, focusing on the modelling efforts to capture a small part of the semantics of SCXML using theories. Here we go further providing an in-depth comparison including the proving efforts of the two styles.

The structure of the paper is as follows. Section 2 gives some background information about Event-B and the Theory plugin. Section 3 summarises the formalisation of SCXML semantics using Event-B standard constructs, i.e., contexts and machines. Section 4 summarises the equivalent formalisation using the Theory plugin. Section 5 discusses the design of proof rules corresponding to the formalisation using the Theory plugin. Section 6 considers the related work and Sect. 7 gives a summary of the paper.

2   Background

In this section, we briefly review the Event-B modelling method, the Theory plugin, and the SCXML modelling language.

2.1   Event-B

Event-B is a formal modelling method for system development [1]. An Event-B model contains two types of components: *contexts* and *machines*.

Contexts represent the static part of an Event-B model and can contain carrier sets (types), constants, axioms, and theorems constraining them.

Transitive Closure as a Constant. Figure 1 shows the specification of transitive closure using two contexts. Context c0_0_states declares the carrier set (type) STATE. Context c0_1_closure_def defines transitive closure of a relation r (a relation between STATE) as the generalised intersection of all the transitive relations containing r (Axiom @def−cl). From the definition of transitive closure cl, we prove (automatically with the help of SMT solvers) several theorems (derivable from @def−cl) about cl including its typing information (@typeof−cl), and that cl(r) is the *smallest transitive relation containing* r (thm1, thm2, and thm3). Further properties about transitive closure are introduced and proved (semi-automatically) in a further extended context c0_2_closure_prop (omitted here).

> **context** c0_0_states
> **sets** STATE
> **end**

context c0_1_closure_def
extends c0_0_states
constants cl
axioms
  @def−cl: cl = $(\lambda\, r \cdot r \in$ STATE $\leftrightarrow$ STATE $\mid$ inter($\{p \mid r \subseteq p \wedge p;p \subseteq p\}$))
  theorem @typeof−cl: cl $\in$ (STATE $\leftrightarrow$ STATE) $\rightarrow$ (STATE $\leftrightarrow$ STATE)
  theorem @thm1: $\forall\, r \cdot r \subseteq$ cl(r)
  theorem @thm2: $\forall\, r \cdot$ cl(r);cl(r) $\subseteq$ cl(r)
  theorem @thm3: $\forall\, r \cdot (\forall\, p \cdot r \subseteq p \wedge p;p \subseteq p \Rightarrow$ cl(r)$\subseteq p$)
end

Fig. 1. Contexts to specify transitive closure

As seen in the example above, contexts can be extended by further contexts (adding more carrier sets, constants, or axioms) allowing to gradually developing complex contexts. Figure 2 shows another context c0_3_tree_def with the formalisation of a tree-shaped structure (of states) based on closure. Here, Tree is a constant, defined using transitive closure, that formalises the definition of tree-shaped structures axiom (@def−Tree) using set comprehension.

Machines capture the dynamic part of an Event-B model as transition systems where the states are represented by variables and the transitions are expressed as

```
context c0_3_tree_def
extends c0_2_closure_prop
constants Tree
axioms
  @def−Tree: Tree = {Sts ↦ rt ↦ prn | Sts ⊆ STATE ∧ rt ∈ Sts ∧
    prn ∈ Sts \ {rt} → Sts ∧ (∀ n · n ∈ Sts \ {rt} ⇒ rt ∈ cl(prn)[{n}])
  }
end
```

Fig. 2. Contexts to specify tree structure

guarded events. An event comprises a guard denoting its enabling condition and an action describing how the variables are modified when the event is executed. In general, an event e has the following form

$$\text{any t where } G(t,v) \text{ then } v := E(t,v) \text{ end} \; ,$$

where t is the event parameters, $G(t, v)$ is the guard of the event, and $v := E(t, v)$ is the action of the event. An important feature of a machine is invariants which are safety properties that must be satisfied in all reachable states. Proof obligations are generated to ·ensure that the invariants are indeed established and maintained by the Event-B machines. To cope with system complexity, machines can be refined. Consistent refinement in Event-B guarantees that safety properties (e.g., invariants) are maintained through the refinement process.

Event-B is supported by the Rodin toolset [2], an extensible open-source toolkit which includes facilities for modelling and verifying the consistency of models using theorem proving.

2.2   The Theory Plugin

The Theory plugin for Rodin [4] enables developers to define new polymorphic data types and operators upon those data types. These additional modelling concepts (datatypes and operators) might be defined axiomatically or directly (including inductive definitions). For example, a theory for transitive closure can be seen in Fig. 3. Here cl is defined as a polymorphic operator (with respect to the type parameter S), with a direct definition. Theorems similar to those in the context of Fig. 1) are declared and proved by expanding the definition of cl accordingly.

Direct Definition for cl Operator. This is shown in Fig. 3. For this first example we have retained the modelling style so that the only difference from the contexts in Fig. 1 is that the theory is polymorphic (with respect to the type parameter S) and can be reused in machines for different modelling situations, whereas the context is specifically defined for the carrier set STATE.

The TREE Datatype. Theories can be imported to develop further data structures and operators. Figure 4 shows the tree theory defining the TREE data

theory closure
type parameters S
operators cl $\widehat{=}$ $(\lambda\, r \cdot r \in S \leftrightarrow S \mid inter(\{p \mid r \subseteq p \wedge p;p \subseteq p\}))$
theorems
  @typeof−cl: cl $\in$ $(S \leftrightarrow S) \rightarrow (S \leftrightarrow S)$
  @thm1: $\forall\, r \cdot r \subseteq cl(r)$
  @thm2: $\forall\, r \cdot cl(r);cl(r) \subseteq cl(r)$
  @thm3: $\forall\, r \cdot (\forall\, p \cdot r \subseteq p \wedge p;p \subseteq p \Rightarrow cl(r) \subseteq p)$

Fig. 3. Theory to specify irreflexive transitive closure

theory tree
imports closure
type parameters NODE
datatypes
 TREE(NODE) $\widehat{=}$
  Cons_Tree(States : $\mathbb{P}$(NODE), Root : NODE, Parent : $\mathbb{P}$(NODE $\times$ NODE)))
operators
 Tree_WD(tr : TREE(NODE)) $\widehat{=}$
  Root(tr) $\in$ States(tr) $\wedge$
  Parent(tr) $\in$ States(tr) $\setminus$ {Root(tr)} $\rightarrow$ States(tr) $\wedge$
  ($\forall\, n \cdot n \in$ States(tr) $\setminus$ {Root(tr)} $\Rightarrow$ Root(tr) $\in$ cl(Parent(tr))[{n}])

Fig. 4. A theory to specify tree data structure

structure with an operator Tree_WD, representing its well-definedness operator. Here, we followed the similar approaches in [13] to split the data structure
TREE(NODE) and its well-definedness condition operator Tree_WD. The definition of TREE(NODE) states that a tree (of NODE) can be constructed from the
set of States, the Root state, and the Parent relationship between Nodes. The
imported theory closure allows the Tree_WD operator's definition to use the cl
operator. Compared to Fig. 2, where Tree is defined as a constant, the Tree_WD
operator essentially corresponds to the conditions inside the set comprehension.
The only difference is that since the argument tr is an element of the TREE data
structure, we need to use the TREE's destructors, namely, States(tr), Root(tr),
and Parent(tr), to get the states, the root, and the parent relationship tr. (This
is enforced by the static checker of the Rodin platform and Theory plug-in).

Inductive Sequence Datatype and its Operators. Datatypes can be defined inductively using the Theory plug-in. An example is the Sequence datatype as seen
in Fig. 5. A Sequence of elements (i.e., members of ELEMENT) is either an
EmptySequence (contain no elements) or appending of a Last element to an Init
sequence. Several operators are defined using recursive definitions on the operators' arguments (case seq), e.g., SeqLength (returns the length of a sequence),
SeqConcat (returns the concatenation of two sequences), SeqContent (returns the
content of a sequence as a set), SeqHead (returns the head of a sequence), and

datatypes
  Sequence(ELEMENT) $\hat{=}$
    EmptySequence   // Base constructor
    // Inductive constructor
    Append(Init: Sequence(ELEMENT), Last: ELEMENT)
operators
  // Returns the length of a sequence
  SeqLength(seq : Sequence(ELEMENT)) $\hat{=}$ **case** seq
    SeqLength(EmptySequence) $\hat{=}$ 0 // Base case
    SeqLength(Append(S, e)) $\hat{=}$ SeqLength(S) + 1 // Inductive case

  // Concatenate two sequences
  SeqConcat(seq1 : Sequence(ELEMENT), seq : Sequence(ELEMENT)) $\hat{=}$
  case seq2
    SeqConcat(seq1, EmptySequence) $\hat{=}$ seq1   // Base case
    // Inductive case
    SeqConcat(seq1, Append(S, e)) $\hat{=}$ Append(SeqConcat(seq1, S), e)

  // Returns the content of a sequence
  SeqContent(seq : Sequence(ELEMENT)) $\hat{=}$ **case** seq
    SeqContent(EmptySequence) $\hat{=}$ $\varnothing$ // Base case
    // Inductive case
    SeqContent(Append(S, e)) $\hat{=}$ SeqContent(S) $\cup$ {e}

  // Helper operator for defining SeqHead
  _SeqHead(seq: Sequence(ELEMENT), elem: ELEMENT) $\hat{=}$ **case** seq
    _SeqHead(EmptySequence, elem) $\hat{=}$ elem // Base case
    // Inductive case
    _SeqHead(Append(S, e), elem) $\hat{=}$ _SequenceHead(S, e)

  // Returns the head of a sequence
  SeqHead(seq: Sequence(ELEMENT)) $\hat{=}$ _SeqHead(Init(seq), Last(seq))
    for seq $\neq$ EmptySequence // Applicable only to non−empty sequence

  // Keep only the elements of the set elems
  SeqKeep(seq: Sequence(ELEMENT), elems : $\mathbb{P}$(ELEMENT)) $\hat{=}$ **case** seq
    SeqKeep(EmptySequence, elems) $\hat{=}$ EmptySequence // Base case
    // Inductive case
    SeqKeep(Append(S, e), elems) $\hat{=}$
      COND(e $\in$ elems, Append(SeqKeep(S, elems), e), SeqKeep(S, elems))

  // Seq(elems) is the set of sequence whose content from the set elems
  Seq(elems: $\mathbb{P}$(ELEMENT)) $\hat{=}$
        {seq | seq $\in$ Sequence(ELEMENT) $\wedge$ SeqContent(seq) $\subseteq$ elems}

Fig. 5. Inductive Sequence datatype and its operators

SeqKeep (returns a sequence by keeping only elements of the input sequence seq and are members of the input set elems). (We omit the definition of SeqTail for brevity). Note that the definition of SeqHead itself is not recursive but relies on a helper operator _SeqHead which is defined recursively. The definition of SeqKeep also used a built-in operator COND(P, E1, E2) representing conditional formula: if P holds, it is the same as E1, otherwise, it is the same as E2. The ability to define inductive datatypes and operators is another advantage of the Theory plug-in over the standard Event-B. In fact, it is non-trivial to define operators such as SeqKeep using set theoretical constructs directly (it is defined axiomatically in [17]). Finally, we define operator Seq(elems) allowing us to construct sequences where their elements are member of the input set elems. We will use this operator later to construct queues of triggers, e.g., internal queues (of internal triggers), external queues (of external triggers).

Rewrite Rules and Inference Rules. In addition to modelling capabilities, the Theory plugin also offers developers the opportunity to extend the reasoning capacity with inference rules, rewrite rules, or expansion of operators' definitions. These rules can be specified for use by the automatic provers and/or for use during interactive proof sessions. Consider @thm1 in Fig. 3, we can define the following (unconditional) rewrite rule @cl_⊆_str_rew and inference rule @cl_⊆_str_inf (Fig. 6). Similarly, the definition of Tree_WD allows us to have the inference rules @tree_root_type_inf and @tree_root_reachable_inf. Rewrite rules allows the prover to replace any formula matching the left-hand side (of ⟹) with the corresponding instantiated right-hand side. Inference rules have zero or more antecedents (above the horizontal line) and a consequence (below the horizontal line). Inference rules can be applied (1) *forwardly*: match the antecedents with the available hypotheses and generate a new hypothesis by instantiating the consequence, or (2) *backwardly*: match the consequence with the current goal and any triggering antecedents (marked with **in_hypothesis**) with the available hypotheses, and generate zero or more sub-goals by instan-

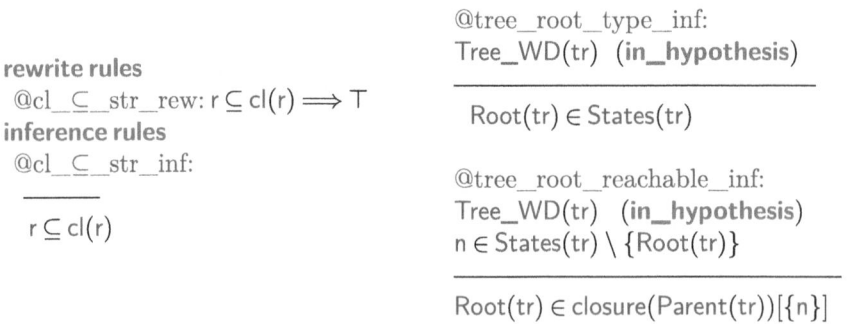

Fig. 6. Example of proof rules of closure and tree theories

tiating the remaining antecedents. We will use the example in Fig. 6 to explain the application of the proof rules further.

Rewrite rule @cl_⊆_str_rew allows to replace formula of the form r ⊆ cl(r) with ⊤. For the @cl_⊆_str_inf inference rule, since it does not have any *triggers* (i.e. in_hypothesis antecedents), it can only be applied backwardly when the goal matches the form r ⊆ cl(r) and it generates no sub-goals. Given a hypothesis of the form Tree_WD(tr), inference rule @tree_root_type_inf can be applied either: (1) forwardly to generate a new hypothesis of the form Root(tr) ∈ States(tr), or (2) backwardly when the goal matches the form Root(tr) ∈ States(tr) (and generates no sub-goals). Finally, @tree_root_reachable_inf can be applied forwardly when there are hypotheses that match both antecedents Tree_WD(tr) and n ∈ States(tr) \ {Root(tr)} (i.e., the remark in_hypothesis only applicable when inference rules applied backwardly). When applied backwardly (given a hypothesis of the form Tree_WD(tr)), the inference rule matches the goal of the form Root(tr) ∈ closure(Parent(tr))[{n}] and generates a sub-goal of the form n ∈ States(tr) \ {Root(tr)}. We will discuss further about the design of the proof rules and configuration of the proof tactics later in Sect. 5.

2.3 SCXML

SCXML [3,15] is a general-purpose event-based statemachine language that combines concepts from Call Control eXtensible Markup Language (CCXML) and Harel State Tables (part of the Unified Modeling Language (UML)). The concrete syntax for SCXML is based on XML. Hence, SCXML is an XML notation for UML style statemachines extended with an action language that is intended for call control features in voice applications. SCXML uses a run-to-completion semantics, also known as macro-step/micro-step semantics. This means that trigger events may be needed to enable transitions. Trigger events are queued when they are raised, and then one is de-queued and consumed by firing all the transitions that it enables, followed by any (un-triggered) transitions that then become enabled due to the change of state caused by the initial transition firing. This is repeated until no transitions are enabled, and then the next trigger is de-queued and consumed. There are two kinds of triggers: internal triggers are raised by transitions and external triggers are raised non-deterministically by the environment. An external trigger may only be consumed when the internal trigger queue has been emptied. This means that an external trigger is only consumed when no transition can be taken without doing so.

3 Approach 1. Using Event-B Contexts and Machines

In this section, we summarise our formalisation of the semantics of SCXML using contexts and machines. A more detailed discussion of this formalisation including discussion of the proofs is presented in [17].

The principle of this formalisation is: (1) to use the Event-B *contexts* to capture the *syntactic elements* of the model with axioms ensuring that the model is well-defined and (2) to use the Event-B *machines* to capture the *semantics* of the models. The verification process helps us to find sufficient conditions for well-defined syntax to guarantee consistent semantic behaviour of such models.

Figure 7 shows our strategy for developing the semantics of SCXML using contexts and machines. SCXML has a trigger-based run-to-completion style of operation, where triggers are used to enable the firing of transitions. To make the formalisation more manageable, we decided to deal with the formalisation of statemachines (without any triggering, i.e., untriggered statecharts) and the formalisation of run-to-completion triggering (without statemachines) as separate issues and then compose these formalisations to achieve a formalisation of SCXML (Triggered Statecharts on the bottom of the figure). The rectangles in Fig. 7 represent Event-B contexts which *extend* each other (i.e. superimpose new sets, constants and properties) to progressively develop a syntactic definition using axioms. The ellipses in Fig. 7 represent Event-B machines which *see* the final context and add variables and events that change those variables in order to define the semantics. After modelling both the statemachines and the run-to-completion in this way, the two are composed using the Event-B *inclusion*

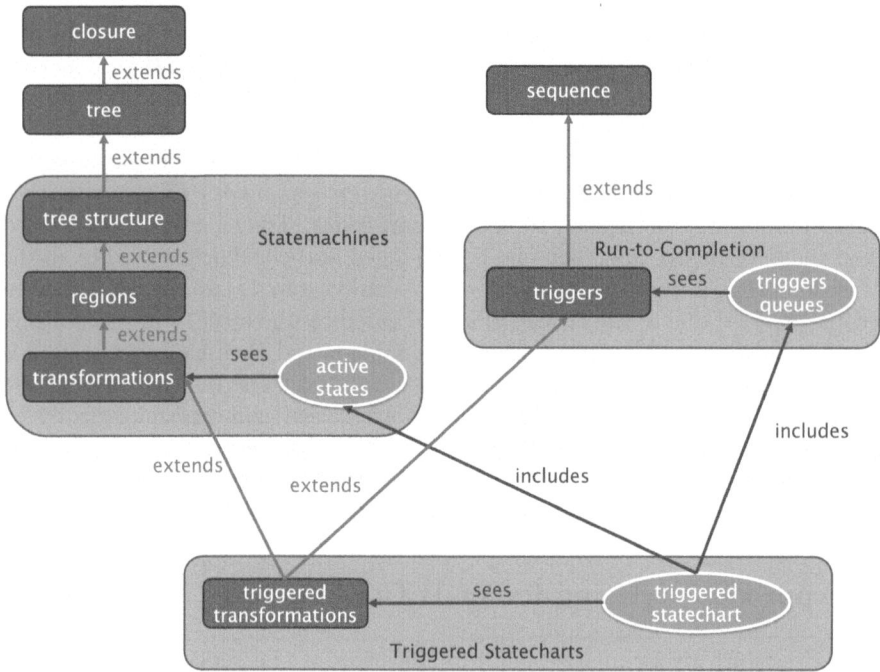

Fig. 7. Formalisation of triggered statecharts using Event-B contexts and machines

mechanism which allows the events of the composed machine to be defined by synchronising events from the two parts.

Here, the focus of this section is the following aspects.

- The use of constants to define the syntactical elements of SCXML.
- The use of context extension to build the syntactic model gradually.
- The use of axioms to define the syntactic constraints.
- The use of variables and events to capture SCXML's semantical elements.
- The use of invariants to specify the semantical consistency constraints.
- The use of composition mechanism to combine different parts of SCXML, namely untriggered statecharts and run-to-completion scheduling.

3.1   Formalisation of the Untriggered Statechart Syntactic Elements

As the syntactic elements of untriggered statecharts are fairly complex, we develop them gradually, together with their well-definedness conditions, using Event-B context extension in the following steps.

1. Model the tree structure of the states.
2. Model the parallel regions.
3. Model the transformations (a generalisation of transitions) between states.

Tree-Structured States. The structure of the states of a statechart is represented by the following constants; states (the set of all states), root (the implicit root state), and container (the relationship between a child state and its parent container). These constants satisfy an axiom stating that they form a tree-shaped structure (here $\mapsto$ is the notation for specifying tuples).

$$\mathsf{states} \mapsto \mathsf{root} \mapsto \mathsf{container} \in \mathsf{Tree}$$

Where, Tree is the constant defined earlier in Sect. 2.1. (In [17], we also include the leaves as part of the definition for Tree, but it is just a "derived" attribute, i.e., $\mathsf{leaves} = \mathsf{states} \setminus \mathsf{ran}(\mathsf{container})$).

Regions. Untriggered statecharts support the parallel composition of two or more nested statechart regions. That is, a single state of a statechart may represent several sub-components, each represented by a corresponding region. We formalise the notion of regions as partitions of the set of non-root states by using the following axioms to constrain the constant regions.

- Regions are subsets of states: $\mathsf{regions} \subseteq \mathbb{P}(\mathsf{states})$
- Regions are disjoint:

$$\forall \mathsf{r1}, \mathsf{r2} \cdot \mathsf{r1} \in \mathsf{regions} \wedge \mathsf{r2} \in \mathsf{regions} \wedge \mathsf{r1} \neq \mathsf{r2} \Rightarrow \mathsf{r1} \cap \mathsf{r2} = \varnothing.$$

- Regions cover the non-root states: $\mathsf{union}(\mathsf{regions}) = \mathsf{states} \setminus \{\mathsf{root}\}$.
- Every region has a unique container:

$$\forall \, \mathsf{region} \cdot \mathsf{region} \in \mathsf{regions} \Rightarrow (\exists \mathsf{parent} \cdot \mathsf{container}[\mathsf{region}] = \{\mathsf{parent}\}).$$

Transformations. Unlike the common definitions of transitions, which map a source state to a target state, we define transformations, which give a hierarchical view of the set of all simultaneously enabled transitions of the system, from one *enabling* state configuration to the next configuration. There are different types of transformation including *forking* (starting from a state and ending in one or more states in different parallel regions), *joining* (starting from two or more states in different parallel regions and ending in a state), *parallel* (updating parallel regions at the same time), and any combination of these types. To model all transformation types, we formalise each transformation by three sets of states.

- enabling: A transformation is enabled (i.e., can be executed) if its (non-empty) set of enabling states is active.
- exiting: The (possibly empty) set of states that the transformation will exit upon execution.
- entering: The (possibly empty) set of states the transformation will enter upon execution.

There are several constraints (well-definedness conditions) relating enabling, exiting, and entering states for a transformation. We identified some of these constraints directly, however, it is important to not over-constrain the syntax. We aim to find the minimal set of constraints for the syntax which will allow the semantic behaviour. Hence most of the constraints were initially omitted and then discovered during the proof of the invariant preservation proof obligations of the semantics.

3.2   Formalisation of the Untriggered Statechart Semantics

Given an untriggered statechart (characterised by the tree-shape structured states, the regions, and the transformation), the semantics of the statechart is characterised by the set of active states during its execution. We can formalise the semantics of the untriggered statechart in a machine using a single variable active satisfying active $\subseteq$ states . The system's functionality is encoded through one event called transformation that captures how the design transitions from one configuration to the next. Essentially, the variable, active provides a discrete characterisation of the information and event transformation represents the operation of the system under analysis.

```
event transformation
any trf where
  @typeof−trf: trf ∈ transformations
  @active−enabling: enabling(trf) ⊆ active
then
  @update−active: active := (active \ exiting(trf)) ∪ entering(trf)
end
```

Guard @active−enabling ensures that the chosen transformation trf is enabled and action @update−active first removes the trf's exiting states then adds trf's entering states. Notice that this action also allows a transformation to exit a state and re-enter that state.

An important aspect for the semantics of statecharts is that it can only transform amongst valid configurations. The following constraints on active specify the valid configuration for a statechart, which we encode as five invariants for the machine.

- There are always some active states, i.e., active $\neq \varnothing$.
- If a non-root state is active then its container is also active, i.e.,

$$\forall s \cdot s \in active \setminus \{root\} \Rightarrow container(s) \in active .$$

- If a container state is active then one of its sub-states must be active, i.e.,

$$\forall s \cdot s \in ran(container) \wedge s \in active \Rightarrow container^{-1}[\{s\}] \cap active \neq \varnothing .$$

Here, the notation r^{-1} denotes the inverse of a relation r.
- There can be at most one active state in a region, i.e.,

$$\forall r, s \cdot r \in regions \wedge s \in r \cap active \Rightarrow r \cap active \subseteq \{s\} .$$

- All parallel regions are inactive (hence active) at the same time, i.e.,

$$\forall r1, r2 \cdot r1 \in regions \wedge r2 \in regions \wedge container[r1] = container[r2] \wedge$$
$$r1 \cap active = \varnothing \Rightarrow r2 \cap active = \varnothing$$

We have to prove that the event, transformation, maintains these invariants using the well-definedness constraints of the syntax. Note that all proofs related to this work were discharged semi-automatically within Rodin.

3.3   Formalisation of the Run-to-Completion Syntactic Elements

To define run-to-completion, we first specify the syntactic elements involved in a context. Triggers are partitioned into either internal or external triggers. We define the internal and external trigger queues as sequences of internal and external triggers respectively. Sequences and their allowed operations (e.g. append trigger, head of sequence) are constructively defined via a series of theorems and axioms in an extended context. The context defining the syntactic elements for a run to completion is shown in Listing 1. An important notion for the run-to-completion schedule is steps. A triggered step is taken when an internal/external trigger is consumed and a non-deterministic number of untriggered steps may be taken subsequently. We will show how these steps relate to triggered/untriggered transitions later.

```
context r2c_ctx extends r2c_c0_2_dequeue
sets Steps
constants InternalTriggers ExternalTriggers Triggers StepTrigger StepRaised
axioms
```

@typeof_IT: InternalTriggers ⊆ InternalTriggerType
@typeof_XT: ExternalTriggers ⊆ ExternalTriggerType
@def_T: Triggers = InternalTriggers ∪ ExternalTriggers
// ↠: Partial function
@typeof_StepTrigger: StepTrigger ∈ Steps ↠ Triggers
// →: Total function
@typeof_StepRaised: StepRaised ∈ Steps → Seq(InternalTriggers)
end

Listing 1. Context for Run-to-Completion Semantics

Here, constant StepTrigger defines the required trigger for a Step (zero or one), and constant StepRaised defines the (possibly empty) sequence of internal triggers that will be raised for a step. Steps that do not have any required trigger, i.e., not in the domain of StepTrigger function, are *untriggered* steps.

3.4 Formalisation of the Run-to-Completion Semantics

Given the syntactic elements defined earlier, the machine defining the semantics for the run-to-completion schedule models the dynamic status of the run-to-completion by the variables for the internal and external queues, the dequeued trigger, and a flag to indicate when the run is completed. When a run is finished, i.e., completed = TRUE, the system may de-queue an internal/external trigger if there are any, and use it to fire a *TriggeredStep* followed by zero or more *UntriggeredSteps*. These steps are represented in the machine by Event-B events that can raise a sequence of internal triggers which is concatenated to the internal queue. External triggers can be raised non-deterministically by an event raiseExternalTrigger and appended to the external queue.

Note that at this stage (without the statemachine), there is non-determinism between untriggeredStep and completion. When we combine the untriggered statechart and the run-to-completion schedule in the next section, we will distinguish the two cases. The model of the run-to-completion schedule maintains its invariants straightforwardly (relying on operations of sequence manipulation).

3.5 Formalisation of Triggered Statecharts

To formalise the complete semantics, we compose the previous two models, of the untriggered statechart (Sect. 3.2) and the run-to-completion schedule (Sect. 3.4). The composition is performed by using the inclusion mechanism built into the CamilleX extension [8] of the Rodin platform.

Triggered Statechart Syntactic Elements. Since a *triggered* statechart is a combination of an *untriggered* one and a run-to-completion schedule, the former is a syntactic extension of the latter two (Listing 2). We introduce some syntactic elements *connecting* the sub-context together. Namely, relationships linking untriggered statechart transformations and run-to-completion steps, to form transitions. Here we need to introduce the notion of discard steps. If a trigger (internal or external) is de-queued, but there is no enabled transformation that can consume the trigger, we need to ensure that the system can still progress. Hence discardSteps are introduced to capture the special steps that discard triggers without linking to transformations.

```
context tstc_ctx extends r2c_ctx utstc_ctx
constants transitions discardSteps
axioms
  // ↣↠: bijective function (bijection)
  @typeof−transitions: transitions ∈ transformations ↣↠ Steps \ discardSteps
  // ◁: Domain restriction
  @discardSteps−Triggers: discardSteps ◁ StepTrigger ∈ discardSteps ↣↠ Triggers
  // r[S]: Relational image of relation r apply to a set S
  @discardSteps−Raised: StepRaised[discardSteps] = { ∅ }
end
```

Listing 2. Context for Triggered Statechart

Axiom @typeof−transitions states that every transition is an ordered pair from a unique transformation and a unique non-discarded step, i.e., transitions is a bijection. For Axiom discardSteps−Triggers, if we restrict function StepTrigger to the discard steps discardSteps, it will be a bijection between discardSteps and Triggers. This means, for every trigger, there is exactly one unique discard step corresponding to that trigger. Finally, Axiom @discardSteps−Raised states that the relational image of StepRaised apply to the set of discard steps discardSteps is a singleton set containing the empty set. It means discard steps will not raise any triggers.

Triggered Statechart Semantics. The semantics of a triggered statechart is captured by a machine that includes both the untriggered statechart and the run-to-completion schedule. We also use a prefixing mechanism (part of the CamilleX extension), so that all modelling elements of the included machines are prefixed accordingly (e.g., with utstc, r2c, etc.).

The following events are *lifted* an unchanged from the run-to-completion machine: raiseExternalTrigger, dequeueExternalTrigger, dequeueInternalTrigger. Essentially, they only concern the management of trigger queues and do not relate to the statechart's status.

```
event triggeredTransition
synchronises r2c.triggeredStep
synchronises utstc.transformation
where
  @grd1: transitions(utstc_trf) =
    r2c_Step
end
```

```
event untriggeredTransition
synchronises r2c.untriggeredStep
synchronises utstc.transformation
where
  @grd1: transitions(utstc_trf) =
    r2c_Step
end
```

Events to model the transitions (triggeredTransition and untriggeredTransition) *synchronise* the events from the untriggered statechart with the events from the run-to-completion schedule. The additional guard of the events ensure that the chosen transformation (from the untriggered statechart) and the step (from the run-to-completion model) corresponds with each other.

As discussed before, we need to introduce the events to discard triggers discardTrigger (in the case where triggeredTransition is not available). This condition is formalised as discardTrigger's @grd3. We also strengthen the guard of completion to ensure that the system will complete a run only when an untriggeredTransition is not available (see completion's grd1).

event discardTriggered
any trigger
synchronises r2c.triggeredStep
where
    @grd1: r2c_Step ∈ discardSteps
    @grd2: trigger = StepTrigger(r2c_Step)
    @grd3: $\forall$trf · transitions(trf) ∈ StepTrigger^{-1}[{trigger}]
        $\Rightarrow \neg$enabling(trf) ⊆ utstc_active
end

event completion
synchronises r2c.completion
where
    @grd1: $\forall$ r2c_Step · r2c_Step ∈ Steps \ dom(StepTrigger)
        $\Rightarrow \neg$ (enabling(transitions^{-1}(r2c_Step)) ⊆ utstc_active)
end

The use of composition as supported by the inclusion mechanism in Rodin results in the triggered statechart semantics inheriting the invariants from the sub-machines without the need to prove them as they are correct-by-construction.

4   Approach 2. Formalisation Using Theories

In this section, we show the algebraic formalisation of the SCXML statecharts using theories[1]. We first consider the formalisation of untriggered statecharts (Sect. 4.1) and then sketch the formalisation of run-to-completion (Sect. 4.2) and triggered statecharts (Sect. 4.3).

---

[1] Available online at https://doi.org/10.5258/SOTON/D3102.

4.1   Algebraic Formalisation of Untriggered Statecharts

Figure 8 shows the comparison between the formalisation of untriggered statecharts using standard Event-B (i.e., contexts and machines) versus using theories. The general structure of the formalisation using the Theory plugin is described by the green boxes in Fig. 8. The modelling starts with theories about transitive closure. The theories about trees import the theory about transitive closure. The syntactical elements of (untriggered) statecharts is specified in the theories about statecharts, which import the theories about trees. Finally, the semantical elements of statecharts is captured as the theories about active statecharts by importing the Statechart theory.

The STATECHART datatype is defined as in Fig. 9. Notice that we decide to define the STATECHART datatype all at once rather than gradually introducing its aspects. The definition of STATECHART(NODE, TRANSFORMATION) states that a statechart (of NODE and TRANSFORMATION) can be constructed by the Cons_Statechart constructor, with the following destructors.

– Tree: a tree-shaped structure of STATEs,
– Regions: a set of set of STATEs representing the different parallel regions.
– Transformation: a set of transformations
– Enabling, Exiting, Entering: representing the set of enabling, exiting, and entering states for invidiual transformation.

We also define the well-definedness operator Statechart_WD, based on some auxiliary well-definedness operators Regions_WD and Transformation_WD), a statechart st is well-defined if its tree-structure Tree(st) is well-defined according to Tree_WD. The regions are well-defined according to Regions_WD, and the

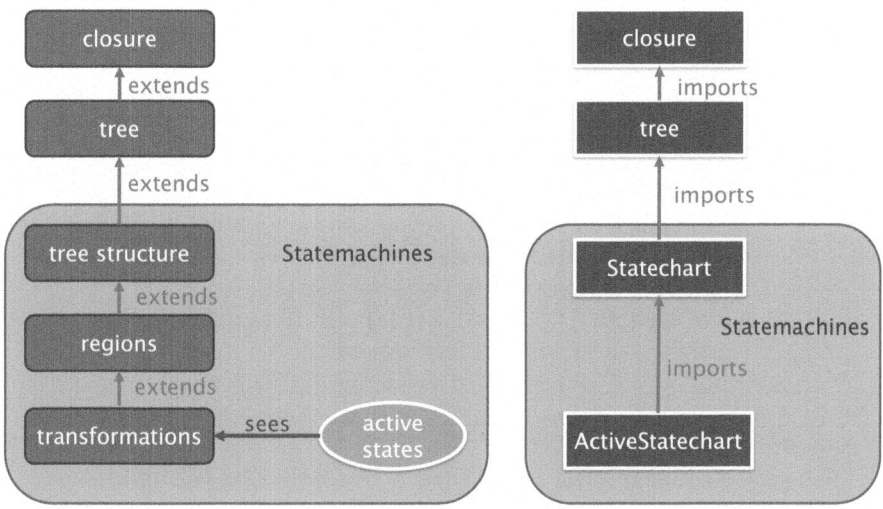

Fig. 8. Formalisation of untriggered statecharts: contexts/machines versus theories (Color figure online)

datatypes

STATECHART(STATE, TRANSFORMATION) $\widehat{=}$

  Cons_Statechart(// Constructor

    Tree : TREE(STATE),

    Regions : $\mathbb{P}(\mathbb{P}(\text{STATE}))$,

    Transformation : $\mathbb{P}(\text{TRANSFORMATION})$,

    Enabling : $\mathbb{P}(\text{TRANSFORMATION} \times \mathbb{P}(\text{STATE}))$,

    Exiting : $\mathbb{P}(\text{TRANSFORMATION} \times \mathbb{P}(\text{STATE}))$,

    Entering : $\mathbb{P}(\text{TRANSFORMATION} \times \mathbb{P}(\text{STATE})))$

operators

Regions_WD(st: STATECHART(STATE, TRANSFORMATION)) $\widehat{=}$

  // Regions are set of set of the states for the input statechart

  $\text{Regions(st)} \subseteq \mathbb{P}(\text{States(Tree(st))})$

  // There are no overlap between any distinct regions

  $\wedge\ (\forall \text{r1, r2} \cdot \text{r1} \in \text{Regions(st)} \wedge \text{r2} \in \text{Regions(st)} \wedge \text{r1} \neq \text{r2} \Rightarrow \text{r1} \cap \text{r2} = \varnothing)$

  // The regions cover all the states for the input statechart, except the root

  $\wedge\ \text{union(Regions(st))} = \text{States(Tree(st))} \setminus \{\text{Root(Tree(st))}\}$

  // Every region has exactly one parent.

  $\wedge\ (\forall\ \text{r} \cdot \text{r} \in \text{Regions(st)}$

       $\Rightarrow (\exists \text{p} \cdot \text{p} \in \text{States(Tree(st))} \wedge \text{Parent(Tree(st))}[\text{r}] = \{\text{p}\}))$

Transformation_WD(st: STATECHART(STATE, TRANSFORMATION)) $\widehat{=}$

  // Every transformation has one or more enabling states

  $\text{Enabling(st)} \in \text{Transformation(st)} \rightarrow \mathbb{P}_1(\text{States(Tree(st))})$

  // Every transformation has zero or more exiting states

  $\wedge\ \text{Exiting(st)} \in \text{Transformation(st)} \rightarrow \mathbb{P}(\text{States(Tree(st))})$

  // Every transformation has zero or more entering states

  $\wedge\ \text{Entering(st)} \in \text{Transformation(st)} \rightarrow \mathbb{P}(\text{States(Tree(st))})$

  // If a parent s of a region r is an exiting state then r has some exiting states

  $\wedge\ (\forall \text{trf, s, r} \cdot \text{trf} \in \text{Transformation(st)} \wedge \text{s} \in \text{Exiting(st)(trf)}$

      $\wedge \text{r} \in \text{Regions(st)} \wedge \text{Parent(Tree(st))}[\text{r}] = \{\text{s}\} \Rightarrow \text{Exiting(st)(trf)} \cap \text{r} \neq \varnothing)$

  // If s is an exiting state in a region r then either s is the unique exiting

  // state or every states in r are exiting states

  $\wedge\ (\forall \text{trf, s, r} \cdot \text{trf} \in \text{Transformation(st)} \wedge \text{s} \in \text{Exiting(st)(trf)}$

      $\wedge \text{r} \in \text{Regions(st)} \wedge \text{s} \in \text{r} \Rightarrow \text{Exiting(st)(trf)} \cap \text{r} = \{\text{s}\} \vee \text{r} \subseteq \text{Exiting(st)(trf)})$

  // If s is a unique exiting state in a region r and r has more than one state

  // then s is also the unique enabling state in r

  $\wedge\ (\forall \text{trf, s, r} \cdot \text{trf} \in \text{Transformation(st)} \wedge \text{r} \in \text{Regions(st)}$

        $\wedge \text{Exiting(st)(trf)} \cap \text{r} = \{\text{s}\} \wedge \text{r} \neq \{\text{s}\} \Rightarrow \text{Enabling(st)(trf)} \cap \text{r} = \{\text{s}\})$

  $\wedge\ ...$ // Further conditions omitted for brevity

  // A statechart is well−defined if its tree−shape structure is well−defined,

  // its regions are well−defined, and its transformations are well−defined.

Statechart_WD(st: STATECHART(STATE, TRANSFORMATION)) $\widehat{=}$

  Tree_WD(Tree(st)) $\wedge$ Regions_WD(st) $\wedge$ Transformation_WD(st)

Fig. 9. Statechart datatype

transformations are well-defined according to Transformation_WD. For brevity, we show only a partial definition of Transformation_WD in Fig. 9, the complete definition of operator Transformation_WD can be found in the development archive.

Comparison to Sect. 3.1. Using Approach 1, essentially the model corresponds to a single statemachine, whereas with Approach 2, we define a datatype for all statemachines. In Approach 1, we utilise context extension, which is a natural way to develop the statemachine's syntactical elements gradually. However, attempts to do this (gradually introduced the details) using theory extensions with Approach 2 results in nested datatypes which are cumbersome to use (see Fig. 9). This is an disadvantage of Approach 2 compared to Approach 1. In both approaches, the syntactical constraints on the models can be represented. These are captured as axioms in the context constraining the syntactical elements (using Approach 1), and as well-definedness predicate operators using Approach 2. The main advantages of using Approach 2 over Approach 1 are (1) the datatype are polymorphic and (2) it is easy to create an instance of the datatype and state and prove the obligations that the instance is well-defined. (Using contexts in Approach 1, it requires "instantiation" of the context which is not yet supported by Rodin[2].)

The ACTIVE_STATECHART Datatype. Figure 10 on the facing page shows the formalisation of the ACTIVE_STATECHART datatype and its WD operator ActiveStatechart_WD. An active statechart encapsulates a set of active states Active. The definition of ActiveStatechart_WD captures the properties of the active states of a statechart, similar to what we have specified in Sect. 3.2, where they are invariants. Compared to [9], our modelling of ACTIVE_STATECHART here does not "wrap" an instance of STATECHART. This has the benefit of separating completely the syntactical and semantical elements of statecharts and avoid the unnecessary nesting of datatype. The semantics of statecharts are captured by the operator transform and theorem @statechart_consistency. The transform operator takes a well-defined statechart, a well-defined active statechart and one transformation of the statechart (the well-defined condition for) and constructs an active statechart by updating the active states to remove the transformation's exiting states and add its entering states. Theorem @statechart_consistency specifies that the result of the transform operator is always a well-defined active statechart. By discharging this theorem, we prove the consistency of the statechart semantics.

Comparison to Sect. 3.2. Semantical properties are also captured in both approaches: as machine invariants in Approach 1, and as theory theorems in Approach 2. Essentially, the transform operator in Fig. 10 corresponds to the transform event in Sect. 3.2, whereas theorem @statechart_consistency corresponds to the invariant preservation proof obligations for the transform event. Here, Approach 1 utilises the mechanisms of Event-B so that reasoning is split into several obligations, one for each invariant. Using Approach 2, one has to do this manually. Nevertheless, Approach 2 presents the consistency explicitly

---

[2] Context instantiation is an on-going work [14].

datatypes
  ACTIVE_STATECHART(STATE) $\hat{=}$
  Cons_ActiveStatechart(Active : $\mathbb{P}$(STATE))
operators
  // Operator has two arguments: the statechart and the active statechart
  ActiveStatechart_WD(
    sc: STATECHART(STATE, TRANSFORMATION),
    asc: ACTIVE_STATECHART(STATE)
) $\hat{=}$
    // There must be some active states
    Active(asc) $\neq \varnothing$
    // The active states must be a subset of the states of the tree
    $\wedge$ Active(asc) $\subseteq$ States(Tree(sc))
    // If a non−root state s is active then the parent of s is also active.
    $\wedge$ ($\forall$ s · s $\in$ Active(asc) \ {Root(Tree(sc))}
        $\Rightarrow$ Parent(Tree(sc))(s) $\in$ Active(asc))
    // If a parent state s active, then one of its child state must be active
    $\wedge$ ($\forall$ s · s $\in$ ran(Parent(Tree(sc)) $\wedge$ s $\in$ Active(asc)
        $\Rightarrow$ Parent(Tree(sc))$^{-1}$[{s}] $\cap$ Active(asc) $\neq \varnothing$)
    // There are no more than 1 active state within a region
    $\wedge$ ($\forall$r, s · r $\in$ Regions(sc) $\wedge$ s $\in$ r $\cap$ Active(asc) $\Rightarrow$ r $\cap$ Active(asc) $\subseteq$ {s})
    // If two regions have the same parent then they are active at the same time
    $\wedge$ ($\forall$r1, r2 · r1 $\in$ Regions(sc)) $\wedge$ r2 $\in$ Regions(sc)
        $\wedge$ Parent(Tree(sc))[r1] = Parent(Tree(sc))[r2]
        $\wedge$ r1 $\cap$ Active(asc) = $\varnothing \Rightarrow$ r2 $\cap$ Active(asc) = $\varnothing$)
  for Statechart_WD(sc)

  transform(sc : STATECHART(STATE, TRANSFORMATION),
      asc : ACTIVE_STATECHART(STATE), tr : TRANSFORMATION) $\hat{=}$
  // Construct an active statechart by removing the sets of exiting states
  // and add the entering states of the input transformation
  Cons_ActiveStatechart((Active(asc) \ Exiting(sc)(tr)) $\cup$ Entering(sc)(tr))
    for Statechart_WD(sc) $\wedge$ ActiveStatechart_WD(asc, sc)
      $\wedge$ tr $\in$ Transformation(sc)

theorems
  // Consistency of the semantics: any transformation maintains
  // the well−definedness of the active statechart.
  @statechart_consistency: $\forall$sc, asc, tr ·
    sc $\in$ STATECHART(STATE, TRANSFORMATION)
    $\wedge$ asc $\in$ ACTIVE_STATECHART(STATE)
    $\wedge$ Statechart_WD(sc) $\wedge$ ActiveStatechart_WD(asc, sc)
    $\wedge$ tr $\in$ Transformation(sc)
        $\Rightarrow$ ActiveStatechart_WD(transform(sc, asc, tr))

Fig. 10. Statechart semantics and its consistency as a theory

as a mathematical theorem, whereas for Approach 1, they are implicit as the consistency of the machine. Regarding the proof for @statechart_consistency, it requires several manual steps. Compared the proofs in Approach 1 and Approach 2, some of the small steps in Approach 1 are now automated in Approach 2 using custom proof rules about the datatypes and operators. However, key proof steps, i.e., instantiation or consider proof by cases, are still the same (unsurprisingly). An example of such key proof steps can be found in [17].

4.2   Algebraic Formalisation of Run-to-Completion Schedule

The run-to-completion syntax and semantics are modelled using datatypes and operators similarly. Figure 11 on the next page shows some snippets of the datatype definitions for TRIGGERED_STEPS and RUN_2_COMPLETION. The TRIGGERED_STEPS datatype concerns the step, what triggers are responsible for the step to happen (StepTrigger), and what triggers are raised when the step is executed (StepRaised). The RUN_2_COMPLETION datatype captures the run-to-completion schedule, i.e., the trigger that has been dequeued (de_q), the internal queue (int_q), the external queue (ext_q), and the completed flag to indicate if the system has finished a run. Several operators are defined to model the evolution of the run-to-completion schedule. We show here the snippet for a triggeredStep that updates the de_q trigger (by consuming the trigger) and the internal queue int_q (by concatenating it with the raised triggers of the input step s). Theorem @triggeredStep_consistency states the consistency of the triggeredStep operator, i.e., maintaining the well-definedness of the Run-to-Completion.

4.3   Algebraic Formalisation of Triggered Statecharts

In Sect. 3.5, the syntactic and semantical elements for triggered statecharts are introduced via a combination of context extension and machine inclusion. Here, we just utilise datatypes to formalise them. Figure 12 on page 22 shows the definition of TRIGGERED_STATECHART datatype and its well-definedness operator TriggeredStatechart_WD. The semantical datatype SCXML combined the semantic ACTIVE_STATECHART, RUN_2_COMPLETION and a reference to the syntactic datatype TRIGGER_STATECHART. The well-definedness operator SCXML_WD ensures that the shared elements for a SCXML are the same.

By this point, we have modelled the syntactical and semantical elements of SCXML through various datatypes. We then combine the operators of untriggered statechart and triggered steps to describe the operators of triggered statechart. For example, Fig. 13 on page 23 shows the definition for operator triggeredTransition, a combination of a transformation and a triggered step. Given a well-defined triggered statechart (the syntatical elements), a well-defined SCXML (the semantical elements), a transformation and a triggered step (see the well-definedness condition for), the operator construct a SCXML semantical elements by applying the transform operator (from Fig. 10 on the preceding page) to the ActiveStatechart component and the triggeredStep operator (see Fig. 11 on the next page) to the Run-to-Completion component.

datatypes

  TRIGGERED_STEPS(STEP, TRIGGER) $\widehat{=}$ // Syntactical elements

  Cons_TriggeredSteps(// Datatype constructor

    Steps : $\mathbb{P}$(STEP),

    StepTrigger : $\mathbb{P}$(STEP × TRIGGER),

    StepRaised : $\mathbb{P}$(STEP × $\mathbb{P}$($\mathbb{Z}$ × TRIGGER)))

  RUN_2_COMPLETION(TRIGGER) $\widehat{=}$ // Semantical elements

  Cons_Run2Completion(// Datatype constructor

    de_q : $\mathbb{P}$(TRIGGER),

    int_q : $\mathbb{P}$($\mathbb{Z}$ × TRIGGER),

    ext_q : $\mathbb{P}$($\mathbb{Z}$ × TRIGGER),

    completed : BOOL)

operators

  TriggeredStep_WD(tstp : TRIGGERED_STEPS(STEP, TRIGGER)) $\widehat{=}$

    // Every step is associated with zero or 1 trigger (partial function $\rightarrow\!\!\!\!\rightarrow$)

    StepTrigger(tstp) $\in$ Steps(tstp) $\rightarrow\!\!\!\!\rightarrow$ TRIGGER

    // Every step is associated with 1 sequence (possibly empty)

    // of raised internal triggers (total function $\rightarrow$)

    $\wedge$ StepRaised(tstp) $\in$ Steps(tstp) $\rightarrow$ Seq(InternalTriggers(tstp))

  Run2Completition_WD(tstp : TRIGGERED_STEPS(STEP, TRIGGER),

    r2c : RUN_2_COMPLETION(TRIGGER)) $\widehat{=}$

    // There is at most one dequeue trigger

    (de_q(r2c) $\neq \varnothing \Rightarrow (\exists t \cdot$ de_q(r2c) = {t}))

    // If there is some dequeue trigger then the run is incomplete

    $\wedge$ (de_q(r2c) $\neq \varnothing \Rightarrow$ completed(r2c) = FALSE)

    // The internal queue contains only internal triggers

    $\wedge$ int_q(r2c) $\in$ Seq(InternalTriggers(tstp))

    // The external queue contains only external triggers

    $\wedge$ ext_q(r2c) $\in$ Seq(ExternalTriggers(tstp))

  triggeredStep(tstp : TRIGGERED_STEPS(STEP, TRIGGER,

    r2c : RUN_2_COMPLETION(TRIGGER), s : STEP) $\widehat{=}$

  Cons_Run2Completion(de_q(r2c) \ {StepTrigger(tstp)(s)},

    Seq_concat(int_q(r2c), StepRaised(tstp)(s)),

    ext_q(r2c), completed(r2c)

) **for** TriggeredSteps_WD(tstp) $\wedge$ Run2Completion_WD(tstp, r2c)

    $\wedge$ s $\in$ dom(StepTrigger(tstp)) $\wedge$ StepTrigger(tstp)(s) $\in$ de_q(r2c)

theorems

  @triggeredStep_consistency: $\forall$tstp, r2c, trigger $\cdot$ TriggeredSteps_WD(tstp)

    $\wedge$ Run2Completion_WD(tstp, r2c)

    $\wedge$ trigger $\in$ dom(StepTrigger(tstp))

    $\wedge$ StepTrigger(tstp)(trigger) $\in$ de_q(r2c)

  $\Rightarrow$ Run2Completion_WD(tstp, triggeredStep(tstp, r2c, trigger))

Fig. 11. Run-to-completion syntactic and semantical elements

datatypes
  TRIGGERED_STATECHART(// Syntactical elements
    STATE, TRANSFORMATION, STEP, TRIGGER) $\widehat{=}$
  Cons_ActiveStatechart(
    Statechart : STATECHART(STATE, TRANSFORMATION),
    TriggeredSteps : TRIGGERED_STEPS(STEP, TRIGGER),
    transitions : $\mathbb{P}$(TRANSFORMATION $\times$ STEP),
    discardSteps : $\mathbb{P}$(STEP))

  // Semantical elements: composing of an active statechart and
  // a run–to–completion
  SCXML(STATE, TRIGGER) $\widehat{=}$
  Cons_SCXML(
    ActiveStatechart : ACTIVE_STATECHART(STATE),
    R2C : RUN_2_COMPLETION(TRIGGER))

operators
  TriggeredStatechart_WD(tst : TRIGGERED_STATECHART(STATE,
    TRANSFORMATION, STEP, TRIGGER)) $\widehat{=}$
    StatechartWD(Statechart(tst))   // Statechart component is well–defined
    // The triggered steps are well–defined
    $\wedge$ TriggeredSteps_WD(TriggeredSteps(tst))
    // Discard steps are valid steps
    $\wedge$ discardSteps(tst) $\subseteq$ Steps(TriggeredSteps(tst))
    // Transitions are one–to–one mappings between transformations and
    // non–discard steps (bijective function $\rightarrowtail\!\!\!\rightarrow$)
    $\wedge$ transitions(tst) $\in$ Transformation(Statechart(tst)) $\rightarrowtail\!\!\!\rightarrow$
                          Steps(TriggeredSteps(tst)) \ discardSteps(tst)
    // Exactly one discard step for every trigger (bijective function $\rightarrowtail\!\!\!\rightarrow$)
    $\wedge$ discardSteps(tst) $\lhd$ StepTrigger(TriggeredSteps(tst))
                          $\in$ discardSteps(tst) $\rightarrowtail\!\!\!\rightarrow$ TRIGGER
    // Discard steps do not raise any triggers
    $\wedge$ StepRaised(TriggeredSteps(tst))[discardSteps(tst)] = {EmptySequence}

  SCXML_WD(
    tst : TRIGGERED_STATECHART(
              STATE, TRANSFORMATION, STEP, TRIGGER),
    scxml : SCXML(STATE, TRIGGER)) $\widehat{=}$
      // The active statechart component is well–defined
      ActiveStatechart_WD(Statechart(tst), ActiveStatechart(scxml))
      // The run–to–completion component is well–defined
      $\wedge$ Run2Completion_WD(TriggeredSteps(tst), R2C(scxml))
  for TriggeredStatechart_WD(tst)

Fig. 12. Triggered Statechart using theories

operators

triggeredTransition(
  tst : TRIGGERED_STATECHART(STATE, TRANSFORMATION, STEP,
    TRIGGER),
  scxml : SCXML(STATE, TRIGGER),
  trf : TRANSFORMATION,
  stp : STEP) $\cong$
Cons_SCXML(
  transform(Statechart(tst), ActiveStatechart(scxml), trf),
  triggeredStep(TriggeredSteps(tst), R2C(scxml), stp)
)
for TriggeredStatechart_WD(tst) $\wedge$ SCXML_WD(tst, scxml) $\wedge$
  // (trf, stp) forms a transition
  $\wedge$ trf $\mapsto$ stp $\in$ transitions(tst)
  // stp is a triggered step
  $\wedge$ stp $\in$ dom(StepTrigger(TriggeredSteps(tst)))
  // the trigger is currently being dequeued
  $\wedge$ StepTrigger(TriggeredSteps(tst))(stp) $\in$ de_q(R2C(scxml))
theorems
  // Consistency theorem for a triggered transition:
  // maintenance of SCXML_WD
  @triggeredTransition−consistency:
  $\forall$tst,scxml,trf, stp ·
    tst $\in$ TRIGGERED_STATECHART(
              STATE, TRANSFORMATION, STEP, TRIGGER) $\wedge$
    scxml $\in$ SCXML(STATE, TRIGGER) $\wedge$
    TriggeredStatechart_WD(tst) $\wedge$
    SCXML_WD(tst, scxml) $\wedge$
    trf $\mapsto$ stp $\in$ transitions(tst) $\wedge$
    stp $\in$ dom(StepTrigger(TriggeredSteps(tst))) $\wedge$
    StepTrigger(TriggeredSteps(tst))(stp) $\in$ de_q(R2C(scxml))
    $\Rightarrow$
    SCXML_WD(tst, triggeredTransition(tst, scxml, trf, stp))

Fig. 13. Triggered transition

We also present the theorem (@triggeredTransition−consistency) stating that any triggeredTransition preserve the well-definedness of SCXML component. The proof is relied on the consistency of the transform operator (Theorem @statechart−consistency in Fig. 10 on the preceding page and triggeredStep operator (Theorem @triggeredStep−consistency in Fig. 11 on the next page) to maintain the well-definedness of the ActiveStatechart and the R2C components, respectively.

5   Proof Rules for the Algebraic Data Types

The Theory plug-in [4] offers the capacity to extend the provers for the new datatypes and operators. There are three main extensions to the prover that can be used: expanding operator definitions, rewrite rules, and inference rules. In this section, we discuss the effect of these prover extensions and potential improvement for scoping these extensions for automatic proofs. We estimated that carefully designing proof rules can help to reduce the complexity of the proof of consistency SCXML semantics. Nevertheless, care should be taken when designing these proof rules. The hierarchy of theories can be seen in Fig. 14. We omitted some intermediate theories for clarity (e.g., those for the properties of transitive closure, etc.). Currently, if Theory A imports Theory B, the operation definitions and proof rules available in B (including from any theories that B imports) will be visible to A.

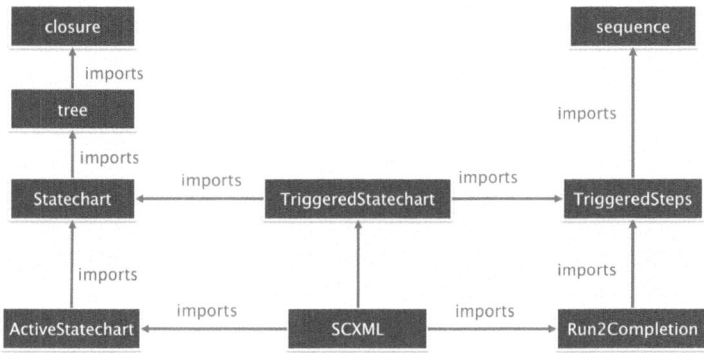

Fig. 14. Hierarchy of theories

5.1   Expanding Operators' Definition

Expanding definitions of operators is often useful when proving some basic properties of the operators. Consider the example of cl in Fig. 3, the proofs of the theorems, e.g., @thm1, @thm2, @thm3 benefit from expanding the definition of cl automatically. Outside of this the closure theory, expanding the definition of cl is not helpful. In fact, proving further properties about closure and any data structure relying on cl often use the proof rules resulting from the theorems. It is therefore important that the theorems sufficiently capture the essential properties of the datatype, allowing us to hide the datatype's definition. As a result, we suggest *only automatically expanding the definition of operators within the same theory where the operators are defined.*

5.2   Rewrite Rules

As shown in Fig. 6, proof rules can be defined for rewriting formulae. For example, the rule @cl_⊆_strengthen_rew allows us to rewrite $r \subseteq cl(r)$ to $\top$. This rewriting will be useful, for example, when the goal matches the form $r \subseteq cl(r)$, thus being rewritten to $\top$ becomes trivial. However, when applying to a hypothesis, this results in information being removed. As a result, automatically applying this rewrite rule is undesirable. A possible solution is to be able to specify that *a rewrite rule should only be applied automatically in a goal.*

Another potential issue with rewrite rules is that they can lead to infinite application of the rules. For example, given the following theorem

$$\forall r \cdot cl(r) = (cl(r);r) \cup r \, ,$$

one might be tempted to define a rewrite rule that expands $cl(r)$ into $(cl(r);r) \cup r$. However, this rewriting can be applied again, to rewrite $(cl(r);r) \cup r$ further into $(((cl(r);r) \cup r);r) \cup r$. The Theory plugin *should detect this simple problem with rewrite rules and prevent users applying these types of rules automatically.*

5.3   Inference Rules

As shown in Fig. 6 on page 7, inference rules can be defined and (depending on the rules) be applied either backwardly or forwardly. At the moment, the Theory plugin does not allow the application of an inference rules to be restricted to be either backward only or forward only. In many cases, an inference rule is only useful when applied backwardly or forwardly, but not both. Consider the following property of transitive closure cl.

$$\forall r, p \cdot r \subseteq p \Rightarrow cl(r) \subseteq cl(p) \, .$$

Here, one might define an inference rule as follows.

$$\frac{r \subseteq p \quad \text{(in\_hypothesis)}}{cl(r) \subseteq cl(p)}$$

The rule can be applied backwardly when the goal is of the form $cl(r) \subseteq cl(p)$ and $r \subseteq p$ is one of the hypothesis and discharge the goal. When applied forwardly, given that $r \subseteq p$ is one of the hypothesis, it generates an additional hypothesis $cl(r) \subseteq cl(p)$ (and this is applied to any hypotheses of the form $r \subseteq p$). This might result in generating irrelevant hypotheses which affects the performance of the provers. As a result, the Theory plugin *should allow the user to specify that the rule can only be applied backwardly automatically.*

Instantiating Theorems. Theorems in theories required instantiation as they are often polymorphic with respect to the type parameters of the theory. However, within the theory itself, the instantiation is straightforward. As a result, the Theory plugin *should instantiate the theorems automatically within the theory where the theorems are declared.* This will be useful for discharging other theorems or proving the consistency of the proof rules.

6 Related Work

Formal verification techniques are ideal to address the inherit complexity associated with design and implementation of digital systems, and the need to exhaustively explore their state space to ensure correctness. Research and development of formal verification approaches have focus on improving the scalability of the verification process via some automation. This automation requires a formalised language to represent the design and the requirements the design must satisfy. Previous work has leveraged Unifying Theories of Programming (UTP) [11] to develop verification workflows for theorem proving models developed with a diagrammatic statemachine language [12]. Not surprisingly, this work has found the need to support both model checking and theorem proving capabilities in an effort to provided not only quick feedback (e.g. problems detection) in the early stages of development, but also support for symbolic techniques that allow for the exploration of the infinite state space of the systems of interest.

The formalisation of the aforementioned language was used to developed, RoboChart, a reactive language used for specifying, simulate and generate code implementations of controllers for autonomous robotic systems [6,19]. Similar to this work, the language formalisation presented in this paper is intended as a means to enable a diagrammatic language that designers can use to specify and verify digital systems of interest. In [6], the untimed subset of RoboChart is formalised in UTP. The selected subset of statemachine contains many features that we did not consider here, including variables declaration, entry/exit actions. Instead our focus for SCXML statemachine is on hierarchical, i.e., parallel regions, nested states. Our motivation is to develop a refinement-based approach for developing SCXML and introducing nested states or parallel regions, which are important for practical development. Similarly, in [18], RoboChart state machines are verified by translation to Z-machines and eventually represented as to Circus semantics in Isabelle. The authors carefully designed a verification strategy for discharging obligations utilising the proof support in Isabelle/HOL. Notice that this approach is for verifying properties of a specific model, while our work focus on the consistency of SCXML semantics in general.

We make use of the Theory plugin for Rodin as the supporting tool for extending the Event-B mathematical language, with the aim of automating the reasoning for consistency as much as possible. An alternative would be to make use of a framework such as Isabelle/UTP [7] to do such formalisation. The main purpose of the Theory plug-in is to extend the modelling language of Event-B and proving support. Nevertheless, the features of the Theory plug-in is quite

Table 1. Comparison between standard Event-B and Theory plug-in

Approach 1. Standard Event-B	Approach 2. Theory Plug-in
– Model a single SCXML statechart	+ Model a datatype of SCXML statecharts
= Syntactical elements are captured using contexts	= Syntactical elements are captured using theories
+ Syntactical elements are gradually added to the model using context extension	– Gradually introduce syntactical elements results in nested datatype
= Syntactic constraints are represented as context axioms	= Syntactic constraints are represented as WD operators
– Combination of different parts of the language using the composition plugin (i.e., outside of standard Event-B)	+ Composition is done by defining composite datatypes
= Semantical consistency is encoded as machine invariants	= Semantical consistency is enconded as theory theorems
+ Consistency proof obligations are decomposed automatically (per individual invariants)	– Must manually construct theorems for decomposing the consistency proof
– No customisation for the provers to discharge proof obligations	+ Define proof rules for the provers to discharge proof obligations
– Model-related properties (e.g., refinement) requires additional tool	+ Model-related properties (e.g., refinement) can be stated as theory theorems

limited compared to general-purpose theorem provers like Isabelle/HOL. The limitation here includes less control of the provers (e.g., restriction for inference rules to apply forwardly or backwardly only, restriction to the scope of the rules, etc.), and the sanity checking of the proof rules (e.g., if not careful in writing proof rules, the Theory plug-in provers can go into infinite loops or lead the proof into complex state). The advantage of using a state-of-the-art theorem prover includes the fact that there is more control over the tactics for reasoning. In particular, we are inspired by the work of the formalisation of Circus in Isabelle/HOL [16], with the ultimate aim of providing a practical tool for systems engineering. In particular, we aim to look at refinement for SCXML statecharts and prove the consistency of refinement laws for SCXML. As such, the experience for developing a verification strategy such as one in [6] is valuable.

7   Conclusion

This paper provides some insights comparing the two modelling styles for formalising semantics of modelling languages: using Event-B contexts/machines (Approach 1) versus using the Theory plugin's theories (Approach 2). Table 1 summarises the comparison between the two approaches. Here the + symbol indicates an approach's advantage, the – symbol indicates an approach's disadvantage, and the = symbol indicates comparable features. We also elaborate some potential pitfalls and suggestions for improvement when designing proof rules in using the Theory plugin.

In the future, we plan to address the following issue: reasoning about refinement using Approach 1 requires duplication of the models (representing the abstract and the concrete statemachines). On the other hand, the explicit representation of statemachines as objects from a datatype in Approach 2 allows us to write theorems in first-order logic about these well-defined objects. We expect that using Theory will help with stating and reasoning about refinement relationships. While we use the example of statemachines to compare Approach 1 and Approach 2, these comparisons are applicable to formalisation of other type of models, e.g., UML-B statemachines, etc.

References

1. Abrial, J.R.: Modeling in Event-B: System and Software Engineering. Cambridge University Press, Cambridge (2010)
2. Abrial, J.R., Butler, M., Hallerstede, S., Hoang, T., Mehta, F., Voisin, L.: Rodin: an open toolset for modelling and reasoning in Event-B. Softw. Tools Technol. Transf. **12**(6), 447–466 (2010)
3. Barnett, J.: Introduction to SCXML. In: Dahl, D. (ed.) Multimodal Interaction with W3C Standards, pp. 81–107. Springer, Cham (2017). https://doi.org/10.1007/978-3-319-42816-1_5
4. Butler, M.J., Maamria, I.: Practical theory extension in Event-B. In: Liu, Z., Woodcock, J., Zhu, H. (eds.) Theories of Programming and Formal Methods. LNCS, vol. 8051, pp. 67–81. Springer, Cham (2013). https://doi.org/10.1007/978-3-642-39698-4_5
5. Ciobanu, G., Hoang, T.S., Stefanescu, A.: From TiMo to Event-B: event-driven timed mobility. In: 2014 19th International Conference on Engineering of Complex Computer Systems, Tianjin, China, 4–7 August 2014, pp. 1–10. IEEE Computer Society (2014). https://doi.org/10.1109/ICECCS.2014.10
6. Foster, S., Baxter, J., Cavalcanti, A., Miyazawa, A., Woodcock, J.: Automating verification of state machines with reactive designs and Isabelle/UTP. In: Bae, K., Ölveczky, P.C. (eds.) FACS 2018. LNCS, vol. 11222, pp. 137–155. Springer, Cham (2018). https://doi.org/10.1007/978-3-030-02146-7_7
7. Foster, S., Baxter, J., Cavalcanti, A., Woodcock, J., Zeyda, F.: Unifying semantic foundations for automated verification tools in Isabelle/UTP. Sci. Comput. Program. **197**, 102510 (2020). https://doi.org/10.1016/j.scico.2020.102510
8. Hoang, T.S., Snook, C.F., Dghaym, D., Fathabadi, A.S., Butler, M.J.: Building an extensible textual framework for the Rodin platform. In: Masci, P., Bernardeschi, C., Graziani, P., Koddenbrock, M., Palmieri, M. (eds.) SEFM 2022. LNCS, vol. 13765, pp. 132–147. Springer, Cham (2022). https://doi.org/10.1007/978-3-031-26236-4_11
9. Hoang, T.S., Voisin, L., Morris Wright, K.V., Snook, C.F., Butler, M.J.: Semantics formalisation - from Event-B contexts to theories. In: Riccobene, E., Leuschel, M., Bonfanti, S., Gargantini, A. (eds.) ABZ 2024. LNCS, vol. 14759, pp. 208–214. Springer, Cham (2024). https://doi.org/10.1007/978-3-031-63790-2_14

10. Hoang, T.S., Voisin, L., Salehi, A., Butler, M.J., Wilkinson, T., Beauger, N.: Theory plug-in for Rodin 3.x. CoRR abs/1701.08625 (2017). http://arxiv.org/abs/1701.08625

11. Hoare, C., Jifeng, H.: Unifying Theories of Programming. Prentice Hall Series in Computer Science. Prentice Hall (1998). https://books.google.com/books?id=WpdQAAAAMAAJ

12. Li, W., Miyazawa, A., Ribeiro, P., Cavalcanti, A., Woodcock, J., Timmis, J.: From formalised state machines to implementations of robotic controllers. In: Groß, R., et al. (eds.) Distributed Autonomous Robotic Systems. Springer Proceedings in Advanced Robotics, vol. 6, pp. 517–529. Springer, Cham (2018). https://doi.org/10.1007/978-3-319-73008-0_36

13. Riviere, P., Singh, N.K., Ameur, Y.A., Dupont, G.: Formalising liveness properties in Event-B with the reflexive EB4EB framework. In: Rozier, K.Y., Chaudhuri, S. (eds.) NFM 2023. LNCS, vol. 13903, pp. 312–331. Springer, Cham (2023). https://doi.org/10.1007/978-3-031-33170-1_19

14. Verdier, G., Voisin, L.: Context instantiation plug-in: a new approach to genericity in Rodin. https://wiki.event-b.org/images/RodinWorkshop2021_Context_instantiation_plug-in.pdf. Rodin Workshop 2021

15. W3C: SCXML specification website (2015). http://www.w3.org/TR/scxml/

16. Woodcock, J., Cavalcanti, A., Foster, S., Oliveira, M., Sampaio, A., Zeyda, F.: UTP, circus, and Isabelle. In: Bowen, J.P., Li, Q., Xu, Q. (eds.) Theories of Programming and Formal Methods. LNCS, vol. 14080, pp. 19–51. Springer, Cham (2023). https://doi.org/10.1007/978-3-031-40436-8_2

17. Wright, K.V.M., Hoang, T.S., Snook, C.F., Butler, M.J.: Formal language semantics for triggered enable statecharts with a run-to-completion scheduling. In: Ábrahám, E., Dubslaff, C., Tarifa, S.L.T. (eds.) ICTAC 2023. LNCS, vol. 14446, pp. 178–195. Springer, Cham (2023). https://doi.org/10.1007/978-3-031-47963-2_12

18. Yan, F., Foster, S., Habli, I.: Automated compositional verification for robotic state machines using Isabelle/HOL. In: Aït-Ameur, Y., Khendek, F., Méry, D. (eds.) 27th International Conference on Engineering of Complex Computer Systems, ICECCS 2023, Toulouse, France, 14–16 June 2023, pp. 167–176. IEEE (2023). https://doi.org/10.1109/ICECCS59891.2023.00029

19. Ye, K., Foster, S., Woodcock, J.: Formally verified animation for RoboChart using interaction trees. In: Riesco, A., Zhang, M. (eds.) ICFEM 2022. LNCS, vol. 13478, pp. 404–420. Springer, Cham (2022). https://doi.org/10.1007/978-3-031-17244-1_24

Author Index

A
Antonino, Pedro   172

B
Burns, Alan   22
Butler, Michael   346
Butterfield, Andrew   203

C
Chakrabarti, Sujit Kumar   233
Chen, Ningning   1

D
D'Souza, Deepak   233
D'Souza, Meenakshi   233
Dong, Jin Song   71

F
Fitzgerald, John   103

H
He, Jifeng   1
Hoang, Thai Son   346
Hou, Zhe   71
Huang, Wen-ling   144

J
Jiang, Kan   71
Jones, Cliff B.   22, 43

L
Larsen, Peter Gorm   103
Lawrence, Jonathan   172
Lecomte, Thierry   329
Leeding, Kent   123
Liu, Zhaoyu   71

M
Ma, Murong   71
Miyazawa, Alvaro   261
Morris Wright, Karla Vanessa   346

O
O'Halloran, Colin   306

P
Pai, Rekha   233
Peleska, Jan   144

R
Ribeiro, Pedro   261
Roscoe, A. W.   172

S
Sachtleben, Robert   144
Schneider, Steve   123
Shi, Ling   71
Simmonds, William   306
Snook, Colin   346
Suresh, Varsha P.   233

T
Talasila, Prasad   103
Treharne, Helen   123
Tudor, Nick   306

V
Voisin, Laurent   346

Y
Ye, Kangfeng   261

Z
Zeyda, Frank   261
Zhu, Huibiao   1

S. Foster and A. Sampaio (Eds.): *The Application of Formal Methods*, LNCS 14900, p. 375, 2024.
https://doi.org/10.1007/978-3-031-67114-2

GPSR Compliance

The European Union's (EU) General Product Safety Regulation (GPSR) is a set of rules that requires consumer products to be safe and our obligations to ensure this.

If you have any concerns about our products, you can contact us on ProductSafety@springernature.com

In case Publisher is established outside the EU, the EU authorized representative is:

Springer Nature Customer Service Center GmbH
Europaplatz 3
69115 Heidelberg, Germany